Doreen Diller Trilogy

The Complete Doreen Diller Mystery Trilogy

Margaret Lashley

Published by Margaret Lashley, 2023.

Copyright

What Readers are Saying About Doreen Diller

"A great plot, exceptional storytelling and a whole new cast of fun characters make this one a must-read."

"What a delightful start to a new cozy mystery series by one of my favorite contemporary Southern authors!"

"Doreen Diller is pretty sure she didn't kill her boss. But, could the last few stressful days have turned her into a psycho-eyed homicidal maniac? Read it and find out!"

"I love books that grab me from the start, make me laugh and cry, and keep me glued to the end. This book is all that and more."

"Ms. Lashley takes loads of quirky characters, a twisty mystery, a pinch of romance, and a heaping helping of humor to create this masterpiece!"

"This book is hilarious. I couldn't believe how funny Doreen is. The craziness in this story was such fun to read. Doreen is my new favorite character."

Book One: Almost a Serial Killer

Chapter One

People in Hollywood don't lead normal lives.

Nowhere on Earth does the fine line between real life and the movies blur like it does in L.A. On any random day you could sit next to Jennifer Aniston in a restaurant. Or stand in line with Johnny Depp in a grocery store. Or pump gas next to George Clooney.

(I once hopped into a cab to find Betty White inside. Nicest, funniest lady ever. Highlight of my life!)

Anyway, because we live side by side with celebrities, news about them touches us deeper—like they're family. I always thought this was unique to Tinseltown. But I was about to find out the hard way that I was totally wrong about that.

The truth is, nobody *anywhere* leads a normal life. And that fine line between reality and fantasy? Well, it's one you cross at your own peril ...

***

"I can't believe you watch that crap," my roommate Sonya said, rolling her eyes as she tied the laces on her worn-out sneakers. "It's so lame."

"Are you *kidding*?" I said, aghast at her heresy. "Tad Longmire is a living god! Just *look* at him."

It was 7:30 in the morning, and I was in the middle of my daily "spiritual harmonizing" ritual. In other words, I was in my pajamas on the couch in front of the TV, gulping down a bowl of Lucky Charms, my eyes glued to Tad Longmire.

Tad played Dr. Lovejoy, the hunky heartthrob surgeon on my favorite daytime soap, *Days of Our Lies*. He was my yogi, messiah, and savior all rolled into one. I knew this because just one look at him made everything right with my world.

"Tad's not *that* great," Sonya said, crinkling her nose.

"Not that great?" I gasped, nearly choking on a mouthful of cereal. "Are you blind? He's tall, blond, and has those amazing, twinkling blue

4

eyes. See how he moves? He's got the suave confidence of a top-shelf movie star. Tell me. What's not to love about him?"

Sonya tugged a gym jacket over her gray T-shirt. "Geez, Doreen. Sounds like you've got a crush on the guy."

I poised midway into shoveling a spoonful of magically delicious cereal into my mouth. "Maybe I do. Is that so wrong?"

Sonya laughed. "Last time I counted the candles, Doreen, you were thirty-nine."

"So?" I frowned and blew an errant lock of brown hair from in front of my eyes. "I'm never gonna give up on my dreams."

Sonya arched an eyebrow. "Good for you. Mine took a one-way bus to the Mojave years ago." She picked up her backpack and opened the front door. "I'm catching a ride to the studio with Derek. See you there. Don't be late. You know how Jared hates that."

"I know. I'll be there soon."

As the door closed behind her, I glanced at the time on my cellphone. My heart skipped a beat. Four days ago, Jared Thomas, big-time letch and small-time Hollywood studio director, had given me a new assignment. As usual, it totally sucked. But for once, my lousy job had an upside. It put me in the same production building as Tad Longmire. That meant in two short hours, there was a chance I might actually meet my dreamy soap opera surgeon face-to-face!

According to *The Hollywood Gossip Gal*, my favorite online blog, Tad Longmire was in L.A. working on the mid-budget action thriller, *Breaking Code*. As a longtime fan of Tad's, I knew in my gut the movie was going to be his big break—the role that would transform him from small-screen beefcake into big-screen dreamboat. And, as a longtime aspiring actress myself, I knew such breaks didn't come along every day.

If ever.

As for me, I was still waiting for my own ship to come in. I'd never admit it to Sonya, but lately I'd begun to fear my ticket aboard the cruise to fame and fortune had been eaten by a horny goat.

If that weren't bad enough, for the past week I'd been having this recurring nightmare. In it, the entire cast of *The Love Boat* waved from the bow as they steamed past me—while I sat in a leaky rowboat wearing a moldy life vest and bailing water for all I was worth. Every time I dreamt it, I'd wake up in a cold sweat, my sheet twisted around my neck like a noose.

That had to mean something, didn't it?

Anyway, today was going to be different. I could feel it in my bones. I put my cereal bowl in the sink, brushed my teeth, and pulled my wavy hair back into a messy bun. I was running late, so I tossed my cosmetics into a makeup bag. I'd have time to fix myself up properly when I got to work.

Being a Girl Friday at a Hollywood film studio might've sounded glamorous. But believe me, it wasn't. Besides the guy who cleaned the toilets, it was the lowest job on the studio rung. But it paid the bills—sort of—while I treaded water and waited for Captain Stubing to turn his blasted ship around.

Hopefully, he'd do it soon. I was starting to get wrinkly.

After fifteen years of acting lessons, dance classes, cattle-call try-outs, bit parts in low-budget community theater productions, bowing and scraping to studio bigwigs, and clearing my aura of karmic negativity, the biggest movie role I'd managed to land so far was stunt-double for a hooker found decapitated in a dumpster. Not exactly a cameo designed to make Hollywood casting directors sit up and take notice.

Jared Thomas had given me that gig six months ago. But only after I'd agreed to go out on a date with him. He'd promised that, if I played my cards right, he could get me a good part in his next project. The only problem was, Jared had been holding an ace the whole time—and it wasn't up his sleeve. Don't get me wrong. Like Jared, I believed in happy endings, too. Just not on a first date.

My failure to perform on demand had resulted in Jared giving the "good part" to a more willing starlet. In return, I'd vented my frustration by shoving a rotten banana down the front of Jared's pants in front of his film crew. After that? Well, let's just say my acting prospects had shriveled up faster than a spider in a microwave oven.

The only thing that had saved me from being fired outright was my SAG membership, which I managed to keep alive playing a random crowd "extra" in whatever low-budget movie would hire me. Because of it, Jared hadn't been able to can me on the spot. So instead, he'd settled for sticking me in a series of dead-end jobs that, I'd come to believe, were part of an evil, passive-aggressive crusade to make me so miserable I'd quit.

Jobs like my latest assignment—personal assistant to Dolores Benny.

Ms. Benny was a plump, googly-eyed actress in her late sixties. And even though she swore like a sailor, chain-smoked Virginia Slims, and looked like Jabba the Hutt in drag, I'd have done just about anything to be *her* instead of me.

Ms. Benny, like Tad Longmire, had made it to the big screen.

As her personal assistant for the past four days, I'd been responsible for attending to the odd-looking woman's every whim. That included hourly ego massages, landmine-filled hair and makeup sessions, death-defying wardrobe wrestling matches, and late-night ice cream-and-cigarette emergencies, which happened more often than you'd think humanly possible.

Most nights, grunt-workers like me and Sonya never even made it back to the flophouse apartment we shared in South Park with two other would-be stars. Instead, we usually took turns napping on the lumpy cots tucked away in a dark corner of the production studio. The ones reserved for "acting tryouts" and sleep-deprived underlings such as ourselves.

On a good night, we'd catch two or three hours of uninterrupted sleep before our cellphones rang, startling us into the next mad dash to the trailer of whichever star we'd been assigned to. On the bright side, the work was excellent acting practice. There was nothing quite like getting up at 3 a.m. to wax somebody's back hair or sort the blue M&Ms from a family-sized bag to help an aspiring thespian dig deep for an ingratiating smile or a cheerful attitude.

People like Sonya and me were the worker bees in a hive with too many queens. To cope, we swapped horror stories in the dark. And we dubbed ourselves the TTC—Trailer-Trash Crew. Why didn't we just quit? Believe me, we contemplated it daily. But there was one perk our jobs offered that made the demeaning tasks worthwhile.

Working there kept our studio passes active.

As long as we retained permission to roam the sacred grounds of a Hollywood production set, we wannabe-actors could still cling to the hope that fate would deliver us our own big break one day.

And with the chance of meeting Tad Longmire on the set today, *this* just might prove to be *my* lucky day.

***

As soon as I stepped out the door of the apartment, my carefully laid plans derailed faster than that horrific train crash in *Unbreakable*. In the movie, Bruce Willis had emerged from the wreckage unscathed. Whether *I* would survive my current catastrophe still remained to be seen.

First off, my car, a battered, drab-green Kia Soul I'll nicknamed The Toad, refused to crank. After opening the hood and beating the solenoid with a socket wrench, it finally coughed to life. But by then, I was running late. Really late.

When I finally got to the studio, I encountered my second glitch. Jared Thomas. The petty tyrant was storming through the studio warehouse on another one of his egomaniacal rampages.

Not willing to find out if I was the cause of or solution to his latest meltdown, I dived into a supply closet. After ten minutes of pressing my ear to the cheap panel door, the angry voices faded. The coast finally clear, I fled, makeup bag in hand, to Dolores Benny's trailer in the studio's back lot.

Escaping Jared's wrath might've saved me a chewing out, but it had cost me more precious time than I could afford. As I reached for Ms. Benny's doorknob, I checked my cellphone. It was nine o'clock on the dot. Today's filming would begin in half an hour.

Crap!

I was going to need every last remaining second to get Ms. Benny ready for her close-up with Tad—not to mention my own. Out of breath from running, I burst into the old woman's trailer. The horrors that awaited me inside made me let out an asthmatic wheeze.

Ms. Benny appeared to be engaged in a fight to the death with a full-body latex girdle.

I'd seen slasher movies that weren't that graphic.

"There you are, girl!" Benny grumbled. "It's about time you got here!"

I winced. "Sorry. Let me help you with that."

I flung my makeup bag on the counter and dived in, yanking at the flesh-squashing undies like the heroine in a low-budget sci-fi movie from the 1950s—*It Came from Planet Spanx*.

Eight minutes later, sweaty and exhausted, I'd managed to encapsulate Ms. Benny into her spandex chrysalis. But my work was only half over. I still had to turn her from a moth into a butterfly.

While she sat in front of the vanity mirror patting pancake makeup over her beet-red face, I opened Ms. Benny's wardrobe bag. Inside hung a purple sequined cocktail dress. It was a size ten—at least four sizes too small. (In Hollywood, "plus size" meant anything over a size two.)

God give me strength.

I slipped the dress off the hanger and unzipped it. "Step in," I said, holding the bottom of the dress open six inches off the floor.

"Gimme a minute," Benny said, snapping her powder compact closed. She set it on the vanity. Then, grunting from the effort, she stood. Gripping my shoulder for balance, she slowly shifted one barefoot, pudgy white leg at a time into the opening of the dress.

"Good job," I said, tugging the sequined gown up the front of her ample torso. That part of *Mission Impossible* completed, I began stuffing her arms into the elbow-length sleeves.

"Cripes," Benny grumbled. "I look like a Liberace sausage in this get-up."

"No way," I cooed. "You look gorgeous. Now let me zip you up."

I went around to the back of Ms. Benny. A long, silver zipper ran up the back of her dress from her butt crack to her neck. Against the dark purple fabric, it resembled a miniature railroad track. Unfortunately, just like in *Unbreakable*, the massive gap between destinations appeared tragically insurmountable.

"Here we go," I said, searching for the zipper pull. I found it protruding from the bottom of her buttocks like a stubby metallic tail. I grabbed ahold of it and tugged with all my might.

It wouldn't budge.

"Umm ... try holding your breath," I said gently.

"Ung," Benny grunted. "Fine. But don't bother holding yours."

"What?" I asked.

"Don't bother holding *your* breath," Benny repeated, letting her Jersey accent slip out. "Look, hun. I know you're not working this job for the perks. You wanna be a star, right?"

"Well, yes."

She shook her head. "Don't take this wrong, but I just don't see it happening."

"What?" I gasped, my fingers going limp on the zipper pull.

"You just ain't pretty enough for leading lady roles." Benny leaned in closer to the vanity mirror to touch up a fake mole on her puffy cheek. "Your only shot at the big screen is with character bits. Like me."

"Oh. I see. Thank you, Ms. Benny," I said. Wounded, I pursed my lips into a vice. If I wanted to see Tad, I needed to keep this stupid job. And to keep this stupid job, I had to keep my mouth shut and get Ms. Benny's zipper up.

I winced out a smile and tugged again with all my might. This time, the zipper shot up to her bulging waist.

"Watch it!" Benny said. Her reflection in the mirror glared back at me. "That pinches!"

"I am *so* sorry, Ms. Benny," I groveled. "Thank you so much for the advice about trying out for character-actor parts. Do you think you could recommend—"

The old woman's cackling laughter drowned out my pandering.

"You know, even landing a character role would take a miracle for you, hun. Your face is bland, girl. *Bland!* You got no *angle.* You got nothing to make you stand out. Those poor casting directors have to wade through a whole *sea* of headshots, you know? You gotta give 'em something to work with!"

Something to work with?

An odd combination of humiliation and rage surged through me. Remembering my acting classes, I *channeled the energy* into forcing the industrial-strength zipper past three rolls of spandex-covered back fat and up to the nape of Ms. Benny's mole-pocked neck.

I hooked the clasp at the top and tried to glean some bit of satisfaction from my Herculean solo performance. But who was I fooling?

As Benny hung earrings from her thick lobes, I studied my reflection in her vanity mirror. What *did* I actually have to offer? Unremarkable brown hair. Unremarkable face. Unremarkable ... *everything*.

Ms. Benny had been rude. But she'd also been *right*.

Crap.

Benny turned around to face me. Her dress was so tight it forced her to move in small, wobbly steps. My mind raced to an image of *ET the Extraterrestrial*—in cocktail attire.

"Face it, girl," Benny said, watching me inventory myself in the mirror. "You're a Plain Jane."

"Looks aren't everything," I said. "What about *substance*?"

Benny arched a drawn-on eyebrow. "Honey, the only *substance* anybody in L.A. cares about comes in pill, capsule, or powder form."

I frowned. "But—"

"How *old* are you, anyway?" She looked me up and down, her oversized eyeballs not quite following the same trajectory.

"Is that really relevant?" I asked, shriveling under her cockeyed scrutiny.

She chuckled. "*That* old, huh?"

I picked up a fake diamond brooch to pin to the front of her dress. Benny took it from my hand, then let out a series of clucking sounds that left no doubt as to what she thought about my prospects for stardom.

"I'll do it myself," she said, dismissing me with a wave of her hand. "I need coffee. Be a dear and go get me my usual, would you ... *Plain Jane*?"

My shoulders slumped beneath the weight of the old woman's casual death blow. "Yes, ma'am. Would you like your usual vanilla éclair to go with it?"

"Yeah. With extra filling. And hurry up. We don't got that much time left."

"Yes, ma'am," I said, reaching for the doorknob, my eyes brimming with tears.

Apparently, some of us never had any time to begin *with.*

***

Five minutes after having my acting prospects squashed like a roach by a pulsing larva in a purple dress, I was in the studio parking lot, dejectedly shuffling my way back to Ms. Benny's trailer. As I contemplated whether or not to add a few drops of arsenic to her double-shot, caramel, almond milk, iced-mocha cappuccino, a young woman burst from the trailer next to Ms. Benny's.

The stunning brunette steamed down the trailer steps and sprinted past me, leaving a trail of tears and curse words in her scorching wake. A second later, to my utter shock, Tad Longmire, my daytime daydream, appeared in the trailer's open doorframe.

He was shirtless.

I was speechless.

"Hey you," he called out, fastening the top button of his jeans. "Don't I know you?"

"Uh ... *me?*" I asked, my cheeks suddenly aflame. "No sir. But I definitely know *you.*"

A corner of his mouth curled into an *of course you do* grin. "What's your name, sugar?"

I swallowed a lump in my throat. "D ... Doreen Diller."

Tad shot me a smile that melted the souls of my sneakers. "Ah, yes. I've had my eye on you."

"You *have?*" I gasped, nearly dropping Ms. Benny's cappuccino.

"Of course," he said. "Who wouldn't?"

"Wha—?" I fumbled, my tongue suddenly an uncooperative lump of meat in my mouth.

My hair was a mess. My makeup was still in a bag on Ms. Benny's countertop. Yet there he was, Tad Longmire, my secret crush, *hitting on me!*

This has to be a dream.

new face of femininity. Strong. Confident. And driven not by the external, but *internally*, by my own sense of justice.

Exhilarated by my newfound freedom, I sat down at Tad's banquette table to read over his employment contract. But I couldn't concentrate. Tad was only a few feet away from me. I couldn't help but keep sneaking furtive glances at him. I mean, who wouldn't?

My brain kept telling me to remain calm and hold onto my wits. But the rest of me wanted to jump his bones.

In a star-studded daze, I watched breathlessly as the handsome hunk slipped a crisp, white, button-down shirt over his smooth, perfect chest. He left it open, offering glimpses of his six-pack abs as he casually milled about in his kitchen—*humming a tune!*

All of a sudden, Tad reached up and took two crystal flutes from a cupboard. I held my breath as he bent over and took a bottle of champagne from his fridge...

Oh. My. God. I'm going to throw back some bubbly with Tad Longmire!

"I've had my eye on you," Tad said again, popping the cork. "You know, I think we could be really good together."

"You do?" I gulped.

"I do."

Tad's words echoed in my head like a bridegroom fantasy. As I envisioned him in a tux next to a big, white cake, he aimed his heart-melting, crooked smile my way.

"All signed, Dorey?"

I nodded, then hastily scrawled my name on the dotted line. Beaming, I held up the contract like a child showing Daddy her crayon drawing of a unicorn jumping over a rainbow.

"All done!" I squealed.

Tad grinned. "Perfect."

I sighed.

Yes, Tad. You totally are.

Mesmerized, I watched as Tad's strong, beautiful hands filled two sparkling crystal flutes with expensive-looking bubbly. With grace and elegance, he swept up one of the slender glasses and shot me a gleaming, toothpaste-commercial smile.

I nearly swooned.

Then, for the second time in under an hour, Tad Longmire said something that would change my life forever.

He nodded toward the trailer door and said, "Get out."

I nearly fell out of my chair. "What?"

"Come back in an hour," he said. "And bring me an In-N-Out Burger, animal style. Large fries." He turned away and took a sip of champagne.

"What?" I gasped as he brushed back his signature blond bangs, admiring his reflection in one of the huge mirrors lining the walls.

"You heard me," he said.

"But Tad, I don't underst—"

A quick rap sounded on the trailer door.

It flew open.

A gorgeous redhead with boobs bigger than her head came flouncing into Tad's trailer. She grinned at him lasciviously, not even bothering to acknowledge my existence.

My face dropped four inches.

"Oh."

The word tumbled out of my mouth like a bitter marble. I grabbed my contract and scrambled from the banquette. Then I slunk past the woman and out of the trailer like a scolded dog.

Outside, in the parking lot, anatomically incapable of kicking my own ass, I settled for biting down hard on my bottom lip.

"What an idiot!" I hissed at myself.

Once again, I'd fallen for the L.A. fairytale—hook, line, and too-good-to-be-true *stinker*.

Stupid, stupid, stupid!

I flopped my butt down on the hard curb and checked the time on my cellphone. According to Andy Warhol, Tad Longmire had just tricked me out of nine of my allotted fifteen minutes of fame.

I hung my head in shame.

Why do I keep falling for the bad guys?

As I sat there commiserating my own idiocy, a brown tabby cat came ambling toward me. A chunk was missing from his left ear. Apparently, I wasn't the only one having a rough life this time around.

The skinny feline rubbed its threadbare chin against my shin and purred. I sat up a little straighter. "You're right," I said. "Strays like us need to stick together."

I stroked its tawny head. It purred louder. I set my jaw determinedly and looked into the kitty's jade-green eyes.

"Tell you what," I said. "You show me where I can get some cat turds for my new boss's lunch, and I'll bring you back a tuna sandwich. Deal?"

The cat winked.

It was on.

Chapter Three

It's a well-known fact that anyone who says they've never fantasized about killing their boss is a liar. Possibly pathological.

After just four days of being Tad Longmire's personal assistant, I was ready to act on my newly revised fantasy about the handsome but lecherous hunk. Instead of dreaming of hitting the sack with Tad and rocking his world, I was ready to hit him over the head with a sack of rocks, then hold his face down in a dirty toilet bowl until his spirit left this world.

Other than that, things had been going relatively well.

Since being hired on Sunday, I'd spent my time alternating between helping Tad rehearse his lines—and then making myself scarce so he could have sexy time with the boobalicious redhead he'd been boinking almost non-stop since I slithered out of his trailer with a contract, but no champagne.

During my "get lost" breaks, Tad had kept me busy running out to get him coffees, smoothies, and In-N-Out Burger takeout. How the man could eat burgers and fries every day and look like he did was a discussion I was saving for when I met God in person. On the flip side, at least I didn't have to wrestle Tad into a girdle. And, I had to admit, Tad was a great actor.

He'd certainly fooled me.

Since Monday, my hunky new boss had been hitting his cues on *Breaking Code* like a superstar. So when I returned to the set on Thursday with Tad's emergency organic acai-and-blueberry green energy smoothie, I was surprised to find him engaged in an intense conversation with a short, hairy, red-faced man. It took me a minute to recognize the guy as the movie's director, Victor Borloff.

"What's going on?" I whispered to the camera guy.

He muted the mouthpiece on his headset, then turned to me and said, "Artistic differences."

"What kind of artistic differences?" I asked, watching a shirtless Tad back away from the director until his broad, tan shoulders were pinned against a wall.

18

"The 'director's cut' kind," the camera guy said.

I frowned. "What do you mean? Are they arguing about Tad participating in extended scenes?"

He smirked. "I guess you could say that."

I frowned. "I don't get what all the fuss is about. I'm sure—"

The cameraman cocked his head and shot me a smirk. "You know that big-boobed redhead Tad's been porking?"

"Uh, Bonnie? Yeah."

He wagged his eyebrows. "She's Borloff's wife."

My gut flopped. "Oh. My. God."

Dumbfounded, I watched in stunned horror as the director's right arm angled backward, then lunged forward. In a flash of red-knuckled fury, Borloff's fist smashed into Tad's once-perfect nose like an angry jackhammer.

"And there it is," the cameraman snorted. "The director's right cut."

***

Back at Tad's trailer, my philandering new boss was standing by the sink, holding an icepack to his swollen nose. I was seated at the banquette, holding his studio contract to my bespectacled eyes, reading through the fine print.

"I can't believe Borloff canned me," Tad grumbled.

I shook my head. "I can't believe he was savvy enough to include 'boning director's wife' as a cause for immediate dismissal. Didn't you even *read* this contract before you signed it?"

Tad rolled his gorgeous blue eyes. "Nobody reads those things, Dorey."

I grimaced.

Touché.

"I know," Tad growled. "I'll sue him for punching me!"

I shook my head. "Can't. The contract clearly states 'boning of said wife in Article 14-A entitles director to one face punch to the offender, any resulting damages of which are to be covered solely by said actor/actress.'"

Tad frowned. "Crap. Directors think of everything."

"At least you have three days to vacate the trailer," I said, reading Article 15. "I think you should use the time to try to mend fences."

"Like some groveling ranch hand?" Tad laughed. "Yeah, right." He flung the ice pack into the sink, grabbed a bottle of Jack Daniels from the countertop, and stormed out the trailer door.

I thought about trying to stop him. But what chance did I have against a raging god? Tad was a head taller than me and outweighed me by at least eighty pounds. Besides, while a broken nose on Tad's face would most likely be viewed as "adding character" and land him more tough-guy roles, a broken nose on *my* face would be deemed an "insurmountable flaw" and destroy whatever slim chance I had left of landing a decent part.

So I didn't run after Tad.

Instead, through the open trailer door, I watched him march across the parking lot toward the production warehouse, chugging whiskey straight from the bottle.

I knew Tad Longmire was no heroic, white-hatted cowboy. But I had no idea just how determined he would be to set himself out to pasture—*permanently.*

＊＊＊

Caught in a trap of his own making, Tad had gone ballistic.

Fueled by whiskey and emboldened by lack of self-reflection, Tad Longmire did *not* take my advice and mend fences. Instead, he set about burning every bridge he'd ever built in Hollywood.

While I cowered in Tad's trailer scouring my contract for a loophole to get out of working with him, news of his exploits buzzed my cellphone like tiny kamikaze pilots. Texts came in hot and heavy from Sonya and other members of the Trailer-Trash Crew.

Tad released a cageful of rats on the film set!
Tad peed all over the catered lunch buffet!
Tad kicked dents in the director's Lamborghini!

Tad took off in the studio owner's Tesla—with his wife!

I sat back and groaned.

Kill. Me. Now.

As Tad's personal assistant, I knew I'd be labeled guilty by association. My reputation in Tinseltown—if I ever *had* one—was officially toast.

Not swanky, chic, avocado toast.

Burnt toast.

Burned-beyond-scraping-the-black-stuff-off toast.

Even worse, according to my contract, I still had eleven months, three weeks, and three days left to serve as the personal assistant to a drop-dead-gorgeous madman.

Chapter Four

Since moving to L.A., I'd lived through plenty of highs and lows. But until now, I didn't know how truly nasty Hollywood gossip could get. Apparently, however, my longsuffering roommate Sonya *did*. Yesterday, after she found out about Tad's tornadic tirade, she'd come home bearing a gift to cheer me up.

"I don't know if this is any good or not," she said, handing me a brown paper bag. "But at this point, it can't hurt."

"What is it?" I asked. "A pack of cyanide capsules?"

"I wish," Sonya said. "I've looked around. Nobody sells those. This is the next best thing."

I opened the bag, anticipating a cobra to pop out and bite me on the neck, allowing me to end my life in a final act worthy of Cleopatra. Instead, inside was a pocket-sized book. Its cover was the yellow-orange color of a caution light. The title read, *Hollywood Survival Guide*.

"It's supposed to have tips on how to get through any occasion or situation," she said. "It says so right there on the cover."

"Geez," I said. "Does it cover how to survive your boss's career-suicide?"

My cellphone buzzed.

Sonya winced. "There it goes again."

I groaned and reached for my phone. For the last day and a half, calls and texts about Tad had been blowing up my phone like a string of Black Cat firecrackers. Some had been helpful. Most had not.

"Somebody says they spotted Tad at the Lost Property Bar," I said, reading the text.

"Better hop to it, then," Sonya said. Then she added sarcastically, "Don't forget your smile."

***

As I pulled up to the Lost Property Bar in my rusty Kia, I got another text saying Tad had moved on and was now making a ruckus at Tramp

Stamp Granny's. After coughing and sputtering my way there in The Toad, a text came in saying Tad Longmire had just left the building.

Crap! Where the hell are you, Tad?

I was about to drive back to the studio and ram The Toad into Tad's trailer when yet another text came in saying he was drunk and disorderly at a bar called Sunset & Vinyl.

By the time I got there, Tad was gone again.

I slumped my head onto the steering wheel. I was exhausted. I'd been white-knuckle driving all night trying to apprehend Tad before he committed a felony. But no matter how fast I'd driven, I'd remained one step behind my boss's wanton trail of destruction.

I was out of leads and nearly out of gas when, at a few minutes to midnight, my phone buzzed again. This time, I recognized the number immediately. It was the In-N-Out Burger on Venice Boulevard.

As one of Tad's daily nutritional requirements, I'd put the fast-food restaurant on speed dial. But the image lighting up my cellphone screen wasn't their late-night burger menu. It was a picture of Tad. Pants down. Passed out in a restroom stall.

The accompanying text read, *"U got 20 minutes. Then I call the cops."*

I ditched The Toad, grabbed a taxi, and made it there in eighteen.

After convincing the restaurant manager not to press charges, I shoved one of Tad's business cards into his palm and promised to pay for any damages. His ruffles soothed by the news, the manager helped me shove Tad's drunken carcass into a taxi. I used my last twenty-dollar bill to bribe the cab driver into helping me drag Tad into the studio trailer and onto the bed.

While Tad lay sprawled out snoring like a sea lion, I spent the early morning hours trying to figure out what the hell to do next. As I fished through my purse for a much-needed chocolate bar, I spotted the little yellow book Sonya had given me. I grabbed it and thumbed through the pages.

According to the *Hollywood Survival Guide*, Tip #2 was: *Always have an escape plan.* (Tip #1 was: *Never trust an actor whose lips are moving.* But it was way too late for that.)

Yes! An escape plan was *exactly* what I needed.

I wonder if Prince Holland Cruise Lines is still hiring. I hear Siberia is nice this time of year.

I glanced over at Tad. His head was snuggled against a goose-down pillow tucked inside a 600-threadcount Egyptian cotton pillowcase. After laying waste to his career and possibly mine, the drunken sailor was smiling as if he didn't have a care in the world.

Jerk!

My jaw clenched. My hands balled into fists. I wanted to punch Tad's lights out. But they were already out. Besides, if I killed him, I'd be out of a job. Then I'd *never* get my big break in showbiz.

I flopped down onto the couch and chewed my thumbnail.

As I sat there wondering how I was going to get Tad out of the trailer by noon and back to his place, I realized I had no idea where Tad actually lived. We'd never discussed it. I rifled through his wallet. It was stuffed with credit cards, slips of paper with hearts and phone numbers on them, and VIP club passes. But no driver's license. And nothing with an address.

Perfect. What the hell am I supposed to do now?

Chapter Five

Tad's terroristic tour of Tinseltown had pretty much assured the number of friends he had left in Hollywood was exactly zero. Unfortunately, my contract as his personal assistant made it my responsibility to "manage" the colossal mess he'd made.

I didn't know what to do. The few friends I had left, I didn't want to call. If I dragged them into this, they might also end up blacklisted by association.

At four in the morning, I gave up searching for help and picked up my contract with Tad. There had to be some way out of it. But after reading through the whole thing, I hadn't spotted a single loophole. The attorney who'd put it together was good. I found his name at the bottom of the last page.

Ralph B. Steinberger, Esq.

Desperate and out of options, I google-searched the attorney's number, then rang him up. To my shock, Steinberger actually answered. Then I remembered the guy was *Tad Longmire's* attorney. He was probably used to late-night emergencies.

"Sorry to call at this early hour, Mr. Steinberger," I said. "I'm Tad Longmire's personal assistant, and this is kind of a crisis."

"Yes," he said wearily. "It always is."

"Uh ... I was wondering ..."

"If there's any way to get out of your contract?"

I winced. "Well ... yes."

Steinberger let out a sigh, then spoke as if he'd memorized the lines by rote. "There are exactly three sets of circumstances by which you can be released from your legal obligation. One, by mutual agreement to end said contract. Two, if Mr. Longmire fails to pay you. Three, if either party dies."

"Thank you," I said. "Any chance he won't pay me?"

"Doubtful. His trust fund is still loaded. And you're set up for direct payments."

My right eyebrow rose an inch. "Tad's forty years old. He's still a trust-fund baby?"

"There's no age limit on arrested development."

You aren't kidding.

I chewed my bottom lip. "What would it take to get Tad to mutually agree to release me from the contract?"

"Are you having sexual relations with him?" Steinberger asked.

"What?" I gasped. "No!"

"Good. My advice? Don't. Find a replacement who will. It's your best hope."

I frowned. "Unless he dies."

"Excuse me?" Steinberger said.

"Nothing."

"I thought so. Good luck, Ms. Diller."

"What about if I—" I said, but I was talking to a dial tone. Steinberger had already hung up.

I glanced over at Tad. He was splayed out on the bed like a sculpture carved by a drunken Michelangelo. I shook my head.

I've either got to find a hot-to-trot replacement, or make a run for it, change my name, and live in a mud hut surrounded by wild dogs.

As appealing as the mud hut was beginning to sound, I knew it wasn't really a viable option. If I left Tad, my dream of a movie career would go with it. At my age, and with Jared Thomas as my only other reference, I wouldn't get another chance in Hollywood. Not even as a personal assistant.

I wracked my brain. What else could I do? All those years of acting lessons had left me virtually unemployable in the real world. And, apparently, in Hollywood, too.

I couldn't sing like Tina Turner. I couldn't dance like J. Lo. I couldn't tell jokes like Margaret Cho. The only true gift I had was my ability to keep my closetful of festering feelings bottled up inside while wearing a fake smile and projecting a false sense of giving a crap.

In other words, I was perfectly suited to working in retail.

Crap!

I chewed my bottom lip. Whether I liked it or not, my star was firm-ly—and legally—hitched to a broken wagon named Tad Longmire.

I glanced around the messy kitchen in his trailer. At least cleaning it up would be someone else's problem at noon. Even so, I couldn't control myself. I picked up an empty bourbon bottle and threw it into the trash. As it slammed into the bottom of the can, the cold, hard truth hit me. If either one of us was ever going to have another shot at the silver screen, I was going to have to get Tad back on the wagon, and *keep* him there.

I caught my reflection in one of his many wall mirrors. The look on my face said it all.

Yeah, right. Good luck with that.

***

At exactly 9:37 a.m., after taking a taxi to recover my car, I returned to Tad's trailer in The Toad, ready to set the rest of my freshly hatched es-cape plan into motion.

Steeling myself, I took a deep breath, gulped my last sip of coffee, and climbed out of the Kia. I stuck my chin in the air, tugged the hem of my jacket for good measure, and marched determinedly into Tad's trailer.

The lout was still in bed, unconscious, just as I'd left him. I let out a huge sigh.

Dammit. How could a drunk jerk who hasn't bathed or shaved in days still look so infuriatingly sexy?

"Wake up, Tad," I said, leaning over the bed and shaking him on the shoulder.

Tad cracked open a bloodshot eye. "Wha?"

"I said, wake up."

His eye clamped shut. "Go away."

I frowned. This wasn't exactly how I'd envisioned my escape plan playing out in my head. It was nearly ten o'clock. Somehow, I had to get Tad's drunken butt up and out of this stupid trailer in less than two hours.

"Please?" I asked, gently jogging his side.

"Why?" he grunted.

"Because your phone keeps ringing."

It was true. Ever since I'd hung up with Mr. Steinberger at 4:15 this morning, Tad's phone had been buzzing like a masochistic moth in love with a sadistic bug zapper.

"Huh?" he grumbled, opening his eyes. They didn't quite focus on me. No doubt he was still lit from his three-day bender.

"What's your phone code?" I asked, holding up his cellphone.

"Why?" Tad groaned and tried to sit up. Only then did he finally notice that I'd tied both his hands to the bedposts.

Yes. *Bondage* was part of my newly hatched plan to get Tad sober.

The way I figured, Tad couldn't drink if couldn't reach a booze bottle. I squeezed the balled-up pair of gym socks concealed in my left hand. They were at the ready to stuff into his mouth if he started yelling.

"Hey," Tad said, tugging playfully on the nylon leggings I'd used to bind his wrists to the posts. A crooked smile broke the crusty corners of his mouth. "Kinky, Dorey. Me *likey*."

"Phone code," I said, sitting down on the edge of the bed beside him. "Somebody's been calling you all morning."

"So?"

"Come on, Tad. Cough it up. You made me give you mine."

Tad grinned lewdly. "Okay, Mistress Dorey. It's T-A-D-1."

I stifled an eye roll.

TAD-1. Of course it's TAD-1.

I punched the code into the phone.

"Hey, I need a Jack and Coke," Tad said, trying to sit up again. "Hair of the dog, you know."

"Yeah. Not happening. It's time your dog learned some new tricks."

"Yeah?" He shot me a lascivious leer. "Now we're talking. Bring it, Mistress Dorey!"

I hesitated for a second. I mean, how often did a gal like me get a chance to have her way with a gorgeous movie star? But then my self-preservation gene kicked in.

I really hated that gene sometimes.

I gritted my teeth, looked away, and hit the button to play Tad's voicemail over the cellphone speaker.

"Hello, Mr. Longmire?" a woman's voice said. "I'm Kerri Middleton from Sunshine City Studios. We're interested in having you audition for an upcoming television series we're putting together. Please contact us at your earliest convenience."

I nearly dropped the phone. "Tad! Someone's calling about a job offer!"

Tad didn't appear quite as excited. Actually, he was passed out cold again. I fought the urge to punch him where the sun didn't shine, and shook him awake again.

"What?" he grumbled.

"Be a good boy and listen to this. If you do, I'll go get you a latte. Okay?"

That perked him up a bit. "With bourbon?"

"No bourbon. Now listen!" I tried to replay the voicemail, but screwed it up. A second message played instead.

"Hi. This is Kerri Middleton calling again. We'd really like to hear from you as soon as possible, Mr. Longmire. We think you'd be perfect for the leading role in our upcoming project. Please contact us as soon as possible."

"Did you hear that?" I nearly squealed. "A job you're *perfect* for!"

Tad frowned. "What kind of perks are they offering?"

I fought back the urge to throttle him. The guy was so drunk he couldn't remember his name, but he remembered to ask for perks. "I don't know, Tad. Probably good ones. Should I call them back?"

Lines creased Tad's beautiful brow. "If they don't include free booze and burgers, I'm not doing it."

My face turned to stone. "Look, Tad. You've basically Blitzkrieged both of our careers. You'll do this audition or I'll ... I'll ..."

My train of thought derailed. Tad was shooting me that sexy grin again. The one that, six days ago, had nearly melted my tennis shoes. While his come-hither smile still made me catch my breath, in view of recent events its effect on me had cooled considerably.

Tad smirked. "Or *what*, Dorey? What are you gonna do?"

I steeled myself, then glanced around the room for something to threaten my new boss's life with. A pair of manicure scissors lying on the nightstand caught my eye. I snatched them up, then sat back down on the edge of the bed.

Tad laughed. "What are you gonna do, Dorey? Trim my cuticles?"

I leaned over Tad's prone body until our faces were inches from each other. "You'll audition for this role, Tad Longmire, or I'll cut your bangs off like that guy in *Dumb & Dumber*."

Tad gasped. "You wouldn't!"

"Try me."

I clicked redial on Tad's phone, praying someone at the studio worked on Saturdays. The phone rang once, then someone picked up. "Sunshine City Studios. Kerri Middleton speaking."

"Oh ... uh ... hello," I said, caught off guard. "I'm Doreen Diller, personal assistant to Tad Longmire."

"Oh. Hello!" the woman said enthusiastically. "Thanks so much for getting back to me. I've been calling for days. I thought Mr. Longmire might not be interested in the part."

Days?

I shot Tad an angry glance. He opened his mouth to speak. I held up the miniscule scissors and savagely cut the air with them like a psychotic barber. He shriveled.

"No, Mr. Longmire is *very* interested," I said. "Could you please email me the terms and audition script?"

"It would be my pleasure, Ms. Diller. Auditions begin on Monday. Does that work for you?"

"Auditions?" Tad grumbled. "Why should I have to—?"

I jabbed the tiny scissors toward his groin, Tad grimaced and drew up his knees.

"That should be no problem, Ms. Middleton," I said cheerfully.

"Excellent! I'll put you down for 3 p.m. on Monday. I'll email the script and terms to you right away. I'm so sorry, but I'm afraid you'll have to find your own accommodations in town. We're running on a tight budget. But we'll reimburse Mr. Longmire if he gets the part." Ms. Middleton's voice lowered to a whisper. "And between you and me, it's a done deal."

Feeling fifteen thousand pounds lighter, I said, "That's fine, Ms. Middleton. But could you keep this on the down-low?"

"Certainly. We'll be filming on a public beach. We'll have enough drive-by gawkers as it is."

"Thank you," I said. "We'll be there."

"Perfect!" she said. "May I recommend The Don CeSar Hotel?"

My left eyebrow rose an inch. "I've never heard of it. What part of L.A. is it in?"

Ms. Middleton giggled. "Oh. We're not in L.A., Ms. Diller. We're in St. Petersburg, Florida. See you on Monday!"

Chapter Six

Well played, Kerri Middleton.

I had to give her this—the woman from Sunshine City Studios had chutzpah. She'd hung up before I could respond to her hidden bomb that her film studio wasn't in L.A., but in St. Petersburg, Florida.

I shook my head. I wasn't sure I could get Tad out of this stupid *trailer* by noon today, much less get him to *Florida* by the day after tomorrow.

But the bigger question was, was it even worth the effort to try? My L.A. peeps always said nothing big ever came out of anywhere but Hollywood. But then again, Tad was nothing big here anymore, was he? And at this rate, I never *would* be.

Crap.

I sighed and glanced over at Tad. The guy was incredible. Despite having both hands bound to the bedposts, he'd fallen asleep again. There he was in all his glory. My fantasy crush reduced to a dirty, drunken ape tied to a mattress in an aluminum-clad cage.

And they say Tinseltown has lost its glitter ...

***

On my way to the coffee shop to pick up Tad's cinnamon mocha, dark-roast Honduran, iced oat-milk latte, I google-searched St. Petersburg, Florida. If memory served, one of my mother's relatives used to live there.

I'd never met whoever it was. But I vaguely recalled catching glimpses of the postcards Ma occasionally got in the mail. Sometimes she would show me the picture on the front. A baby alligator. An orange tree. Old people on green benches.

Based on that, I expected my google search to reveal a collage of shabbily dressed seniors waiting for a bus to catch the early-bird buffet. Instead, the images I found surprised me. White-sand beaches. Sunlit street festivals. Thriving downtown food and entertainment scenes. St. Pete looked like a mini L.A.—without the choking smog or the celebrity snobs.

Intrigued, I looked up Sunshine City Studios. It was one of a handful of small, independent production houses in the area. Online, the studio had decent ratings from several local businesses who'd hired them for what I assumed were TV commercials and recruitment videos.

Huh. I wonder what kind of project they have in mind for Tad.

***

I picked up Tad's order at the coffee shop. As I walked back, I sipped my cappuccino and began to warm to the idea of a trip to Florida.

I mean, what would be the harm?

As I reached Tad's trailer, my phone pinged. It was the email Kerri Middleton had promised. I set Tad's iced coffee on the front steps and glanced around to make sure no L.A. spies were watching. Then I sat down beside his frosty latte and opened the email.

To my surprise and delight, Tad's pay and terms were much better than I'd expected. The project, on the other hand, was much worse. Kerri's studio was shooting a pilot for a new TV series apparently aimed at drunken beach bums. Its working title was *Beer & Loathing in F.L.A.*

My nose crinkled.

I scrolled through the sample script and groaned. It read like a cross between *Two-Headed Shark Attack* and *Dude, Where's My Car?*—without any of that annoying plot stuff.

I blew out a disgusted breath.

Beer & Loathing was more of the same mindless, misogynistic rubbish that made women like me—of a certain age and IQ—abandon all hope for the evolution of mankind. It was exactly the kind of crap I'd made my goal in life to eradicate, once I made the bigtime.

If I made the bigtime.

I closed my eyes and let out a huge sigh.

The script was totally wrong.

But Kerri Middleton was totally right.

Tad Longmire was absolutely perfect for the role.

***

"I dunno," Tad said as I finished reading him the studio's proposal.

After making him promise to behave, I'd freed his right hand. Tad was sitting up on the edge of the bed, calmly sipping his iced latte through a straw—as if being tied to the bedpost happened to him *every* Saturday.

Yuck. Maybe it did.

"What do you mean, you don't know?" I asked, hiding my frustration under an ever-thinning veneer of syrupy sweetness. "This is an excellent offer!"

Tad shrugged, his dirty blond hair sticking up like a cockatoo's crest. "TV again? I'm not so sure it's a good career move."

My face went slack.

And boning the director's wife was?

I plastered on the extra-special personal assistant smile I kept in a jar for emergencies. Seeing as how Tad had destroyed my other prospects, I *had* to keep in his good graces. He was the only life raft I had left.

If Tad went down, I went with him.

The way I saw it, I could either stab a hole in the raft, or get busy inflating Tad's ego. I chose the latter, but kept the little cuticle scissors handy, just in case.

"Look, Tad," I cooed. "You were fabulous as the heartthrob doctor on *Days of Our Lies.*"

He shrugged. "I know. But it was just a daytime soap opera for old ladies."

My eyebrows shot to my hairline. "I watched it all the time!"

"Hey, if the orthopedic shoe fits, wear it," Tad said with a smirk.

I'm younger than you, you philandering jerk!

I was about to give Tad a piece of my mind when I remembered *Hollywood Survival Guide* Tip #3: *If all else fails, start slinging compliments like an angry chimp at the zoo.*

I reset my attitude and cleared my throat. "Look. *Days of Our Lies* got you a lot of great exposure, Tad. Don't forget, George Clooney got his big break after doing that TV show *ER*. And you have to admit, the salary for this project is pretty generous."

Tad took a sip of latte and shrugged. "Yeah. But—"

"Come on, Tad. It's just three weeks of shooting. Think of it as a little vacation from L.A. You know. Time to work on your tan and let things cool down a bit."

"Cool down?" An indignant line creased the brow of Tad's impossibly handsome face. "What exactly are you implying needs to 'cool down'?"

I gritted my teeth into an Emmy-worthy smile.

Your nuclear meltdown, perchance?

"Give them time to miss you," I said smugly. "Make them come crawling back."

Tad nodded slowly, a sly grin formed on his lips. "Hmm."

"The show is set on the beach," I said in the kind of voice mothers used to woo kids into eating strained peas. "Doesn't that sound like fun? It'll be filmed on location in a quirky little beach shack."

Tad frowned. "A shack?"

"I meant *cottage*."

"Uh-huh. What's my role?"

You play a drunken, burned-out, misogynistic dirtbag. I know it'll be a stretch. But with your magnificent acting talents, I think you can handle it.

"The lead, of course!" I said brightly.

Tad nodded and chewed the straw sticking up from the lid on his latte. "I gotta think about it."

We've got to be out of this freaking trailer in 30 minutes. We don't have time for you to think about it, you pompous, pampered, freak of nature!

I took a deep breath. It was time to sell this idea like my life depended on it. I leaned in closer and played my ace in the hole.

"Did I mention that you'll be surrounded by gorgeous beach bunnies in teeny-weeny bikinis?"

Tad licked his lips.

I winked and grinned. "Say yes and I'll untie your other hand."

Tad smiled. "Okay, Dorey. Yes."

I clapped my hands. "Excellent decision, Mr. Longmire!"

I reached over the bed and used the manicure scissors to cut the nylon legging binding Tad's left hand.

"Now, mister," I said. "*You* get in the shower and clean yourself up. *I'll* make all the arrangements for Monday."

"Okay, Dorey." Tad's freed hand landed on my waist. He glanced up at me with those bedroom eyes of his. "What would I do without you?"

I swatted his hand away. "Just about *anything*, I'd say."

Tad studied me for a second, then laughed. "You're probably right."

A tentative smile curled my lips. "You made the right decision, Tad. Now be a good boy and scoot!"

"Okay. But call a limo for me. I'm not going anywhere in that butt-ugly car of yours."

"Yes, sir."

As Tad yawned lazily, then slowly stood, the seconds we had left before Jared had us forcibly thrown from the trailer ticked off in my head.

Apparently, Tad wasn't bothered by such minutia. He continued to languidly stretch his beautiful torso for what seemed like half an hour. Then, finally, he dragged himself off to the bathroom like a teenager heading to the principal's office.

As soon as the bathroom door closed behind him, I snatched up my phone and got busy dialing.

Phase one of Escape Plan A is complete. Now, all I have to do is get Tad to Florida and under contract before they find out what a jerk he is. If that fails, I'll resort to Escape Plan B.

I'll drown Tad in the Gulf of Mexico myself.

Chapter Seven

Traveling with Tad Longmire was like holding onto the leash of an irresistibly adorable, but totally untrained puppy. Every woman old enough to drive stopped to gush over him—but those who lingered too long were in danger of getting their legs humped.

It was Monday morning, and I'd been in Tad's employ for exactly one week. Yesterday, at his ultra-fabulous apartment, he'd proven to be quite the hands-on boss. Even so, I'd followed Tad's lawyer's advice and thwarted my new boss's flirty advances.

Thank goodness there'd been a lock on the guestroom door.

Actually, I was fairly certain Tad was enjoying the conquest challenge I presented. He probably considered me a shag to save for a rainy day. But now that I'd discovered the charming puppy was actually a rabid wolf, it would take a typhoon to get me under the sheets with him.

During the five-hour flight from L.A. to Tampa, I kept Tad out of trouble by going over the audition script for the pilot episode of *Beer & Loathing*. All was going well until nature called. When I returned from the bathroom, I discovered a star-struck flight attendant slipping Tad her phone number—along with a little something extra in his Coca Cola. By the time we landed in Florida, Dr. Jekyll was displaying telltale signs of Mr. Rye.

Totally not good.

"I can't believe all the women that keep throwing themselves at you," I whispered as Tad downed his fourth Coke, which I was certain had been spiked with bourbon.

He grinned. "Can I help it if I'm irresistible?"

Can I help it if I want to punch you in the gonads?

Given how much he'd drank, a normal person would've probably needed a wheelchair to get off the plane. But professional drunken letch that Tad Longmire was, he managed to stagger his way through the terminal with me, drag his luggage off the carousel, and tumble into a cab under his own steam.

"Downtown St. Petersburg," I said to the cabby as I climbed into the backseat with Tad. "How long is the ride?"

"Twenty, maybe twenty-five minutes."

Crap. It's already 2:25. Thanks to Tad's inebriated bumbling, we're cutting it way too close.

"Thank you," I said to the driver. "We're supposed to be downtown at three o'clock. Can you make that happen?"

The cabbie eyed me in the rearview mirror. "I'll do my best." He smiled and hit the gas pedal, sending me tumbling into Tad's lap.

"*Now* we're talkin, Dorey," Tad said, grinning at me lewdly.

"Ugh," I grunted, scrambling out of his arms. I rifled through my purse for something that might sober up my drunken disaster of a boss. I figured mace would only aggravate him. And unfortunately, I'd left my Taser at home...

"Here, eat these," I said, pulling out a bag of airline peanuts.

"Kiss me, first," he said.

Any other time I'd have probably gone for it. That's how infuriatingly hot the guy was—even with a nose still swollen from Borloff's right-handed punch. But, as usual, my timing was impeccably bad. If I didn't get Tad under control and pronto, my last chance at a career in showbiz would go right down the toilet along with his.

"Settle down, hotshot," I said. "Now, be a good boy and open up for a peanut."

"Make me." Tad pursed his lips and giggled like a naughty child.

"Zoom zoom, here comes the peanut train," I said, wishing I had a vise to crack his nuts with. Tad grinned and let me pop a peanut into his baby-bird mouth. "Good boy."

"Ooo, water," Tad said, crunching the peanut and gawking out the cab window. I glanced out and realized we were crossing a long bridge over what I assumed was Tampa Bay.

"Yes. Pretty," I said, nodding at the shimmering water. But I didn't really see it. I was too busy praying the peanuts would work a miracle on Tad's blood-alcohol and render him coherent enough for the impending audition.

Tad put a hand on my thigh. I let out a sigh.

Geez. I'm totally *not getting paid enough for this crap.*

***

Either my prayers had been answered, or Tad was a bigger pro than I'd given him credit for. By the time the cabbie pulled up to the address I'd handed him, Tad was sitting up straight. He'd also regained control of nearly all of his facial muscles.

"This is it," the taxi driver said.

Tad shot me a confused look. "Where are we?"

Oh. Dear. Lord.

"I hope you're joking," I said, grabbing him by the shoulder and yanking him out of the cab. "Please. For the love of God, try to act sober, would you?"

As the taxi drove away, I realized we weren't in a warehouse district, like I'd expected. Instead, Tad and I stood in front of an unassuming, faded red door attached to a two-story brick building. There was no placard on the door. Uncertain, I checked the address Kerri Middleton had given me. The numbers matched.

"This must be it," I said. "Sunshine City Studios."

"You sure?" Tad asked.

No, I wasn't. Oddly, the building was on Central Avenue, in the middle of an old-fashioned, main-street type area. To either side of the studio stood an eclectic mix of small, glass-storefront boutiques, trendy coffee shops, and mom-n-pop diners. My stomach sank. Was this place a dive? Had I just made a huge mistake?

Then I remembered *Hollywood Survival Guide* Tip #4. *Never EVER look back. Especially on a first date.*

"Of course this is the place," I said, straightening Tad's tie. "Now, smile."

I knocked on the door, half expecting it to be answered by some shuffle-footed, dirty-haired Millennial with a nose ring and tat sleeves. But I was wrong—again.

"Welcome to Sunshine City Studios," said a tall, slender, elegantly dressed woman in her mid-fifties. She opened the door wide, then beckoned us in with a graceful swoop of her hand. "You're right on time. I'm Kerri Middleton."

"Oh! Hello," I said. "We're—"

"Hurry. Don't let the mosquitos in," Kerri said, tucking a lock of silver hair behind her ear.

"Come on, Tad," I said, grabbing him by the arm and scurrying inside.

Kerri shut the door behind us, then assessed us with sharp, hazel eyes. "You must be Tad," she said, skimming over him quickly before turning her attention to me. "And you must be Doreen Diller."

"Yes," I said. "We're glad to be—"

"Is this where we'll be filming?" Tad asked, crinkling his swollen nose hard enough to make him wince in pain.

"No. Just the auditions," Kerri said. "We do most of our filming on site. Please, follow me."

Kerri turned and marched down a hallway, her shiny, kitten heels clicking on the hardwood floor. She led us to a room with exposed brick walls and a cozy sitting area furnished with a teal couch and two white leather chairs.

"Have a seat. I'll let Marshall know you're here. Would you like something to drink?"

"Yeah," Tad said. "I'll take a—"

"Coke, if you've got it," I said. "Two Cokes?"

Kerri's eyes crinkled as she offered us what appeared to be a genuine smile. I wasn't sure, having not seen one since I moved to L.A.

"Coming right up," she said. "I won't be long."

As soon as Kerri left, I shot Tad a death-ray glare. "No more drinking! Not until you've got the part. Don't ruin this for us!"

"*Us*?" Tad laughed. "I thought this was *my* audition."

"It is, but—"

"Who's Marshall?" he grumbled.

I took a deep breath and fought the urge to hit Tad over the head with my purse. "Marshall Lazzaro. He's the director of the project you're auditioning for. We've been over this a dozen times! Now, what are the rules?"

Tad's handsome head cocked to one side. "Rules? I don't know about—"

I thrust my hand two inches from his face and made scissoring motions with my first two fingers. Then I grabbed a lock of my bangs with my free hand and used my finger scissors to cut the hunk of hair off at my scalp.

Tad blanched. "Okay already. The rule is, no drinking."

"Right. *And?*"

"No boning the director's wife."

"Good boy." I patted his leg. "Play nice and land the job, okay? It'll be fun. You'll see. Like a beach vacation."

Kerri returned holding two cans of soda. She noticed my hand on Tad's knee. I jerked it away and took the Coke she offered.

"You look just like your headshot," she said, handing Tad his can of Coke. "Except for the nose."

Tad frowned at his soda. She hadn't opened it for him. "Yeah, well—"

"Just allergies," I said, cracking the tab on my can of soda. I quickly switched it with Tad's before he could make a fuss.

"I see," Kerri said. "Well, I think we can work around it. Actually, Tad, why don't you go on in? Marshall is eager to meet you."

Tad stopped mid-slurp. "Huh? Oh. Okay."

"He's just through there," Kerri said, motioning toward a solid oak door.

"Thanks for the soda," I said, standing up to join Tad.

Kerri put a hand on my shoulder. "Just Tad. For now."

"Oh. Okay." I shot Tad a thumbs up. "Show them what you've got, superstar!"

"Right-O, Dorey." Tad wagged his eyebrows. "I'll knock 'em dead."

I turned my worried cringe into a smile, then watched Tad amble casually toward the door, my entire future riding on his wobbly steps.

You'd better knock 'em dead, Tad Longmire. Or I'll kill you myself.

Chapter Eight

"So," Kerri said, turning to face me as Tad disappeared behind the director's door at Sunshine City Studios. "How did you get tangled up in this mess, anyway?"

"You mean showbiz?" I asked.

"I mean Tad Longmire."

I blanched. "You ... you *know* about Tad?"

Kerri's left eyebrow arched. "Anybody with an internet connection knows about Tad Longmire. Why else do you think we figured we had a chance at hiring him?"

I grimaced and fiddled with the tab on my Coke can. "Well, I think the whole story about him going ballistic was blown out of proportion. You see—"

"Loyalty," Kerri said, cutting me off. "I like that. But listen, sister. You can save the excuses. I'm a big girl. I know a player when I see one. Tad and Marshall? They're two of a kind. They'll get along fine. It's the people like us—the ones who do the actual *work*—who need to watch each other's backs."

I stared up at her, wide-eyed. Kerri Middleton didn't play around. That was fine by me. I was used to blunt. But was there a chance she was actually sincere as well? That she actually played fair?

I thought back to something I'd read in my *Hollywood Survival Guide*. Tip #6: *Nothing is fair in love, war, or movie making.*

I chewed my lip, wondering whether to trust Kerri. She was in movie making, but then again, this wasn't Hollywood. It was St. Petersburg. Maybe the rules were different here. Plus, there was something about Kerri that drew me to her. I just couldn't quite put my finger on it ...

"So, what's the real score with Tad?" Kerri asked.

"Honestly?"

Kerri smirked "Of course. Aren't you *always*?"

I blushed. "I have to admit, when it comes to being frank, I'm a bit out of practice. L.A. stands for Liars Anonymous, in case you didn't know."

"Really." Kerri smiled. "I always wondered about that."

"You've never been?"

"No. But I'd like to visit a Hollywood studio someday. It's on my bucket list."

"Well, don't bother," I said. "Whatever you might have imagined goes on behind the scenes of making a movie, add to it a horny, hairy-backed director, a bowl of cocaine, and—god help me—a bubble machine."

Kerri laughed. "Yet you somehow managed to survive with some integrity intact."

I stared at her, stunned, as if I'd just been blessed by the Dali Lama. "Why do you think I have integrity?"

"Easy," Kerri said. "You can still blush."

"Oh." I let a smile curl my lips. "Thanks." Then, all of a sudden, it hit me. That was it! That odd thing about Kerri I couldn't place. She'd just named it herself.

Integrity.

Kerri seemed to have it. Off the bat, I couldn't think of another person in my life who did. Quite possibly not even *me*—not much, anyway. I decided right then that Kerri Middleton deserved to know what she was getting into by hiring Tad, warts and all.

"Okay, here's the honest truth," I confessed. "Tad Longmire is gorgeous, obviously. And he's actually a really decent actor. But when it comes to discretion? Forget it. Tad puts the 'pro' in inappropriate."

"What do you mean?" Kerri asked.

"He can be demanding. Whiny. Hot-tempered. And most of all, lecherous. But he's not all that horrible unless he drinks. Then? Well, all bets are off."

Kerri's eyes narrowed. "Does he use hard drugs?"

"No," I blurted. "Well, I've only been his assistant for a week. So, none that I'm aware of. As far as I can tell, his main weaknesses are brown liquor and red-headed bimbos."

Kerri pursed her lips and nodded slowly. I steeled myself for rejection. Good thing I'd purchased flexible return tickets. I sighed. This time tomorrow, I'd be back in L.A., resuming my pathetic life as a stand-in for headless dumpster-hookers.

"Okay," Kerri said. "I can work with that."

"Really?" I said, nearly springing from my chair.

"Yes, really."

"Oh! Thank you, Kerri!" I squealed, shaking her hand. "I promise I'll do my best to keep Tad on track."

"Good. Now, one final question." Kerri locked eyes with me. "How do you feel about the project, based on the sample script?"

Aww, crap! The script was total kaka. Another idiotic, shiftless beach bum who—for some inexplicable reason—is a magnet for hot beach babes. What a crock of ...

I swallowed hard, recalling the sage advice in the *Hollywood Survival Guide*. Tip #7 read: *The path to stardom is lined with lies—fling them around like pavers.*

I could feel Kerri's hazel eyes scrutinizing me. "I ... uh ...," I fumbled.

Come on, Doreen! Just say you like the stupid thing and the job is in the bag. JUST DO IT!

I hesitated, looking for a clue in Kerri's face. The woman could've won a national poker playoff.

Screw it.

"Honestly, Kerri?" I said, mentally pulling my bags off the luggage carousel back in L.A. "Nothing personal, but the script is infantile rubbish. *Beer & Loathing* is just the kind of sexist crap that makes me want to stab the author in the gonads."

Kerri snorted—something I'd never have expected from someone who looked so proper and elegant. "You certainly don't mince words, do you?" she said.

"I'm sorry," I said, wanting to kick myself. "I thought that—"

Kerri held her palm out, a signal for me to stop talking. "No need to apologize, Doreen. I appreciate your candor. So I'll be frank, too. Marshall wrote the script himself. I agree, its total garbage. But he's the boss. His father bought him this studio, along with all the assorted toys and gadgets. So, like it or not, Marshall has final say on the project."

I sighed. "Just like Tad."

Kerri smiled tiredly. "In a lot of ways, it's still a man's world, isn't it?"

"Yeah. As much as I'd like to change that."

"I would, too." Kerri pursed her lips, then locked eyes with me again. "So, can I count on you to keep a good attitude, even though the project is a boatload of crap?"

I let out a short laugh. "Believe me, if L.A. has taught me anything, it's how to steer my gondola through a sewer and still belt out a love song."

Kerri grinned. "I can believe that." She cocked her head. "I'm curious. Why do you stay with Tad if he's such a lout? Are you two, you know...?"

"No!" I said. "Nothing like that. I ... I stupidly signed a twelve-month contract as his personal assistant." I smiled sheepishly. "Only fifty-one more weeks to go."

Kerri winced. "Ouch. Why'd you do it?"

I shook my head and sighed. "Tad promised to make me a star."

Kerri's bright hazel eyes dulled. "Just like in the movies."

"I know," I groaned. "I should've known better, for crying out loud. I'm 39 years old and I'm still a total sap. It's just that ... it's hard to give up on your dreams, you know?"

"Yes," Kerri said. "Believe me, I know exactly how you feel."

The convincing tone of her words made me sit up straight.

"Okay," I said. "You know why *I'm* here. Let me ask you the same question. You seem like a smart, well-put-together woman. How'd *you* get tangled up in the production of something called *Beer & Loathing*?"

Kerri shot me a tired smile. "Someone in the room has to be the designated grown-up."

My eyebrows rose an inch. "Excuse me?"

Kerri sat down in the leather chair next to mine. "I'm here as a favor to an old friend. Marshall's mother and I were best pals before she passed away seven years ago. Marshall was just sixteen. His father, Dave Lazzaro, well, he kind of left Marshall to run wild."

I fidgeted with my can of Coke. "Oh. I'm sorry to hear that."

"Thank you. Anyway, after Marshall flunked out of college last year, Dave set him up in this studio. He was hoping to give his son something productive to focus on. Dave hired me to help keep an eye on both Marshall and his own financial investment." Kerri shot me a wry smile. "So, basically, my job is to make sure Marshall doesn't swing naked off a cliff and take Dave's bank account down with him."

"Wait," I said. "So this whole studio is just some privileged brat's *hobby*?"

"No. I didn't mean that at all," Kerri said. "We aim to make a serious go of it. We've already filmed several commercials and training videos for local businesses. *Beer & Loathing* will be our first stab at a real production, though."

"So, no one here has any experience?" I asked, trying not to groan.

Kerri shook her head. "No, that's not correct. We have a decent cameraman on salary. And we hire professional staff on a temp basis. You know, for makeup and set production, that kind of stuff."

"But with a 23-year-old kid directing, how—"

Kerri locked eyes with me. "Just so you know, Dave didn't hire me for my mothering skills. I've never had children of my own. What I bring to the table is direct industry experience, along with tons of local connections."

"Oh," I said. "What did you do before?"

"I was the co-anchor for Channel 22 news for 15 years. But like an idiot, I had the audacity to age." She shook her head. "Last year, the powers that be decided I'd gotten a bit too old for the job. They handed me a silver parachute to match my hair. You know how it goes."

I sighed. "Yeah, I do."

Kerri's perfectly glossed lips formed a wistful smile. "Funny thing is, my male co-anchor is ten years older than me. Paul looks like a walrus in a cheap suit, but he's still on the air and going strong."

"They were fools to let you go," I said. "You're so beautiful. And ... *elegant*."

"Thank you," Kerri said. "But to be honest, this job at Sunshine City Studios suits me fine. It's fun. There's a ton less bureaucratic bull to deal with. And there's no pressure to look like a plastic supermodel all the time." She grinned and leaned in closer to me. "Want to know a little secret?"

"Uh, sure," I said.

She winked. "Carbs are delicious."

I laughed. "Yes. They *totally* are."

Kerri sat back and sighed. "I only wish this project Marshall wants to do was less ... what would you say?"

"Sophomoric?" I offered. "Neanderthal?"

Kerri laughed. "Exactly."

The door to the director's office flew open. Tad and Marshall came tumbling out, slapping each other's backs like they'd just won the NFL playoffs.

"Looks like we've found our leading man," Marshall said, beaming at Tad.

Tad wagged his eyebrows at me mischievously and said, "I'll drink to that!"

Chapter Nine

"That takes care of the paperwork," Kerri said, handing me a red folder. Inside were two copies of the contract Tad had just signed with Sunshine City Studios. "We start shooting the pilot in the morning."

"So soon?" I asked, winking at Kerri.

At my request, she'd convinced Marshall to agree to the ultra-quick start, arguing it would save money on production. While that was true, the real reason was my need to keep Tad in check. By beginning filming tomorrow, my wayward boss wouldn't have enough time to get into any real trouble—fingers crossed.

I smiled at Tad. "Well, this is exciting! I guess we should get over to our hotel and rest up for the big day tomorrow. You've got lines to rehearse."

"What?" Marshall objected, his freckled, college-boy face aghast. "Don't you want to see where we'll be filming? It's right on the beach!"

"That's right," Tad said as if he'd just remembered we were in Florida. He high-fived Marshall. "I'm in. Let's go!"

"Well ..." I hesitated, feeling a bit like Tad's parole officer.

"I'll drive," Marshall said. "How about that, Doreen?" He slid a pair of expensive-looking aviator sunglasses from atop of his strawberry blond head and onto the bridge of his suntanned nose.

I grimaced. "Well, it's just that—"

"Come on," Marshall said. "It's not far from where you're staying at the Don CeSar. I'll drop you there afterward. I promise. It'll be fun!"

I glanced over at Kerri. She shrugged. The corners of her mouth crinkled upward, betraying a stifled grin. I was about to object again, but suddenly my feet lifted off the floor.

"Lighten up, Dorey," Tad said, sweeping me up into his arms. "Marshall, you get the luggage. I've got the girl."

Marshall grinned. "Tad, I bet you *always* get the girl."

Tad squeezed my thigh and winked. "You better believe I do."

***

48

Tad and Marshall hooted like frat boys as we cruised down Central Avenue in his shiny red Mercedes convertible. Florida's tropical sun beamed warmly on our faces. The guys were stretched out in the front seat. I was crammed into the tiny afterthought of a backseat. Tad had unceremoniously dumped me into it after I'd opted out of sitting in his lap. Kerri had opted out of the trip.

Well played yet again, Kerri Middleton.

As we sped along, the wind whipped my shoulder-length brown hair around like a palm tree in a hurricane. "How far is it?" I asked, swiping at an errant lock of hair flitting around my eyes.

"Not far," Marshall said. "Relax, Dorey. Enjoy the ride."

"It's *Doreen*," I said.

Marshall appeared confused. "But Tad calls you—"

"Tad writes my paycheck," I said, cutting him off. "When *you* do, you can call me whatever you like."

Marshall's back stiffened. "Yes, ma'am."

I winced. "Except for *ma'am*."

Marshall's brow furrowed. "No? What should I call you, then?"

"Sorry," I said, softening my tone. "It's just that I hate ... never mind. How about just calling me *Doreen*?"

Marshall nodded. "You got it, Doreen."

"Geez," Tad said. "Chill out, Ms. Minion. Boss's orders."

"Jerk," I muttered to myself, sinking lower into the narrow wedge masquerading as a back seat. I glanced in the rearview mirror. The small cluster of high rises that made up downtown St. Petersburg were fading farther and farther from view as we followed the sun westward.

After a few miles, the colorful, renovated shops and storefronts of St. Pete's Grand Central District gave way to generic, neglected strip centers. The startling contrast had me wondering how long the shiny new façade of friendship between the two men in the front seat would last.

Tad was nearly twice Marshall's age. On the other hand, just as Kerri had hinted, the two men shared something in common with each other *and* the section of town we currently traveled. They all appeared to be suffering from the same problem of arrested development.

"Ooop!" I blurted as we sped across a small bridge. Flying over the span had, for a second, sent the Mercedes airborne—along with my stomach.

"Welcome to Treasure Island," Marshall said, beaming proudly. He gestured toward the right side of the road.

I glanced that way and spied a lifesize cutout of an old-timey pirate. Dressed in full regalia—from feathered hat to peg leg—the swashbuckler stood astride an open treasure chest full of orange citrus fruits.

"Treasure Island," I whispered to myself. A vague memory played hide-and-seek with my brain. "Cute," I said, as an unexpected smile tugged at my lips.

We crossed another bridge and the west-bound lanes abruptly dead-ended. Marshall pulled up to the stoplight and said, "Doreen, let me be the first to welcome you to the best beach in the whole entire world."

"What? Where?" I asked. Then I spotted it. Straight ahead. Peeking out from behind the 1950's-era Thunderbird Hotel, the sparkling Gulf of Mexico twinkled like blue diamonds in the golden sun.

"Not L.A., but pretty nice," Tad said, glancing around as we waited for the light to turn green.

"It's *better* than L.A.," Marshall said, ribbing Tad with his elbow. "Wait till you see the tiki bars!"

Tad grinned. "*Now* we're talking. Carry on, my wayward son."

Marshall hooted, then turned the convertible left onto Gulf Boulevard. As the sun beat down, we cruised south along a strip of low-rise hotels, funky gift shops, and kitschy restaurants catering to the tourist trade.

The sidewalks lining both sides of the road were filled with a steady procession of deeply tanned people dressed mainly in bathing suits and beach cover-ups. Many of them dragged small canvas wagons behind them, laden down with beach chairs, umbrellas, and coolers.

I'd seen Elvis movies set in beach towns like this. But I'd never believed they really existed. Growing up in the Pacific Northwest, our beaches were cold and gray and dangerous. If you weren't careful, you'd be swept out in a fast-rising tide. Or crushed between huge, water-soaked logs.

The only danger I spotted on Treasure Island was getting sunburned.

The thought made me touch my nose. It was warm and tender. I was just about to ask Marshall to stop and let me buy a sunhat when he turned right onto a small side road. He drove a couple of blocks past a few condos and houses, then pulled the tiny red convertible up to a small bungalow that could've been plucked from a fantasy in my mind.

The adorable cottage was painted turquoise blue. Its high-gabled roof was clad in sheets of tin. Lemon-yellow shutters lined the large, sunny windows. A set of wide French doors opened onto a front porch that ran the length of the cottage. In the shade of the porch, wicker loungers beckoned invitingly, each fitted with comfy-looking cushions in pastel tropical prints.

"What do you think?" Marshall asked, cutting the ignition on the Mercedes.

"What do I *think*?" I asked. I caught a glimpse of myself in the rearview mirror. My nose was red, but I was grinning from ear to ear. "I *think* this will do just fine, Marshall."

We climbed out of the convertible. I was dying to take a peek inside the cottage, but Marshall led us away from it and toward the beach. Across a wooden boardwalk flanked by sea oats lay a wide expanse of sugar-white sand and the glistening shore of the Gulf of Mexico.

I had to stop and admire the contrast. Treasure Island was the polar opposite of the beaches I'd grown up with along the Washington coastline. Here, the sand was warm—and gleaming white. The tide was calm and playful. And instead of tangles of deadly driftwood waiting to drag you to your death, countless seashells dotted the sand like confetti, as if inviting you to a non-stop party.

As I took in the gorgeous view, I spotted a huge, pink, castle-like building along the shoreline a mile or so south of us. I recognized it from the internet. It was the famous Don CeSar, our destination for the night. Tad had insisted on first-class accommodations. From what I could see, the hotel certainly fit the bill. Suddenly, the urge for a warm shower, clean cotton sheets, and sushi delivery overwhelmed me.

"The location looks great," I said to Marshall. "But we should get going. We need to check into the Don CeSar. It's been a long day and I'm exhausted."

"Can't we just stay here at the cottage?" Tad asked. He pointed to a thatched-roof structure a few doors down. "Look. There's a beach bar right over there!"

Marshall chewed his lip, then shrugged. "Well, I guess so. Sure. Why not? But I gotta warn you. There's not much in the fridge. And there's no room service like you're used to in L.A."

"Sure there is," Tad said, draping his arm across my shoulder. "I've got Dorey right here."

Chapter Ten

Sometime around ten o'clock, I left Tad and Marshall swapping war stories from their barstools at the Crooked Conch. That was the kitschy name of the open-air tiki bar Tad had spotted when we'd first arrived at the beach cottage late that afternoon.

Thankfully the bar was only a hundred yards or so down the beach from the little turquoise bungalow where we were staying. And even though I was dragging tired from jet lag when I'd set off alone, I enjoyed the peaceful walk back to the cottage.

The feel of the soft sand on my bare feet. The warm salt air in my lungs. The starry sky overhead. The absence of Tad and all the other L.A. noise. They all intertwined to soothe me like a lullaby.

With Marshall babysitting Tad, I was finally free to let my guard down a little and relax. And I knew exactly how I wanted to spend my "me" time. I brushed my teeth, washed my face, slipped into my pajamas, and snuggled into the fluffy feather bed in the guest room.

Ahhh!

The last thing I remember was picking up Marshall's script, reading the first line, and then promptly nodding off to sleep.

***

What is that weird noise?

I cracked open an eye. Faint bluish morning light was peeking through the slits between the bedroom-window blinds.

The strange noise repeated itself.

Mwack. Argk. Yark.

It sounded like a cat coughing up a hairball. I got up and padded into the kitchen, looking for a wayward beach kitty. What I found instead was a tomcat named Tad.

He was dry-heaving into the kitchen sink.

Lovely.

"Morning," Marshall said, startling me.

53

I whirled around to find the young director sitting at the kitchen table sipping a can of energy drink and snickering.

"Gotta excuse Tad," he said. "He had a rough night."

I shot a worried glance at Tad. "What did you do to him?"

"Tequila shots. My bad. I thought he was a pro."

I grimaced. "Tad is. He's just ... not as young as you are."

"No kidding," Marshall said. "From here on out, I promise to go easier on the old man."

"Old man!" Tad grumbled. "I'm not—" But he couldn't finish his thought. Interrupted by another wave of nausea, he doubled over the sink again and imitated coughing up a mouse.

"What are we going to do?" I asked Marshall. Bright-eyed and grinning, apparently he'd bounced back from a night of drunken debauchery like a shiny rubber ball. "Don't we start filming any minute?"

Marshall shrugged. "No worries, Dorey. I mean, *Doreen*. Look. The opening scene is just Tad in bed, hungover."

"I guess that's not too far a stretch," I said, glancing over at Tad.

"No stretch at *all*," Marshall said. "Actually, the way he looks now is *perfect*. Tad won't need makeup or a wardrobe. And he's already got a wicked case of bedhead." He smirked at me. "You know what, Doreen? You should be paying *me* for doing *your* job."

I smiled wryly. "I would, but I don't think you'd be impressed with the wages."

Tad groaned into the sink. "A little help here, please?"

Marshall laughed. "I'll get the old guy in bed. You get him some coffee. I already got a pot going."

"Oh." Surprised at not having to deal with Tad for a change, Marshall's offer was one I couldn't refuse. I grinned. "Okay. You got yourself a deal."

***

After tucking Tad in bed with some aspirin and a cup of coffee, I joined Marshall back in the cottage's cozy kitchen for my own badly needed cup of java.

"Good thing all Tad has to do is lie in bed with two girls," I said, pouring coffee into a bright yellow mug. "Inside scoop. It's one of his specialties."

Marshall laughed. "I *bet* it is. He does all right for an old guy."

I thought about telling Marshall to stop calling Tad *old*, but I was getting way too much enjoyment out of how it made Tad wince.

"I started reading your script last night," I said, dumping cream into my coffee.

"And?" Marshall asked.

Crap.

I mentally kicked myself for bringing it up. From what I'd read so far, the freckled frat boy's screenplay was a jumble of mismatched ideas. A heap of incoherent crap. I winced, shoveled a spoonful of sugar into my coffee, then forced a smile and turned to face Marshall.

He was leaning back in his chair, sporting a smug expression that told me he was bracing for an avalanche of compliments. While I *did* feel like unloading on him, compliments weren't exactly what I had in mind. I bought myself a few seconds to think by stirring the sugar into my coffee.

"Well?" he asked.

"Uh ... to be honest, I don't exactly get the plot, Marshall," I said, joining him at the table.

His head cocked slightly. "What don't you get about it?"

Cornered, I stared into the swirling void of my coffee. "Well, Tad shags a bunch of women, all of whom end up getting eaten by a shark."

"Right."

"I don't see the connection. The only thing that kind of makes sense is the ending. You know, where he winds up in a gutter alone, clutching his Teddy bear."

"Oh, man," Marshall said. "Haven't you seen that movie *Inception*?"

I looked up at him. "With DiCaprio? Of course. I'm from L.A. I've seen every movie ever made. But I—"

"It's just like *that*, only different." Marshall's eyes gleamed with creative spark—either that or depravity. L.A. had taught me the two were surprisingly close bedfellows. "You see, in *Inception*, DiCaprio can't tell if he's in a dream or not. So he keeps a dreidel in his pocket. If he can spin the top, he knows he's awake."

"Uh ... okay. But what's that got to do with *your* project?"

"Don't you see?" Marshall said. "Tad spins a beer bottle to see if he's dreaming or not. But whoever it lands on ends up dead. Did he kill the girls? Or did the shark get them? Then Tad wakes up in a ditch clutching his childhood Teddy bear, thinking it's all been a dream."

My nose crinkled.

Don't you mean nightmare?

"Err ... has it been?" I asked. "A dream, I mean?"

Marshall grinned, then winked. "Who knows? Tune in next season to find out."

"Think *Inception* meets *The Beach Bum* meets *Jaws*," a familiar voice said behind me.

I turned in my chair to see Kerri Middleton standing in the front hallway. She was wearing a crisp, cotton sundress and clutching a white paper sack that read *Fray's Donuts*.

My eyebrow shot up. "Okay," I said. "But the script reads like a patchwork of disjointed ideas."

"Kinda," Marshall said. "But I want *Beer & Loathing* to do something that's never been done before."

"Uh ... so did Dr. Frankenstein," I said. "And see where that got him?"

"Oh!" Marshall said. "That's *it*, Doreen! We could add a monster!"

Kerri shot me a pained glance and put a finger to her lips. I got the message.

Don't add more nuggets to the flaming poo poo platter.

I dropped the topic, and Kerri dropped the bag of donuts on the table. "Hey," she said. "If there's an audience for *Sharknado V*, there's bound to be an audience for *Beer & Loathing*, right?"

I cast a concerned eye at Kerri. "Uh, sure. But all those films you guys are referencing are movies. This is a *TV series*. It's a whole different animal."

"In what way?" Kerri asked as Marshall dug into the bag of donuts.

"Well ... in just about *every* way," I said. "Story length. Continuing story threads. Audience expectations. Even distribution channels. I mean, how do you plan on marketing this to the major networks?"

"Kerri's got connections," Marshall said, as if that answered everything. Then he bit into a powdered donut.

"I'm working on that," Kerri said. "If all goes to plan, I think I have a fairly good shot at convincing the local station manager at Channel 22 to switch out reruns of *Gilligan's Island* for *Beer & Loathing* in the 2 p.m. time slot."

I caught my mouth before it fell open. Was Kerri serious? In showbiz, "small potatoes" didn't come any smaller than that.

"Uh ... Tad won't be happy about that," I said.

Kerri's lips pressed to a white line. "Look, Doreen. We're not paying Tad to be happy. We're paying him to draw an audience. As you know, the only thing that talks in this industry is money. I know for a fact that Channel 22's ad revenues are down. *Way* down."

"So?" I said.

"*So*, if I can convince them that Tad Longmire can increase their viewership, Channel 22 will get the audience numbers they need to justify an increase in the rate they charge their advertisers for that time slot. Tad gets paid. You get paid. We get paid. The station makes money. Everybody wins."

I nearly dropped my coffee cup. Not only was Kerri smart. She was as shrewd as a circling shark. But hell. Maybe she really *could* make this garbage scow of a show float. Anyway, that was *her* job, not mine. Why should I care one way or the other?

"You're right," I said, feeling the pressure ease from my shoulders. "Like you said, everybody wins."

"I hope the station manager is as easy to convince as you were," Kerri said, her back to me as she fixed herself a cup of coffee. "But I can't even begin the negotiations without a decent pilot to show them."

"Hey, don't sweat it," Marshall said. "We're gonna start working on it today, like you wanted."

"I know," Kerri said. "But I have some pressing news. I spoke with an old friend at Channel 22 last night. One of the execs decided to take a vacation next week. So yesterday they moved up the planning meeting to schedule the summer rerun lineup."

"So?" I said.

Kerri nervously tapped a manicured nail on her coffee mug. "So, that means that if we're going to have a shot at being considered, we've now got to have the pilot episode filmed, edited, and available for their review by tomorrow at three."

I nearly spewed my sip of coffee. "You're *kidding*!"

Kerri sighed. "I wish I was. But I'm not. So, I guess that means we'd better get busy, eh? Any more questions before we start setting up for filming?"

"Nope," Marshall said, springing up from his chair. "I'll go wake up Tad."

"Uh ... I have a question," I said to Kerri after Marshall disappeared down the hallway. "If by some miracle we actually get this thing filmed, the station approves it, and it bumps Gilligan off his 2 p.m. timeslot, does *Beer & Loathing* really have a chance at boosting Channel 22's revenues? I mean, who'll be watching at that hour?"

Kerri shrugged. "I don't know. Probably just unemployed deadbeats, stay-at-home moms, and little old ladies."

"Then how can it—"

"Look," Kerri said, cutting me off. She glanced around, then whispered, "I just said all of those things to boost Marshall's morale. Whether any of this actually works out or not, we'll just have to wait and see. There's no guarantee on any of it. But does it really matter to you? Tad gets paid one way or the other."

"Sure, that's true," I said. "But for your sake, I'd like for it to be a success, just the same."

Kerri shot me a pained smile. "Thanks. I appreciate that. So, will you help me? Will you work with me and do what you can to help make that happen?"

"Of course!" I chewed my lip. "But we have to make one change right away."

"What's that?"

"I noticed in the script that Marshall is using the cast's real names. We can't have Tad's character actually be named Tad Longmire in the show."

"It's not," Kerri said. "It's Tad *Love*mire."

"Oh." I picked up my copy of the script again. "I must've missed that. Still, it's a little on the nose, isn't it?"

Kerri sighed. "Marshall's an on-the-nose kind of guy. But take my word for it. Letting the cast keep their real first names is going to make filming a whole lot easier."

"It is? Why?"

Kerri smirked and shook her head. "Let me put it this way. Marshall didn't pick these people for their Mensa scores."

"Morning, Kerri!" a man's voice called out.

I looked up to see a slim, bald man in his mid-thirties walking into the kitchen. In his left hand he carried a gray metallic case. A camera tripod was slung over his right shoulder.

"Doreen, this is Tommy Bigelow," Kerri said as he joined us. "Our cameraman and editor extraordinaire."

Tommy grinned at me. "Thanks, but I think Kerri meant *debonair*."

Kerri laughed. "Tommy, this is Doreen Diller. She's Tad Longmire's personal assistant."

"Oh." He grimaced. "My condolences."

I smirked. "Hey. *Somebody's* got to lead the glamorous life."

The three of us shared a brief laugh, then Kerri handed Tommy the bag of donuts.

"Thanks," he said, fishing out a cruller. "We're setting up in the bedroom, right?"

"Yes," Kerri said. "The opening scene has Tad in bed with two women."

"Of course it does," Tommy said, shaking his head. "From Marshall, I would expect no less."

Chapter Eleven

The opening scene was Tad "*Love*mire" waking up in bed with a pair of beach bimbos named Candy and Honey. By the time we finished filming, I realized Kerri hadn't been joking about the actors' IQs. While the two young women were indeed knock-outs, they were so ditzy I'd have bet good money the pair thought Grape Nuts was an STD.

"Hold that pose," Tommy directed Candy, her lips puckered on Tad's cheek. The canned overhead spotlights glared off the cameraman's bald head as he slowly panned his equipment out for a wide-angle shot of the cozy threesome propped up on bed-pillows. "Okay! I think that'll do it. Cut!"

"Yes! It's a wrap," Marshall said. "Great job, everyone!"

"You're the best, Marshall," Candy Liebowitz (aka Candy Lipps) cooed. The irritatingly gorgeous young redhead climbed out of bed wearing a thong bikini that would've been declared illegal in most undeveloped countries.

I sighed and took consolation in the fact that, according to the script, she would be the first to die.

"Yeah, thanks, Marshall," Honey Thompson (aka Honey Potter) said. She'd played the blonde bombshell occupying the left side of Tad's bed. Tad leered at Honey's taut, skimpily clad butt as she stood and ran a tanned hand through her long, golden tresses.

What did I care? I knew Honey was destined to be the second bimbo to become fish food for an inflatable shark. I smirked.

I wonder if plastic sharks like silicone …

"You girls were great," Marshall said as the twin bombshells cornered him and simultaneously kissed him on either cheek, lifting a leg like pin-up models. "You two take twenty, then meet us out at the beach in your bikinis."

"Ah, break time," Tad said, flashing his blue bedroom eyes. "So, which one of you two lucky ladies wants to come join me for a sleep-over?"

"Hold on, Romeo," I said to Tad. "We've got a tight schedule to follow."

"Yeah, so do *I*," Tad quipped, smiling appreciatively at Honey's derriere.

"Sorry, Tad," Marshall said. "Doreen's right. Let's forget the break. Everybody into wardrobe, then out to the beach in five. It's time to feed Candy to the shark!"

***

I walked with Marshall toward a tent set up on the beach, listening as he eagerly discussed the next shot. In it, Candy was to get crushed in the jaws of a Great White.

I had to admit, the thought had me excited, too. I'd planned to argue that Great Whites weren't in the Gulf of Mexico. But a quick Google search had set me straight. According to a marine research group, there were currently nine Great Whites circling the Gulf of Mexico, the largest of which weighed in at 2,076 lbs.

So much for my plans for a quick dip after lunch.

"And then she sinks under the water in a bloody cloud," Marshall said. "What do you think?"

"Uh, groovy," I said, having missed half the conversation due to rewriting the scene in my head. "Question. Do implants float?"

"Trevor! Blake!" Marshall shouted toward the tent, apparently not hearing my question. "How goes it with the star of the show?"

Under the shade of a large blue canopy, two hot young men in tropical print swim trunks were wrestling with something large and rectangular. As we got closer, I realized it was a cardboard carton containing an air pump.

"Not so good, Marshall," the taller of the two men called back. "How're we supposed to get the box open?"

"With the box cutter I left you," Marshall said. "It's right over there on the table behind you."

"Oh. Yeah," the other guy said, picking up the blade. "Okay, dude. We're on it!"

I stifled an eye roll. "Where'd you find *those* two?"

"Longtime friends," Marshall said. "They're not too bright, but they're always up for a good time. And best of all, they work for beer."

"Ah." I watched the two stud muffins slice open the carton. "That explains so much."

Apparently the smartest member of this cast is from China—and arrived in a box labeled Super Monster Fish Killer Shark ...

"So," I asked, "What can I do to—"

"Somebody help me!" a woman shrieked. I turned to see Candy Lipps, the beautiful redhead, holding a hand over her nose as if it had just been cut off.

"Could you see what's up with her?" Marshall asked. "She's kind of high maintenance."

You think?

"What's wrong?" I asked, sprinting over to Candy. She was on her knees in the sand, wringing her free hand while the other covered her nose.

"I think I feel a pimple coming on," she whined. "My nose feels all hot and stuff."

"Oh. Well, maybe you should put some sunscreen on it," I offered.

"That stuff makes me all itchy," she said. Candy glanced over at Marshall, then pulled me to the side and whispered, "Does this bikini make me look fat?"

"Seriously?" I had more fat under my chin than she had on her entire body. "You look fine," I said. "But the sun's hot today. Let's get you into the shade before your makeup melts."

I led Candy over to the canopy. Trevor and Blake were gone. In their place, Marshall and Kerri were trying to attach the air pump hose to the inflatable shark's posterior region.

"There! Got it," Marshall said. "Let's fill it up."

Kerri flipped the switch on the air pump. The plastic beast began to inflate. We all stood and watched in amazement as the apex predator of the ocean took shape. Unfortunately, it only took a couple of minutes to become painfully apparent that *Super Monster Fish Killer Shark* wasn't quite living up to the hype.

The label on the side of the carton displayed the image of a menacing man-eater with a mouthful of razor-sharp teeth. In reality, the plastic shark was about as scary as a Disney princess.

Instead of the promised mouthful of lethal, slashing incisors, the shark's balloon-like teeth formed a hokey, cartoonish smile reminiscent of Donkey in *Shrek*. What were supposed to be black, menacing eyes were as goofy as ... well ... *Goofy's*.

If that weren't bad enough, the inflatable shark's dorsal fin drooped like a bad comb-over. And the end of its nose was concave, as if it had just lost a bar fight with Mike Tyson. To be honest, I hadn't seen a monster prop this bad since *Attack of the Eye Creatures*.

"Aww, crap," Marshall grumbled. "This stupid shark looks bogus, doesn't it?"

I pursed my lips. *Bogus?* More like *ridiculous*. The only believable way that shark could kill someone was if they died laughing at it.

I stifled a snicker. "Er ... can't you get the nose to inflate?"

"I'm trying," Marshall said. "But I think Trevor and Blake must've cut a hole in it when they sliced open the box. Crap! What are we gonna do now?"

"Yeah," Candy whined. "I can't work with that thing. I'm a professional!"

My eyebrows rose an inch.

Wow.

Marshall kicked the shark in the side. It squeaked like a dog toy and rolled belly-up in the sand. "Man, this really sucks!"

Kerri chewed her lip. "I'm sorry, Marshall. If we're going to get this over to Channel 22 tomorrow, we don't have time to order another one."

"Yeah," I said, rubbing my index finger across my bottom lip. "Anyway, I don't think another one of those things is the answer."

"Then what *is*?" Marshall asked, his normally happy-go-lucky face red with anger and frustration. "We need a solution. *Now!*"

"He's right," Kerri said. "It's almost noon. We've only got the rest of the day to get this done or we miss our chance."

"I *know*," I said, chewing my lip. "Hey. Wait. I've got an idea. Why don't you just have a *person* kill Candy?"

"A person?" Kerri asked, as if she'd never heard of such an outrageous idea.

"Like, who?" Marshall asked. "We don't have anybody on cast who looks like they could be a killer."

"Then how about a *secret* killer," I said. "One you won't reveal until the end of the season?"

Marshall kicked the sand. "Yeah. Maybe." He looked up at me. "But for it to work, we'll need somebody *weird*. You know, somebody who really stands out in a crowd."

"You mean like a hunchback?" I asked.

"Or someone with a scarface?" Kerri offered.

"No," Marshall said. "I was thinking more like somebody with super-huge ta-tas."

My lips pursed into a sour line. "Of course you were. But where—"

"I know!" Marshall said. "I'll call Angel Santos!"

"Is that an escort service?" I asked sarcastically.

I bet the kid has it on speed dial.

I rolled my eyes. A pain shot through my left socket, making me wince. "Ouch!"

"Did you get sand in your eye?" Kerri asked.

"No." I wiped my watering eye. "I think my contact lens got hung up in the socket."

"I didn't know you wore contacts," Kerri said.

"Only one," I said, trying to hold open my burning eye. "Kerri, could you take a look, see if you see it up in there?"

"Sure."

Kerri peered into my face. Suddenly, she gasped.

Then Marshall gasped.

When Candy screamed, I knew they'd all seen it.

The secret I'd kept hidden since I was old enough to talk.

I blew out a long breath.

Great. Now I'll never get a job in Hollywood.

Chapter Twelve

"What's going on with your eye?" Kerri asked. "Should I call an ambulance?"

"No," I said, squeezing my left eye shut. "I have *Heterchromia iridum*."

"Wicked!" Marshall said. "Is it contagious?"

"No," I grumbled, both angry and slightly afraid. The secret I'd tried to hide under a contact lens for nearly 40 years was finally out in the open.

"I was born with one brown eye and one pale blue one," I explained. "It's a family genetic trait."

"Oh," Kerri said. "Does it hurt?"

"Not normally," I said. "Only when my contact lens decides to take a trip up inside my head."

Candy's beautiful face puckered in horror. "Gross! Your eye looks so creepy! I think I'm gonna throw up." She grimaced and turned away.

I ground my teeth and thought about all the times my mother had warned me about the cruelty of ignorance. What would someone like Candy know about imperfections? The girl was flawless.

Ma had been right to homeschool me until I was old enough to tolerate a contact lens. People could be stupid. And cruel. And complete asswipes. Up until now, I'd been able to escape the trauma wrought by uncaring idiots. But now, the gig was up. Thankfully, I was mature enough to handle it—I hoped.

"Sorry if my eye disturbed you," I said to Candy. I tried to put my hand on her back. She squealed and shrank away from my touch like I was an escapee from a leper colony.

"Well, I think your eye is cool as hell, Doreen," Marshall said.

"What?" I asked, blinking up at him. "You think my milky white eye is *cool*?"

"Yeah!" He stared at me. A grin spread across his freckled face. "Oh, man, you look freaky! Like you're possessed or something."

"Thanks," I said sourly. "I'm glad you find me so entertaining." I turned to go. I really needed to find a washroom so I could coax the contact lens out of my eye socket and back onto my cornea. "I'll be back in a few minutes."

"Wait!" Marshall said. "That's it!"

I turned around. "*What's* it?"

Marshall grabbed me by the shoulders. "Doreen, with those eyes of yours ... you'd make the perfect psycho killer for *Beer & Loathing*!"

Kerri, who'd been staring at me like a concerned mother hen, suddenly burst into an enthusiastic smile. "Marshall's right!"

"No way," I said, jerking away from Marshall. "Kerri, please. Come with me back to the cottage and help me get this contact lens back in the right place."

"Aww, come on, Doreen," Marshall whined as Kerri put an arm over my shoulder. "Be our killer. Please? Pretty please?"

"It would solve a world of problems for us," Kerri whispered in my ear. "And we'll pay you for the bit."

The bit.

Kerri's words transported me back to Ms. Benny's trailer, and the words of wisdom the googly-eyed woman had dropped on me like a ton of bricks. *"Your only shot at the big screen is with character bits, like me."*

I stopped in my tracks. Maybe I should give up on the idea of trying to live up to society's idea of beauty and perfection. Maybe I should embrace my shockingly weird left eye. Maybe it's not a flaw holding me back, but the *angle* that could propel me forward!

Maybe I was born to play the bit of a crazed psycho killer!

"You okay?" Kerri asked.

I nodded, then gently pulled Kerri's arm from my shoulder. I glanced around the beach for Tad. What would he think of the idea of me taking the role?

I spotted my boss across the sand over by the makeup tent. His wandering hand was on the thigh of the giggling blonde named Honey. A petite brunette with a pixie haircut eyed Tad with disdain. I recognized her as Leslie, the makeup woman Kerri'd hired for the project.

I nearly groaned with disgust.

Screw Tad. I don't need his permission.

"You know what?" I said, whirling around to face Kerri. "Sure. I'll play the part. Why the hell not?"

"Woohoo!" Marshall hooted. "Now we're just gonna need a body double."

"For what?" I asked.

Marshall cocked his head like a confused puppy. "For the boobs, of course."

I shot Kerri a sideways *WTH* glance.

"Marshall," Kerri said. "I think we may need to make a few concessions. Doreen's saving our bacon here. Can't she do it with a pair of 36Cs?"

They're 34Bs, but what the heck.

"Sure," Marshall said, looking me up and down. "I guess I can roll with that."

***

It took a pair of tweezers and a whole bottle of Visine to retrieve the wayward contact lens from way up inside my eye socket, but it was finally out. When I emerged from the bathroom triumphant, Kerri and Marshall were at the table eating lunch, busily working on rewriting the script.

"Got you a tuna on rye," Kerri said. "Hope that was okay."

"Fine," I said. "I'm starved!" I sat down at the table and tore into my lunch bag. "So, how's it going?"

"We're a bit stuck," Kerri said. "The shark didn't have any lines."

"Only Candy screaming at it," Marshall said.

"We need something to leave them wanting more," Kerri said. "What we need is some kind of twist at the end."

Marshall started to speak. Kerri shut him down. "And I don't mean a twist of the knife, Marshall. Having a woman killing off our characters is unusual, but not exactly innovative."

"Kerri's right," I said, munching a mouthful of sandwich. "What about if the killer spoke?"

"Earth to Doreen," Marshall said. "I think that's been done before."

"I know," I said, wracking my brain for ideas. Then I remembered *Hollywood Survival Guide* Tip #8: *If all else fails, tell a joke.*

"Hey," I said. "What if the killer was a wiseass?"

"Huh?" Kerri and Marshall uttered in unison.

I took a sip of soda to wash down the sandwich. "Hear me out. Instead of just stabbing the victims, what if we gave the psycho killer a few lines to say? It could add a kind of macabre humor to the end of each episode. You have to admit, it would be totally unexpected, right?"

"Uh ... I guess," Marshall said.

"Like, what did you have in mind?" Kerri asked.

I picked up a carrot stick and held it like a knife. "Picture this. What if, when the killer stabs Candy, she says something corny like, 'Revenge is sweet, Candy.' Then the killer lets out a sinister laugh and says, 'Looks like I got you *good and plenty.*'"

Kerri snickered. "God, that's bad."

Marshall laughed. "It's so bad it's great! I love it!" He set down his soda. "So, like, what would you say for Honey Potter?"

I grinned. "How about, 'Bee brave, Honey. This might sting a bit.'"

Marshall hooted and high-fived me. "Now *that's* what I'm talking about!"

Kerri's face lit up. "Yes! It's brilliant! And given the ridiculousness of the rest of the characters, by the end of each episode, the viewers might actually *be rooting* for the serial killer."

I smirked. "I agree the motivation is definitely there."

"This is perfect," Kerri said, shooting me a big smile. "It takes care of the shark problem, and we can continue shooting the rest of the pilot today." She leaned over and hugged me. "Thank you! You're a lifesaver!"

"Well, that's rather ironic," I quipped, "considering you just hired me to *take* lives."

Marshall and Kerri stared at me for a second. Then the joke hit home. As we all shared a chuckle, a thought hit me.

"Wait," I said. "There's a problem. If we film my face—I mean the face of the *killer*—the viewers will know it's not Tad, and there won't be any surprise reveal at the season finale."

"She's right," Marshall said. "Hey, wait. What if you wore some kind of mask? You know, like Jason did in *Friday the 13th*? Then all people would be able to see is those crazy eyes of yours!"

Kerri chewed her lip. "That could work. But what about the voice? They'll know the killer's a woman and not Tad."

"I know," Marshall said. "We could use an *electronic* voice. You know, like Siri. That way, the killer could still be Tad, or another dude, or even a woman. And if it all turns out to be a dream, the electronic voice would just make everything even weirder."

"Okay," I said, a conflicted smile crooking my lips.

Geez. I finally get a real role in a production and they don't want my face or my voice on the screen. Awesome.

"This is good stuff," Kerri said, making notes on a pad. "We'll save the reveal of the killer's face for the final scene of season one."

"Yeah," Marshall said, turning to me. "Then we blast the viewers with your face with those crazy eyes of yours! Oh! And instead of ending up in a ditch, we can make Tad go spinning down the drain in your pale blue eye!"

"Perfect!" Kerri said, scribbling in her pad.

I wasn't quite sure what either one of them was talking about, but I figured we'd work it all out along the way.

"Works for me," I said.

"Great. Now all we need is a name for our killer," Marshall said, slapping me on the back. "How about Doreen *Killigan*!"

I glanced over at Kerri. The smirk on her face made me burst out laughing.

So bad it's good? From Marshall's lips to God's ears.

***

It was time for the after-lunch shoot, and I couldn't find Tad anywhere. He was integral to the shot, as it was the bar scene where he was to spin the beer bottle, thus marking Candy for certain death.

After scrambling around the beach, the prep tent, and the Crooked Conch, I was just about to panic when I spotted him lying on one of the loungers on the front porch of the cottage. As I ran toward him, I realized he was drinking a bottle of beer he'd actually opened himself. For Tad, that practically counted as a DIY project.

"There you are," I said, too excited to even be mad at him for day drinking.

"You found me," he said. "Damn."

"Get up," I said, grinning down at him. "It's time for the shoot. By the way, you're looking at the newest member of the cast."

Tad's smirk lost a bit of smugness. His brow furrowed. "They gave you a role?"

"Yes. As the killer."

He snorted. "Ha! You gonna wear a shark-skin suit, or what?"

"No. We changed the killer to a person."

"Oh." He looked me up and down. "So you're gonna kill me, are you?"

I shrugged. "That depends."

"On what?"

"On whether you keep drinking on the set. Remember, you're under contract."

Tad frowned. "You told me this project was just a piece of crap, and we were really on holiday."

"I know." I frowned and fidgeted. "But now ... well, this might actually end up being something good. Don't blow it. Please?"

Tad eyed me like a predator toying with its prey. "I see what you're doing here. You think this little sideshow is gonna make you a star, don't you, Dorey Diller?"

"No," I protested. "I'll be in a mask. Nobody will even know it's me. Look, Tad. Kerri should be coming by with my contract in a few minutes. You don't see any issues with me doing it, do you?"

He shrugged. "I guess not. Just so long as you keep my smoothies and lattes coming. And you help me rehearse my lines. And don't bust my balls over a beer."

"Okay. Anything else?"

"Yeah. Don't let this gig go to your head and get all dreamy on me."

I shot him a facetious smile. "Why? Jealous I might make it into a movie before *you* do?"

Tad snorted. "Me? Jealous of a *woman*? Now I *know* you're dreaming, Dorey."

Chapter Thirteen

After Tuesday's filming finished at sunset, Tommy and Marshall took off like stray bullets. They had a long night of editing ahead to transform the raw footage they'd shot today into a pilot worthy of showing to Channel 22 executives tomorrow.

Despite our best efforts, we'd run out of daylight before we could film the final scene. The guys said they'd be back at the beach cottage at the crack of dawn tomorrow to shoot it, then hightail it to the studio to edit it into the first episode and get it to the station by three o'clock.

For once, I was glad I had *my* job instead of *theirs*.

As they climbed into their cars to go, I wished them luck. They were going to need it. Then I snuck back to the cottage to call my mother. I wanted to share my news about my bit part in *Beer & Loathing*. Lord knows, she'd waited long enough for news I'd finally landed a role.

I wasn't a celebrity yet, but it was a start.

Funny, since moving to Hollywood over 15 years ago, I'd grown accustomed to people comparing everyone to celebrities.

"That guy's got crazy eyes like Jack Nicholson in *The Shining*."
"He's got a frizzy red fro like Jon Heder in *Napoleon Dynamite*."
"She laughs like Julia Roberts in *Pretty Woman*."

Granted, the resemblances weren't always spot on—but you got the gist of what they meant in a second, and in a way no amount of words could adequately convey.

As I dialed Ma's number, I lay back on the feather bed and took a deep breath to brace myself. You see, my mother, Maureen Diller, was the spitting image of Chloris Leachman in *Young Frankenstein*. But in pretty much all other ways, Ma channeled Roseanne Barr in *She Devil*.

She was cautious, plotting, and paranoid. As her child, I'd always felt like an inconvenience—a dim-witted, bumbling, sidekick she'd had to watch like a hawk to keep me from sticking a fork in a light socket or drowning in the rain.

"Hi, Ma," I said.

"Who is this?"

"Doreen. Your offspring."

"Oh. I'd given you up for dead."

"I called two weeks ago."

"A lot can happen in two weeks."

"I know."

Sensing a chance to detour from our usual dead-horse soundtrack, I blurted, "I got a new job!"

"What? The studio fired you?"

Not exactly...

"No. Ma, I got a role in a new TV series!"

"You're kidding."

"I'm not. And it's an *important* role, too."

"Huh. What is it?"

"I play a killer."

"Oh. What kind of killer?"

"Uh ... the kind that kills people?"

"More than one, huh?" Ma grunted. "So, a serial killer."

I hadn't thought about it, but yeah. "Yes."

"Lemme guess. You showed them your crazy eye."

I gritted my teeth. "It was an accident. Anyway, what's the big deal?"

Ma let out a sigh that could've been heard from Snohomish without the phone. "So you're a psycho killer now. I'm so proud. Where are you?"

"St. Petersburg."

"Russia?"

"Florida. It's so nice here—"

"Your Aunt Edna lives there," Ma blurted. "Have you seen her?"

"No. Why would I—"

"You should contact her while you're in town."

"But you told me she was dead."

"I never said that."

"Then Aunt Edna's still alive?"

"Of course she is," Ma said. "If you weren't so caught up in yourself all the time, you'd know that. Now be a good person and take an hour out of your *busy acting career* and go visit her. It's time. Here's her phone number, 7-2-7—"

"Ma, I can't write it down right now. Could you text it to me after we hang up?"

She sighed. "I suppose. I have to do *everything* around here. Hey. So these people flew you to Florida for this gig?"

"Well, sort of. I came here with Tad Longmire. I'm his personal assistant now."

"Tad Longmire?" my mother gasped. "Dr. Lovejoy on *Days of Our Lies*?"

I smirked. "The very one."

"Why would *he* be hanging around *you*?"

My smirk vanished. "I was the one who convinced him to take the starring role in the project here in St. Pete. We're fellow cast members now."

"Why didn't you tell me this before?"

"It all happened kind of last-minute. We just got here yesterday. We've been busy filming ever since."

"Uh-huh."

I could hear my mother's devious mind whirring on the other end of the line. I didn't want to be around for what finally came flying out. "I gotta go, Ma."

"Hold your horses, Dorey. I heard about Tad's blowout in Tinseltown."

I gulped. "You did?"

"Of course. It was all over the tabloids. So I get why he was available on short notice. And you? Well, you've had an empty dance card since you left Snohomish."

"Is there a point to this, Ma?"

"Yeah. Why were there these openings in the first place?"

"What do you mean?"

"I mean, who were the two suckers cast for the roles before *you two* suckers replaced them?"

Arrgh!

"I gotta go Ma."

"Don't be rude. Call your Aunt Edna," I heard her yelling as I clicked off the phone.

A few seconds later, Ma texted me a phone number. I stared at it blankly. I'd never met my Aunt Edna. And if she was anything like Ma, with any luck I never would.

Chapter Fourteen

Wednesday arrived way too early, and stayed way too late.

Between keeping up with Tad's whims, keeping his hands off the beach babes, and keeping my chin up through eleven takes of the pilot finale featuring yours truly as Doreen Killigan, the whole harried morning melted into a frenzied blur.

Except for two things.

One—being startled awake by an old man in a bingo cap. And two—being jolted by a blast of ice-cold seltzer water to the face.

The day had started off with a knock on my bedroom door. Before I could rouse myself to total consciousness, the lock began to jiggle. Then the door cracked open and an old man stuck his shriveled head inside.

"What the!" I yelled, pulling the bedcovers to my chin.

"It's me," the old man said. "Marshall." Then, like a scene out of *Total Recall*, he pulled off his face. He'd been wearing a gnarly rubber mask.

"Marshall!" I gasped. "You nearly scared me to death!"

He shrugged. "Sorry. I was testing a theory."

I sat up in bed. "What are you talking about?"

"Our killer needs a mask, right?"

"Uh, yeah."

"So, what do you think of this one?" Marshall stepped inside my bedroom and held up the latex head like the victor in a rubber sword fight to the death.

I squinted at the severed rubber head. It was as pasty-white and wrinkly as an albino raisin. A pointy, hook nose protruded from above a wide slit of a mouth. A pair of flabby ears stuck out on each side like jug handles. Deep, sunken eyeholes stared blankly at me from beneath a ball cap that read, *I Love Bingo*.

Still half asleep, I didn't know what to think. I chewed my lip and stared studiously at the mask, buying time while my mind scrambled to recall something I'd read in the *Hollywood Survival Guide* about just such a situation. Ah, yes! Tip #9: *When stuck for an answer, ask, "What's the concept?"*

"What's the concept?" I asked.

Marshall grinned. "Think about it. What's the opposite of an attractive, but scary-looking woman? A harmless, ugly old man."

Attractive? You think I'm attractive?

I shot him a smile. "You know, that whole irony thing could work."

"All right!" Marshall said. "I was hoping you'd say that. Now get up. We've got a scene to shoot!"

***

Three hours of frenzied filming went by in a flash. Before I knew it, we were on the 11th take of my killer's last scene. My arm was tired from all the stabbing, and I was beginning to feel like Bill Murray in *Groundhog Day*—except I kept killing the same dummy over and over again ...

"Action!" Tommy yelled.

The camera zoomed in. I plunged the eight-inch collapsible knife into the bulbous, bikini-clad chest of Candy Lipps. Right on cue, Leslie, the makeup woman, squirted fake blood from a squeeze bottle onto both of us. Candy began screaming, and I made googly eyes at the camera through the holes in the old-man bingo mask covering my head.

This was usually the point where Tommy yelled, "Cut. Let's do it again." Then we'd all race around like mice, trying to get cleaned up for another take.

But this time, Tommy yelled something different.

"Yes! It's a wrap, folks!"

Marshall followed with a hearty, "Woohoo!"

"All right!" I joined in, tired, but elated. I pulled off the sweaty rubber mask and ran a hand through my damp hair. Suddenly, cold water spurted onto my forehead and ran down my nose.

Marshall had shot me in the face with a seltzer gun.

"What the?" I said, water dripping from my chin.

Marshall laughed and handed me a towel. "It's supposed to be good luck."

I laughed. But still, I eyed him suspiciously.

Good luck? I hadn't read anything about that *in the* Hollywood Survival Guide.

After the hit-and-run filming session, Tommy and Marshall took off like lightning bolts. It was already past 11 a.m., giving them precious few hours to edit the final act into a pilot worthy of showing Channel 22 at three o'clock.

After they left, Kerri gathered her things to make a hasty getaway. "I need to supervise those two," she said, climbing into her Jaguar. "And I've got to prep for the meeting at three."

"Good luck," I said, squeezing her shoulder.

"Thanks. Keep your fingers crossed. And take the rest of the day off. You earned it!"

***

With nobody else left at the cottage but Tad, I took him to lunch at the Crooked Conch. I felt like celebrating my first real action shoot, but Tad decided to be a spoilsport and refused to even raise his beer to the toast I'd made for the success of the project. Disgusted, I left him at the bar with his beloved bourbon and bimbos.

Fine by me. I can think of better ways to spend my time than babysitting Tad's humongous, fragile ego.

As I shuffled along the beach on my way back to the cottage, my cellphone chimed a funny ringtone. It was the special ring Sonya and I used for gossiping with each other back at the Hollywood studio. We'd nicknamed the tone, "Drama Alert."

I checked my phone for her text.

> *News flash! Boobie Bonnie's husband sent her packing from the set today.*

I texted back.
What happened???

Borloff caught her in the supply room with one of the camera grips. Her punishment? A vacation in Miami. Geez. Where do I sign up for that life?

Seriously. Some people have all the luck.

How's it going in St. Pete?

Actually, pretty good. Tad's being a jerk, of course. But get this. I actually got a role in the production. A good one, too! I get to kill bimbos!

Wow! Good for you! So what you're saying is that for us to get a job in the movies, we have to leave Hollywood?

It would appear so.

Life is too weird to contemplate, D. Must drink wine and consume massive amounts of air-popped popcorn.

Got to watch that figure.

Always. Later!

It was almost 2 p.m.—nearly deadline for the guys back at the studio editing their butts off. I didn't want to bother them, but I just had to know if we were going to make the time crunch. I hit speed dial for Sunshine City Studios.

"How's it going?" I asked Marshall when he picked up.

"Thanks to Tommy's perfectionism, we got some excellent footage," he said. "Like he keeps saying, 'Better a good take than a bad fake.' But let me tell you, Doreen, the real magic happens in editing."

"Right," I said. "Is there anything I can do to help?"

"Yeah. Pray for magic."

I grimaced. "Uh ... okay. Will do."

Chapter Fifteen

A thunderstorm kicked up the wind last night. Tucked safely inside the downy womb of my soft, goose-feather bed, I'd drifted off to sleep to the sound of thunder and ocean waves tumbling onto shore. When I awoke this morning, the sky had cleared. I hoped it was a portent of good things to come.

I sat up and thought about the conversation I'd had with Kerri yesterday afternoon.

"Hey, Kerri. How'd the meeting go?"

"Well, they didn't say no, so that's good."

"What *did* they say?"

"Well," Kerri had hesitated. "They were impressed we'd gotten Tad Longmire to star in it. So be sure and thank Tad."

"Uh ... I will. He's not here right now."

"Oh. Well, anyway, they said they'd let me know as soon as they made a decision. The meeting for that is at 2 p.m. tomorrow. They won't call before then. So we can all quit holding our breath."

"Hard to stop," I'd said.

"Agreed. Look. We're all exhausted here at the studio. I told Marshall and Tommy to take tomorrow morning off. We're too nervous to work, anyway. Sleep in and I'll call you tomorrow. Okay?"

"Okay," I'd said. "But I'd like to see the pilot if you don't mind."

"Oh! Sure. I'm sorry. It slipped my mind. I'll arrange something for tomorrow and let you know."

I yawned and stretched. Tomorrow was now today. A jolt of nervous energy surged through me. Today I'd get to see the pilot episode of my first official acting gig! I pressed my eyes closed and giggled excitedly.

So this is what it feels like to be a movie star!

I lay back in bed for another moment, planning my lazy morning ahead. First, as a treat I'd have breakfast somewhere I could dig my toes into the sand. Then I'd stroll the beach collecting shells, thinking up punchlines for upcoming episodes, and keeping my fingers crossed Channel 22 would give us the green light.

My stomach gurgled. Daybreak was peeking through the blinds. The room was so quiet I could hear the clock ticking on the nightstand. I breathed in deep and drank in the silence. No car horns beeping. No tires squealing. No roommates bumbling around in the kitchen. No Tad barking orders at me.

Tad!

I sat up and checked my cellphone. Somehow, it had switched itself off. I powered it back up and stared at the screen.

Messages from Hollywood directors? Zero.

Messages from Tad? Eighteen.

Eighteen!

I leapt out of bed. Hazy memories of yesterday afternoon pinged in my brain like drips from a leaky faucet. After filming had wrapped up yesterday morning, Tad and I'd shuffled over to the Crooked Conch for fish tacos. He'd tried to turn it into a drinking match. Disgusted, I'd left the jerk to fend for himself.

All afternoon and evening.

And Tad had been calling me over and over ever since!

What has he done now? Geez, I hope it doesn't involve the police!

"Tad!" I hollered, then scurried out of my room and ran down the hallway like the cottage was on fire.

When I got to Tad's bedroom, the door was open. The bed was still made. Tad was nowhere in sight. Panic shot through me. An image of Tad in an orange prison jumpsuit flashed in my mind. I shook my head like an Etch-a-Sketch to clear it away.

"Tad!" I yelled down the hallway. "Tad! Where are you?"

I raced through the cottage. He wasn't passed out on the bathroom floor. He wasn't dry-heaving into the kitchen sink. He wasn't sprawled face down on the living room sofa.

OMG. This is so not good!

In a few hours, we'd know the fate of *Beer & Loathing*. And while everyone else had been working their butts off to make that happen, I'd gone and lost the leading man!

I flung open the French doors and ran outside. Two steps onto the porch, I nearly tumbled over a pile of stuff heaped up near the front door.

"Ouch!" a voice sounded from somewhere under the jumble of pillows and cushions.

"Tad?" I asked.

"Who else?" he grumbled. A hand emerged from the pile and pulled a chenille throw-blanket from his face. Sometime between yesterday's lunch and now, Tad had acquired a black eye.

"Dear lord!" I cried out. "Are you okay?"

"You missed it," Tad said, his lips pouting above his unshaven cleft chin.

"Missed what?" I asked. "The ambulance?"

"No. The party."

"Tad, there's only so much tequila a girl can take. What happened to you? How'd you get the shiner?"

"Shiner?" he asked. "I dunno. I fell down, I think."

I groaned. "Why didn't you come inside last night?"

Tad frowned at me. "The door was locked. You didn't answer your phone. I didn't have a key."

I winced.

Oops.

Tad yanked back the blanket, revealing his complete asset package.

"Why are you naked?" I gasped, unable to stop myself from staring.

"I always sleep in the raw, Dorey." He rubbed his forehead. "My head hurts. Help me up."

He reached a hand toward me. Sensing a trap, I hesitated.

"And have you pull me down into your naked lair? I don't think so."

Tad laughed. "Eh. It was worth a try."

"Geez, Tad. Look at you! Get up. We need to get you showered and shaved. Then we've got to cover up that shiner."

"You're no fun," he said, hauling himself up. "All work and no play will get you nowhere."

"So will all play," I countered.

Tad's brow furrowed as if trying to think made his head hurt.

That would explain so much ...

He stumbled to his feet. Then he reached out and hugged me, pressing all six feet of naked man-hunk against me. My mind screamed "NO!"

But despite everything I knew about the jerk, my traitorous body screamed, "YES! YES! YES!"

Thankfully, Tad himself came to my rescue. He opened his mouth and extinguished my libido with six little words.

"Dorey, get me a latte. *Now*."

My cellphone rang. "Hold on, Tad. It's Kerri."

"Doreen, hey, it's Kerri. If you're interested, I wanted to invite you and Tad to the studio at one o'clock to see the finished pilot reel. Then we can sit around and chew our nails off until the callback from Channel 22 at two."

Tad frowned. I cut the air between us with my finger scissors.

"That sounds fantastic, Kerri. We can't wait!"

***

Sobering up Tad and concealing his black eye took most of the morning. By the time he was washed, fed, and fit to be seen in public, it was time to hail a limo to Sunshine City Studios. But at the last minute, Tad backed out, saying he had other things to do.

I wasn't about to argue. I'd simply said, "Fine," and left without him.

I arrived at the studio a minute after one o'clock. The faded red door was unlocked. As I stepped inside, I heard people talking. I followed their voices to the conference room. There, Tommy and Marshall were seated across from each other at a large, rectangular table. Both were staring at a large TV screen mounted on the wall.

"Doreen!" Marshall said, turning to face me when I walked in. "Where's Tad?"

"Uh ... I left him at the beach ... in the care of a local redhead."

I'd wanted to add, "Sorry about Tad. Not sure if he's an asset to the project or just an ass." But from the look on Marshall's face, he was figuring that out all by himself.

"Come have a seat," Marshall said, pulling out a chair for me. "We're getting ready to watch the pilot reel again."

"Awesome." I slipped into the chair next to Marshall. Kerri poked her head in the door and joined us.

"Any word from Channel 22?" I asked.

"Not yet," Kerri said, chewing a fingernail.

"Why do you think we're watching this thing again for the fourth time?" Tommy asked.

"Anyway, it's too soon," Kerri said, glancing at a clock on the wall. "They're probably still reviewing the pilot. After that, they'll consider what to offer us."

"*If* they like it," Tommy said.

"Right," Marshall said. "If they don't, well, it's done."

Suddenly, the conference landline jangled. The four of us jumped as if a bomb had gone off.

"You gonna get that?" Tommy asked, eyeing Marshall with trepidation.

Marshall glanced at me, then snatched up the receiver. "Hello?"

"Is it Channel 22?" Kerri whispered.

Marshall shook his head. "Pizza guy. I left the door open for him. Somebody closed it."

"Sorry," I said. "That would be me."

"Well, at this point," Kerri said, "Let's hope no news is good news."

Chapter Sixteen

While Tommy let the pizza guy in, Marshall and I grabbed some sodas from the breakroom at Sunshine City Studios and microwaved some popcorn. With the fate of *Beer & Loathing* in the hands of the Channel 22 gods, we decided to blow off some steam and watch the pilot episode in style.

"Okay, here goes," Tommy said, clicking the remote as we all settled into our chairs around the conference table.

The big screen flickered on. Bongo-beat tropical music played as the words *Beer & Loathing in FLA* appeared against a beachy backdrop. The camera panned to an outside view of the idyllic beach cottage.

Suddenly, the scene shifted to an unshaven Tad Longmire, nose still red from Borloff's special director's right cut.

Tad leered at us drunkenly from his bed. On either side of him, two mysterious lumps under the duvet moved from his groin area up toward his head. The faces of two gorgeous women popped out from under the covers. A blonde and a redhead.

I closed my eyes and prayed it would get better from there.

It did not.

After twenty minutes of Tad horn-dogging women around the beach and into his bed, Marshall elbowed me out of my disgusted stupor.

"Here it comes," he said. "Your killer scene!"

I sat up straighter. The camera honed in on a close-up shot of Candy Lipps. Her bronze, bikini-clad body lay sleeping, uncovered, atop the bed. She clutched a Teddy bear.

I stifled a groan.

I guess I should be grateful she isn't sucking her thumb.

Suddenly, the wrinkly, rubber chin of the bingo man mask appeared next to her ear. "Revenge is sweet, Candy," my digitized voice whispered.

A jolt of horror-movie soundtrack jabbed the silence, making me jump. A flash of light stabbed my eyes. Suddenly, a hand jutted into the air, gripping a gleaming knife. It plunged downward savagely. When it rose again, the blade and the killer's hand were completely soaked in stage blood.

I'll admit it. I gasped.

The next shot was of Candy's lifeless eyes staring into space. (I figured she conjured up the look by trying to multiply 347 by zero.) Candy's once-nubile chest was now a bloody pool of multiple stab wounds.

Let's hope she didn't spring a silicone leak.

The camera panned over to my character, Doreen Killigan. Dressed in black from neck to toe, it was impossible to tell whether I was a man or a woman. I stood over Candy, the bloody bingo man mask concealing my identity.

Suddenly, the camera zoomed in close on the mask. Behind the rubber eye holes, my brown eye was hard to see. But my pale blue one was as visible as the moon in a cloudless sky—and was darting around like a paranoid schizophrenic.

A chill went up my spine. I finally saw myself like everyone else did.

I shivered in my seat.

In the midst of the macabre scene, a sinister laugh cut the silence. My digitized voice followed, landing the final line, "Looks like I got you good and plenty."

The screen faded to black.

Marshall hooted. "Wicked, man! I'm telling you, that's wicked with a capital W!"

As a movie buff, I'd seen a crap-load of films. So, in all honesty, I had to admit I'd seen worse. To his credit, Tommy's camera work was surprisingly good. So was the acting, considering how disjointed both the script and the filming had been.

I sat back and smiled. If I were a movie critic, (a kind one) I'd have written that "*Beer & Loathing* could best be described as the beachside prequel to *Idiocracy*—with a dash of *I Married an Axe Murderer.*"

"Well?" Marshall asked, his eyes eager with anticipation. "What do you think, Doreen?"

Knowing this moment would come, I'd already plucked a gem from the *Hollywood Survival Guide*. Tip #22. *When at a loss for words, you can't go wrong with "interesting."*

"Interesting," I said. "And, I have to admit, unexpected."

"In a *good* way, right?" Marshall asked.

"Totally," I said, improvising.

"God, I wish Channel 22 would call already," Tommy said, wringing his hands. "The suspense is killing me. I'm gonna take a walk to calm my nerves."

"Good idea," Kerri said. "Mind if I join you?"

I was relieved when Tommy left the conference room. He'd drummed his bitten-to-the-quick fingers on the table during the whole viewing. If the guy didn't let out some nervous tension soon, I was afraid he might next start pulling out his eyelashes.

As soon as Tommy and Kerri left, I grabbed my chance to be alone with Marshall. "So, I wanted to ask you something."

Marshall leaned back in his chair and locked his fingers behind his head. "Sure. Shoot."

"I ... I guess I'm just curious about something. When did you first write *Beer & Loathing*?"

"Oh. Last year. Why?"

"No reason really. I just thought, you know, given the last-minute casting, that it was a recent project. You only cast Tad for it four days ago. That doesn't seem like Kerri Middleton's way of doing things."

Marshall smirked. "But it *does* seem like mine, huh?"

I shrugged and smiled. "Well, kind of."

"Look," Marshall said, unoffended in the slightest. "I know everybody thinks I'm just a kid. And maybe this project isn't the greatest story ever told. But everybody's got to start somewhere, right?"

"Sure. I didn't mean—"

"And to answer your question, we *did* have another guy lined up for the role before Tad."

Crap. Ma had been right. I hated it when she was right!

"So what happened?" I asked.

Marshall shook his head. "I don't know. Brent—my high school buddy, Brent Connors? He was all stoked up about doing it."

"So, what happened?"

"Like I said, I'm not sure. After the audition, he met with Kerri to sign the contract and the next thing I know he'd dropped out of the project."

My eyebrows knitted together. "Did Kerri say why?"

"No. She was as baffled as I was."

"Why baffled? Everybody's entitled to change their minds."

"Sure," Marshall said, lowering his hands to the armrests. He leaned in close to me. "But not everybody just disappears off the face of the earth afterward."

I blanched. "Brent *disappeared*?"

"Yeah. He won't return my calls. His car isn't at his apartment. He used to come to the beach every day. I haven't seen him since he quit."

"When was that?"

"Last week. Wednesday or Thursday, I think."

Whoa. Kerri Middleton is smart and ambitious. But is she smart and ambitious enough to throw Brent under the bus? Or to get rid of him for good when she found out Tad was available for the leading role? No. That couldn't be possible. Could it?

I needed more information from Marshall. "What about—"

The conference door squeaked open. I dropped my thought as Kerri stepped in, looking excited but worried.

"So what have you two been talking about?" she asked.

Oh, nothing. Just whether or not you might be a two-faced murderer ...

Marshall pursed his lips. "We were just—"

"Discussing the pilot," I interjected. "You think we have a chance with Channel 22?"

"All I can say is, it's in their hands now," Kerri said, heaving a sigh. "But based on their reactions, I'd say they liked it."

"Really?" Marshall asked, fishing for a compliment. "Which part did they like best?"

Kerri smirked. "I believe it was the part about the audience numbers Tad's been generating for *Days of Our Lies*."

***

Too nervous and wound up to go home, at 4:30 Marshall, Kerri, Tommy and I were still sitting around the conference table in the studio downtown. We'd been killing time re-watching the pilot episode of *Beer & Loathing* and wafting pros and cons back and forth about whether or not we'd get the nod to be in the summer time slot on Channel 22.

After watching Kerri the whole time, I decided she couldn't have harmed Brent. But then again, I used to think Tad was a dreamboat.

"Enough gabbing already," Kerri said. "We can wish and pray all we want. But the decision about *B&L* boils down to Bob Johnson, the guy in charge at 22."

"*B&L*?" Marshall asked.

"Oh. That's Johnson's nickname for the series. I did my best to persuade him. Geez. I promised him everything but the moon."

"Let's just hope he didn't think you were full of cheese," Tommy quipped.

"That's funny," Marshall said. "Hey, Doreen, you should have the killer say something like that."

"I could," I said. "But I've already worked out the lines for the rest of the bimbos."

"Oh yeah?" Tommy said. "Let's hear them."

"Yeah," Marshall said. "What's the line for Penny Nichols?"

I sat up and tried to imitate the digital version of my voice. "I cents it's time for a change, Penny. But I can see you're already spent."

Kerri laughed. "I love it! What about Cookie Baker? What do you tell her when you're stabbing her to death?"

I smirked and gave them my best Mae West. "So long, sugar Cookie. Let the chips fall where they may."

"Wicked," Marshall said. "That just leaves the season finale bimbo. What do you say to Fanny Tight?"

I opened my mouth.

The conference phone rang.

The three of us jumped like victims in a horror movie.

Kerri was the first to un-freeze. She snatched up the handset on the conference landline.

"Kerri Middleton speaking." Her eyes grew wide. "Oh, hello, Mr. Johnson. Yes. Now's a good time. Actually, I and the other studio principals were just finishing up a meeting. Shall I put the call on speaker? Very good, then."

Kerri eyed us wildly, then mashed the speakerphone button.

"Hello," Johnson's voice boomed through the speakerphone. "I don't exactly know what to call this thing you've all made. It's quirky. Kind of like *Baywatch* meets a female *Dexter*."

"We call it a daytime serial," I said, then cringed and wanted to kick myself.

Johnson laughed. "You! You're the voice of the mysterious serial killer, aren't you? I love that dry sense of humor of yours."

"Uh ... thank you, sir," I said, still cringing.

"Are those eyes real?" Johnson asked. "I mean, brrr! Really spooky special effects!"

Kerri shot me an apologetic grimace. "So, Bob. Don't keep us in suspense. All joking aside, we're dying to know. Is it a 'go' or is it a 'no'?"

"Like I told you in the meeting, Kerri. I can't answer that until you tell me whether *B&L* is ready for airtime."

"Right," Kerri said. "Hold on a second. Let me get the latest update from production."

Kerri leaned over and jabbed the speakerphone button to shut it off. Her eyes darted from Tommy to Marshall and back again. "Listen, guys. In the meeting? I ... I *lied* to Johnson."

"What?" Marshall said.

Kerri winced. "I had to. I thought he was about to greenlight us. Then, all of a sudden, he sideswiped me with this requirement to have five complete episodes ready before he could approve it."

"What do you mean?" I asked.

"What I mean is, for *B&L* to be considered for a timeslot, we have to have five episodes ready to air. Anyway, the thing is, I panicked and told him a lie. I said filming was finished on all of them, and production was nearly complete." She turned to Marshall and grimaced. "I'm sorry. It was either lie, or the project was dead in the water. I should have—"

"What's the harm?" Marshall said, putting a hand on her shoulder. He glanced over at Tommy. "We can crank them out pretty quick, right?"

"Yeah, sure!" Tommy said. "We've got the prototype done!"

"So we're agreed?" Kerri asked.

Marshall nodded. "Agreed."

Kerri clicked the speakerphone back on. "Mr. Johnson? Don't worry. We're very close to finalizing the project," Kerri said.

"Hmm," Johnson growled. "How close?"

"Um ... we just have to finish editing the last episode. My production team sees no problem with it. In fact, everything should be in the can and ready for airtime by tomorrow afternoon."

"I see," Johnson said. "In that case ... it's on."

A collective gasp filled the conference room.

"What was that?" Johnson asked.

"Nothing," Kerri said. "A faulty air-conditioner vent."

"Oh," Johnson said. "Okay. Listen. I'll clear that spot at 2 p.m., like we discussed. We'll air the first episode on a Friday, and let the media buzz build over the weekend. If it's good, we'll run the first episode again on Monday to catch more viewers. The remaining four episodes of *B&L* the following Tuesday through Friday."

"That's fabulous," Kerri said. "Which Friday are you thinking of to air the first episode?"

"*Friday* Friday," Johnson said. "As in *tomorrow*."

Kerri gulped. "Um ..."

"Is there a problem?" Johnson asked.

"No problem at all, sir," Marshall blurted.

"Good. So tell me," Johnson said. "Do we have a deal?"

We glanced around at each other, then nodded like a collection of bobble-head dolls.

"Bob?" Kerri said. "We have a deal!"

Chapter Seventeen

After promising the moon, it was my new friend Kerri and I who were left seeing stars. As the only two bona fide grownups on board the *B&L* ship of fools, it was up to us to figure out how to produce four episodes in under four days.

At 7 a.m. Friday morning, she and I were already hard at work at The Frog Pond diner, trying to slap together a production schedule between panic attacks.

I nervously drummed my fingernails against my coffee cup. "How are we going to wrangle Tad and a bunch of pouty, pampered starlets into cramming two weeks' worth of filming into what basically amounts to one long weekend?"

"First things first," Kerri said, downing half a cup of coffee like it was a shot of whiskey. "We need to fix the scripts. They need more dialogue."

"Are you sure?" I countered. "Given the cast, the less they have to say, the faster filming will go."

Kerri's face grew serious. "You've got to help me, Doreen. I have a reputation in this industry. I really didn't think Marshall's project would get this far. But now that it has ..." She looked away and shook her head. "My *name's* going to be associated with this."

I grimaced. "What can I do?"

Kerri locked eyes with me. "You've seen the scripts. Help me fix this disaster before it happens."

Over coffee and croissants, we did our best. Mainly, we beefed up Marshall's skimpy plots with more tongue-in-cheek dialogue from Doreen Killigan, my murderous alter ego.

To be honest, by the time we were done, my character had practically become the star of the show. It was a little embarrassing and self-serving. But I had to admit, it was also a bit of an ego rush. I, Doreen Diller, was single-handedly ridding the world of five hapless bimbos.

"Okay, that's the last one," I said. "Fanny Tight is finished."

"Good lord," Kerri said, glancing at her watch. "We better get a move on. The entourage should be arriving at the beach cottage any minute now."

I motioned for the waitress to bring the check. When it arrived, Kerri snatched it up.

"This is on me," she said, relief returning a bit of sparkle to her hazel eyes. "I owe you, big time. The load of zingers you wrote almost makes up for the idiocy of the rest of the script."

"Almost?" I asked.

Kerri smirked. "That's what I said, didn't I?"

Chapter Eighteen

As they say in Hollywood, time flies when you're killing bimbos.

From Friday to Sunday, in four frenzied days of filming, I'd stabbed three additional starlets to death with a butcher knife the size of a hothouse cucumber. As gruesome as that sounded, I'd enjoyed every second. It beat lying headless in a dumpster any day.

My fledgling acting career wasn't the only thing looking up for me. Other than catching Tad with some mysterious redhead at the beach cottage when I got home from the studio on Thursday night, I'd managed to keep Tad on mark with his lines and out of any major trouble.

Believe me, accomplishing this had required every spare second I had between film takes. Tad Longmire was such a diva that his idea of "roughing it" was lukewarm French fries. Despite Tad's numerous attempts to woo Kerri to his boudoir, she'd remained completely immune to his smarmy charms. I loved that about her.

And now, here it was. Monday morning. The last day of filming. After the past three 15-hour days, I was exhausted before I even climbed out of bed.

Despite feeling that my limbs were made of lead, the sound of tires crunching on the gravel outside the beach cottage sent me springing up out of the covers for a peek through the blinds. I spotted Kerri's silver Jaguar pulling up to the front porch.

She rolled down the window and waved.

I blanched.

Can she see me?

Then I realized she wasn't looking at me. She was waving toward the front of the cottage. My mind raced. It was barely daybreak. The sun was just coming up. Who could be out there at this hour?

OMG! Tad! Had he slept on the front porch again—naked?

I shot out of my bedroom and down the hallway. But it was too late. Through the French doors, I could see Tad's firm, meaty buttocks glowing in the pink rays of dawn. He was standing on the porch steps grinning and waving at Kerri.

94

God. Give. Me. Strength.

I bolted out the French doors, grabbed a pillow from a lounge chair, and placed it strategically over Tad's loins.

Calmly, Kerri climbed out of the Jag carrying a cardboard tray of Starbucks coffees. "Good morning, you two," she said, walking up and handing me a coffee.

As she passed by on her way toward the French doors, Kerri cocked her head and took a good, long look at Tad's naked ass. She didn't even smirk.

Man, that Kerri Middleton had poise.

***

"Sorry again about Tad," I said.

Kerri and I were sitting on the porch sipping our coffees, waiting on the rest of the crew to arrive. "I do my best to keep an eye on Tad, but I'm not a machine. I have to sleep sometimes."

"I understand," Kerri said. "Perhaps staying at the cottage was a bad idea. We'll get you into the hotel when we wrap up filming today."

"No," I blurted, then caught myself. "Uh ... what I mean is, I actually like it here. And since you're renting it for the production anyway, it's a lot cheaper than us staying at that fancy hotel, right?"

"You're right about it being cheaper," Kerri said. "But we're not renting the cottage. Marshall's father owns it. So it's not actually costing us anything."

"Really?" I said, nearly choking on a sip of coffee. "The guy must be *loaded.*"

"There's no 'must be' about it," Kerri said, laughing. "Actually, if you want to stay a few extra days, I don't think he'd mind. Want me to arrange it?"

"I'd love to," I said. "But Tad can't wait to get out of here. I've already got our flights booked back to L.A. tomorrow morning."

"He doesn't like the beach?" Kerri asked, frowning. "I know we've been pushing him hard, filming the whole series in under two weeks. But he still gets his full pay. I thought he'd be pleased."

"It's not that," I said. "It's just that ... well, St. Petersburg isn't L.A."

"Really? What's L.A. got that we don't?"

"Something vital to Tad's quality of life," I said.

Kerri's eyebrow arched. "What?"

I leaned closer to Kerri. "There's no In-N-Out Burger."

She laughed. "I see."

I rolled my eyes. My contact lens slipped again.

"Ouch!" I muttered. "Stupid contact lens! Can you help me out?"

"Sure," Kerri said. "Then we'd better tell the emperor to put on some clothes. It's time to get this last day of filming in the can."

Chapter Nineteen

With the clock ticking down to D-day, everyone was scrambling around the set like fire ants trying to rebuild a kicked-in nest. Everyone *except Tad*, that was.

As usual, the "star of the show" had demanded every last one of his contractual perks and breaks—including his In-N-Out Burger substitute—a Wendy's shake, a Burger King Whopper, and a supersized McDonald's French fries.

But as it turned out, it wasn't Tad who'd ended up being the biggest pain in the butt on our final day of marathon filming. That distinction fell to the final femme fatale of the series, Fanny Smith—aka Fanny Tight. She was every bit the prima donna Tad was, with one exception.

Fanny was abysmal at acting.

After screwing up her line, she'd nearly ruined her makeup by spritzing herself with coconut water. I'd rushed to Fanny's aid with the special organic blotting tissues she'd demanded. While tamping her petulant forehead, Fanny spotted my pale blue eye, screamed, and shouted she was going to call 9-1-1 and report a zombie invasion.

Yeah. That really happened.

By the time the other crew members got her calmed down, I was pretty certain the only real assets Fanny had brought to the table were those 38 double-Ds in her bikini top.

Her part in the final scene couldn't have been simpler. Fanny was supposed to scream, then lie there while I stabbed her and delivered my punchlines. In my mind, it should've taken all of fifteen minutes to film. But even though the woman only had one line (a scream, no less), she kept screwing it up by breaking into a giggling fit.

We were now on hour four of shooting—and tempers were starting to flare. At 3:00 p.m., Marshall angrily announced that if we didn't get the shot completed within the next ten minutes, we were going to miss the deadline to deliver the four remaining episodes of *B&L* to Channel 22 by five o'clock today.

According to Marshall, if we didn't deliver on time, the project was dead. All I knew was that if I didn't get out of that sweltering old-man mask soon, *I'd* be dead as well.

Frustrated, I was ready to kill Fanny with my bare hands if she giggled again. I wasn't the only one for whom Fanny had lost her luster. Tommy and Marshall had stopped staring at her chest and begun glaring at her face. I took it as a sure sign the apocalypse was at hand.

"Come on, people, we can do this," Kerri announced, trying to inject some calm into the stormy set. She glanced at her watch and gulped.

"Are we too late?" I asked through the mask.

"Maybe," Kerri said. "Maybe not."

Fanny giggled.

"Dammit, Fanny!" Marshall hissed. "This isn't funny!"

"Look," Kerri said. "It's past three. Channel 22 just finished replaying the same pilot episode that aired Friday. At this point, they're pretty committed to running *B&L*. I'm going to call Bob Johnson and beg for an extension. I mean, what can he say?"

"Good idea," Marshall said.

"Good luck," I said as Kerri scurried out the door.

While Kerri begged for leniency, we kept filming. And, infuriatingly, Fanny kept giggling.

Talk about your incentive to murder someone ...

I think Marshall was about ready to stab Fanny himself when he was interrupted by Kerri's return.

"Bob's agreed to give us more time!" she beamed.

"Yes!" we all cheered.

"Don't celebrate just yet," Kerri said, holding up a finger. "The extension is based on one condition. Bob said that as long as the three new episodes we've finished are delivered to Channel 22 by five today, he'll give us until five tomorrow to deliver the final episode."

"You've got wicked negotiating skills, Kerri!" Marshall said, patting her on the back. "You saved us!" He turned to Fanny. "That should be no sweat, *right*?"

Fanny smiled sheepishly. "Sure." Then she giggled.

I gritted my teeth and glanced out the window. The sun was setting outside. We were all exhausted. Would this dingbat woman ever quit giggling like an idiot and give us a freaking break?

"Come on, crew," Tommy said. "This is the final scene for the series. Let's nail it with this next take, then go celebrate, okay?"

We all mumbled in agreement and took our places on the set. Fanny lay on the bed. I stood over her with the collapsible knife. But as soon as I raised my hand to stab her, Fanny giggled.

Again.

For the millionth time.

"Once more, from the top," Marshall said wearily.

I contemplated asking Marshall for a real knife. Then I recalled a nugget of the wisdom I'd gleaned from the *Hollywood Survival Guide*. Tip #39. *When you're ready to stick a fork into another cast member's eye, channel your rage into character inspiration.*

I envisioned Fanny lying headless in a dumpster.

"You know, Fanny dear," I said, raising the knife above her ridiculous, bulbous breasts for the umpteenth time. "You can be a *real* pain in the ass."

Fanny's lips began to curl into a smile. Before she could giggle again, I ripped off the rubber bingo-man mask and leaned over her until my bare, sweaty face was mere inches from hers. I glared into her mascara-laden peepers with my ghostly, pale-blue eye and hissed like a snake.

Fanny gasped. And I don't think she was acting.

Like a lightning strike, I raised the fake knife and plunged it into her chest. Tommy zoomed his camera in for a close-up of the action. I turned my face to the camera and let out a maniacal laugh, whirling my weird, mismatched eyes for all I was worth.

Suddenly, something cold and wet spurted across my face. Right on cue, Leslie the makeup girl had squeezed a rubber ketchup bottle full of fake blood at me. It splattered across my face in a perfect line.

"Yes! Yes! Yes!" Tommy screamed. "It's a wrap!"

"Wicked!" Marshall yelled. He rushed over and hugged me, getting fake blood on his expensive Hawaiian shirt.

"Sorry about ripping the mask off," I said. "But I figured we already had enough takes of it the other way. All we needed was to get the final shot without Fanny giggling like a deranged hyena."

"Great save, Doreen," Tommy said. "I don't think we could've gotten through this without you."

"What about me?" Tad said from his comfy chair in the corner. He was sipping an organic shake, his arms folded across his chest. "*I'm* the real hero here."

"Of course you are," I said, barely containing my disdain. "*Everyone* knows that."

"Here you go, *hero*," Leslie said, then shot Tad across the chest with the fake blood.

I smirked. I guess I wasn't the only one fed up with my boss's holier-than-thou crap.

"This is silk!" Tad growled. "The dry cleaning is coming out of *your* paycheck."

"It was worth it," Leslie said, and squirted Tad again.

"Uh, okay," Marshall said, grabbing Leslie by the arm. "We're all beat. Let's go home and get some rest."

"Fine by me," Tad grumbled.

He shot the two young girls a lewd look. They turned to each other, fake-gagged, and headed for the door. On their way out, I heard Leslie whisper to Fanny, "What a pig."

Marshall turned to me, grinning from ear to ear. "We got some great footage that time, Doreen." He leaned in and whispered in my ear, "Fanny may be a pain in the ass, but she really brought out your killer instinct! Your face on that last take was a real money shot!"

Uh, okay...

I glanced over at Tad, expecting him to be happy that I'd done so well. Nope. His face was the color of a ripe pomegranate. Or was that a ripe grenade?

Geez. I just survived a marathon filming session and now I have to soothe Tad's ego? This is bull hockey!

"I was merely the sideshow," I said loud enough for Tad to hear. "We all know the *real* star is *Tad*."

Tad sneered.

Seriously? Ugh. Grow up!

I turned to Kerri. "When you talked to Bob, did he mention anything about last Friday's audience numbers for the pilot?"

"Yes he did," Kerri said. "He said they weren't bad. But coming from Bob that could mean anything."

"Oh." I suddenly felt deflated. Kerri must've noticed.

"Chin up, Doreen," she said. Then she leaned in and whispered in my ear. "Johnson told me that if the audience gathers steam by the time the final episode airs this Friday, he may decide to run the whole serial again. Maybe even pick it up for another season."

My eyebrows rose an inch. "Seriously?"

"Yes, seriously. But keep that under your hat for now." Kerri turned and spoke loud enough for everyone else to hear. "You know, it wouldn't hurt for us to try and create some publicity for the show."

"Like what?" Tommy asked.

"Whatever might get us some traction on social media. Any ideas?"

"Yeah," Tad said, eyeing me angrily. "We could kill off Dorey."

"What?" I hissed. Anger shot through me. "How about we kill off *you*!"

"We need Doreen for next season," Marshall said, stepping between us. "If we get picked up, I mean."

Tad's eyes narrowed. "Won't you need *me*, too?"

"Of course," Kerri blurted. "That goes without saying."

I shot Kerri a *maybe it's time for you to get out of here* look. She got the hint. She reached out and shook Tad's hand. "Thank you for everything, Mr. Longmire."

Tad sighed. "Whatever."

Kerri turned to me. "We best be going. We've barely got more than an hour to get those episodes over to the station."

"I wish you luck," I said, the words catching in my throat. I'd been so busy the last three days I hadn't had time for the realization to sink in that the job with Sunshine City Studios was over. Most likely, I'd never see any of these people again. Except Tad, of course. I couldn't get rid of the jerk even if I wanted to. Life really could stick it to you sometimes.

"It's been great working with all of you," I said.

"The pleasure was ours," Kerri said. "I'm sorry to see you go."

"Yeah," Marshall said, handing me a beer. "I planned an after-party to celebrate tonight. I thought we'd be finished. But as long as we don't get too wasted, we should have enough brain cells left to finish editing the final episode tomorrow and get it to the studio by five, right Tommy?"

Tommy nodded. "Yeah, sure."

"So we'll see you and Tad at the Birchwood rooftop downtown for the party, right?" Marshall said. "Say, nine o'clock?"

I cringed. "I'm sorry. We can't. I glanced over at Tad. He was checking his cellphone and chugging a beer. "Uh ... our plane leaves for L.A. in the morning. I need to get Tad back to the cottage. We've got a long day of travel ahead."

"Of course," Kerri said. "We'll clear out of here and let you two get some rest." She took my hand. "Thanks again for convincing Tad to take the role. And for helping make the project a success. Let's stay in touch. I mean it."

"Okay," I said.

She shot me a friendly, maternal smile. "Have a safe journey home." She hooked Marshall by the arm. "Now we better go deliver those three episodes to Channel 22!"

"Get going, you two," Tommy said, then walked up and placed a hand on my shoulder. "Nice working with you, Doreen. I'm just gonna get a few shots of the outside of the cottage at sunset and I'll be out of your hair." He turned to Marshall and Kerri. "I'll see you at the Birchwood."

"I'll be out of reach most of tomorrow," I said as the three stepped off the porch and headed for their vehicles. Oddly, I already missed them. "But I'm available for a video meeting on Tuesday," I called out like a spinster hoping for a second date. "I'd love to preview the finale. I can't wait to see how it ends!"

"Wouldn't it be great if this turned out to be a hit?" Marshall yelled as he climbed into the passenger seat of Kerri's Jaguar.

I grinned. "It sure would."

Tad snickered behind me. "That load of crap? I wouldn't get my hopes up."

"Hush," I hissed.

"It sure would be great if it was a hit!" he said, mocking my voice. "You're such an ass kisser, Dorey."

I pursed my lips. "It's called *caring*, Tad. You should try it some time."

"Ha ha," he sneered. "Oh, by the way, speaking of *caring*, Dolores Benny cared enough to call me a couple of days ago."

My face went slack. "Ms. Benny? What did she want? She didn't accuse me of stealing something, did she?"

"No." A cruel smirk curled the corners of Tad's handsome mouth. "The crazy old bat asked me if I'd recommend you to play some stupid part in *Breaking Code*."

My mouth fell open. "What?"

Tad let out a sharp laugh. "Yeah. I told her you weren't interested. You were too busy doing your silly serial-killer side gig."

"You *what*?" I screeched.

Tad snorted. "Come on, Dorey. You're not big-screen material. You should be grateful Marshall wanted you for that lousy bit part in his TV series."

"That's not fair!"

"Isn't it?" Tad's ice-blue eyes cut through me. "Isn't that exactly what you told *me* to get me here? Isn't that why I'm in this stupid town filming this piece of crap?"

Insulting *me* was one thing. Insulting my friends and my acting career was quite another.

"Tad Longmire, I could *kill* you!" I screamed.

I raised my hand in anger, then realized the fake knife was still in it. I plunged the collapsible blade into his chest, almost wishing it were real. "You're a first-rate jackass! You know that?"

Tad laughed and grabbed my arm. "At least *I'm* first rate at *something*. Doesn't look like *you'll* ever be."

A car horn beeped. I glanced into the yard. Kerri's silver Jaguar was halfway down the drive. Marshall hung his head out the passenger window and yelled, "Everything okay over there?"

I fake-smiled and waved. "No," I muttered under my breath. "Not by a longshot."

Chapter Twenty

Screw the *Hollywood Survival Guide*. Sometimes when you've got nothing left to lose, you just freaking lose it.

After ripping into Tad with everything I had, he snatched my rubber knife from my hand. I jerked free of his grip and ran toward the beach. Halfway to the shoreline, I began frantically dialing Dolores Benny, hoping it wasn't too late to audition for the part she'd talked with Tad about in *Breaking Code*.

Two hours later, she hadn't returned any of my 38 messages.

I was so mad at Tad Longmire I could barely breathe.

For Kerri and Marshall's sake, I'd worked hard to keep my dirtbag boss in line. But filming was over. And so was my patience. Tad could now officially fall off a cliff for all I cared. I thought about Brent, the young man who should've had the role in *B&L*. Where was he now? Geez. Even if Kerri Middleton had chopped him into little pieces, I'd still think she was a better human being than Tad.

Still fuming, I marched over to a nearby convenience store and bought a bottle of wine to try and dull my anger. Afterward, I skulked back to the cottage, locked myself in my bedroom, packed my bags, and set the alarm for 6 a.m.

I tried calling Ma again, to let her know I was heading back to L.A. She didn't answer. I didn't leave a message. Instead, in desperate need of a good friend and a better mood, I surfed through Netflix until I found my old standby, *Bridget Jones' Diary*. I settled into bed and hit play.

Then, my good buddy Renee Zellweger and I downed a bottle of cabernet sauvignon and commiserated about men until I passed out cold.

***

BUZZ.

I groaned.

Go away.

BUZZ BUZZ.

I rolled over in bed. My brain thumped against my skull.

BUZZ BUZZ.

I leaned over and slapped the little travel alarm clock until it finally shut up. I groaned again, then rolled over onto my back. My head throbbed with every pulse of my heart. To distract myself from the pain, I stared up at the ceiling and counted the tiles. Thirty-eight. That done, I did a bit more math in my head.

I didn't like the outcome.

I still had eleven months and eight days left to serve on my sentence as Tad Longmire's personal assistant.

Crap!

I sat up in bed. My head pounded as if it had just been slugged with a rubber mallet.

Ugh. With any luck, the plane to L.A. will crash and put me out of my misery ...

In a hangover daze, I got up and stumbled to the kitchen for some much needed coffee.

Why on earth hasn't someone invented a coffee IV bag already?

As I fumbled with the coffee filters, I noticed it was 6:15. Mercifully, there was still plenty of time to let the aspirin do its work before Tad and I had to catch the limo to the airport. It was scheduled to arrive at 7:30.

For ten minutes, I sat at the kitchen table, my head in my hands, and let the coffee and pain relievers kick in. Feeling slightly better, I shuffled over to Tad's bedroom door in my fuzzy slippers.

"Get up, Tad," I shouted through the door. "It's time to get going!" Not my most brilliant move. Yelling at him had set off the throbbing in my head again.

Through the door, Tad muttered something I couldn't make out. Knowing him, it was an obscenity. I leaned an ear against the door and listened to be sure. I heard a grunt. Then a woman giggle. My teeth began to grind.

You've got a girl in there? You've got to be kidding me!

"Wrap it up in there," I said. "We have to be out of here in an hour."

"Unbelievable," I muttered over and over as I took a quick shower. I dreaded the trip back to L.A. with Tad. The guy couldn't keep his hands to himself if his life depended on it. And what a control freak! If I had my way, I'd dress for today's travel day in comfy yoga pants and a t-shirt. But as Tad's assistant, he insisted I always appear "professional and sexy," so as not to tarnish his image as a player, I guess.

I begrudgingly pulled on a pair of slacks, a silk shirt, and strappy heels. After fixing my hair and applying the minimal obligatory amount of eyeliner and lipstick, I closed my suitcase and dragged it out into the living room. That done, I glanced over at the coffee I'd set on the kitchen counter for Tad. He hadn't touched it.

Geez Louise! What a turd!

I marched back to Tad's bedroom in a fury. The grunts and groans emanating from behind his door could've made the perfect soundtrack for a porno film. Disgusted, I raised my fist and banged on the door. It swung open.

Cringing, I hazarded a peek inside, hoping I wouldn't get an eyeful of something I couldn't un-see. Tad was still in bed, moaning and sighing. Mercifully, the covers were pulled up over him, so at least I didn't have to un-see *that*.

Anger surged through me anew as I wondered which of the beach bimbos he'd lured into his bed *this* time. My money was on Fanny Tight, the big-boobed pain in the ass. She was a dye-job redhead and dumb as a box of rocks.

Perfect Tad bait.

"Get up, Tad," I grumbled. "You've only got a little over half an hour left to get ready."

He didn't respond. I glanced over at the TV. A dirty movie was playing. I gritted my teeth.

The stupid jerk is pranking me!

"Ha ha. Very funny," I spat. "I get it. The joke's always on me. Now get up. We've got a limo to catch!"

I jerked back the duvet. Tad stared up at me, a stupid, googly-eyed expression on his face. His hands were wrapped around the handle of the fake knife, which he pretended was stuck in the middle of his chest.

"Seriously, Tad?" I growled. "This isn't funny. If you're not ready when the limo comes, I'm leaving without you. I'm serious!"

Tad just stared at me, that stupid grin on his face. Then I saw it. The blood-soaked sheets underneath him.

"Tad!" I screamed. "Tad! Are you all right?" I tried to loosen the knife from his hands and pull it out of his chest. But Tad's hands were cold and stiff. The knife wouldn't budge.

Oh. My. God! This is real!

Panic shot through me like ice water.

Someone's murdered Tad! Are they still here?

Am I next?

I gulped against the hard knot in my throat and slowly backed out of the room. The second my backside hit the doorjamb, I turned and fled down the hall, my heart pounding in my ears like an underwater drum solo.

I gotta get out of here! I gotta call someone!

With the last grain of wits I had left about me, I grabbed my purse off the kitchen table and bolted for the French doors.

I never made it.

Three steps from safety, I slammed into a dark figure in the living room. He grabbed me by both arms and wouldn't let go.

Chapter Twenty-One

"Let me go!" I screamed as I struggled with the unknown intruder in the dim light of the beach cottage's living room.

"Calm down, lady!" the man said, holding me by the wrists as I squirmed, trying to break free.

"Please!" I pleaded. "Don't kill me!"

"Kill you?" the man said. "Come on, my driving isn't *that* bad."

"Wha??" I asked, confused and on the verge of hysteria.

"I'm the limo driver," he said. He released one of my wrists from his vice-like grip. As I stared at him like a stunned sheep at the slaughter-house gates, he reached into his jacket. I flinched, expecting a gun or a knife. Instead, he pulled out a business card.

"I'm Darryl Fin. From Florida Limos. Somebody called about a ride to the airport?"

I nearly fainted from relief. "What are you doing here so ... so *early*?"

"Trying to beat rush-hour traffic," he said. "The door was open. I thought I might come in and get some coffee while I waited. But then I heard someone screaming bloody murder, and you came running at me."

"Oh. Sorry." I felt both stiff and limp at the same time—as if I couldn't move, but might collapse on the floor any second.

The driver let go of my other wrist and I nearly toppled over. "You okay?" he asked. "Wait. What's all over your hands?"

I looked down. It was blood. My hands were covered in Tad's blood.

"Help," I whispered, suddenly unable to breathe. "Call the police. Somebody murdered my boss."

The driver eyed me as if I might be deranged. "Where?"

"In the bedroom."

"Uh ... stay here. Don't move." He slipped past me and cautiously made his way down the hall to Tad's bedroom. I watched, frozen in place, as he took a peek inside.

"Holy hell!" he yelled. "I'm calling 9-1-1!"

***

Darryl the limo guy stayed with me until the police arrived. He stood beside the limo, nervously smoking one cigarette after the other. I sat on the front steps of the cottage, shivering and blinking back tears as I watched the sun rise on a new day without Tad Longmire in it.

After what seemed like forever, two police cruisers came racing up the driveway. A tall, slim black man in a blue uniform jumped out of the lead car.

"Where's the victim?" he asked.

"He's in there," I said weakly, pointing to the French doors.

The cop looked me over for a moment, then sprinted inside the cottage, gun drawn. The second cop stood guard over Darryl and me, his hand at the ready on his revolver.

After a minute or so, the first cop reappeared on the cottage porch. "All clear, Rainy," he said to the other cop. "One DB. Second door to the left. Call forensics." He knelt down on one knee beside me on the steps. "What's your name?"

"Uh ... Doreen Diller."

"I'm Sergeant McNulty." He glanced at my hands. "Are you injured?"

"Uh ... no. I don't think so."

"Okay. Tell me what happened, to the best of your recollection."

I glanced over at Darryl. "Where do I start?"

"Rainy," McNulty said, shooting the other cop a stern look. "Take the driver's statement over by your patrol car."

"Yes, sir," Officer Rainy said, then led Darryl out of earshot.

Sergeant McNulty watched them go, then turned his attention back to me. "Do you know the man inside?"

"Yes. He's Tad Longmire."

"What's your relationship to him?"

"He's my boss."

"Can you explain what happened to him?"

"No. I found him like that this morning. I thought it was a joke."

"A joke?"

"You see, last night I was playing around with the knife. I told Tad I wanted to kill him. So when I found him I thought he was pranking me ..."

I stared at the blood on my hands and crumpled. "Can I go wash my hands? Please?"

"No. Not yet." McNulty took me by the arm and stood me up on the steps. "Come with me." He walked me over to his police cruiser and opened the back door. "Get in, Ms. Diller."

"Where are we going?" I asked.

"To the police station."

I cringed. "What for?"

His brow furrowed. "Lady, do you really have to ask?"

Chapter Twenty-Two

"So let me get this straight," Sergeant McNulty said, his knuckles ashen as they pressed against the metal interrogation table he was leaning across. "You're telling me you slept through a homicide that occurred in the bedroom right next to yours?"

"Well, yes," I said.

Technicians had already confiscated my purse, swabbed my hands, collected fingerprints, and stripped me nearly naked to check for fresh wounds and bruises. Then they'd photographed me both front and sideways for what I assumed were *not* new headshots for my acting portfolio.

After processing was done, I was carted off to a very small room that smelled of stale coffee, urine, and desperation. Still numb from the shock of Tad's death, I rubbed my trembling, purple fingertips together. To stop my thighs from shaking, I wrapped my ankles around the front legs of the hard, metal chair I'd been directed to sit on.

"How is it possible you didn't hear a thing?" McNulty asked.

I looked up at the police sergeant. "Well, you see, I'd been watching TV and ... uh ... drinking."

He blew out a breath. "What were you watching and drinking?"

"*Bridget Jones* ... and a very nice bottle of cabernet sauvignon."

A vein on McNulty's temple began to pulse. "Right. So you're saying you got drunk and fell fast asleep. Then what?"

"My alarm went off at six. I got up, made coffee, and took a shower."

"Not hearing or suspecting a thing."

I nodded. "That's right."

"So, did you stab Mr. Longmire *before* or *after* you took the shower?"

I blanched. "What? Neither! I mean ... that doesn't make sense. Why would I take a shower and wash off the blood only to get myself all bloody again?"

The corners of McNulty's mouth curled slightly upward. "So you took the shower to wash off the blood *after* the attack."

"No! That's not what I meant! I was only saying it makes no sense—"

The hard look on McNulty's face made my voice trail off.

"Look," I said. "When I first went to wake up Tad, I heard groaning. And a woman giggling. I thought Tad was having sex. He ... uh ... did that a lot. So I yelled through the door for him to hurry up or something like that, then I went and got a shower."

"Hurry up?"

"We have ... uh *had* ... a flight at ten this morning back to L.A."

McNulty eyed me carefully. "Ms. Diller, were you and Longmire lovers?"

I nearly choked. "He was my employer."

"That's not what I asked."

"No. We weren't lovers."

"Never? Not even once?"

I shook my head. "Not even once."

McNulty scrutinized me with his dark brown eyes. "I hear the guy is some kind of TV heartthrob. It must've been hard to resist his charms."

"Okay," I said. "I'll admit it kind of was. Before I met Tad, I had a crush on him for years. But that ended when I got to know him. He's actually a real jerk."

"What do you mean by 'real jerk'?"

"He's mean-spirited. Lecherous. And a philanderer. And yesterday I found out he cost me a big acting role back in L.A. It quite possibly could've been my big break!"

McNulty's tone sharpened. "So you were angry at him."

"Yes."

"Angry enough to stab him in the heart with a butcher knife?"

I stared, wide-eyed. "Come on. You don't really think—"

"I'm not sure *what* to think, Ms. Diller. "That's why we're having this conversation."

The way he was looking at me, I had a feeling McNulty already knew *exactly* what to think. And it didn't appear I was winning his vote for the Miss Goody Two-Shoes Award.

Backed into a corner, I desperately rifled through the *Hollywood Survival Guide* in my mind. Tip #67 popped up. *Before you dig your own grave, call a lawyer with a sharper shovel.*

"I ... I don't want to say any more without someone here with me," I said.

McNulty let out a disgusted-sounding grunt. "Are you requesting legal representation, Ms. Diller?"

"Shouldn't I?"

The cop's eyes narrowed. "If that's the way you want to play it."

"Play it?" I gasped. "I'm not *playing* anything! Hey, don't I get a phone call or something?"

"No."

"Why not?"

"Because you're not under arrest."

I blanched. "I'm *not*?"

"Not *yet*, no," McNulty said.

I frowned. "What's *that* supposed to mean?"

"It means you're free to go—for now, Ms. Diller."

"I am?"

"Unless you'd like to recant your request for legal representation."

I shook my head. "I don't know. I need to think about it."

"By law, that *is* your right." McNulty opened the door to the tiny room. "Thank you for your cooperation. I'd advise you not to leave town until we've cleared you to do so. I have a feeling we're going to need you for more questioning."

"Uh ... okay," I said, scrambling up from the chair.

McNulty handed me a business card. "We'll be in touch. In the meantime, you can reach me here if you have further information you'd like to share."

"What about my purse and my cellphone?" I asked as I brushed by him and out into the hallway.

"They should be done processing them by now. You can pick up your personal effects at the reception window on the way out."

***

Out in the hallway, I stumbled into Darryl Fin, the limo driver. He was dumping the contents of a manila envelope into his hands. Out tumbled his wallet, a watch, and his cellphone.

"I see they took *your* phone, too," I said.

"And my black shirt I needed for work." Darryl pulled at the tight black T-shirt he'd worn underneath his other shirt. "They confiscated it for evidence. It had your bloody handprints on it."

"Oh. Sorry," I said. "Do they think you're a suspect?"

He grimaced. "If they don't, they sure left me wondering. How about you?"

"Yeah. I feel the same. Guilty until proven innocent."

"Tough break for us," he said. "Hey, if you ever need another ride, do me a favor and *don't* give me a call. The last one totally wasn't worth it."

"Geez!" I said. "I totally forgot. I need to pay you for the ride to the airport."

He shot me a pained smile. "Don't sweat it. Send me a get-out-of-jail-free card instead, and I'll do the same for you."

***

As I waited in line to pick up my cellphone, Kerri walked into the station. I nearly leapt for joy at seeing a friendly face.

"Kerri!" I called out. "You came!"

She saw me, winced out a smile, and came rushing over, her arms open wide. "It's so awful about Tad. I came as soon as I heard."

"Thanks. I ... I don't know what happened. But I'm pretty sure the police think I did it."

"Seriously?" Kerri said. "Why?"

"Who's this?" a voice sounded behind me. I turned to see Officer McNulty eyeing Kerri.

Kerri straightened to her full height. "I'm Kerri Middleton."

McNulty's eyebrow angled upward slightly. "And your relationship to Ms. Diller?"

"Work colleague. And friend."

"Right," he said. "Would you mind stepping inside my office for a moment?"

**

I sat on a hard bench in the corridor of the police station for half an hour, watching what passed for humanity come and go through the front door. But who was I to talk? I was a stranger in a strange town, and had just been declared a murder suspect! I'd never felt so small and lost and afraid.

I was about to start bawling when Kerri finally returned, escorted by McNulty. She looked pale.

"Keep my card handy," McNulty said, then shot me a dubious look. "You may need it."

"What did he say to you?" I asked as he walked away.

Kerri leaned close and whispered, "Not here. Come with me."

"Where are we going?" I whispered back. She didn't answer.

I followed Kerri down the corridor like an orphaned puppy. "McNulty told me not to leave town," I whispered. "I guess I need to find a place to stay for a few days."

"I'm sorry, but you can't go back to the beach cottage," Kerri said as we walked past a line of people sitting in the front lobby. "Marshall called and said it's a crime scene now. It's swarming with police investigators. I guess that just leaves my place."

I cringed. "I know it looks bad for me, Kerri. And you barely know me. If you don't want to take me into your home, I totally understand."

Kerri turned and put a hand on my shoulder. "Look. Being a news anchor taught me that people are capable of just about anything." Her eyes darted around. "This place is living proof."

"I hope you don't count me in this lot," I said.

Kerri looked into my eyes. "Let me tell you this, Doreen. You don't work in the business as long as I have and not learn how to tell a good guy from a bad guy. You just don't strike me as a murderer."

My knees nearly buckled from relief. "Thank you!" I cried. "Thank you for believing me. I only wish Sergeant McNulty did."

"Come on," Kerri said. "Let's get out of here before the news channels pick up on this and all hell breaks loose."

She swung open the door to the police station.

A barrage of blinding lights flashed in our faces.

A crop of microphones crackled to life.

Then a pack of reporters fell upon us like ambush predators closing in for the kill.

Chapter Twenty-Three

I stood, mouth agape, and stared in utter shock and awe at the crowd of reporters racing toward us like Kerri and I were the finish line. I'd often dreamt of being chased by the paparazzi—but that had been for winning an Oscar, not for being the prime suspect in a celebrity murder.

Not quite the same thing.

"Are you involved in the Tad Longmire case?" one of the news crew shouted from the gathering horde.

"Crap," Kerri hissed. "The word is out."

She shoved me back inside the police station, snatched a magazine from a table in the lobby, and said, "Here, cover your face with this."

"Got it," I said. Mimicking all the celebrity duck-and-cover videos I'd seen, I tucked my head and buried my face behind the magazine.

"Here we go," Kerri said, grabbing my hand to guide me. She kicked open the door and yelled, "Run!"

Then she nearly yanked my arm off.

Together we raced toward the parking lot, worming our way through the gauntlet of reporters' elbows and the cameras and microphones they jammed into our faces. Somehow, we made it to Kerri's Jaguar. We scrambled inside and locked the doors. Hands and faces filled the windows like a scene from *The Twilight Zone*.

"Now what?" I asked, confused and out of breath.

"Get down," Kerri said calmly.

She motioned for me to crouch down onto the passenger-side floorboard. I obeyed. A second later, she punched the gas and peeled out of the lot, trailing a ragtag parade of news vans and sketchy vehicles behind us.

***

Crammed into the space between the passenger seat and the dashboard, it wasn't long before my left calf began to cramp. I looked up from Kerri's

Gucci pumps mashing the gas pedal and said, "I think my foot is turning gangrenous."

The tension in Kerri's face relaxed a notch. "Sorry. Looks like we've lost most of the press. You can get up now. We're almost there."

"Thanks for saving me," I said as I extricated myself from the floorboard of the Jaguar and slowly straightened my body up and into the passenger seat.

To my surprise, Kerri was pulling up to an impressive, stucco guardhouse surrounded by tropical foliage. A huge iron gate blocked our entry into what appeared to be a hoity-toity paradise for the rich and famous.

"Ms. Middleton," a man in uniform said, smiling at her as she rolled down the window. "Nice to see you. Who's your guest?"

"Hi, Charlie. She's an old friend. Hey, I'm in a bit of a hurry today. No time to chat."

Charlie nodded and scribbled something onto a clipboard. "No worries. You two have a nice day." He reached over and punched a button. The massive metal gate swung open. Kerri sped inside, then stopped. She watched in the rearview mirror until the gate closed and locked back into place.

"Whew," she sighed. "Looks like we lost them."

"Thank you again," I said. "Without you, I'd be on the front page of every tabloid still in print."

"Bad news travels fast," Kerri quipped.

I glanced around. "Wow. This place is really posh!"

All around, lush tropical palms and flowering bushes formed oases in the sea of emerald-green grass. A fountain spouted water in a scallop-shell pattern from the middle of a small lake.

"It's all right," Kerri said, hitting the gas. "But the best part about Scallop Lake is that it's safe." She blew out a breath. "You know, I never was one for gated communities until I landed the job as a news anchor. Once you get a little famous, the psychos seem to come out of the woodwork."

"I know what you mean," I said, gawking at the elegant, Spanish-style mansions lining each side of the road. Everything—even down to the length of the grass blades—was perfect.

"The general public is bad enough," Kerri said, pulling into the driveway of a two-story Mediterranean house covered in swirly, pink stucco. "But give somebody a press pass and a microphone, and you have the makings of a petty dictator."

"Whoa. I never thought about it like that."

Kerri cut the ignition and turned to me. "Be careful what you ask for, Doreen. Take it from me. Fame, no matter how fleeting, can be a real bitch."

***

Safe inside Kerri's beautiful home, I'd spent Monday afternoon making phone calls to friends and associates back in L.A. to let them know Tad was dead. Oddly, none of them seemed that surprised—especially Tad's attorney, Ralph Steinberger.

"I was expecting something like this," he said.

"You were?" I asked. "Why?"

"Let's just say Tad knew how to irritate people."

I grimaced. "I can't argue with that. I guess that means I'm freed from my contract?"

"Yes. I'll send you a letter to that effect. Email okay?"

"Yes. Thank you. Will I get paid any kind of severance?"

"Don't worry, Ms. Diller. I'll make sure you get what's coming to you."

"Uh ... thanks."

"Good day," he said, then clicked off the phone.

"Who was that?" Kerri asked as I hung up.

"Tad's attorney. He's going to make the arrangements for his body to be shipped back to L.A. once it's released from the coroner's office."

"Will there be a funeral?" she asked.

I shook my head sadly. "No. Just a memorial service. He said Tad was too famous to have a funeral. What did he mean by that?"

"Too many nut jobs," Kerri said. "Like I told you, fame can be a mixed blessing. You hungry? I ordered pizza."

I suddenly realized I was famished. "Pizza sounds great!"

The doorbell buzzed. Kerri smiled. "I told Charlie to let the pizza guy through. That must be him now." She walked over to the front door and looked through the peephole. She frowned, then she mashed an intercom button. "Who's there?"

"Pizza guy," a voice sounded through the speaker.

Kerri's nose crinkled. "Take off the hoodie. Let me see your face." She shook her head. "Nice try, Brad. But I'm not opening the door."

"Come on, Kerri," the man said. "Just five minutes. That's all I'm asking."

"Not happening. Leave the pizza on the steps and I won't report you to the guard *or* your boss." Kerri stared through the peephole for another minute or so, then opened the door. She grabbed the pizza, and quickly shut and locked the door behind her.

"Who was that?" I asked.

"Brad Teller from Channel 7," she said. "Just your typical second-string reporter willing to sell his soul to make it to the next rung."

I nodded. "That was a pretty clever trick."

Kerri laughed. "Yeah. Can't say I haven't done the same thing myself. As a former reporter, I know all their sleazy tactics. I also know they have the upper hand on me."

"What do you mean?"

"They know where I live."

"Oh. So, what do we do now?" I asked.

"Keep the drapes pulled and we should be okay."

I followed Kerri into the living room. She put the pizza box on the coffee table in front of the sofa. "You want a Coke?"

"Sure. Let me help."

"Nothing to it. Help yourself to a slice before it gets cold."

"Thanks." When Kerri came back with the sodas, I hung my head.

"I'm so sorry about inconveniencing you like this, Kerri. I'd leave on the next plane out, but Sergeant McNulty told me I couldn't. I think I'm his main suspect. They found me with Tad's blood on my hands. It doesn't look good for me."

"Don't give up on yourself just yet," she said.

I tried to look nonchalant, but I was dying to know. "What did he ask you about back at the station?"

Kerri opened the pizza box and took a slice. "He asked me what I knew about Tad's and your relationship."

"What did you say?"

Kerri winced. "I had to be honest with him, Doreen. I told him the afternoon before the murder, I'd offered to put you up in a hotel, but you wanted to stay at the cottage."

"That's fine," I said. "It's true."

"I also had to tell him that the last time I saw Tad alive, you were screaming in his face that you were going to kill him."

My jaw dropped. "I'm doomed."

"Not if you're innocent."

"I am! But the evidence doesn't look good. I was in the room next to him when it happened. I slept through him being stabbed! Why didn't they stab me, too?"

I shook my head. "My hands were bloody from touching the knife in his chest, Kerri. And the only alibi I have is that I was watching Netflix, drunk. The media is going to crucify me!"

Kerri scrunched her face sympathetically. "Maybe not. Let's turn on the news and see what they know."

She clicked the TV remote. The screen blinked on, revealing a news desk with the emblem Channel 22 on it. A guy with a walrus moustache and matching waistline was sitting next to a stunning young blonde.

"That's anchorman Paul Fenderman," Kerri said, disdain marring her usually serene face. "I used to occupy the seat next to him until I aged out. Did I tell you his breath smells like sardines and day-old coffee?"

"Police report they have suspects, but they're not saying who," Fenderman's voice boomed from the screen. "What have you been able to find out, Tegan?"

"*Tegan*?" I said as if it were a curse word. "Ugh."

"Exactly," Kerri said.

"Yes, Paul!" Tegan gushed. "What was Tad Longmire, bad-boy heart-throb of *Days of Our Lies* doing in St. Pete?" Her voice squealed with naughtiness. "Some are specul ... speca ... *thinking* he was here on a secret rendezvous."

Kerri turned to me. "Could Tad have been meeting someone in secret while you were here?"

"Hardly," I said. "Tad had plenty of uh ... *rendezvous*, as you no doubt bore witness too. But Tad didn't keep secrets. He never thought anything he did was wrong, so where was the need? That's the reason he lost his last job, you know. He was caught boning the director's wife in broad daylight."

"I heard," Kerri said. "I'll be honest with you, Doreen. You sound angry. And perhaps even a bit jealous. Are you being straight with me when you say you and he didn't have something going on?"

"Yes," I said. "I'm angry because the guy ruined my life! Why would you even *think* that I'd sleep with him?"

"Well, I saw your hand on his knee once. Then Tad was naked on the front porch the other morning. Not to mention the constant barrage of innuendoes he kept flinging at you. Then there was the punched nose. The black eye ..."

"You think ... I never *hit* Tad!" I shook my head, bewildered. "Look. Sure, I had a crush on him at one time. But it took me less than an hour to figure out Tad was a horn-dog. For him, getting lucky with the ladies is just a numbers game. I felt like punching him out plenty of times. But I never acted on it."

Kerri nodded. "Okay. So, explain to me why you were screaming that you wanted to kill him last night?"

I crumpled back onto the couch. "I've been waiting *fifteen years* for someone to offer me a part in a movie. Last week, someone called Tad asking him for a recommendation for me. It was for a part in an action flick being filmed right now in Hollywood called *Breaking Code*. That part could've been my big break, Kerri. Maybe my only chance to hit the big time. But Tad blew them off, saying I wasn't interested."

Kerri blanched. "What a jerk! Why would he *do* that?"

"Out of spite, maybe. Or jealousy."

Kerri shook her head. "I don't understand."

I looked up at Kerri. "Tad was peeved that I was getting more attention from you guys than he was."

Kerri blew out a breath. "Men."

"There's no way I'd sleep with Tad. Like you said, he was a jerk. Besides, keeping Tad out of my pants was job security insurance number one."

Kerri's eyebrow rose. "Usually in this business it's the other way around."

I locked eyes with her. "I didn't say he didn't *try*."

"Well, once you reach my age, you won't have to worry about that anymore."

"As beautiful as you are? I'd say I find that hard to believe, except I've done the math."

"The math?"

"Yeah. Did you see the latest movie by Paramoral Films, *Baby my Baby*?"

Kerri shook her head. "No."

"Don't bother. Here's the gist. Gorgeous, blonde, 29-year-old hottie falls for 58-year-old barely passable gasbag twice her age. He's a lout and a loser, but she can't get enough of him."

Kerri groaned. "Not another one."

"Yep." I shook my head in disgust. "Ugh! I'm *so sick of it*! If the roles were reversed, the guy would have to date someone *116 years old*. We're talking *Tales from the Crypt*, here!"

"Typical misogynistic bull crap," Kerri sighed.

"Exactly. Tad's 40. I'm 39. I'd be lucky to get a part playing his mother!"

"You're right. But take my advice. *Let it go*."

"Let it go? Why?"

"Because, in case you forgot, we have bigger fish to fry at the moment. You look worn out. Why don't you try and get some sleep?"

"Who can sleep with this going on?"

"I know," Kerri said. "But we're all exhausted from four days of nonstop filming. We can't think straight. I realize things look bad right now, but don't forget, you have an ace in the hole."

I blanched. "I *do*?"

"Yes," Kerri said. "You're innocent."

Oh. Right.

"You *are* innocent, aren't you?" Kerri asked.

I smiled weakly. "Of course. Of course I am!"

Chapter Twenty-Four

"Who would want to kill Tad?" I asked Kerri, putting voice to the question that had been silently plaguing both my thoughts and my dreams since finding my boss stabbed to death yesterday morning.

Kerri was perched on a barstool at her spotless granite kitchen counter, sipping coffee and tapping away on her laptop. Even though it was barely dawn, she was glamorously put together in a matching pink-satin loungewear ensemble. By comparison, I was dressed in rumpled sweatpants and T-shirt, looking as if I'd just tumbled out of a dirty clothes hamper at a homeless shelter.

"The question is who *wouldn't* want to kill him?" Kerri asked, looking up from her computer.

"What do you mean?" I reached for the cup she'd set out for me on the counter next to the coffee machine.

"Come look at this." She spun the laptop around so I could see the screen. "There's an entire AboutFace page dedicated to *Tad's a Cad*—a fan page for Tad Longmire haters."

I gawked at an image of Tad in an unflattering, leering, drunken pose. "Geez. There's like, over a thousand members!"

"Yes," Kerri said, her eyes darting up to mine. "See? Fame cuts both ways." She grimaced. "Sorry. I didn't mean to make a pun."

"Huh? Oh. It's okay." I shook my head. "I still can't believe Tad's really dead."

"Me, either. Well, he certainly won't be starring in any more episodes of *B&L*."

"Oh my gosh!" I blurted. "I completely forgot. What about the edits for the series finale? Weren't they due yesterday?"

"Yes. But don't worry. Marshall said he took care of it." Kerri looked away and smiled wistfully. "You know, that's one advantage of being young ... and a man. Ambition can overcome emotion. If it had been up to me alone, I'm not sure I could've gotten through the edits yesterday."

"I don't think I could either," I said, pouring myself a cup of coffee.

Kerri smiled wistfully. "Anyway, I'm proud of Marshall. He supervised Tommy through the entire editing process. The two of them got the project delivered to Channel 22 all on their own."

She let out a small laugh. "Maybe I'm not the only grownup in the room after all."

I smiled and touched her arm. "Thank you again for saving me yesterday. I'm sorry you missed out on supervising the final episode."

"It's fine, really. I was there for the first part of it."

"And?" I asked.

Kerri shrugged. "Honestly? It was just like the others. A bit hokey, a bit sexy, and no brain cells were harmed in the making of it."

I laughed. Kerri smiled at me. "You know, Doreen, without the wry humor we wrote into your killer's lines, to me the whole project would be ultimately forgettable. But do you think that you or I will get any credit? I, for one, am not holding my breath."

I crinkled my nose. "Maybe it's just as well if *B&L is* forgotten. Without Tad, the series is dead anyway, whether the station offers to pick it up or not."

Kerri's hazel eyes found my mismatched pair. "That's what happens when you kill off the heartthrob, Ms. Killigan."

Even though I was pretty sure Kerri was just joking, her words jabbed at my heart, rekindling the panic I'd felt yesterday after Sergeant McNulty had insinuated I was responsible for Tad's death. I didn't do it. But who did?

I needed to figure that out in order to save my own skin. So far, the only other lead I had was sitting across from me. If Kerri did away with Brent, she could certainly do-in Tad as well. It felt weird to even entertain the thought. Kerri had been so nice to me. But then again, according to the documentaries I'd watched, serial killers could seem absolutely normal.

"You know," I said, "I've been meaning to ask you about the guy who Tad replaced. Brent something? Whatever happened to him?"

Kerri pursed her lips. "Well, I—"

My cellphone rang. "Hold on," I said as I grabbed it up. The screen showed it was the St. Petersburg Police Department. "I better get this."

Kerri nodded. "Go ahead."

"Hello?" I said into the phone.

"Ms. Diller? Sergeant McNulty here. I need you to come in today at one o'clock for more questioning."

"Uh ... sure. Have you found something else?"

"Like what?"

I cringed. "I don't know. That's *your* job, isn't it?"

"We're working on it. So, I'll see you at one?"

"Sure. Anything I can do to help."

"Good. When you come, bring any receipts you have with you. Travel vouchers, airline tickets, and the like. We'll need to verify your whereabouts on Monday afternoon through Tuesday morning."

"Uh ... sure thing."

McNulty clicked off. I looked up at Kerri. Her face was lined with worry.

"What's wrong?" I asked.

"Look, I'm sorry to ask, but have you got anywhere else you can go?"

"I ... uh ... I guess so," I said.

The look on Kerri's face knocked the wind from my sails. I'd begun to worry she might be Tad's murderer. Now I was afraid she thought *I* might be. Geez. Tad had been dead for barely a day and suspicions were popping up everywhere like toadstools after a rain.

"Are you worried that I killed Tad?" I asked.

"What? No!" Kerri said, shaking her head. "We just need to get you out of here. While you were on the phone, Charlie at the front gate called. The entire entrance is overrun with news vans."

"Oh." I cringed. "What are we going to do? They know your car. And I don't have one."

Kerri's lips twisted in thought. "How do you feel about bagels?"

***

It was another clever idea from Kerri. She called a food delivery service. Twenty minutes later, a guy who barely spoke English came to the door with a bag of bagels. Tempted by a crisp fifty-dollar bill, Paco was more than happy to smuggle me out of Kerri's place in the trunk of his car.

"Message me when you get there," Kerri said as I lugged my suitcase into the junk-filled trunk of Paco's light blue Chevy Caprice.

"I will," I said. I handed him a slip of paper with an address, then climbed into the trunk next to my bag.

Kerri waved goodbye. As Paco closed the trunk lid, I saw her note down his license plate—in case she never heard from me again.

The address I'd given Paco was the only other one I knew in St. Petersburg. As he took off, I bounced around inside the dark, smelly trunk, chewing on a mouthful of onion bagel. The absurdity of my situation made me laugh, albeit with a tinge of hysteria.

To calm myself, I used my phone light to search through my *Hollywood Survival Guide*. I wanted to see if it offered any advice on what to do when trapped inside the trunk of a car.

Surprisingly, it did.

Tip #84 read: *When forced into a car trunk, call 9-1-1. No phone? Search the crevices for a weapon to whack your abductor with when he lifts the lid.*

I found a weapon, just in case. Then, in lieu of 9-1-1, I dialed the number Ma had texted me a week ago. As it rang, I crossed my fingers and said a short prayer.

Hopefully, Aunt Edna would be a lot more accommodating than my own mother had been.

Chapter Twenty-Five

It was nearly ten o'clock when Paco's Chevy Caprice came to a lurching halt. Uncertain if I'd just been driven to Aunt Edna's place or to a serial killer's lair, I followed the advice in the *Hollywood Survival Guide* and armed myself with a rusty old wiper blade.

Fortunately, I didn't need to use it. True to his word, Paco opened the trunk and helped me out, no questions asked. As he drove away, I texted Kerri the code we'd agreed upon if all had gone according to plan.

The chick has hatched.

My phone pinged immediately with her reply.

Hope the new coop is nice. Keep me posted.

After being unceremoniously dumped from Paco's trunk, I glanced around. The neighborhood looked decent enough. Not nearly as posh as Kerri's place, but it was well-kept.

I could see the top floors of some high-rise condos at the end of the street and realized it was an older, mixed-use suburb near downtown St. Pete. On either side of the road, two-story block apartment buildings sat tucked amidst rows of cute, wood-frame bungalows in various states of renovation.

As for the address Aunt Edna had given me, it turned out not to be a house at all, but a collection of four small, single-story cottages encircling a common courtyard. A small, wooden sign by the walkway read, *Palm Court Cottages. No Solicitors.*

When I'd talked to her over the phone, Aunt Edna had said she was number one. I thought she'd been bragging or telling some kind of joke that had gone over my head. Now, seeing the place, I figured she must've meant she lived in cottage apartment number one.

Not wanting to show up on her doorstep toting luggage like some transient hobo, I stashed my suitcase behind an azalea bush. That sorted, I tugged the hem of my shirt to straighten out the wrinkles I'd gotten from lying next to a bag of kitty litter in Paco's trunk. Then I took a deep breath and poked my chin up.

Here goes nothing.

As I walked through the courtyard past a huge mango tree, I wondered if Aunt Edna looked like Ma. She'd sounded a lot like her when she'd invited me to tea and cookies. Funny thing was, besides the ancient postcards, I couldn't remember Ma ever talking about her sister Edna.

I wonder why.

"You must be Doreen," a woman's voice sounded from somewhere nearby.

A movement caught my eye. At the end of a rectangular table in the center of the courtyard, a filigreed metal chair swiveled around. A thin, older woman was sitting in it. She eyed me carefully from behind a pair of wrap-around sunglasses. Her face was narrow, punctuated by a large, pointy nose. Her head was capped with curly short hair the color of pewter.

"Aunt Edna?" I asked.

She laughed. "Lord, no. I'm Jackie Cooperelli. I live here. Come on, I'll take you to your aunt."

"Thanks." I followed Jackie to the first cottage on the right. Apartment number one. Jackie banged on the door with a boney fist and yelled, "She's here!"

The door flew open. A woman who looked like Shirley MacClaine in *Steele Magnolias* eyed me up and down. "So you're Doreen, are you?"

"Uh, yes ma'am. Thank you for seeing me on such short notice."

"Not at all. Come on in," Aunt Edna cooed. Slightly plump and wearing a flower-print house dress, she stood to the side and let me pass. "I made snickerdoodles. I hope you like them."

"I do," I said, shooting her a smile. It was a good sign. Ma *never* made snickerdoodles. "But you didn't have to go to any trouble."

"No trouble at all," Aunt Edna said. "Hey, Jackie. You want a snickerdoodle?"

"Yeah, sure," she said, and followed me inside.

The apartment was neat as a pin. But it looked as if it hadn't been updated since VCRs were invented. Harvest gold appliances filled the kitchen. The couch was avocado green velveteen. Three gold chenille cushions on the sofa matched the urine-colored glass of the lamp bases flanking either side of the couch. The lamps sat atop knobby-legged end tables straight from a vintage Sears catalog.

"Have a seat," Aunt Edna said. I took a step toward the couch. "No. Take the easy chair. It's the best seat in the house."

"Thank you," I said, then settled into the huge, overstuffed vinyl recliner. I stared at the gold tassels on the green velour curtains while Aunt Edna poured the tea. "Uh ... nice place you've got here."

"Glad you like it," she said, handing me a dainty teacup. "I put two sugars in it. That's how Maureen ... uh, your *mom* likes it."

"Yes. Thank you," I said, taking the cup.

"Have a snickerdoodle," Jackie said, shoving a plateful at me.

"Thanks." I took a cookie and set it on my plate.

"How about a toast?" Aunt Edna said, raising her teacup.

"Yeah, a toast," Jackie said.

"Sure," I agreed. I smiled and raised my cup.

"To new acquaintances," Aunt Edna said, then drained her cup in one gulp. She shot me a crooked smile. "Come on, drink up. It's a Diller tradition."

I grinned. "Okay. Here goes nothing." I downed my cup.

A moment later, Aunt Edna's huge balloon hand reached out and took the empty cup from me.

She grinned.

The room began to spin around her.

My mouth fell open.

I tumbled forward.

Then I got an up-close-and-personal look at Aunt Edna's green, sculptured-shag carpeting right before the world went black.

Chapter Twenty-Six

I woke up in a strange bed with my arms over my head. I tried to move them but couldn't. Then I realized my hands were tied to the bedposts.

I guess it was true—what goes around comes around.

"She's awake," I heard someone say.

I flinched in fear as Aunt Edna came into the room and stood over me, studying me with narrow, accusing eyes. I spotted a rolling pin poking from her apron pocket. A knot the size of a fist formed in my throat. I was beginning to see why Ma and Aunt Edna had lost touch ...

"Who are you *really*?" Aunt Edna asked, her head cocked sideways at me like an angry parrot.

"Huh?" I stuttered, still recovering from whatever she'd drugged me with. "I ... I'm your *niece*, Doreen Diller."

"Yeah, right." She plucked the rolling pin from her pocket. "You usually travel around inside the trunk of a Chevy Caprice?"

"Uh ... no."

"Spill it. Who sent you?"

"*Ma* gave me your address. Your sister. Maureen Diller?"

Aunt Edna eyed me with suspicion while her friend Jackie took up position by the door, armed with a flyswatter and a can of Raid.

"Huh," Aunt Edna grunted. "From what I hear, my niece Doreen is living in L.A. And she's a lot fatter than you."

I was suddenly wide awake. "Ma told you I was *fat*?"

"I got my sources," Aunt Edna said, folding her arms across her chest.

I frowned. "I'm not fat. I'm big-boned. And nobody sent me. I'm here in town because I'm doing a film out at the beach."

"Uh-huh. I ain't buyin' it toots." Aunt Edna began to slap the rolling pin in her left palm like she was warming up to slam a homerun through my right temple.

I flinched. "I *swear* I am! How can I prove it to you?"

Aunt Edna sneered. "If you was really my niece, you'd have a bum eye."

I gasped. "How do you know about that? Ma told *nobody*!"

"I was there for Doreen's birth," Aunt Edna said.

"You were?"

"Yeah. Scared the poop outta the doctor. Pulled her out and nearly dropped the child on her head. Me and Maureen knew right then we had to hide the eye if the poor girl was gonna have a chance at a normal life. We'd both seen what it did to Sammy."

"Sammy?" I asked.

"Our cousin, twice removed. Sammy the Psycho. He had them crazy eyes, too. Made his childhood miserable. Turned him mean. Nuts, even. Last I heard, Sammy was a serial killer up in Wisconsin."

"He always did love cheese curds," Jackie said.

Aunt Edna smiled wistfully. "Yeah, he did."

I blanched.

Is that why Ma had home schooled me until I learned how to wear a contact lens?

"Look, Aunt Edna. Untie me and I'll show you my eye."

"Ha," she laughed. "You're a slick one. Just like Sammy." She motioned to her accomplice who was still standing guard by the door. "Jackie, you check her eye. I'll hold the pin on her."

"You got it." Jackie set the flyswatter and bug spray down on a white-and-gold French provincial vanity. Then, with two boney fingers, she pried open my right eye and clawed at it with a fingernail.

"Ouch!" I cried out. "No. It's in my *left* eye!"

"Oh. Sorry." Jackie let go of my eyelids and tried the left side. She peeled off my contact lens and gasped.

"Well, I'll be damned," Aunt Edna said. "Sorry, Dorey. A girl can't be too careful these days."

Says the woman who just drugged me, kidnapped me, and nearly clawed my eye out!

"Yeah, right," I said.

"So what'd you say you're in town for?" Aunt Edna asked, as if she'd just sat down next to me on a bus. "Some kind a film?"

"Yes." I blinked my watery eyes, hoping there was no corneal damage. "It's called *Beer & Loathing*. What time is it?"

She frowned. "Quarter to two. You got someplace to go?"

"The program," I said. "It'll be on soon. On Channel 22. Untie me and I'll show you."

Aunt Edna gave a quick nod. "Okay, go ahead Jackie. Untie her. I'll turn on the boob tube." She took a step toward the door, then turned back. "Wait a minute. Is that the one that bumped *Gilligan's Island* off the air? The one with Tad Longmire in it?"

"Yes," I said. "You *saw* it?"

"Hubba hubba," Jackie said. "That Tad Longmire's a real dish!"

"Stop!" Aunt Edna shouted, slapping Jackie's hand away from my restraints. "Don't untie her. The girl's working with Sammy!"

"What?" I gasped. I tried to tug my arms free. They wouldn't budge. I closed my eyes.

Dear god! Aunt Edna's bingo-wing crazy!

"The old guy in the bingo cap," Aunt Edna said.

"What?" I repeated. I opened my eyes and nearly gasped again. Aunt Edna's face was hovering inches above mine. She was so close I could make out the thin, black hairs sprouting above her upper lip.

"The guy in the bingo cap," Aunt Edna repeated. "He looks a lot like Sammy. Admit it. You two are in cahoots to kill us, aren't you?"

"No!" I cried. "That's *me* in the mask."

"Ha! I knew it," Aunt Edna said. She turned to Jackie. "See how I tricked her into confessing?"

"Nice work," Jackie said, pulling my restraints tighter.

"So it's *you* who wants to kill us," Aunt Edna said.

"What?" I cried. "No. I'm not a criminal. I swear!"

"No?" Aunt Edna pulled a cellphone from her pocket. "Well, how about I call the cops. Just in case."

"No!" I yelped.

"Why not?"

"They're ... uh ... kind of looking for me."

Aunt Edna nodded smugly at her partner in crime. "See? What'd I tell you, Jackie? That cop line works every time."

Chapter Twenty-Seven

I was trapped inside the plot of a Steven King movie. I couldn't decide which was worse—being held captive by deranged relatives, or knowing that I was floating along beside them in the same gene pool ...

"I knew it!" Aunt Edna said. "You *are* a criminal."

"No, I swear!" I said, tugging at the restraints binding my hands to the bedposts.

"Then why'd you say the cops are after you?" Aunt Edna asked.

"I didn't *say* that." I tried to sit up, but couldn't. "I mean ... the cops want to *question* me. I have an interview—" My jaw went slack. "Aww, crap! I *had* an interview at the police station at one o'clock. Thanks to you two, I missed it. Now the whole force is probably out looking for me!"

Aunt Edna's eyes narrowed. "So, what do they want to *question* you about?"

I cringed. "Uh ... somebody murdered Tad Longmire."

"In the movies?" Jackie asked.

"No. For real," I said. "And they think it was me."

"That don't surprise me none," Aunt Edna said, shaking her head. She stared at me. Suddenly her hard face softened and went pale. She wobbled on her feet, then collapsed onto a chair beside the bed. "I was hoping we'd saved you, Dorey," she said. "But I guess not."

"Saved me?" I asked.

"Yeah. Me and your ma. We tried to hide the eye. You know, so nobody knew you were cursed. Who do you think told Maureen to dress you like a pirate in all your baby pictures?"

"Huh?" I shook my head. "Wait. I'm *cursed*?"

"Yeah," Aunt Edna said. "You got the Diller Killer Curse, honey. You're doomed to be a serial killer, just like Sammy the Psycho. You can't help it. It's in your genes. You inherited it along with the Psycho Eye."

"Psycho Eye?" I gasped. A wave of indignation shot through me. "Look. I just have a genetic disorder, see? *Heterochromia iridum*."

"Look out!" Jackie said. "She's trying to put a curse on us!"

"No, I'm not!" I yelled. "That's the Latin name for my eye condition. Lots of folks have it."

Jackie screwed up her face and stared at me. "Oh, yeah? Like who?"

"Uh ... Demi Moore," I said. "Dan Aykroyd. Christopher Walken. Kiefer Southerland. Look it up yourself if you don't believe me."

"Those are all actors," Aunt Edna said. "So, you're saying psychopathy and acting are related?"

Huh. I never thought about that.

"You're missing the point," I said.

"So, what *is* the point?" Aunt Edna asked.

"The point is, I was born with an eye condition. Otherwise, I'm perfectly normal."

My aunt's eyebrow shot up. "Except for this little 'killing Tad Longmire' thingy?"

I winced. "I didn't do it. I'm not lying!"

"Huh," Jackie grunted, looking up from her cellphone. "The girl's tellin' the truth, Edna. All them actors have this hexachromia thing. Even that guy Benedict Arnold Cucumber Patch."

"Benedict Cumberbatch," I said.

Jackie nodded. "Yeah. That's the one."

"So, will you untie me now?" I asked.

"Not yet," Aunt Edna said. "You still have to pass the sniff test."

I blanched. "The *sniff* test?"

"Yeah. Jackie, go get Benny."

"Benny?" I grimaced in horror, imagining some liver-spotted old man with a nose like Burgess Meredith smelling me from head to toe. *Ugh!*

"Here we go," Jackie said, returning to the room. Tucked in her arms was an ancient, gray-faced pug with googly, mismatched eyes and a gap-toothed underbite.

"What are you gonna do with *him*?" I asked.

"*Her*," Jackie said, shooting Aunt Edna a knowing smile. "This here pooch has a talent a lot of folks would kill for. You see, ol' Benny here smells dead stuff."

I blanched. "What?"

"You know. Like that kid in *Sixth Sense,*" Aunt Edna said. "The one that saw dead people."

I winced in confusion. "Wha ...?"

Aunt Edna tapped a finger to her temple. "Benny here is like that. Only she can smell deadbeats."

Jackie dropped the dog onto the bed by my feet. It wandered up to my crotch and had a good sniff. Then the pooch ambled up to my head. It smelled my mouth, then tried to French kiss me with a tongue that stunk like roadkill.

"Ugh!" I grunted, pulling my face away.

"Well, what do you know?" Aunt Edna said. She grinned at me. "I guess you're okay after all, Dorey. Untie her, Jackie."

***

"So, you want another cup a tea?" Aunt Edna asked as I rubbed my wrists and stared at the little dog who'd just tried to get to second base with me.

"No thanks."

Aunt Edna chuckled. "Guess I can't blame you there." The dog barked and wagged its stub tail. "Benny likes you."

"Benny?" I asked. "How'd she get that name?"

"On account a she looks like Dolores Benny," Jackie said, setting down her teacup. "You know, that actress who played Danny DeVito's ma on *Throw Momma from the Train.*"

"That was Anne Ramsey," I said.

"Ha!" Aunt Edna laughed. "Told you, Jackie. You owe me fifty bucks."

Jackie scowled. "Crap."

"But you're right," I said. "That pug *does* look like Dolores Benny."

"You *know* her?" Jackie asked, her eyebrows almost to her hairline.

"Yes," I said smugly. "I was her personal assistant."

For four whole days.

"No kidding!" Jackie scooted to the edge of her seat on the couch. "You gotta tell me. Is that mole on her cheek real?"

I shook my head. "Nope. Drawn on with eyeliner."

Jackie scowled. "Crap!"

Aunt Edna laughed. "Looks like you owe me another fifty, Jackie."

"I can't win for losing." Jackie hauled herself up off the sofa and headed for the kitchen. "Hey Doreen, too bad we missed your TV show. We'll catch it tomorrow, okay?"

"No worries about that," Aunt Edna called after Jackie. "I recorded it on the VCR. We'll take a look at it after my niece here finishes her important call." She smiled at me and winked. "By the way, I got a spare bedroom if you need a place to stay. You'll be safe here. And it'd be nice to catch up on the family gossip."

There it was. The offer I'd come here looking for. But after being run over by Aunt Edna's version of the "welcome wagon," I was a tad dubious. Still, I'd survived. And things could only get better from here on out, right?

"Thanks," I said. "I appreciate that."

My aunt handed me my cellphone. "Here you go. Better call that cop and reschedule before he sends out a search party." She turned and cupped a hand to her mouth. "Jackie!" she yelled. "Be a doll and go get Doreen's suitcase she stashed in the azaleas!"

"You got it," Jackie said, filing out of the kitchen.

I followed Jackie out into the tropical courtyard, hoping to find a quiet spot to speak with Officer McNulty in private. As Jackie jerked my suitcase out of the bushes and rolled it back toward Aunt Edna's apartment, a thought clicked in my mind.

Wait a minute. I'll be safe *here? What did Aunt Edna mean by that?*

Chapter Twenty-Eight

I found a secluded spot in the tropical courtyard beside a palm tree and tried calling Ma. I wanted to thank her for not bothering to tell me our family was a bunch of lunatics. I also was keen to find out if Aunt Edna's brand of crazy was the harmless or the lethal kind.

I counted off ten rings. Ma didn't answer. I blew out a breath, then checked my recent calls in search of McNulty's number.

"Which cop you calling?" Aunt Edna's voice sounded from behind me, startling me so badly I jumped.

"Uh ... McNulty," I said, whirling around to face her.

Her lips snarled. "Ugh. McNutsack. He's a real ball buster. You should ask for Brady. He's a good cop. Try to switch to Brady."

"I don't think I get a choice here," I said.

"Then you better get your story straight before you say another word to McNulty."

My eyebrows rose an inch. "How do you know all these cops, Aunt Edna?"

She shrugged. "Eh. We go back a ways. Hey, when you're done, come back inside. It's half past three. I gotta get dinner going. You like linguini with clams?"

"As long as the clams aren't laced with arsenic."

"Ha!" Aunt Edna threw back her head and laughed. "You know, I like you, kid."

Jackie grinned. "Don't worry about dinner, Dorey. If Edna wanted you dead, you'd already be sleeping with the snitches."

"It's *fishes*, Jackie," Aunt Edna said, shaking her head. "How many times I gotta tell you that?"

"As many as it takes." Jackie shot me a wink. "You already passed the sniff test. You've got a shoe in, hun."

I glanced over at my aunt. She was pinching her nose like she felt a migraine coming on. "It's *shoe-in*, Jackie."

"That's what I said!" Jackie shot back.

"*You're* a *shoe-in*," Aunt Edna said. "Not you've *got* a shoe in."

Jackie cocked her head. "That don't make no sense. How could Doreen be in a shoe? She ain't exactly an old lady with a bunch a kids, like in that nursery rhyme."

Aunt Edna sighed and locked eyes with me. "What am I gonna do with her?"

"Don't look at me," I said. "I just got here."

***

"So, what's the plan?" Aunt Edna asked, setting a plate of linguini on a wobbly TV tray in front of me.

While she'd made dinner in the kitchen, Jackie and I'd sat in the living room drinking Cokes and listening to the grandfather clock tick. According to Jackie, dinner was always served at 4:00 p.m. on the dot, and Aunt Edna preferred to cook alone—as in, "Enter the kitchen at your own risk."

"I have an appointment with McNulty in the morning," I said, taking the plate from Aunt Edna.

She scowled. "Not Brady?"

"No. I felt weird about asking McNulty. I mean, what could I say to him? My aunt thinks you're a nut sack?"

She shrugged. "I see your point." She turned and headed back toward the kitchen.

"I guess I could've told him you tried to kill me," I called out after her. "Maybe he'd go easier on me."

Jackie elbowed me. "Like we told you, if we wanted you dead, hun, you'd be dead already."

"Really?" I grimaced. "Were you really gonna kill me with a flyswatter and bug spray?"

"Jackie could make it happen," Aunt Edna said, setting a plate of linguini on Jackie's TV tray. "Dorey, you don't know it, but you're looking at the last crumbs of the Cornbread Cosa Nostra."

"The cornbread *what*?" I asked.

"Cosa Nostra," Jackie said. "It's mob lingo for *The Family*."

My nose crinkled. "*Whose* family?"

Jackie grinned. "The Dixie Mafia."

Aunt Edna searched for a glimmer of recognition in my eyes. "Come on. The Biloxi Brigade, Dorey." She shook her head and sighed. "How soon they forget, Jackie."

"Forget *what*?" I asked as my aunt's backside disappeared into the kitchen again.

"The women," Jackie said.

"The *women*?" I asked.

"Like me and Jackie," Aunt Edna said, emerging from the kitchen again with her own plate of pasta. "We're the gals the gangsters left behind. All the dons and made-men and hotshots. They're either dead or spending the rest of their days at Parchman Farm."

"Huh?" I grunted.

"MSP," Aunt Edna said. "Mississippi State Prison?"

"It ain't fair," Jackie said. "The guys get free room and board for life, but nobody ever thinks about the women they left behind."

"That's us," Aunt Edna said, sticking a thumb in her chest. "The Collard Green Cosa Nostra."

My mouth fell open. "Ma never said a word to me about *any* of this."

Aunt Edna's eyebrow shot up. "And for good reason. We're the original *Fight Club*, Dorey. Rule number one? You don't talk about the Collard Green Cosa Nostra."

Jackie crossed herself.

Aunt Edna locked eyes with me. "From now on, it's the CGCN. Got it?"

"But what about Ma—" I began.

"Enough said." Aunt Edna ran a finger across her neck. "You need to know more, I'll tell you. But only if there ain't no other choice."

"We operate on a need-to-know basis, hun," Jackie said. "And right now, you don't need to know nothin' else."

I poked a fork at some green stuff on my plate. "What's this?"

"Collard greens," Aunt Edna said.

"I have to eat this?" I asked. "Why? Is this some kind of club initiation?"

"No," Aunt Edna said. "Collard greens are good for you. They've got tons of calcium. No need for any of us to catch osteoporosis like your poor cousin, Marcie."

"Oh." I eyed the greens with a smidgen less disgust.

"Plus, they stink when you cook them," Jackie said. "Good for covering up the smell of blood and stuff."

I stifled a cringe. "So, uh ... how'd you ladies end up here in St. Petersburg?"

"Florida's a nice, warm place to die," Aunt Edna said. "Plus, it offers almost as good a cover as the moon."

"Huh?" I asked.

Jackie winked. "With so much weird stuff going on around here all the time, it's easy to live under the rainbow."

"Under the *radar*," Aunt Edna corrected.

Jackie's nose crinkled. "Who'd wanna live under a freakin' *radar*?"

"Forget it," Aunt Edna said. She grabbed the TV remote and clicked on the old set. "Okay, everybody. Put a sock in it. We're gonna take a look at this fakakta show of yours, Dorey."

"Fakakta?" I asked.

"Sorry," Aunt Edna said. "I picked that up from Morty. This guy I used to date."

***

The pasta was in our stomachs and the show credits were rolling on the TV screen. Episode three of *Beer & Loathing* had made its world debut.

"Huh. You're a regular wise guy," Jackie said, grinning at me.

I nearly blanched. "I am *not* a mobster."

She laughed. "No. I meant with the *jokes*."

"Oh."

"Sammy always did like a good joke," Aunt Edna said, a faraway smile on her lips. Suddenly, she pointed to the TV. "Ha! There's your name on the credits, Dorey. But it don't say what for. Unless your stage name is Miss Cellaneous."

"That's because the killer's supposed to be a secret," I said.

Aunt Edna crinkled her nose at me. "That was really you in that rubber mask? Your voice didn't sound right."

"They digitally enhanced it to sound gender neutral," I explained.

"Yeah?" My aunt snorted. "Well that Honey Potter's been enhanced too, but I wouldn't say it's gender neutral."

Jackie scrunched her face in disgust. "If you ask me, that blonde bimbo had it coming." She elbowed me. "If I were you, I'd a stabbed her, too."

I nodded and sniffed.

"Hey. You crying?" Jackie asked.

"No." I blinked hard. "It's my eye. It hurts pretty badly. I think it got scratched."

"Oh." Jackie winced. "Sorry about that." She scooted closer to me on the couch and patted my back. "We'll put some Mercurochrome in it. It'll be good as new tomorrow. You'll see."

Horrified, I glanced over at Aunt Edna. She smiled and shook her head. "I think Visine should do the trick. So, Doreen, what other movies have you starred in?"

"Did you see *Trailer Trash Mama*?" I asked.

"Oh my gawd!" Jackie yelped. "That's my favorite movie of all time!"

I blanched with surprise. "Seriously? Uh, do you remember the character Darla Dingworth?"

"Of course. Wait. That was *you*?"

"No. I was the stunt double. That was me in the dumpster with my head cut off."

"Wow," Jackie said, beaming at me. "You really *are* a movie star!"

Chapter Twenty-Nine

"How'd you sleep?" Aunt Edna asked as I dragged myself into her harvest gold time-warp of a kitchen.

I shot my unpredictable aunt a wary glance.

With the door locked and a chair wedged under the doorknob, just in case. That's how.

"Fine," I said. "I can't believe I went to bed at 7:30 last night. I must've been exhausted. Or did you put a little something extra in the peach cobbler?"

"Around here, you never can tell," Jackie said with a laugh. She was sitting at the kitchen table dishing sugar into her coffee cup. She turned to face me and smiled dreamily. "But you know, there's something about watching *Wheel of Fortune* that can wear a girl out. That Pat Sajak is one hot number."

Seriously?

Feeling slightly disoriented by my new surroundings and possibly mild sedatives, I glanced up at the ornate, gold-leaf clock on the wall. Like a prop from a *Godfather* film, it was a Rococo relief of a fat-cheeked cherub. It stared down at me accusingly. According to the clock dial wedged in its chubby-armed embrace, it was ten minutes past eight.

"Coffee?" Aunt Edna asked, holding up the carafe.

"Yes, please," I said with a grateful groan.

"So, what's your story?" my aunt asked as she poured me a steaming cupful.

My brow furrowed. It was way too early for twenty questions. "What do you mean?"

"You know. What's the story you gonna tell Sergeant McNutsack today?"

"Oh. I'm not sure yet."

"Well, then, we need to work on that." She handed me the cup of coffee.

"I say it was one of those bimbos on the show who killed Tad," Jackie said.

"She's got a point," Aunt Edna said as we sat down with Jackie at the dining table. "Who would want to frame you for murder, Dorey?"

"Nobody that I can think of," I said. "Besides, no one needed to. I did a pretty good job of doing that all by myself."

"What are you talking about?" Jackie asked.

I drummed my nails on the coffee cup. "Well, for one, I was alone with Tad at the cottage the night he got stabbed. Then I was the one who found him dead in his bed the next morning."

"So?" Jackie said. "That don't sound too bad."

I cringed. "When I found Tad, I panicked and tried to pull the knife out of his chest."

"Oh, crap," Aunt Edna said, shaking her head. "Amateur move."

"It gets worse," I said. "The last time Tad was seen alive he was with me. And I was stabbing him with a fake knife and screaming that I wanted to kill him."

My aunt grimaced. "Any witnesses to that?"

"Yes."

She blew out a breath. "Geez."

"Can we make them go away?" Jackie asked.

"Huh?" I asked. "Who?"

"The witnesses."

I blanched. "What? No. Besides, they've already told the cops."

"Bad break," Aunt Edna said.

"Did I mention that they found me with Tad's blood on my hands and a one-way ticket to L.A. for ten in the morning?"

"Okay, okay. We get the picture. It looks bad," Aunt Edna said. "Let's go through your alibi."

"Yeah," Jackie said. "When did these deadbeat witnesses leave you alone with Tad?"

"I guess it was about four o'clock Monday afternoon," I said.

"Gotta be more specific," Jackie said. "Cops like specific."

"How?" I asked. "Oh, wait. I remember the sun was going down."

"Aha," Jackie said, scrolling through her phone. "Sunset on Monday night was 4:23 p.m."

"Good," Aunt Edna said. "Let's start the timeclock there. What did you do next?"

"I left Tad at the cottage and went and bought a bottle of wine at the liquor store a couple of blocks away."

She nodded. "Okay, the cashier can back you up. You got a receipt?"

"Yeah. In my purse."

"Okay, so then what happened?"

"I went back to the cottage, packed my suitcase, and locked myself in my bedroom. Then I drank the bottle of wine watching *Bridget Jones*."

"So there you have it," Jackie said. "Just call this Bridget girl and get her to vouch for you."

Aunt Edna pinched her nose. "*Bridget Jones* is a movie, Jackie."

Jackie winced. "Oh. So then what happened?"

I threw up my hands. "*Nothing*. I stayed in my room all night until the alarm went off at six a.m."

"You didn't even get up to pee?" Jackie asked.

"No."

Jackie shook her head. "Lucky duck."

"Not *so* lucky," Aunt Edna said. She locked her earnest eyes with mine. "Doreen, are you *sure* you didn't kill this Tad guy?"

"Yes." I stiffened with indignation. "Why would you even *think* such a thing?"

"Because I've heard Sammy give pretty much the same alibi," she said. "Except his program of choice was *The Ed Sullivan Show*."

I blanched. "What?"

"Don't get me wrong. Sammy was a nice guy," she said. "Until he got angry. If something really pissed him off, he'd get drunk. But for Sammy, that one-two combination was bad news."

"What do you mean?" I asked.

Aunt Edna pursed her lips. "That mixture of anger and alcohol turned Sammy into a raging psycho. You know, kind of like Bill Bixby in *The Incredible Hulk*. Sammy'd get mad, then he'd get soused. Then he'd disappear for a while to sleep it off. Next thing you know, somebody got murderized. Sammy always swore he didn't know nothing about it."

Jackie bared her teeth. "Geez. That don't look too good for you, Dorey."

I winced. "Are you saying you think the same thing happened to *me*?"

"Huh?" Jackie grunted. "No. I mean your eye. It's all bloodshot."

"Oh. Yeah, right," I said, sitting up straight. "That's what I meant, too." I glanced over at Aunt Edna. Her lips were still pursed. "I can't wear my contact lens today. It hurts too much."

"I'll get you an appointment with the eye doctor for this afternoon," Aunt Edna said. "In the meantime, you can't go see McNutsack with your eye looking like that."

I chewed my lip. "You think they'll figure I injured it fighting with Tad?"

"I dunno about that. But if they get a good look at that pale blue marble rolling around in your head, they could get a bad vibe about you."

"Yeah," Jackie said. "We don't need any more bad juju around here."

"So, what can I do?" I asked.

"Hold on," Aunt Edna said. "I think I got something that'll work." She got up and ambled out of the dining room.

"What am I gonna tell McNulty?" I asked, turning to Jackie.

She shrugged. "The truth. They always find it out anyways."

"Here you go," Aunt Edna said, tossing something onto the kitchen table. One look at it made me question her sanity—yet again.

"Are you serious?" I asked.

"It's just a suggestion," she said. "Or you can show up at the police station looking like Sylvester Stallone at the end of *Rocky IV*, then explain to the cops how you couldn't hurt a fly."

Chapter Thirty

"You okay to drive like that?" Aunt Edna asked, chewing her bottom lip and giving me the once-over as I prepared for my meeting with Sergeant McNulty at the police station.

"Sure," I said. "I'm used to driving in L.A. traffic."

"No, I meant in that getup," Aunt Edna said.

I glanced over at Jackie. "Well, I don't have much choice, do I?"

Jackie grimaced. "Sorry, I owe you one for the laundry thing."

After breakfast, while I was taking a shower, Jackie had taken it upon herself to gather up every stitch of clothing I'd brought with me and dump it into Aunt Edna's washing machine. I'd stepped out of the bathroom to discover that the only things I owned that weren't sopping wet were my sandals, a pair of pumps, and my fuzzy bedroom slippers.

With no time to dash to a 24/7 Walmart, I'd been forced to don an orange terrycloth robe and follow Jackie to her apartment. There, we rifled through her closet in search of something I could wear to my interview with Sergeant McNulty.

Given the sketchy alternatives Jackie had on offer, I'd settled on a pair of black yoga pants and a leopard-print pullover shirt with open shoulders and elbow sleeves. (It'd been a toss-up between that or a souvenir "WTF"—Welcome to Florida—T-shirt.)

Afterward, Aunt Edna had pumped my eye full of Visine and helped me put on her solution for hiding my 'Psycho Eye' problem.

It was a child's black Petey the Pirate eyepatch.

"I better get going," I said, taking the car keys from Jackie. Like a pair of stray cats, she and Aunt Edna followed me out of the apartment all the way to the street.

"Which car is yours?" I asked.

"The green Kia," Jackie said, pointing to a vehicle almost identical to The Toad, the POS car I'd left back in L.A.

Dear lord. Maybe I really am related to these people.

"You know how to drive one?" Aunt Edna asked. "That thing's kind of tricky."

"Yeah," I said. "I got this." I opened the driver's door. "Where's the socket wrench to beat on the solenoid?"

I glanced over at Aunt Edna. She was beaming at me like I'd just graduated from Harvard. "It's under the passenger seat, Dorey."

I nodded and climbed in. "Thank you ladies. Wish me luck."

"Good luck, hun," Jackie said.

"Don't forget to stop by Dr. Shapiro's on your way back," Aunt Edna said. "I put his number and address in your phone."

"How did you unlock—? Never mind."

"The last thing you need is a tardy slip to go with your demerit for skipping school yesterday," Aunt Edna called out as I fastened my seatbelt.

Right. I only hope McNulty isn't the evil headmaster I fear he might be.

"Gotta go," I said, and shifted into drive.

As I pulled away, I glanced back in the rearview mirror. Aunt Edna was waving at me like Aunt Bea in *Mayberry RFD.*

An odd wave of nostalgia, either real or imaginary, made me wave back hesitantly. The last 48 hours had seemed like a surreal blur. But as I rounded the corner and headed for my second-ever police interrogation, I had a feeling things were about to get *very real*—very soon.

***

Jackie and Aunt Edna had shooed me out the door early, ensuring I had plenty of time to make my 10:00 a.m. appointment with Sergeant Mc-Nulty.

As I cruised down 4th Street, I glanced in the rearview mirror at myself. Between the eyepatch and the leopard print shirt, I looked like a one-eyed cougar on the prowl. I grimaced and adjusted the Petey the Pirate eyepatch. Somehow, my effort made it look even worse.

How is that even possible?

I sighed, hit the gas, and headed for my showdown with McNulty. It was just 9:25 when I spotted the police station on the corner of 1st Avenue North and 13th Street. I was 35 minutes early. Not wanting to be arrested for loitering or solicitation, I drove on past and looked for a place to kill half an hour.

A few blocks down, I spotted a coffee shop with a drive-thru. I pulled up to the window and ordered a latte. "It'll be a minute," the young woman said. "Pull on into the lot and I'll bring it to you."

I drove Jackie's old Kia into a parking spot and turned off the ignition. As it coughed its way off, I practiced saying *McNulty* in my head. Thanks to Aunt Edna, I now kept stumbling over the sergeant's name, just like my pal Bridget Jones had with Mr. Fitzherbert-Titspervert. *McNutly. McNulty.*

"Good morning, Sergeant McNutly," I said to my reflection in the rearview mirror. "Crap! I mean, good morning, Sergeant Mc*Nulty*."

"Nice eyepatch," a voice sounded beside my open car window. Startled, I realized it was the girl from the coffee bar drive-thru window.

"I bet my kid would love one of those," she said. "Where'd you get it?"

"It was a gift," I said, my face suddenly as hot as the cup of coffee I took from her hand. "I gotta go." I rolled up the window and turned the key in the ignition.

Nothing happened.

Then, like a punchline on a bad joke, a fat raindrop hit the windshield.

Seriously? What next? A freaking asteroid?

On the bright side, at least I was close enough to walk to the police station.

I pulled the lever to pop the hood on the Kia, and grabbed the socket wrench from under the passenger seat. I flung open the door, got out, and pried open the hood. As I was about to beat the solenoid to death, a flash of movement caught my eye.

I looked up to see someone dressed in black dive headlong into the open driver's door of the Kia. Before I could utter a sound, he scurried back out of the car and took off for the alley, my purse tucked under his armpit.

"Come back here, you scumbag!" I screamed and hurled the socket wrench at him.

It missed and bounced onto the asphalt. I ran over and picked it up. As I tried to take aim at the robber again, somewhere behind me, a cop-car siren blasted out a single, soul-crushing note.

I froze, then slowly raised my hands over my head. As I turned around, a patrol car containing a man and a woman lurched to a stop in the parking lot beside me. The man, a uniformed officer, jumped out of the driver's seat.

"You okay?" he asked.

"I just got robbed!" I screeched. "He stole my purse. A guy in a black hoodie. He ran that way!"

The cop bolted in the direction I'd nodded. With my arms still raised like a criminal, I watched him disappear into the alley as the drizzling rain melted my hair like wet cotton candy.

"Hey you," a woman yelled.

"Huh?"

I turned around, wild-eyed, socket wrench still firmly in my raised right hand. The woman who'd been riding in the patrol car's passenger seat was now hanging halfway out the door. She had a video camera trained on me.

"What the?" I said.

"Shirley Saurwein, *Beach Gazette*," she said from behind the camera. "Nice eyepatch, cougar. You going to entertain some old men in the hospital in that getup?"

"What? No. It's ... uh ... a long story. One I'd prefer didn't end up in your newspaper."

"Ooo," she squealed. "That's even more attention-grabbing than that sexy leopard-print shirt of yours. What's your name?"

I grimaced. "I don't have to tell you, do I?"

"Sorry. Looks like he got away," the officer said, huffing as he sprinted up to us. He looked to be about forty, and in good shape. Impressive biceps pulled at the fabric of his short sleeves, and there was no hint of a donut paunch.

"I see you met Shirley," he said.

"Uh ... yes."

"And you are?" Shirley asked again. She lowered her camera, revealing a hard, suntanned face. Her ice-blue eyes took notes while she chewed a thin bottom lip covered in bright-red lipstick.

"I'm nobody," I said.

"You want to file an incident report?" the cop asked. "I can take it down back at the station. It's just down the block."

"Yeah," Shirley said, smirking at me. "It's no problem at all."

"Uh ... no, that's okay," I said. "There wasn't much of value in there anyway."

"You sure?" he asked. His face, almost boyish, seemed genuinely concerned. "Looks like you've got car trouble?"

"No, it's all fixed." I unlatched the hood and let it freefall with a loud *clang*. "I really need to go."

"Sounds like she's got a prior engagement," Shirley said to the cop. "I can't wait to see where she leads us next."

"Leave her be, Shirley," he said, "or this is the last time I let you ride along on patrol." He turned to me. "Here's my card. I'm Officer Gregory Brady. If you change your mind about filing a report, give me a call."

"Thanks, I will." Out of habit, I reached toward my side to tuck the card into my purse.

The purse I no longer had.

I smiled weakly, then waved and climbed into the Kia. Thankfully, the keys were still in the ignition. I tucked the socket wrench back under the seat, and watched the patrol car cruise down the street. Once it was out of sight, I tried the Kia's engine again.

Nothing.

I scrambled out of the car, slammed the door, and ran for all I was worth in the rain toward the police station and my meeting with Sergeant McNutly.

Argh! McNulty!

Chapter Thirty-One

It was 10:00 a.m. on the dot when I burst into the police station. Dripping, I ran up to the reception desk. "Help!" I yelled, then remembered where I was and tried to compose myself. "I mean ... uh ... hello, there. I have an appointment to see Sergeant McNutly."

"You mean McNulty?" she asked.

Argh!

I poked my chin higher. "That's what I said."

"Diller?" a voice sounded behind me.

I whirled around to see Sergeant McNulty eying me like Damon Wayans in *Major Payne*.

"Yes, sir!" I said, stopping short of saluting.

"You nervous?" he asked.

"No, sir!"

"Then why are you all sweaty?"

"I ... uh ... it's raining out."

"And what's with the eyepatch?"

"Scratched cornea, sir."

"Really. Let me see."

He reached for it. I stepped back.

"Can't," I lied. "Doctor's orders. It's all gooped up with salve."

"I see," he said. "Which doctor?"

"No, sir. An ophthalmologist. Dr. Shapiro."

The hard edges around McNulty's eyes softened slightly. "On 12th?"

"Central."

"Okay. Follow me."

McNulty led me back to the same interrogation room as before. I assumed the position on the hard metal chair. He stood across from me, leaning over the table on his knuckles, just like last time.

"So, here's what we've got so far," he said. "We found your prints in blood in the hallway and on the driver's shirt."

"I told you—"

He held up a finger to silence me. "But curiously, there was no blood in the shower. Not even a speck of a Luminal hit. That means you couldn't have cleaned yourself up in there after the attack. So you were being truthful in that statement."

A glimmer of hope flickered inside me. I nodded eagerly. "Like I told you, why would I shower and then go incriminate myself by getting bloody all over again?"

"I can think of one reason. To make the crime seem fresh," McNulty said, extinguishing my hope he was on my side. "But that wouldn't have worked. According to the initial crime scene reports, all the blood samples collected were coagulated. That means Tad Longmire was murdered hours before you allegedly 'found' him."

I blanched. "*Allegedly*?"

"Unfortunately, all the evidence still appears to point to you, Ms. Diller. Help me out here. Besides the blood evidence, you're the only one in town who actually *knew* Longmire, right?"

"Uh, as far as I know, yeah."

"And you admitted to being livid with him over ruining your chances at a movie role." He shot me a sympathetic smile. "Missing your big break after fifteen years of auditions must've stung pretty hard."

I sighed. "You have no idea."

"The night before his death, you were seen fighting with Longmire, threatening to kill him. There are witnesses to you actually stabbing him with a fake knife. And you were the last known person to see him alive. I'm sure you can appreciate why this would make you our prime suspect."

"Appreciate being called a murderer? No, I don't appreciate that! Come on. I was just angry and venting my frustrations. I ... was just play-acting when I stabbed him."

"The first time, perhaps," McNulty said. "Maybe that was just practice for the real thing?"

"What? No! I swear!"

"According to the autopsy, Mr. Longmire was killed with a single stab to the heart. The blade cut his aortic valve clean through. Do you have medical training, Ms. Diller?"

"No."

"Then that was one lucky stab, I'd say."

I shook my head. "Give me a break. Do I look *lucky* to you?"

McNulty's dark eyes moved from my black eyepatch to my goosepimply shoulders sticking out of Jackie's secondhand leopard blouse. The cruel smirk on his lips evaporated.

"Surely I'm not your *only* suspect," I said.

"Okay, fine. Care to name another for us to investigate?"

My mind raced.

Kerri? No. She's been so nice.

"Uh ... there were like a *dozen* other people working with me on the set. What about the other cast members?"

"They were at an after-party," McNulty said, pulling out a metal chair and sitting down across from me. "I've got the pictures and bar bill to prove it. I'm curious. Why didn't you and Tad attend the party?"

"He didn't want to. And we had tickets to leave for L.A. in the morning."

McNulty's eyebrow rose. "Tad Longmire didn't want to party? That doesn't sound right, from what I heard about him. Maybe he didn't go because *you* wouldn't let him."

"Well ..."

"Kerri Middleton told me that's what you said. That Tad couldn't go because you didn't want him to. She also told me Tad showed up on the set the first day with a swollen nose. Then later in the week with a black eye. Ms. Diller, do you like to punch men who don't do as you say?"

I gasped. "What?"

McNulty smiled cruelly. "Let me tell you what I think. You and Tad had a thing going. But he couldn't keep his hands off the beach bunnies on the set. Let's face it, you can't exactly compete with a twenty-three-year-old silicone sister."

"How dare you!"

"What are you going to do? *Punch me* in the face?"

"No." I crumpled into my chair. "But I swear, I didn't hit Tad. He got that swollen nose in L.A."

"How?"

"He'd just been fired from filming *Breaking Code* for 'having rela- tions' with the director's wife. That's why he took this job in St. Peters- burg in the first place. That director in L.A. is the one who punched Tad. You can ask anybody working on the set that day."

"This director have a name?"

"Yes. Victor Borloff."

"That certainly was on the tip of your tongue."

"You don't forget the man who derailed all your hopes and dreams."

"I thought Longmire did that."

"He *did*. For *me*. But Borloff was the one who ended *Tad's* dreams."

"You don't say." McNulty leaned back in his chair.

"Wait," I said. "Maybe *Borloff* flew here and killed Tad. Or maybe he sent a hitman to do his dirty work!"

"Right," McNulty said. "You've been watching too many mafia movies, Ms. Diller. That kind of thing rarely happens in real life."

I bet my Aunt Edna would disagree.

"Come on," I begged. "There's got to be *somebody* else you can inves- tigate besides me. What about the person who gave Tad the black eye?"

"That makes more sense. Whoever punched him had to be local. So, who did it?"

I cringed. "I have no idea." I slumped back in my chair. Then I re- membered something Kerri told me. "Hey. Did you check on About- Face? There's a whole pile of people who hate Tad on there. It's called—"

"Tad the Cad," McNulty finished. "Yes, we're aware of it. Our cyber forensics crew is combing through the list for leads now. But from what I hear, the group is based mainly in Hollywood."

"So?"

"Again, the murder took place *here*, Ms. Diller. Hollywood is over twenty-five hundred miles away, on the other side of the country."

With the last lead I could think of summarily debunked by McNulty, I let out a defeated sigh.

I wonder if there'll be worms in the prison food, like in Shawshank Re- demption ...

"Ms. Diller?"

McNulty's voice burst my thought bubble.

"Yes?" I gulped. Then I laid my hands on the table so McNulty could cuff me. But to my surprise, he offered me an olive branch instead.

"You've been helpful," he said. "So I'll share something with you. We *do* have a couple more leads we're following up."

I perked up a bit. "You *do*? Who?"

"That's confidential information. But be assured, just like with you, we're gathering evidence that will either exonerate these individuals or incriminate them."

"Good," I said, feeling a tiny wave of relief. "Let me know if I can help."

"You can," he said.

"How?"

McNulty's raven eyes locked on mine. "By taking a polygraph."

"Oh. Uh ... sure. When?"

McNulty smiled. "As they say, there's no time like the present."

Chapter Thirty-Two

Flop-sweat dribbled down my temples. It pooled along the black elastic band that secured my Petey the Pirate eyepatch to my head.

I was strapped into a chair, six clothespin-like sensors clipped to my fingers. I was trying to remain calm and focus on my breathing, but Jackie's borrowed bra was itching my left boob, and her leopard-print shirt was casting a weird reflection off the metal base of the polygraph machine.

I closed my eyes and sighed.

This is so not *how I pictured the final scene going down in* The Life & Times of Doreen Diller ...

"Okay, that's it," the technician said. "You can relax. We're done."

"Really?" I asked. "Did I pass?"

The woman's lips smiled, but the rest of her face must've missed the cue. She glanced down and said, "I'll leave that to Sergeant McNulty to discuss with you."

"But—"

"I have to go," she said, ripping a sheet of paper from the polygraph machine. She scrambled for the door, nearly tripping over her chair. She flung open the door, raced out, then quickly pushed the door shut behind her. It closed with an ominous *click*.

I sat there stunned.

Was she afraid of me?

It seemed pretty clear the polygraph technician hadn't believed my version of events. I could barely blame her. After what Aunt Edna had told me about Psycho Sammy, I was beginning to question it myself.

I thought back to all the murderous thoughts I'd had. Like the time I'd considered putting arsenic in Dolores Benny's latte. And when I'd tied Tad to a bed and threatened him with the cuticle scissors. Good grief! I'd even been prepared to stuff socks down his throat if he'd hollered! To top it off, three nights ago, I'd actually stabbed Tad with that fake knife!

But they'd all been nothing more than idle threats. Jokes, even. Right?

Geez, Louise. What if they hadn't been? What if they'd all been steps leading me down a slow progression toward psycho-eyed homicide?

My eyes grew wide at the thought. I struggled in the chair, wanting to break free and run. But from whom? And to where?

What if there's some evil killer twin living inside me? What if I stabbed Tad for real in a drunken, Hulk-like rage like Sammy the Psycho?

Suddenly, the door to the polygraph room cracked open. I stifled a gasp. McNulty entered, gave me a solemn nod, then sat down across the table from me.

I smiled sheepishly. "Everything turn out okay?"

"According to the technician, you've been truthful," he said.

I nearly fell out of my chair. "Thank god!"

"With one exception," he added. "When asked if you had any involvement in Tad Longmire's death, the results came back inconclusive."

I closed my eyes.

Dear God. I'm a psycho killer. This can't be happening.

"What do you think would cause an inconclusive result?" I asked, my voice squeaking as it squeezed through my tight throat.

"Guilt, for one," McNulty said. "But it could be due to a conflicting memory relating to a prior incident."

"Prior incident?" I gulped.

Dear god! How many people have I killed that I don't know about?

"Yes," McNulty said. "When you stabbed Longmire with the fake knife, the memory of that could have caused you to react, thus registering a false positive on the polygraph. Or perhaps there was yet another incident involving Tad? Tell me, have you ever threatened Tad Longmire with a *real* weapon?"

I gulped. "Uh ... do cuticle scissors count?"

"This is no time for jokes." McNulty said. "In case you're not aware, you're in serious trouble, Ms. Diller."

"Believe me. I'm aware."

McNulty shook his head. "Still, something doesn't add up. Why would an otherwise law-abiding citizen such as yourself suddenly decide to stab a man to death? Stabbing is usually a rage killing. And highly personal. In my line of work, murder motives usually fall into three categories—sex, drugs or money. You say there was nothing sexual going on between you and Mr. Longmire."

"That's right."

"Regarding drugs, you've openly admitted to alcohol abuse."

"Wha?"

"But one bottle of wine rarely leads to homicide. Do you take prescription drugs?"

"No, sir."

"Street drugs?"

"Absolutely not!"

"So if we took a blood sample from you right now, it would come back clean?"

I opened my mouth, then snapped it shut. Aunt Edna had put something in my tea yesterday. Would it show up on a blood screening? I didn't want to lie to Sergeant McNulty, but I didn't want to get my aunt in trouble, either.

"I don't give myself drugs," I said.

"Okay." Sergeant McNulty studied me carefully. "That leaves money. What were your financial arrangements with Tad Longmire?"

I sat up primly. "I was his personal assistant. So when you think about it, it makes no sense for me to kill him. I'd be out of a job."

"So, you enjoyed working with Mr. Longmire?"

I grimaced. "I've had worse assignments."

"I see." McNulty pressed his fingertips together. "Then explain something to me. Why, on the very same day after you were hired, did you place a call to Longmire's attorney asking if you could be released from working with him?"

My throat went dry. "You spoke to Ralph Steinberger?"

"Yes. He told me you two had quite an interesting conversation at three in the morning." McNulty flipped through a notebook full of scribblings. "Here it is. You'd called him asking if you could quit. Steinberger explained there were three circumstances in which you could be released from the contract."

"Yes," I said. "Tad tricked me into—"

"Hold on," McNulty said, reading from the notebook. "Steinberger said, and I quote, 'One, by mutual agreement to end it. Two, if Mr. Longmire fails to pay you. And three, if either party dies.'"

"I remember the terms," I said. "What's your point?"

"Steinberger also said he explained to you that the probability of Tad agreeing to let you go was extremely low. He said you might be able to get Longmire to do so if you found a replacement willing to engage in sexual relations with him."

"Yes, that's right," I said.

McNulty frowned. "Longmire sounds like a real creep."

I nearly blanched. Could McNulty be softening to my side of the story? "Uh ... yes. Tad was definitely no choir boy."

McNulty leaned in toward me, his eyes narrowing. "Steinberger said you then made a joke about Tad Longmire's impending death."

I gasped. "I did *not!*"

"No?" McNulty leaned back and picked up his cellphone. "Let me refresh your memory. Steinberger sent me a recording of your actual conversation."

"He did? Is that *legal*?"

McNulty hit a button on his cellphone. Steinberger's voice came through clearly on the speaker.

> *"Are you having sexual relations with him?"*
> *"What?"* I heard my voice say. *"No!"*
> *"Good. My advice? Don't. Find a replacement who will. It's your best hope."*
> *"Unless he dies."*
> *"Excuse me?"*
> *"Nothing."*
> *"I thought so. Good luck, Ms. Diller."*
> *"What about if I—"*

The recording cut off.

"What about if you *what?*" McNulty asked, his dark eyes staring right through me. "What about if you *stab him to death with a butcher knife?*"

Chapter Thirty-Three

I raced out of the police station, my heart thumping in my ears. I was both terrified *and* hopping mad. First Kerri had ratted me out. Now Steinberger. God only knew what Marshall and the others had said about me during *their* interviews! Even my Aunt Edna thought I was a chip off the old psycho. Geez. I was beginning to question the possibility myself.

Not knowing where to turn for help, I shuffled back toward where I'd parked Jackie's ugly green Kia. At least the rain had stopped harassing me. And, for the moment at least, all the evidence McNulty had against me was still circumstantial. Merely he-said, she-said stuff. He had no solid motive for me to murder Tad Longmire, other than the guy was a complete douchebag.

I think even *McNulty* was beginning to realize *that*.

Why else would the sergeant have freed me on my own recognizance? Still, I knew my freedom might not last. Once the DNA results came back, they'd show for sure that I'd touched the knife sticking out of Tad's chest. Unless I could prove that somebody else stabbed Tad, that DNA was going to be game over for me. Do not pass go. Do not collect two-hundred dollars.

Go directly to jail.

I thought about wormy porridge in *Shawshank Redemption* again and nearly heaved. Where was Morgan Freeman when you needed him? I walked back to the car, just another broken-spirited woman wearing an eyepatch and an old lady's man-catcher clothes.

Cut me a break, universe! Who else around here would want Tad Longmire dead?

My cellphone rang. I fished it from my shirt pocket. It was an L.A. number.

I nearly choked on my own spit. Could Dolores Benny finally be calling me back about that part in *Breaking Code*? Was my career in show business about to be resuscitated from the dead?

"Hello?" I said, trying to sound cheerful. I *was* an actress, after all.

"Ms. Diller?" a man asked.

"Yes. This is Doreen Diller. How may I help you?"

"It's Ralph Steinberger."

"You!" I hissed. "Thanks for throwing me under the bus. Are you recording *this* conversation, too?"

"Look. The police called asking about you. I sent them the tape. I didn't record it with the intent to harm you. I *always* tape conversations that come in between midnight and five a.m. It's the only way I can remember them clearly."

"Yeah, right," I grumbled. "What do you want?"

"I just got into town last night to make Tad's um ... travel arrangements. I'd like to meet with you, if possible."

"What for?"

"It's nothing I want to discuss over the phone."

"Too incriminating?" I sneered.

"No. Too *important*. Can we meet?"

"Right now?" I asked.

"Yes, if possible. I've got a tight schedule. I need to catch a plane back tomorrow night. Where are you staying?"

Somewhere between a patch of collard green crazies and the trunk of a Chevy Caprice ...

"I'm out at the moment," I said. "Pick me up at the coffee shop at the corner of 1st Avenue North and 15th Street?"

"Perfect. I'm only a few blocks from there now. See you in a minute."

I ambled back to Jackie's beat-up Kia and leaned against the dented hood. A minute later, a white Mercedes convertible pulled into the lot. A burly man with a full head of salt-and-pepper hair and a beard to match waved at me.

"Doreen Diller?" he asked.

I adjusted my eyepatch and walked over to his car. "Maybe I am. Maybe I'm not."

"Look, lady," he said. "I'm not in the market for a hooker right now. I'm meeting someone."

"Hooker!" I growled. "I'm Doreen Diller!"

"Why didn't you say so?" He looked me up and down. "Wow. You sure don't look like your headshots. I guess it was the eyepatch that threw me off. What's up with that?"

I scowled. "Long story. Can we just skip it and you tell me *yours*?"

"Sure. Climb in. Hey, did you drive that Kia all the way here from L.A.?"

"Are you crazy? No. It's a loaner."

He smirked. "If I were you, I'd loan it to somebody else."

"Hilarious," I said as I settled into the plush leather seats.

Damn, this car is nice.

Steinberger fished around in his briefcase. "Here, hold this for a minute." He handed me a fistful of papers. The one on top was a rental car agreement.

"Geez," I said, reading it. "Two hundred bucks a day? That's ridiculous."

"I know. Good thing I only need this baby for three days. I take her back tomorrow."

I picked up a cardboard tube rolling around on the floorboard at my feet. "What is this? Generic oatmeal?"

"Tad. I had him cremated."

"Oh." Then it dawned on me what I was holding. "Eew!" I laid Tad back on the floorboard. "I thought Tad wanted to be buried in Hollywood Forever Cemetery, next to Rudolph Valentino."

Steinberger shook his head and laughed. "He *would*."

"Pompous jerk," I said to the container.

"Well, life doesn't always turn out like we planned, does it?" Steinberger said.

I blew out a breath. "You can say that again."

Steinberger pulled a folder from his crammed briefcase. "Here we go. This is the paperwork regarding your remuneration for the dissolution of the contract between you and Tad Longmire—"

"*This* is what you wanted to meet me about?" I said, annoyed at the inconvenience. "I thought you were going to email all that stuff."

"Yes, well, that was before I came across a stipulation in Tad's will."

"A stipulation?" I shot him a dirty look with my good eye. "Are you trying to screw me out of my severance money?"

Steinberger looked taken aback. "No. Just the opposite, actually. I thought you knew, Ms. Diller. Mr. Longmire recently changed his will to provide $25,000 to his personal assistant at the time of his demise, whoever that may be. Which, according to my records, is you."

My stomach sank. "How recently did he make the change?"

"The day before he died," Steinberger said. "He faxed me the paperwork himself."

I grabbed the paper and studied it. There it was, in black and white, just as Steinberger said. Tad Longmire, bane of my existence, had managed to gut punch me one final time right before he kicked the bucket.

Somehow, even from beyond the grave, Tad had found a way to deliver a crystal-clear motive for me to murder him.

For the money.

Chapter Thirty-Four

At least at the ophthalmologist office, Dr. Shapiro couldn't tell I'd been crying. I'd blamed my tears on my scratched left eye. (The *real* reason—that at any moment I could be snatched by the cops and hauled off to jail for murder—had seemed rather off-topic.)

After removing my Petey the Pirate eyepatch, Dr. Shapiro had diagnosed me with a pretty nasty corneal abrasion. He'd cleaned my eye and given me a little plastic bottle of ocular lubricant, along with instructions not to wear my contact lens until my cornea had completely healed.

On the way out the door, Dr. Shapiro told me to give his regards to Aunt Edna. He also informed me that the Visine and eyepatch she'd given me had probably saved my eye from getting infected and possibly ulcerated.

Gee. Maybe Aunt Edna and her Collard Green Cosa Nostra aren't out to get me after all ...

As I drove back to my aunt's apartment with a sterile bandage the circumference of a grapefruit covering my left eye, my cellphone buzzed.

It was Sergeant McNulty.

My gut lurched. I envisioned him and Tad's stupid attorney Steinberger sitting around like a pair of villains in a *Batman* movie, rubbing their hands together and laughing maniacally at my twenty-five thousand new reasons to kill Tad Longmire.

Unnerved, I let McNulty's call go to voicemail. As I steered Jackie's Kia down 4th Street, I finally spotted a friendly face. A liquor store. Like a responsible citizen, I turned on my blinker.

Then I pulled into the lot.

It was time to stock up while I still could.

***

I parked the Kia on the street in front of the Palm Court Cottages and grabbed the canvas tote from the liquor store. As I ambled toward Aunt

Edna's apartment, I grunted under the strain of hauling ten bottles of wine.

"I see you traded in your eyepatch," Jackie said, spying me from her usual spot in the shade of the umbrella-covered table in the center of the courtyard garden. "How'd it go with Dr. Shapiro?"

"Not so great. He cleaned my eye out and put some drops in it. He says I might have posterior uveitis."

Jackie's eyebrow arched. "That dirty old man did a pelvic exam on you?"

"Huh? No. Posterior uveitis means swelling in the back of the eye."

"Oh. So your peeper's gonna be okay?"

"Probably, yeah." I set the heavy tote full of wine on the table. "He said I've got to be careful, though. If I get uveitis, it could last for years. I might not be able to wear a contact lens ever again."

"That'd be a tough break," Aunt Edna said, coming up the path with a garden hose. "How long do you have to wear that bandage?"

"Just overnight. Then I have to protect my eye from bright light while it heals for the next couple of days."

"Uh-huh." Aunt Edna aimed the hose at a patch of flowers. "Jackie, don't you have a pair of those wraparound glaucoma sunglasses?"

"Sure do."

"No offense, ladies, but I look old enough as it is," I said, tugging at the hem of Jackie's leopard-print shirt. "Anyway, keeping my eye a secret probably won't matter soon, when the cops haul me off to jail."

"What?" Aunt Edna gasped. "What did McNutsack say to you?"

I grimaced. "He had me take a polygraph."

Aunt Edna scowled and shook her head. "Damn. You should've called me, Dorey. You should *never* take a polygraph!"

"Why not?"

"Because if it comes back clean, the cops don't believe it. If it comes back dirty, they never quit riding your ass."

"So were you clean or dirty?" Jackie asked.

"Clean," I said.

"All right!" Jackie cheered.

"Uh ... except for when they asked if I stabbed Tad," I said sheepishly. "That came out inconclusive."

"Ha! I can tell you why that happened," Aunt Edna said.

I cringed. "Because I really *did* go psycho and stab Tad like Sammy the Psycho?"

Aunt Edna's face puckered. "Huh. Well, I was gonna say it was because your mind got all confused about stabbing Tad with that fake knife the night before. But what you said could work, too."

I shook my head and flopped into a chair across the table from Jackie. "Believe it or not, that's not the worst thing that happened while I was out."

"No?" Jackie asked. "What could be worse than failing a polygraph?"

"I ran into Tad's attorney," I said. "He told me Tad changed his will the day before he died. He left me $25,000 in the event of his death."

Jackie whistled. "That's a lot a dough. Congratulations!"

Aunt Edna squirted Jackie with the hose. "That ain't good news. Now she's got even more reason to have murdered him."

"Oh," Jackie said. "Tough break."

"What's in the bag?" Aunt Edna asked.

I sighed. "Wine. Lots of wine."

"Amateur move," Aunt Edna said. "This obviously calls for gin."

***

While Aunt Edna made dinner, I sat at the table in the courtyard and got busy opening the first bottle of cabernet.

"Thanks for lending me the clothes," I said, pouring Jackie a glass. "I should probably go finish up my laundry before I'm too drunk to do it."

"It's all done, hun. Washed. Folded. Hanging in your room."

"Seriously? Wow. Thank you. I mean, Ma stopped doing that for me when I was ten."

"When you're retired like me, you got time. Hey, what's your ma have to say about all this Tad business, anyway?"

"I don't know." I set down my glass. "I haven't been able to get ahold of her on the phone."

Jackie chewed her lip. "I was afraid this would happen."

"What do you mean?"

Jackie did a sharp little inhale. "Oh. Nothing." She glanced over toward Aunt Edna's cottage. "Better talk to your aunt about that. But not now. Not while she's cooking veal parmigiana."

"She might get angry?" I asked.

Jackie shook her head. "She might screw it up. She makes the best I've ever tasted."

"Oh." I played with my glass. "I wish I knew what to do."

"Hey, I know," Jackie said, her face brightening. "It never hurts to have some character witnesses. What about your friends here? You got anybody who can vouch for you?"

"Besides you two?" I asked.

"Yeah. About that. I don't think we'd be much help."

"Because you don't know me," I said.

"Well, besides that. Let's just say when it comes to the local cops, we got a little trouble with credibility."

"Why? Because of the Collard Green Cosa—"

Jackie's face flashed in horror. She raised a finger to her lips. "Don't say it. And no, that ain't it."

"Then what?" I asked.

"It's on account of our neighbor Wanda. She ain't quite right in the head. She calls the cops every other day about something. She's like, you know, the boy who cried wharf."

"Wolf?"

"No. *Wanda.*" Jackie's brow wrinkled. "Hey, what about that lady who put you up? The one who sent you here in the trunk of that Caprice?"

"Kerri Middleton," I said. "Last time I talked to Ma, she thought something was sketchy about her."

"Like what?"

"Well, I told Ma I thought Kerri was a real professional. She had everything so organized, you know? But then Ma said if that was true, why did Kerri call us at the last minute to work on the project here in St. Petersburg."

Jackie nodded knowingly. "Your Ma always was one to spot the files in the ointment."

Flies.

"Anyway, I asked Kerri about that. She told me she'd called on a whim after reading about Tad Longmire getting fired, figuring he might be available. I thought, okay, that makes sense. But later, when I talked to Marshall, the studio director, he told me the guy who had the role before Tad was a friend of his, Brent Connors. He said Brent quit right after talking to Kerri."

Jackie shrugged. "So? Maybe Kerri thought Tad would be better, so she fired this other guy."

"Maybe. But Marshall said he hasn't been able to get ahold of Brent ever since. He said it was like he disappeared off the face of the earth."

Jackie's eyebrow shot up. "You don't say. Maybe that's what was supposed to happen to Tad, too. But you interrupted her before she could get rid of the body."

"What?" I gasped. "You think Kerri might—"

"What does this Kerri lady say happened to this Brent guy?"

I frowned. "I don't know. I've tried to ask Kerri a couple of times, but she keeps evading me. Or something happens and we have to drop the topic."

"Uh-huh," Jackie said, obviously unconvinced. "So, what's stopping you from picking up the topic right now? Go on, give her a call."

My back straightened. "You're right, Jackie. I'll do that right now."

I pulled my cellphone from my pocket and unlocked the screen. It was one minute to four. Kerri was probably still in the office. I moved my thumb to the dial icon for Sunshine City Studios. I was about to press the button when the door to Aunt Edna's apartment flew open.

She stuck her head out and yelled, "Dinner's ready!"

Chapter Thirty-Five

"Here," set these on the table outside," Aunt Edna said, handing me a stack of melamine dinner plates covered in a daisy pattern. "And Jackie? Go inside and get the nice placemats. The ones with the manatees on them."

"Why are there four plates?" I asked, setting them down on the table beside the tote full of wine.

Aunt Edna shrugged and turned back toward the apartment. "Eh. I invited a friend."

"A friend?" I asked.

"That's right," she said, turning back to face me. "From what I hear, you don't have too many around. So I thought I'd help you make some. You'll like him. He's a nice fella."

"He?" I asked. "You're not setting me up on *a date* are you? Right in the middle of a murder investigation? Look, I'm trying to keep a low profile here—"

"Aww, would you look at that," Aunt Edna said, looking past me over my shoulder. "Here he comes now."

I turned to see a fit man in jeans and button-down shirt walking toward us carrying a bouquet of daisies.

Coincidence, or has he eaten with these ladies before?

I realized his face was oddly familiar. Then the bulging biceps gave him away. It was Officer Brady, the cop who'd tried to run down the guy who stole my purse earlier today.

"These are for you," he said, handing Aunt Edna the flowers. He offered me a warm smile—one without a glint of recognition.

I sighed.

It's official. I really am totally forgettable.

"This is my niece, Doreen," Aunt Edna said. "She's new in town."

"Nice to meet you," I said, grateful that at least I'd had the chance to change out of Jackie's cougar shirt and into a pink tank top. Then I remembered I was wearing that big honking bandage over half my face.

Argh!

"Nice to meet you, too," he said, lingering a little too long over the bandage. "Are you here visiting a medical clinic?"

"No," Jackie said. "That's my fault. I nearly scratched her eye out. But it's gonna be all right. Right Doreen?"

"Sure." I smiled tightly, feeling my face heat up. "Oh, gee. I think the red wine is giving me rosacea." I cringed, realizing Brady must've thought I was either a hypochondriac or decrepit and falling apart at the seams.

Desperate to divert attention off myself, I turned to my aunt. "Aunt Edna. The food smells fabulous."

"It always is," Officer Brady said, smiling over at my aunt. "What can I do to help?"

"Sit down by Doreen," Aunt Edna said, patting the back of a chair. "You two have a nice little chat while Jackie and I bring out the food."

I objected. "But—"

It was no use. Two women were already giggling and scampering back toward Aunt Edna's cottage. I turned back to Officer Brady, feeling a bit like a trapped animal. At least it wasn't a *cougar* this time.

"Please. Allow me," he said, pulling out a chair and motioning for me to sit.

"I can do it," I snapped. "I'm not old or infirm."

"I'm sure you're not," he said. "You know, I almost didn't recognize you without your leopard shirt and Petey the Pirate eyepatch."

I flopped into the chair and groaned.

Brady laughed and sat down beside me. "It appears you failed to inform them that we've already met."

I grabbed his arm and whispered, "Please, let's keep that our little secret. I don't want them to know that I got robbed. I've already given them enough to worry about."

He eyed me coyly. "What do you mean?"

I shook my head, then noticed Aunt Edna coming out the door with a plate loaded high with veal parmigiana. "It's a long story," I said. "Maybe I'll tell you later."

"So," Aunt Edna said, putting the platter down on the table. "Did my niece Dorey tell you about how she might end up in the slammer for murder?"

***

After laying out the whole story between mouthfuls of the best veal parmigiana in the entire history of the world, Aunt Edna turned to Officer Brady and asked, "So, can you help our girl?"

He let out a low whistle. "I'll ask around and see what I can do. But McNulty usually likes to run the ship his way."

Aunt Edna frowned. "And that's fine, just as long as he doesn't shipwreck our niece here."

"You got to help our girl," Jackie said. "Look at her. She's a delicate flower. She won't last a day in the hoosegow."

"And the way she put away my veal, she's an eater," Aunt Edna said. "She'll starve in prison. I hear the meatballs in there are as tough as Titleist golf balls, but what do I know?"

"I'll see what I can do." Brady turned to me. "I agree with McNulty. It makes sense the murderer would be someone who held a grudge against Tad. Most likely a lover. Or one of the cast or production crew he might've pissed off. Did he tell you when the murder took place?"

"No. But he said it had to have happened quite a few hours before I reported finding Tad at six-thirty that morning. So probably sometime around midnight? Maybe three a.m. at the latest."

"Okay, good."

"Oh, and McNulty said the night of the murder, all the cast and crew were at an after-party at the Birchwood downtown. He said he had evidence to substantiate their claims."

"Is the evidence their *word*, or surveillance tapes?" Brady asked.

"I don't know."

He nodded. "Okay. Get me a list of everyone involved in the production of this *Beer & Loathing* project. I'll see if I can find out from forensics the exact time of death. Once we know that, I'll see if I can get my hands on any surveillance footage from the Birchwood and see if anyone's missing. Or if anyone left in time to commit the murder."

My jaw went slack. "You'd do that for me?"

Brady glanced over at Aunt Edna, who was busy pretending not to be listening. "For you and Edna. She and I go way back. But that's a story for another day." Brady cleared his throat. "Thank you for a lovely dinner, ladies, but I best be on my way."

"Always a pleasure," Aunt Edna said. "Dorey, walk the nice man out to his car."

Too grateful and embarrassed to object, I did as I was told. As we reached Brady's car, I said, "Thank you for anything you can do to help. My aunt means well, but I know you can't get involved in someone else's investigation."

"No, but I can volunteer my time. No cop ever turned down free help with paperwork."

I smiled up at him, and was surprised to see he was smiling back. "I appreciate it," I said. "What can I do to help, Officer Gregory Brady?"

"Two things, to start. One, call Kerri Middleton and see what she has to say about Brent Connors. I'm curious about her."

"Okay." I watched him climb into his Ford pickup. "And the second thing?"

"Brady," he said, climbing into the seat. "Don't call me Gregory. Call me Brady. I only use my full name for official *Brady Bunch* business."

I grinned. "Yes, sir. I can do that. Brady it is."

***

Lovers.

For some reason, my conversation with Officer Brady—or just Brady as he'd asked me to call him—had me thinking about Tad and his many lovers. I shivered at the thought of what perverted horrors awaited the police techs who had to wade through the lecherous text messages on Tad's cellphone.

Victor Borloff had punched Tad in the nose over his wife Bonnie. I wondered if another jealous husband was the cause of the black eye I'd found Tad with on Thursday morning.

Thursday was the same day I'd caught a glimpse of Tad canoodling with a red-headed woman on a lounger on the porch of the beach cottage. At the time, I'd assumed it was Candy Leibowitz from the shoot.

Could the mystery red-head have been Bonnie Borloff, back for more?

I shook my head.

Love is such a ridiculous thing. Who needs it? All it does is drive people crazy.

Drive ... Hold on a second!

If Bonnie had flown to Miami and rented a car, she could've driven it anywhere. Including right here to St. Petersburg for another rendezvous with Tad. And who's to say Victor wasn't hot on her heels?

Chapter Thirty-Six

"I thought you said you were trying to keep a low profile," Aunt Edna said, tossing a newspaper on the breakfast table beside my coffee and onion bagel.

"What's this?" I asked, staring at the top half of a folded newspaper called the *Beach Gazette*.

The front-page article featured a shot of two dolphins swimming beside a boat being captained by a couple of bearded, shirtless, beer-bellied guys with herniated navels. The headline read, *Another Day in Paradise*.

Well, that's one *version of it, anyway.*

"You know these guys?" I asked.

"The other side," Aunt Edna said.

I flipped the paper over. The bottom right quarter panel was taken up with another large photo. A picture of a woman in a leopard print shirt wielding a socket wrench. A Petey the Pirate eyepatch covered her eye. A maniacal expression covered the rest of her face. The caption read, *Cougar Pirate Robbed During Booty Call*.

"So," Aunt Edna said. "It says a local streetwalker got robbed yesterday. Were you not going to mention this?"

I cringed. "Somebody stole my purse, that's all. With everything else that's going on, I ... uh ... I forgot."

"You forgot you got mugged? Or you forgot you were a prostitute?" Aunt Edna shook her head. "Geez. Life in L.A. must be tougher than I thought."

"I'm not a hooker!" I said, then wilted. "I only played one on TV. Once. A headless one ... in a dumpster."

Aunt Edna kept shaking her head.

"Look," I said, trying to explain. "Compared to failing the polygraph and then Tad leaving me $25,000 worth of rope to hang myself with, somebody jacking my purse yesterday didn't seem like such a big deal."

"Okay, I get it. Sort of. But why aren't you eating your onion bagel? I thought you liked them. You reeked of one when you first got here."

"I actually prefer cereal for breakfast. Lucky Charms."

Aunt Edna smirked. "Oh yeah? And how's that been working out for you so far?"

My shoulders stiffened.

Ouch. Point taken.

My aunt flicked a hand at the newspaper on the table. "That Shirley Saurwein is a piece of work. At least she had the decency not to use your name."

"Only because I didn't give it to her," I said sourly. "That's probably the only thing that went *right* yesterday."

"Besides meeting hunky Officer Brady, you mean," Aunt Edna said, smirking.

"More like besides tasting your *veal parmigiana*. One bite and I felt like I'd wasted the last forty years of my life without it."

Aunt Edna beamed. "Eh. I do what I can."

"I see you two survived the bathtub gin party," Jackie said, sailing into the kitchen.

Funny. I never even heard her knock.

"Bathtub gin?" I asked. "Are you saying you made that stuff we drank last night *in a tub?*"

"Oh, no. That's just something my father—" Jackie's voice trailed off, obliterated by the lasers shooting from Aunt Edna's eyes.

"Never mind," Jackie said. She walked over and stood behind my chair and put her hands on my shoulders. "Looks like you're a regular celebrity, Doreen. First I seen you kill off that bubble-headed blonde girl yesterday on Channel 22. Now you're gracing the cover of the *Beach Gazette*. So, which bimbo do you murderize today?"

"Shirley Saurwine," I hissed. "If I can find her."

"Eh. Shirley? Don't worry about her," Aunt Edna said. "By this afternoon, every copy of that rag she writes for will be wrapped around fish guts or lining a bird cage."

"Yeah," Jackie said. "Besides. That picture's no good for business. You ain't even showing any cleavage."

I blanched. "What?"

"It's boobs what sells, Doreen," Jackie said. "Socket wrenches? Not so much. I figured you'd know that, given your line of work."

I opened my mouth to explain. My cellphone rang. I gave up and checked the screen. It read *McNutsack*.

I said a silent prayer of gratitude that the cops had already examined my phone for evidence. Then I glanced over at Aunt Edna. "Seriously?"

I'd already blown off McNulty yesterday. I didn't dare piss him off again. "I gotta get this." I got up and sprinted back to my bedroom and clicked the answer button. "Hello?"

"Is that you on the front page of the *Beach Gazette*?" McNulty asked.

I cringed. "I'd hoped nobody would notice. How did you figure it out?"

"I saw you in that outfit, remember? And, in case you forgot, I'm a detective."

"I didn't forget. Are you calling to tell me I'm under arrest?"

"No. Not yet. I wanted you to know I checked out your lead on Victor Borloff. Nobody by that name flew from L.A. to Tampa. At least, not within the three days prior to Longmire's murder."

"Maybe Borloff didn't use his real name."

"That's pretty tricky to pull off these days," McNulty said. "Plus, it seems like a longshot that a Hollywood director would take the trouble to fly all the way across the country to kill Longmire. Why not just wait until he got back to L.A.? You said you were heading back there the following morning, correct?"

"Yes. But I don't think Victor Borloff would've known that. Actually, I don't even think he knew Tad was here in St. Petersburg. Not unless someone told him."

"How could he have found out?"

I scratched my head. "Maybe my roommate Sonya? But I doubt it. Wait a second. The first episode of *Beer & Loathing* aired on the Friday before Tad was killed."

"How is that relevant?" McNulty asked.

"In that episode, Tad hooks up with a redhead who looks an awful lot like Victor Borloff's wife, Bonnie. Sonya told me last week that after Borloff caught Bonnie with Tad, he sent her to Miami to keep her off the set."

"I'm still not following you."

I sat down on the bed and chewed my lip. "What if Victor thought Bonnie had traveled from Miami up to St. Petersburg for another rendezvous with Tad? If they started up their affair again, that'd be motivation enough for Victor to catch the first plane out, wouldn't it?"

"It would be for me," McNulty said. "But I've already checked the commercial flight manifests. No Borloff."

"What about a private charter? Borloff could certainly afford it. Or he could've flown into Miami to surprise her, but then the surprise turned out to be on him."

"Hmm. Okay. I'll look into it."

"Really? Thank you. I ... I appreciate that."

"This is an investigation, Ms. Diller. Not a witch hunt. I follow all leads."

I nodded, even though he couldn't see me. "I'm glad to hear that, Sergeant McNulty. Because somebody's got to have killed Tad—besides me, I mean."

"Your willingness to cooperate speaks well of you," McNulty said. "And to be frank, I'm finding it hard to see sufficient motivation on your part for such a gruesome murder."

"Uh ... thank you," I said hesitantly.

"I sense a 'but' coming," McNulty said.

I cringed. I was finally making headway on my public relations campaign with Sergeant McNulty. And now I was about to blow that ship out of the water. I didn't want to say what I was about to say, but not saying it would make it even more incriminating if McNulty heard it from somebody else.

"Uh ... did you happen to talk to Steinberger lately?" I asked.

"Longmire's attorney? No. Should I?"

"He told me yesterday that I'm in Tad's will. I just found out I stand to inherit twenty-five grand."

McNulty cleared his throat. "I see. And you didn't know about this until yesterday?"

"That's right. I swear. I know it looks bad. But Borloff still looks worse than me, right?"

"I'll refrain from commenting on that for now."

Crap.

"Okay, I understand. But what about other leads? What about all those Tad haters on AboutFace?"

"We've skimmed through the profiles. Not a single one lists St. Petersburg as their home address."

"So?" I said. "As we were just discussing, people travel."

"Yes. For business or pleasure. But not usually to commit crimes. They tend to do those in familiar places."

"What about Tad's phone?" I asked. "Were there any leads on that?"

"We haven't been able to open it yet. We're still trying to crack the code."

"Oh. Well, if you need the password, I know it."

"Why would you know his phone code?" McNulty asked, his tone taking a turn for the worse.

I winced. "Uh ... we exchanged codes in case of emergency."

"I'd say this is an emergency, wouldn't you?"

"Yes, sir."

"So, what's the code?"

"T-A-D-1."

"Thank you, Ms. Diller. I'll get the techs on it right now. Perhaps you're correct and there are some incriminating messages on it. Or do you already know that?"

"Huh?" I gulped. "No. I never snooped on his phone. It wasn't like that."

"I'll take your word on that for now. But I still think we're looking for someone with the proximity to perpetrate."

"What does *that* mean?" I asked.

"It means that for now, our suspect list remains local and short."

I bit my lip. "How short?"

"Very short. Look, Ms. Diller. I appreciate you being forthcoming with information about the phone and your pending inheritance. And I'll check the private air charters for Borloff's name. But I'm fairly certain this will all sort itself out when the DNA results come back tomorrow."

"Right. Tomorrow," I whispered, suddenly out of breath.

What hope remained inside me fluttered in my stomach like a battered moth.

Unless I can figure out who did this by tomorrow, I'm toast.

Again.

Chapter Thirty-Seven

"Kid, you look like you just saw a ghost," Jackie said after my call with McNulty.

"Pretty accurate, considering I'm fairly certain I just dug my own grave." Like a zombie, I flopped down at the table in front of my cold coffee and bagel and stared at them listlessly.

Jackie eyed me funny. "What are you talking about?"

"I told McNulty about Tad's will. Like you said, Jackie, they're gonna find out the truth anyway."

Jackie picked up my cold coffee. "Why don't you just not take the money? That'd show them you weren't gonna get nothing from Tad's death."

"Too late. It's already been deposited into my account."

"How's that possible?" Jackie asked, pouring my cold coffee down the drain and rinsing the cup.

"Tad paid me by direct deposit."

"Oh."

"But that's not the only nail in my coffin," I said. "McNulty thinks the killer has to be somebody who *knew* Tad. But besides the *B&L* cast, who else would've even been aware Tad was here in St. Pete? We kept it pretty hush-hush. After all, this was supposed to be a low key project. Almost a vacation."

"Well, it ain't no vacation no more," Jackie said, handing me a fresh cup of coffee. "Tad's been all over the news ever since he went and got himself killed."

"Right," I said. "But all that publicity didn't start until *after* he was already dead."

"Hmm. Maybe McNutsack's wrong," Aunt Edna said, joining us at the table. "Maybe the killer *didn't* know who Tad was. They could've hated this creep just the same. I mean, you said Tad was a first-rate jerk, right?"

I frowned. "I suppose so. But what if McNutsa—McNulty's right? What if I really *am* the killer? What if I'm just like Sammy the Psycho and I turn into a raging green Hulk without knowing it?"

Jackie stood over me and put a hand on my shoulder. "That ain't possible, hun."

"It's not?" I asked, a smidgen of hope glimmering in my good eye.

"Naw. You can't be the Hulk. You ain't got the biceps. The most you could turn into is Gamora. That green lady on *Guardians of the Galaxy*."

I wilted. "Thanks, Jackie. I feel a lot better now."

Jackie patted me on the shoulder. "Any time, kid."

I turned to my aunt, who was busy working a crossword puzzle in the newspaper. "Aunt Edna, I've been trying to reach Ma. She's not answering. Jackie said to ask you about it."

Aunt Edna looked up from her puzzle and shot Jackie a look. "Maureen's probably busy right now." She turned her gaze to me, her expression switching to a soft smile. "What about that Kerri lady? You reach her yet?"

"No. I left a message for her to call me." I hung my head. "What's going on? Why doesn't anybody want to talk to me?"

"*We* do," Jackie said. "What's on your mind, hun?"

I nearly blanched.

Seriously?

"Well, for starters, when the DNA results come in tomorrow, I'm finished. My prints are all over the knife." I slumped into my chair. "Honestly, maybe I really *did* kill Tad in a drunken rage."

"Nah," Jackie said. "I think you're innocent."

I looked up at her. "Really?"

She shrugged. "Yeah. If you'd a killed Tad like Sammy the Psycho, you'd a stabbed him at least a dozen times."

"Gee, thanks."

"Jackie's right," Aunt Edna said. "If you turned into that green lady from Gamora, you'd have been outta your gourd, right?"

I grimaced. "Uh ... I suppose so. Is this supposed to be helping my case?"

"Yes," Aunt Edna said. "So listen up. If you were nuts, Tad's murder would've been a crime of passion. One lousy stab seems more like a business transaction to me. A calculated hit." She rubbed her chin. "If you ask me, whoever killed Tad with one jab either got really lucky, or they knew exactly where to stick him. In other words, this was no amateur move."

I wanted to ask Aunt Edna how she knew about where to stab someone, but then again, I wasn't sure I really wanted to know.

"Uh-huh," I offered as a form of non-committal response.

"Either that, or they hired a killer," Jackie said. She eyed me slyly. "Hey, Dorey, this driver who just happened to be at the cottage when you found Tad. Who hired *him*?"

"Uh ... Kerri did. Why?"

"Again with the Kerri lady," Aunt Edna said, her eyes narrowing. "Any reason *she* might want Tad dead?"

I shook my head. "Not that I can think of."

"You sure about that?" Jackie asked. "I mean, how well do you know these studio folks, anyway? Could they be blowing sunshine up your ass?"

My face suddenly went slack. "Publicity." The word leaked from my mouth like a slippery secret. I jumped to my feet. "Oh my lord. That's *it*!"

"What's it?" Aunt Edna asked.

"Marshall and Kerri told me we needed *publicity* for the series. Something that would go viral!"

"But Tad didn't die of no virus," Jackie said. "Unless the stab wound got infected. Or he had the flu and they gave him the jab wound just for show."

"Go viral on *social media*," I said.

"Ah! *Murder*," Aunt Edna said, shaking her crossword newspaper in the air. "Now *that* sells papers!"

I stood beside the table motionless for a moment, frozen by a mixture of elation and horror. I was elated at the prospect of someone else besides me being the murderer. I was horrified that it could be Kerri and Marshall.

I shot a desperate glance at Jackie and Aunt Edna. "So, what should I do now?"

The two women exchanged knowing glances. Then Aunt Edna turned to me and said, "Sounds to me like it's time to hire a limo driver."

Chapter Thirty-Eight

I reached for my imaginary purse again. "Crap. Darryl's card was in my purse that got stolen."

"Who's Darryl?" Jackie asked.

"He's the limo driver Kerri hired. The one who found me with Tad."

"Well, ain't that a coincidence," Aunt Edna said. "He's there at the crime scene, gives you a business card, and then your pocketbook goes missing."

I blanched. "You think Darryl stole my purse so I wouldn't have his phone number anymore? That doesn't make sense. I mean, if that's the case, why would he have given it to me in the first place?"

"Criminals make mistakes all the time," Jackie said, shooting Aunt Edna a knowing glance.

"But the police interviewed him," I said. "Plus, all I have to do is call Kerri to get his number again."

"Maybe that's why she isn't answering your calls," Aunt Edna said. "She's still trying to get her story straight."

"I dunno," I said. But Aunt Edna's reason made more sense than anything else I could come up with.

Aunt Edna shrugged. "I'm only saying, it all sounds kind of hinky to me, Dorey."

"Yeah," Jackie said. "Hinky dinky."

Aunt Edna locked eyes with me. "Okay. You listen to me, Doreen Diller. I think it's time you gave that studio woman another call. And don't take no for an answer this time. But also, you know, don't let on like you're suspicious she hired a hitman. Capeesh?"

"Hitman?" I swallowed hard and picked up my phone. "Uh ... okay. I'll try."

Aunt Edna smiled like I'd just earned a gold star. "You do that, Dorey. In the meantime, I think I'll bake some cookies."

***

"Doreen!" Kerri nearly shouted over the phone. "It's you!"

"Uh ... is this a bad time?" I asked.

"No. It's *perfect*. There's um ... there's something I need to talk to you about. Urgently."

"What?" I asked.

"I don't want to discuss it over the phone. Can we meet face to face?"

Why? So you can stab me to death, too?

"Uh, sure," I said. "But not right this minute. I'm in the middle of something."

"Okay. How about at noon? I can pick you up. Give me your address."

No way I'm telling you where to find me.

"Um, I have another idea," I said. "Why don't we meet for lunch downtown?"

"Too many prying eyes," Kerri said. "The media's in a frenzy. How about the boat launch at Coffee Pot Park?"

Should I bring my cement shoes with me?

"Sure, Kerri," I said, trying to sound breezy. "Hey, you wouldn't happen to have Darryl the limo driver's number, would you? I can't find his card."

"Oh. Sure. Hang on a second. I think I have it here handy."

I bet you do.

I'd no sooner hung up with Kerri when McNulty called.

"Yes, sir?" I answered.

"I want to ask you about a curious phone message on Longmire's cellphone."

"Just one?"

He sighed. "I'll admit, there's plenty to curl your toes on there. But only one that looked truly suspicious."

"What did it say?"

"It's a text message from someone asking to meet up with Tad on Sunday night. Do you know anyone with the initials BS?"

"I most certainly do," I said. "Victor Borloff's wife. Her name is Bonnie Sutherland."

Chapter Thirty-Nine

"I know desperate times call for desperate measures, but this is not what I signed on for," I said, staring in wide-eyed horror at the latest felonious scheme baked up by Jackie and Aunt Edna.

Jackie laughed. "Hey, like Yogi Bear says, 'It's déjàvu all over again.'"

"That was Yogi Berra," Aunt Edna said. "The manager of the Yankees."

"Oh. So who's in charge of the Confederates?"

"Ladies, could we please *focus*?" I asked, teetering on the edge of hysteria.

"Oh. Sorry," Jackie said.

"Thank you." I turned back to Darryl, the limo driver. He'd been knocked out cold by Aunt Edna's tea. Sprawled on my bed, we'd zip-tied him to the same bedposts I'd been lashed to on Tuesday, a mere three days prior.

It seemed like another lifetime ago.

"Geez Louise," I muttered, checking the zip-ties. "You two must spend a fortune on these things."

"Nah," Jackie said. "They come free with the garbage bags. And you can't beat 'em for tensile strength. Flexible nylon polymer's the best. Right, Edna?"

"Right," Aunt Edna said. "Here, Dorey. Wake him up with this. She opened the lid on a small, brown bottle. Suddenly the air smelled like a chorus of dead frog farts.

"Whew! Smelling salts?" I asked.

"Fermented collard green juice."

I grimaced and stuck the vile brown tonic under Darryl's nose. He bolted awake like Frankenstein's monster.

"What the hell?" he yelled. He took a second to surveille his surroundings, then began pulling at the restraints like a hog about to be branded.

"Calm down and keep quiet," Aunt Edna said. "Unless you wanna drink some of that stuff in the bottle."

Darryl went slack and silent. With what sounded like a mixture of terror and curiosity, he whispered, "What do you want from me?"

"Who hired you?" I asked.

Confusion flashed across his face. "*You* did."

I winced. "No. I meant Sunday morning, when you came to pick me up."

"Uh ... *you* did."

"Tsk-tsk. Amateur," Aunt Edna clucked. She grabbed the bottle of collard green juice from me, shoved me aside, and plopped down on the edge of the bed. "Look, Darryl, if that *is* your real name, we just want to know how you know Marshall and Kerri."

"Uh ... I give them rides. I'm a limo driver."

Aunt Edna blew out a breath. "We *know* that, genius. But why, of all the Uber and Lyft drivers in the world, do they use *you*?"

Relief registered on Darryl's face. I wasn't sure if it was because he thought he was out of the woods now, or because he finally knew the answer to one of our questions.

"Oh," he said. "I went to school with Marshall. We're high-school buddies."

Aunt Edna grinned wickedly. "Buddies enough to *kill* for each other?"

Darryl gasped. "What?"

"Doreen said you had blood on your shirt when Tad got murdered."

"Yes, ma'am." Darryl looked my way. "That woman there got it on me when she ran into me."

"Uh-huh," Aunt Edna grunted. "But she says when you took that shirt off, you had a T-shirt on underneath it."

Darryl looked at Aunt Edna like she was crazy. He was probably aping the expression on *my* face.

"Yeah, so?" he said.

"Get real," Aunt Edna said. "Nobody from Florida wears a T-shirt under their shirt. It's too hot. Who are you really? Some kind of Yugoslavian hitman?"

Darryl's eyes grew wild. He glanced up at me, most likely in search of a sane voice in the wilderness.

Yeah. Good luck with that.

"Look," I said to Darryl. "I'm in big trouble. Everybody thinks I killed Tad, but I didn't."

At least, I hope I didn't.

"Oh, I get that," he said, trying to appease his captors.

"Thanks," I said. "Look. Do you think Marshall or Kerri would be capable of killing Tad?"

"What? No," he said. "But hey. I'm no great judge of character, as you can see." He eyed Aunt Edna. "What'd you put in those cookies lady?"

"Forget the cookies," I said. "It was the tea. Anyway, did you pick up anybody else for Marshall and Kerri the Sunday night before Tad was killed?"

Darryl shook his head. "No. I swear."

"Okay. Did you pick up anybody before you came to my place Monday morning?"

"No. Geez, lady. I wasn't even supposed to *do* your job Monday morning. I just swapped fares with another driver because I was already at the beach."

My brow furrowed. "Why were you at the beach?"

"Why do you think?" he said. "I had a fare."

"An affair?" Jackie asked. "With who?"

I groaned. "He said, 'A fare.'"

"Oh," Jackie said.

I turned back to Darryl "But you just told us you didn't have any customers that night."

"No. I said I didn't pick up any fares for Marshall and Kerri."

"That's true," Jackie said. "Semantically, that's what you asked him."

"Okay, thank you for the clarifications, everyone," I said, trying to hide my rising frustration. "So, Darryl. Who was the customer you took to the beach Sunday night?"

He shrugged. "I don't know. Some guy. I dropped him at the Crooked Conch around midnight. He asked me to wait around for him, but he never showed up again. I ended up falling asleep in the parking lot. Woke up when one of the other drivers Kerri uses buzzed me about picking you up."

"This guy you dropped off at midnight. Was he young? Old? Fat? Skinny?"

"An old guy. At least forty."

I stiffened with indignation. "Was it Tad Longmire?"

"The guy who got stabbed? No. This guy was no movie star."

"What did he look like?"

"I dunno. I wasn't exactly keeping score."

"This is important," I said. "My life may depend on it."

"Okay, okay." Daryll closed his eyes tightly and licked his lips. Suddenly, his eyes flew open. "Uh ... I think he had dark hair. And was packing some extra pounds. He kind of looked like an ancient Seth Rogen."

O.M.G! That sounds suspiciously like Victor Borloff!

"Hold on a second," I said.

"Like I got someplace to go?" Darryl said, pulling on the zip-ties.

I grabbed my cellphone and google-searched the director's name. I shoved a headshot of Borloff at Darryl. "Is this the guy?"

"Yeah, sure. That was him."

"Ha! *Bingo!*" I yelled.

Jackie cocked her head. "Is it Friday night already?"

"Look," Darryl said. "Can I go now?"

"Oh. Sure." I turned to my aunt and whispered, "We're *are* going to let him go, aren't we?"

"Of course," Aunt Edna said.

I turned back to Darryl. "Sorry about the unconventional interview tactics."

He scowled at me. "That's what they're calling kidnapping these days?"

"Look, Darryl," I said as I cut off the zip-ties. "The cops are on my ass for killing Tad. If you were in my shoes, what would *you* have done to find out the truth?"

"I dunno," he said, rubbing his wrists. "Asked nicely?"

I winced. "Here's a hundred bucks for your troubles. Hope there's no hard feelings."

"Worth every penny," Aunt Edna said. "You're a prince, Darryl. You just helped clear my niece of murder."

Darryl's shoulders straightened. "Oh. Thanks. You know, I guess I'd have done the same thing to get out of a murder rap." He pocketed the money. "Funny thing. I always thought about becoming a detective myself."

"You'd be a natural," Aunt Edna said. "I'll put in a good word next time I see Officer Brady."

To my amazement, Darryl actually smiled.

"Really?" he beamed at Aunt Edna. "You'd do that? Thanks." He turned to me. "But I'd rather you put in a good word with Kerri and Marshall at the studio. Maybe they have a part for me?"

Why do I suddenly feel like I'm back in L.A.?

"I'll do that," I said. "You know, as long as they don't turn out to be murderers or anything."

"Snickerdoodle?" Aunt Edna asked, holding out a paper sack.

Darryl eyed the bag. "No thanks."

I took the sack from Aunt Edna and shoved it into Darryl's hands. "Go ahead. Take them. Like I said, it was the *tea*."

Darryl grabbed the bag reluctantly. "Can I go now?"

"Oh. Sure." I stepped aside. He scurried toward the door.

As I unlocked it and let him go, Darryl whispered, "Does this kind of stuff happen a lot in your house?"

I winced. "I'd like to say no, but I've never been a very good liar."

Chapter Forty

I called McNulty's office to inform him about what Darryl had just told me regarding dropping Borloff at the Crooked Conch, but his voicemail said he was out of the office. Pinning a murder on someone didn't seem like the type of thing to leave on a recorder, so I asked McNulty to call me back instead.

It was fifteen minutes to noon. If I hurried, I'd have just enough time to get the Kia started and make it to the waterfront park to meet Kerri. After what Darryl had told me, I was fairly confident Kerri wasn't planning on sending me to a watery grave. Even so, I reached under the passenger seat, grabbed the socket wrench, and tucked it away in my back pocket, just in case.

Following doctor's orders, I still had a bandage over my eye, but it was smaller, and mostly hidden by Jackie's glaucoma sunglasses. They weren't fashionable, but at least this time I got to wear my own clothes.

Even though things were looking up a bit, as I drove to the park, my desperation rose again about the impending DNA evidence. McNulty had made it clear that the results would most likely be the deciding factor in the case.

And that factor was most definitely *not* in my favor.

If the evidence I'd gathered so far failed to implicate Borloff, I'd still be on the hook for Tad's murder. But then again, so would whoever else was on McNulty's suspect list. Including Kerri Middleton.

I drummed my thumb on the steering wheel. It was literally do or die time. I needed to gather every incriminating fact I could on Kerri, no matter the risk. Emboldened by desperation and the socket wrench in my back pocket, I decided it was time to go for broke and confront Kerri about Brent Connors, the young man who was cast to star in *Beer & Loathing* before Tad and I ever got involved in the project.

If Kerri got rid of Brent, maybe she got rid of Tad, too.

***

"Doreen!" Kerri yelled when she spotted me pull up in the parking lot of Coffee Pot Park.

I took a deep breath and set my jaw to determined mode.

Here we go.

I climbed out of the Kia and waved at Kerri. Then I picked my way toward her across a wide patch of grass where a set of swings and a slide stood at the ready for neighborhood kids to play on.

Kerri was at the opposite end of the park, on a sidewalk that ran along the edge of a waterway called Coffee Pot Bayou. She sprinted toward me, a smile on her face. Hopefully there was no knife behind her back to go with it.

"Hi, Kerri," I said as she drew near. "What a crazy week, eh?"

"You said it. I've been trying to shake the press since Monday. What a nightmare! So far, the police have kept your name out of the papers, thank goodness. But I saw that photo of you with the eyepatch in the *Beach Gazette*. What happened there?"

I shook my head. "Long story. And not that interesting, relatively speaking. I'd rather talk to you about Brent Connors, if you don't mind."

"Brent?" Kerri eyed me funny. "What about him?"

I swallowed hard and went for it. "Marshall says you had a meeting with him after his audition. And that he quit the project after it, and was basically never seen again."

Kerri's face went dark. "Oh."

"What's up with that?"

She winced and locked eyes with me. "You don't think Brent got jealous and stabbed Tad, do you?"

Whoa. I did not see that coming.

"Not until you just mentioned it," I said.

"Well, I don't think he'd do it," Kerri said. "Brent was a nice kid."

"You said 'was.' Is he dead?"

"What?" Kerri seemed startled. No. It's just that ... he left the project due to 'artistic differences.'"

"Kerri, I'm from L.A. That can mean *anything*. Can you give me more details? My life is, you know, kind of at stake here?"

She grimaced. "Okay. But this is just between you and me, okay?"

"Okay."

"This could take a minute," Kerri said, leading me to a picnic table. She sat down and motioned me to join her. I sat down across from her, at a distance I hoped was out of stabbing range.

"Brent is a friend of Marshall's," Kerri said, nervously twisting her thumb in her palm. "He's a nice looking young man. So when he wanted to audition for *B&L*, I let him. I had him take a few quick scenes with Candy Leibowitz."

"The red-headed rocket scientist," I said.

Kerri smiled wryly. "That's the one. Anyway, after he shot a scene with her in bed, I pulled him aside and asked him to wear a cup. He refused."

"A cup?"

"Yes." Kerri looked down. "To hide his uh ... *masculine enthusiasm.*"

"Oh."

"Well, Brent got embarrassed and stormed out. I never saw him in the studio again."

"That explains him leaving," I said. "But why isn't he returning Marshall's calls?"

Kerri's nose crinkled. "I don't know. But I can look into it."

"Thanks. And thanks for sharing that with me."

Kerri reached out and took my hand. "Sure. Anything to help."

I smiled, relieved that Kerri hadn't killed Brent, Tad, or me. "So, you said you had something you wanted to tell me?" I said.

Kerri winced. "Yes. It's about the series."

"*Beer & Loathing?*"

"Yes." She swiped at an errant lock of gleaming silver hair. "You may not be aware of this, but since news of Tad's death hit the press, the ratings have sort of ... *skyrocketed.*"

Part of me was elated. Part of me was mortified. I could tell Kerri's feelings were mixed as well.

"I wasn't aware," I said. "I've been tied up—uh, working on trying to clear my name."

She nodded, a sympathetic smile on her face. "I know it's morbid, but Tad's death has been good for us. Can you see that?"

"Good for you. Not so good for me. I'm the one people think murdered him."

Kerri bit her lower lip. "Um ... that's what I want to talk to you about."

"I didn't do it, Kerri!" I blurted. "Geez! Why won't anyone believe me?"

"No!" Kerri said. "I believe you! What I meant was, well, with Tad dead, we had to make some adjustments to the final episode. He won't be coming back for another season, you know?"

"Not unless there's some parallel dimension I don't know about," I said.

Kerri shot me a tight smile. "Of course, due to the unfortunate circumstances, we couldn't get any new shots of Tad, so we had to rework the ending with stock footage."

"I get it. You did what you had to do."

Kerri let out a huge sigh of relief. "Thanks for understanding. Anyway, I wanted you to see the final episode before it airs today. I meant to do it sooner, but it's been such a crazy week."

"I totally understand," I said. "And I appreciate you taking the time. To be honest, I've been so busy with my ... uh ... *relatives* ... that I haven't had time to think about it."

"They showing you the sights?" Kerri asked as she reached into her purse and pulled out a small laptop.

"Uh ... in a manner of speaking, yes."

She fired up the tablet. "You've already seen most of this before. I'll skip through to the last five minutes. That's where we had to make the biggest changes."

"Okay."

Kerri found the spot on the video she wanted me to see, then turned the laptop around so I could see the screen. The first thing I saw were Fanny Tight's breasts bouncing as she ran for her life from an as yet unseen psycho killer. She tripped and fell in the sand, of course, right on cue.

I grimaced with expectation at what I knew would come next. I was about to catch up with Fanny in the cottage bedroom, stab her in the chest, and deliver my "You're a real pain in the ass," line. But to my surprise, suddenly Tad was there, helping Fanny to her feet.

"What?" I said as the camera cut to a shot of Fanny running up the steps of the beach cottage and through the French doors. The camera cut again to an image of Tad sprinting toward the camera. Suddenly, the angle went wonky. The shadowy image of two figures scuffling in the sand came into view.

Suddenly, to my utter horror, my face appeared on the screen—my completely unmasked, recognizable, crazy-eyed face.

I glanced up at Kerri. "What's going on? That's the shot I did to make Fanny quit giggling!"

Kerri nodded, her lips pursed into an apologetic grimace. "This is where we had to write Tad out," she said.

I looked back down at the laptop screen to see my image say, "You know, Taddy dear."

I gasped. The studio had dubbed in "Taddy" for the name "Fanny."

"Wha?" I said, staring at the rewritten scene. I watched myself raise the knife above my head.

"You can be a real pain in the ass," my psycho-killer persona said. "I won't be the butt of your jokes anymore."

And then, there it was. The coup de grâce.

I was standing next to Tad on the front porch of the cottage, red-faced and screaming, "Tad Lovemire, I could kill you!"

Then I plunged the fake knife into Tad's bare chest.

Chapter Forty-One

Oh my god! Tommy must've filmed Tad's and my fight that night when he was outside getting shots of the cottage at sunset.

And those creeps used it in the final episode!

The stabbing had looked so real on the screen. Stunned, I watched the shot switch back to my maniacal, cackling, weird-eyed face. A squirt of fake blood splatted across my cheek in a perfect line.

The screen went black.

I thought it was over, but then up flashed an outside shot of the beach cottage—complete with crime scene tape and cop cars with blue and red lights blazing.

Finally, mercifully, the credits started rolling.

I slowly looked up at Kerri. "What did you do?" I gasped. "You can't ... put that on the air."

Kerri cringed and snapped the laptop closed. "Tommy and Marshall pieced this together without us, Doreen. It's already been approved by Bob Johnson at Channel 22. We can't change it."

"But it makes me look even more guilty!"

"I know it wasn't what you were expecting," Kerri said, putting the laptop back into her purse. "But you have to admit it works. And this surprise ending could send the show off the charts!"

And me to jail.

"Kerri, please. I'm begging you. Don't air this."

Kerri shook her head. "I can't stop it, Doreen. It's too far in motion. It airs in like, an hour and a half from now."

Anger shot through me. "I could sue you for character defamation!"

"No. You can't," Kerri said coolly. "According to your contract, Sunshine City Studios has the right to use stock footage as they see fit for programming and publicity purposes."

Damned contracts!

"But ... I thought we were friends," I said.

Kerri cringed. "We are. And I'm sorry, Doreen, I truly am. I had no idea about this until it was already too late."

"But don't you see? This makes me look like Tad's murderer! Did Tommy and Marshall do this on purpose to frame me?"

Kerri blanched. "On *purpose*? What do you mean?"

I stood up and leaned over the table on my fists like I'd seen McNulty do. "I mean, are *they* the real murderers? Are they trying to point the finger at me and disguising it as some horrible publicity stunt?"

"How could you say that?" Kerri gasped.

"Because I'm desperate! I'm being accused of murder, Kerri. *Murder*!"

"I know. And I'm sorry."

The tears in Kerri's eyes took the steam out of my sails. I flopped back down onto the picnic bench. "Are you absolutely sure they didn't have a hand in killing Tad?"

Kerri shook her head. "I've learned you can never be absolutely sure about anything, Doreen. Even so, I can't imagine those two being involved in a real-life murder."

"Only a fake one on screen."

Kerri nodded.

I blew out a breath. "Okay. Call me if you hear anything that could exonerate me. The sooner the better."

A tear streamed down Kerri's cheek. "I will. I promise."

***

Still reeling from Kerri's death blow, I was dragging myself back to the Kia when my cellphone rang. It was Sergeant McNulty.

"I think I know who killed Tad," I said before he could get a word in edgewise.

"Ms. Diller?"

"Yes."

"You don't sound like yourself."

"I've had a long day."

"It's lunch time."

"Whatever," I said. "Look, I think Borloff really could be the killer. If Tad met Bonnie on Sunday night, he'd have blown his stack. I've seen the man in action."

"Okay. But right now, all we have to go on is circumstantial at best."

"Not anymore. I've got a witness."

"To the murder?" McNulty asked.

"Not exactly. You remember Darryl, the limo driver you guys interviewed?"

"Yes."

"He told me he dropped off a guy who fit Borloff's description at the Crooked Conch around midnight the same night Tad was killed. It's just a short walk to the beach cottage from there."

"Interesting. Can you get Darryl to come in and make an official statement to that effect?"

I envisioned Darryl fleeing Aunt Edna's apartment with a hundred dollar bill and a bag of snickerdoodles, compliments of his kidnappers.

"Uh, sure," I said.

"Good. I'm in my office all afternoon waiting on the DNA results. They're supposed to be here anytime now."

I hung up the phone. "Easy peasy," I muttered to myself. Then I raised the hood on the Kia and beat the life out of the poor solenoid.

Chapter Forty-Two

"I'm doomed," I said, then took a savage bite of the humongous sandwich Aunt Edna had waiting for me when I got back from talking with Kerri at the park.

"Why do you think you're doomed?" Aunt Edna asked, heaping pastrami on rye bread for her own sandwich.

"If the DNA comes back as a match, I know McNulty's gonna arrest me today for probable cause."

"Hmm." Aunt Edna took a bite of pastrami and chewed it while she talked. "Better if you turn yourself in before they come and haul you away. Trust me on this one."

"Thanks for the vote of confidence," I said sourly.

Aunt Edna slapped her sandwich together. "I was joking. Don't lose hope yet, Dorey. DNA is just a piece of the puzzle. It doesn't tell the story. Like they say on those cop shows, 'It's not the whole narrative.'"

"It isn't?" I poised mid-bite. "What do you mean?"

"If you have a good reason for your DNA to be on the knife, then that can introduce reasonable doubt."

"Yeah," Jackie said, fixing her own sandwich after Aunt Edna was through. "And you have to be proven guilty *beyond a reasonable doubt.*"

"I touched the knife because I thought Tad was pulling a prank on me," I said. "Does that sound reasonable enough?"

Jackie shrugged. "I'd buy it, maybe."

I turned to Aunt Edna. "What about you?"

She shrugged. "Eh. But you were living there, right? So your DNA could've been on the knife before the killer touched it, eh?"

"Yeah, I suppose so." I sighed and set down my sandwich. "But now McNulty wants me to try and get Darryl the limo driver to come with me to the police station and testify he saw Borloff. How am I gonna do that? Since we tied him to the bed and threatened him with collard green juice, I doubt he'll come anywhere near here again."

"Some people are touchy that way," Jackie said.

"I don't know if any of that matters anyway," Aunt Edna said. "From what I remember, Darryl didn't exactly say the guy he saw was Borloff."

"Yes he did," I argued. "When I showed Darryl the picture of Borloff, he said it was him."

Aunt Edna laughed. "I saw that picture. I gotta say, Borloff looks like half the poor slobs in the world, Dorey." She sighed. "And, sadly, every man I've ever gone out with."

I wilted. "So, it really *is* like I said at the beginning. I'm doomed."

Aunt Edna walked over and wrapped her arm around my shoulder. "Not yet, you aren't. It ain't over until I've hit the high notes."

***

As my bellyful of pastrami digested, I contemplated whether to turn myself in to the police *now*, or wait and be hauled out kicking and screaming later. As for Aunt Edna, she was calmly thumbing through the tattered yellow-pages of a phone book that had to contain ads for Burma-Shave.

While she searched for an attorney she knew who wasn't already disbarred or taking an extended dirt nap, I fished a quarter from my pants pocket and walked over to the kitchen counter.

Heads I turn myself in. Tails I make a run for it in Jackie's Kia.

I tossed the quarter. It bounced off the counter, hit the floor rolling, and disappeared under the harvest-gold refrigerator.

Just my luck.

I sighed. I was officially out of time and out of ideas. McNulty would have the DNA results in his hands any second now, and then my fate would be sealed for good. Where else could I turn for advice?

Suddenly, I remembered my *Hollywood Survival Guide.* I sprinted to my bedroom, grabbed it off the dresser and thumbed through the pages. I stopped at Tip #48. *Whatever you decide to do, make sure you look fabulous doing it.*

That's it! If I'm going to jail, I'm going there in style.

I jumped in the shower, washed and blow-dried my hair, and slathered on my best body lotion. I slipped into my fanciest white silk shirt and gray slacks. Then I pulled out my cosmetic bag and prepared my makeup like I was going to the Emmy's. When I was done, I slipped on Jackie's glaucoma glasses and stared at myself in the mirror.

I barely recognized myself.

That's when the idea hit me.

Eureka!

I grabbed my purse. "Gotta run," I said to Aunt Edna and Jackie. Then I bolted out the door.

***

Five minutes ago, I'd sprinted out of Aunt Edna's apartment and over to Jackie's next door. There, I'd made a quick call on her landline using my best impersonation of Fran Drescher on that sitcom, *The Nanny.*

Now I was standing on the street corner five blocks away, waiting.

"Is that the Cougar Pirate of Penzance?" a man's voice sounded behind me.

I whirled around. Officer Brady was grinning at me. He was in uniform, straddling a ten-speed bicycle.

"What are you doing here?" I asked.

"I was headed to your aunt's to give you the update on the alibis of your cast and crew. You going to a Hollywood party? Or are you making a quick getaway?"

"Oh, this? Just didn't have anything else clean." I glanced around warily. "So, tell me what you found out. But do it quickly."

"You in a hurry?"

"Yes. And being seen with a cop right now could blow my cover. So, come on. What did you find out?"

Brady shrugged. "In a nutshell? Everybody's alibis check out."

I frowned. "What about Tommy and Marshall?"

"They left the party early, like you thought they might've. But surveillance cameras on Central have them entering Sunshine Studios at eleven p.m. They didn't leave until daybreak on Monday."

"Yeah," I said sourly. "Apparently, they had some editing they needed to finish up."

"Everyone else stayed at the party until three. They didn't have time to kill Tad."

Crap.

"Okay. Thanks for the info, Brady. Now, could you do me another favor?"

"Sure, what?"

"Beat it. Scram. *Now.*"

His eyebrow arched. "Yes, ma'am. You got it."

Officer Brady had barely rounded the corner when my target approached. I waved down the limo, crawled in the backseat, and laid on the Drescher accent. "Police station. And make it snappy."

"Okay," the driver said. He pretended to adjust the rearview mirror while he checked me out. Suddenly, his mouth fell open.

I'd been made.

"Hi, Darryl," I said in my normal voice.

"What? *You* again?" He slammed on the brakes. "Get out! *Now!*"

"Hear me out," I said. "No funny business this time. I swear. I just need a ride to an interview. Fifty bucks for a ten-minute ride."

"Geez," Darryl muttered. "Fine. But only if you promise never to call me again." He scowled for a moment. Then his face brightened like a lightbulb just went on. "I mean, unless it's about a part at the studio, I mean."

"Will do," I said.

Not wanting to aggravate the situation, I kept my mouth shut on the ride to the station. Once there, I handed Darryl the fifty bucks and said, "Come in with me."

He shook his head. "Not on your life."

"Come on. I thought you wanted to be a detective. You're here. Why not take a look around the place? Fill out an application?"

"No."

"What about taking a look around to get a feel for a movie role as a cop? My interview won't take long. And I hear there's free coffee and donuts inside."

He crossed his arms over his chest. "Not happening."

"How about for another fifty?"

He cracked open the driver's door. "Twenty minutes and I'm out of there."

"Deal."

We got out of the limo and headed into the station. Once inside, I latched onto Darryl's arm like a rabid Chihuahua.

"Let go of me!" he growled under his breath.

"No way. You're coming with me. It'll take you five minutes to corroborate my story about Borloff to Sergeant McNulty, then you're free as a bird and I'll never bother you again."

"Why should I?" he said.

"Because I'm desperate. Do you know how hideous I'd look in an orange jumpsuit?"

"Diller, is that you?" McNulty's voice rang out across the lobby.

"Yes!" I practically squealed. "And I brought the limo driver like you asked me to."

"The same one you accused of stealing your purse so you wouldn't have his card anymore?" McNulty asked.

I grimaced. "Uh ... no. I was wrong about that. I'm thinking now it was just a reporter trying to get the goods on me. Anyway, Darryl's here to back me up about Borloff."

"Right. Follow me." McNulty turned and headed down a dim hallway that was already way too familiar for my taste. Halfway down the corridor, Darryl tried to make a run for it, but I had him hooked by the elbow. I dragged him along behind McNulty, whispering, "It's too late to turn back now."

McNulty put us in a room slightly bigger than the original interrogation room. I hoped that it was where they put the nice, innocent people.

"So, what do you have for me?" McNulty asked as we took seats around a small, round table.

"Darryl here can confirm he picked up Victor Borloff late Sunday night and dropped him off around midnight at the Crooked Conch. It's just blocks from the beach cottage Tad was murdered in."

"Is that so," McNulty said. His eyes shifted to Darryl. "I'd like to hear the story in your own words."

The young man squirmed in his chair. "Look, I'm sorry, but I lied."

"You what?" I squealed.

"I ... I just said that the guy I picked up looked like the guy you showed me so you and your old-lady kidnapping crew would let me go. I mean, my *life* was at stake."

"But—" I muttered.

Darryl turned and glared at me. "You said it yourself. You'd do the same thing if you were in my shoes."

Something crumpled inside me. The way McNulty was glaring at me, I had a feeling that whatever had just crumpled would soon be ablaze.

"Kidnapping? Lying?" McNulty asked.

"I can explain," I said.

McNulty shook his head. "Don't bother, Ms. Diller. I've already spoken with Victor Borloff. He has an iron-clad alibi. He was in L.A. the entire weekend."

McNulty's eyes narrowed in on me. "But now I have a whole new lead. *You two.* How interesting that the only two people found at the scene of the crime should work together to point the finger at someone else." He laughed and shook his head. "I should've seen that coming."

"That's not how it is, sir," Darryl blurted. "I had nothing to do with that guy's murder. I just showed up and found this lady all bloody and screaming, just like I said before."

"And then you two bonded and became best pals," McNulty said. "How nice for you. And how convenient that you should remember picking up the guy she needs to pin this on. One of life's true miracles."

"It's true," I whimpered with so little conviction I barely believed it myself.

McNulty let out a tired sigh. "Let's start from the top again. Ms. Diller, you said you were here filming a TV series called *Beer & Loathing,* correct?"

"Yes, sir."

"What exactly is it about?"

I winced. "It's crap. A low-rent version of *Dude, Where's My Boat?* Only not as thoroughly thought through."

"Excuse me?" McNulty said, rubbing his temples.

"Um ... it's just a silly TV drama," I said. "A little beach murder-type thingy. It's hard to explain."

McNulty glared at me. "Try."

"Wait," Darryl said. "Marshall told me the final episode airs today, right?"

I grimaced. "Yes."

"What time?" McNulty asked.

"I think it's already over," I answered.

"No," Darryl said. "It's only 2:45. Actually it's on right now. Turn on that monitor, Sergeant. If you're quick, we can catch the tail end of it."

McNulty picked up the remote and switched the monitor on above our heads. "What channel?"

"Twenty-two," I said, feeling the life drain out of me.

Oh, please, God. Let the show be over already!

It wasn't. McNulty switched to Channel 22 just in time to see the train wreck that was my life jettison fully off the rails and into a giant cesspool.

There I was, in all my unmasked, crazy-eyed glory, grinning like Glen Close in the bathtub in *Fatal Attraction.*

Darryl gasped and withered in his chair.

McNulty stared at the screen, open mouthed. "Is that *you?*"

"You know, Taddy dear," my image on the TV screen said, raising the glinting knife above my head. "You can be a real pain in the ass. I won't be the butt of your jokes anymore."

My life flashed before my eyes, waiting for what I knew came next. And there it was. Me standing with Tad on the front porch of the cottage.

"Tad Lovemire, I could kill you!" The knife plunged into Tad's chest. Blood squirted across my maniacal, cackling, weird-eyed face. Then the beach cottage appeared—caught up in crime scene tape and flashing cop cars.

"Wait a minute," McNulty said. "That's footage of the real crime scene. Did you *plan* this all along? For *ratings*?"

"No!" I cried. "I promise. I had nothing to do with the ending!"

"That's not the way it looked to me," McNulty said.

"Me either," Benedict Darryl said.

Just when I thought things couldn't possibly get any worse, the TV crackled with a breaking news report. McNulty turned up the volume.

A hard-faced woman sporting red lipstick and a microphone leered into the camera like a vulture at a kill. "I'm Shirley Saurwein," she said. "And I'm standing in front of the beach cottage where soap-opera heart-throb Tad Longmire was murdered. In an eerie twist of fate, life imitates art here in St. Petersburg, Florida."

A picture of my crazy-eyed serial-killer mug flashed on the split screen while Saurwein continued her commentary.

"Los Angeles actress Doreen Diller, who played the serial killer Doreen Killigan in the local production of *Beer & Loathing*, has been accused of murdering Tad Longmire, the star of the—pardon the pun—*short-lived* daytime TV drama. Fans might recognize Longmire as Dr. Lovejoy in *Days of Our Lies*. As for Doreen Diller, this may be her first and last memorable role."

As the three of us sat there stunned, the door to the conference room cracked open. A cop stuck his head in. "Sarge, you've got a phone call."

"Take a message," McNulty said. "Can't you see I'm in the middle of something here?"

"Um ... I think you'll want to take this, Sarge. Someone on the line says they witnessed the murder of Tad Longmire."

"Did they name the perpetrator?" McNulty asked.

The cop's eyes darted to me. Then he leaned in and whispered, "She's sitting right across from you."

Chapter Forty-Three

Did I really kill Tad in a psychotic, blackout rage?

As I sat there wondering if my only friend would be a blackbird I raised from a chick by feeding it the worms in my prison porridge, Mc-Nulty burst back into the interrogation room.

"I knew she did it!" Darryl squealed like a rat. "Don't leave me in here with a murderer!"

McNulty eyed him with disgust. "Save it," he said.

"Am I going to prison?" I asked.

"Not yet," McNulty said. "The witness was ... confused. She said she saw the murder ... ahem ... on Channel 22."

I couldn't tell if McNulty was blushing. I hoped he couldn't tell I'd just peed my pants a little.

As we sat there in awkward silence for a moment, another rap sounded at the door. The same cop poked his head back into the room. "Uh, Sarge, you've got a visitor. Says you've been expecting a package from him?"

"Finally," McNulty said, letting out a long breath. "I had the DNA results couriered over."

McNulty glared across the table at me and Darryl. "Take my advice, you two. Sit tight. And keep working on that story of yours. So far, the plot is total garbage."

***

"Lady, you are certifiably nuts," Darryl said, turning on me as soon as Mc-Nulty left the room.

"Tell me something I *don't* know," I said, laying my head on the table. "Could you do me a favor and turn that stupid TV off?"

"We're both going to need good attorneys," Darryl said, clicking the remote.

"Correction. We're both going to need *fabulous* attorneys." I sighed and lifted my head. "The only one I know is Ralph Steinberger, Tad's

211

lawyer. You think it would be a conflict of interest for him to represent me?"

"I dunno," Darryl said. "But maybe he'll represent *me.*"

I gritted my teeth. "Lawyers. They'll do anything for money. Maybe we can talk him into a two-for-one deal."

"Seriously?" Darryl said.

"Either that, or I can call my Aunt Edna and see who she dug up from the 1965 yellow pages."

Darryl groaned. "Geez. So go ahead and call the guy already!"

I pulled out my phone. "Okay. Here goes." I rang Steinberger's number. He didn't answer.

"That's weird. This guy *always* answers his phone."

A phone rang out in the hallway. I hung up and tried Steinberger's number again, in case I'd gotten a bad line or something. Oddly, right on cue, the phone in the hallway rang again.

"Wait a minute," I said. I got up, cracked open the door, and peeked outside. Ralph Steinberger was standing in the hallway talking to Sergeant McNulty.

I nearly choked on my own spit.

"Mr. Steinberger!" I yelled. "Boy am I glad to see you!"

"Get back in there," McNulty said, reaching over to shut the door on me.

Before he could, Darryl pushed past me and burst through the opening. "Please, Mr. Steinberger. You gotta help us!"

Darryl took another step toward the two men and froze. His eyes grew large. "Hey, wait a minute. Aren't you the guy I picked up at the Don CeSar a couple of days ago?"

"Me?" Steinberger said, shaking his head. "No. Couldn't have been."

"Yeah," Darryl said. "I remember you because of the weird request. You wanted a ride to the airport, but you didn't want to catch a plane. You wanted to rent a car."

Steinberger shook his head. "Sorry, son. You've got me confused with someone else."

"No, I don't think so," Darryl said. "I asked you, 'Why go to the airport to rent a car when there's places at the beach to do it?' You told me it was the only place with white Mercedes convertibles in stock."

"What?" I said.

"When was this?" McNulty asked Steinberger.

"He told me he got here on Wednesday," I said.

"I did," Steinberger said. "You saw the car rental receipt yourself."

My eyes narrowed. "Yeah, I did. You made darn sure I got a good look at it, didn't you? You wanted me to think you didn't arrive in St. Pete until Wednesday. But you were already at the Don CeSar when Darryl picked you up."

"That's right. I'd just gotten in," Steinberger said.

"If you'd just gotten in, why didn't you simply rent a car while you were at the airport?" I asked. "Or did you drive all the way here from L.A. and then your car broke down?"

"I don't have time for this nonsense," Steinberger said, turning away from me. "McNulty, thank you for signing the paperwork. Now, I have a plane to catch."

"Not so fast," McNulty said. "Let's all go have a seat in the conference room. I want to hear what these two have to say."

***

McNulty sat and studied the three of us like we were lab rats. I glared at Steinberger from across the conference table. Now that I thought about it, the guy really *did* look like an older, liver-spotted Seth Rogen.

"Hey Darryl," I said. "Could Steinberger here also be the guy you dropped off at the Crooked Conch on Sunday evening?"

"It's possible," Darryl said. "It was dark. And like I said before, the guy never came back. But one thing's for sure, whoever the guy was, he was a real cheapskate."

"Well, then, it couldn't have been me," Steinberger said. "I'm not cheap. I always go first class."

"Is that so?" Darryl said. "Funny. That's *exactly* what the guy told me who stiffed me Sunday night."

My eyes narrowed at Steinberger. "You told me that, too, when we were in your Mercedes." Suddenly a passage from the *Hollywood Survival Guide* popped into my head. Tip #62. *Where there's a will, there's an attorney.*

"Cardboard," I said, voicing a thought out loud.

"What?" McNulty asked.

I turned to the sergeant, the thread of a thought weaving into a tapestry in my mind. "Tad Longmire once told me he wanted to be buried in Hollywood Forever Cemetery. Next to Rudolph Valentino. But Steinberger over there had him cremated and stuck Tad's remains in a cheap, cardboard tube."

"I fail to see your point," Steinberger said. "There's nothing illegal about being cremated."

"Maybe not," I said. "But you're in charge of Tad's affairs, right?"

"Yes."

"So, if you can change his burial arrangements, why not change his will, too? Why not give me twenty-five grand?"

Steinberger blanched. "Why would I do *that*?"

"To make me look guilty," I said. "To throw some shade on yourself. Given what Tad told me about his trust fund, twenty-five grand would be chicken feed to pay."

McNulty's eyes narrowed on Steinberger. "You have a copy of Longmire's will in that briefcase of yours?"

"It's not public domain," Steinberger said, tightening his squeeze around the briefcase he held against his chest.

"Maybe not," McNulty said. "But with a warrant it will be. And I already have the airline manifests handy to check out passenger records for the past week. Do you spell Steinberger with an E or a U?"

"An E," I said. "And might I suggest you start with first class."

Chapter Forty-Four

As it turned out, a passenger manifest showed that Steinberger had flown to Tampa not on Wednesday as he'd claimed, but four days earlier. And, true to his word, the attorney had traveled first class. The registry at the Don CeSar hotel recorded Steinberger as checking in on Saturday, the day before Tad's demise.

While those points of evidence were circumstantial and could be explained away as a business trip or vacation, the DNA results proved to be a little trickier to deflect. While they confirmed my DNA on the murder weapon, they also detected an unknown male's DNA as well.

When Sergeant McNulty discovered Steinberger had been "in proximity to perpetrate," he'd insisted on fingerprinting Steinberger and collecting a DNA sample. After running the attorney's prints through AFIS, the Automated Fingerprint Identification System, no one was more surprised than me when they got a hit.

Steinberger's thumbprint was a perfect match to the bloody print found on the light switch in Tad's bedroom. DNA results are still pending, but let's just say it's not looking too good for poor old Steinberger.

It was kind of ironic, but we might never have identified Steinberger's thumbprint if he hadn't insisted on trying to pin Tad's murder on *me*. He could've handled the dissolution of my contract with Tad by email, like we'd discussed over the phone. If he had, there's a good chance we would never have known he'd even come to St. Petersburg.

But Steinberger's desire to provide a solid motive for me to murder Tad for the money was his undoing. The $25,000 inheritance document had been meant to seal *my* fate, not his. Instead, it helped us catch him in his web of lies.

As Aunt Edna says, that's the way the snickerdoodle crumbles, sometimes.

As for what the cops found in Steinberger's suitcase, it hardly matters now. Even if he forged more than that inheritance document he tried to snag me with and set himself up as Tad's sole beneficiary, no amount of money could save him from a murder rap. And dollars don't matter much when you're locked in the slammer.

I hear there's no first class in Sing Sing.

As for that note on Tad's phone from BS? It turned out that Steinberger's middle name was Brutus. Man, that guy just couldn't catch a break.

***

You might not believe this, but when McNulty let me and Darryl go, he actually smiled at me. What was even more unbelievable was that I was able to talk Darryl into giving me a ride back to Aunt Edna's in his limo.

There were terms, of course.

The main demand from Darryl was a stop at Sunshine City Studios on the way. He wanted me to chat him up to Marshall and Kerri for acting gigs. Considering I owed Darryl big time for helping put the spotlight on Steinberger, it was the least I could do.

"Doreen!" Kerri said as she opened the faded red door to let us into the studio. "I was just about to call you. I finally got in touch with Brent Connors' mother. She said he's been working on an oil rig in Texas. No phone reception out there. So all is well. He couldn't have killed Tad."

"It doesn't matter now," I said. "Darryl and I figured it out. It was Tad's attorney, Steinberger."

"Really? That's crazy," Kerri said.

"I couldn't have solved it without Darryl, here. He's got quite the talent for ... acting and stuff."

Darryl shot me the look of an unsatisfied customer. I upped my game.

"I mean, you should use Darryl in your productions," I said. "He's a real team player!"

Kerri eyed Darryl. "Are you interested in working here?"

"Yes, ma'am. I know a lot more than how to drive a limo."

Kerri smiled. "Okay. I'll see what I can do. In the meantime, Marshall and Tommy are in the editing suite, if you want to say hi."

"Thanks!" Darryl beamed, then took off down the hall.

Kerri turned to me. "You know, I can think of someone else I'd like to work here."

"Who?" I asked.

She grinned. "I could use another adult to play with. We can't offer you full-time work. Not yet, anyway. But I'd love to have you around for production jobs and acting parts, when it works out. I might even have something for you coming up next week. This local—"

"Gee, thanks, Kerri," I said. "But I need to get back to L.A."

She nodded. "I understand. Well, if you change your mind, my door is always open. I see your eye is healing up. No eyepatch today."

"No. Just these lovely geriatric glaucoma glasses."

Kerri smirked. "They're not *that* bad." She took me by the hand. "And Doreen? I wanted to say again, I'm really, truly sorry about how the final episode of *Beer & Loathing* turned out."

"I know it wasn't your fault. It was—"

"There she is!" Marshall said, coming toward me with open arms. Tommy and Darryl came trailing behind him. "The star of my show!"

I bristled, then decided to let my feelings go. What was done was done. "Hi, Marshall."

"Did Kerri tell you the good news?" he asked.

"What? No, I don't think so."

"The viewers are wild about the show! The station wants to air Beer & Loathing again during the summer, and maybe even pick up a new season in the fall!"

My mouth fell open. "Seriously? That's ... something."

Marshall laughed. "Are you kidding? It's *fantastic*! Hey, I saw that picture of you in the *Beach Gazette*. Kind of funny, eh?"

My nose crinkled. "What do you mean?"

"When you and Tad first got here, I showed you that pirate on Treasure Island. You know, the one with the oranges in the treasure chest?"

"Yes. But I—"

"And then you go and become a pirate for real! Where'd you get that Petey the Pirate eyepatch anyway? I've only ever seen them on vintage memorabilia sites."

"My aunt gave it to me."

"Man, she must've kept that in a drawer for like, forty years!"

"Yeah, I guess so. Well, Darryl, I guess we better get going."

"Let's keep in touch," Marshall said. "I may need you for the next season of *B&L*."

I grimaced. "Yeah, I don't know about that."

"Oh, come on. You were perfect for the role." He shot me a grin. "You know, not everybody's *cut out* to be a serial killer."

I cringed and shook my head. "Are you really gonna go there?"

Marshall cocked his head. "What? Too soon?"

Chapter Forty-Five

For the last time, I found myself being unceremoniously dumped in front of Aunt Edna's place—but at least this time I'd ridden there in a backseat instead of a trunk.

I waved goodbye to Darryl, then trekked through the tropical courtyard of the Palm Court Cottages up to my aunt's little bungalow.

As I reached the door to her apartment, I noticed the brass palm-tree door knocker below the peephole. A vague recollection overcame me. A déjàvu feeling—as if I'd been here and done this all before. A long, long time ago. When everything seemed, I dunno, *bigger* somehow.

"Is this the home of the Cougar Booty Call Lady?" a man's voice rang out behind me. I turned to see Officer Brady walking up the path toward me, a smile on his boyishly handsome face.

I smirked. "On that, I plead the fifth."

He studied me playfully, his eyes twinkling. "No eyepatch today, I see."

"Um, no. Just the glasses."

He grinned. "And boy, are they ever *fab-u-lous*!"

"They're for glaucoma."

Brady cringed. "Oh. Geez. Sorry. That would just ... uh ... I feel like a big jerk."

I let him squirm for a few seconds, stifling the smile eager to curl my lips. "Eh, you're not *that* big," I quipped.

The lines creasing Brady's brow vanished. He laughed. "I guess I deserved that. Hey, I heard you solved the murder of Tad Longmire. Congratulations."

"News travels fast around here."

He waggled his eyebrows. "You have no idea. McNulty told me. He said he never took you as a serious suspect."

"What?" I blinked hard. Twice. "That's not how *I* read him. What did he say to you?"

Brady shot me a devilish grin that kind of reminded me of Tad's. Whether that was a good thing or bad, I wasn't sure. "McNulty told me he knew from the start that you were too big a klutz to pull off a murder."

I folded my arms across my chest. "Well, what a relief to know *somebody* believed I was innocent."

"He also told me to tell you he prefers McNulty over McNutly. What's that all about?"

"Long story. Anyway, what are you doing here again?"

The question seemed to catch Brady off guard. "I ... um—" he stuttered.

Suddenly, the café curtains in Aunt Edna's kitchen window jerked to the side. Jackie's face peered at us from behind the bug screen.

"He's here because—" Jackie managed to utter before a hand clamped over her mouth and pulled her from the window like a cane jerking a bad act from the stage.

The curtains swished closed. Either Aunt Edna had shut Jackie down again, or some hapless kidnap victim had gotten loose from the zip-ties. Oddly, neither prospect seemed to bother Brady ... or me.

"Will you be staying here in St. Pete?" Brady asked.

I chewed my bottom lip. "I don't think so. I've got a career back in L.A."

Or do I?

Besides Sonya's Trailer-Trash Crew calls, I hadn't heard a peep from anyone in Hollywood for the three weeks I'd been in St. Pete. And as far as a paycheck went, my only remaining source of income was now quite inconveniently sitting in a cardboard tube in the police station's evidence room.

"Seems to me you've been putting down roots here," Brady said. "I know your aunt and Jackie are glad you're here."

My right eyebrow rose. "They said that?"

"Sure. In their own special way."

I laughed. "Well, I only hope nobody was harmed in the process."

***

"What were you doing in the window?" I asked Jackie as I set my purse on the kitchen counter.

"About to blab a secret," Aunt Edna said.

"What secret?" I asked.

Jackie opened her mouth, then shut it again after getting a gander at the stern look on Aunt Edna's face.

Aunt Edna came over and put an arm around my shoulder. "Secrets are like character flaws, Dorey. You don't go blurting them out all at once. You gotta let them leak out here and there. Slowly. Like molasses in winter."

My nose crinkled. "What are you talking about?"

"Secrets," Aunt Edna said. "Pay attention! What I mean is, you've got to let a person *habituate to the information*. Let them ease into the concept until it becomes their new normal."

"Sounds ominous," I said, crinkling my nose. "What secret are we talking about here?"

Jackie laughed. "Oh, there's plenty more than just *one*."

Aunt Edna shot Jackie a death ray, then turned back to me, her face transformed into a sunny smile. "Come into the living room, Dorey."

"Uh, okay."

Aunt Edna's arm dropped from my shoulder. I followed her down the hall and into the 1970s time capsule she called a living room.

"Sit in the good chair," Aunt Edna said, motioning to the big, overstuffed vinyl recliner. As I settled in, she said, "Jackie, go get the box."

"The box?" I asked. "Uh ... what's going on here?"

"You like it here, don't you?" Aunt Edna asked, smiling down at me.

"Sure. But I need to get back—"

"Well, we like you here, too." She turned and yelled, "Jackie! Come on with the fakakta box already!"

Jackie stumbled out of Aunt Edna's bedroom carrying a shoebox and a pair of meat scissors. A shot of cold adrenaline surged through me.

Maybe I really am *in a Steven King movie.* Misery. *Come to think of it, Aunt Edna looks a bit like Kathy Bates ...*

I gulped down a knot in my throat. "What are you going to do with those meat scissors? Cut off my toes so I can't get away?"

"Huh?" Aunt Edna shook her head. "You been watching too many weird movies, Dorey."

"Then what's in the box? And what are those cutters for?"

"See for yourself," Jackie said, handing me the box.

I opened it slowly, bracing for a severed horse head or some gruesome body part. Instead, I was greeted by a pair of gleaming pink flip-flops.

"What the?" I asked.

"The scissors are to cut the tag," Jackie said. "I wasn't sure if you was a size six or seven. We might have to exchange them."

"Oh." I held up the plastic sandals. "I don't get it."

"It's a little celebration gift for beating the murder rap," Aunt Edna said. "Pink flip-flops are the official leisure footwear of the Collard Green Cosa Nostra."

"Seriously?" I snorted. "I mean ... uh ... *thanks.*"

"Don't tell me you haven't noticed," Aunt Edna said.

I looked down at the women's feet. Both were sporting a pair of flip-flops identical to the ones in my hands. "Uh ... sure. I just thought they had a sale on them at Walmart or something."

"*Walmart?*" Aunt Edna said with a huff. "These are high-class Gucci pinks." She shook her head. "We've got to work on your observation skills, Dorey."

My nose crinkled. "Why?"

"'Cause you got some big shoes to fill, that's why," Jackie said. "Go ahead. Try them on."

"Whose shoes?" I asked.

"Molasses," Aunt Edna said, handing me the scissors.

"Fine." I cut the zip-tie holding the flip-flops together and slipped them onto my feet. They fit perfectly. "Gee. I wonder if this is how Cinderella felt," I quipped.

"Ha," Jackie said, elbowing Aunt Edna. "Size seven. You owe me fifty bucks."

Aunt Edna opened her mouth to speak, but was interrupted by a sharp rap on the front door.

"That must be my fairy godmother now," I cooed. "Should I click these things together? Or take them off and slap somebody in the face with them?"

"Check who it is, Jackie," Aunt Edna said, ignoring me.

Jackie peeked out the peephole, scrunched her face, then unlocked the door and flung it open. "Ain't nobody here," she said, glancing around. "Oh, wait. Somebody left us a package."

"What is it?" Aunt Edna asked.

Jackie bent over, then stood up and showed us the small Styrofoam box she'd found. "It's a cooler," she said. "Did you order more pastrami, Edna?"

"No." Aunt Edna eyed the cooler warily. "Open it."

For the second time in under two minutes, I was afraid I was about to get a gander at a dismembered body part. I flinched as Jackie slid the top off the cooler and reached inside. She pulled out a clear plastic bag stuffed with globs of white, gooey-looking stuff.

"Oh my god!" I said. "What *is* that? Somebody's cerebellum?"

Jackie's face went as white as the stuff in the bag.

"No," Aunt Edna said. "It's cheese curds."

"Cheese curds?" I asked. "What's up with that?"

Aunt Edna motioned me toward the recliner. "Sit down, Dorey. We've got something we need to tell you."

Book 2: Almost A Clean Getaway

Prologue

I'd fantasized about accomplishing a lot of things before I turned forty. Escaping a murder rap wasn't one of them. Neither was discovering that I had a secret family in Florida with ties to the mob. Did I mention that one of them was a serial killer?

Sammy the Psycho.

And he was on the lam.

Fun times.

If that weren't enough to curl a girl's hair, in less than a week, I, Doreen Diller, would turn the big four-oh. That meant I only had *five days left* to become a movie star, marry Keanu Reeves, and cure cancer.

Yeah. Like any of that was gonna happen.

Anyway, if life really *did* begin at forty, I was going to need a do-over like the Titanic needed more life rafts. Because, as I was about to find out, despite all the crazy crap that went down with my new family last week, I'd barely seen the *tip* of the lunatic iceberg bobbing around in their gene pool ....

Chapter One

"Cheese curds?" I asked, then sank back into the hideous brown recliner my Aunt Edna referred to as "the good chair."

The old Barcalounger had come off the assembly line well before I was born—and, as I mentioned, I was no spring chicken. Aunt Edna might've been an immaculate housekeeper, but she hadn't redecorated her living room since Disco Duck gasped out his last *quack*.

"Yeah, cheese curds," my aunt said, her gaze fixated on a clear plastic bag full of gooey white globs.

The nasty things reminded me of somebody's cerebellum.

Yuck!

The bag of curds was dangling from the geriatric hand of Jackie Cooperelli, my aunt's squirrely sidekick. The thin, pewter-haired woman was smiling and holding the gross-looking blobs up as if they were gold-fish she'd just won at the county fair.

From what I'd observed in my brief time with these ladies, Jackie possessed the slightly dim-witted, yet annoyingly cheerful disposition of Edith Bunker in *All in the Family*. And, like Edith to Archie, Jackie's perpetual good mood rankled Aunt Edna to no end.

A sturdy, no-nonsense woman, my aunt had shown herself to be one incredibly tough cookie. But at the moment, the bag of cheese curds appeared about to push her to the verge of crumbling. She wiped her palms on her apron and took a step toward me. Wobbling unsteadily, she grabbed ahold of the back of the avocado-green couch for support.

"You okay?" I asked.

"Huh? Yeah," she muttered absently, her voice husky and strained. She turned to her companion. "Hey, Jackie. Anything else come with those curds?"

"Lemme check." Jackie peeked inside the small Styrofoam cooler.

The lumps of white cheese had arrived mere minutes ago. Someone had dropped the box on the front doorstep, rapped hard with the knocker, then taken off before we could catch a glimpse of them.

"Yeah, there's a note," Jackie said. She plucked a damp piece of paper from the cooler with her long, bony fingers. "Now ain't that nice!"

"Gimme that!" Aunt Edna leaned forward and snatched the note from Jackie's hand. As she read it, her face took on the kind of hopeless, slack-jawed expression generally seen in doomsday films, right before the asteroid struck.

"What's it say?" Jackie asked, beating me to it.

Aunt Edna's hand fell limply to her side. "It says, '*Atta girl.*'"

Jackie cocked her narrow head sideways like a curious hound. "Who's Atta?"

Aunt Edna didn't answer. But based on the scowl tightening her jaw-line, I figured she was contemplating sending Jackie back to the pound. Or maybe to a kill shelter ...

"Uh ... is that some kind of congratulatory note?" I asked, trying to break the tension between the long-suffering pair.

Aunt Edna pursed her lips. "That's *one* way to look at it, I suppose."

My upper lip snarled. "What's the *other* way?"

Aunt Edna grimaced. "Sammy *knows.*"

My eyes opened wide. "Sammy? As in that psycho dude Sammy?"

"That's the one," Jackie said merrily.

"What do you mean *he knows*?" I scooted to the edge of the recliner. "Knows *what*?"

My aunt's lips were a thin, white line. "I dunno. Maybe nothing. Maybe everything." She turned to me and sighed. "Dorey, there's a lot you don't know about this family."

"No kidding. I only found out ten days ago that you guys even *existed.*"

"Not our fault," Jackie said, wagging a finger at me.

She was right. The blame for that fell squarely on the shoulders of my mother, Maureen Diller. Until a week and a half ago, I'd been under the assumption my mother was an orphan. It wasn't until I'd told her I was in St. Petersburg, Florida filming a TV show that she'd ever mentioned a single word about having relatives here.

Ma had given me Aunt Edna's number. To be honest, I hadn't exactly been in a hurry to make the call. I'd figured that if Ma hadn't kept in touch with her sister, why should I? But before I could pack my bags and skip town back to L.A., fate had intervened—in the form of a murder rap.

Yeah. A murder rap.

The night Sunshine City Studios wrapped up filming of their hokey slasher serial set on St. Pete Beach, life had imitated art. Someone had stabbed to death Tad Longmire—my boss and star of the show. Since I was the only one in town who knew Tad, the local cops had pinned me as the prime suspect. They'd also advised me to stick around while they conducted the homicide investigation.

Unfortunately, their suggestion hadn't come with an offer to pay for my room and board. Being a hot tourist town, St. Petersburg's hotel prices could blaze a hole through a wallet faster than the new girlfriend of an A-list celebrity.

Seeing as how I was both freshly unemployed and not-so-freshly broke, I was so desperate at the time that staying at a relative's house had sounded like a good idea. So, I'd rung up Aunt Edna.

When she'd politely invited me for tea, I'd been relieved. Excited, even. On the way to her house, I'd envisioned having a gentile chat with Maggie Smith from *Downton Abbey*. What I got instead was bush-whacked by Anne Ramsey from *Throw Momma from the Train*.

Before I knew what hit me, Aunt Edna and Jackie had drugged my tea, tied me to a bedpost, and interrogated me with a rolling pin and a can of Raid. The pair had thought I was a hit-woman sent to "rub them out."

After finally convincing them that I was Maureen Diller's daughter, I found out why Ma had never talked about her family. According to Aunt Edna, it had been against "Family" rules. Which Family? A little-known southern branch of the mafia referred to as the Cornbread Cosa Nostra.

Once the two had removed the zip-ties from my wrists, my aunt had explained the whole situation to me. Back in the 1970s and '80s, their entire limb of the mafia had been cut down by the long arm of the law. Nearly every single one of the Cornbread mob men had either been killed or were busy finishing out life sentences in Sing Sing.

But the mob *women* were still very much alive and kicking—and they wanted to stay that way. (At least, that's the reason they gave me for our not-so-cute meet-cute. Though I suppose, to be fair, it hadn't helped that I'd arrived at their doorstep in the trunk of a Chevy Caprice. But that's another story.)

Given how it had ended for their men, the women left standing after the Cornbread Cosa Nostra crumbled had sought to shield themselves from unwanted attention. As part of their cover, they'd moved into Palm Court Cottages, a small apartment complex in an older neighborhood near downtown St. Petersburg, Florida. They'd also renamed themselves the Collard Green Cosa Nostra, or the CGCN for short.

Jackie Cooperelli and Aunt Edna were two such women. And although both of them were pushing seventy, they still carried a healthy fear of mobsters.

One in particular.

Sammy the Psycho.

And, unfortunately, he just happened to love cheese curds.

Chapter Two

I sat up in the old recliner and studied my aunt. She was staring blankly at the bag of gooey cheese globs still dangling from Jackie's hand. Her face had taken on the same sickly shade of green as the sculptured carpeting beneath her feet.

"Do you really think Sammy the Psycho sent those things?" I asked.

"Maybe." Aunt Edna gnawed her bottom lip. For the first time since meeting her, my aunt appeared to have lost the pep that fueled her typical steamroller personality.

"I thought Sammy was dead," Jackie said, gawking at the plastic bag full of white, lumpy goo. She hoisted it up to eye level again for our viewing pleasure.

"Maybe he *is*, maybe he *ain't*." Aunt Edna collapsed onto the velvet couch and shook her head slowly. "The last news I got on Sammy was over two years ago."

"Oh, yeah?" Jackie crinkled her long, thin nose. "What news was that?"

Aunt Edna sighed. "I heard a rumor he's in a vegetative state."

Jackie gasped. "Sammy's in *Idaho*?"

Aunt Edna glared up at Jackie. A pained look flashed across her face. She spoke in a weary, half-whisper. "Seriously, Jackie. I've got a bad feeling about this."

I leaned closer to my aunt. "Isn't there someone you can call to find out?"

She shook her head. "Sammy's not somebody you can just casually bring up in a conversation."

"Why not?" I asked.

Jackie twirled a finger next to her temple. "They don't call him Sammy the Psycho for nuthin', you know."

I squirmed in my seat. "So why exactly *do* they call him that?"

"Molasses," Aunt Edna said.

Molasses was the code word my Aunt Edna used for secrets. Or, more accurately, how secrets should be revealed.

Slowly. Drip by drip.

According to my aunt, it was better to give people time to gently soak in bittersweet information by giving them just a little sample. That way, they could acquire a taste for it without losing their appetites completely. She'd tried her method on me. But after already having swallowed a bellyful of family secrets, I was craving something more akin to a shot of Kentucky Bourbon.

"Come on," I said. "Just give it to me straight."

Jackie folded her arms across her chest. "Edna, if you don't tell her, I will."

Aunt Edna blew out a breath that could fill a hot-air balloon. "Okay, okay. All right, already." She locked eyes with me. "Dorey. Get comfy. This could take a while."

***

As I sat on the couch and munched homemade snickerdoodles, Aunt Edna settled herself into the good chair and proceeded to lay out a tale that would've been hard to swallow even *with* a bourbon chaser.

According to her, Sammy the Psycho had been an on-again, off-again hitman for the Cornbread Cosa Nostra. And she'd meant that quite literally.

If Aunt Edna was to be believed, Sammy had performed his "services" in an altered state of consciousness, like some Southern-fried *Manchurian Candidate.* She'd explained that during their childhood years, Sammy's fellow teen-mobsters-in-training had discovered they could turn his murderous talents on and off like a switch.

"On the surface, Sammy was your average Joe Mafioso," Aunt Edna said. "But the guys found out that when he got boiling mad—and then drunk as a skunk—Sammy turned into a murderous, *Hulk*-like monster capable of just about anything."

"But here's the *real* kicker," Jackie chimed in. "Afterward, Sammy couldn't remember a thing."

My nose crinkled in disbelief. "Seriously?"

"You're darn tootin'," Jackie said. "The mob guys used Sammy like a Polaroid camera. Just pointed him and said, 'Shoot.'" She winked and shot me with a bony finger gun.

"I know it sounds crazy," Aunt Edna said, wiping an errant strand of gray hair from her face. "But it's true. As you can imagine, Sammy's blackout brain came in pretty handy during police investigations. Not being able to remember nothin', he could sail through interrogations and polygraphs like a pigeon through a wind tunnel."

I gulped. "So, what happened to him?"

"Nothing," Aunt Edna said. "Despite a boatload of suspicions, the cops could never pin so much as a jaywalking charge on Sammy."

"Wow," I said. "Sounds like he was one lucky guy."

Jackie shrugged. "Not really. Sammy avoided the slammer, but then the Family started avoiding *him*."

My right eyebrow shot up. "Why?"

"Because," Aunt Edna said. "If *our* men could use him to get rid of their enemies, what was to stop someone else from flicking Sammy's switch to get rid of *us*?"

"Sammy was a ticking time bomb," Jackie said. "And nobody wanted to get caught holding the magic eight-ball."

My brow furrowed. "I don't get it. It seems to me that all you guys had to do was keep Sammy away from the booze and he'd be fine."

"Yeah," Aunt Edna said. "And all you gotta do is drain the ocean and you got anchovies." She shook her head. "Look, Dorey. Maybe what you said could've worked. But nobody was willing to put their life on the line to find out. Besides, there was more to Sammy than your typical, rage-filled booze hound."

My nose crinkled. "What do you mean?"

Aunt Edna tapped a finger to her graying temple. "Maybe the booze wiped out his memory. *Or* maybe, just maybe, *Sammy was faking it all along.*"

"Faking it?" I frowned. "How could he? I mean, beating all those polygraphs and stuff?"

"I can think of *one* way," Aunt Edna said.

"Oh!" Jackie piped up. "Was it because he wore a disguise?"

Aunt Edna ground her teeth. "No." She turned to me. "Maybe Sammy played us all because he knew in his rotten little mind that he could beat the system. Maybe he really *is* a bona fide psychopath."

My mouth fell open. "Are you saying you think Sammy *knew* what he was doing when he killed people?"

"How could he *not*?" Aunt Edna scowled. "But enough about him. Talking about Sammy is bad luck." She pursed her lips and crossed herself.

"Bad luck?" I asked. "How could it be bad—"

"Edna's right," Jackie blurted. "It's bad luck because *Sammy* was bad luck. Talk about him and his bad luck finds you. You know, like the Dim Reaper."

Aunt Edna shot me a tired look. "I rest my case."

I frowned. "Come on. That doesn't make any sense."

"Sure it does," Jackie said. "Everybody knows Sammy was a natural-born killer. The poor guy was doomed from birth. You know. On account of the 'Curse of the Psycho Eye.'"

Jackie beamed at me, then shrunk back and grimaced. "Oh. No offense, Dorey."

My shoulders slumped. "None taken."

The "Curse of the Psycho Eye" Jackie had referred to was the fact that Sammy had been born with one brown eye and one pale-blue one.

Just like *I* had.

Heterochromia iridum (mismatched irises) ran in the Family. I'd inherited a nearly identical pair as Sammy's. Whether I'd *also* inherited the drunken-rage-serial-killer trait was still up for debate. But I had no plans to hang around to find out.

Just a little over an hour ago, Sergeant McNulty of the St. Petersburg Police Department had cleared me of all suspicion in the death of my old boss, Tad Longmire. Given the insanity I'd just been through with the cops and my wacko new mob family, all I wanted now was to make a hasty exit back to my pathetic, but comparatively quiet life as a would-be actress back in L.A.

"Anyway, Dorey," Aunt Edna said. "Now that the news about your eye is out, we need to keep an eye out for Sammy."

What the?

I was going to ask her why, but decided not to. Instead, I stood up and said, "Well, ladies, it's been fun. As much as I'd love to help you find Sammy, I better get back to—"

Bam! Bam!

A loud knock sounded at the door.

The three of us froze.

"It's Sammy!" Jackie squealed. "He found us!"

"Hush!" Aunt Edna whispered. "I *told* you it was bad luck to say his name!"

"What are we gonna do?" Jackie whispered.

"Pull yourself together!" Aunt Edna barked, rocking herself to standing. "Run to the kitchen and get the bug spray—and bring me back my rolling pin!"

"What about me?" I asked.

"Go put Jackie's sunglasses on. If it ain't him, we don't want to be scaring any Girl Scouts to death."

Chapter Three

The knock sounded again at the door—louder and more insistent this time. Apparently, Sammy the Psycho not only had no conscience, but no patience to boot.

I glanced at my aunt and Jackie and nearly groaned out loud. Armed with nothing but household gadgets, the three of us stood poised to do battle with a psychotic killer.

We were doomed.

All six of our knobby knees shook as Aunt Edna crossed herself, then gave the "go" signal to her reluctant sidekick. Jackie gulped and nodded.

Slowly, one of her bony hands raised, then hovered over the doorknob like a hairless, liver-spotted tarantula. Her other hand had a white-knuckle grip on an industrial-sized can of Raid.

"Who's there?" Jackie squealed into the gap in the front door.

A trickle of sweat ran down my back. The three of us held our breath, waiting for a reply.

"Me," a man's voice answered.

Jackie gasped and turned to us. Horror sagged her usually sunny expression. "Edna! That sounds just like Sammy!"

"Crap!" I said. "What are we gonna do?" My hand was shaking so badly I nearly dropped the weapon they'd given me—a toilet brush.

"Hush! Lemme think!" Aunt Edna hissed. "Jackie, whatever you do, don't open the door."

Jackie grimaced. "Are you sure?"

"Yes!" Aunt Edna and I said simultaneously.

"Okay, here goes," Jackie said.

She grabbed the knob and flung open the door.

"Ack! Noooo!" I screeched. I slammed my eyelids shut and braced for the oncoming hail of bullets from a Tommy gun.

"Gee. Am I *that* repulsive?" a man's voice asked.

My eyes sprung open. Instead of a mad serial killer in a double-breasted suit, a cop in a blue uniform stood just outside the doorframe. A very handsome cop. One who'd helped save my bacon when it was about to fry for the murder of Tad Longmire.

"Brady!" I yelled. "What are *you* doing here?"

"I could ask you the same thing," he said. "I thought you were on your way back to L.A."

"Oh. I was," I fumbled, suddenly flustered. "I mean, I *am*. This evening."

"Unless we can convince her to stay," Aunt Edna said, no hint of fear left in her voice. "You got any ideas?"

"Well, you could start by not making her clean the johns," Brady quipped.

"What?" I followed his gaze up my raised arm, where the toilet brush hovered like a club in my hand. "Oh." I let out a nervous laugh and lowered the brush.

Jackie laughed. "Dorey was getting ready to clean your clock, Brady."

"Remind me not to hire her as a maid, then," he quipped.

Aunt Edna and Jackie laughed. But I was dumbstruck—and impressed.

"Geez, Brady," I said. "You didn't even *flinch* at the sight of three armed women. That's pretty impressive."

Brady grinned. "You forget. This isn't my first ride on the Palm Court Express."

I smirked. I hadn't forgotten.

As a friend of the family, Officer Brady made a habit of dropping by once or twice a week to check up on, and sometimes share a meal with, the elderly women living at Palm Court Cottages. From what I could tell, it was a mutually beneficial arrangement. Aunt Edna provided the main course in the form of delectable Italian cuisine. In return, Brady provided dessert—in the form of mouth-watering eye candy.

Blessed with a full head of mink-brown hair, a muscle-man's physique, and a boyish, friendly face, Officer Brady was quite the dish, all right.

"Well?" Aunt Edna asked, nudging Brady with her rolling pin. "You gonna get Dorey to stay, or what?"

"I can't exactly cuff her to the bedposts," he said. "But I might be able to think of something to persuade her."

Brady shot me a grin that made me wonder if the whole cuffing thing might not be such a bad idea after all.

My cheeks grew hot. If Brady noticed, he didn't show it. Instead, he turned to Jackie and said, "That is, if you ladies don't *exterminate* me first."

"Oh," Jackie giggled at the can of Raid still locked in her bony grip. "Sorry. We thought you was somebody else."

"Who?" Brady asked. "The abominable Orkin man?"

"Close," I said. "Sammy the Psycho."

"Can it!" Aunt Edna hissed, jabbing an elbow into my ribs.

"You sayin' I should spray Brady?" Jackie asked.

"No!" My aunt shook her head. "That's it, Jackie. Tomorrow we're getting you fitted for a Miracle Ear."

"Wait a minute," Brady said, his grin evaporating. "Are you serious? You thought I might be some kind of psycho?"

"No!" Aunt Edna protested too loudly.

Brady's eyes made a quick study of us all. "Then what's going on here?"

Aunt Edna softened her tone. "It's just that, you know, somebody sent us some cheese curds. That's all."

"Ah. The case of the killer curds," Brady said. "Why didn't you say so in the first place?"

"It's no joke," I said. "They think they came from Sammy the Psycho."

Aunt Edna shot me a dirty look. Brady noticed. His friendly voice switched to no-nonsense policeman mode. "Where are they?"

Jackie grimaced. "They? There's just *one* Sammy, right Edna?"

"The curds are in that cooler over there," Aunt Edna said, pointing to the Styrofoam box on the floor beside the door. "They just got here ten minutes ago."

Brady knelt by the cooler and opened the lid. "No return address?"

"Nope," Jackie said. "Kinda rude, eh?"

Brady carefully picked up the baggie of curds and studied them. "Hmm. They appear to be direct from Wisconsin."

Jackie stared at Aunt Edna. "I thought you said *you-know-who* was in *Idaho*."

The tendons in Aunt Edna's neck grew taught. She closed her eyes and turned away from Jackie. "Brady, how do you know those things came from Wisconsin?"

"Well, it's a little known fact," he said. "But I happen to have majored in cheese-curd forensics."

"Really? Wow!" Jackie said, the whites of her eyes doubling.

Brady laughed. "Well, *that* and there's this nifty little label on the bag. It says, *Waylan's Famous Wisconsin Cheese Curds*. Also, based on the dry ice in the cooler, these curds have traveled a long *whey*. Get it?"

Jackie laughed. Aunt Edna and I groaned.

"So they weren't sent locally?" I asked.

"It doesn't appear likely," Brady said. "Otherwise, they'd have used regular ice. Tell me, ladies, did this psycho of yours send any kind of message along with these weapons of mass arterial destruction?"

"Yeah," I said. "A note—"

"Saying to enjoy them in good health, that's all," Aunt Edna said, her voice drowning out my own. "But it wasn't signed."

"Hmm." Brady eyed the lumps of cheese. "Well, if you ask me, these curds either got delivered to the wrong address, or they were likely meant as a gift for one of you. Anybody have a special occasion coming up?"

Jackie perked up. "Hey, maybe—"

"Nope. Nobody," Aunt Edna said, slipping the rolling pin back into her apron. She dusted off her hands and shot me and Jackie her distinctive *shut your trap* glare. "So, I guess that's that. It was just an innocent little mix-up at the post office."

"Uh, yeah," Jackie said. "That's it."

"Okay," Brady said, but the look on his face said he wasn't buying it.

"Oh well, their loss is our gain," Aunt Edna said, trading her angry glare for a brilliant smile. She beamed up at Brady and said, "So, who's up for some nice cheese curds and tea?"

Chapter Four

"You always wear sunglasses?" Brady asked me.

"Doreen's a big star in Hollywood," Aunt Edna said, shoving us out the front door and into the courtyard. "Doesn't want to get recognized by the paparazzi."

He smirked. "I see."

"I bet you do," Aunt Edna said, then ushered Brady and me to the wrought-iron picnic table that stood at the center of Palm Court Cottages' tropical courtyard. The small, jungle-like oasis was surrounded on all sides by quaint, single-story wooden cottages, each nestled amidst a riot of colorful foliage on the verge of going rogue.

"Sit right here," my aunt said, and motioned to two chairs right next to each other. She set a platter of Ritz crackers and gooey cheese curds down on the table. "Now, you two make yourselves comfortable and enjoy your snacks."

As we settled into our cushioned seats, Jackie came strolling down the paved path toward us, humming *Strangers in the Night*. In her hands was a tray laden with two plates, two sets of silverware, and a pair of tall glasses filled with iced tea.

"Here you go," she said, setting the tray down in front of Brady and me.

"Well, doesn't that look delicious?" Aunt Edna said, winking at Brady. "Oh, dearie me. I forgot something on the stove."

"You did?" Jackie asked. "That ain't like you, Edna."

Aunt Edna rolled her eyes. "Geez, Jackie. Too bad they don't make a Miracle *Brain*." She hooked Jackie's arm in hers and tugged her, begrudgingly, back toward their cottages.

Brady and I watched as they disappeared into the fading light of dusk. A few seconds later, a string of festive party lights blinked on over our heads.

Brady laughed. "So much for subtlety."

I smirked. "I don't think my aunt knows the meaning of the word. Still, I'm glad to catch a moment alone with you."

Brady's dark brown eyes brightened. "You are?"

"Yes. I'm surprised at you. Making light of Sammy the Psycho. Aunt Edna and Jackie seem genuinely worried about him. Is their safety all a joke to you?"

Brady blanched. "Not at all. It's just that ...." Brady chewed his bottom lip for a second. When he spoke again, his tone was more serious. "Let me put it this way, Doreen. I've known these ladies a lot longer than you have. I've learned to humor them, okay?"

My back bristled. "*Humor* them?"

"Yes." Brady picked up a fork, stabbed a cheese curd, and doled it onto my plate. "Let's just say the women in your family appear to be blessed with *exceptional imaginations.*"

My right eyebrow angled sharply. "Am I supposed to take that as a compliment or an insult?"

Brady grinned. "Use your imagination."

My jaw tightened. "I'm serious! Those two are acting as if their lives are at stake."

"I understand," Brady said. "But what you don't know is, their lives are *always* at stake."

I nearly choked on a sip of iced tea. "*What?*"

"There's always *something* going on with them. Last month, Jackie was sure the neighbor's dog was wearing a wire. The month before that, your aunt was convinced someone had sent her a death threat on a potato chip."

The indignation went out of my righteousness sails. "Oh." I grimaced. "And?"

Brady smiled softly. "In Jackie's case, the poor pooch had gotten tangled in an old telephone cord."

"And the potato chip?"

"Edna told me the chip had the perfect outline of a coffin burned onto it."

My upper lip snarled. "Did it?"

He shrugged. "I don't know. Jackie ate it before I had a chance to see it."

"Geez." I slumped into my chair. "So, you think Sammy the Psycho is just something they made up?"

"More likely a figment of their paranoia," Brady said. "Actually, this is the first time I've ever heard of him."

I locked eyes with Brady. "Do you think he could actually exist?"

"Theoretically, sure." Brady put a cheese curd on his plate. "As a cop, I've learned virtually anything, no matter how improbable, can be possible. On the other hand, after you've heard as many tales as I have, they all tend to sound suspiciously familiar."

"What do you mean?" I frowned and watched a moth flittering around the party lights above our heads.

Brady stabbed another curd with his fork. "Okay. Let me guess. Sammy murdered a bunch of people, right?"

My shoulders stiffened. "Yes."

"And he's on the lam?"

I blushed. "Uh ... yes." I poked a fork at the nasty lump of cheese on my plate. "But there's more to it than that."

Brady put a cracker on my plate. "Like what?"

I frowned. "Well, according to Aunt Edna, Sammy can be programmed to kill."

One of Brady's thick eyebrows ticked up slightly. "Programmed? How?"

"By getting him all fired up with alcohol and rage."

"I see." Brady put his fork down. "Well, I hate to break it to you, Doreen, but there's nothing unusual about that. Especially here in Florida."

"Maybe not," I argued. "But Sammy's different."

"How?"

"He ... well, Aunt Edna says that after Sammy kills someone, he says he can't remember a thing."

"Wow," Brady said, tapping a finger on his chin. "A criminal who can't recall his crimes. I've never heard *that* one before."

I groaned.

Brady grinned at me. "Sorry, Diller. You've got to do better than that."

"Okay, fine! He's got the Curse of the Psycho Eye, okay?"

Brady blanched. "Excuse me?"

I whipped off my sunglasses and scowled at Brady. "Sammy's got a wonky eye. Just like mine. Jackie says that means he's a natural-born killer."

Brady's face lit up with horror. "Oh my God!"

His eyes darted maniacally around in the fading light, causing my heart to quicken. He grabbed my hand and whispered, "Anything else you can tell me about this hideous, murdering, Frankenstein mobster?"

"Argh!" I jerked my hand away. "Yes. He loves cheese curds!"

Brady burst out laughing. "Well, that proves it."

I eyed him with suspicion. "Proves *what*?"

"That you're not like Sammy, if that's what you're so worried about."

I nearly gasped. How did he know my secret fear?

I winced. "So my eye doesn't gross you out?"

Brady shook his head. "I'm a cop, remember? I've seen it all. If it makes you feel any better, I can show you the hairy mole on my back."

I gave him half a smile. "Thanks, but I'll pass." I locked eyes with him. "But tell me, how can cheese curds prove I'm not like Sammy?"

"Because you obviously *hate* them," Brady said. "At least, that's what I gather from the look on your face." Brady nodded at my plate. "Go on. Prove me wrong."

I glanced down at my plate. My nose crinkled at the thought of the slimy, white goo touching my lips. But I wasn't going to wimp out in front of Brady.

"Fine." I steeled myself and stabbed a cheese curd with my fork. I lifted it to my nose and took a whiff. It smelled like sour milk.

Eeew!

"Go on," Brady coaxed. "Be brave. Take a bite."

Battling my pride *and* my gag reflex, I took a nibble. To my surprise, the disgusting glob *squeaked* against my teeth. I nearly heaved.

"Gross!" I blurted, spitting out the rubbery white morsel.

Brady laughed. "And there's your proof. You hate cheese curds. It's official. Doreen Diller is no Sammy the Psycho."

I smiled. But inside, my gut was summersaulting.

To my utter horror, that disgusting-looking cheese curd had tasted even better than Aunt Edna's clam linguine.

Chapter Five

Last night, I'd had every intention of asking Brady take me to the airport after our less-than-subtle set-up by Aunt Edna. But while the cheese curds she'd served us had been flown in from Wisconsin, my aunt had neglected to inform either of us that the *iced teas* had come directly from Long Island.

"Great," I grumbled.

I held my thumping skull together with my hands and slowly crawled out from under the covers. Careful not to lean over far enough for my brain to slosh out of the top of my cranium, I grabbed ahold of the handle on my ratty suitcase and hoisted it up onto the bed.

I yanked open the zipper. The case was empty.

WTH?

"You up in there?" Aunt Edna's voice boomed through the bedroom door.

"Uh ... yes!" I yelled back, causing my head to pulse along to the beat of my heart.

I blinked my bloodshot eyes at the baby-pink walls and yellowing French provincial furniture that had been my home base for the last week and a half. As dated as the room was, it still beat the one I shared in a rundown flat in a crappy area of South Park, California.

"Then you'd better get a move on," Aunt Edna bellowed. "You wouldn't want to miss your flight back to L.A. now, would you?"

"My flight last night!" I gasped. "I missed it!"

"Don't worry," she said through the door. "I helped you rebook it for 9:45 this morning. You know you giggle a lot when you're drunk?"

"So I've heard."

I glanced at the clock radio on the nightstand. It was 9:38 a.m. I nearly choked on my own spit. Even with a *Star Trek* transporter, I couldn't make it on time. Thank goodness my ticket was exchangeable.

I flopped back onto the bed. The sudden jerking motion jarred my brain, causing it to thump like an angry orangutan against my skull. I couldn't believe it. Once again, my aunt had rendered me unconscious. Only this time, her drug of choice had been alcohol.

Geez! Is everyone in Florida bonkers?

I lay back on the bed pillows and sighed. The people I worked with back in L.A. were odd. But actors and producers were *predictably* weird. It didn't take a lot of work to peg them as phonies, narcissists, or egomaniacs. But here in St Petersburg, my powers of perception had turned as vague as what's covered by an insurance policy.

Florida seemed to possess its own unique brand of weirdos. From what I'd been able to ascertain so far, Jackie Cooperelli was a harmless one. Granted, she was a lamebrain who thought dogs were capable of both espionage *and* sniffing out deadbeats, but harmless nonetheless.

Aunt Edna, on the other hand, was proving trickier to diagnose. Though she seemed relatively normal on the surface, I suspected her culinary mastermind could be peppered with more than a mere pinch of delusional paranoia. And I had to hand it to her. She sure knew how to incapacitate a gal.

Then there was the annoyingly attractive Officer Gregory Brady. Where he fit into this goofball crew was still a total mystery to me.

Brady was handsome, smart, and cared about my aunt and Jackie. That was obvious. But what secret cards was he holding close to his vest? And what was up with that warped sense of humor of his? Was it an unavoidable side effect of being named after a TV character?

I pictured Brady's face amongst the tic-tac-toe vignettes on the opening jingle to *The Brady Bunch* and laughed out loud.

What a bunch of nut balls. Geez. If Sammy the Psycho really does *exist, he might turn out to be the sanest one of us all.*

***

"Why didn't you wake me up?" I asked, stumbling into the kitchen in my pajamas.

"Do I look like your personal valet?" Aunt Edna asked, barely glancing up from the newspaper crossword puzzle. "You're a grown woman, Dorey."

Unable to argue her point so soon after regaining partial consciousness, I settled for the consolation of a cup of coffee and a bowl of Lucky Charms. As I sipped and munched across the table from my aunt, I got busy thumbing through my phone for flights back to L.A.

"What's a seven-letter word for a guest who don't pay?" Aunt Edna asked.

I glanced up at her. "Is that part of your puzzle, or are you trying to make a point?"

Aunt Edna laughed. "You know—"

A sharp creaking sound interrupted her. Someone had just opened the front door.

"Who's that?" I asked, lurching back in my seat. The sudden movement made me wish some of those marshmallow thingies in my cereal were aspirins.

"Anybody home?" Jackie's voice rang out, answering my question.

"We're in here," Aunt Edna said. She smirked at me and quipped, "My, you're jumpy this morning. Guilty conscience?"

Before I could answer, Jackie came bouncing into the dining room. She was wearing white shorts and a golf shirt so orange it forced me to shut my eyes.

"Morning!" she said. "Any coffee left?"

"In the pot," Aunt Edna said. "Like it always is."

"Fantastic!" Jackie grinned with such cheer that both Aunt Edna and I winced.

"Hey, did you see the news?" Jackie asked, holding up a rolled newspaper as if she were about to use it to swat a fly. "Another old-timer bit the dust at Shady Respite."

I shrugged. "What's so unusual about that? Isn't Florida God's waiting room?"

"If you ask me, somebody's getting tired of waiting," Jackie said, arching a drawn-on eyebrow. "This is the third one in less than a month."

"You're kidding," Aunt Edna said, looking up from her crossword.

"Nope." Jackie tapped a bony finger on the folded paper. "Says so right here in this article."

"Lemme see that." Aunt Edna snatched the paper from Jackie's hand. As she unrolled it, I recognized the title running across the top of the page. It was a local tabloid called the *Beach Gazette*.

I watched silently as Aunt Edna chewed a mouthful of bagel and read the article circled by Jackie with a red marker. Suddenly, her eyes grew wide. She dropped the paper and sprang to her feet.

"This is worse than I thought," she said. "We need to talk to Sophia. *Now!*"

I stuck my spoon into my magically delicious cereal. "Who's Sophia?"

My question seemed to startle Aunt Edna, as if she'd forgotten I was there. She shook her head. "Molasses."

"No molasses," Jackie said sternly. "It's time Doreen got to know the Family."

Aunt Edna let out a groan and closed her eyes. "Fine. Sophia's the head of the CGCN. The Queenpin, so to speak."

My right eyebrow arched. "So, she's like ... Cosa Nostra *royalty*?"

An image of Michelle Pfeiffer in *Scarface* popped into my mind—an elegant woman in a sleek, sequined ball gown, lying atop a piano smoking a cigarette with one of those long, tapered holder-thingies.

"Sorta," Jackie said.

I perked up at the opportunity to meet a real, live mob queen in action. I figured I could gather a few useful tips for future auditions back in L.A.

"Okay, I'm in," I said. "As long as you can get me back to the airport in time, that is. I just rebooked my flight for this evening at seven."

Aunt Edna shrugged. "Sure. It shouldn't take too long."

I smiled. "Cool. So, where does Queen Sophia live?"

"In apartment three, across the courtyard," Jackie said, returning from the kitchen with a cup of coffee. "But at the moment, she's ... um ...." Jackie's voice trailed off. Her eyes darted left, then right. She cupped a hand to her mouth, leaned over and whispered in my ear, "She's in a *facility*."

I blanched.

Geez. This seals it. This whole family is 100% nuts!

"Drug rehab or mental breakdown?" I asked, imagining a crazed, big-eyed Bette Davis holed up in the attic in *Hush, Hush, Sweet Charlotte*.

"Neither," Aunt Edna said. "Convalescent center. Busted hip. Sophia's about to turn a hundred years old."

"Oh." My image of the CGCN Queenpin degenerated from 'dapper diva' to 'dowager in Depends.'

Jackie smiled coyly and winked at me. "Rumor has it Sophia came over from Sicily in a wooden ship."

I frowned, my former curiosity replaced with suspicion. "Rumors seem to run rampant around here."

Jackie smirked and clapped a hand on my shoulder. "Dorey, you got no idea."

I grimaced. "That's what I'm afraid of. You know what? You guys go ahead without me. I think I'll just stay here and re-pack for my trip back to L.A. Speaking of which, who unpack—"

"Come on," Jackie pleaded. "One little Family visit won't hurt nothing. Then we'll come straight back here and get you to the airport on time. I promise."

I chewed my lip. "Well ..."

"Oh, crap!" Aunt Edna bellowed. "Would you look at the clock? It's almost lunchtime and I got nothing in the oven!"

I glanced at the gaudy cherub clock casting aspersions at us from the wall above our heads. The dial in its pudgy, golden arms registered quarter past ten.

In Aunt Edna's world, lunch was served promptly at eleven, followed by dinner at four o'clock. I didn't know if the early-bird arrangement was her own personal preference or a CGCN regulation. Either way, I'd learned not to ask if I could help out with the preparations. Setting foot in the kitchen when Aunt Edna was cooking was a risky proposition. The woman had a cleaver and she knew how to use it.

Aunt Edna wrung her hands. "Geez, Louise. Good thing I already got most of it together. I'll pop the cacciatore in the oven and we should still be able to make it in time."

"In time for what?" I asked.

"Saturday lunch with Sophia," Aunt Edna said, sprinting toward the kitchen. "It'll sweeten the pot."

My brow furrowed. "*What* pot?"

Aunt Edna shrugged. "Sophia can be cranky when it comes to surprises."

"What's the surprise?" I asked.

"You," my aunt said.

"Oh." I glanced over at Jackie. She was already licking her lips in anticipation. I couldn't blame her. Aunt Edna might've been rigid when it came to rules, but her cooking could steal the "Bam!" right out of Emeril's envious, drooling mouth.

Looking at Jackie made me think of my own mother. She was a total disaster in the kitchen. The best recipe she'd ever come up with was a tin of tuna dumped into a can of cream-of-something soup, poured over a box of macaroni and cheese and microwaved until the plastic bowl half-melted. To be honest, until I'd met my aunt, my idea of a gourmet meal had been a Denny's Grand Slam. I wasn't even sure there was a functioning stove in my apartment back in L.A.

I drained my coffee mug and chewed my lip. While I tried to decide whether Aunt Edna's cacciatore was worth missing my flight over, Jackie reached across the table and patted my hand.

"Come with us and meet Sophia," she said. "It'll be fun."

"I dunno," I said. "I don't even know her."

Jackie made googly eyes at me. "Hello? Earth to Doreen. *Meeting* Sophia is how you *get* to know her."

I hesitated. The delectable aroma of Aunt Edna's cacciatore was busily eroding my resolve.

"Do it for your Aunt Edna," Jackie said. "Do it for your *Family*."

My eyebrows shot up. "The same family that drugged me, hog-tied me to a bed, and nearly scratched my eye out?"

Jackie shrugged. "Hey. We didn't know you was Family then. Besides, ain't that exactly what *you* did to that soap-opera hunk boss of yours?"

I frowned. "I never *drugged* Tad."

Jackie smirked. "No. You just threatened to cut off his body parts."

I winced, caught in my own trap. "Just his *bangs*. And cuticle scissors never killed anybody!"

Jackie smirked. "Honey, a good hitman can turn a *broken toothpick* into a deadly weapon."

I grimaced.

Geez. I wonder how she knows that?

Chapter Six

That '70s Show had nothing on Aunt Edna's living room.

I parked my butt in her brown Barcalounger and stared blankly at the urine-colored lamps flanking either side of the green velveteen couch. While I waited for the two women to get ready for our trip to visit Godmother Sophia, I found myself caught in an internal debate—one I couldn't win despite the fact that I was arguing both sides.

My brain kept telling me to leave this whole Collard Green Cosa Nostra craziness behind while I had the chance. Just call a cab and get my butt to the airport. But the smell of Aunt Edna's chicken cacciatore baking in the oven had my traitorous stomach shredding through my sensible escape plan like a tornado in a trailer park.

Admittedly, I *was* more than a smidgen curious about meeting the CGCN's leading lady. And I couldn't deny a niggling sense of duty to Ma's family, no matter how nutso they were.

I chewed my lip, then let out a sigh.

What would be the harm in staying a few more hours? Face it, Doreen. The only cook waiting for you back in LA is Chef Boyardee.

"So, you coming or not?" Jackie asked.

I nodded, letting the deciding point go to the cacciatore. The aroma alone made me feel as if I'd died and gone to Sicily. "Okay," I said. "I'm coming."

"All right!" Jackie hooted. "Edna, she's going with us!"

Aunt Edna stepped out of the kitchen and beamed at me. "Good girl! Now, let's get a move on, you two. Jackie, you carry the casserole dish. Dorey, you grab the keys. You're driving."

"I am?" I asked.

"Yes." She looked down at my bare feet. "Put on those new flip-flops we gave you."

I didn't argue. What was the point?

***

As I scooted into the driver's seat of Jackie's ancient, olive-drab Kia, my mind flashed back to my suitcase. I'd left it lying open at the foot of the bed like a gutted fish. I needed time to repack before my flight back to L.A. this evening. Would we make it back in time?

I glanced over at Aunt Edna climbing into the passenger seat beside me. An unfamiliar emptiness shot through me. I told myself it was a hunger pang, but it felt more substantial than that. She and Jackie had been kind enough to feed and house me for well over a week, asking nothing in return. I'd never known such selflessness. Nobody in L.A. did *anything* without an ulterior motive. The least I could do was drive them over to have lunch with this Queenpin lady.

I turned the key in the ignition. In a minor miracle, the car coughed to life without having to be beaten about the solenoid with a socket wrench. But as I shifted into reverse, something felt off to me.

Neither of the other two women appeared overly excited about the trip.

Aunt Edna was staring blankly out the window, chewing her thumbnail to the quick. In the backseat, Jackie anxiously drummed her fingers on the side of the harvest-gold casserole dish nestled on a dishtowel in her lap.

"You two look nervous," I said, reversing out of the parking space. "Anything wrong?"

"Not a thing," Aunt Edna said. "I just hope Sophia likes her lunch, that's all."

"Don't worry," Jackie said. "Chicken cacciatore is Sophia's favorite. She'll love it. Unless she went and lost her dentures again. Then all bets are off."

Aunt Edna sighed. "If it weren't for us, I swear that poor woman would starve to death in that place."

"Why?" I asked, steering the Kia onto the street. "Is the food that bad in there?"

Aunt Edna shrugged. "I dunno. I've never tried it."

"Sophia won't touch it either," Jackie said. "She thinks somebody's trying to poison her."

I nearly drove the Kia into the curb. "*Poison* her? Why would she think *that*?"

Aunt Edna shot me a cockeyed glance. "When you're the Queenpin of the CGCN, your head's always on the chopping block."

I grimaced. "It *is*?"

"Hello?" Aunt Edna said. "Welcome to the mafia, Dorey. Sophia's rivals have been trying to do her in since before you were born."

I shot a paranoid glance in the rearview mirror at Jackie. "If that's so, how does Sophia know you haven't put cyanide in that chicken cacciatore of yours?"

"Because we've been taking care of Sophia for over thirty years," Aunt Edna said wearily. "If I wanted to poison her, I'd have done it by now."

"Sophia's not just our *boss*," Jackie said. "She's our cash cow, too. She knows she can trust us 'cause if *she* dies, the money dies with her."

I blinked hard at Aunt Edna. "Is that true?"

My aunt shot Jackie a dirty look in the rearview mirror, then turned to me. "Yeah, pretty much. Unfortunately, we mob women were better at *hiding* dough than *making* it."

"Then where does Sophia get *her* money?" I asked.

Aunt Edna frowned and stared at the road ahead. "The Family Fund. And to be honest, I think they're getting tired of shelling out the greenbacks for her."

Jackie snorted. "I'm pretty sure they hadn't counted on Sophia living to be a bazillion."

Aunt Edna smirked sourly. "As they say, nothing ensures longevity like a monthly stipend."

"Huh." I turned right onto Fourth Street. "So, who's in charge of the Family Fund?"

"I think it's—" Jackie blurted.

"Can it, Jackie!" Aunt Edna yelled. "Look, Dorey. All you need to know right now is that keeping Sophia alive keeps *us* alive. Now, no more questions. Capeesh?"

I grimaced. "Capeesh."

Geez. This pair have more secrets than a call girl's condom box.

I shut my mouth and stared at the road ahead. As I drove, I mentally repacked my suitcase to beat a hasty retreat back to L.A. before I became a Cosa Nostra casualty myself. The two women in the car may have looked harmless, but I knew better. I didn't want to stick around and feel the wrath of Jackie's Raid ...

My head still hummed from my "iced tea" hangover. And my ghostly left eye still ached from when Jackie had accidently scratched my cornea during our "get acquainted" interrogation. It was still too irritated to conceal with a contact lens like I normally did. As a makeshift alternative, I'd been forced to don Jackie's huge, wraparound glaucoma sunglasses instead.

I glanced at myself in the rearview mirror and blanched.

Geez. I'd better get out of here fast. All I need is a blue-tinted wash-n-set, and I'll be one of them!

Chapter Seven

At the reception window at the convalescent center, we showed our IDs to a bored, middle-aged medical tech clad in dingy gray scrubs. Ms. Rodriquez eyed us up and down and said, "None of you are afraid of dogs, are you?"

"No," Aunt Edna said. "Why?"

"We got a lady making the rounds with a therapy dog," she explained, pushing her mountain of frizzy black hair away from her face. "It's good for the patients' mental health. Unless, of course, they're terrified of dogs." She stared at us with dull, disinterested eyes. "It happens more than you'd think. That's why I have to ask. It's a matter of liability."

"Liability?" I asked.

"Yeah." Rodriquez sighed. "I thought it was stupid, too. But I looked it up. Dogs kill like 25,000 people a year."

"Geez," Jackie said. "I better be nicer to Benny."

"I'm okay with dogs," I said. "What about you two?"

"Sure," Aunt Edna said.

"Me, too," Jackie said.

Rodriquez nodded. "Okay, then. Go on through. Ms. Lorenzo is in room 113."

Jackie, Aunt Edna, and I made our way down the dreary beige corridor. The hallway hummed with the insect-like buzz of dying fluorescent lightbulbs hanging from the drop ceiling. Pine-scented disinfectant assaulted our noses.

Even the flapping noise generated by our pink flip-flops seemed to add a foreboding eeriness to the dank passageway. Our rubber sandals were the official leisure footwear of the CGCN. Aunt Edna had insisted we wear them as a sign of respect to the Queenpin.

According to Aunt Edna, the only thing Sophia hated more than being disrespected was being surprised. And while she had the hearing of a bat, the Queenpin couldn't see squat without her bifocals. Thus the flapping of our sandals would provide Sophia with fair warning of our approach.

I'd shrugged at the news. Given the crap I'd had to put up with as a Girl Friday back in L.A., it seemed a more than reasonable enough request.

"Here we go," Aunt Edna said as we reached room number 113. She cautiously rapped her knuckles on the door in a kind of SOS-like code.

Tap. Tapity-tap. Tapity-tap. Tap. Tap.

"Enter," a quavering voice said from the other side.

Suddenly I felt silly, as if I were auditioning for a bit part in a comical mobster movie. I giggled—a nervous habit—then took a step toward door number 113. Aunt Edna put a hand on my shoulder and held me back.

"Listen, Dorey," she said. "No stupid questions, okay? And no sudden moves. Smile and be humble. You think you can handle that?"

Smile and be humble?

I nearly laughed out loud.

My old job at the L.A. production studio had entailed catering to stars' outlandish whims at all hours of the day and night. As a "human gopher," I'd once been summoned at 2 a.m. by a D-List celebrity who'd insisted I smell his armpits and "describe the aroma in the voice of an android sent from the future." Like all my assignments, I'd done it with a smile—albeit a fake one.

I nodded at my aunt. "Yeah. I think I can handle it."

She looked me up and down. Worry lines etched her face. "Okay. But keep Jackie's sunglasses on, for crying out loud. We don't want to give Sophia a heart attack with that wonky eyeball of yours. Capeesh?"

"Capeesh." I pushed Jackie's huge glaucoma glasses up higher up on the bridge of my nose. "Ready when you are."

Aunt Edna nodded solemnly. "Okay. We're going in."

Like all L.A.-trained actors, I instinctively took a deep breath to center myself. Then I straightened my posture, set my attitude to *Can do!* and followed the two women into the nursing-home lair of the reigning Queen of the Collard Green Cosa Nostra.

Doña Sophia Maria Lorenzo.

Chapter Eight

The heavy metal door creaked open to Doña Sophia Maria Lorenzo's room at the convalescent center. Aunt Edna licked her lips nervously, cleared her throat, and pushed the door open a bit wider.

"Doña Sophia?" she said softly, aiming her voice at the backside of a wheelchair. It had been turned to face a small window in the stark, hospital-like space. "I'd like you to meet my niece, Doreen Diller."

A mechanical buzz sounded, as if in reply. It reverberated oddly off the blank, white walls as the wheelchair swiveled slowly around to face us. As it turned, it revealed its occupant—a shriveled, milky-white old woman shrouded in a black crocheted shawl.

If there'd been an audition for the part of Vito Corleone's grandmother in *The Godfather*, Doña Sophia would've been a shoe-in for the role.

A shiny silver turban sat atop the ancient woman's ghostly head like a bulbous, comical crown. But there was nothing funny about the dour, narrow face staring at us from beneath the Jiffy-Pop headdress. I recognized Doña Sophia's countenance well. "Regal disgust," was a popular attitude among celebrities.

The wheelchair buzzed to a stop. Doña Sophia jutted her sharp chin upward and studied the three of us silently with a pair of green, cat-like eyes.

Her intelligent, humorless visage reminded me of Celia Lovsky, the woman who played the Vulcan leader T'Pau in the *Star Trek* episode *Amok Time*. (The one where Spock fought Kirk to the death, driven mad by a desire to get laid. *Et tu*, Spock?)

For a moment, my eyes scanned the room, wondering if a hormone-crazed Vulcan might be hiding behind the bathroom door, preparing to lunge at me with a double-sided axe.

The mechanical buzz of Sophia's chair sounded again, drawing my wandering attention back to her. One of her gnarled fingers was pressing a button on the arm of her customized wheelchair. Slowly, the seat rose up, enabling Doña Sophia to look down her nose at us through a set of bejeweled bifocals.

"So you're Maureen's daughter, Doreen," she said slowly, apprising me with her almond-shaped eyes.

"Yes, your majesty." I curtseyed awkwardly, unsure of how to address the queen of the CGCN. "It's a pleasure to meet you."

"She came here all the way from L.A.," Aunt Edna said.

"Hmm." Sophia's eyes dulled, apparently unimpressed by my curtseying skills or my place of residence. Her attention shifted over to Jackie. "What's in the casserole dish?"

"Chicken cacciatore," Jackie answered. "You hungry?"

"Yes. Prepare me a plate."

"Yes, your Queenship," Jackie said reverently.

While Jackie carefully arranged a plate for Sophia, the old woman leaned her thin frame toward the small table beside her hospital bed. A spidery arm jutted from under her shawl and mashed a call button on an old landline phone.

"Freddy?" she said into the intercom. "Come over. *Now*."

Before I could even ask who Freddy was, an old guy in a hospital gown tapped twice on the door, then stuck his pasty, half-bald head inside.

"Come in," Sophia said, offering him the first smile I'd seen grace her thin lips.

"Yes, ma'am," Freddy said, bowing as he entered. The old man was small and wiry. Not much bigger than Sophia herself.

"Here you go, my dear," Sophia said. "Have a plate of homemade cacciatore. Compliments of my Family."

The old man's eyes lit up. He grabbed the plate from Jackie. "Thanks, Soph. You're the best!"

"Yes. I know," she said dully. "Now run along and eat it before it gets cold." She shooed him out of the room with a flick of a blue-veined wrist.

Confused, I turned to Jackie and whispered, "What's going on?"

"Shh!" Aunt Edna hissed.

"Freddy is my food tester," Sophia said, eyeing me intently as she smoothed the lap of her black dress with a ghostly, liver-spotted hand.

I nearly blanched. "Food tester?"

Aunt Edna walked over and wedged herself between me and Jackie. "Yeah, in case someone tries to poison her," Jackie said, earning her an elbow in the ribs from Aunt Edna.

My mouth fell open. "Are you serious? People are willing to risk their lives like that for *money*?"

Doña Sophia tutted as if I'd amused her. "Don't be ridiculous, Doreen. Freddy's not getting *paid*. Except, of course, with some of Edna's excellent Italian cuisine."

My nose crinkled. "But .... I mean, how did you get him to put his life on the line like that for you?"

"Easy," Sophia said, the right corner of her mouth angling upward. "He doesn't know."

"Wha—" I managed to utter before Aunt Edna's elbow knocked the wind from my lungs.

Sophia's smirk broadened into a thin-lipped smile. "Take it from me, young Doreen. A woman can never be too careful, or a man too dumb to be useful."

"But surely you must know by now that Aunt Edna's food is safe," I said.

"Of course." Sophia sighed as if my protestations bored her. "I can't kill every man with every morsel I offer. Word would get around."

"*Every* man?" I asked, my throat suddenly dry. "You've done this *before*?"

Sophia sighed. "Freddy's the third tester I've had this month. The other two didn't, shall we say, *pass the test*."

I gasped. "You *killed* them?"

Suddenly, the room went wonky. I tilted on my heels. Aunt Edna reached out and grabbed my upper arm.

"Thanks," I said, assuming my aunt had taken hold of my arm to keep me from falling over. But then I felt a sharp pinch. She was squeezing my upper-arm flab!

"Ouch!" I whined, pulling my arm away. "What'd you do *that* for?"

Aunt Edna hissed through her fake smile. "Cool it with the twenty questions already."

"*I* didn't kill those two men," Sophia said indignantly. "Whoever was trying to kill *me* is to blame. Besides, they could've died of natural causes. In a place like this, you can never be too sure."

"But ... why would someone want to kill *you*?" I asked.

Aunt Edna grabbed my arm flab again. "Like I said, lay off with the inquisition, okay?"

"Heavy is the head that wears the crown," Sophia said. She sighed dramatically and shook her head. "Didn't these two tell you?"

I glanced at Aunt Edna, then Jackie. "Tell me what?"

"Whoever kills me gets to take over the Family." Sophia reached up and adjusted her silver turban. "Believe me, Doreen. You don't last as long as I have by being careless. You might not believe this young lady, but I'm about to turn a hundred on Tuesday."

Actually, that was the easiest thing to believe that I'd heard since arriving in St. Petersburg.

"Tuesday?" I said. "Wait. That's June twenty-first, right?"

"Yes."

I smiled. "Huh. What do you know? Looks like you and I have the same birthday. Only, *I'll* be forty, of course."

"Humph," Sophia snorted. "I've got corsets from Sicily older than you. Take off those sunglasses, child. Let me see your face."

I glanced over at Aunt Edna for her consent. She grimaced, then gave me a tiny nod.

Slowly, I pulled off the wraparound glaucoma glasses, revealing my ghostly left eye. To my surprise, Sophia didn't even so much as a blink. Instead, the ancient Queenpin sat up straighter in her wheelchair and said, "Come closer."

I blanched. "What?"

Aunt Edna pushed me forward. I took a single, cautious step toward the mysterious, possibly murderous queen of the CGCN.

"Closer," Sophia said, beckoning me with a curl of her gnarled index finger.

I swallowed a dry knot in my throat. Hesitantly, I inched forward another half-step. Fear pricked my spine.

What does this old lady want from me? Is she going to stab me with a silver dagger hidden under her shawl? Or—God forbid—hand me a specimen bottle to take to the nurse's office?

"Closer!" Sophia demanded.

"I ... uh ... I'm right here, Doña Sophia," I stuttered, taking another infinitesimal step. It landed me about foot and a half from her wheelchair. Not daring to come any closer, I asked, "Can I do something for you?"

"Yes, Doreen. You can." The old woman reached a dry, withered hand from under her shawl and grabbed ahold of my forearm.

"What do you want?" I nearly squealed.

"I'm hungry," she said, then flashed a set of ivory dentures at me.

I gasped.

Dear lord! Is she about to taste-test me?

I stared, frozen in horror as Sophia's other arm emerged from beneath her inky shawl. Her ancient, knobby hand reached out and softly patted my own.

"Now then," she said. "Be a dear and go see if Freddy's dead or not."

Chapter Nine

After escaping my own brush with death with the spooky Queen-pin—whether imagined or not—I was relieved to find Freddy was also still alive and well. The old man was in the convalescent center's cafeteria, scarfing back a plateful of fish sticks and tater tots. Apparently, the wiry little guy could really pack away the grub.

"Looks like Freddy survived the chicken cacciatore," I announced as I returned, albeit somewhat reluctantly, to Sophia's room.

I studied the three women's expressions, looking for a glimmer of mirth that would tell me I'd just been sent on a wild goose chase—that this had been some silly CGCN prank of theirs. If that was the case, nobody was letting me in on it. At least, not yet.

"Good to hear," Aunt Edna said, waving me over. "Now, let's eat!"

The trio were hovered over a small table in the corner of Sophia's room, admiring the cacciatore as if it were a newborn baby. As I walked over to them, Aunt Edna grabbed a large spoon and began portioning the casserole onto plates. After serving Sophia, Jackie, and herself, she picked up my dish.

"That's okay," I said. "Have a rest. I'll serve myself."

Aunt Edna surrendered the spoon, but not her watchful gaze. "Take another scoopful," she said after I'd already heaped my plate with enough chicken and pasta to choke a goat.

"Yeah," Jackie said. "You don't eat enough to keep a Dodo bird alive." She winked at me. "That's why they went extinct, you know."

Feeling a little more at ease, I smirked. "The only thing extinct about *me* is my size-six thighs. I'll never see *those* babies again."

"Ha!" Aunt Edna said. "You can say that again."

Balancing a mountain of steaming cacciatore on my plate, I took a seat beside Aunt Edna at the cheap, laminate-topped card table. After a quick round of crossing themselves, the three women dug in like rabid wolves.

"Well, here go my size *eight* thighs," I said, and joined in the feast.

***

Sophia's room at the convalescent center might've been dreary, but the conversation was anything *but*.

Between mouthfuls of delectably cheesy chicken and pasta, Doña Sophia loosened the reins on her dour, regal persona and regaled us with recollections of what she referred to as the "Golden Age"—the time when the Cornbread Cosa Nostra ruled most of Florida.

"We were as untamed as the swamp gators back then," the Queenpin said, her green eyes sparkling with a faraway glow. "It was the Wild West all over again—only instead of rattlesnakes and cactus, we had mosquitos and palm trees."

Seeing the softer side of the Queenpin caused my worry about being on the old woman's hit list to dissipate considerably. I grinned at her. "Florida must've been something to see back then, Doña Sophia."

"Oh, it was. Believe me." Sophia sighed and shook her head sadly. "If only I could wave a magic wand and go back to the days before RICO, when the booze was flowing and the bolita balls were still rolling."

"Bolita balls?" I asked, a forkful of cacciatore poised halfway to my mouth.

"Yeah," Aunt Edna said. "It was a gambling game. Kind of like the state lottery. But back then it was run by the Family."

My eyebrows rose half an inch. "Seriously? I've never heard of bolita."

Sophia tutted softly. "Nowadays, nobody has. Bolita's gone the way of the Dodo bird and your skinny thighs, young lady. But back in the day, let me tell you. Bolita was *huge*."

"She ain't lying," Jackie said. "You could buy a bolita ticket at every street corner, grocery store, and backroom bookie in the state."

"Backroom bookie?" I asked. "So bolita was a scam?"

"No!" Sophia slammed a gnarled hand on the table. Her sharp eyes narrowed in on me. "No more than that stupid state-run lottery is today!"

"I'm sorry," I backpedaled. "I didn't mean to upset you."

Sophia crumpled into her wheelchair. The four of us sat in silence for a few minutes, as if paying respects to a dearly departed friend. When Sophia finally spoke again, her voice was still fiery, but it had lost a significant bit of its spark.

"Bolita was better than the lottery," she said. "Way better. Back then, it didn't cost an arm or leg to play. You could place a bet for as little as a penny."

"That seems like a good deal," I said, mainly to appease her. "So, how did bolita work exactly?"

"Simple." Aunt Edna set down her fork. Italian to the core, she used her hands to demonstrate as she spoke. "Every week, people would bet on a number from one to a hundred, hoping their number would be picked. On Saturdays, the heads of the bolita games would draw from a bag with a hundred numbered balls in it. The lucky winners got paid. The bolita runners kept the rest."

Sophia sighed. "Rain or shine, the Family always won the biggest pot."

"With penny bets?" I smirked. "I bet those 'pots' were *humongous*."

Sophia jabbed a fork into her cacciatore. "I'll have you know, young lady, those pennies added up."

"To *what*?" I snickered, imagining some kids in old-timey clothes sorting through a wheelbarrow full of dirty pennies.

"A *lot*," Sophia grumbled.

"Okay," I said. "So, how big was the take on an average week?"

Aunt Edna shrugged. "Well, you've gotta remember this was back in the fifties and sixties, so everything is relative. But back then, I'd say it was around half a million a week."

My shoulders straightened. "Pennies?"

"*Dollars*," Sophia said, trumping my smirk with a bigger one of her own.

My gut fell into my shoes. "Holy crap!"

Sophia grinned like a fox with a bellyful of hen-house chickens. "Crime might not pay, Doreen Diller. But *organized* crime sure does." She sighed. "Or, at least, it *did*."

I shook my head. "Geez. You can say that again."

"Organized crime used to pay," Jackie said brightly, earning her another dirty look from Aunt Edna.

Sophia frowned and picked at her cacciatore with her fork. "Like all good things in life, bolita didn't last." She glanced up at me. "I was a mere slip of a girl like you when it all started to go belly-up. In fact, I remember the exact day the grits hit the fan, so to speak."

"You do?" I asked.

"Of course I do." Sophia's face grew dark again. "It was the summer of 1961. I was in the kitchen helping my mother make pasta e fagioli. My father came home and announced that Congress had formed that blasted BATFE. Ma dropped the pot of soup right on the floor." She shook her head. "Two complete disasters in one day."

"BATFE?" I whispered to Aunt Edna while Sophia stared at her plate and ruminated. I didn't want to ask another stupid question and tick off the old Queenpin even more. After all, if Jackie knew how to kill someone with a broken toothpick, what could Sophia do with that fork in her hand?

"The Bureau of Alcohol, Tobacco, Firearms and Explosives," Aunt Edna whispered back. "It was really bad news for bookies."

Sophia muttered into her cacciatore, oblivious to the other passengers on board as her trip down memory lane derailed. She shook her head. "Then they passed that damned RICO act and went after the Family with a vengeance!"

Aunt Edna must've read my face. She leaned over and whispered, "Racketeer Influenced and Corrupt Organizations Act. That's what really did the Cornbread Cosa Nostra in."

"That's right!" Sophia said. She banged her bony fist on the table. "When that blasted Bureau got going, there was no stopping them! Before we knew it there was a Fed on every corner and a G-Man in every pot!"

The old woman sighed and stared out the window. "In less than twenty years there was nobody left standing but us women folk. Us and the handful of man-rats who beat the rap by selling the others down the river."

"Wow," I said softly. "I get why you'd be so angry. Was Sammy the Psycho one of those rats?"

A loud, shattering *crash* sounded right beside me.

I whirled my head to the left to see Jackie frozen in place, her face aghast. Her half-eaten plate of cacciatore lay in a tomato-covered heap on the floor like the victim of a drive-by pasta shooting.

"Sammy wasn't never no rat!" Sophia bellowed.

I blanched with confusion. "But ...," I stuttered. "I ... I didn't mean anything by it. I just thought he might be. You know, since he's trying to kill you, and everything."

"What?" Sophia hissed.

"She don't know what she's talking about," Aunt Edna said, her elbow rocketed sideways into my ribcage. "Stuff a sock in it, Doreen!" She turned to Jackie. "Go get a mop! Now!"

Jackie bolted for the door. Aunt Edna sopped up the sauce on the table with her napkin.

I turned to Sophia. "I'm sorry. It's just that, well, if *Sammy's* not trying to poison you, who *is*?"

Sophia leaned forward until her face was mere inches from mine. "*Humpty Bogart*, that's who."

"What?" My mind whirred with confusion. Either I hadn't heard her right, or Sophia was totally off her rocker. I glanced over at Aunt Edna for a clue. Her stern, angry face offered no conclusive evidence one way or the other.

"Humph," Sophia growled. "Why on earth would you think *Sammy* would want to poison *me*?"

I chewed my lip, unsure of how to proceed. No matter what I said, I figured it would earn me either a hard elbow to the ribs or a fork in the eye.

I am SOOO going back to L.A.

I clamped my mouth shut. Then a thought hit me.

If I'm leaving tonight anyway, why not go for it? What have I got to lose?

"Well," I said, "it's just that Aunt Edna looked pretty upset when we got those cheese curds last night."

Sophia choked on a sip of water. "What did you say?"

"Someone sent us cheese curds," I repeated. "They came with a note that said, 'Atta girl.' What do you think that means?"

Aunt Edna stopped cleaning, closed her eyes, and groaned.

Sophia set her fork down and slowly straightened to perfect posture. Her glowering gaze shifted to Aunt Edna. "What's she talking about?"

Aunt Edna squeezed on a painful-looking smile. "I was going to mention it after we ate."

"Then your timing's perfect," Sophia said, her face puckered with anger. "I've suddenly lost my appetite."

***

"Err ... the curds arrived in a cooler yesterday evening," Aunt Edna explained, her tone soft and apologetic. "Along with the note, just like Dorey said. But it was already way past visiting hours here at the facility, see? So we waited until this morning. I wanted to tell you in person. We headed over as soon as I got the cacciatore ready. A good cacciatore takes time, as you well know, Doña."

Sophia glanced down at her plate. Her angry countenance barely softened. "That's true. But still, you should've called me as soon as you knew."

"Knew what?" I asked.

"Molasses," Aunt Edna growled at me.

"No molasses," Jackie said, sweeping up the broken plate of cacciatore at her feet.

"What's with this *molasses* business?" Sophia demanded. "This some kind of new code, Edna? Something *else* you haven't bothered to tell me about?"

"No. It's nothing. I swear," Aunt Edna said. "But with all due respect, I have to ask, Doña Sophia. Do you think Sammy might've sent the curds? We're not sure of his ... um ... current *state of health*."

Sophia studied the three of us as if trying to decide which to kill first. Finally, she said, "It could've been *anybody*."

"Does that mean Sammy's still alive?" I asked.

Jackie let out a squeak, then nearly dropped her dustpan full of man-
gled cacciatore on the floor again.

"Maybe," Sophia growled. "Or maybe somebody just wants you to
think he's still alive."

I frowned. "What about—"

"Anybody got a roll of duct tape?" Sophia growled, glaring at me. "If
I hear another question out of this one's mouth, I'm gonna stuff a sock in
it!"

Aunt Edna grabbed me by the arm and yanked me toward the door.
"Sorry about all the bother, Sophia. We'll be going now. You need your
rest. I'll be back tomorrow with a nice linguine Alfredo."

The old woman frowned and waved a dismissive hand at us. "If I live
that long."

"Take care, Queenie," Jackie said, bowing and scraping as she backed
herself out the door. She waved the broom handle like a magic wand.
"May you remain forever in good health."

What the?

As Jackie cleared the doorframe, Aunt Edna jerked me by the elbow
into the hallway.

"Ouch!" I said, wincing. "What did *I* do?"

"I told you not to ask dumb questions! Nobody's allowed to ask
Sophia about Sammy."

My nose crinkled. "Why not?"

"There you go with your dumb questions, again," Aunt Edna said.
"Sophia's touchy when it comes to Sammy."

"But why?" I asked.

Aunt Edna frowned. "Molasses!"

"But—" Jackie protested.

This time Aunt Edna held her ground.

"I *said* molasses!"

Chapter Ten

"I've never seen Sophia so pissed off," Aunt Edna said, gingerly tiptoeing away from the door to the Queenpin's room at the convalescent center. "We need to get outta this joint and let her cool down." She shot me a *this is all your fault* glare that sent a twinge of panic racing along my spine. "You got a big mouth, Dorey."

I cringed. "Sorry!"

Great going, Doreen. Now you've gone and ticked off the head of the southern mafia! What happens now? Is Sophia already dialing H for hitman on that ancient landline of hers? Am I about to be fitted for a pair of cement shoes?

I gotta get back to L.A. — A.S.A.P.!

"Don't just stand there like a couple of knuckleheads," Aunt Edna barked. "Come on." She turned on her pink heels and headed down the hallway.

"We're coming!" Jackie said, ditching the dustpan in the corridor. She grabbed me by the arm and yanked me along. "Come on, Dorey. Let's go!"

I scrambled to keep up with the women's quick pace. As we rounded a corner in the hallway, I spotted a ray of sunlight glaring through the set of glass exit doors. Feeling bad about blowing it big time with Sophia and my aunt, I was eager to make amends before I ended up on the wrong side of a poisoned gelato.

I sprinted past the two women, intent on opening the door for them to show my respect. But just as my fingers touched the push-handle on the exit door, an old woman sitting on a bench nearby sprang to her feet. She raised a huge, purple umbrella over her head, then sent it crashing down on my unsuspecting noggin.

"Argh!" I cried out, shocked by her unexpected attack. "What'd you do that for?"

"Because you're a murderer!" she yelled.

I flinched. "What?"

She jabbed at me with the umbrella. "You killed my boyfriend!"

My mouth fell open. "Uh ... I'm sorry, but I didn't—"

I glanced around for a dementia nurse. No such luck.

"I *saw* you do it," she grumbled. "On TV!"

"Ma'am, I assure you ..." I said. Then something clicked inside my brain. My voice trailed off.

Today is Saturday.

Yesterday afternoon, the last episode of *Beer & Loathing*, the TV show I'd come to St. Pete to film with Tad Longmire, had aired on Channel 22. In it, I'd played a mysterious, unidentified, crazy-eyed psycho killer.

But in the final episode that aired yesterday, the rubber mask I'd worn to conceal my identity had been ripped away. The face of my murderous character, Doreen Killigan, had finally been revealed to the world—just as I'd fake-stabbed Tad Longmire to death.

Killigan's face was also *my* face. Wonky eye and all.

I groaned.

Somehow, the old woman had the mental wherewithal to recognize me, but not enough to tell the difference between reality and TV.

Given the current state of the world, I kind of got that. But what I *couldn't* understand was how the old woman had pegged me as Killigan. My wonky eye and half my face were hidden behind Jackie's giant glaucoma glasses.

Or were they?

I nearly slapped myself on the forehead. After giving Sophia a look at my face, I'd forgotten to put the stupid sunglasses back on.

"You killed Tad Longmire!" the old woman yelled, confirming my theory. She reared back and swung her umbrella at me again. This time, I was able to deflect it with my forearm.

"Sheesh, lady! I'm no killer," I said, rifling through my purse for Jackie's glasses. I slapped the big, black frames onto my face. "That was just a role I played on TV."

A deep

scowl creased the suspicion already lining the elderly woman's face. "Yeah. That's what they *all* say." Then, for good measure I suppose, she raised her umbrella and beaned me with it again.

"What's going on here?" Aunt Edna yelled as she and Jackie came flip-flopping up to us.

"Help me nab her, ladies," the old woman yelled. "She's a killer!"

Jackie and Aunt Edna both stopped in their tracks and stared at me.

"Ha! I knew it!" Jackie said.

I gasped. "I'm not! I didn't! Geez. It's just ... uh ... This is just a funny *misunderstanding*."

"If you say so," Aunt Edna said. She shot Jackie a dubious glance, then the pair took off out the exit door like buckshot from a double-barreled rifle.

"Hey! Wait!" I yelled after them.

Hot on their heels, I chased them through the parking lot as they made a mad dash toward the battered old Kia. "Why are you running?"

"Like Queenie says, a girl can ever be too careful," Aunt Edna said as she reached the Kia. She leaned on it, huffing and puffing.

"You really think I'm a killer?" I asked.

"Unlike you, I don't ask questions I don't want to know the answer to," Aunt Edna said. "Now unlock the fakakta car and let's get the H-E double toothpicks out of here before some wiseguy gets a bead on us!"

I gulped, not sure if she was serious or not. Unwilling to wait around to find out, I scrambled into the driver's seat.

The old Kia creaked and bobbed like a rickety old boat as the three of us piled in. I slammed the door, locked it, and scanned the parking lot for snipers.

"What are you waiting for?" Aunt Edna said. "*Hit it*, Dorey."

I shot her a worried look. "You really think someone's after us?"

Thwack! Thwack! Thwack! Thwack!

"What the?" I screeched, as a hail of bullets riddled the windshield.

Chapter Eleven

"Oh my gawd!" I squealed and ducked for cover between the seat and the dashboard. "Somebody's shooting at us!"

"Those ain't bullets," Jackie said, craning her long neck for a better look from the backseat. "Just acorns. That nutso umbrella lady's throwing them at us."

"Really?" I asked, staring up at Aunt Edna.

She smirked down at me. "Yes, really. "I remember when I had reflexes like that."

I felt my face heat up. I scooched myself up from the floorboard and back in the driver's seat. The "shell casings" littering the hood of the Kia were green and brown—and wore cute little caps with stems at their centers.

Jackie snorted with laughter. "Thank goodness that old geezer ain't packin' an Uzi. She's got deadly aim."

I scanned the parking lot. In the shade beneath a huge oak tree, I spotted the old lady with the purple umbrella—or, more accurately, I spotted her backside. She was bent over gathering another handful of ammunition.

"Start the car already, Dorey," Aunt Edna said.

"Oh. Right." I turned the key in the ignition. All three of us let out a collective sigh of relief when the hunk of junk started on the first try.

Aunt Edna crossed herself. "Thank you, Saint Frances of Rome."

"Saint Frances of Rome?" I asked, backing out as another hail of acorn artillery blasted the side of the car.

"Yeah." Aunt Edna shrugged. "She's the patron saint of car drivers. Closest I could come up with on short notice."

"I'll take it," I said, shifting into drive. "Right about now, I could use a little help from above."

"Couldn't we all," my aunt said. "Now step on it. That dingbat old woman's almost done reloading again."

I reversed out of the parking spot and hit the gas so hard it plastered Aunt Edna flat against the passenger seat. I glanced in the rearview mirror at Jackie. She was grinning from ear to ear.

"Woohoo!" she giggled. "That was one for the bucket list! I ain't never been attacked by a rabid squirrel in a muumuu before."

My nose crinkled.

Who ever had?

Aunt Edna snorted despite herself. "Jackie's right. Dorey, you sure know how to bring out the *animal* in people."

"Ha ha," I sneered. "You two laugh all you want. But it's not funny. Sophia hates me. And now some crazy old woman recognized me from TV. She thought *I killed Tad*!"

"You *did*," Aunt Edna said.

I frowned. "I mean *for real.*"

"You *did* for real," Jackie said. "With those tiny little cuticle sciss—"

"Okay, Okay!" I said, drowning out Jackie. "Enough with the jokes on me, already! Can we change the subject?"

"Fine with me," Aunt Edna said, stifling a smirk.

"And you're wrong about one thing," Jackie said. "Sophia don't hate you."

"She doesn't?" I asked.

"Naw," Aunt Edna said. "I mean, no more than she generally hates everybody."

"Good to know," I said. "Mind if I ask a question?"

Aunt Edna shot me a look. "*Now* you're gonna ask my permission?"

I winced. "Sorry about asking about Sammy," I said. "I was just trying to look out for you. You know, because of the curds. You two looked so worried when they came."

"Thanks, kid," Aunt Edna said. "But we can look out for ourselves. So, what do you want to know?"

I cleared my throat and tried to sound casual. "When we were leaving Sophia, I heard Jackie call Sophia *Queenie*. I thought she was the *Queenpin*."

"I didn't say Queenie," Jackie said. "I said Queen '*E*'. You know, like Queen Elizabeth."

My brow furrowed. "I don't get it."

"Sophia's like Queen Elizabeth," Aunt Edna said, staring out the windshield. "And we're like a bunch of Prince Charles's."

My eyebrows rose an inch. "Prince Charles's?"

"Yeah." Aunt Edna sighed. "We've been waiting around so long for Sophia to die that in the meantime, we've all turned into old coots ourselves."

"Oh." My brow furrowed. "But why is everybody waiting around? I thought whoever killed Sophia got to be the new leader."

"Not everybody's ready to murder to get their own way," Jackie said, then shot me another wink.

I scowled. "Gimme a break." I pulled up to the exit for the parking lot. "For the millionth time, I didn't kill—"

Suddenly, my voice died in my throat. I'd been struck dumb by the sign for the convalescent center we were leaving.

It was Shady Respite.

Chapter Twelve

Shady Respite! That's the name of the place where those three people died. Good gawd! Could this whole poisoning nonsense be real after all?

I stared, wide-eyed, at the sign for the convalescent center.

"What are you waiting for?" Aunt Edna asked. "The lane's clear."

"Oh. Right," I muttered, and steered the battered old Kia onto the highway. I punched the gas pedal to the floorboard. But as we made a hasty getaway from the potential scene of three poisoning deaths, I suddenly felt more in danger than ever.

"Wait a second," I said to Jackie and Aunt Edna. "You guys never told me Sophia was staying where those other people died. Is that the *real* reason we came here? Not for lunch, but to make sure nobody had poisoned her?"

Aunt Edna cocked her head. "Well, we sure as heck didn't come here to check out the vacation rentals. Right Jackie?"

Jackie grinned at me. "Look at you, Miss Detective. You figured it out all on your own!"

I shook my head. "Why didn't you just tell me that in the first place?"

"Because Edna still ain't a hundred percent sure about you," Jackie said. "You might still be a hitman. Only you're after Sophia instead of us."

I turned and stared at my aunt. "Is that true?"

She shrugged. "Naw. Well, maybe it *was*. But not anymore." She patted me on the shoulder. "Nobody who knows nothing about the Family would've talked to Sophia that way."

"You had her on the ropes," Jackie said. "Sophia will either love you or hate you for that."

"How will I know which one?" I said sourly.

Aunt Edna laughed. "Good question. At least we know now you're not after Sophia." She grinned at me. "Turns out *you're* the one with a price on your head. Or is that *an acorn*?"

Jackie snorted.

I gritted my teeth and turned back to the road ahead. "I'm so glad you two find my death threat so amusing."

"Sorry," Jackie said, drying tears of laughter from her eyes. "But you gotta remember, we're used to 'em. Somebody's always trying to bump us off. Now more than ever."

Like that stray dog wearing a wire? Yeah, right.

"Anything *else* pertinent I should know?" I asked.

"Yeah," Aunt Edna said. "You found us at a pivotal moment in CGCN history, Dorey. As you might've noticed, Sophia can be a real pain in the bunions. But if she manages to live to her hundredth birthday, Family rules say she can step down peacefully and name her own heir."

"So?" I said. "What's so pivotal about that?"

"Like I said, *timing*," Aunt Edna said. "If some wiseguy wants to be head of the CGCN, they've only got until Tuesday to bump off Sophia and claim the crown. It's now-or-never time. After Tuesday, she can live in peace, without a target on her head."

Jackie reached forward and put a hand on my shoulder. "That's why we was so suspicious when you showed up last week in the trunk of that Chevy Caprice. See?"

"Okay," I said. "I kind of get that."

Jackie winced. "Sorry again about your eye."

"Thanks." I turned to Aunt Edna. "So, who's your number one suspect for poisoning Sophia? Sammy?"

She shrugged. "No. He's already waited this long. Why would he want to kill his mother *now*, with just a few days to go?"

I nearly wrecked the Kia. "Wait. Sammy is Sophia's *son*?"

"Yeah," Aunt Edna said.

I shook my head. "Another tiny fact that would've been good to know. So that means we can probably rule him out."

"Why do you say that?" Jackie asked.

"Seriously?" I asked. "She's his *mother*!"

Aunt Edna shot me a sideways glance. "You never thought about killing your own ma, Maureen?"

I cringed. "Look. Surely, if Sammy's alive, Sophia will name him to take over, right? So there's no need for him to kill her."

"You'd think so," Aunt Edna said. "But in case you weren't listening, Sammy's loyalties aren't exactly what you'd call 'predictable.' He could go nutso and take any of us out at any time. Why do you think the Family's been hiding from him all these years?"

My heart skipped a beat. "And now you think he's found you? Because of the cheese curds?"

"That's his calling card," Jackie said. "Like E.T., he just phoned home."

I grimaced. It made sense now why they were so worried. "So, how do you think Sammy figured out where you are?"

Jackie shrugged. "Maybe he got the Google on us."

"Or it could be that Sophia summoned him home for her big birthday party," Aunt Edna said.

I chewed my lip. "That would make sense, I guess, if she's going to name him as the new Kingpin."

"Sammy the Psycho our Kingpin?" Aunt Edna hissed. She crossed herself. "God forbid!"

"Nobody wants him in charge," Jackie said. "Not even Sophia!"

"Then why in the world would she tell him where you are?" I asked.

"I didn't say she *did*," Aunt Edna said. "It's just a theory."

"A theory that doesn't hold water," I said.

"Sure it does," Aunt Edna said. "Look at it this way. Say Sophia *is* gonna name somebody besides Sammy as the new leader of the CGCN. She could be leading him on, telling him she's gonna name him Kingpin. Then pow! She names somebody else during the party. Dropping news like that, she's gonna need protection."

My nose crinkled. "Protection?"

Aunt Edna tapped a finger to her temple. "Think about it, Dorey. If Sammy finds out the news with an audience around, it'll be harder for him to kill Sophia on the spot."

Geez. And I thought my mother was a cold fish.

"But it's just a theory," Jackie said. "I got one, too. Wanna hear it?"

Before either of us could object, Jackie told us anyway.

"What if Sammy caught old-timer's disease, and wants a chance to be Kingpin before he forgets how to bowl?"

Aunt Edna and I groaned simultaneously.

"I've got a question," I said.

"What a surprise," Aunt Edna said. "You ask more questions than a kid in a candy store."

I shot her some side eye. "What if Sophia dies of natural causes before she turns a hundred? What are the Family rules then?"

Aunt Edna sat up straight. "Sammy would take over automatically. Why do you think we work so hard to keep her alive?"

"Poor Sophia," Jackie said. "For her, Sammy's always been a double-edged swordfish."

I shot a glance at Aunt Edna. "What does she mean?"

Aunt Edna shifted in her seat. "On the one hand, Sammy's Sophia's good-luck charm. Nobody dares bump her off for fear of Sammy taking over and exacting his revenge."

"And the other hand?" I asked.

"Sammy's a nut case. Sophia's had to hide out from him just like the rest of us. That's why she won't tell nobody whether he's still alive or not. If people knew for sure he was dead, it'd be open season for her."

I frowned. "But Sophia told me people are *always* trying to get her."

Aunt Edna's lips twitched to one side. "About that. We kind of ... feed her *stories*."

My eyebrows rose an inch. "Stories?"

Aunt Edna shrugged. "That's how we keep her in check. Otherwise, she'd be wandering the streets, accusing the neighbors of working for the FBI. We'd be found out in a heartbeat."

Jackie giggled. "Sophia thinks everybody's after her lucky charms—just like that little gnome on your cereal box."

"Leprechaun," I said.

"Lepers, cons, whoever," Jackie said. "Sophia thinks *everybody's* out to get her."

I sighed.

I guess that runs in the Family, too.

Chapter Thirteen

On the drive back to Palm Court Cottages, I mulled over the bizarre events of the last few hours.

I'd met a mafia Queenpin in a turban who was convinced she was being poisoned by Humpty Bogart. I'd spied on a hapless food taster to see if the old man had survived Aunt Edna's cacciatore. I'd found out Sammy the Psycho is real—and that he's Sophia's son. And I'd been attacked with an umbrella and acorns by an old lady in a muumuu.

If I'd have written this as a screenplay, Hollywood producers would've laughed me off the set. It was all just too absurd to be plausible. As I pulled up to a red light, it finally dawned on me.

That's it! The only way this makes sense is if it's all an elaborate joke on me.

"Okay, I need you to be honest with me," I said, turning to Aunt Edna in the passenger seat. "I'm not mad. But did someone put you up to this?"

She turned and studied me. "Up to what?"

I threw my hands up. "This whole thing! Ever since those curds arrived last night, I've felt like the only one not in on the joke. Are you pranking me? Did my roommate Sonya back in L.A. put you up to this?"

"I don't know what you're talking about," Aunt Edna said. "I swear, Dorey, none of this is a joke. I wish it was."

"She ain't lying," Jackie said from the backseat. "Believe me, the CGCN ain't got that good a sense of humor."

I frowned. If the joke wasn't on me, maybe it was on someone else. "Aunt Edna, you said you tell Sophia stories to keep her in line. This whole poisoning thing. Is it one of those?"

My aunt shot me a hard look, then her face softened a notch. "To tell you the truth, Dorey, I don't know anymore. When Sophia first brought it up, I thought it was just another one of her paranoid delusions. That is, I did until this morning, when Jackie showed me that article in the *Beach Gazette*."

"What did the paper say, exactly?" I asked, then hit the gas.

"Nothing specific," she said. "Just that there'd been a rash of deaths. Three in less than two weeks. That's unusual, even for a place like Shady Respite."

"And don't forget, Edna," Jackie chimed in. "Sophia said the old geezers who died were all her taste testers."

I shot my aunt a look. "Yet *another* fact that would've been good to know."

"Excuse me," Aunt Edna said, "but your ears work better than mine. You were there when Sophia said that. Whether it's actually true or not, who knows? The newspaper didn't name names."

I grimaced, then nodded. "Okay, fair enough."

"Humph," Aunt Edna grunted. "All I know for sure is that we need to keep Sophia alive until she turns a hundred."

"I second that emotion," Jackie said.

I gripped the steering wheel tighter. "Okay, ladies. Let's get hypothetical here for a minute."

"What do you mean?" Jackie asked.

I chewed my lip. "Let's say Sammy *is* in town. And that he wants to do in Sophia. He'd need to kill her before Tuesday, right? Because after she turns a hundred, Sophia sure isn't going to name him Kingpin herself. Correct?"

"Yeah, I guess so," Aunt Edna said. "What's your point?"

"My point is, I don't see how poisoning Sophia would be Sammy's method of choice."

"Why not?" Jackie asked.

"Too risky." I tightened my grip on the steering wheel. "What if the poison only made her sick? Sophia could still live long enough to name somebody else as heir to the throne."

"Hmm," Aunt Edna said. "Yeah, I suppose that could be a problem."

"I know, right?" I said. "Sammy would want to make sure she was a hundred percent dead before Tuesday. And from what you've told me, Sammy was more of a gun guy anyway."

"Another good point," Aunt Edna admitted.

"Wait a minute," Jackie said, piping up from the backseat. "If Sammy's not trying to poison Sophia, who is?"

"That's what we need to find out," Aunt Edna said. She looked my way. "Got any more ideas, Miss Detective?"

I nodded. "One. But it's kind of weird. Sophia told me she suspects some guy named Humpty Bogart is the one trying to do her in. No disrespect, but could Sophia be as psycho as her son?"

Aunt Edna's eyes narrowed. "Why would you say that?"

"Uh ... didn't you hear me? Sophia told me she thought *Humpty Bogart* was trying to kill her."

Aunt Edna locked eyes with me. "Like I said, lots of folks wish they could bump off Sophia."

"Right. But *Humpty Bogart*?" I shook my head. "You've got to admit, that name is well ... *ridiculous*. I think Sophia could be suffering from the same thing as that old lady with the umbrella."

"Old timers?" Jackie asked.

"No," I said. "Well, maybe a little bit. I'm referring to her confusion over what's real and what's something she watched on TV."

Aunt Edna shot Jackie a look in the rearview mirror. "Eh," she grunted. "You could be right, Dorey. Take the next right onto Fourth Street."

I did as instructed and steered the Kia south in the direction of Palm Court Cottages. As I drove, a boatload of questions swirled in my mind, but I decided to keep my mouth shut. After all, what did it matter? I'd be back in L.A. tonight.

Yep. In a few short hours, this would be their *circus.*

Their *psycho monkeys.*

Even so, I just couldn't resist finding out what else might be lurking under the CGCN Big Top.

"Besides Sammy, who else would want to kill Sophia?" I pondered aloud. "She seems nice enough. You know, besides using Freddy as a human guinea pig and all."

Neither Aunt Edna nor Jackie said a word.

"Sophia's just a little old lady," I tried again. "How hard could it be to bump her off?"

"Like we told you," Aunt Edna said. "Everybody's afraid of what Sammy would do. Paybacks are hell when a psycho's holding the purse strings."

"That's why everybody's dying to find out whether Sammy's still alive or not," Jackie said. "If he really *is* out of the picture, Sophia's throne is up for grabs *right now*—for *any* of us—with nobody standing in the way."

"Except Sophia," I said.

"Well, yeah," Aunt Edna said. "That goes without saying."

I shook my head. "I still don't get it. If Sophia's such a pain in the butt, why hasn't someone at least taken a pot-shot at her by now?"

"And if they missed?" Aunt Edna said. "They'd be found out and fall from Sophia's good graces forever. Even if they survived Sammy's revenge, they'd lose any chance of being picked to take over the reins."

"Then it makes no sense for someone to be trying to *poison* her," I said.

"Sure it does," Aunt Edna said.

I crinkled my nose. "How do you figure that?"

"Because poisoning is *anonymous*. If it fails, well, nobody's the wiser. But if it *works*, and Sammy doesn't show up and chop the culprit's head off, the killer can step up, take the credit, and grab their prize."

My left eyebrow ticked up a notch.

Geez. What's wrong with my world that that kind of makes sense?

Aunt Edna turned her gaze to the windshield. "Let me tell you something, Miss Detective. Sophia may be old, but she's one tough broad. Take my word for it, the woman is harder to kill than Rasputin."

My right eyebrow shot up to meet the left. "You've *tried?*"

Aunt Edna scowled, then muttered something under her breath.

I'd have sworn it was the word, "Molasses."

Chapter Fourteen

As I steered the Kia past the shops and strip centers along Fourth Street, my mind boiled with burning questions about Sammy the Psycho.

I'd have already chalked the whole crazy business up to the demented suspicions of a couple of old ladies except for two things. First, the cheese curds were definitely real. I'd seen them with my own eyes. But even if they were Sammy's calling card, anybody could've sent them. Second, Aunt Edna and Jackie seemed genuinely worried about Sammy.

Is he still alive? Is he the one who sent the cheese curds? Is he really psycho? Is he here to kill his mother and take the title of Kingpin? Or is he just a figment of what Brady had referred to as my relatives' "exceptional imaginations?"

I turned to my aunt. "If Sammy—"

"Enough talk about him already," Aunt Edna barked. "Everybody put a sock in it before his bad mojo finds us again."

"Fine." I turned my attention back to the road.

What do I care? I'll just to keep my trap shut and wave goodbye to this whole mess from the plane back to L.A.

"Take a right here," Aunt Edna said. "Let's stop by Morty's bakery."

I blanched. "What? I thought we were going straight home."

"We are. Right after this. It won't take a minute. I wanna see how the *torta alla panna* is coming along for Sophia's birthday party."

"The tortellini *what?*"

"Torta alla panna," Aunt Edna repeated. "Traditional Italian birthday cake. Didn't Maureen teach you anything?"

The corner of my mouth curled downward.

Nope. Not even about Betty Crockeroni.

Aunt Edna blew out a breath and shook her head. "If it were *my* party, I'd personally rather have a nice peach cobbler. But Sophia's a stickler for the old ways."

"What's this torta thing made of?" I asked.

"Finally, a question I don't mind answering," Aunt Edna said. "Okay. First, you start with a *pan di Spagna*—uh, sponge cake. Then you fill it with vanilla pudding and cover it in homemade whipped cream. If you want, you can top it with seasonal fruits."

That's handy, considering how there's no shortage of seasonal "fruits" hanging around.

"What's your favorite fruit, Doreen?" Jackie asked from the backseat.

"Uh ... strawberries, I guess. Why? I won't be there for Sophia's party."

"You won't?" Jackie asked.

"No. That reminds me. Who keeps unpacking my suit—"

"You can't leave now!" Jackie blurted. "And miss Sophia's big centennial bash?"

"She's right," Aunt Edna said. "Now that you've met her, the Doña would consider it extremely rude of you to skip out on her big celebration. And believe me. You don't want to see Sophia when she's ticked off."

My eyebrows shot up. "I thought I already had. She threatened to duct tape my mouth shut, remember?"

Jackie giggled. "That's nothing. When she mentions a chainsaw? *Then* you start worrying."

I gulped. "Chainsaw?"

"Jackie's just pulling your leg," Aunt Edna said. "Anyway, what will it hurt to stay a few extra days? You can meet the Family at the party. Then we can have a little celebration right after, just for *your* birthday."

I chewed my lip. "I dunno."

"Maybe Miss Bigshot's got bigger plans waiting for her back in Hollywood," Jackie said.

Aunt Edna turned and studied me. "*Do* you?"

I thought back to my thirty-ninth birthday and cringed. I'd been working in Hollywood on the set of a low-budget western. As the two lowest grunts on the totem pole, my roommate Sonya and I'd been assigned to "trailer-trash crewing." In other words, we were doomed to satisfying the weird whims of the celebrities cooped up in trailers in the back lot.

Given our luck, we'd been assigned the worst shift—6 p.m. to 6 a.m. As we'd started work that night, Sonya had surprised me with a chocolate cupcake with a candle sprouting from the center of its gooey frosting. Desperate to catch a few badly needed winks, I'd blown out the flame and wished for no middle-of-the-night celebrity meltdowns.

My birthday wish had not been granted.

Around 3 a.m., my cellphone had buzzed. For a brief second, I'd thought it was Sonya pulling a birthday prank.

No such luck.

Instead, I'd been summoned to the trailer of octogenarian Arthur Dreacher. As usual, the dirty old man had answered his trailer door wearing nothing but a pair of saggy cotton underpants. After beckoning me inside, between slugs of Old Milwaukee he'd laid out to me his urgent, life-or-death emergency.

The creep had wanted me to clip his thick, fungus-yellow toenails.

The job had required bolt cutters.

"Ugh," I grimaced aloud, still scarred by the disgusting memory.

"Is staying with us so bad?" Aunt Edna asked.

"What? No." I winced. "I was just—"

Jackie tapped my shoulder from the backseat. "The light's green, hun."

"Oh, right." I hit the gas. "Uh ... regarding my birthday, I think my friend Sonya might have something planned for me, that's all."

"Call her and find out," Aunt Edna said. "We need a headcount for Morty."

Jackie laughed. "So you're turning the big four-oh, eh? You know, by the time I was your age, I'd been divorced twice already. Figuring out how to kill dirtbag losers and get away with it was pretty much all I ever thought about back then. I couldn't get enough of *Forensic Files*. But look at you. You're way ahead of me. You've already gone and done it."

My shoulders stiffened. I glanced at Jackie in the rearview mirror. "You know I didn't *actually stab* Tad Longmire. Right?"

"Right." She shot me an exaggerated wink. "You only tied him up and threatened to cut off his body parts if he didn't do what you said."

I groaned. "For the millionth time, they were *cuticle* scissors. And I only threatened to cut off his—"

"Slow down!" Aunt Edna grunted. She pointed to her right. "Turn in here."

I glanced over at a generic strip center. Painted on the glass display window of one of the shops were the words, *Morty's Bakery*. I pulled into the narrow lot.

"You guys go on inside," I said, shifting into park. "I'm gonna call Sonya."

"You do that," Aunt Edna said. "Then come and join us inside."

I nodded. "Will do."

I waited until the Kia coughed itself out and the two women had ambled into the bakery.

Then I made a call.

But it wasn't to Sonya.

Chapter Fifteen

After spending a crazy morning with my new mob Family, I needed a reality check that wasn't going to bounce.

I needed to talk to Officer Brady.

Last night, during our sketchy date over a plate of cheese curds and Ritz crackers, I'd had so many things I'd wanted to ask Brady about my aunt and Jackie. But I'd been sidetracked by two rather unexpected developments.

First, I'd lost my nerve after the cheese curds had turned out to be freaking delicious. And second, I'd lost my train of thought after chugging down my tea as I pretended to wash the "horrible" taste from my mouth. Little had I known that Aunt Edna had replaced Lipton with her special Long Island blend.

I still wasn't sure how I'd made it to bed last night. And I wasn't sure I wanted to find out. But now, in the sober light of day, as I sat in Jackie's old Kia in front of Morty's Bakery, I figured it was time for a dose of reality. And Brady was the only one I knew of who could possibly deliver.

I raised my index finger to punch in his number, then hesitated. What was I going to say to him?

It was barely three o'clock and I'd already lived through a quadruple dose of the *Twilight Zone*. Sophia the Queenpin. Sammy the Psycho. Freddy the food taster. And an unnamed acorn assassin.

Geez. The guy's gonna think I'm nuts.

I shoved the phone back into my purse and crossed my arms.

But hell. I'm leaving anyway. What does it matter?

I dug my phone back out of my purse and called Brady's number before I lost my nerve. When it went directly to voice mail, I felt both disappointed and relieved.

Just as well. I mean, what could I say to him that would make any sense, anyway?

"Brady here. Leave your message at the tone," his recorded voice said.

Beep!

288

"What?" I gasped. "Oh! Uh ... Hi. It's just me, checking to see if I'm insane or not, hee hee. But seriously ..."

Oh, God! Hang up, Doreen! Hang up now!

I clicked off the phone and groaned. My face was the temperature of the sun. Panic shot through me. I closed my eyes and took a deep breath.

It's okay. With any luck, he won't know it was me.

But even *I* wasn't buying it.

Who do you think you're talking to, Doreen? With any luck? Since when have you had any luck?

"Crap!" I muttered, then tossed my phone into my purse.

I gulped in another lungful of oxygen to calm myself. Then I grabbed the phone again and quickly punched in another number before I had time to analyze what just happened with Brady and go throw myself under a bus.

The phone rang. This time, it didn't go to voicemail. Accustomed to dealing with non-stop emergencies, Sonya answered on the first ring. "Hello?"

"Sonya, it's me, Doreen. How's it going?"

"Uh ... okay. I heard you beat the murder rap. Good for you."

"Well, if by 'beat the rap' you mean that I didn't kill Tad, then yes. I beat it. Uh ... listen. I'm thinking of coming back home today."

"Today? Uh ... about that. Well ...."

"Well what?"

"Okay, I'll just say it. I sublet your part of the apartment."

I blanched. "You *what*? Why?"

"You lost your job. You missed the rent. I thought you were going to jail. Sorry."

I slumped into the seat. "Sorry for renting my space? Or for not believing in me?"

"Uh ... both? But hey, if you need to, you can bunk with me. Still better than the studio cots, right?"

I pursed my lips in frustration. Sonya could be such an airhead. But at least she'd always remembered my birthday.

"So ... anything *special* going on next week?" I asked, trying to drop a hint.

"Not that I know of," Sonya said. "Oh, wait. There is *one* thing."

I grinned. "What?"

"I hear Arthur Dreacher might drop in at the studio. He always asks about you, you know."

My stomach turned. That was one encore performance I never cared to see again. "Gee, thanks. Hey Sonya? Could you do me a favor?"

"Sure. What?"

"Could you box up all my stuff?"

"Already done. Just tell me where to send it."

I nearly dropped my phone. "Seriously? I just meant so the new person doesn't mess with my junk."

"That's why I did it," she said unconvincingly. "So, you coming back or not?"

I frowned. "I'll have to get back to you on that. But don't lease out the other half of your bed just yet, okay?"

"I'll try. But if I run into Johnny Depp, all promises are null and void."

"Got it. Thanks."

I clicked off the phone and sighed. L.A. was a fickle place. Hollywood was even crueler. If you made it big, you were only as good as your last acting role. If you *didn't* make it big, you were only as good as your last rent check.

I glanced through the windshield at the dismal-looking strip center in front of me.

Would it just be more of the same here in St. Pete?

I blew out a breath and stared at the luscious desserts in the bakery's display window.

Geez. Maybe my best bet for a real birthday cake is in Morty's hands after all.

Chapter Sixteen

As I walked up to the glass storefront to Morty's Bakery, I could see Aunt Edna and Jackie inside. They were chatting up a plump, sweaty guy wearing a crisp, white apron tied around his belly. He bore the crooked mug of an ex-prize fighter. I immediately thought of Vic Tayback, the guy who played Mel, the diner cook on that 1980s sitcom, *Alice*.

I pushed open the door, causing a bell affixed to the top to clang. Jackie, my aunt, and the aproned guy looked my way and clammed up. A millisecond later, they unfroze and shot me a trio of smiles that seemed way too enthusiastic for the occasion.

Even over the heavenly scent of vanilla and cinnamon, I smelled a rat. Were they secretly plotting together to rub Sophia out? Or were they merely haggling over the price of baguettes? Or, worse yet, was I turning into a paranoid schizophrenic like the rest of them?

"Hey. What's going on?" I asked, trying to sound breezy.

"Nothing," Aunt Edna said. "Morty, this here's my niece Doreen from L.A. Doreen, this here's Morty."

"From Brooklyn," he said, then offered me a hand as big as a baseball glove.

I smiled sheepishly and shook it. "Hi."

"You should try Morty's famous cannoli," Jackie said.

"Yes, she most definitely should." Morty grinned at me. "Hold on a second."

He snatched a small sheet of wax paper from a dispenser on the counter, then reached into the display case and plucked out a golden-brown, tubular pastry. He held it out for me. "A cannolo for the beautiful young lady."

"Cannolo?" I asked. "I thought Jackie called it a cannoli."

"*One* cannolo, *two* cannoli," Morty said, his smile never wavering. "Little known fact. Go on. Take a bite."

I sunk my teeth into the crispy pastry. An unusual flavor tickled my taste buds. "That's delicious," I said. "But what's the cream—"

"They're filled with banana pudding!" Jackie blurted.

My eyebrow shot up. "Whoa. That's unusual. I've never heard of that before."

Morty beamed. "That's because *I* invented it. I like to take the best of Italian and Southern cooking and combine them into something fresh and new."

"Well, this is a match made in heaven," I said. "Who knew the two could blend so well?"

"*I* did." Morty stuck out his chest and hooked his thumbs into the armpits of his apron. "Actually, when it comes to food, you'd be surprised how close the two countries are. Take grits for example."

"Grits?" I took another bite of cannolo and studied Morty. I'd been right. Up close, he was the spitting image of Mel, the rough-and-tumble hash slinger.

"Yeah," he said. "Think about it. Grits are just polenta you eat for breakfast."

"Huh." I smiled. "I never thought about that."

"Hey, Dorey," Aunt Edna said. "You know what the *real* difference between polenta and grits is?"

"What?" I asked.

She smirked. "About ten dollars a bag."

"Ha!" Jackie cackled. "Good one, Edna!"

The bell on the front door clanged again. We all turned to look.

The door flew open. A balding, sixty-something man with a round belly walked into the shop. He could've been Morty's twin, except that he was about a foot shorter than the baker, and as bald as a boiled egg.

"Morty!" the man called out chummily. "I'm here for my ... *usual*."

"Got it all ready for you," Morty said, his smile growing less generous. He reached for something behind the display counter.

"So, what are you three old hens clucking about?" the man asked.

"Grits," I said.

Morty handed the guy a white paper bag. "That's right. I was just saying how you should put basil in your grits. You know, the good, sweet basil from Italy."

The man took the bag. "Really? I'll have to give it a try."

"You be sure and do that, and let me know what you think." Morty scrambled past us to the door and held it for the man. He ushered his customer out, then closed the door behind him.

"Basil in grits?" I asked Morty. "I'd have never thought about doing that. Is it good?"

"Did I *say* it was good?" Morty shook his head. The ingratiating smile he'd worn for the man was gone. "Actually, it's disgusting. But then again, so is *that* douchebag."

My eyebrows rose an inch. I turned and stared through the display window, watching the roly-poly figure of a man climb into a Lincoln Continental.

"Who is he?" I asked.

Morty shook his head and spat, "That piece of work there? You're looking at none other than the dirtbag we call Humpty Bogart."

Chapter Seventeen

"You mean Humpty Bogart *isn't* a figment of Sophia's imagination?" I asked, dumbfounded as I slid the keys into the Kia's ignition.

"Why would you think that?" Jackie asked from the backseat.

Uh ... why wouldn't *I?*

I shrugged. "I just thought Sophia was trying to get me off the topic of Sammy the—"

"Shhh!" Aunt Edna hissed. "Enough with him, already! We don't need any more bad luck! You want to know about the jerk who came into the bakery? Fine. His real name is Humphry Bogaratelli."

After saying his name, Aunt Edna turned her head and pretended to spit.

"Geez," I said. "What's so bad about the guy?"

"Didn't you hear him call us a bunch of old hens?" Jackie groused. "I'd like to turn him into Al *Capon*!"

I smirked. "Wow. That's pretty foul, Jackie."

"Humpty ain't no joking matter," Aunt Edna said. "The guy's a total shyster. When the Feds were busy busting the Family apart in the '70s and '80's, Humphry told us he was working on putting the pieces of the Family fortune back together. But what did he *really* do? He bogarted most of the money for himself."

"That's why we call him Humpty Bogart," Jackie said. "Get it?"

"Got it." I turned the key in the ignition. The Kia made a clicking sound, but didn't start.

"Fantastic," Aunt Edna grumbled. "Here we go again."

"Sit tight." I leaned over and grabbed the socket wrench from the floorboard beside her feet. "I'll be right back."

I climbed out of the Kia and lifted the hood. Leaning over the engine, I gave the solenoid a solid whack with the wrench. As I raised my hand to deliver a second blow, I called out to Aunt Edna. "Hey. What do think was in the bag Humpty picked up from Morty?"

"Lemon bars." The man's voice sounded so close behind me that I jerked upward and banged my head on the hood.

"Geez!" I yelped, turning to see Morty standing less than two feet away. "Where'd you come from?"

"The bakery. Where else?" He pointed a meaty thumb back toward the storefront. "I practically live there. So, solenoid, eh?"

"Yeah."

Morty leaned sideways so he could see past the Kia's open hood and into the passenger compartment. "I told you two to get a decent vehicle already. This fakakta thing is a piece of kaka!"

"Hey, you wanna pay for us a new car, we'll be glad to have it," Aunt Edna shot back.

Morty took the wrench from my hand and tapped the solenoid on the side. "Go give her a try now."

I hopped into the driver's seat. The Kia cranked to life. I leaned my head out the window. "Thanks!"

Morty closed the hood and handed me back the wrench. "Some things just need a man's touch." He waggled his grey eyebrows at me.

"Careful Morty," Aunt Edna said. "Dorey's got a wrench and she knows how to use it. And in case you haven't noticed, she's half your age."

"I'm not *eighty*," Morty said. "Geez, Edna. Gimme a break."

"I'd love to," she quipped. "We talking femur or kneecap?"

Morty smirked, causing his large nose to dent in at the tip. "You still got the fire, Edna. But you and me don't got the spark no more."

Aunt Edna scowled. "Maybe not. But we all know my niece here is a real fireball. She's already shown us some pretty slick moves. So watch your step around her, Morty. And no more funny business. Capeesh?"

I smiled sheepishly. "Uh ... nice to meet you, Morty. Thanks for the cannolo."

He smiled and winked. "Plenty more where that came from if you play your cards right."

Unsure whether to smile back or slap his face, I rolled up the window. Then, as quickly as I could, I reversed the Kia out of the parking lot.

Morty watched us intently as we pulled away. He certainly appeared to be longing for something, all right. But what? Me? Aunt Edna? Or something else entirely?

"Schmuck," Aunt Edna muttered.

"What's the deal with you and Morty?" I asked as I steered the Kia down the street. "Did you two used to date or something?"

"Or something," Aunt Edna said. "Now, no more questions about Morty."

"What about Sam—"

"Or him, either."

I frowned. "I thought you wanted me to get to know the Family."

"I do," she said. "I just need some time to think about *what* I want you to know."

Chapter Eighteen

Aunt Edna wasn't the only one who needed time to think things over. When we got back to her cottage apartment at half past three, it was crunch time.

I needed to decide whether to risk hanging around a few days for my birthday, or repack my suitcase and catch the red-eye back to L.A. before I ended up dating Morty the ex-con faced baker—or I got whacked to death by a random old lady who couldn't tell the difference between reality and a lousy TV show.

Geez. I'm not sure which would be worse ...

I needed advice. *Sane* advice. With Brady unavailable and Sonya dumping me like a hot-to-trot potato, I was left with only one real choice.

Dear old Ma.

Like I said before, my mother Maureen was what you might call a "cold fish." Distant. Secretive. And hard to catch—especially in a good mood.

To be honest, ever since seventh-grade biology class, I'd been fairly certain Ma was the spawn of one of those weird, sharp-toothed, big-eyed creatures that lived in the darkest depths of the ocean. She was beautiful to look at, I'd give her that. But anyone who tried to get too close fell prey to her painfully sharp barbs.

On the other hand, what Ma lacked in warmth she more than made up for in cold rationality. And a sane voice in the wilderness was exactly what I desperately needed right now. My life back in L.A. was disintegrating by the second. If I stayed here with Ma's family, my life might not last another minute.

Ain't life grand?

I plopped down on the chenille bedspread and fished my cellphone from my purse. I wanted to get Ma's take on whether her sister and her friends were really dangerous, or merely delusional.

While I was at it, I also wanted to ask Ma why she'd never told me that her family were mobsters. And, more importantly, *why on earth* she hadn't used her mafia connections to get me a decent acting gig in Hollywood? I mean, what was the good of being a mob moll if you couldn't throw your weight around a little?

I pushed her speed-dial button and held my phone to my ear. While I could never depend on Ma for cuddles, I could always rely on her to answer her phone. I listened to her line ring five times, then go to voicemail. I didn't leave a message.

Great. Now what?

I grabbed my purse and rifled through it for my *Hollywood Survival Guide*. A gag gift from Sonya, the little book had actually helped me out a few times since I'd gotten to St. Pete. Maybe there was some bit of sage advice inside that would set me on the right path now, as well. At this point, what the heck did I have to lose?

I flipped through the little volume with a cover the color of a yellow caution light. Tip #53 seemed appropriate, but vaguely unhelpful:

> *When you come to a fork in the road, pick it up and eat cake with it.*

I crinkled my nose.

What the heck is that *supposed to mean?*

My phone rang, startling me. I snatched it up. "Ma?"

"Not exactly," a man's voice said. "But I *am* calling to check up on you."

My face ignited into flames. "Brady! What do *you* want?"

"Just to see if you survived the Long Island iced tea massacre. When you called earlier, you sounded ... well, a bit flustered?"

I cringed, too mortified to speak.

"Sorry," Brady said. "Is this a bad time?"

"Huh? No. It's just that ...."

My voice trailed off. After the scatterbrained voicemail I'd left him earlier, maybe the less I said now, the better.

"You still there?" Brady asked.

"Yes."

"Something you want to talk about?"

Only a gazillion things. All of which would prove to Brady once and for all that I was a complete nut job. No thanks. I was definitely going back to L.A. The sooner, the better.

"No, nothing," I said. "Listen, I've got to go. I still have to pack for my flight."

"So you're leaving?"

"Yes."

"I see. Well, have a good flight. "It was nice meeting you."

"Thanks. You, too."

***

Frustrated and bummed out, I padded into Aunt Edna's living room. The green sculptured carpet was truly hideous, but it felt good on my bare tootsies. Aunt Edna was parked in the old Barcalounger, sipping a glass of iced tea. She appeared lost in thought.

"Aunt Edna? Sorry to bother you, but I can't get ahold of my mother. I haven't talked to her in over a week."

"Geez, Louise," Aunt Edna said, setting her glass of tea into the plastic cup holder hooked to the armrest of the vinyl recliner. "I forgot to tell you. Maureen called this morning. She's in Anchorage."

"Alaska?"

"Yeah. She went on one of those summer solstice cruise deals. Said the phone reception there is terrible. I could barely make out what she was saying. Anyway, she said to wish you happy birthday."

"Oh. Okay."

She shot me a weak smile. "How's about a nice iced tea?"

"Uh, sure. Thanks."

I followed Aunt Edna into her kitchen domain, feeling like a lost child.

"Don't worry. Maureen always *was* her own girl," Aunt Edna said, pouring me a glass of strong, brown brew. "So, you staying a while?"

"I don't know yet," I said, not wanting to hurt her feelings.

"Well, just so you know, me and Jackie would like it if you did."

"Really? I ... I just need a little time to think."

"Take all the time you want." My aunte winked at me. "Your plane doesn't leave for another three hours."

"Oh. Right."

She patted me on the shoulder. "Well, I better get busy with dinner. Let me know if I should set a place for you or not."

"I will. And thank you for your hospitality. I really appreciate it."

"You're family, Dorey. Hospitality is for strangers. And there's no need to thank me. It's been my pleasure getting to see how Maureen's daughter turned out."

I hugged my aunt, but when she opened a kitchen cabinet and reached inside, I sniffed my tea for alcohol. Aunt Edna might be sentimental, but if I'd learned anything about her and Jackie, it was that the pair were craftier than they looked.

And I didn't particularly feel like waking up tied to the bedposts again.

***

I toted my glass of tea outside into the tropical courtyard at the center of the cottage apartments. I pulled out a chair and sat down at the wrought iron table to think things through. Even though it was sweltering outside, under the shade of the massive, yellow umbrella overhead it felt at least ten degrees cooler.

As I glanced around at the cute cottages and colorful foliage, I suddenly felt as hollowed-out as a Halloween pumpkin. Palm Court Cottages wasn't posh by any means. But compared to the ramshackle apartment I shared with four—make that *five*—other would-be actresses back in L.A., this place looked like the Ritz.

And *here* I had my own bed. And I didn't have to live out of boxes. Just a suitcase.

A magical, self-unpacking suitcase.

I took a sip of tea and wiped a trickle of sweat from my forehead.

How can it be that I'm about to turn forty and I have absolutely nothing to show for it?

I shook my head slowly. Hitching my wagon to Tad Longmire had been a colossal mistake. When his acting career went off the rails, it had taken mine down with it.

Who are you kidding, Doreen?

My career hadn't exactly been going gangbusters *before* I met Tad. Actually, after fifteen years in the cutthroat world of Hollywood, I hadn't been able to land a real *friend*, much less a real movie role.

I chewed my bottom lip and pondered my options.

One, I could go back to Snohomish and live with my mother until I figured things out. Two, I could go back to Hollywood and beg sleazebag Jared Thomas to give me back my crappy job at the production studio as a human grub. Three, I could stay here with Aunt Edna for a few more days and see how it goes. Or four, I could go back to L.A. and throw myself into the La Brea Tar Pits.

I took another sip of tea and looked up at the palm leaves waving softly in the late afternoon sky. As I stared into space, a weird, déjàvu feeling overcame me. It felt as if I'd been here and done this all before. I shook my head.

Geez. I wonder how many lives I've led as a total loser.

Aunt Edna and Jackie had made a life here in St. Pete. It was a weird life, sure. But a bona fide life, nonetheless. Not like my fake-it-till-you-make-it life back in L.A. I'd faked it and faked it and faked it. When did the "make it" part kick in?

Would it ever?

I blew out another long, hot breath.

Should I stay? Should I go? Should I throw myself under a bus?

I closed my eyes and said a silent prayer to whoever might be listening.

Please. If anybody's up there, I need a sign.

Suddenly, my cellphone buzzed. I bolted upright in my chair and stared at the display.

The caller ID read: *Unknown.*

Chapter Nineteen

I couldn't take my eyes off my cellphone. It was ringing on the picnic table next to my frozen hand.

Panic shot through me. Had my prayer been answered? If so, was God going to tell me to go back to my mother in Snohomish?

Please, no! Anything but Snohomish!

I quickly promised God that I'd never swear again or stick my chewing gum under another bus seat if *only* I didn't have to go to Snohomish. The pact sealed, I swallowed hard and clicked the answer button on my cellphone.

"Hello?"

"Doreen? Hi! It's me!"

I nearly melted with relief. The voice on the other end of the line wasn't God. It was Kerri Middleton.

Kerri was the manager of Sunshine City Studios. She was also the reason I'd come to St. Pete in the first place. She'd hired Tad Longmire to star in *Beer & Loathing*. As his personal assistant, I'd been obligated to come along to keep the gorgeous lout both on his mark and off the booze.

Kerri was also who I had to thank for my first real acting gig. (Unless you counted playing a decapitated hooker in a dumpster, but that's another story.) When the original killer in the *B&L* script—an inflatable shark—had burst before its maiden performance, quick-thinking Kerri had cast me as its replacement. That's how I'd ended up playing a serial slasher on TV.

Come to think of it, that's *also* how I'd become the unwitting victim of an old lady's purple umbrella. I guess fame really did have its plusses and minuses.

"Doreen? Are you there?" Kerri asked, interrupting my trip-and-fall down memory lane.

"Oh. Yes. Sorry," I said. "How are things at the studio?"

"Not bad. Actually, I'm calling to see if you're still in town."

"Yes. But I'm getting ready to—"

"Excellent! I've got another job offer for you!"

"What?" I nearly choked on my own tongue. "A new season of *B&L*? Did Channel 22 pick it up after all?"

"It's related," Kerri said. "More like a spinoff. Can you come in on Monday and talk about it?"

"Uh ..."

"Great. See you at ten thirty?"

"Err ... okay."

She clicked off the phone before I could ask any more questions.

Typical Kerri. Cut and run while she was ahead.

I frowned.

Huh. Maybe I should do the same.

But as I glanced up at the palms gently swaying in the afternoon sky, it dawned on me that I'd already made my decision. I'd stay. At least for a few more days, anyway.

I looked up at the clouds. The universe had given me my answer after all. I smiled and mouthed the words, "Thank you."

"How's the tea," Aunt Edna asked. She'd walked up the courtyard path while my gaze had been skyward.

I looked at her smirked. "Not as strong as *last night's*."

She laughed and pulled out a chair. "Southerners love a ton of sugar in their tea. I guess that's where the Italian in me draws the line."

"I like it unsweetened, too," I said, raising my glass to her. "Besides, I don't need the extra calories. I'll save those for Sophia's birthday cake."

Aunt Edna's face brightened. "So, you're staying?"

I nodded. "At least through Tuesday. Actually, I might have another film gig here. I'll know more on Monday."

"That's excellent news," Aunt Edna said. "Now, how about a nice piece of veal scaloppini?"

I grinned. "I thought you'd never ask."

***

After dinner, Aunt Edna and I sat out in the courtyard and watched the sky turn pink. It was Jackie's turn to do the dishes, and we both were grateful for a little silent star gazing.

As the streetlights came on, Aunt Edna turned to me. "So, a job at the studio, eh?"

"Yes," I said brightly.

"Doing what?"

"I'm not sure yet. But it's an acting role, not grunt work."

Aunt Edna beamed. "I'm glad for you Dorey. You know, we could really use—"

"Really?" I squealed, surprised at my own enthusiasm. I sat up straight. "You know, I was thinking that if things work out with this offer, maybe I could move into Sophia's apartment. While she's not using it?"

Aunt Edna's smile evaporated. She glanced around the courtyard, then leaned over and whispered, "No way. If I let you into her place, Sophia would kill us both."

Brrrzz!

The cellphone in Aunt Edna's apron pocket blared like a time's-up buzzer, startling us both. She pulled her phone out and glanced at the display. Her face turned to stone. "It's Sophia."

I flinched. "Geez! Has she got this place bugged or something?"

"I dunno." Aunt Edna cleared her throat and answered her phone. I could hear Sophia's voice on the other line.

"Sophia. Everything okay?"

"Edna! Thank goodness you picked up. I've got bad news."

"What?"

"Freddy's dead."

Aunt Edna's jaw dropped. "I swear it wasn't the cacciatore!"

"I know that," Sophia said. "Freddy keeled over ten minutes after I gave him a cookie. It came from the Neil Mansion."

"The funeral home on Central?" Aunt Edna asked.

"Yeah," Sophia said. "Either those grave diggers put a hit out on me or they've come up with one hell of a new marketing strategy."

Aunt Edna grimaced. "What kind of cookies were they?"

"Sneaky bastards," Sophia hissed. "They sent my favorite. Lemon bars."

Chapter Twenty

Aunt Edna clicked off the phone and slammed her fist on the picnic table, causing my iced tea to nearly topple off onto the ground.

"Lemon bars!" she hissed. "Who *does* that?"

I gulped and grabbed my glass just before it fell.

Oh, no! That's what Morty told me he'd given Humpty Dumpty at the bakery!

Aunt Edna and Morty definitely had some past chemistry. I needed to tread carefully. "Um ... you don't think Morty and Humpty are working together to bump off Sophia, do you?"

Aunt Edna eyed me, incredulous. "No way. Morty and Humpty *hate* each other."

Jackie stepped out of the shadows like a gray-haired ghost. She pursed her lips and said. "Maybe they do, or maybe they don't."

"What do you mean?" I asked.

Jackie sat down in the chair next to me. "You know the old saying, 'The enemy of my enemy is my fiend?'"

"*Friend*," I said. "It's Sanskrit."

Jackie's nose crinkled. "You got a friend named Sand Grits? Is he related to Joey the Sandman?"

My nose crinkled. "Uh ... I don't think so."

Aunt Edna groaned and shook her head. "Listen. If you two are done with the Abbott and Costello routine, we need to get serious here. Apparently, somebody really *is* trying to poison Sophia."

"Holy cow," Jackie said. "So, what's the plan?"

Aunt Edna glanced around the courtyard, then leaned in and whispered, "We need to bust Sophia out of Shady Respite. She's not safe in there anymore."

"You got it," Jackie said, springing up out of her chair. "Let's go!"

"We can't right now," Aunt Edna said. "Visiting hours are over for the night. That place will be locked up like Fort Knox."

"Oh," Jackie said. "Then we ride at dawn. Or as soon as breakfast is over. Whichever comes first."

Aunt Edna nodded, then locked eyes with me. "You in, Dorey?"

"Uh ... *sure.*"

Like I had a choice.

***

We didn't actually ride at dawn. It was more like 8:45. Visiting hours at Shady Respite didn't start until nine o'clock.

Even though this was supposed to be a covert operation, Aunt Edna had insisted we wear the neon-pink flip-flops that branded us as members of the CGCN. Her rationale was that she didn't want to confuse Sophia so early in the morning, in case her meds hadn't had a chance to kick in yet.

We arrived at the convalescent center armed not to the teeth, but more like to the ankles. Aunt Edna had her trusty rolling pin tucked into her pocketbook. Jackie had her can of Raid hidden under a lime-green vest. As for me, I carried a very bad feeling in the pit of my stomach ...

As I shifted the Kia into park, my nerves began to unravel like a cheap sweater.

If I help kidnap Sophia from Shady Respite, is that considered a felony in Florida?

I chewed my lip.

I just beat a murder rap a couple of days ago. If Sergeant McNulty finds out, he'll throw the book at me!

"You coming?" Aunt Edna asked as she climbed out of the car.

I hesitated in the driver's seat, my fingers gripping the steering wheel like a life ring in a Nor'easter. "Uh ... I don't know about this."

If all I do is drive the getaway car, will my jail sentence be shorter?

"Dorey," Aunt Edna said softly. "We could really use your help. Freddy's dead. Sophia could be next."

I swallowed hard and unclenched my fists.

"Okay. I'm coming."

***

"Where's the lemon bars?" Aunt Edna shouted as she burst into Sophia's room, her rolling pin at the ready.

"Oh, it's you," Sophia said, sitting up in bed. "Thank God. I thought it was that stupid woman with that therapy mutt again. It's getting to where a person can't die in peace anymore."

"You're not dying. Not yet, anyway," Aunt Edna said. "And you won't be on my watch. We're here to get you out of this place."

"It's about time." She threw the covers off her torso and scooted to the edge of her bed. She was fully clothed—all the way to her sensible shoes.

"I see you were expecting us," Aunt Edna said dryly. "So, where are these deadly lemon bars?"

"Under the bed," Sophia said, brushing a wrinkle from the skirt of her black dress.

Aunt Edna turned to me. "Dorey, get down there and grab them."

I cringed. "Why *me*? Because I'm the most expendable?"

"No. Because you're the one most likely to be able to get back up off your knees." Aunt Edna reached into her pocketbook. "Here, wear these rubber gloves, just in case the poison leaked through the sack." She whipped out a pair of latex dishwashing gloves as pink as our CGCN flip-flops.

I dutifully slipped them on, got on my hands and knees, and looked under the bed. I half expected to see some kind of homemade bomb-like contraption oozing icky green poison. Instead, lying amongst an impressive collection of dust bunnies, was a decidedly *unimpressive*, crumpled white paper bag.

It was the same kind I'd seen Morty hand over to Humpty Bogart.

"Uh, I think I see them," I said.

"Congratulations," Aunt Edna said. "Now be a dear and actually get them out from under there."

I grimaced and inched my arm and shoulder under the bed until I could reach the bag. I snatched it with my gloved hand and dragged it out from under the box springs.

"Here you go," I said, holding it out to Aunt Edna.

"Not so fast," my aunt said. "Open it first. To be sure."

Sure of what? That it's not going to explode?

I gulped, then cautiously opened the paper sack. To my great relief, it didn't detonate.

"Uh ... they look like ordinary lemon bars," I said.

"Right." Aunt Edna turned to Sophia. "How do you know these things came from the Neil Mansion? Did one of your moles tell you?"

"No." Sophia sat down in her wheelchair and wrapped her shawl tighter around her thin shoulders. "The delivery man said so himself."

Aunt Edna's face grew red. "They let a delivery guy into your room?"

Sophia scowled. "That's what I just said, didn't I?"

"You sure did, Queen E," Jackie said, grinning and nodding like a bobble-head toy. "Hey, Edna. Maybe we should *both* go get Miracle Ears!"

Aunt Edna's jaw flexed. "The security here is ridiculous," she growled to Sophia. "Why didn't you call us earlier? During visiting hours? We could've come for you yesterday."

"I called you right after he left," Sophia said. "Someone let the delivery man in last night, after visiting hours were over."

"What?" Aunt Edna bellowed. Tendons protruded from her neck. She glanced around the room. "They probably have your room bugged, too."

"Those dirty cockroaches," Jackie said. "Where are they? I'll spray them in the face with Raid!"

"That's *it*," Aunt Edna growled. "We're not waiting around for someone to take another potshot at you. We're busting you out of here. *Right now.*"

Sophia shrugged. "Well, okay. If you insist."

Chapter Twenty-One

Here's a tip that should've been in my *Hollywood Survival Guide*:

If you ever need to make a clean getaway, don't wear flip-flops.

After wheeling Sophia out of her room, the four of us burned rubber as we raced down the dreary corridor of Shady Respite convalescent center. The ruckus our flip-flops made was enough to wake the dead—which was ironic, considering we were trying to sneak Sophia out of there before she bit the dust herself.

I'd been assigned to "Queenpin detail," which involved pushing the cantankerous old lady down the hall in her fancy throne wheelchair as fast as my legs could take us. Aunt Edna and Jackie had taken up positions on either side of us. Their job was to guard our flanks using their signature weapons of choice, a rolling pin and a can of Raid.

If I'd been asked to star in this movie, I'd have turned it down.

Our mission, though outwardly ridiculous, wasn't without tactical thought. Aunt Edna had chosen to strike at precisely 9:45 a.m., twenty minutes after the convalescent center served breakfast. According to my aunt, that was when the hallway would be at its most quiet.

I'd asked her how she knew that, then had instantly regretted it.

According to Aunt Edna, a quarter to ten was peak hour for patients to be occupied with what she called their "post-coffee constitutionals."

My aunt had a strategy for the staff, as well. They'd been lured away to the breakroom by the plate of Snickerdoodles she'd drop off at the reception desk.

As I pushed Sophia's chair with all my might, I could scarcely believe my aunt's crazy plan had actually worked. We'd made it all the way down the hallway without being noticed by a single soul.

But our luck didn't last. Fifteen feet from the exit doors, a silver-haired fly buzzed into our ointment.

The sour-faced head of an old woman poked out of a doorway as we flapped noisily by. She looked me up and down and snarled. My gut dropped. It was the same muumuu-clad lady who'd beaned me with her umbrella yesterday.

"You!" she screeched. Then she hobbled out into the hallway and yelled, "Look out, everybody! Killigan's back to kill again!"

My back bristled. I stumbled to a stop. "Look, ma'am. We're just here to—"

"Help!" the old lady hollered as I turned toward her. Her high-pitched voice reverberated down the empty corridor. "Help! Killigan's kidnapping an old lady! She's gonna murder her, too!"

I'd had enough of her crap. I frowned. "Ma'am, if you would just let me—"

But the old lady didn't stick around to hear my argument. Having completed her public service announcement about a killer in the hallway, she ducked back inside her room and disappeared behind the metal door like a geriatric cuckoo clock.

"That's just fantastic," Sophia said. "Now we've got about three seconds before Gloria hits the emergency button in her room."

"Gloria?" I asked.

Sophia elbowed the back of her wheelchair, poking me in the gut. "Don't just stand here, girl! Get going before she rounds up her walker posse!"

I grimaced. "Her *what?*"

"Step on it!" Aunt Edna yelled.

I did as I was commanded and kicked into high gear. The four of us raced out the exit while Jackie held the doors open wide. We'd just made it out the door when an alarm bell sounded.

"Shizzle!" Sophia grumbled.

I winced. "What should we do now?"

"Keep going," Sophia ordered. "Hopefully they'll think Gloria is nuts and ignore her."

"What are the chances of that?" I asked, pushing her down the sidewalk toward the parking lot.

"Pretty high," Sophia said. "Because she *is.*"

"Save the conversation for tea and crumpets," Aunt Edna yelled. "Get a move on!"

**

Maneuvering the wheelchair through the parking lot was relatively easy. But once we got to the Kia, I suddenly felt at a loss as to what to do next. How was I supposed to get frail-looking Sophia the Queenpin inside the car without breaking her?

"Don't just stand there," Aunt Edna said. "Lift her up and put her in the passenger seat. Jackie and I'll fastened her wheelchair to the tow hitch in the back."

I glanced over at the entrance to the convalescent center. A mob of gray-headed avengers was forming. "Uh ... I'm not sure we have time for all that."

"Oh, geez," Sophia said, hopping out of her wheelchair. "Stop complaining already. Help those two stuff this thing into the trunk. I'll get in the car on my own steam."

"You're getting' in the steamer trunk?" Jackie asked.

Sophia shook her head. "Mother Mary. Maybe I'm better off here at this crappy old folks' home."

"Let me help you," I said, reaching for Sophia's arm.

"Mitts off," she said, then hit a button on the wheelchair's armrest. To my surprise, the chair folded down to a rectangle the size of a large suitcase.

"There they are!" someone hollered from across the parking lot.

I looked over and spotted the top of a purple umbrella bobbing toward us from between the parked cars.

Not again!

"Everybody in! Now!" I yelled. "I'll get the chair."

While the others scrambled into the Kia, I heaved the wheelchair into the trunk. I managed to wedge it inside, then I scrambled for the driver's seat. Once behind the wheel, I crossed my fingers and said, "Okay, everybody. Hold your breath."

I turned the key in the ignition. The car fired right up.

"Halleluiah," Aunt Edna yelled from the backseat. "Now get us the H-E double toothpicks out of here, Dorey. That nutcase is almost on top of us!"

She wasn't kidding. Umbrella-toting Gloria was only about ten feet away. She raised a fist and flung it our way. Acorns blitzed the side of the car.

Jackie rolled down the back window. "Come any closer and you'll get a faceful of Raid!"

"Oh, yeah?" Gloria yelled back. "Bring it, Killigan! I ain't afraid of you!"

I did, in fact, *not* bring it. Instead, I peeled out of the lot before Jackie could get off a killer shot of bug spray.

"Sheesh. That was a close one," Aunt Edna said as we sped away. "Good driving, Dorey."

"That Gloria Martinelli is a real piece of work," Sophia said. She glanced over at me from the passenger seat. "Who's Killigan?"

"That's the name of a character I played on TV."

Sophia's green eyes narrowed. "Wait a minute. You mean the serial killer who took out Tad Longmire?"

My face went slack. "You saw that?"

"Of course." Sophia took a parting glance back at the convalescent center. "In that place, you only have two choices to pass the time. TV or Tiddlywinks. And let me tell you, young lady. Most of the folks in there haven't got the brains for Tiddlywinks."

"Come on, Dorey," Aunt Edna said, putting a hand on my shoulder. "Step on it."

"Okay, okay!" I shook my head to clear it. "Where to?"

"Home," Aunt Edna said. "We'll get Sophia settled, then we'll go check out this Neil Mansion funeral home that sent these fakakta lemon bars."

"There's no need to curse," Sophia said. "I've got another idea. I've been cooped up in that smelly old nursing home for weeks. I need some fresh air. I'm coming with you."

I glanced in the rearview mirror. Aunt Edna was scowling, but she gave a quick nod. I don't think she had much choice in the matter. I was beginning to know exactly how she felt.

"Yes, ma'am, your Queenpin," I said.

"Now *that's* what I like to hear." Sophia reached over and placed a gnarled hand on my thigh and squeezed it.

"Punch it, Killigan Girl," she said. "Let's see what this baby can do."

Chapter Twenty-Two

According to Jackie, the Neil Mansion funeral home was run by the same family that owned the discount baby goods chain known as Babies or Bust.

"These Neil folks got the perfect racket going," she said from the backseat of the Kia.

The four of us were speeding down the road, having just busted Sophia out of Shady Respite convalescent center. I felt like I was starring in a low-budget remake of *Thelma and Louise*—and, as much as I hated to admit it, I kind of liked it.

"What do you mean by the 'perfect racket'?" I asked, locking eyes with Jackie in the rearview mirror.

"They get your first dollar coming into this world, and the last one leaving it," she said. "It's a real 'cradle to gravy' operation, as they say."

My eyes shifted in the mirror to Aunt Edna. She rolled her eyes and turned away from her backseat companion. Apparently, my aunt wasn't in the mood to fight over semantics. Neither was Sophia. She simply sighed and shook her head.

"You probably don't know this, Doreen," Sophia said. "But the Neil Mansion really *is* an old mansion."

"It's true," Aunt Edna said. "It used to be a fancy estate. Sat on some nice acreage, too. But then the government took the land around it by eminent domain."

"Why?" I asked.

"So they could build that fakakta interstate," Aunt Edna said. "Now the poor old house butts up to an exit ramp." She shook her head. "A lousy, postage-stamp lot. That's all the government left the poor owners."

"It was a real tapestry of justice," Jackie said. "But one man's disaster is another man's treasure. The Neils bought the place for cheap and turned the dance parlor into a casket showroom. Now if that ain't using your noodle, what is?"

"In your case, we may never know," Sophia said. "But I agree. Neil Mansion is still the best place in town to hold your send-off. When my time comes, I want the works."

My jaw nearly dropped. "What? Even though they just tried to poison you with those lemon bars?"

"We don't know that for sure, Dorey," Aunt Edna said. "That's what we're going there to find out. And we need to do it without ticking them off."

"Why?" I asked. "What does it matter?"

"It matters because Sophia's final send-off is all arranged and paid for with them, that's why." Aunt Edna reached over from the backseat and laid a hand on Sophia's shoulder. "When your time comes, you don't have to worry about a thing."

"Except the dying part," Sophia muttered.

"Here it is, coming up on the right," Jackie said.

Just left of the 1-275 overpass, I spotted a stately, three-story, Victorian-style mansion. It was painted the purplish-black color of a semi-ripe eggplant. The ornate trim was mint green. Against all odds, the combination just ... well, *worked*.

"Okay, we're here," I said, pulling into the parking lot. "What's the plan? Hold a pastry gun to their heads until they confess?"

"I wish," Sophia said. "Back in the day, when this whole place was nothing but dirt roads and pine trees, you could get away with stuff like that."

Aunt Edna's hand moved from Sophia's shoulder to mine. "Dorey, the plan is for you to go in. *Alone*."

I blanched. "Me? Alone? Why?"

"Because they don't know *you*," she said, squeezing my shoulder. "You can go in without raising suspicion. So hop out and snoop around while we wait in the Kia."

My eyebrows met my hairline. "Snoop around? What am I? A Basset Hound?"

"Of course not." Aunt Edna lifted her hand from my shoulder.

"If Benny was here, she'd sniff out the backstabbing deadbeat from a hundred yards," Jackie said, referring to her ancient pug.

"You're absolutely right," I said. "I'm definitely no deadbeat-smelling dog. And I'm no Sherlock Holmes, either. Look, ladies. I have *no clue* how to 'snoop around.' I've never investigated a murder before."

"Sure you have," Jackie said. "The one you just got away with."

I turned and stared at the pewter-haired woman in the backseat. "I've told you a ... *argh*! Forget it. Look, what am I supposed to say to these funeral people? 'Read any good books lately about how to poison lemon bars?'"

Sophia snickered.

"No," Aunt Edna said. "You never want to confront a suspect outright like that."

"Not unless you're packing heat," Jackie said.

My brow furrowed. "Why not?"

"Amateur move." Aunt Edna tutted and shook her head. "Rule number one, Dorey. Never let a suspect know you're onto them. You gotta keep your cool and use it to your advantage."

Somebody shoot me now.

I closed my eyes and let out a breath. "And how do I do that?"

"Easy." Aunt Edna shrugged. "Just keep it casual. Strike up a nice little conversation. You know, about funeral arrangements and stuff. And then see what happens."

"*See what happens?*" I balked. "That hardly seems like—"

"Look," Aunt Edna said. "I didn't want to say this in front of the head of the CGCN, but you need *training*, Dorey. If you're gonna make the cut, you've gotta develop an eye for detail. No pun intended."

"Make the cut for *what*?" I argued. "And excuse me, but I believe I already *have* an eye for detail. No pun intended."

Aunt Edna smirked. "Okay, then. If you're so smart with the details, answer me one simple question and you're off the hook."

"Fine." I folded my arms across my chest. "Go ahead."

Aunt Edna waggled her eyebrows. "What's my last name?"

I grimaced. "Uh ... *Diller*?"

Aunt Edna snorted. "Heh. That's what I thought. Now, get going, Killigan Girl."

Chapter Twenty-Three

"So, this is your basic midrange model?" I asked, knocking my knuckles on the smooth, polished oak of a casket labelled *Settler's Rest*.

"Yes," Neil Neil answered. "It's our most popular choice."

I'd almost done a double-take when the man had introduced himself as Neil Neil. I'd thought maybe he had a stutter. But then I'd spotted the name placard on his desk and realized his only impediment was being born to a set of parents with either no imagination or a twisted sense of humor.

I was certain Neil Neil himself couldn't have possibly inherited those unappealing attributes—or any flaws at all, for that matter. From outward appearances, the man running the Neil Mansion funeral home was absolutely *perfect*.

Neil Neil's shiny blond hair and clean-shaven face were impeccably groomed. Dressed in an immaculate blue suit with fashionably coordinating tie, he appeared ready to step into a *GQ* magazine photoshoot.

Tall and slim, he was head and shoulders above most of the schleps I'd auditioned with back in Hollywood. If he had any flaw at all, it was that he reminded me of how irritatingly gorgeous Tad Longmire had been.

In other words, Neil Neil was just my type. But the wedding picture of him and his husband displayed on his desk informed me that I was definitely not *his*.

"How much?" I asked, slapping a palm on the shiny hull of the Settler's Rest.

"For the casket or the whole service?" Neil asked, raising his chin as if he found my question distasteful.

I crinkled my nose.

What is it with doctors and undertakers? Are we not supposed to ask how much it costs to live or die?

"The whole shebang," I said. "How much?"

The prospect of a big sale made the pinched look on Neil's handsome face disappear. The corners of his perfect mouth curled upward slightly.

"Let me check." He sat down at his desk and began punching a calculator as if his life depended on it. After a minute or so of banging away, he stopped.

"Okay, here we go," he said. "The casket, plot, ceremony, and premium burial service come to $15,355."

I nearly swallowed my tonsils. "Holy smokes!"

"No," he said dryly. "Cremation is $595 extra."

I laughed. Neil smiled.

"Good one," I said. "I guess ... well, I'm sorry. I just had no idea funerals were so expensive."

"I agree it can be a real *eye* opener," he said, dropping a hint for me to remove Jackie's giant glaucoma shades that were hiding my mismatched eyes.

Not happening.

"Indeed," I said.

Neil cleared his throat. "That's why we recommend the prepaid plan. With all your arrangements preset, your relatives can't blow your burial budget on things like tattoos and marijuana edibles."

My left eyebrow shot up.

Neil closed his eyes and nodded. "Happens a lot more than you'd think."

"Hmm. That's something I never considered. But I can see how prepayment makes sense."

Neil stared up at me patiently from his desk, his perfect smile brightening the otherwise slightly morbid space. He and I both knew it was my turn to make a move. But I wasn't sure what to do. I had to get busy grilling him for information about the lemon bars. Otherwise, he might charm me into becoming the next owner of my own shiny, satin-lined Settler's Rest.

A tinge of panic swept through me as we faced off within the pregnant void. I wracked my brain to think of a way to steer our conversation toward the true goal of my mission.

I couldn't exactly ask Neil Neil outright why the Neil Mansion had delivered poisoned lemon bars to Sophia at the nursing home. Besides the fact that Aunt Edna had warned me not to give away that I knew anything about it, if he was the murdering type, Neil Neil could easily stuff me into the Settler's Rest never to be seen again. Then again, the coffin was probably more comfortable than the cot waiting for me back in L.A. But still, it wasn't exactly how I'd pictured my grand finale panning out ...

"So, are you ready to put together a plan?" Neil asked brightly. "We offer layaway."

My upper lip twitched. "*Layaway*? That seems rather—"

"Not for *bodies*," Neil said. "I was referring to monthly payments toward future funeral services."

"Oh. Uh ... do you guys ever have any promotions?"

"You mean *sales*?" Neil appeared a bit horrified. "Sometimes, I suppose. On outdated models."

My nose crinkled. "Just exactly how does a casket get outdated?"

Neil's brow furrowed. "I beg your pardon?"

"Sorry." I shot him a tentative smile. "I guess this whole death business makes me a little nervous. What I *meant* was, how do you get your customers? Do you, I dunno, maybe hand out business cards at churches? Or at *old folk's homes*, perhaps?"

Neil's chin raised a full inch. "We're undertakers, not ambulance chasers. But occasionally, we do extend tokens of community goodwill."

"Really?" I perked up. "Like what?"

Neil exhaled sharply. "We sponsor races. Donate to school sports programs. Things like that. Why?"

"I was just wondering if you ever use local caterers. Or maybe supply food to senior centers?"

Neil stiffened. "Are you here seeking a donation?"

I seized on the lead he'd handed me. "Well, now that you mention it, I *am* thinking about putting together food baskets for elderly shut-ins. And those poor old folks in nursing homes and convalescent centers."

"I see. Well, we generally avoid programs where food is involved."

My eyebrow shot up. "Really? Why's that?"

"In a word? *Liability*. Food is wrought with dangers, Ms. ... I'm sorry. What was your name?"

"Diller," I said, then kicked myself for not coming up with an alias. "Dangers? What kind of dangers?"

"All kinds." Neil pulled a sheet of laminated paper from his desk drawer. It was an article he'd clipped from a magazine.

"See here?" he said, pointing to the plasticized sheet. "In any given year, over forty-eight million Americans get food poisoning. Five-thousand die from choking on food alone!"

He slapped the article down on his desk and looked up at me. "Don't even get me *started* on deaths related to obesity and diabetes."

"Geez," I said. "You sure know a lot about how people die."

"I should. It's my business."

You don't say ...

"Oh. Of course," I said. "So, what if you became aware of an upcoming death? You know, someone on their last legs. How much notice do you need to get a funeral together?"

"Well, we can't exactly *plan* these things, now can we?"

The tone of Neil's voice told me his patience was growing thin. I could barely blame him. I studied him as he blew out a breath and glanced out the window beside him. All of a sudden, his handsome jaw went slack.

I followed his gaze out the window and nearly choked on my own spit.

In the parking lot, ten yards away, stood the beat-up old Kia. From the open passenger window, Sophia glared at us like an angry cadaver sporting a Jiffy-Pop wig.

Holy crap!

Neil turned a hardened face toward me and glared. "We don't take *early delivery*, either, Ms. Dither, if that's what you're after. We serve the *dearly* departed here. We're not a boarding kennel for the *nearly* departed."

"Uh ... of course you aren't," I backpedaled. "That's not what I meant ...."

"So, exactly what *can* I do for you today?" he asked, his lips a tight, white line. "Or are we through here?"

"Uh ... just your business card will do for now." I plucked one from the stand on his desk. "Thank you for your time. I'll be in touch."

***

"Neil told you his company doesn't mess around with food?" Aunt Edna asked as I drove us back to Palm Court Cottages. "That's all the goods you got on that crew?"

"Like I told you," I said. "I'm no murder investigator."

"Maybe it's that crappy nursing home that's behind all this," Sophia said. "So many old geezers die in there they've got a conveyor belt from the lunchroom to the morgue."

"I knew it!" Jackie said.

"Knew what?" I asked.

"*Shady Respite*," she said. "Never trust a company with *shady* in their name. Am I right?"

"Well, at least we've got the lemon bars for evidence," Aunt Edna said, holding up the bag.

"That's right," Sophia said. "We can use Kitty to test them for poison."

I blanched. "Now you're going to poison a *cat*?"

"No," Jackie said. "Kitty lives in apartment four. She's our resident gardener and potioneer."

My nose crinkled. "Potioneer?"

"She cooks up stuff," Jackie said. "Like the knock-out drugs we used on you." She shot me a grin. "Pretty effective, eh?"

Sophia nodded her determined-looking face. "Kitty will be able to tell us what's in the lemon bars that shouldn't ought to be there. Let's get her going on that as soon as we get home."

Aunt Edna cleared her throat. "Um ... Doña Sophia? I've been meaning to tell you. Kitty took a short vacation while you've been away. She should be back any day now."

Sophia frowned and crossed her thin arms across her bony chest. "What *else* are you not telling me, Edna?"

"Nothing," Aunt Edna said. "I swear."

"Humph," Sophia grunted. "Today's Sunday. We talking today or to-morrow? You know how much I hate to wait."

"Yes, I know," Aunt Edna said. "But—"

Aunt Edna's phone buzzed. She glanced at the display. "Crap. It's Shady Respite. They must've figured out Sophia's flown the coop."

"Don't answer it!" Sophia barked.

"I've got to," Aunt Edna said. "You don't want the cops poking around your place, do you? I'll just tell them we checked you out early."

"Humph," Sophia grunted.

Aunt Edna clicked on the phone. "Hello? Uh-huh. Oh, no. She's fine. Yeah, sure." She put her hand over the speaker and said, "Sophia? Someone wants to talk to you."

"Who?" the grumpy Queenpin asked.

Aunt Edna glared at her. "He says his name is Freddy."

Chapter Twenty-Four

"All right," Sophia admitted with a shrug. "So I may have exaggerated a smidgen about the current state of Freddy's health. But I did give him some lemon bars this morning, so I couldn't exactly be sure."

"I thought you said you gave them to him last night," I said. I glanced in the rearview mirror at Aunt Edna. Her face was so red I feared it might explode like a rotten tomato.

"Does it matter?" Sophia said, raising her skinny arms in a *what's the big deal* gesture. "Look. I needed to get out of that crap hole to save my own skin. When that punk with those lemon bars showed up last night, I figured the clock was ticking on me biting the big one in there."

I grimaced. "So you really think someone's trying to poison you?"

"Absolutely." Sophia folded her arms across her bony chest. "Either that, or kill me by pure mental torture. I'm telling you, if I had to hear Gloria Martinelli talk about her gallbladder one more time, *I'd* be the one up on murder charges. Besides, all the nurses in that place do is walk around and check who's asleep—so they can wake us up and jab us with needles. God only knows what they've got in those syringes of theirs."

My shoulders stiffened. My fingers curled into a death grip on the steering wheel. "Hold on a minute. Are you saying I just humiliated myself at the Neil Mansion *for nothing*?"

"Nobody told you to humiliate yourself," Sophia said. "That's on *you*."

My jaw dropped. If I'd been searching for a sympathetic ear, I'd definitely paddled up the wrong auditory canal. I glanced back at Aunt Edna. She leaned forward and whispered, "Welcome to *my* world, Dorey."

***

By the time I pulled the Kia up to Palm Court Cottages, I found myself once again seriously debating whether to skip town while I had the chance.

On the one hand, on Monday I had a potentially career-making acting job waiting for me here with Kerri Middleton at Sunshine City Studios. On the other hand, I was currently bunking with a posse of sketchy mob molls and it was three days to the showdown at the Sophie Corral.

I parked the Kia and turned off the ignition. Before I could say a word, Aunt Edna began barking orders from the backseat like a drill sergeant.

"Doreen! You get Sophia's wheelchair ... I mean *throne* ... out of the trunk. Jackie! You get Sophia settled into her cottage while I make lunch."

"No!" Sophia protested. "I want *Doreen* to help me."

I glanced back in the rearview mirror. Jackie appeared just as shocked as I was. Her mouth was opening and closing like a fish out of water. As for Aunt Edna, the fact that Sophia had taken a shine to me had seriously dulled the usual glint in her eyes.

"Fine," Aunt Edna said, her face puckering. "Jackie, *you* get the throne out of the trunk. And Dorey, *you* get Sophia back to her cottage. It's number three, in case you forgot."

***

As I'd pushed Sophia and her wheelchair down the path past the courtyard picnic table, I'd pictured the inside of her apartment as a dusty, gray hovel laden with crocheted doilies and cobwebs. Possibly even a skeleton lying in a corner. But to my surprise, the hard-nosed Doña's apartment turned out to be quite the opposite of my dreary machinations.

If Aunt Edna's place was stuck in the 1970s, Sophia's cottage was a portal back to the 1950s.

The living room sported a brilliant teal sofa flanked by two lemon-yellow armchairs. The kitchen was furnished with vintage pink appliances and a matching dinette set. I hadn't seen that much chrome since Henry Winkler played The Fonz on *Happy Days*.

"Set my purse on the table," Sophia ordered.

"Yes, ma'am. I hear you came over on a boat from Sicily," I said in a nervous attempt to make conversation.

"You did, did you?"

I cringed. "Uh ... that must've been quite an adventure."

Sophia chortled, but said nothing as I helped her to the low-slung, peg-legged couch.

I glanced around the place as she settled herself into the cushions. Uncertain whether I was supposed to stay and keep her company or leave and let her be, I suddenly realized just exactly how much I knew about Cosa Nostra etiquette.

Exactly diddly squat.

"I guess I'll be going," I said, and took a step toward the door.

"Stay."

I looked over at Sophia. She was staring at me with those cat eyes of hers as if she expected something.

"Uh ..." I fumbled.

"Uh, what?" Sophia said. "Speak up, Doreen Diller. I don't care for mealy-mouths."

I found another inch of backbone. "Okay. I was wondering. Why did you ask *me* to help you instead of Jackie?"

Sophia shrugged. "I need to get a feel for you. Don't get me wrong, but the rest of my crew is a bunch of goomahs."

I nearly blanched. "*Goomahs?*"

She smiled at me like I was a bug and she was an entomologist. "You like them, don't you?"

"I guess."

"Mealy-mouth."

I straightened my shoulders. "Yes, ma'am. I think they're nice ladies."

"Nice ladies," she repeated as if it amused her. "Now, don't get your hackles up, Doreen. Goomah is just what we call mob wives and mistresses. Jackie and Edna are good women. They both bring their own skills to the table. But neither of them has ever been *made*."

She studied me for a moment. "I'm not sure any of the goomahs left in the Family have the gumption I'm looking for to take over the Collard Green Cosa Nostra. You catch my drift?"

Uh ... not really.

The first time I'd met them, Jackie and Aunt Edna had drugged me, tied me up, and interrogated me before I'd known what hit me. Sure, it'd been an ambush. And their weapons of choice had been garbage-bag zipties, a rolling pin, and a can of Raid. Nevertheless, they'd definitely held the upper hand on me. If that wasn't gumption, what was?

"Well ..." I managed to utter before Sophia cut me off.

"You see, Doreen, the mafia is like a bunch of hermit crabs."

I blanched. "*Hermit crabs?*"

"Yeah." Sophia picked a piece of lint from the lap of her black dress. "When one crab finds a bigger shell, the whole lot get in line. You know, to trade up." She locked her green cat eyes with mine. "But you can't have the bigger shell unless you fit. And to fit, you have to prove yourself."

I winced out a fake smile. "So, how do you prove yourself?"

The ancient Queenpin cocked her turbaned head. "By making your bones. Don't you know *anything?*"

I grimaced. Apparently not.

"Making *my bones?*" I asked.

"Bumping somebody off." Sophia smiled coyly. "From what I hear, you already *did* that."

***

After fetching Sophia some water, an aspirin, and her pocketbook, I left her resting on the couch in her cottage and returned to Aunt Edna's. As usual, my aunt was busy in the kitchen. And *I*, as usual, began obsessing about what I should do next.

I was short on cash, but long on apprehension. From what I could tell, the whole CGCN mob was convinced I'd actually whacked Tad Longmire and gotten away with it scot free. And they also thought I had "big shoes to fill."

A thought hit me between the eyes like a stray bullet.

O.M.G! Do they expect me to be their new hitman? Am I supposed to take over for Sammy the Psycho?

I jumped up off the couch and took a flying step toward the bedroom. If that was the case, I needed to pack my suitcase and get my butt out of Dodge! As I made my way to my bedroom, another thought froze me in place.

But what if that acting role Kerri Middleton has for me is my big break? If I leave now, I'll be throwing fifteen years of acting lessons, humiliation, and grunt work down the drain!

I nearly groaned out loud.

What am I gonna do?

As I agonized in my petrified state, a third thought wormed its way into my seesawing mind.

Kerri let me stay at her place once before. Now that she knows I'm not a murderer, she might let me again. I can throw my crap in my suitcase and be out of here in ten seconds flat!

I glanced around to make sure the coast was clear. Then I pulled out my cellphone, dialed Kerri's number, and scurried into the spare bedroom where I'd been staying. As I closed the door behind me, the call went straight to voicemail.

Crap!

I glanced around for secret listening devices, then I cupped my hand to my mouth and whispered an urgent message for Kerri to call me back, A.S.A.P.

Then I opened my suitcase and started flinging my junk into it like my life depended on it.

Chapter Twenty-Five

"Lunch is ready!" Aunt Edna called out down the hallway.

Startled, I slammed my crammed suitcase shut and stuffed it under the bed as if I were hiding a murder victim. My mind reeled with trepidation. Would going to Kerri's place hurt Aunt Edna's feelings? Would it turn the whole CGCN against me?

If it meant escaping a future as the new Sammy the Psycho, it was a chance I had to take—right after I finished off a plate of my aunt's ridiculously good food.

"Coming!" I yelled.

Geez. Why am I such a sucker for Aunt Edna's cooking? Is her secret recipe cocaine or something?

I cautiously stuck my head into the kitchen, expecting to find my sketchy aunt sprinkling mysterious white powder onto plates of linguine. Instead, I found her humming away, dutifully rolling paper napkins around sets of silverware.

She looked as wholesome as June Cleaver.

My nose crinkled. Guilt washed over me. Had I read these ladies wrong? I mean, June Cleaver would never hire a hitman, would she?

The only way to be sure was to stay for lunch and pump these ladies for more information. It was only right to give them a fair shake, right? Plus, whatever was cooking in that huge pot on the stove smelled absolutely divine.

"Smells great in here," I said, taking a cautious step into the carefully guarded domain of my aunt's kitchen.

She smirked. "It's my new perfume. Eau de garlic and onions."

I smiled. "Heavenly. Hey, can I ask you something?"

"Sure. As long as you lend a hand while I answer."

"Of course."

Aunt Edna handed me a napkin and set of silverware to roll. "So, shoot."

"Well, first off, I'm curious. Why do you call Sophia the Queenpin? I thought that, you know, *technically*, she's the Godmother."

329

Aunt Edna sighed tiredly. "She is. But when you're the Godmother, people call you what you *tell* them to call you. If Sophia wants to be Queenpin, you call the lady Queenpin. Or Doña. She likes that, too."

"Good to know." I laid the rolled silverware on the counter and picked up another set. "So, how does this whole CGCN thing work?"

"What part?" Aunt Edna asked, her tone sharpened a notch. She plucked four bowls off the shelf of a fake woodgrain cupboard, then eyed me carefully as she handed them to me.

"Well ... the *hierarchy* part, I guess," I said, taking the bowls.

"You doing some kind of research on us, Dorey? You a monkey eager to climb up the Family tree?"

"No!" I blurted. "I ... I was just wondering, you know, how you all ended up here together. Taking care of Sophia. I mean the *Queenpin*. She told me that to get bona fide, you have to crush somebody's bones."

Aunt Edna snorted. "You mean you have to make your bones."

"Yeah, that's it." I looked her square in the eye. "Have *you*?"

"If you're asking me if I've ever whacked somebody, the answer is no." Aunt Edna stacked four laminated placemats atop the bowls in my hands. "But there are other ways to prove your worth, Dorey. How else do you think I got to be the Capo?"

"The Capo?"

Aunt Edna shook her head. "Geez. I forget how green you are to all this. The *Capo* is the one who leads the crew when the Godmother's not around. I'm second fiddle to Sophia, so to speak."

"Oh. What about—"

"No more questions. We gotta get lunch on the table before the Queenpin has a meltdown. She gets crabby when she's hungry." She winked at me. "And she's *always* hungry."

"I've noticed."

Aunt Edna chuckled and shoved the rolls of silverware into my free hand. "Go set the table in the courtyard. It's good weather. We'll eat outside today. And while you're out there, do me a favor and go see what nonsense Jackie's up to. She should be rounding up Sophia."

I smirked. "I'm on it, Capo."

Aunt Edna laughed and swatted me on the butt with the kitchen towel. "That's right. And don't you forget it!"

***

Out in the courtyard, I found Jackie on her hands and knees under the picnic table, spraying the ground with Raid.

"Hey, Jackie," I called out, then coughed. I waved a hand in front of my face to whisk away the fumes. "Aunt Edna says lunch is ready."

"Good. I'm starving. I'll go get the Queenpin."

As I watched Jackie sprint down the pathway, I thought twice about setting the dining ware down in a cloud of toxic bug spray. I toted them back into Aunt Edna's cottage.

"What's going on?" she asked, glancing down at the bowls and place-mats still in my hands.

"Uh ... technical difficulties," I said. "Does Jackie always blast the courtyard with Raid?"

"Ugh!" she groaned. "I told her not to."

"Is it to keep away the mosquitoes?"

Aunt Edna closed her eyes and let out a long, slow breath. "That woman. Who needs mosquitoes when Jackie's already sucking the life out of me?" She opened her eyes and shook her head. "I swear. Raid is that woman's answer to everything. One of these days she's gonna do us all in with that stupid bug spray of hers."

I cocked my head. "Then why do you put up with her? After all, you're the Capo."

Aunt Edna shot me a sly look. "Think about it, Dorey. Then take a guess."

I shrugged. "Out of loyalty and friendship?"

Aunt Edna sighed. "Eh. Partly. But think harder. A successful mob leader always has a good reason for everything she does."

My eyes widened. "Don't tell me you keep Jackie around for the jokes!"

Aunt Edna laughed. "I said *good* reason." She grinned. "I'll admit, that's part of Jackie's 'charm'—and I used that term loosely. But no.

Think *strategically*, Dorey. Like a wiseguy. This is the *Family* we're talking about here."

I grimaced. "Because she's your *sister*?"

Aunt Edna crossed herself. "Heavens no! We're no relation, thank God."

Suddenly the front door flew open. A second later, Jackie burst into the kitchen. "What's taking so long?" she asked. "Sophia's out there chomping at the bit like a pierogi-fish in the Amazon."

I shot Aunt Edna a pursed-lip smirk. "Sorry, Jackie. It's my fault. I've been holding up Aunt Edna with questions about the CGCN."

"Oh, *have* you now." Jackie's shoulders broadened. "Well, I say it's high *crime* you learned all about the Family." She snickered. "High *time*—high *crime*. Get it?"

"We got it," Aunt Edna said. "Jackie, you take the place settings out to the table. Tell Sophia that Doreen and I are coming right behind you with the food."

"You got it." Jackie grabbed the bowls, placemats, and rolls of silverware from my hands, then winked at me. "Looks like you'll have to save your questions for the dinner table, Doreen. The Doña's getting restless."

Aunt Edna watched Jackie go, then handed me a pot full of soup. "Okay. So you want to know the main reason I keep Jackie around?"

I nodded eagerly. "Yes. I really do."

"It's simple." She tapped a finger to her temple. "Pretend you're Sophia. Between me and Jackie, which one would *you* choose to be the Capo?"

My right eyebrow shot up.

Well played, Aunt Edna. Well played.

Chapter Twenty-Six

"Where's the linguini already?" Sophia grumbled as Aunt Edna brought out a gorgeous, magazine-worthy platter of ripe, red tomato slices. A slab of milky mozzarella was sandwiched between each juicy slice, accompanied by a healthy sprinkling of bright-green, aromatic basil leaves.

"The linguini's for *dinner*," Aunt Edna said. "For lunch we're having a nice caprese salad and a bowl of my homemade minestrone. They're good for your constitution."

Sophia frowned. "My mouth was all set for linguini."

I frowned. So was mine.

"But I guess I can make do," Sophia said.

"Much appreciated," Aunt Edna deadpanned. "Now let's eat."

I doled out the soup with a ladle, then sat down and dug in with the rest of them. One mouthful of Aunt Edna's minestrone and I forgot all about my packed suitcase stuffed underneath my bed like a stiff.

"Geez, this is fabulous," I said to Aunt Edna. "What's your secret?"

"She'd tell you, but then she'd have to kill you," Jackie quipped.

I laughed and glanced over at Aunt Edna. Her Mona Lisa smile sent mixed signals as to the seriousness of Jackie's statement. I supposed thirty years of Jackie's bad jokes and Sophia's bad temper had taught my aunt how to cloak her true feelings better than a Klingon bird of prey.

"Ah," Sophia said after guzzling her soup like a starving hobo. "It's good to feel the sunshine on my face again. And smell the fresh air at last."

I smirked. "Wow. The way you talk, people would think you just did a stint in San Quentin instead of Shady Respite."

"What's the difference?" she grumbled. "I barely got a wink of sleep in that old-folks warehouse." She sniffed the air. "Hey. What's that flowery bouquet I smell?"

"Beats me," Jackie said. "If Kitty was here, she'd know."

I sniffed the air.

I believe it's called a Raid blossom.

"Enjoy the outdoors while you can, Queenpin," Aunt Edna said. "After lunch, you're on lockdown. We need to keep you under wraps until your birthday celebration at the Coliseum."

I blanched. "The *Coliseum*? In *Rome*?"

"Naw," Jackie said. "The one over on Fourth Avenue."

"Wait till you see it, Dorey," Aunt Edna said. "It's grand."

"It is?" I asked.

My aunt nodded. "Yeah. It's a classy dance hall built back in the roaring '20s. Wood floors. Crystal chandeliers. Domed ceiling. It's really something to see."

"I met my husband there at a USO dance," Sophia said, her eyes fixed on some faraway point in time and space.

"Really?" My eyes lit up. "Was he in the military?"

"No," Sophia growled. "Harvey was in the waste management business. I thought you knew that."

My nose crinkled. "The garbage business?"

Aunt Edna leaned over and whispered, "That's a euphemism for organized crime."

"Oh." I smiled at Sophia. "Was it love at first sight?"

An infinitesimal smile cracked Sophia's pale lips. "You could say that. Let me tell you, Harvey Lorenzo was quite the Dapper Dan."

"He sure was," Aunt Edna said.

"This one's gonna be a party for the history books, Doreen," Jackie said. "We're pulling out all the stops! Everybody in the business is gonna be there vying for the Queenpin's favor. Ain't that right, Edna?"

"That's right," my aunt agreed. "Everybody who's anybody will be there."

Aunt Edna smiled and raised her glass of tea to Sophia. "Think of it. At the stroke of midnight, our very own Sophia Maria Lorenzo, Doña of the Collard Green Cosa Nostra for the past forty years, will turn one hundred years young."

Sophia stuck her chin up proudly. "And then, young Miss Doreen, all bets are off. At the stroke of midnight, I'll no longer be a moving target for every two-bit goodfella trying to make his bones and take my throne."

"Here, here," Aunt Edna said as we all chinked our glasses together.

Sophia grinned smugly. "I'll be *untouchable*. And I can name my own heir." She laughed. "After that, instead of every goombah in town trying to *kill* me, they'll be falling all over themselves to pay tribute and win my favor."

As my glass clinked with Jackie's, my face froze into a grimace. I wasn't sure whether to be glad for Sophia or afraid for her. My mind's eye envisioned an old-fashioned ballroom filled with a conga line of hermit crabs—each toting machineguns in their claws and scrambling for a shot at the biggest conch shell before the clock struck midnight.

I'd once had a hermit crab as a pet. When it died, it had stunk to high heaven. Was this party going to end the same way?

Sophia cackled. "It's going to be like Oscar night. And I'm a shoe-in for best director."

I gulped.

Or it's gonna be like Apocalypse Now *at an all-you-can whack crab-leg buffet.*

***

While Jackie tucked Sophia securely away in cottage number three, I helped Aunt Edna by washing up the lunch dishes. She was busy rummaging through the cupboards for the ingredients for the linguini Alfredo she'd promised Sophia for tonight's supper.

The thought of missing out on her pasta sent a ting of disappointment through me. So did the fact that once I heard from Kerri I'd be skipping out on her and the CGCN crew. But after hearing about the time bomb ticking down to the Queenpin's party, I was more convinced than ever that the prudent thing to do was to, as my aunt would say, "Get the H-E double toothpicks outta here."

I'd checked my cellphone after lunch. Kerri still hadn't returned my call.

"I'm curious," I said, dawdling over a dirty soup bowl in the sink.

"That you certainly *are*," Aunt Edna said, then chuckled.

"I'm serious," I said. "Are you really so worried about somebody trying to bump off Sophia that she has to go on lockdown until the party on Tuesday?"

Aunt Edna pursed her lips. "It could happen. There's still over two days to go."

"Come on. Do you really think someone poisoned those lemon bars, or is she just paranoid?"

My aunt set a package of flour on the counter. "Nobody's tried to pop Sophia in years. I think most of her competitors got too old to give a damn anymore. To be honest, half the people she wanted me to invite are already dead."

"Oh."

She eyed me up and down. "Now that I think about it, it's been pretty quiet until *you* showed up. You got plans you're not sharing with us, Dorey?"

"What? Me? No!"

Aunt Edna laughed. "Okay. If you say so."

I dawdled with the dishtowel. "If Sophia is in danger, why'd you let her stay at Shady Respite in the first place?"

Aunt Edna shrugged. "She fractured her hip. I'm too old to lift her. What else could I do? Besides, I thought Shady Respite was safer for her than this place. That is, I did until that guy with the lemon bars showed up in her room last night."

"How do you think he was able to get in after hours?"

"I don't know. Either somebody let him in, or he actually came before visiting hours were up. As you've seen for yourself with Freddy, with Sophia the truth is like a bra strap. Adjustable to suit her needs."

"Are you saying she's a *liar*?"

"I'm only saying that the whole lemon bar story could be just part of her scam to make us get her out of that place."

"And the food testers, too?"

"Bazinga."

"But she actually *had* the lemon bars," I said.

Aunt Edna yanked a dozen eggs from the refrigerator. "She could've ordered them over the phone."

"True." I hadn't thought about that. "But according to the *Beach Gazette*, three people really *did* die in Shady Respite during the time Sophia's been in there."

"Yeah, but *which* people? The article didn't say. And one of them *wasn't* Freddy, obviously."

"Fair enough."

Aunt Edna's phone rang. She pulled it from her apron pocket. "It's Shady Respite. I better get this."

While I dried glasses and put them away in the cupboard, I eavesdropped on her conversation, but only caught dribs and drabs.

"Uh-huh, I see," Aunt Edna said. "Yes, we'll take care of it. Thank you for letting us know. Goodbye."

"What did they want?" I asked.

"The usual." She slipped the phone back into her apron pocket.

"The usual?"

"They want us to pay the final bill and go pick up Sophia's stuff."

"Oh."

Aunt Edna put her hands on her hips and scowled at the sack of pasta flour on the counter. "Sheesh. I can't believe it."

"What's wrong?" I asked.

"Sophia."

She plucked her rolling pin from her pocket and slammed it onto the counter. "I gotta hand it to her. That woman always keeps me on my toes."

My nose crinkled. "What did she do now?"

"Nothing. Or maybe everything."

I grimaced. "What do you mean?"

Aunt Edna shook her head and stared at the kitchen counter. "According to the lady at Shady Respite, Freddy's dead. For *real* this time."

Chapter Twenty-Seven

I nearly dropped the glass I was drying. I set it down and grabbed Aunt Edna by the arm. "Sophia *wasn't* lying? The lemon bars really *are* poisoned?"

"Either that or something *else* got Freddy."

She turned and stared blankly into the open cupboard. Worry lines creased her brow. "I didn't take Sophia seriously when she told me she was using the old guys at the nursing home as taste testers." She hung her head. "I guess I should've."

"How could you have known?" I put my hand on my aunt's shoulder. "Besides, the deaths might be totally unrelated. Like you said about Freddy. It wasn't necessarily *poison* that killed them. They could've died of *anything.*"

Aunt Edna pursed her lips. "Two might be a coincidence, Dorey. But *three*? That's a much harder pill to swallow." She sighed tiredly. "Anyway, now with Freddy dead too, I'm beginning to think Sophia was right. Somebody really *was* slipping something into her food at Shady Respite."

I cringed. "It seems so ... *implausible.*"

Aunt Edna locked eyes with me. "Get this straight, Dorey. Sophia may stretch the truth sometimes, but she's no fool."

I bit my bottom lip. "Okay, suppose she's right about someone trying to poison her. Who would do such a thing? I'm pretty sure Neil Mansion had nothing to do with it."

"With the clock ticking down on Sophia's hundredth birthday, my money's on somebody in the Family. Anybody who's got their heart set on being the new boss is running out of time to seal the deal."

"I thought we agreed that poisoning wouldn't be the method of choice for someone wanting to make sure she died before Tuesday."

Aunt Edna scowled. "Ever hear the term, 'Desperate times call for desperate measures'?"

Yeah. Pretty much every day of my life.

I frowned. "Sophia thinks Humpty Dumpty is behind it. And, I didn't want to say anything, but Morty gave him a sack of lemon bars. He told me so himself."

"My Morty?" Aunt Edna eyed me funny. "When?"

"When we stopped at his bakery yesterday."

"Impossible," Aunt Edna said.

"Look, I know you and he had a thing—"

"Ancient history. And that ain't why it's impossible."

"Then why not?"

"Morty don't make lemon bars."

My shoulders straightened. "Yes, he does."

"No, he don't."

"But he told me so himself," I argued. "I asked Morty what he gave Humpty in that paper sack. He said it was lemon bars."

Aunt Edna's furrowed brow went slack. She laughed. "That's a euphemism for *cash*, Dorey. Little golden bars. Why do you think it's Sophia's favorite cookie?"

"Oh." I frowned sourly. "If they're Sophia's favorite, why doesn't Morty make them?"

"He used to. But they were never good enough for the Queenpin. Morty's no masochist."

Crap. There goes my theory about Morty the Masher.

"If Humpty didn't get the lemon bars from Morty, he still could've gotten them from somewhere else."

"Eh." Aunt Edna plucked a can of roasted roma tomatoes from the cupboard. "I'm not saying it couldn't be Humpty. But there are plenty more suspects where he came from."

My eyebrows shot up. "Like who?"

"Well ... Vinny Zamboni, for one."

"Who's he?"

"A bagman. Like Humpty."

"Bag man? Those guys are *homeless*?"

Aunt Edna's lips puckered. "Hardly. A bagman is what we call a money runner. Sort of like a banker who makes house calls, if you catch my drift."

"Huh?"

"Humpty and Vinny pick up and drop off loot for the Family. That's all I'm saying. Capeesh?"

"Capeesh. Why do you think Vinny would want Sophia dead?"

"Who knows? She's not exactly Mother Teresa now, is she?" Aunt Edna set a large pot on the stove. "Maybe the Family's tired of paying Sophia's widow's pension and gave Vinny a little 'extra homework' assignment."

"Or maybe he wants to be Kingpin himself?"

"Vinny?" Aunt Edna shook her head. "I don't see it. He ain't what I'd call *management material*. When it comes to work, he's more like a fireman."

My brow furrowed. "A fireman?"

"Yeah. He likes to drop and roll. No time for chit-chat."

"Just like Humpty. He got his sack of so-called 'lemon bars' from Morty and took off with barely a word."

"Exactly. In their line of work, the less said, the better." Aunt Edna plucked a wooden spoon from a canister on the kitchen counter.

"You know what? Maybe the lemon bars weren't poisoned. Maybe Freddy just died of natural causes. Then there'd be *nobody* to blame, would there? All of this could just be a figment of Sophia's imagination."

Aunt Edna blew out a big sigh. "Sure. That could be true. But unless we can figure out what actually killed those old geezers at Shady Respite, we're just a bunch of cuckoos on a wild goose chase."

"Well, the first thing to do is find out their names," I said.

"Yeah, I guess you're right." Aunt Edna pursed her lips. "Geez. I wish Kitty was back already. She could test the lemon bars and we'd have our answer to—"

The creaking sound of the front door opening caused Aunt Edna to stop mid-sentence. She pushed me behind her protectively and snatched up her rolling pin.

"Who's there?" my aunt called out.

"It's me," a voice said from just beyond the kitchen door.

The hair on the back of my neck pricked up.

Oh, no. Here we go again!

Chapter Twenty-Eight

I had a death grip on Aunt Edna's apron strings I peeked over her shoulder as the sturdy old woman stood her ground, rolling pin at the ready. Slowly, a head peeked into the kitchen door frame.

If it was Sammy the Psycho, he'd arrived in drag.

"Kitty!" Aunt Edna exclaimed. "You and your silly tricks. It's about time you got back."

Kitty laughed. "I came as soon as I got your message. What's 'gone all fakakta' on you?"

Aunt Edna reached around and pulled me from my hiding place behind her. "Dorey, meet Kitty Corleone, our resident prankster and chemical engineer."

"Chemical engineer?" I stared at the woman. The job title seemed so ... *unlikely.*

Judging from the lines on her face, Kitty Corleone was in her late sixties. Petite and busty, she was dressed from head to toe in pink—from her blousy shirt and leggings all the way to her sunglasses, purse, and coordinating pink rinse in her silver hair. Oh, and, of course, her obligatory pink flip-flops.

So much for better living through chemistry.

"Nice to meet you," I said, woozy with relief that I was shaking her hand and not dying in a blaze of Sammy's gunfire.

The lady in pink grinned. "Likewise. I hear you're settling in well here. Welcome to the Family."

"Uh ... thanks." I shot her a sheepish smile. "So, what's 'chemical engineer' a Family euphemism for?"

Aunt Edna and Kitty exchanged knowing glances.

"Nothing," Kitty said, peering at me through the top of her heart-shaped sunglasses. "It's just Edna's fancy title for what I do. Which is mostly tend the posies and make magic potions. So, what's your job around here? Or haven't they told you yet?"

"She's our new associate in training," Aunt Edna blurted.

I blanched.

I am?

"And *she's still got a lot to learn*," Aunt Edna added in a tone that implied Kitty should be careful what she said around me.

"I see." Kitty lowered her sunglasses and studied my face. "Spooky pair of peepers you've got there, Doreen."

I frowned. "Thanks for noticing."

She laughed. "So you want to become a garbage woman, huh? Well, let me be the first to welcome you to waste management 1-0-1, collard-green style. How do you like it so far?"

"It's been an experience," I said.

"I bet it has." Kitty's mischievous eyes darted back and forth between me and Aunt Edna. "So, what were you two busy gossiping about? From the looks on your faces, I don't think it was the recipe for linguini Alfredo."

"No," Aunt Edna said. "Lemon bars."

***

While Aunt Edna brewed the tea, she brought Kitty up to speed about our theory on who might be trying to poison Sophia. Exactly four minutes later, my aunt poured the steeping tea into dainty cups. We each took one and moved to the living room so Kitty could fill us in on what *she'd* been up to.

"I don't know anything about Freddy," Kitty said. "But neither of the other two taste-tester guys Sophia used keeled over while I was on watch."

"While you were on watch?" I asked.

Kitty glanced at Aunt Edna, then said, "Yeah. The three of us took turns watching over Sophia while she was at Shady Respite. One week on, two weeks off for vacation. Didn't Edna tell you?"

"No, she did not." I looked over at Aunt Edna. "Are you saying you guys put Sophia in Shady Respite so you could have *a vacation*?"

My aunt crossed her arms. "You've met Sophia. Can you blame us?"

I frowned. "What about the fractured hip?"

"Eh, cover story," my aunt said.

My brow furrowed. "But—"

"I used to date a guy in the X-ray department," Kitty said. "You've seen one busted hip, you've seen them all. Dr. Mancini didn't even notice."

Aunt Edna shrugged. "As they say, no harm, no foul."

"But what if somebody had actually managed to bump off Sophia while she was in there?" I asked.

"They couldn't have," Kitty said. "Believe me, we took turns keeping a close eye on everything going on in the place. Especially the food."

"But four people have died at Shady Respite in the past two and a half weeks," I said. "And at least one of them was Sophia's taste-tester."

"Two of them were," Kitty said.

I gasped. "What?"

"Take it easy, kid," Kitty said. "Two of Sophia's testers died on my watch. But they didn't die of poisoning. Charlie choked on an apple fritter. And poor Ernie strangled to death on a cheese Danish."

"How is that possible?" I asked.

"Hazard of the trade." Kitty shrugged. "Look, Doreen. You can't choose a picky eater as a taste-tester. You need somebody with what you call a 'healthy appetite.' Charlie and Ernie were the kind of guys that if you give 'em a free pastry, you gotta count your fingers afterward. You know what I meant?"

"Not really."

Kitty ran her fingers through her pink hair. "You'd think they never ate in their lives. Believe me. For them, choking to death was just a matter of time."

Aunt Edna scowled at Kitty. "Why didn't you tell me about them dying?"

"I didn't want to worry you unnecessarily," Kitty said, setting her teacup down on the coffee table. She leaned toward us. "I figured the whole poisoning thing was just another one of Sophia's paranoid imaginings."

"Ha! Me, too," I said.

Aunt Edna's back stiffened. "That's not why—"

"Wait. I'm not finished," Kitty said. "Edna, I'm no sloppy Sally. I did my due diligence. When those two gluttonous guys died, I chatted up Dr. Mancini. He's the attending physician at the joint. He told me both of them died of old age, exacerbated by insufficient oxygen."

"Oh," Aunt Edna said.

Kitty turned to me and wagged her silver eyebrows like Groucho Marx. "Choking on food will do that to a person."

"Is that what their autopsies said?" I asked.

Kitty shook her head. "As far as I know, none were ordered. Dr. Mancini said there was no point, seeing as both were well into their eighties. He chalked them up to age-related disease."

"*Life* is an age-related disease," Aunt Edna said, shaking her head. "That diagnosis could mean anything."

"Sure." Kitty shrugged. "But the bottom line is this. No foul play equals no autopsy. Same with the old lady that died. Eunice, I think. But she had a heart attack."

I glanced over at Aunt Edna. Kitty noticed. "Wait a minute," she said. "Why the sudden interest in these two old dead guys?"

"Because another one died today," Aunt Edna said. "A guy named Freddy Sanderling. And he just happened to be—"

"Don't tell me," Kitty said. "Sophia's latest 'taste-tester.'"

"Bazinga," Aunt Edna said.

Kitty's perfectly arched eyebrows knitted together. "As they say, when it comes to coincidences, three's a crowd."

Aunt Edna nodded. "My sentiments exactly. Something's up. It's gotta be."

"So, what do we do now?" I asked.

"First things first," Kitty said, picking up her teacup. "I'll drop by Shady Respite tomorrow and talk to Dr. Mancini. Maybe with Freddy being number four, he'll be doing an autopsy."

"Good." Aunt Edna set down her cup. "And while you're there, I need you to pick up Sophia's stuff and pay the bill. Let me tell you, it's pretty hefty."

Kitty smirked. "But worth every penny, right?"

Aunt Edna nodded. "Best two weeks of my life."

"What'd you do with *your* free time?" Kitty asked.

Aunt Edna grinned. "Read books and ate Thai take-out every night. I'm telling you, there were cobwebs in the kitchen."

Kitty laughed. "Good for you." She turned to me. "I went to Miami. Took a class in botany."

"To each his own," Aunt Edna said. "But now it's time to pay the piper."

Kitty pursed her lips. "We're gonna need to get the money from Sophia. I'll see if I can squeeze it out of the old cash cow at dinner."

"Dinner!" Aunt Edna yelped. "I forgot all about it! I gotta get the sauce going for the linguini!" She gripped the sides of the old recliner and began rocking herself up and out of it.

Kitty shot me a smirk. "In case you don't know it yet, kid, we need to stay the hell out of Edna's kitchen."

"By threat of death," I said. "It's the first thing she taught me."

"Hey, don't talk about death to *me*," Aunt Edna said, pulling herself to standing. "If anybody knows how to kill somebody, it's Kitty. Why do you think I don't want her in my kitchen while my back is turned?"

"You could poison somebody a lot easier than me," Kitty said. "You're the cook."

"True," Aunt Edna said. "And my food is so good it'd be worth dying for. Right, Doreen?"

I blanched.

Kitty laughed. "From the look on the kid's face, Edna, I'd say she's pleading the Fifth."

Chapter Twenty-Nine

A few short hours ago, I'd made up my mind to stay in St. Pete, albeit with Kerri Middleton if she'd have me. But as I stood there listening to Aunt Edna and Kitty Corleone casually volley back and forth about which one of them was better at poisoning people, I kind of felt like it'd be better to put some distance between myself and them.

Like, 2,549 miles to be exact, according to Google.

I chewed my lip nervously and wondered if I could still catch a flight back to L.A. tonight. I might not become a star, but at least I'd still live to audition another day.

"Uh, I'm not feeling so well," I said as Aunt Edna headed for the kitchen. "I need to go to the restroom."

"Edna's food can do that to a person," Kitty quipped.

"I heard that!" Edna bantered back.

I smiled wanly. "Excuse me."

I sprinted down the hall to the bathroom and shut the door. Once out of their sight, I crossed my fingers and checked my phone, hoping Kerri had called. I was out of luck.

I chewed my lip and wondered, was the woman in pink merely an eccentric old lady, or a deadly hit-woman in disguise? What about Aunt Edna? She'd just called me an "associate in training." Did that mean they were planning on teaching *me* how to kill so they could retire to Florida?

Wait. They already *were* in Florida ...

Crap!

What do I actually know about any of these CGCN women? Do I really want to be around for Sophia's party? What if her birthday bash turns into a midnight massacre?

No. I needed to get out of Palm Court Cottages before the CGCN thought I knew too much. Once I'd crossed that line, I had a feeling there would be no turning back.

But without Kerri Middleton to run to, where could I go? Thank goodness I'd already packed. All I had to do was sneak out to the street and grab a taxi to the airport. Heck, I could sleep in the ladies' room if I had to!

Like a ninja, I sprinted out of the bathroom, across the hall, and into the spare bedroom. Carefully and silently, I closed and locked the door behind me.

After kicking off the pink flip-flops Aunt Edna had given me, I yanked my suitcase out from under the bed. It was so light it flew across the room and banged into the wall.

What the?

I pulled the old suitcase to me and unzipped it. It was empty. Someone had unpacked my luggage. *Again.*

I glanced around the room. From my toothbrush to my underwear, everything I'd crammed into my suitcase a few hours ago was now neatly tucked back inside the closet, drawers, and atop the bureau.

Suddenly, I knew how Bill Murray felt in *Groundhog Day.* The only difference was, I knew who was pulling the strings. Now, how did I get them to stop?

"Doreen?" Kitty's voice sounded at my bedroom door, startling me. "You in there, hun?"

"Um ... yes."

"I've got something I want to show you."

"I'm kind of busy," I said.

"Well, get un-busy. Edna says it can't wait."

My knees went weak. I flopped onto the edge of the bed.

Crap! Did I already know too much?

Chapter Thirty

Kitty rapped harder on my door. "You okay in there? What's taking you so long?"

I sat on my bed and chewed my thumbnail to the quick.

Just a major panic attack, that's all.

When I'd arrived at my aunt's doorstep last week, she and Jackie had suspected me of being an assassin sent there to kill them and Sophia. Now I was worried the crafty old ladies had turned the tables on me. Had they hired Kitty Corleone to bump *me* off?

No. That's crazy.

Are you sure about that? Aunt Edna did claim to see a coffin in a potato chip...

I glanced around wildly for a weapon. Thanks to the mystery suitcase unpacker, everything I'd brought with me was within easy reach. I grabbed my cuticle scissors from atop the bureau. They'd come in handy once before. Besides, it was either them or my hairbrush. I'd watched every horror movie ever made. Not once had I ever seen anyone bite the dust from a hairbrush.

I palmed the tiny scissors, then cautiously opened the door. "Yes?"

Before I knew what hit me, Kitty grabbed my free hand and tugged me out of the room. I couldn't help but notice she had a dark leather bag in her hand. Was her hit-man gear inside?

"Come on, Doreen," Kitty said, yanking me into the hallway. "I don't have much time."

Does that mean I don't, either?

"Where are you taking me?" I squealed.

"While we're waiting for Edna to get dinner ready, she says I should give you the nickel tour of my place."

A trickle of relief worked its way into my stunted lungs. "Oh. Okay."

Kitty grinned. "That's a good girl! By the way, did you know you can kill somebody with a nickel?"

***

The first thing I saw when I entered Kitty's spare bedroom was a whole roll of red biohazard bags. They were hanging casually on a spool—as if we'd just entered the homicide section of the local grocery store.

I gasped and glanced around. On every wall, clear jars of what appeared to be dried herbs and pickled roots were lined up neatly on open, wooden shelves. Next to a stainless steel sink big enough to conduct an autopsy in, stood a Bunsen burner and an impressive collection of brown and blue glass bottles.

I hadn't seen so many test tubes since I'd flunked high school chemistry.

"What is this place?" I asked.

"My lab," Kitty said. "What did you think?"

You don't want to know.

Kitty plunked her leather bag onto the smooth, concrete countertop and grinned at me. "I guess it's time to get to work."

"Work?" I asked.

Kitty unclicked the latch on the bag. My body stiffened. I doubled down on my death grip on the cuticle scissors hidden in my hand. "What do you mean by 'work'?"

"The lemon bars," Kitty said. "It's time we got to testing them for poison. You can be my assistant."

"Oh," My tight gut let go a tiny bit. "Uh...sure."

Kitty pulled on a pair of rubber gloves. "Any time we suspect poisoning, that's when *I* kick into gear."

My nose crinkled. "Why don't you just send the lemon bars to a professional lab?"

Kitty pulled a white paper sack from the leather bag. "Poison, by its very nature, is a covert business, Doreen. Its success lies in its *anonymity*. You don't exactly send nudie pictures to get developed at Kodak, now do you?"

"No."

At least, not for the last twenty years, anyway.

Kitty cocked her head. "The authorities tend to get suspicious if you keep sending in samples, if you catch my drift."

I nodded. "I get it."

"Good." Kitty grabbed a pair of tongs from a drawer, wiped them with a cotton swab dunked in alcohol, then opened the paper sack. "Besides, those so-called professional lab tests only cover your run-of-the-mill poisons."

"Run-of-the-mill poisons?" I asked.

"Yeah. Your everyday cyanides, arsenics, heavy metals, stuff like that." She scoffed. "Amateurs."

My nose crinkled. "What other kinds of poison *are* there?"

Kitty laughed. "Tons of things."

"Like what?"

Kitty playfully snapped the tongs at my nose like a lobster claw, then used them to pluck a lemon bar from the paper sack. She carefully placed it in a sterile petri dish.

"Doreen, poison is all around you," she said carving off a small sample of lemon bar and dropping it into a test tube. "All you've gotta do is know where to look."

A knock sounded on Kitty's front door. A second later, Jackie appeared in the doorframe.

"Playing doctor again?" Jackie quipped. "F.Y.I., Edna says to let you know dinner will be ready in exactly five minutes."

"Got it," Kitty said, but Jackie was already gone.

"Okay, we better hurry, Doreen. Take a sample from each bar and put it in a separate test tube. I'll mix up the reagent."

"Does this make me a partner in crime?" I asked, only half joking.

"No." Kitty reached for one of the brown bottles. "That is, not unless you plan on stabbing me with those cuticle scissors you've got hidden in your hand."

Chapter Thirty-One

"You did good for a first-timer," Kitty said, pulling off her rubber gloves. "We should have the results from the lemon bars after dinner."

I smiled. "Thanks. Sorry about the cuticle scissors. I just—"

"No worries. I'm used to not being trusted."

"Sorry," I said again. "So, how did you get into this … uh … profession?"

"Natural curiosity." Kitty ushered me out of her lab and shut the door behind her. She snapped closed the padlock. "Doreen, poisons don't just come from some diabolical chemist's lab, you know."

"They don't?" I asked, following her down the hall and out into the tropical courtyard.

Kitty stood on her front porch and put her hands on her hips. "Look around you. From where I stand I can see maybe a dozen things I could poison you with."

I blanched. "Are you serious?"

"Serious as a heart attack," Jackie said, appearing out of nowhere. "Kitty here has a degree in botulism."

"*Botany,*" Kitty said tiredly. "Speaking of which, you'd better go get Sophia before we end up on Botany Bay."

"I'm on it," Jackie said, and disappeared.

"Are you referring to that *Star Trek* episode where they wake up Khan and his crew and they try to hijack their ship?" I asked.

Kitty laughed. "Yes. That's the one. *Space Seed.* You a Trekkie?"

"Kind of."

"Me, too." Kitty held her hand up, then spread her fingers into the shape of a V. "Here's to living long and prospering, Doreen."

"Thanks. It'd be really nice to do both."

"You worried you won't?"

I eyed her with suspicion. "*Should* I be?"

Kitty laughed again. "Good answer. But let me tell you, kid. No matter where you go or what you do, life doesn't come with any guarantees."

I frowned. "I know that."

"Do you? Then follow me and I'll prove it."

My gut flopped again. I trailed a few steps behind Kitty as she walked down the paved path toward the center of the courtyard, where, if I survived the trip, dinner awaited us.

Suddenly, Kitty stopped. "Look, Doreen. See this cute little palm with the small, feathery-looking leaves?"

"Yeah."

"It's called a Coontie."

I smiled. "That's a cute name."

"Deceptive, isn't it? The little devil should be called *Killer* Coontie."

"Why?"

"Eat a seed pod and drop dead."

I grimaced. "Geez. I had no idea an innocent-looking plant could be so lethal."

Kitty shrugged. "Few people do. But toxic plants are everywhere. Especially here in Florida. See that tree over there with the yellow flowers hanging down like bells?"

I spotted a slim, fleshy-trunked tree about eight feet tall. A mass of yellow flowers hung face-down from its limbs like frilly-edged blowhorns. "Yeah. So?"

"That's an angel trumpet tree. Mash up the flowers to make a tea, and you can hear God calling you home." Kitty smirked. "Maybe you survive the hallucinations. Maybe you don't."

"Wow." I glanced around, wondering what else might be waiting to kill me in the courtyard. "What about this vine?"

Kitty laughed. "That's poison oak. Despite the name, it won't kill you. But touch it and you'll itch until you wish you were dead. As far as a potential homicide weapon, it's not a good candidate. But you could sure get even with somebody by rubbing it on their undershorts."

I studied Kitty's face. "Are you speaking theoretically or from experience?"

Kitty chuckled. "Like I said before, poisoning is a *covert* business." She knelt down next to a row of colorful plants lining the pathway. "See these fun little guys here?"

"Yes." I smiled at the heart-shaped leaves speckled with splotches of pink and white, as if they'd just been sprinkled with confetti. "Caladiums, right?"

Kitty's eyebrow shot up. "Very good, Doreen. But did you know they're also called Heart of Jesus?"

"No. Why?"

Kitty winked. "Nibble on a bulb and the only way you'll live through it is to be born again."

"Geez, Louise!" I shook my head. "I had no idea I was walking around in a tropical courtyard of death."

"Hmm," Kitty said, rising to her feet. "'Tropical courtyard of death.' I like that. Sounds like a euphemism for life itself."

I frowned. "What do you mean?"

Kitty locked her blue eyes with mine. "Like I said. Life doesn't come with guarantees. Never forget, kid. Everything survives by killing something else."

I grimaced. "How do you figure that?"

An insect landed on Kitty's arm. "Think about it. We're all just like this little ladybug here." Kitty's face lit up like a child's as she played with the ladybug, allowing it to crawl along the top of her index finger.

"How so?"

"Everybody's got to eat to live," she said. "And whatever you eat—animal or vegetable—has to give up its life energy for your survival."

I let out a breath. "I can't decide if that's poetic or bleak."

"It's neither," Kitty said. "It's just nature's way."

She blew on the ladybug. It flew away. "Doreen, we only exist in the tiny moment of time allotted to us by our parents. And by that, I mean Mother Nature and Father Time. While we're here, we need to make the most of it."

"By growing poisonous plants?"

Kitty stroked a bush that had long, blade-like leaves dotted with yellow. "If that's what it means to follow your heart? Then, yes. By growing poisonous plants."

"To each their own, I guess," I said. "Have you got any more felonious foliage to show me?"

Kitty laughed. "I sure do. A whole greenhouse full behind my cottage. Want to see?"

"Uh ..."

"Dinner's ready!" Aunt Edna hollered into the courtyard.

Kitty turned and winked at me. "How about right after we eat?"

I smiled weakly. "Uh ... sure thing."

Chapter Thirty-Two

Instead of eating dinner outside in the courtyard, Aunt Edna insisted that it be served promptly at four o'clock inside the confines of her drab dining room.

We took our places around her old, oak dining set. A beige vinyl tablecloth covered the table, while five dung-brown placemats marked the place settings. Atop each ugly laminated rectangle sat the most hideous melamine dinner plates I'd ever seen. Dull beige, they were rimmed in a brownish-gold hue that perfectly matched the twin wheat-stalk motif stamped onto their centers.

I'd seen L.A. homeless shelters with more ambiance.

Was everybody back in the '70s tripping on acid or something?

While I poured the tea, Aunt Edna dished out the pasta. On the wall above us, a picture of Mother Mary watched over us, her hands clasped in prayer. Beside her, wrapped in swaddling clothes, baby Jesus stared down at the linguini with envy.

"My compliments to the chef," Sophia said, eagerly swirling a forkful of pasta around the bottom of a spoon. "Edna, I do believe this is your best Alfredo yet."

"Eh," Aunt Edna shrugged nonchalantly, but the pride on her face was unmistakable.

"Absolutely delectable," Kitty said, wiping her mouth with a napkin. "I lost four pounds while I was gone. I think I'm gonna find them all again right here on this plate."

"Four pounds? Ha! That's nothing," Sophia said, a forkful of pasta poised inches from her mouth. "I think I dropped twenty in that stupid nursing home. I've got to make up for lost time."

Kitty nodded. "Speaking of nursing-home food, I heard you lost a third food taster today, Sophia. A guy named Freddy, right?"

"Men." Sophia shook her head. "You were there for the first two, Kitty. First Charlie chokes on that apple fritter, then Ernie bites it on a cheese Danish. Such weaklings. While you were gone, the goons tried to get to me with my favorite."

"Freddy was your favorite?" I asked.

Sophia eyed me as if I'd just fallen off the collard green truck. "No. *Lemon bars.*"

"So you never took a bite of the other desserts?" Jackie asked.

"Nothing doing." Sophia's shoulders broadened. "I did like Kitty told me. After giving the guys a sample, I waited to see what happened. Good thing, too. Or right now I'd be six feet under along with the rest of them."

"What did the guys say when you gave them the desserts?" Jackie asked.

"What do you think?" Sophia grumbled. "Thank you."

Kitty cleared her throat. "I think what Jackie means is, did any of them mention any symptoms or problems after eating them?"

Sophia frowned and shook her head. "Nothing that I can recall." She twirled more pasta on her fork. "Except for Freddy." She smiled. "For a small guy, he sure could pack away some food."

"What do you mean, 'Except for Freddy.'?" I asked.

Sophia shrugged. "After I gave Freddy a lemon bar, he was back in a flash for more. He went on and on about how delicious they were. He was such a pest I gave him two more just to shut him up. And then, just like that—bam!"

I gasped. "He died on the spot? But I thought—"

"No!" Sophia grumbled. "Before I could stop him, Freddy laid one on me. Right on the kisser!" She shook her head in disgust. "God knows what he would've tried if you guys didn't come get me out of there. Anyway, the next thing I hear, that jerk's dead, too."

"Gee. I'm sorry for your loss," I deadpanned.

"Loss, schmoss," Sophia said. "I think that horny toad gave me herpes!" She pulled down her lower lip to reveal a blister on her gums.

Aunt Edna let out a deep, soulful sigh. She leaned over and whispered in my ear, "Probably from her caustic tongue."

"What was that?" Sophia demanded, her green cat eyes narrowing to slits.

"I said it was probably caused by some ... uh ... caustic agent," Aunt Edna said. "Did you switch from Crest to Pepsodent again?"

"No!" Sophia scowled. "You think I'm crazy or something?" She turned to Kitty. "Pussycat, what did you find out about the toenail clippings?"

I nearly spewed my mouthful of linguine. "Toenail clippings?"

Sophia eyed me funny. "Kitty took samples from all my tasters. To test for poison. Ain't that right, Kitty?"

"Yes," she answered softly.

My nose crinkled. "Gross! Why not just get hair samples?"

Kitty sighed. "Both Charlie and Ernest were bald as billiard balls."

"Well?" Sophia demanded. "What did the lab results say while you were out having a big time on vacation?"

"I was gone *four whole days*," Kitty said.

"Excuse me?" Sophia said.

Kitty wilted. "Sorry, Queenpin. The results haven't come back yet. But if Charlie and Ernie died within hours of ingesting poison, the toxin wouldn't show up in their hair or nails anyway. For that, we'd need blood or urine for analysis."

"Don't look at me," Sophia said. "The only adult diapers *I'm* touching are my own."

Aunt Edna groaned. "Could we can it with the—"

"Anyway, it's a moot point now with those two," Kitty said. "No autopsy was conducted on either man. And Charlie and Ernie were both cremated."

"How do you know that?" I asked.

"Obits, honey," Kitty said. "There's no way to get samples from them now. But Freddy's still fresh. There's a chance we could still nab some swabs from him."

"Good thinking," Aunt Edna said. "You can do it while you're there paying the bill in the morning. Take a sneak peek in the morgue for Freddy. And while you're at it, ask around about who was working the late shift. Somebody might've let that creep with the lemon bars in after visiting hours."

"You got it, Capo," Kitty said.

Aunt Edna chewed her bottom lip. "Look, guys. We've only got a couple of days to figure this out. If somebody's trying to poison Sophia, they need to have their invitation to the party revoked."

My back stiffened.

Was that a mob euphemism for murder?

***

After dinner, I checked my cellphone. Still no word from Kerri. What was up with that?

While we cleared the dinner dishes and set the table for dessert, Jackie helped Sophia to the bathroom. With the Queenpin out of earshot, I had a few delicate questions I wanted to ask. I set a clean dessert plate on the table and took my shot.

"Excuse me, Kitty," I said. "I'm curious. Freddy either ate the lemon bars last night or this morning. But he didn't die until this afternoon. Is there a poison that takes hours to kill someone?"

"Sure." Kitty laid a fork beside my plate. "Poisoning someone isn't like in the movies where somebody up and dies in seconds. Most poisons take time. Only strychnine and cyanide can kill you in a flash. Well, them and the bite of a Fer de Lance."

"Fair de what?" I asked.

"A snake that lives in Central America. But that's not important right now."

"Oh."

Aunt Edna came in carrying a key lime pie. "Feast your eyes on this beauty," she said. "Homemade with love."

"Just so long as that love isn't the lethal kind," Kitty quipped. She tapped a pink fingernail on the table. "You know, Edna, the tartness of those key limes would make an excellent cover for a bitter toxin. So would that linguine sauce, come to think of it."

Aunt Edna laughed. "You got some imagination, Kitty."

She grinned. "It runs in the family."

My aunt's face turned somber. "Listen, you two. I didn't want to say this in front of Sophia, but I'm worried somebody's gonna take a shot at her before Tuesday. That's why we're eating inside tonight. I didn't want to take the risk."

Kitty nodded solemnly. "I think you're right to play it safe, Edna. This close to her centennial party, Sophia's like a sitting duck in the posies. Does this mean we're going back to overnights?"

"Yeah."

"Overnights?" I asked.

"We're all gonna have to do guard duty at Sophia's cottage overnight," my aunt explained. "To keep the wolves at bay."

"So we'll split the time into four shifts?" Kitty asked.

"No. *Three.*" Aunt Edna put a hand on Kitty's shoulder. "You can't do a shift. You'll be busy analyzing those lemon bars. Dorey will take up the slack."

Kitty nodded. "You got it, Capo. Thanks, Dorey."

I grimaced. I guess my fate was sealed for the night. I couldn't exactly ditch them in their time of need, could I? Besides, what had I been thinking? All I had to do was get through tonight, then I could ask Kerri about staying with her when I saw her tomorrow for the interview at ten thirty.

That settled in my mind, I turned to Kitty. "I'm curious. Did you test the apple fritter and the Danish?"

"Nope."

My eyebrows shot up. "Why not?"

"Nothing left to test. Sophia only got one of each. She gave them both to the guys."

My jaw dropped. "If Sophia only got one apple fritter and one Danish, why didn't she just throw them away, instead of making those guys eat them?"

"Sophia never lets down her guard," Kitty said. "That's why she's managed to live for so long."

"That's an important lesson for you, Dorey," Aunt Edna said.

I frowned. "What lesson?"

Aunt Edna's eyebrow crooked. "Monkey business usually starts way before the circus tents show up."

Kitty nodded. "She's right. And if you ask me, the clowns are circling the wagons as we speak."

Chapter Thirty-Three

After dessert, Kitty left with Sophia to get her settled for the evening in her apartment. Meanwhile, Jackie and I got busy cleaning up the dinner dishes under the watchful eye of Aunt Edna. She was also sorting out the shifts for overnight guard patrol of the Queenpin's cottage.

"So, Dorey, you familiar with the undertaker's friend?" my aunt asked.

My nose crinkled. "Neil Neil? Not really. I just met him this morning."

Jackie snorted.

Aunt Edna shook her head. "Undertaker's friend is mob-speak for a *gun*, Dorey. You ever shoot one?"

I grimaced. "Uh ... no."

Aunt Edna smirked. "Oh yeah. I forgot. You prefer *knives*."

Jackie hooted. "Ha! Good one, Edna!"

I blew out a breath and shook my head. "Whatever."

"You're gonna take the amateur shift, Dorey. You're on from 3 a.m to 6 a.m. So you better get some shuteye soon."

I eyed her with suspicion. "*Amateur* shift? Is that mob-speak for the *worst* one?"

Aunt Edna grinned. "No. Not *this* time, anyway. Statistically, it's actually the *easiest* shift. Three to six in the morning are the hours when it's least likely for a violent crime to go down."

I frowned. "How do you know that?"

"When you're in the garbage business, you learn the schedule," Aunt Edna said.

"That's right," Jackie said. "And we're smack dab in the deadliest month of the year."

"June is the deadliest month?" I asked.

"Yep." Jackie grinned. "And the time you're most likely to get murderized is from midnight to three in the morning. I thought everybody knew that."

I stared at Jackie as if I'd just spotted a horn growing out of her forehead.

"She's not kidding," Aunt Edna said. "Summer is high season for homicide. The only deadlier time is December." She shot Jackie a sideways glance. "Probably because of all the relatives visiting."

I sighed. "I heard *that*."

"Anyway," Aunt Edna said, "even in the heat of summer, things cool down after three in the morning. They pick up again after sunrise. So there you go, Dorey. Three to six. The amateur shift."

I shook my head. "The things you two think are common knowledge blow my mind. I guess the next thing you're going to tell me is that Sunday's the deadliest *day*, too?"

"Ha! It sure is, kid!" Jackie said with glee.

"Unfortunately, Jackie's right." Aunt Edna's face pinched with concern. "Another reason we need to keep a tight watch over Sophia."

Jackie studied her wrist. "How can I, Edna? I haven't worn one since 1999."

I crinkled my nose. "Worn what?"

"A watch," Jackie said. "I threw mine in a dumpster on New Year's Eve. How was I supposed to know Lionel Ritchie was just kidding about 2000 being the end of time?"

Aunt Edna groaned. "Don't listen to her, Dorey. At any rate, your shift doesn't technically start until tomorrow. And Monday's the least deadly day of the week."

"Huh," I said. "I'd have thought the existential dread of having to go to work would've bumped it up at least higher than say, *Tuesday*."

"Yeah, you'd think so," Jackie said. "Poor working stiffs." She laughed at her own joke. "Stiffs. I guess all that killing on Sunday wears a homicidal maniac out. They need their rest on Monday."

Aunt Edna rolled her eyes. "Enough claptrap already. Jackie, go start your shift." She reached into a gap between the wall and the refrigerator. "Here, take Kate with you." She handed Jackie a shotgun.

"You got it, Capo." Jackie grabbed the gun and headed for the door.

"The gun's name is Kate?" I asked, slack-jawed as Jackie disappeared out the door.

"Yeah. Any more questions? Or can I go take a load off now before I have to start *my* shift?"

"Uh, sure. But could I ask just one more little question? Who keeps unpacking my suitcase?"

Aunt Edna laughed. "That would be Jackie. She's our resident ninja. You might not believe this, Dorey, but that woman can move like the wind. She's also got a photographic memory."

I shook my head. "You're right. I don't believe it. That woman is a walking malapropism."

"Excuse me?" Aunt Edna growled defensively. "You calling Jackie maladjusted?"

"No! Not at all! A malapropism is when you switch a word with one that sounds similar, but isn't right. You know. Like when she said mobs-macked instead of gobsmacked."

Aunt Edna's stern face softened. "Oh. Well, yeah. Jackie ain't too great on remembering words. But she's like one a them idiot savant people. Jackie can take one look at something and remember every single little detail."

"Like where every item in a suitcase goes?" I said sourly.

She smirked. "Exactly."

"And yet she can't seem to remember that I'm going back to L.A." I shook my head. "From the looks of it, Jackie doesn't want me going anywhere."

Aunt Edna took my hand in hers. "None of us do, Dorey. Don't you know that by now?"

An odd twinge pricked my heart. "Really?"

"Yeah, really. It'd be nice to have you around, kid."

I swallowed a lump in my throat. "Thanks."

"You're welcome. Now get your ass in bed." She swatted me on the butt with a dishtowel. "You're gonna need your sleep. Three o'clock will be here before you know it."

"Okay." I turned to go.

"Hold up a minute, you two," Kitty said, poking her head in the door. "I took a look at the lemon bar results."

"And?" Aunt Edna asked.

"There's something in them, all right. But I gotta say, this one's got me stumped. I'm gonna have to run some more tests."

Aunt Edna pursed her lips. "So Sophia wasn't making this up."

"It would appear not," Kitty said.

My aunt's broad shoulders slumped. "Be sure and tell Jackie we've got a live one, eh?"

"I will." Kitty turned to me. "Oh, here, Dorey, take this for a bedtime story." She handed me a beautiful, leather-bound journal.

"What's this?" I asked.

"My life's work. I didn't have time to give you a tour of the greenhouse tonight, so I thought I'd bring the greenhouse to you."

"Oh." I opened a page of the journal. Inside was a beautiful, hand-painted watercolor illustration of a plant. "Wow. You did this?"

"Yeah. It's a curated collection of my favorite deadly plants. It'll make good reading while you're on shift."

I flipped to another page and shook my head. "Geez. Who knew there were so many ways to die?"

Kitty grinned. "*I* did."

***

I never heard the alarm go off at quarter to three. Instead, I was awakened by a gentle nudge on the shoulder and the smell of fresh-brewed coffee. I opened my eyes to find Jackie standing over me, holding a white coffee cup. It seemed to glow like a lantern in the darkness.

"Rise and shine," she said softly.

I sat up with a start. "Did something happen to Sophia?"

"Nope. All's quiet on the Southern front. But if you're one second late for your shift, it won't be. Edna can get pretty vocal when she's grumpy."

"You don't have to tell *me* that." I smiled and took the coffee. "Thank goodness it's a short commute."

Jackie laughed softly. "Take my advice. Wear your pink flip-flops over to Sophia's. As a safety precaution. They're in your closet, right next to your black pumps."

"Okay," I said sleepily.

"Those things practically glow in the dark, you know. You can best bet Edna's got her eyes peeled on the walkway, and it's still pretty dark out there."

"Okay, will do. Thanks for the coffee."

"You got it, kid. Glad to have you on board."

Jackie slipped out the door and closed it behind her. I sighed, thankful for a brief moment of privacy. I took a sip from my cup. Suddenly, my eyes bulged in their sockets. The coffee was so strong and bitter it sent a jolt racing through my body.

Either that, or I'd just been done in by the CGCN.

I bolted to sitting and swung my legs over the bed. My dangling feet hit something roundish and hard on the floor beneath my feet. My mind went haywire.

Oh, lord! Is that a severed head beside my bed? Or—worse yet—the head of an assassin waiting to do me in?

My heart thumped in my chest like a kettle drum. I leapt out of bed and over the severed head. In the dim light, I raced to the light switch and flipped it on.

Then I wanted to kick myself in the ass.

The object on the floor wasn't a head—detached or otherwise. It was the round corner of my suitcase peeking out from under the bed. I'd put it there myself after scrounging my toothbrush and pajamas from it. The rest I'd left packed, waiting on Kerri's call.

As I walked over to haul my suitcase onto the bed and grab some yoga pants, I spied my favorite sweatshirt hanging on the back of the door.

What the?

I glanced over at the bureau. My hairbrush and toiletries lay on top of it, all neatly organized. My clothes were stowed away in the closet—including the pink flip-flops.

Right next to my black pumps. Just like Jackie'd said.

I shook my head.

How does she do that?

***

"Keep your eyes peeled like boiled eggs," Aunt Edna said, handing me the shotgun at the front door of Sophia's cottage at three in the morning. "I'll send Jackie over to relieve you at six. Keep your phone handy, just in case."

"Okay." I took hold of the shotgun as if it were a venomous snake. "Where's Sophia?"

"In her bedroom sawing logs. She could sleep through a hurricane. With any luck, she might just snooze right through to the end of your shift."

A sudden wave of apprehension swept through me. I'd never spent more than a few minutes alone with the Queenpin.

"What do I do if she wakes up?" I asked.

"Whatever she tells you to do. Capeesh?"

I nodded. "Capeesh."

I stared out the front window and watched Aunt Edna slowly amble along the courtyard path in the dark. I kept my eye on her until I saw the glow of her front door opening, then closing behind her. A weird mixture of relief and pride and something else I couldn't name caused my heart to feel oddly warmer in my chest.

I glanced up at the sky. Beneath a nearly full moon, huge, feathery palm leaves swayed in the amethyst sky. The moon was so bright it glinted off the glass candleholders on the picnic table in the center of the courtyard. In the warmth of the night, the tropical foliage surrounded the tiny apartment homes like a leafy hug—albeit a potentially lethal one.

I let out a long, slow breath.

Maybe Kitty was right. Life doesn't come with any guarantees. You just have to make the most of the hand you're given.

And, unlike me, these women had found a way to do just that.

Chapter Thirty-Four

Despite my fear that crazed mobsters would descend in hordes upon Sophia's cottage during my watch, except for a wayward possum that tripped a motion-activated light on the courtyard path, all remained quiet on my "amateur shift."

Until a few minutes before six, that was.

I'd been sitting by the front window, trying to stay awake by skimming through Kitty's poison journal. It was full of impressive illustrations of deadly plants, and even more impressive lethal recipes that could be made from them. All in all, the tome was what I imagined Charles Darwin would have written if he'd been a serial killer.

Annihilation of the Species.

Suddenly, I heard a strange rustling coming from behind Sophia's bedroom door. Immediately, my thoughts flashed back to Tad Longmire. I'd heard noises in his bedroom too—right before I'd found him stabbed to death!

I sprinted toward Sophia's bedroom, my heart racing faster than my feet. As I skidded to a barefoot stop in front of her door, I realized I didn't know the proper etiquette for addressing the Queenpin in such a situation.

Should I bang on her door? What if I startle the poor old woman and give her a heart attack! If she died, would I have to take over the CGCN? Holy Crap!

I put my ear to the door's cool, wooden panel. I heard the faint rustling again.

"Sophia?" I called out in a voice just a notch above a whisper. "Are you okay in there?"

The rustling sound ceased. In the silent void, I could hear my heart thumping in my ears.

"Sophia?" I said a little louder. "It's me, Doreen. Are you okay?"

No answer.

Holy crap! Someone's in there trying to murder her!

I grabbed the doorknob and tried to turn it. It was locked.

What were you going to do if it opened? Scream for them to go away? Go get Kate, you dolt!

I scrambled back to the living room and grabbed the shotgun leaning against the wall. I skittered back to the bedroom and rapped my knuckles hard on the door this time.

"Sophia? Are you awake?"

"I am *now*," I heard her grumble from behind the door. My shoulders drooped.

Oops.

"I want coffee," she said, her voice gravely from sleep. "Get me some."

"I ... I can't," I said, reeling with relief. "I can't leave you alone in the cottage."

"You ever heard of a coffee pot? I got a kitchen, you know."

I winced. "Yes, ma'am. I'm on it."

***

After perking a pot of coffee, I went back to find Sophia's bedroom door cracked open a few inches. I tapped lightly on it, then slipped inside with a cupful. Sophia was sitting up in bed.

"Good morning," I said brightly, setting the coffee on her nightstand. "Need help getting up?" I reached toward her.

"Don't touch me!" she hissed. "I can get up on my own. I'm not an invalid!"

"I know that. It's just—"

"Plump my pillows," she demanded, sitting up on her elbows. "And then hand me my coffee."

I did as she commanded. "Anything else?" I asked, leaving off an unspoken *"your majesty."*

Sophia settled into her warm nest of cushions. "Yeah. Pull up a chair. I got something I want to say to you."

Oh, no! Did she detect my hint of sarcasm? Am I about to face the wrath of Khan?

"Uh, sure. I'll be right back."

I scurried into the living room and grabbed my cup of coffee and gulped down a mouthful. Fortified with caffeine, I dawdled slowly back to Sophia's room, feeling like a child who was about to get her butt spanked.

As I enter her bedroom, Sophia nodded, wordlessly, toward a wicker chair in the corner. I picked up the chair and strategically placed it arms-length away from the side of her bed. I wasn't going to give the crotchety old woman a chance to grab me again.

I took a moment to survey her lair. Sophia's bedroom was surprisingly small. To accommodate her full-sized bed, the other side of it had been positioned mere inches from the wall. In the middle of that wall, just above the chenille of her bedspread, was a window covered in lace curtains.

"Ahem," Sophia said, clearing her throat. She eyed me up and down.

"Yes, your Queenpin." I braced myself for a lecture about the atrocities of waking her up too soon. Or, possibly, of some other offense of which I had yet to be made aware.

"Doreen, I don't know what the others have told you about me, but I'm no liar."

Realizing this wasn't about me, I perked up like a kid being released from detention. "I know tha—"

"Don't interrupt me," she barked. "I'm not crazy, either. Charlie and Ernie were poisoned. Freddy, too. You know how I know?"

I stared into her green cat-like eyes. Uncertain whether to answer with a reply, or follow her orders to not interrupt, I settled for a small shake of my head.

"Because the same guy who brought me the apple fritter and cheese Danish also dropped off the lemon bars."

"Oh." Shocked, I asked, "Do the others know this?"

"Not yet. I want you to tell them."

"Why me?"

"Because I got my pride," she said. "I know they just stuck me in that old folks' home so they could have a break from me."

I winced. "You don't miss much, do you?"

"Ha!" Sophia said, sitting up straight in her bed. "So I'm right!"

Crap. I've just been outwitted by a lady in a Jiffy Pop turban. Some detective I am.

***

"So that's why I didn't try a lemon bar, even though they're my favorite," Sophia said and drained her coffee cup. "I knew it was the same guy."

She shook her head and sighed. "Back in the good old days, the bad guys wore normal hats. Take my advice, kid. Never trust a guy in a hoodie. You can't get a good look at him. What's he trying to hide?"

"Do you think you could make out the delivery guy in a lineup?"

Sophia scoffed. "Who are you? Joe Friday? I just told you I couldn't see his face."

I flinched, recalling Aunt Edna's warning right before I met Sophia for the first time at Shady Respite. *Don't ask stupid questions.*

Too late. But then again, maybe Aunt Edna didn't ask *enough* questions. I dared another.

"There's got to be some other way to identify the guy. Did he walk funny? Have any kind of nervous ticks or something?"

Sophia frowned. "No. But he *did* act all haughty-like."

Haughty like? In a hoodie?

"What do you mean?" I asked.

"You know. All fancy-schmancy. Like he was too good for the likes of me."

"Anything else?"

Sophia's brow furrowed. "Now that I think about it, I could see his chin poking out of the hoodie. It had a cleft. And like I said, the jerk sounded all hoity-toity when he spoke."

I blanched. "He *spoke*? What did he say?"

Sophia's nose crinkled as if she'd just smelled a skunk. "The creep stuck his nose in the air and said, 'I hope you enjoy these sweet treats M' Lady, compliments of the Mansion Neil.'"

"You mean Neil Mansion?" I asked.

"That's what I said," she grumbled.

My mind flashed back to Neil Neil at the funeral home. Of all the people I'd met to date, he was by far the most pretentious of the lot. But his handsome chin definitely didn't have a cleft. I tried to recall details of the picture of him with his husband. Had his partner's chin been cleft?

"Hmm," I said. "What about—"

All of a sudden, the bushes outside the window above Sophia's bed began to quiver. I leapt out of the chair. In the moonlight, I caught a glimpse of a ghostly hand reaching toward the glass.

"Duck, Sophia!" I yelled.

"What?"

Instinctively, I grabbed the shotgun and leapt into bed on top of the old Queenpin.

"What the hell!" she yelled, squirming underneath me.

"Hush!" I leaned across Sophia and took a tentative peek between the lace curtains.

I was right. Somebody *was* out there.

And whoever it was had a knife.

Chapter Thirty-Five

So much for this being the "amateur shift."

Just before my watch guarding the Queenpin was about to be over, I spotted someone in the bushes right outside her bedroom window. And they had a blade in their hand.

I was so freaked out I'd jumped in the bed with Sophia.

"Quick! Get under the bed!" I whispered.

"With you on top of me?" Sophia grumbled. "How am I supposed to do that, genius?"

I rolled off of her. "This is no time for jokes. I'm serious. There's an assassin out there with a knife!"

"Look again," Sophia said, reaching for her turban on the nightstand. "Is this 'assassin' of yours wearing pink?"

"What?"

I pulled back the lace curtain a crack and took a cautious peek, hoping not to get stabbed between the eyes. The hitman was indeed wearing pink.

The tension in my gut went limp. "How'd you know?"

"Because that's Kitty. She's on morgue patrol."

I blanched. "Morgue patrol?"

I flung the curtains open wide. Sure enough, there stood Kitty, a huge pair of garden shears in her hand. I felt like a complete fool.

"Who died?" I asked, rolling over and practically spooning Sophia.

"Nobody. *Yet*." Sophia pushed me away. "Unless this is purgatory and nobody told me."

Geez. Stuck with Sophia through eternity? I'd rather go back to Ma in Snohomish. I think ...

"So, what's morgue patrol?" I asked.

Sophia shrugged. "Every morning I don't wake up dead, I open the curtains a little to let the crew know I'm still alive. Kitty likes to peek in and wave." Sophia shook her head. "She's one of those annoying morning people."

I glanced back out the window. As if on cue, Kitty waved. Like an idiot, I waved back. Kitty turned away and started clipping the leaves on a bush.

"What's she doing out there messing around in the dark?" I asked.

"Checking on her plants. They're the same as people to her. Now do me a favor, kid."

"Sure. What?"

"Get out of my bed!"

"Oh. Yes, ma'am."

I scooted down the side of the bed against the wall, using the shotgun like an oar. As I reached the foot of the bed, I heard the front door to the cottage open. I sprung up off the mattress and scrambled to cock the shotgun.

"Shift's over!" Aunt Edna hollered, her voice echoing down the hallway. "It's quarter to six. Breakfast will be on the table in fifteen minutes!"

I nearly melted from relief. I relaxed my finger on the trigger and stood there, heart racing, feeling like a fool for the third time in under two minutes.

Behind me, I heard the mattress creak. I turned to see Sophia crawling out of bed in her turban and a flannel nightgown I'd swear I once saw on an episode of *Gunsmoke*. After planting both feet on the floor, she grinned up at me. I braced myself, expecting her to bust my chops again.

"Well aren't you a little miss Quick-Draw McGraw," she said, patting me on the shoulder as she passed by. "Good thing I was already done with my coffee."

As she took a few steps down the hallway, I heard her say, "Thanks, kid."

I nearly dropped the shotgun in my hands.

Had I actually done something *right* for a change?

Chapter Thirty-Six

Thanks to Aunt Edna, in less than two weeks I'd become as food-motivated as a lab rat. Like Pavlov's dogs, just the sound of my aunt's voice yelling, "Food's ready!" caused my mouth to salivate.

After hearing breakfast would be ready in fifteen minutes, I'd rushed back over to Aunt Edna's and taken a quick shower, trying not to drool from the aroma of cinnamon buns baking in the oven. I pulled on a sundress, put my hair in a ponytail, and headed for the kitchen.

"Can I do anything to help?" I called through the door.

"Go get Sophia," Aunt Edna called back. "We're eating in the courtyard."

"I'm on it!" I dashed out the door.

After my little talk with Sophia, I was no longer filled with trepidation. That is, I wasn't until I spotted someone leaving Sophia's apartment and running out the back gate.

He was wearing a hoodie.

I nearly swallowed my own tonsils.

Oh my God! The poisoner is back!

I ran toward the frail old Queenpin's cottage and onto the porch. I flung open the door, expecting to find Sophia lying dead on the floor, some kind of pastry shoved halfway down her throat. What I found instead surprised me even more.

The old lady was humming to herself as she poured a takeout Starbucks coffee into a ceramic mug.

"Ack!" she hissed as I barged in. "Close the door!"

"What?' I gasped. "Why?"

The queen of the CGCN glared up at me. "One word of this to Edna and you're a dead woman. Got it?"

I cringed. "But ... I don't—"

"Ah!" Sophia said after taking a sip from the steaming cup. "Now *that's* a real cup of joe."

"Don't drink that!" I yelped. "It could be poisoned!"

Sophia chuckled, then looked me up and down. "Hardly. What can I say? When I was at Shady Respite, I got hooked on Starbucks."

My mouth fell open. "What?"

Sophia took another sip. "Don't get me wrong, kid. When it comes to pasta, your aunt is Michelangelo with a spoon. But her coffee is the pure devil's handiwork. Even worse than yours. Now, promise on your mother's grave you won't say a word about this."

"But my mother's not dead. She's in Alaska."

The Queenpin stared at me for a second. Then the old woman burst out laughing so hard she sloshed her Starbucks coffee onto the floor.

***

If anything could help calm my nerves after two false murder attempts, it was cinnamon rolls, bacon, and scrambled eggs. This perfect trifecta of breakfast foods was what awaited us in the courtyard. Starving after a morning full of adrenaline rushes, not even the ugly wheat-patterned melamine dishes could dull my appetite.

"Good morning. *Again*," I said to Kitty as I led Sophia to her seat at the head of the table.

"Good morning," she said, setting a centerpiece bouquet on the table.

The blooms were simple, five-petal flowers of canary yellow with pink centers. Even over the aroma of Aunt Edna's breakfast feast, I could smell their heavenly fragrance—as sweet and buttery as raw sugar-cookie dough.

"What are those?" I asked.

"Plumeria Apocynaceae," Kitty said. "Also known as Frangipani, or Hawaiian lei flower."

"Kitty knows everything about plants," Jackie said, pulling up a chair.

Kitty smiled, then glanced to her right and waved. I followed her gaze and spotted an old woman waving back from a second-story window across the back alley.

"Don't encourage her, Kitty," Aunt Edna grumbled. "That busybody is worse than Mrs. Kravitz on steroids. Sit down, already. So we can eat. Any luck with the lemon bars?"

"A little," Kitty said, shifting the seat cushion on her chair. "I found something unusual in a couple of the samples. But we can definitely rule out arsenic or cyanide."

"How?" I asked.

Kitty shot me a grin. "Either one of those two and Freddy would've dropped dead practically where he was standing."

"Well, we know *that* didn't happen," Aunt Edna said, her eyes darting to Sophia as she jabbed a fork into her scrambled eggs.

"Kitty, what happened to your hand?" I asked, noticing a Band-Aid on her right index finger. "Cut it with the pruning shears?"

"No." Kitty stared at it absently. "I must've brushed it up against my Bunsen burner."

"Oh." I thought back to dissecting frogs in high school science class, then wished I hadn't. "That reminds me, I'd still like to see your greenhouse."

"That's gonna have to wait," Aunt Edna said, unrolling a chunk of cinnamon bun. "After breakfast, I need you two to go to Shady Respite and pay up before they send the bill collectors out on us."

"Yeah," Jackie said, shooting us a wink. "We don't want them coming out and repossessing Sophia, now do we?"

Aunt Edna pursed her lips and muttered, "If only."

"No problem," Kitty said. "Well, *one* problem. How are we going to pay the bill?"

"This ought to cover it," Sophia said. She reached into the bosom of her thin, cotton dress and pulled out a roll of bills big enough to choke an elephant.

I gasped. "Holy Moses! Where'd that come—"

But I didn't get to finish. The dire looks on the faces of the other ladies caused my voice to dry up in my throat.

As usual, there was a lot more going on around me than I had any clue about. In fact, these ladies were virtually swimming in their own secrets.

The only thing I knew for sure was, wherever that money had come from, it sure wasn't Sophia's change back from buying Starbucks.

Chapter Thirty-Seven

On the way to Shady Respite to collect Sophia's things and pay the bill, Kitty filled me in on yet another thing I had no clue about—the Queen-pin's subtle reign of terror over the other residents while she'd been at the convalescent center.

Kitty shook her head and laughed. "I'm sure everyone in there was glad to see her go."

"I can only imagine," I said, steering the old Kia down Fourth Street.

"Sophia had a whole harem of men doing her bidding in there." Kitty cracked her gum. "I don't know how she does it, but Sophia can make a man eat shredded cardboard if she wants."

"Or poisoned lemon bars," I deadpanned.

"Exactly." Kitty studied her pink fingernails. "Don't let her fool you. Sophia can't see squat without her bifocals, but her tongue is still as sharp as Occam's razor. It has to be some kind of miracle for her to have made it this long, right?"

"That and Aunt Edna's food."

"Oh, yeah." Kitty patted her stomach. "There's nothing like it. I'm gonna miss it when I die and have to eat whatever crap they serve in Heaven."

I laughed, then caught myself. "I feel sorry for those poor guys who died being her food tasters."

"Charlie and Ernest? Don't feel too bad about them. At their age, good food was one of the last pleasures left in life."

My brow furrowed. "What do you mean?"

"Listen. If all you had to look forward to was a steady diet of lumpy porridge and mushy green peas, I bet you'd be ready to cash it all in for a good cheese Danish, too."

Geez. In a way, I kind of already am. Is that what happens when you turn forty and have nothing left to live for?"

"I guess," I said. "But that hardly seems charitable."

"Don't judge. You weren't there." Kitty frowned. "Charlie was always hungry. Poor guy wandered the halls looking for scraps."

I blanched. "He did not!"

"Wanna bet? When Sophia told Charlie about the apple fritter, he was at her door before she hung up the phone." Kitty shook her head. "Anyway, the plan was to only give him one bite. But before I knew it, he'd wolfed the whole thing down while I clipped his toenails."

"Gross!"

"You're telling me! Gluttony is one of the seven deadly sins, you know."

"I mean about the toenails." I cringed, fighting back the urge to retch. "You said at dinner last night they wouldn't show evidence of poisoning. So why did you ... ugh ... *clip* them?"

Kitty blew out a breath. "Sophia's orders. Believe me, it wasn't my idea."

"Sophia's orders?"

"Yeah. Sometimes you have to take one for the team, kid." She looked out the window. "Sophia had this great idea for me give her 'boy-toy tasters' pedicures while they ate. It was a ruse she thought up so I could watch for symptoms. I have to say, her idea was both diabolically clever and absolutely disgusting at the same time."

"You aren't kidding." I swallowed the bile rising in my throat. "I suffer psychological trauma every time I even *think* about ADT."

Kitty's head cocked to one side. "You got issues with home security systems?"

"No. ADT is my code for Arthur Dreacher's Toenails."

"Huh?"

I shivered with disgust. "Long story. Just suffice it to say that 'toenails' has become a trigger word for me."

"Ah." Kitty laughed. "Well, take it from me. Trigger words are a hell of a lot better than having a *real* trigger pointed at you, that's for sure."

***

As we approached the front desk at Shady Respite, I began to wonder how Kitty had ended up with the CGCN. Dressed in soft pink from head to toe, she seemed more intellectual and introverted than the others. Mild-mannered and meek didn't seem like attributes that would be highly sought after by the mafia. But then again, what did I know?

I followed behind Kitty as she walked up to the receptionist's window. She smiled like a pink cherub at the haggard woman sifting through papers at her desk.

"Good morning!" Kitty cooed. "I'd like to speak with Dr. Mancini, please."

The receptionist peered up at her through her bifocals. "You have an appointment?"

"No, honey. I'm afraid I don't."

The woman at the desk turned her attention back to the stack of papers on her desk. "Sorry, but the doctor is only available by appointment."

"Oh, dear," Kitty said sweetly. "It's kind of urgent."

The receptionist blew out a tired breath. "It always is. Which patient is this regarding?"

"Mr. Freddy Sanderling."

The woman's tired face grew pinched. "Are you a relative?"

"Why, no, ma'am," Kitty said softly. "My, what a lovely necklace you have on!"

"Look lady. You want to speak with Dr. Mancini, you're going to need an appointment."

"No. *You* look, sweetheart," Kitty said, still smiling sweetly. "I'm here to see the doctor. Then I'm going to pay the bill for Sophia Lorenzo's stay. In that order. *And in that order only.* Got it?"

The woman's brow furrowed in anger. She stuck her nose up. "Like I said—"

"Listen, honey," Kitty said sweetly. "You work hard for a living. Don't make the job even harder on yourself."

"What are you talking about?" the woman asked.

"This." Kitty pulled Sophia's wad of cash from her purse and laid it gently on the counter in front of the hole in the Plexiglas window. "Do you really want to have to explain to your boss why you turned away a customer and their twenty grand in cash?"

The woman gulped. She shook her head.

"Oh, you don't want it?" Kitty asked, snatching up the money. "Okay, have it your way, Miss. Good luck with the unemployment paperwork."

Kitty turned on her heels to face me and shot me a devious wink. "Come on, Doreen. We did our best to avoid the impending catastrophe. It's in God's hands now."

"Wait!" the woman cried out, leaping up from her desk. "Let me make a quick call."

"Oh, that'd be swell," Kitty said, beaming from ear to ear. "You're an angel!"

I watched in awe as the receptionist jabbed digits on her landline phone. If she really had been an angel, she sure as heck didn't play the harp. Her true talent appeared to be grinding glass to dust with her teeth.

I exchanged glances with Kitty. Not only was this odd woman in pink a botanist and potioneer. She was also the smoothest talker I'd come across since my date with Lenny Hobovitz back in 1999.

The receptionist hung up the phone. "Dr. Mancini is on his way," she said. "Now, hand over the cash. I mean, pay your bill."

"Not so fast," Kitty said. "Doctor first. Cash second."

I smiled, amused with my new friend's style and poise.

Whoa! Miss Kitty's got claws.

Chapter Thirty-Eight

After dodging two assaults from umbrellas and acorns, hijacking a mob Godmother in a getaway wheelchair, and now participating in soft-core extortion with a mob moll in pink, I really didn't think Shady Respite could possibly hold any more surprises for me.

Boy, was I wrong.

While Kitty and I stood waiting at the reception area for Dr. Mancini to arrive, a tall, thin woman in jeans and a t-shirt walked up to the window. Something about her made me do a double take.

Lying across her shoulders beneath her short, bleach-blonde hair was a huge, gray-green lizard. The languid reptile sat there motionless, draped around her neck like the world's most hideous neck shawl.

"Hi, Melanie," the receptionist said. "And who have you got for us today?"

"My old pal Iggy," she said, petting the lizard's head. "Where do you want us?"

"They're all waiting for you in the rec center."

"Okay, then." Melanie turned her head and spoke to the lizard. "We better get to it, hon."

"Uh, excuse me," I said, rolling my tongue back into my mouth. "What's up with the lizard?"

"Iggy's not a lizard," Melanie said. "He's an iguana. From Guatemala. Wanna pet him?"

"Ick. I mean ... no thanks. Why is he ... you know, *here*?"

Melanie laughed. "He's a therapy animal."

Kitty's nose crinkled. "I thought therapy animals were supposed to be cute and fuzzy."

"That's pet discrimination," Melanie said. "A social issue I'm trying to change. Here, have one of my flyers." She reached into her purse and handed me a yellow slip of paper. Across the top was a headline that read, *Dander Danger*.

"Dander danger?" I asked.

"Yeah. It's a real thing. A lot of folks are allergic to dander. Makes them choke and wheeze. Iggy is furless, so he doesn't cause a reaction."

"Right," I said.

Unless you're allergic to freaking ugly giant lizards.

"Can you believe people actually eat these poor little things?" Melanie asked, stroking the horny fringes on the iguana's head.

"No." I watched Iggy's pink tongue flick in and out of his mouth. "I absolutely can't believe it."

"Oh. Here comes Dr. Mancini," Kitty said, grabbing my arm.

"I gotta go," Melanie said. "Come to the rec room if you want to see Iggy in action."

I smiled weakly. "Sure thing."

What's he gonna do? Barf up a beetle?

***

"I appreciate your concern, Ms. Corleone," Dr. Mancini said in a tone that implied the exact opposite.

The skinny, fastidious physician had whisked us into his office after spotting the hoagie-roll-sized wad of cash poking out of Kitty's purse. Having just seen my colleague work her magic with the receptionist, I decided to hang back and let Kitty do the talking.

"Why thank you, doctor," Kitty said sweetly. "You see, I'm worried about what happened to Freddy Sanderling. He was a good friend of my mother's."

"Uh-huh." The doctor studied her from behind his thick glasses. "Well, I believe your concerns are totally unfounded. Unfortunately, elderly gentlemen choking to death is a rather common occurrence. Mr. Sanderling is just the latest statistic."

Kitty shot him a look of doe-eyed concern. "What did his autopsy say?"

"That's none of your .... Ahem, that's *confidential*. Besides, I saw no need to conduct one. I've already ruled Frederick Sanderling's death as due to natural causes."

One of Kitty's claws came out. "What *kind* of natural causes?"

"Mr. Sanderling was eighty-four," Dr. Mancini said dismissively. "He was underweight and frail. It's my belief his heart stopped due to complications exacerbated by aspiration."

"Huh. That wouldn't be the first time aspiration killed somebody, would it?" Kitty said, wagging her eyebrows.

"Good one," Dr. Mancini said without a trace of amusement. "Mr. Sanderling swallowed improperly chewed food that then lodged in his throat and blocked his airway."

"What was the food?"

"Nothing we served here at Shady Respite, of that you can be assured," Dr. Mancini said indignantly. "We don't allow our patients to eat sugar-laden foods. Mr. Sanderling choked on contraband goods. Macerated lemon bars, I believe."

"Oh," Kitty said as innocently as *Betty Boop*. "Why do you believe it was lemon bars?"

"Because Mr. Sanderling told me so himself." Dr. Mancini's face drew pinched. "He even offered me one, but I refused." He patted his flat stomach. "What kind of example would that have set?"

My eyebrow arched.

I dunno. A human *one?*

"So you had the chance to save him from eating contraband food, but you didn't," Kitty said.

Meeoow!

"I ..." Dr. Mancini fumbled.

"Don't worry about it," Kitty said, smiling up at him. "So, did Freddy complain about the taste of the lemon bars?"

Sweat began to trickle down Dr. Mancini's right temple. "No. Not that I recall. Wait." He stuck his chin in the air. "I remember Mr. Sanderling saying they were delicious. The best he'd ever had."

"And that's when he choked to death on your watch?" Kitty asked sweetly.

How many claws did that make now? I've lost count.

"No!" Dr. Mancini gulped. "Mr. Sanderling returned to his room to take a nap. Unfortunately, he never woke up."

"How tragic." Kitty tutted and shook her head. "What a comfort it will be for my mother to know this. Thank you, Dr. Mancini."

He eyed her dubiously. "Uh ... you're welcome."

"So," Kitty said. "Where is dear Freddy now?"

Dr. Mancini appeared confused. "Um...heaven or hell, I suppose. I'm a doctor, not a judge."

"I meant his *body*." Kitty shot him a brilliant smile.

Dr. Mancini's eyebrow rose an inch. "I assume it's still in the morgue downstairs. He's slated for pickup and cremation today. Thankfully, Mr. Sanderling had made his pre-arrangements with the Neil Mansion."

"You don't say," I said to Kitty.

"Well, thank you so very much for your precious time," Kitty said, shaking Dr. Mancini's hand. She thrust the wad of cash into his palms. "We'll be going now." She patted his hand. "Just mail us a receipt, hon. I trust you."

Kitty spun on her heels. I tagged along after her, leaving Dr. Mancini standing in the corridor with his mouth hanging open.

"Where are we going?" I asked, trotting up to her side.

"Where do you think?" she whispered out of the side of her mouth. "To the morgue."

"What? Without the doctor?"

"That old tomcat has a new toy to keep him occupied. So now the mice can play."

"But why not just ask—"

"The good doctor?" Kitty scoffed. "You saw that pretentious jerk. He'd never let me in there to see Freddy. So why bother asking and arousing suspicion?"

I grimaced. "But ... how will we get in?"

"Don't you worry about that." She patted her purse. "I've got the key right here."

Chapter Thirty-Nine

As it turned out, the key to the morgue wasn't made of metal, but paper.

"You've got five minutes," the orderly said, counting out the bills in his hands. "Follow me."

"A couple a Ben Franklins can open a lot of doors," Kitty said, shooting me a wink.

The orderly led us into a room so cold it made Jackie's glaucoma sunglasses fog up instantly. I didn't dare take them off and give the guy a look at my wonky eye. He'd probably think I was a zombie. So I stood back and watched through the hazy lenses as the morgue attendant wheeled out a long, narrow table covered in a white sheet.

He pulled back a cloth. "This the one?"

Kitty glanced over at me. "Well?"

"I'm not sure," I said. "It's hard to see."

"Then get over here and take a closer look," Kitty said.

I stepped up to the corpse and stared at the lifeless body of Freddy Sanderling. "Yes. That's him."

"Okay," the orderly said. "I'm going on smoke break. When I get back, you two are gone. Correct?"

"Absolutely," Kitty said.

"Geez. Now what?" I asked, watching the orderly slip out of the room.

"I check for poisoning symptoms and *you* clip his toenails."

"What!" I nearly screeched.

Kitty laughed. "Just kidding. You really *do* have toenail PTSD."

I cringed. "Please stop saying *toenails* and I'll do whatever you want."

Kitty grinned and tutted. "How easy the young ones cave."

She picked up Freddy's arm and let it drop. "Good. No rigor mortis. That makes it easier."

I grimaced. "Easier to *what*?"

"Steal his wallet." Kitty shook her head at me. "What do you think? Get the samples!"

"Oh. Right."

"Okay, now. Doreen, you hold his mouth open while I put a penlight down his throat."

I suddenly felt woozy. "Uh ... can I retract my last statement and clip his toenails instead?"

"Quit grumbling or you'll do *both*." Kitty whipped out two pairs of rubber gloves from her purse. "Here. Put these on first."

"Thank you," I said, truly meaning it. I quickly donned the gloves, swallowed a retch, winced until my eyes were almost shut, then pried open Freddy's mouth. The unexpected smoothness made my eyes open a notch.

"Geez!" I said, startled. "All his teeth are gone!"

Kitty shrugged. "Eh. They usually recycle the spare parts off a cremee. Take my advice. Don't buy your dentures at a thrift store."

The hair on the back of my neck stood up. "Are you serious?"

"Yeah, but that's not important right now."

"Huh?"

Kitty leaned over Freddy's body and aimed the small flashlight in her gloved hands at his head. "Hold his mouth open as wide as you can. I'm going in."

A shiver went down my spine as Kitty shoved the penlight down Freddy's throat and leaned in for a look. Any closer and her right eyeball would've been inside his mouth.

"Huh. Would you look at that," she said.

"What is it?" I asked, not wanting to know.

"See those blisters on his tonsils?"

"Err...no."

"Get closer."

I winced. "Do I have to?"

"Grow up, Doreen. You want to be in the Family, you gotta learn the biz."

"I never said I wanted—"

"Look, hun," Kitty said, shooting me a look. "The clock's ticking. I don't have time for a philosophical discussion about your life right now. Just be a good do-bee and stick your face in there and get a good look, okay?"

I held my breath, sucked up some courage, and did as I was told. In retrospect, I probably shouldn't have closed my eyes as well. As I leaned over his body, I accidently bumped noses with Freddy's corpse.

"Arrgh!" I squealed, and lurched back in revulsion.

"Did you see the blisters?" Kitty asked.

"Uh … yeah," I lied. "I absolutely, most certainly did."

Kitty nodded and chewed her lip. "I figure they had to be caused by some kind of caustic agent."

My nose crinkled. "You mean like battery acid?"

Kitty laughed. "You watch too many mafia movies, Doreen. Life ain't like the movies. I'd say it was more likely Draino. Or a rodenticide."

"A *what*?"

"Rat poison."

"Oh." I slapped my sunglasses back on. "But wouldn't Freddy have tasted it? The doctor said he told him the lemon bars tasted good."

Kitty shrugged. "Like I said before, lemon is a strong flavor. Good for masking unpleasant tastes." Kitty took another look down Freddy's throat and grunted.

"What now?" I asked.

"There's nothing blocking his windpipe. Freddy couldn't have aspirated."

"Maybe they cleared his throat up during the examination."

Kitty pursed her lips. "Maybe. But only if they shoved a garden hose down his throat."

I cringed at the imagery. "Are we done here?"

"Almost. Open wide one more time, Freddy." Kitty shot me a look. "By that, I mean *you*, Doreen."

"Oh."

I grimaced and pulled Freddy's jaws apart again. Kitty pulled out a pack of cotton swabs on foot-long stems.

"Okie dokie, now," she said. "Just gonna get some nice little samples of his throat skin, and some of that juice inside those blisters."

Bile boiled up in my throat. "Fine. But could you do it *without the commentary*, please? And hurry!"

"Sure thing." Kitty laughed. "I forgot this is your first time."

Despite trying not to watch, my eyes kept returning to Kitty and her grisly task. I saw her place six different cotton swabs into six separate plastic tubes.

"I think we're done here," she said, peeling off her rubber gloves. "That's two of our three chores completed. Now all we've got to do is ask around about who worked the late shift for the last two nights."

"Thank God," I said, tossing my gloves into the hazardous waste bin. "Let's get out of here before that creepy orderly comes back."

"Aww, he wasn't that bad. You should see the guys working down at the city morgue. Talk about *Invasion of the Body Snatchers.*"

My eyebrows met my hairline.
What the?

***

After leaving the morgue, Kitty and I crossed the hall and rode the elevator up to the second floor. The doors opened right across from the entrance to the cafeteria.

I blanched.

Geez. Maybe Sophia's right. Maybe this place really does *have a conveyor belt directly from the cafeteria to the morgue. Or at least a dumb waiter ...*

"Why are we going to the lunch room?" I asked Kitty. "I, for one, have absolutely *no* appetite right now."

Kitty laughed. "You're a riot, Doreen. I just want to check on what they served in the cafeteria the last couple of days. See if those blisters might be from food allergies."

"Oh." I glanced around the cafeteria at the old folks busily gumming their plates of ground hamburger steak, instant mashed potatoes, and broccoli cooked to a slimy green mush.

"I think we can rule out a reaction to seafood," I said. "They probably only serve shrimp and lobster on Tuesdays."

"Heh, heh," Kitty giggled. But then her lip snarled as an old man walked by with his tray. She leaned over and whispered in my ear, "You're right, Doreen. From the looks of the food they're serving, allergic reaction is a long shot. I bet they don't let a peanut within fifty miles of this place."

Suddenly, a loud shriek rang out from across the cafeteria. "Murderer!" a woman yelled.

My eyes darted to across the room and landed on the sour face of Gloria Martinelli. The old woman jumped to her feet and begin waving a purple umbrella at me menacingly.

"Oh, crap," I said. "Not *her* again."

"I'm gonna get you, Killigan!" Gloria screamed, causing the old man next to her to spit out a chunk of watermelon.

"Whoa," Kitty said. "What'd you do to Gloria Martinelli?"

"You *know* her?"

"You catch on quick," Kitty quipped. "So, what happened between you two?"

I shook my head and took a step toward the door. "Long story. Now, can we just get the hell out of here? Please?"

Kitty grinned. "You got it, killer."

Chapter Forty

"And that's why that crazy old lady thinks I'm a murderer," I said as I steered the Kia down Fourth Street.

Kitty laughed. "Because Gloria saw you stab a guy on a TV show? Ha! What a hoot!" She shook her head. "What's this world coming to, when people can't tell fact from fiction anymore?"

"I blame reality TV."

"Yeah, I can see where that crap could blur the lines. Especially if you're already skating on thin ice. Mentally, that is."

"What a misnomer. Reality TV is about as far from reality as it gets." I grimaced. "At least, I *hope* it is."

Kitty shot me a knowing look. "You and me *both*, kid."

I pulled up to a traffic light and turned to Kitty. "So how do you know Gloria Martinelli, anyway?"

Kitty shrugged. "She and Sophia used to be good friends when they were young. Not many people who remember are still alive, but as a teenager, Gloria had her heart set on marrying Harvey Lorenzo."

"Sophia's husband?"

"Not at the time, but yeah. But, too bad for Gloria. Harvey met Sophia and ditched her like a cold cannelloni."

"That explains a lot." I hit the gas. "But that was like—a gazillion years ago. You'd think the two would've kissed and made up by now."

Kitty laughed. "You really *don't* know anything about the mafia, do you?"

"Not much," I admitted. "But I feel like I've been taking a crash course the past few weeks."

"I bet."

"Hey. I've got another question for you. How could it be that Dr. Mancini never noticed the blisters in Freddy's throat?"

Kitty stared out the windshield. "Could be any number of reasons. Laziness. Oversight. Or maybe he saw them, but didn't think they were relevant."

"Are you saying you think he's incompetent?"

Kitty shrugged. "Not exactly. But I wouldn't rule it out. They guy's up to his knees in sick, ornery old people every day of his life. Maybe to him, Freddy was just a frail old man whose time was up. Aspirating on food was as good a cause of death as any. I bet ruling it natural causes saved him a lot of paperwork."

My eyebrows inched together. "That's diabolical!"

"Don't throw the doctor in the slammer just yet," Kitty said.

"Why not?"

"Just going out on a limb here, Dorey. But maybe he's actually right and Freddy really did just choke to death on a plain old lemon bar."

My brow furrowed. "I don't buy it."

Kitty sighed. "Me neither. Just trying to be objective."

"Come on. You said yourself you detected something strange in the bars when you tested them last night. That has to mean foul play, right?"

"Not until we know for sure what it is. Right before breakfast, I set up some secondary tests in my lab. I'm hoping they'll tell us more when we get back."

"Good."

Kitty drummed her pink fingernails on the door panel just below the window. "In the meantime, let's do a quick review of the facts. The doc said Freddy ate the lemon bars and told him they tasted good. Then Freddy went to his room, laid down, went to sleep, and died sometime during the night."

"That sounds about right."

"Yeah. Too bad it's wrong."

"What do you mean?"

Kitty blew out a breath. "That story doesn't pan out with the evidence."

"Why not?"

Kitty pulled up a picture on her phone and shoved it in my face. "With all those blisters?"

"Gross!" I yelped, and pushed the phone away.

"No way. Freddy's throat would've felt like it was on fire. Who could sleep through that?"

"Maybe he had help nodding off," I said.

"Like somebody suffocated him?"

"Uh ... I was thinking more along the lines of Freddy complaining and a nurse giving him a sleeping pill."

"Oh." Kitty chewed her bottom lip and nodded. "That could work. Good thinking, Dorey."

"Thanks." I pulled up to another traffic light. "So, where to now?"

"A drugstore." Kitty held up a half-gallon baggie containing the tubes of sampling swabs. "I'm fresh out of drug-testing kits."

I glanced at her quizzically. "But you have your own testing lab."

"That's right. But for *poisons*, not drugs. Why bother with all that hocus-pocus when, for fifty bucks, I can buy a drug-screening panel that tests for over a dozen legal and illicit drugs in one fell swoop?"

"So you think some kind of *drug* caused those blisters in Freddy's throat?"

"Maybe. Maybe not. What you said earlier got me thinking. You may be onto something, kid."

"On to what?"

Kitty wagged her eyebrows. "Maybe somebody not only helped Freddy die—they also made his death a little easier to swallow."

***

I waited in the car while Kitty went in the drugstore. I needed time to think, and to check my phone. Somehow, it had gotten switched off. I turned it back on, and was excited to see a text message from Kerri Middleton. After reading it, however, I wasn't so excited.

Where are you? It's nearly 10:30.

"What?" I said aloud.

Suddenly, I felt the color drain from me. In all the confusion over the past few days, I'd forgotten today was Monday. And, according to my phone, it was now 10:45.

"Oh, crap!" I yelled.

I scrambled to dial Kerri's number, my fingers trembling on the keypad. It rang once. Twice. Three times.

Come on, pick up!

After the fourth ring, it went to voicemail. I groaned.

I can't believe my own stupidity! There goes my best chance at an acting career.

Desperate, I sent Kerri a text.

> *I'm so sorry! I had a few family matters come up. Set up another meeting anytime, anywhere, and I'll be there. I promise! And I'll take the part, whatever it is.*

I pressed *Send*, then drummed my nails on the steering wheel and stared at my phone display. Nothing.

As I obsessed about whether I'd ever hear back from Kerri, a movement outside the Kia made me look up. Kitty had come waltzing out of the drugstore swinging a plastic bag and grinning, like a kid who'd just scored a bag full of candy. For her, life looked as rosy as the outfit she had on.

As for me? Not so much.

Chapter Forty-One

"There you two are," Jackie said as Kitty and I pulled up in front of Palm Court Cottages. "I was about to send out a search party. I thought you might've gotten jacked, carrying around all that loot, you know."

"No," Kitty said. "Everything was smooth sailing. We just had to stop at two different drug stores before I found one with the test kits I needed. Who knew drug testing was getting so popular?"

Smooth sailing? Popular? I wish I could say the same about my *life. At this point, I'd settle simply for not going down the drain.*

I shook my head.

Geez. I just met a damned lizard *with a better job in the entertainment industry than I have. What's wrong with me?*

"Well, I better get to my lab," Kitty said, waving her drugstore bag.

"Uh, can I go with you?" I asked. "I kind of want to see how it all works."

Plus, I suddenly find myself in need of a new career.

Kitty beamed. "Sure, kid. Maybe I can teach you a thing or two."

"Lunch is ready!" Aunt Edna bellowed from the courtyard.

"It's eleven already?" Kitty shot me a wink. "How about right after we eat?"

I sighed. "Sure thing."

As I followed Kitty and Jackie toward the courtyard, my phone buzzed. It was text from Kerri.

Tomorrow. 10 a.m. sharp. No excuses!

My knees nearly buckled as relief washed through me. Maybe I wouldn't be outdone by a lizard after all.

***

In the courtyard. Aunt Edna was busy putting lunch on the table. At her feet, Benny, Jackie's ancient pug, was begging for scraps.

"So, everything all settled at Shady Respite?" Aunt Edna asked as she doled out heaping helpings of fragrant mushroom risotto, along with a side of steaming collard greens.

I was salivating before the food even hit my plate. So was Benny. Either that, or she always had drool hanging out of the corners of her mouth. The threadbare little pooch hobbled along with every step my aunt took, an eternally hopeful glimmer shining in her big, bulging eyes.

"All done," Kitty said. "I paid Sophia's bill in full. They're sending a receipt."

"Good. We'll need it for taxes," Aunt Edna said, then chuckled and almost tripped over Benny. "And the Freddy business?"

"Done, too," I said, not wanting Kitty to get started with any gory details and ruin my appetite. "We're running tests right after lunch."

"What about my *things*?" Sophia asked. "Where are my cherished belongings you were supposed to pick up?"

I glanced over at Kitty and winced. "Crap. We'll have to go back."

Sophia shook her head. "I swear, Kitty. You'd forget your head if it wasn't attached."

"Hey, remember that time she did?" Jackie said.

"Geez, not with the pumpkin head again," Kitty said. She turned to me. "My colleagues at the lab I used to work for gave me a retirement-slash-Halloween party. I went as Ichabod Crane, but I forgot to bring the pumpkin head. I come home later and find these three had murderized it and stuck it under my bedsheets for a joke." She looked at the other women. "Ha ha."

A round of laughter emanated from Jackie, Sophia, and Aunt Edna. After a moment, Kitty shrugged and joined in. "Hey. Nobody's perfect. At least *I* had a *real* career."

"What's that supposed to mean?" Jackie asked.

Kitty smirked and wagged her eyebrows at me. "Oh. Excuse me. Ms. Jackie Cooperelli over there majored in 'cocktail waitress' at a Biloxi casino," she said, air-quoting the term with her fingers.

"*Head* cocktail waitress," Jackie corrected.

Aunt Edna laughed. "Hey, Dorey. You know how you can tell who the head waitress is?"

I shook my head. "Uh ... no."

Aunt Edna snorted. "She's the one with the dirty knees."

Raucous laughter filled the courtyard. Jackie laughed along with us. "Hey, a girl does what she can to make a living. No shame in earning money the hard way."

"Just exactly how *hard* was it?" Kitty quipped.

Sophia chuckled, then took a bite of her risotto. "Hey. Speaking of too hot to handle. Edna, you were a little heavy with the pepper today."

Aunt Edna took a bite of risotto and frowned. I tried it as well. Sophia was right. It was a bit spicy, but still delectable in my book.

"My apologies," Aunt Edna said unapologetically.

Sophia raised a hand to her throat and dramatically downed half a glass of iced tea. I braced myself for more deprecating banter, but Sophia set her glass down and chewed the corner of her mouth as if in deep thought.

"What's wrong?" Aunt Edna asked. "You need a Tums or something?"

"No." Sophia frowned. "I just remembered something about when I gave Freddy those lemon bars. He came back for more, saying they went down sweet, and that he liked the peppery aftertaste."

"The lemon bars that came from the Neil Mansion?" Jackie asked.

"No," Sophia said. "The ones that came from the moon. Isn't that where people who wear hoodies come from? The moon? And speak in British accents?"

Jackie shrugged. "How should I know? I ain't never been there."

"Wait a minute," I said. "The guy in the hoodie spoke with a British accent?"

"Yeah," Sophia said. "I thought I told you that."

"No. You said the guy spoke all hoity-toity."

Sophia shrugged. "What's the difference?"

I opened my mouth to answer, but thought better of it. "You know, when I talked to Neil Neil at the funeral home, he sounded kind of haughty. Do you think it could've been him?"

"Maybe," Sophia said. "What's Neil's voice sound like?"

"Medium, I guess. Kind of nasally pitch."

Sophia shook her head. "This guy's voice was deep. Gravelly, even. He sounded like that snooty butler on *Downton Abbey*."

"What do you mean?" Kitty asked.

"Like when he said m'lady," Sophia said. "And instead of saying the lemon bars were compliments of the Neil Mansion, he said it like the Brits—*the Mansion Neil*."

Kitty choked on her iced tea. "The Mansion Neil? Are you sure that's what he said?"

"I may be old, but I've still got my marbles," Sophia grumbled.

Kitty shook her head. "This makes total sense now."

"What are you talking about?" Aunt Edna asked.

"The lemon bars were poisoned, all right." Kitty said, "And they didn't come from the Neil Mansion or the Mansion Neil. I'd bet dollars to donuts that whoever sent them laced the bars with poison from the *Manchineel* tree!"

I nearly dropped the forkful of risotto poised at my lips. "What are you talking about?"

Kitty gasped. "Nobody take another bite! The risotto could be poisoned!"

"No way," Aunt Edna said. "Not on my watch!" She hung her head. "Okay, already. So I might've accidently dropped the pepper container into the—"

"Thank the lord!" Kitty said, holding a hand to her heart.

Aunt Edna scowled. "You don't gotta be so dramatic about a little extra pepper, Kitty."

"You don't understand." Kitty rose to her feet. "The Manchineel has a peppery taste. It's one of the deadliest plants in the world. If you ingest too much of it, you're a goner. Even standing under one in the rain can cause your skin to blister."

"Geez!" I pushed my plate away.

"What makes you think this Manchineel plant is to blame?" Aunt Edna asked.

"Because of the symptoms," Kitty said. "Upon first eating the fruit, it tastes sweet. Kind of like a plum. Then the toxic juice turns peppery in your mouth. A few minutes later, it burns like drain cleaner down your throat."

My mouth fell open. "That sounds like what happened to Freddy!"

"Exactly," Kitty said. "I'll run some tests in my lab, but I'm quite certain that's what killed him."

"Hold up," Sophia said. "So you're saying this blister on my lip isn't from Freddy giving me herpes?"

Kitty's eyes made half a roll. "Probably not."

"But how would somebody get ahold of a Manchineel plant?" I asked.

"Actually, they're native to Florida," Kitty said.

Aunt Edna shook her head. "I've lived here my whole life. How come I never heard of it before?"

"Probably because they're really rare. And they're not of much commercial value," Kitty explained.

"Commercial value?" I asked.

Kitty shrugged. "They're homely to look at, and they're really hard to grow. The Manchineel needs tropical conditions to thrive. Nowadays, they're only found in a handful of places down south, where their natural habitat hasn't been destroyed."

"I dunno," Aunt Edna said. "This whole thing seems like a longshot to me. You said this plant is nothing to look at. And you gotta go traipsing through the jungle to find it. It doesn't add up. Why bother? Besides, who would even know about it besides a plant nut like you?"

"Yeah," Jackie said. "How would some average Joe lay his hands on a machine eel around here?"

Kitty winced. "Uh ... I have one in my greenhouse."

"Geez Louise!" I gasped. "Should we call the cops and tell them about it?"

"No need," a man's voice sounded behind us.

I turned to see a familiar face staring at us from behind the mirrored lenses of a pair of aviator sunglasses.

I closed my eyes in disbelief.

Oh, dear God. Not again.

Chapter Forty-Two

"McNutsack," Aunt Edna muttered under her breath.

"What are *you* doing here?" I asked.

Sergeant McNulty, the man who'd accused me of stabbing my old boss Tad Longmire to death, eyed me with a familiar suspicion. It'd been less than a week since I'd been cleared of charges in that case. As he stood there in the courtyard staring at us, I could almost hear him opening another file on me in the computer of his mind.

"I'm responding to an anonymous tip," McNulty said. He folded his arms across his chest and scowled. I sensed his dark brown eyes noting every detail, even from behind the mirrored lenses of his sunglasses.

"Anonymous tip?" I asked.

"Yes." He unfolded his arms. "Someone reported that seniors were being murdered at Shady Respite, and that the person behind the killings was hiding out at this address."

"That's preposterous," Aunt Edna scoffed.

"Is it?" McNulty's eyes scanned each of us seated at the table. "From what I just overheard, the potential murderer and murder weapon are still on the premises."

"What are you talking about?" Aunt Edna growled.

McNulty turned his attention to Kitty. "What's your name?"

"Uh ... Kitty Corleone."

"Well, Ms. Corleone, I think it's time I had a look inside that greenhouse full of poisonous plants I heard you talking about."

***

"Officer McNulty, I'm a trained botanist," Kitty explained as she led him toward the greenhouse behind her cottage. Aunt Edna and I followed closely behind, leaving Jackie in the courtyard to watch over Sophia.

"Is that so?" McNulty said. "I'll be sure and make a note of it."

"What I mean is, I'm a *responsible scientist*," Kitty said. "I keep all my specimens under lock and key."

As if to prove her point, Kitty stopped in front of the greenhouse and pointed to an impressive looking padlock still hanging on the entry door. "See?"

"Unlock it," McNulty said.

Kitty reached for the padlock. It fell apart in her hands. "Oh my word!" she exclaimed.

McNulty stepped forward and examined the metal pieces that had fallen onto the concrete paver path. The heavy duty lock had been cut clean through.

"I ... I secured the greenhouse before I left for my trip," Kitty stuttered. "I swear I did."

"Well, from the looks of it, someone *un*secured it," McNulty said.

He pushed on the door. As it slowly creaked open, a steamy blast of ultra-humid air walloped us like an ocean wave.

"I don't see any footprints inside," he said, turning to Kitty. "Shall we go in?"

"Yes, sir."

We all took a step toward the greenhouse. "Not you two," McNulty said to me and Aunt Edna. "Stay outside. But don't go anywhere." He turned back to Kitty. "Okay, Ms. Scientist. Which one is the machine eel?"

"Manchineel," Kitty said. "If you have a hard time pronouncing it, you can call it by its common name. Beach apple."

"Do you take me for some kind of simpleton?" McNulty asked.

"No sir!" Kitty said.

He shot her a sour look. "So which one is it?"

"That one." Kitty pointed to a small tree over in the back right corner.

I peered inside the eight-by-twelve greenhouse, craning for a look. Beyond the tables crammed with pots of herbs and orchids stood a small, scraggly looking tree with oval, yellowish-green leaves. If Charlie Brown was to ever have a tree named after him, this one would be it.

"That pathetic-looking thing is a deadly Manchineel?" McNulty asked.

"Yes." Kitty winced. "It may not look like much, but the *Hippomane mancinella* is considered to be the most toxic tree on Earth. If you don't believe me, check the *Guinness Book of World Records.*"

"I'll take your word for it." McNulty eyed the tree. "Does it appear to have been tampered with?"

Kitty studied the tree for a moment, then her jaw went slack. "Oh. My. Word."

"What is it?" McNulty asked.

"The tree was full of ripening fruit when I left on my trip. Now they're all gone!"

"I see," McNulty said. "Well isn't *that* interesting. Now, just who do you think would break into your greenhouse and take nothing except the fruit from an obscure tree nobody but you has ever heard of?"

"Could rats have eaten the fruit?" I called out from the doorframe, trying to be helpful.

"No." Kitty scanned the ground around the base of the tree. "At most, they would've nibbled one, died, and left the others."

"From what I hear, rats aren't good with bolt cutters, either," McNulty said sourly.

Kitty stared at the tree, then shook her head. "There were eleven fruits on it when I left. Now they're all gone."

"Eleven?" McNulty's eyes focused like lasers on Kitty. "That seems peculiarly precise. Did you have *plans* for these fruits, Ms. Corleone?"

"Uh ... not particularly. I just like to keep an accurate inventory."

"Why bother with an inventory unless you had plans?" McNulty asked. He shook his head. "I don't understand why you'd have such a deadly plant in your possession for no purpose whatsoever."

"For curiosity, I guess," Kitty said. "I love plants. Like I said. I'm a botanist. Or, I used to be."

"Humph." McNulty reached toward the tree.

"No!" Kitty cried out, swatting his hand away. "It's not just the fruit that's deadly. The sap is, too. Just touching the leaves or branches can inflame your skin. Even blister it."

"Is that so?" McNulty eyed Kitty carefully. "Well, then. Let me have a look at your hands."

"Whose hands?" I asked.

McNulty turned to face me. "All three of you."

My nose crinkled. "What for?"

"Don't play dumb, Diller." McNulty turned back to Kitty. "You said it yourself. You believe this plant was used to murder someone. If that's true, I need to know who handled it. Now show me your hands."

"But—" I started to object.

"Or should I come back with a warrant and charge you all with conspiracy to commit murder?"

I wilted. "No, sir."

Aunt Edna held up her hands like she was about to be arrested. McNulty gave them a cursory scan. "You're clean."

"See?" Kitty said. "We're not—"

"Not so fast." McNulty grabbed Kitty's right hand and held it up. "What have we here?"

I gulped. I already knew what he'd found. A blister on her index finger. The burn Kitty told us she'd gotten from her Bunsen burner.

Crap.

It wasn't looking good for Kitty. I hung my head for her. As I did, I caught a glimpse of my own hands. The skin between my right index finger and middle finger had turned red. And rising up from the inflamed area was the pale, circular, unmistakable form of ... a blister.

You've got to be kidding me.

Chapter Forty-Three

Something was desperately wrong with my life.

Instead of being recognized as a fancy VIP customer at fine dining establishments and posh day spas, I'd just been clocked as a repeat offender at the police station—by none other than Shirley Saurwein, ruthless busybody reporter for the *Beach Gazette*.

"Back again so soon?" she cackled, cracking gum between her bright-red lips. She looked me up and down as McNulty herded me across the lobby. "Oh, wait," she called out. "Don't tell me. Another fashion crime?"

As Saurwein's hideous laughter echoed off the industrial-green walls of the police station lobby, I knew what awaited me—and it wasn't a gourmet meal or an aromatherapy massage.

Not even close.

Soon, I'd be sitting in a small, stark room with no windows, feeling like a mongrel mutt at a kill shelter. Geez. At least this time I had litter mates. McNulty had hauled in everyone who had blisters on their fingers. That included Kitty, me, and, oddly, Jackie Cooperelli as well.

"Okay, ladies," McNulty said as we took positions around a metal table in a windowless room that might've once been a storage closet. "After seeing the Manchineel tree myself, I'm of a mind to believe it would take a trained botanist to even *identify* the plant, much less be aware of its deadly potential."

The cop's eyes narrowed in on Kitty. "And you just happen to be one. Isn't that correct Ms. Corleone?"

Kitty swallowed hard. "Yes."

McNulty's eyes narrowed even further on the petite woman in pink. "And you just happen to have all the symptoms of Manchineel poisoning on the tip of your tongue *and* your fingers. My, my. That seems like quite the coincidence."

"It's not like that," I said, coming to Kitty's defense. "We were just discussing different kinds of poisons over lunch."

McNulty's eyebrows rose a notch. His attention diverted to me. "And why would *poison* be a topic of lunchtime conversation?"

I grimaced. "Because we've been trying to figure out if someone tried to poison Sophia while she was at Shady Respite."

"Sophia?" McNulty said. "Does she have a last name?"

"Lorenzo," Kitty said.

McNulty eyed us with suspicion. "I'm investigating the deaths of Charles McDaniels, Ernest Jones, and Fred Sanderling. What's this Sophia Lorenzo woman got to do with it?"

"Uh ...," Kitty fumbled. "Freddy was a friend of hers while she was at Shady Respite."

"That's right," I said, nodding perhaps a bit too eagerly.

"And her taste-tester, too," Jackie added, causing Kitty and me to wilt.

McNulty's left eyebrow arched into a triangle. "Taste-tester?"

"Yeah," Jackie said. "You see, Sophia's our Quee—"

"Quickly about to turn a hundred years old," Kitty blurted over Jackie. "On Tuesday. That's why we've been ... uh ... diligently trying to make sure she ... *stays healthy*. We didn't want her to get food poisoning while she was in Shady Respite recovering from a fractured hip."

McNulty's eyes shifted between us. "I don't follow."

Kitty shot him a beaming smile. "It's kind of silly, you see. While Sophia was there, someone kept delivering sweets to her. She's pre-diabetic. So she gave the treats away to her friends there. She jokingly called them her taste-testers."

"Uh-huh," McNulty grunted. "And now the taste-tester named Freddy Sanderling is dead."

"And Charlie and Ernie, too," Jackie said, nodding cheerfully.

McNulty's eyes grew wide. "Are you saying *all three* men who died were Mrs. Lorenzo's taste-testers?"

I grimaced.

We are now.

Kitty cocked her head innocently. "Gee. I guess so, now that you mention it."

McNulty frowned. "Apparently *somebody* had to." He glared at each of us in turn. "But sugar intake alone doesn't usually kill someone."

"I know, right?" Jackie said. "That's why we think they were poisoned."

"Poisoned," McNulty repeated. "By the fruit of a Manchineel tree."

"Yes." Kitty's jawline tensed. "But there's no way to prove it in the case of Charlie and Ernie. They've both been cremated."

"Another convenient fact you strangely seem to know all about." McNulty crossed his arms and glared at Kitty. "I'm advising you that anything you say from here on out can be used against you."

Kitty blanched. "Are we under arrest?"

"No. Not yet." McNulty uncrossed his arms. "But what you've told me so far has done nothing to exonerate you and *everything* to incriminate you."

"We're just trying to be helpful," I said. "We want to catch who did this just like you do."

McNulty shot me a dubious look. "If that's true, then I need you all to be completely honest with me. Now, before anyone says another word, let me remind you that lying to a police officer is tantamount to perjury."

"Yes sir," the three of us said.

"Okay, then." McNulty turned to Kitty. "You said handling any part of the Manchineel causes skin irritation, correct?"

Kitty nodded. "Yes."

"Then explain to me how the three of you came to have blisters on your fingers."

"I must've gotten mine handling the poisoned lemon bars," Kitty explained. "There must've been a hole in my rubber gloves."

"So you admit to making the lemon bars?" McNulty asked.

Kitty's eyes grew wide. "No! I ..."

"I gave her the bars," I said. "I got them from Sophia's room at Shady Respite. Kitty was just testing them in her ...uh—"

"I was preparing samples to send away for testing," Kitty said, picking up where I'd trailed off. "That's when I got the hole in my glove."

"Right." McNulty turned to Jackie. "And you, Ms. Cooperelli?"

"I didn't use no gloves when I handled them," Jackie said.

Kitty gasped. "You handled them?"

Jackie smiled sheepishly. "I couldn't help myself. I reached into the bag and squeezed one before I gave them to you."

Kitty shook her head. "Why?"

Jackie shrugged. "I dunno. I'm Italian. I guess I just wanted to see if they were as moist as the ones my mama used to make."

McNulty blew out a breath and shook his head. "Enough already." He turned to me. "And you, Ms. Diller? How did *your* fingers come to be blistered?"

I grimaced and glanced at the small pustules forming on the red skin between my fingers. Had I gotten contaminated while prying open Freddy's jaws in the morgue? If so, how the heck was I going to explain *that*? Talk about incriminating myself!

"Uh ... I have no idea," I said.

"I see." McNulty scribbled on his notepad. I could tell by the gleam in his eye that whatever he wrote down was most definitely *not* in my favor.

He looked up from his notepad. "So let me get this straight. Your 'friend' Sophia Lorenzo was at Shady Respite recovering from a fractured hip. While she was there, three men designated as her 'taste testers' died, while she remained in good health."

Kitty nodded. "That's right."

"That doesn't make sense," McNulty said. "Why would you all take it upon yourselves to investigate the cause of three strangers' deaths?"

"To find out if somebody's trying to bump off Sophia," Jackie blurted. "And then figure out who the dirty bird is."

"That's why I was testing the lemon bars for poison," Kitty said, pressing her shoe down softly on my foot. "You know, with *one of those kits you can get at the drugstore*."

"I see," McNulty said. "And?"

"The initial results were inconclusive. But now that I know what to look for, I can run a test specifically for Manchineel poisoning."

McNulty's eyes narrowed on Kitty. "And exactly how are you—"

"Uh, I'm sorry, but I really need to pee," Kitty said. "My bladder isn't what it used to be. If I don't go soon, it could get ugly in here."

McNulty grimaced. "Go ahead."

"Uh, mister officer?" Jackie said, raising her hand. "Me, too."

He blew out a breath. "Fine. Go."

I got up to join them.

"Not so fast," McNulty said. "I have a couple of questions for you."

I gulped and watched the two women disappear out the door. "What kind of questions?"

He shook his head as if in disbelief. "Like, who are these people? And how in the world did you get tangled up in a mess like this again?"

Because the Universe hates me?

"I was staying at my Aunt Edna's place while we sorted out the Tad Longmire case," I said. "Sophia and these two women are just little old ladies who live in my aunt's apartment complex."

"What's their relationship with Ms. Lorenzo?" McNulty asked.

"Friends. They all are. Just a bunch of unrelated women taking care of each other. You know, like the *Golden Girls*."

"I don't recall an episode where the *Golden Girls* poisoned people."

"Well, that's exactly my point. They didn't. I'm pretty sure of it. I honestly think it had to be somebody not in the Family."

"The *Family*?" McNulty's eyes locked like lasers on mine.

Crap!

"You know, the little family unit they cobbled together."

McNulty studied me. "I see. Why should I believe you, Diller? Your fingers are just as blistered as theirs."

"Why shouldn't you? I proved I was innocent of Tad's murder, didn't I?"

McNulty shrugged. "Yes, I suppose so. But—"

"So, can *I* go use the john now?"

"Yes. But hurry up."

***

I scurried to the ladies room to confer with Kitty and Jackie on what our next move was. But when I burst through the door, nobody was there.

"Hello?" I called out. My voice echoed off the empty stalls.

Have I just been ditched and left holding a bag of poison beach apples?

I slunk back out to the lobby. It was empty, too, except for Shirley Saurwein. Through the glass exit door, I saw a flash of green go by. I ran over and flung the door open—just in time to see Jackie's Kia speeding off down the road.

My heart sank.

So much for Family loyalty.

"What's the matter, Diller?" Saurwein said. "You look like you just lost your best friend."

I scratched the itchy red blisters welling up on my hand.

Even worse. I just lost my only alibi.

Chapter Forty-Four

I slunk back to the ladies room and sat in a stall for as long as I could, waiting for the huge lump in my throat to go down. I'd just been hung out to dry by the Collard Green Cosa Nostra.

Bamboozled by a bunch of old ladies.

What an idiot I am!

Wait a minute. If they plan on throwing me under the bus, why not beat them to the punch?

After all, Kitty was a more likely suspect than me. I could tell McNulty about her secret lab. And how I'd seen her messing around in the courtyard early this morning. What had she really been doing there? She never let me into her greenhouse. She could've been in there taking those beach apples herself—to cover her tracks!

I stood up and reached for the stall handle, then had a change of heart.

If I turned her in, I'll be a rat just like Humpty Bogart.

I thought back to that day in the bakery, and recalled the disgust on the faces of Aunt Edna and Jackie when he'd come through the door. Was that what I wanted for my future?

I heard the main door to the bathroom open.

"Hey, Diller," McNulty called out. "You die in there or something?"

"Uh ... no. Just constipated."

"Well, hurry it up!"

"I will," I said. Then I flushed the rest of my self-esteem away and resigned myself to my fate.

***

After stalling another ten minutes in the bathroom, I gave up and poked my head back inside McNulty's interrogation room.

"It's about time," he said, glancing at his watch. "Where are the others?"

"Uh ... I'm afraid—"

The doorknob to the interrogation room jiggled. Kitty came bursting in.

I nearly gasped as my heart fluttered back to life.

"Sorry I'm late," Kitty said. "Jackie crapped her pants. I had to take her home so she could—"

"Spare us the details," McNulty said. "Is she here?"

"No. I took a taxi back. I don't drive."

"Right," McNulty said sourly. "You should be glad I didn't send some officers out to apprehend you."

"Your officers are the ones who should be glad," Kitty said. "If they'd seen Jackie's backside they'd have been scarred for life. Worst case of diarrhea I've ever seen. I gave her some—"

McNulty cringed. "Like I said, spare us the details. *Please.*"

"Of course," Kitty cooed. "Anyway, good news! When we got home, I found out the lab results on the lemon bars had arrived."

"Really." McNulty's face pinched with suspicion. "Show me the report."

"Sure thing. I got it right here." Kitty began digging around in her giant purse. "According to the lab, the test came back positive for Eserine."

"Eserine?" McNulty said. "I've never heard of it."

"Neither had I," Kitty said, still rifling through her huge purse. "I had to Google search it. Come to find out, there's only two naturally-occurring sources of Eserine. The Calabar bean, and the fruit of the Manchineel tree."

"Interesting," McNulty said.

"Sure is." Kitty looked up from her purse and shot me a surreptitious wink.

"What about this Calabar bean option?" McNulty asked.

"Unlikely," Kitty said. "It only grows in West Africa."

McNulty's hard face softened a notch. "And you believe Eserine is the poison used in the lemon bars."

"I *know* it," Kitty said. "Based on the test results. It's a done deal. The Manchineel is to blame."

"It's not the Manchineel that's to blame," McNulty said. "It's whoever used it to poison the victims with."

"Yes, sir," Kitty said. "That's what I meant."

I glanced at the fiery red blisters swelling up on my hand. They were really itching now. "Uh ... Kitty? We're not gonna die from touching it, are we?"

Kitty shook her head. "No. You need a pretty hefty *internal* dose for Manchineel poisoning for it to be deadly. We'll be fine with a little topical steroid cream. But elderly people like Freddy and Sophia most likely wouldn't survive a major ingestion."

McNulty cleared his throat. "Ms. Corleone, you seem to know an awful lot about the Manchineel."

"Nothing you can't find on an internet search."

"Fair enough," McNulty said. "You told us the symptoms of Manchineel poisoning are a sweet taste, followed by peppery, then by blistering of the throat."

"That's exactly right," Kitty said. "You're a great listener!"

"Uh-huh. So tell me, how did you know Freddy Sanderling's throat was blistered?"

"Uh ... lucky guess?" Kitty said, barely missing a beat. "It's a natural progression of the—"

"We went to the morgue at Shady Respite and examined his body," I said.

McNulty's shoulders straightened. "So I shouldn't be surprised to find your DNA on his body, then. That makes for quite a convenient excuse, now doesn't it?"

"Seriously?" My jaw tightened. "We're trying to be *helpful* here, and all you're doing is trying to trip us up, like we're guilty already. Well, how's *this* for convenient? How *convenient* is it that you should get an *anonymous* tip about us being murderers?"

"Well," McNulty said. "I can't—"

I crossed my arms. "I bet it was from an old lady, right?"

McNulty's eyes widened a notch. He sat up straight. "Like I said, it was anonym—"

"And I bet her name was Gloria."

McNulty's eyebrows rose an inch. "How could you possibly know that?"

"Gloria Martinelli is a patient at Shady Respite." I blew out a breath. "The woman is nuts. She saw me on that stupid TV show where I stabbed Tad Longmire." I shook my head. "She keeps calling me a murderer every time I go over there."

"So you admit you've been to Shady Respite numerous times," McNulty said.

The saddle on my high horse slipped. I grimaced. "Uh ... yes."

"We *all* have," Kitty said, patting me on the shoulder. "To visit Sophia."

I stuck my chin in the air. "That's right. Visiting the sick isn't a crime, is it?"

"No," McNulty said. "But only *one* of you has been suspected of murder *twice* in the last two weeks." He turned his laser glare toward me. "Since you arrived in town, Ms. Diller, people seem to be dropping like flies."

"What?" I shrunk back. "Why in the world would I want to kill some old guys at a nursing home?"

"And *I* might ask why you'd want to sneak into a nursing home morgue?" McNulty fired back. "To relive the thrill of killing your victims?"

"What? Gross!" Anger boiled up inside me. "Look. I wasn't even *in town* when the other two guys died."

"That's right!" Kitty said.

McNulty leaned forward. "So, Diller, your accomplices killed the first two men, providing you with an alibi. Then you returned the favor."

"Dream on!" I hissed. "That's insane!"

"She's telling the truth," Kitty said. "Doreen only went to the morgue because I asked her to accompany me."

McNulty's eagle-eyed glare shifted to Kitty. "If you had suspicions about Mr. Sanderling's death, why take the matter into your own hands? Why didn't you simply check with the attending physician?"

"I *did*," Kitty said. "His name is Dr. Mancini. When I asked him about how Mr. Sanderling died, the guy didn't seem concerned about foul play in the slightest. I might add that it was Dr. Mancini who ruled all three men's deaths to be from natural causes."

"People die of natural causes all the time," McNulty said. "Why didn't you take his word for it?"

"Maybe the first two I could chalk up to what you said, that people, you know, kick off from natural causes all the time." Kitty shook her head. "But when the third guy, Freddy died, I couldn't just sweep it under the rug."

McNulty frowned. "So you went and looked under the sheets instead."

Kitty nodded solemnly. "In a manner of speaking, yes. It may have been unorthodox, I'll give you that. But what we did proved that Freddy Sanderling was murdered. And, if you ask me, Dr. Mancini is either negligent or incompetent."

"Or complicit," McNulty said.

"Yes, or that, too."

McNulty rubbed his chin and stared at the table for a moment. When he glanced up at us again, the accusatory look in his eyes had faded a bit. "What did the coroner's report say? I assume you got your hands on a copy of that, too?"

"No," Kitty said. "Dr. Mancini didn't order an autopsy."

McNulty nearly blanched. "No?"

Kitty shook her head. "Look. Whether the doctor is in on the deaths or not, I don't exactly have the authority to demand an autopsy on Mr. Sanderling. But *you* do."

"Believe it or not, we're on the same side as you," I said to McNulty. "We want to know who killed Freddy and the other two men just as badly as you do."

"Okay. Fair enough," McNulty said. "But I'll need more facts before I upset Sanderling's family with the news he may have been murdered."

"An autopsy would give you those facts," Kitty said.

McNulty nodded. "Agreed."

"Then you better hurry," I said. "Because Dr. Mancini is having Freddy's body shipped to Neil Mansion today for cremation. Probably as we speak."

McNulty's eyebrow angled. "How do you know that?"

"He told us so himself," Kitty said. "A couple of hours ago. Right before we examined Freddy's body."

"Without his permission, I assume?" McNulty said.

"He would never have given it," Kitty said. "What choice did I have?"

"Wait here." McNulty jumped to his feet. "I need to make a phone call."

Chapter Forty-Five

"It's too late," McNulty said, returning to the interrogation room. "Sanderling's body is already being cremated."

"Talk about *convenient*," I quipped. "That Neil Mansion crew sure didn't waste any time."

"You think the funeral home might be in on it?" McNulty asked.

"I don't know." I frowned. "But it makes me wonder. Why would they be in such a hurry to get rid of the body?"

McNulty sighed. "It's summer. In Florida. Do the math."

I did. And it added up to *gross*!

"Do any of you own a pair of bolt cutters?" McNulty asked.

"No." Kitty shot me a smirk. "But Doreen told me she used a pair to clip a guy's toenails back in L.A."

I shook my head. "Why do you ask?"

McNulty formed a temple with his fingers. "Someone would've needed a pair to cut through the padlock on the greenhouse."

I blanched. "Are you really back to focusing on *us* again?"

McNulty closed his eyes for a moment. "Okay. Let's put a pin in that for a moment."

"Yeah, let's," I grumbled.

"You seem to have done a lot of homework on this case already," McNulty said. "What other facts or evidence have you ladies ... ahem ... *assembled*?"

"These." Kitty reached into her purse and pulled out a baggie with the tubes containing the long-stemmed cotton swabs. "I used these to take samples from Freddy's throat this morning."

McNulty took the baggie, then frowned at its contents. "We can't use them."

"Why not?" Kitty asked.

"Because the chain of evidence collection can't be confirmed," he said. "The samples could've come from anywhere. You could have altered them." He shook his head. "If you'd called the police instead of taking matters into your own hands—"

"We wouldn't have any samples at all," I said.

"Maybe," McNulty admitted. "What else have you got?"

I glanced at Kitty. "I know! Sophia's description of the guy who delivered the lemon bars to her room at Shady Respite."

"That's right," Kitty said. "Sophia told us the man wore a hoodie and spoke in a gravelly, English accent."

"Not great, but it's something to go on," McNulty said.

"Maybe, maybe not," I argued. "Anybody can fake an English accent." I straightened my shoulders, lowered my voice, and gave it a try. "Well blimey, fancy a pint at the pub?"

McNulty shook his head. "You know that's not helping your case, don't you?"

I cringed.

"Okay," McNulty said. "Let's say Freddy Sanderling was poisoned, possibly even accidently while serving as Sophia Lorenzo's taste-tester. What I want to know now is why someone would want to kill an old woman with a fractured hip in the first place?"

I gulped.

Uh ... because she's a mafia Queenpin?

Before I could think of an answer, Kitty stepped up to the plate.

"Have you ever met Sophia?" she asked. "As they say, to know her is to loathe her."

McNulty smiled cruelly. "Okay, then. We're finally getting somewhere."

"What do you mean?" Kitty asked.

"You just supplied me with your motive to poison her."

***

After delivering his bombshell, McNulty left the interrogation room and locked the door behind him.

"Geez, Kitty," I said. "If loose lips sink ships, Jackie would be the lead singer on the Titanic. She practically told him about the Family and everything! Why would she do that?"

"What can I say? Jackie's brain is wired different from the rest of us."

"You mean that whole photographic memory thing?"

"Well, yes, partly. But there's more to it than that. Jackie is ... sort of incapable of abstract thought."

"What do you mean?"

"She can't bend reality to suit her own perceptions, like the rest of us. That's what gives Jackie her clear sight, I think." She let out a sigh. "It also means she can't lie. Depending on the situation, that can be her biggest strength *or* her biggest weakness."

I blew out a breath. "You aren't kidding."

Kitty shook her head. "You saw for yourself, you definitely don't want Jackie in an interrogation room, even if she's on your side. That's why I begged off and took her back home—that, and to get the test sample results."

"So you weren't just making up the Eserine results?"

"No. Why would you think so?"

"You never gave McNulty anything to substantiate the results."

Kitty smiled. "You noticed."

"Yes."

"*And* you kept your mouth shut." Kitty grinned and patted me on the back. "You know what, Doreen? You just might contain a little bit of the best of all of us."

"Really?" I glanced at the growing red patch on my hand. "I finally do something right, and now I'm going to die."

Kitty laughed. "What are you talking about?"

"My hand. I somehow got poisoned when I pried open Freddy's mouth."

"Let me see that." Kitty grabbed my hand. "You didn't happen to touch that poison ivy I showed you in the garden, did you?"

I grimaced. "Uh ... maybe."

"Uh-huh," Kitty grunted. "Thought so. You didn't touch anything *else* with that hand, I hope."

I shrugged. "No. Only my fork and glass at lunch."

"What about during the restroom break? You wipe with your left hand or right?"

"Uh ... right."

Oh no.

Either it was a case of perfect timing—or the power of suggestion took hold—but at that very second, my butt-crack began to itch.

I cringed. "What do I—"

The door flew open.

McNulty came in.

I couldn't help but notice he was carrying two pairs of handcuffs.

Chapter Forty-Six

I raced out into the lobby of the police station. It wasn't exactly a clean getaway. But like choosing the least-stained shirt in a pile of dirty clothes, it was the best I could do on short notice.

"Over here," Jackie called out.

She and Aunt Edna were loitering close to the exit door, as if they feared going into the station any further might seal their fate, too. I'd never been so glad to see two women's faces in my entire life.

"Coming!" I yelled.

"Hey!" a woman's voice rang out, interrupting my beeline toward my aunt and Jackie. I turned to see a too-tanned, too-blonde woman come rushing out of a hallway.

"Well, if it isn't the fugitive from justice," Shirley Saurwein said. "Did they let you go, or are you making a prison break?" She turned to Jackie and winked. "Oh, and thanks for the tip, doll. I'll see you all at the soiree on Tuesday."

I sneered at Shirley. "What are you talking about?"

Shirley's red lips twisted into an evil grin. "Didn't you know? I'll be covering Sophia Lorenzo's hundredth birthday party for the *Beach Gazette*." She looked me up and down. "Let me guess. You'll be wearing an orange jumpsuit?"

Crap!

"Come on," Aunt Edna said. "Let's get outta here."

I shoved open the door and followed them toward the parking lot. "Looks like Jackie's loose lips sank another ship," I grumbled.

My aunt eyed me funny. "What do you mean by that?"

"She told McNulty way too much."

"She's right," Jackie said, hanging her head. "Sorry."

"Hey, nobody's perfect." Aunt Edna stopped in her tracks and locked eyes with me. "But that don't mean they got no worth, Dorey. Don't you ever forget that."

I scoffed. "Tell that to my Ma."

"No. I'm telling it to *you*." Aunt Edna put her hands on my shoulders. "I don't know what Maureen taught you, or what you learned from all those schmucks in Hollywood. But around here, we don't slit each other's throats over some tiny mistakes."

I winced. "I didn't mean—"

Aunt Edna moved one hand to Jackie's shoulder. "Jackie here may be a blabbermouth, but I'll give her this—she's who you want to have around if you're in a crowd full of strangers."

My nose crinkled. "What do you mean?"

"Who needs Benny the pug?" Aunt Edna said, smiling at Jackie. "She's the *real* genius when it comes to sniffing out deadbeats. Ain't that right?"

Jackie shrugged, her usual perky smile beginning to curl her lips again. "Yeah, I guess so."

"Wait a minute," I said. "When you had Benny sniff me up and down after interrogating me, what was that? A sick joke?"

Jackie smirked. "Sort of. Hey, after we found out you was legit, I kinda felt like the situation called for some comic relief, you know? Anyway, I had Benny do it to make her feel useful. We all need to feel like we've got a purpose in life, right? Even mutts like Benny."

My heart pinged. "Sure."

"What about *your* lips, Dorey?" Aunt Edna said. "How'd you beat the rap when Kitty didn't? You didn't rat us out, did you?"

"No, ma'am. Kitty got me off. She explained the blisters on my hand were from poison ivy. She convinced McNulty to let me go."

"Just like that?" Aunt Edna eyed me funny. "That don't sound right."

"No," I said. "She also confessed that she was the most likely suspect and turned herself in. For desecrating a corpse."

"What?" Aunt Edna screeched.

"She took one for the team," I said. "So I could go free."

"So, I gotta know," Aunt Edna said. "You playing for our side, Dorey?"

I nodded. "Yes, ma'am."

"Good. Because up to now, I wasn't a hundred percent sure."

I grimaced.

Neither was I.

"All right then. Now, let's get to work." Aunt Edna turned and began marching toward the Kia, muttering and shaking her head. "Kitty's in the slammer and Sophia's about to turn a hundred tomorrow. I don't know which disaster to start plugging the holes in first."

"I do," I said. "Let's go back to Shady Respite."

"What for?" Jackie asked.

"To collect Sophia's things." I smiled coyly. "And to do a little bit of housekeeping of our own."

Chapter Forty-Seven

"Does McNutsack really think we're trying to kill our own Queenpin?" Aunt Edna asked as we pulled away from the front of the police station in the rusty green Kia.

"Pretty sure, and I can't blame him," I said, adjusting the driver's seat. "The blisters on our hands might as well have been blood stains."

Aunt Edna groaned. "Aye aye aye."

"But don't get too worried," I said. "I don't think things look all that bad for Kitty."

"How do you figure that?" Jackie asked.

I gripped the steering wheel tighter in an attempt to fight the urge to scratch myself in private places. Kitty had been right. In the bathroom, I'd used my right hand to wipe myself. And now it was coming back to haunt me in all the wrong places.

"Uh," I said, squirming in my seat. "It seemed to me like McNutsack ... McNulty ... was starting to come around to our idea that Dr. Mancini from Shady Respite could be involved in the whole scheme, and is covering up Freddy's death along with the other guys."

Aunt Edna shook her head. "If that's the case, we gotta prove motive. Why would Mancini want to kill Sophia? It don't make sense to me."

"I don't know," I said. "The guy's got the bedside manner of a baboon. Maybe he's got a deal worked out with Neil Mansion funeral home."

"You mean like a 'kickbacks for stiffs' kind of scheme?" Jackie asked from the backseat.

"Why not?" I said. "Neil Neil told me the basic funeral package at his place costs over fifteen grand."

"Sheesh," Jackie said. "That's a lot a dough per capital head."

"You aren't kidding," Aunt Edna said. "I'm in the wrong line of work."

Jackie reached up from the backseat and patted her shoulder. "No you ain't, Edna. I hear it's a dying business."

I groaned. "Sophia said she thought Shady Respite had a conveyor belt running from the cafeteria to the morgue. What if she's right?"

"What?" Aunt Edna said. "No way. Sophia was just being sarcastic. This ain't no *Soylent Green* situation."

"I don't mean it *literally*," I said. "When Kitty and I were there this morning we didn't see an actual *conveyor belt*. But the elevator opened up right in front of both the cafeteria and the morgue, making it only steps to move a body back and forth to the two locations."

"Hold on a second," Jackie said. "If Neil Mansion *is* in on this poisoning scheme with Dr. Mancini, why would they bother with Sophia?"

"For the money," I said. "Fifteen grand a head. I thought I just explained that."

"You did," Aunt Edna said. "But you forgot one thing, Dorey. Sophia's funeral is already paid for."

"That's right," Jackie said. "There ain't no loot in it for them. When Sophia dies, it'll cost Neil Mansion out of their coffins. Right Edna?"

"*Coffers*, but yeah," Aunt Edna said. "But that don't rule out Dr. Mancini."

"It don't?" Jackie asked. "Why would he want to murder her then?"

"Not to reduce his workload," I said. "He'd just get new patients to replace them."

"True enough," Aunt Edna said. "But it still don't rule him out."

"Why not?"

Aunt Edna turned and locked eyes with me. "Because, Dorey. Maybe Mancini is one of those creeps who gets his jollies killing people. You know. The way some people like collecting poisonous plants. Or sniffing out deadbeats. Or pretending to be an actress."

Wait a minute ... ouch.

***

"Should I wait in the car, in case we need to make a quick getaway from Gloria and her deadly acorns?" Jackie quipped as we pulled up to Shady Respite convalescent center.

"Good one," Aunt Edna said. "But no. We go in strong. We go in together."

"Let's make this quick," I said, climbing out of car. "Afterward, I need to stop at a pharmacy. My fingers are itching like mad."

"Itchy fingers, eh?" Jackie smirked. "You got a desire to steal something, Dorey?"

"Huh?"

"Old wives' tale," Aunt Edna said. "Not this time, Jackie. I'm pretty sure it's just the poison ivy."

"If you say so," Jackie said.

"Here." Aunt Edna handed me a pink bottle. "It's calamine lotion. Try it."

I put some on my fingers. The relief was instant. "Thanks."

Aunt Edna reached over to take the bottle back. I resisted. "Uh ... mind if I hold onto it? In case the itch comes back?"

She shrugged. "Sure. Now, let's roll."

***

Thankfully, the receptionist who'd caved to Kitty's extortion routine this morning wasn't the same one working the desk when we went back in. It was the harried Ms. Rodriguez. She seemed in a perpetual state of dishevelment.

"Excuse me," I said. "We're here to pick up the personal belongings of Sophia Lorenzo. She was ... um ... *discharged* yesterday?"

Jackie laughed. "That's one way to put it."

Rodriquez let out a huge sigh and dug through a plastic tub full of boxes and envelopes. "Hmm. I don't see anything here with that name."

"Look again," Aunt Edna said.

"I'm sorry," Rodriquez said. "But we've had a rash of things go missing lately."

Jackie glanced at my hand. "Who would want to steal a rash?"

"I understand," I said to the receptionist, and shot her my best smile. "Could you please tell us who was working the late shift on Saturday and Sunday?"

"Sorry," Rodriquez said and picked at a yellow stain on her scrubs. "We don't release employee records."

Aunt Edna huffed. "Well, that's a bust."

"No it ain't," Jackie said. "That glob of mustard's on a fat roll, not a boob."

"Excuse me?" Rodriguez said, glaring at us.

"Nothing." I herded the women away from the window. I'd considered putting up more of a fight with the receptionist, like Kitty would have. But, unfortunately, I had an even more pressing matter to attend to.

"Um...I need to use the ladies room," I said. "Wait here. I'll be right back."

Before they could reply, I sprinted down the hall. My lady parts were itching like mad. I slipped into the bathroom, yanked open a stall and slammed it behind me. The only thing on my mind at the moment was covering my private areas with the calamine lotion I'd stashed in my purse.

As I pulled down my pants and twisted off the bottle cap, the main door to the bathroom opened. A strange tapping sound traced along the floor. It grew nearer and nearer. Then it stopped right in front of my stall.

Perfect.

Quickly, I poured some lotion onto a wad of tissue, then assumed the position to wipe myself. Just before I reached my fanny, I froze. From under the stall door I spotted the pointed end of a purple umbrella.

Gloria! You've got to be kidding me!

Beside the umbrella tip were two sets of feet. One was clad in squeaky red loafers. The other one wore ugly, beige orthopedic shoes. I held my breath, afraid to move, even though it felt as if I were hosting a flea convention between my thighs.

Suddenly, one of the women spoke.

"Why don't you just do like the doctor said?"

"And look like a weak, old woman?" Gloria said. "No, way."

"You'd have gotten out of here sooner if you'd just done what you were told."

"Humph," Gloria grunted. "I did what he asked me to do, okay? It's not my fault if it didn't work."

"Well, I'll tell you this. He isn't happy one bit about the delay. I'm not sure how much longer I can keep—"

"Do you smell calamine lotion?" Gloria asked.

I froze mid-wipe. A millisecond later, my stall door flew open like it had been kicked by a mule.

"You!" Gloria yelled.

"Who?" the other lady asked. I couldn't see her face, and I prayed she couldn't see my fanny.

"It's *her*!" Gloria screeched at the other woman. "The one I told you about. The one who's trying to murder me!"

"It was a TV show!" I squealed, yanking up my drawers. I covered my head with my arm and dodged the swing of Gloria's umbrella.

"Come back here!" she yelled as I squeezed past her and scrambled out the bathroom door.

Still hitching up my jeans, I made a mad dash down the corridor. As I rounded the corner, I almost slammed into Jackie and Aunt Edna.

"What's going on?" Jackie asked.

"Hurry," I yelled. "Crazy Gloria is after me again!"

"Geez," Jackie said. "That woman needs a hobby, if you ask me."

***

The old Kia bounced like a squeaky balloon house as the three of us scrambled inside and slammed the doors.

"Here, hold this," Aunt Edna said, shoving the brown bag into my lap. "I need a Tums."

"What's this?" I asked.

"Sophia's cherished possessions," she said sourly. "That ditzy receptionist found them after all."

As my aunt fished through her purse, I took a peek inside the bag. "A ratty bathrobe and worn-out slippers? I risked my life for *these*?"

"Hey," Jackie said. "When you reach a certain age, a soft robe and a comfy pair of shoes are worth more than all the teak in China. Am I right, Edna?"

Edna shrugged. "Jackie makes a good point. Now drive, Dorey. Before Gloria makes it rain again with those blasted acorns of hers."

Chapter Forty-Eight

We were halfway back to Palm Court Cottages when Jackie discovered a piece of paper in the pocket of Sophia's well-worn fuzzy bathrobe.

"What's this?" she asked, waving the paper at us from the backseat.

"Lemme see that." Aunt Edna grabbed the paper. "It's a list of people Sophia wanted to invite to her party."

I stopped the Kia at a red light and glanced over at the paper. "If that's the case, I see *I* didn't make the cut."

"Sophia made this before she knew about you," my aunt said. "You're definitely invited, kid."

"Thanks," I deadpanned. "Seems like a short list for such a big party."

"What else could it be?" Jackie asked. "It sure ain't no shopping list."

A thought hit me. "What about a list of *suspects*? You know, people she thought were trying to poison her?"

Aunt Edna's brow furrowed. She studied the list again. "Morty?" She shook her head. "We know it ain't him."

I glanced over at my aunt. "Just because you went out with him doesn't get him off the hook."

Aunt Edna glared at me. "It ain't him. Capeesh?"

I glanced down at the list. "Humpty Bogart is on here. Why would she invite him to her party if she doesn't like him?"

"This party ain't no popularity contest," Aunt Edna said. "It's about paying your respects. With gifts. Sophia likes gifts. And with most of the people she knows dead or dropping like flies, she's not in a position to be choosy."

I shrugged. "Fine. Who's Victor Ventura?"

Aunt Edna snorted. "Victor the Vulture. Clean-up man. You need to make a body disappear, he's your guy."

My upper lip snarled. "I'll keep that in mind."

"You do that," my aunt said.

"What about Dr. Mancini?" I pointed to the name on the list. "Why would she invite *him*?"

"Who has more money to buy her a nice gift than a doctor?" Jackie asked.

"Plus, she likes him," Aunt Edna said.

I frowned. "What about that last guy, Gordon?"

"Never heard of him," Aunt Edna said.

A horn honked. The light was green. I hit the gas.

As we traveled along, I thought about the names on the list. I kept coming back to Morty. What if he and Humpty really *did* have some kind of scheme going on together? Morty used to go out with Aunt Edna, so surely he'd have known about Kitty's greenhouse. And it would be super easy for him to bake the poison Manchineel apples into a dessert.

Easy as pie.

I glanced over at Aunt Edna. She was still staring at the list. Should I bring up Morty again? Why was she so touchy about him? I suspected it was because she was still in love with him. If that was the case, she'd just make more excuses for him.

"Look," I said. "If that *is* a list of people trying to kill Sophia, don't you think we should get some professional help sorting them out?"

"You mean like hire our own hitman?" Jackie asked.

"No," I said. "Hire our own cop. Officer Brady."

Jackie's eyebrow arched. "Like put him on our payroll?"

"No." I shook my head. "Get him on our side. Sergeant McNulty sure isn't."

"Dorey's right," Aunt Edna said. "Call Brady. Have him meet us at home in an hour. In the meantime, we got one more stop to make along the way."

"Where?" I asked.

"Morty's bakery," Aunt Edna said. "I need to check on the cake for the party. Plus, I got a hankering for a fresh cannolo."

Huh. I wonder what that *means...*

***

"Delicious, as always," Aunt Edna said, finishing off the cannolo. "I'll take a dozen to go."

"No can do," Morty said from behind the pastry counter. "I snuck that one out of an order just for you."

"What order?" I asked.

"For the Neil Mansion." Morty wiped the glass-topped bakery case with a dishtowel. "I do a lot of their catering. That cannolo was headed for the Sanderling service."

"Fred Sanderling?" I glanced around the display case. I saw cookies, brownies, cupcakes, éclairs, and croissants. But no lemon bars. Maybe Aunt Edna wasn't just covering for him when she'd said he didn't make them anymore.

"Yeah," Morty said. "You know him?"

I frowned. "No. Do *you*?"

"Not a clue," he said.

"When's his service taking place?" Aunt Edna asked.

Morty glanced at a clock on the wall. "In about an hour. Why?"

My heart thumped in my chest. "Come on, ladies. We better get going."

"Right." Aunt Edna gave me a quick nod, then turned to Morty. "You got everything on track for Sophia's party tomorrow?"

"Absolutely. You don't got to worry about a thing. I got everything taken care of."

"Humph," Aunt Edna grunted. "That's what they all say."

It was like she'd read my mind.

Chapter Forty-Nine

It wasn't hard to convince Aunt Edna and Jackie to take a detour to the Neil Mansion to attend Freddy's memorial service. We were eager to check out the crowd for potential suspects.

As for me, I had a secondary agenda as well. I wanted to see if Morty just happened to make a few lemon bars for the service.

Aunt Edna had told me he didn't make them anymore. Maybe he didn't—for Sophia. But that didn't mean he couldn't be baking up "special" batches for "special" occasions. And who knows? Maybe Sophia broke up the love affair between Aunt Edna and him, and now he wanted his revenge.

On another note, I still hadn't ruled out the folks at the Neil Mansion, either ...

"Aunt Edna, I noticed Neil Neil wasn't on Sophia's list."

"Why would she invite an undertaker to her birthday bash?" she asked.

"What if Jackie's right and that's a list of suspects?" I nodded toward the slip of paper still in my aunt's hand. "Sophia would never suspect the funeral home of being in on killing her, would she?"

"What would be their motive?" Aunt Edna asked. "It don't make no sense. Sophia's funeral is already paid for."

I frowned. "I don't know."

As I drove along, I wracked my brain for the answer. During my frenzied attempt to investigate my boss Tad's death a few weeks ago, I'd learned some valuable lessons from Sergeant McNulty. The biggest one was to look for the motivation behind the crime.

McNulty's words rang in my head.

"In my line of work, murder motives usually fall into three categories—sex, drugs or money."

Given the age of the suspects involved, sex and drugs seemed off the table. Unless the drug was Viagra. The mere thought made my stomach churn.

No. It has to be the third thing.

Money.

O.M.G.

"What if Sophia wasn't the main target?" I said.

Aunt Edna turned and stared at me. "What are you talking about?"

"What if Neil Neil and Dr. Mancini are poisoning random people after getting them to sign up for funeral services? I'm pretty sure Neil's husband has a cleft chin."

"You don't say," Aunt Edna said. "That could make sense, Dorey."

"I don't know much about the suspects on Sophia's list," I said. "But I *do* have an inkling about who has the most to gain from old people dying."

"At fifteen grand a pop, the answer's pretty obvious," Jackie said. "Even to me."

Chapter Fifty

When the three of us walked up to the front door of the eggplant-colored Victorian house, I wasn't surprised to see Neil Neil standing at the entrance ready to greet us. I *was* surprised, however, to see him handing out business cards.

"You two go on inside," I said to Jackie and Aunt Edna. "Check out who showed up, and if anyone looks suspicious. I want to question Neil Neil."

"You got it," Aunt Edna said. She nodded her respects to Neil Neil as she passed by, tugging a gawking Jackie along with her into the funeral home.

"Busy drumming up business?" I asked.

Neil Neil looked down his nose at me. "Excuse me, but aren't you the woman who wanted me to put an old lady on layaway?"

I winced. "That was a misunderstanding."

"Either way, you're too late."

I gulped. "Too late?"

"Yes. I'm sold out of Settler's Rests."

"Oh. So, will your husband be attending?"

Neil practically blanched. "What? No. Not that it's any of your business."

"You're right. It's not." I offered him an apologetic smile. "Look. I'm sorry, Neil. We got off on the wrong foot. It's just that I saw a picture of your husband. He has very striking features."

Including a cleft chin, I think ...

"Oh. Thank you."

"So, where did you two meet? Is he *British*, per chance?"

"No," Neil said sourly. "And if you must know, he's getting his teeth fixed."

"What? I didn't mean—"

A car horn tooted. I turned to see a white van pull up in the parking lot. A sign on the side read *Shady Respite Courtesy Van.*

"Look at that," I said. "Isn't it nice of the folks at the convalescent center to come and see Freddy off?"

"Right," Neil said curtly. "Those old vultures are just here to gobble up the free food and coffee." He looked me in the eye. "Why exactly are *you* here?"

I smiled inside, pleased with myself for having already come up with a line just in case he asked. "I wanted to see what your customers get when they pay for 'the works.'"

"This service certainly isn't the works," he said. "But we do what we can with every budget."

I nodded and smiled. "Good to know."

Neil glanced to his left and let out a big sigh. "Great. Here comes Mrs. Martinelli. That woman wouldn't miss a free meal if it were her own funeral."

I gulped. "Gloria Martinelli?"

"Who else?"

I turned and snuck a peek. Sure enough, the purple-umbrella crusader was making her way toward us, gnashing her teeth. Practicing for the cannoli, I figured.

"Uh, thanks, Neil," I said, then turned and scurried inside the funeral home.

***

While Aunt Edna mingled with the crowd to eavesdrop on conversations, I slipped into the second row of pews right beside Jackie. Her job had been to get us seats as close to the front as possible. Once in position, she would serve as my wingman and dish the dirt on anyone she knew who attended the service.

"Where's the cleft-chin wonder?" she asked.

"Not here," I whispered.

Jackie shook her head. "It's Monday. Like I said, even a homicidal maniac needs a day of rest."

I glanced around. "See anybody you know?"

"Not yet." Jackie cocked her head and smiled. "Hey. What's that music they're playing?"

I listened, expecting it to be *Amazing Grace*. It wasn't. But it did sound vaguely familiar. As I strained my ears and my brain, it finally dawned on me. It was the Musak version of an old Motown hit.

A Curtis Mayfield tune called *Freddie's Dead*.

My jaw went slack. Either the music choice was one hell of a coincidence, or someone had a truly sick sense of humor.

I was about to whisper to Jackie when a man said, "Is this seat taken?"

I looked up to see the tall, slim, imposing visage of Sergeant McNulty. I nearly swallowed my tongue.

"What are *you* doing here?" I asked.

He sat down beside me. "I was about to ask you the same thing, Diller. I came here to check out the crowd. Killers sometimes like to attend their victims' funerals."

My nose crinkled. "Why?"

"Because they're sick bastards," McNulty said. "They want to see the pain they've caused. Some of them get their jollies from being so close to their victim again. Reliving the crime somehow, I would assume."

"Well, that's not why *we're* here," I said.

"I didn't say it was." McNulty eyed me even more suspiciously.

As I scrambled to think of something to say that wouldn't bury me even deeper in McNulty's eyes, Neil Neil approached the podium at the front and tapped on the microphone.

"Good afternoon, everyone," the gorgeous funeral director said. "The Sanderling family thanks all of you for coming. Fred Sanderling was a wonderful man. He will be sorely missed. We'd like to offer time for those who knew him best to come up and share a favorite memory of him."

"Oh, oh!" a woman's voice rang out. "Me first!"

A busty redhead who'd have fit right into Tad Longmire's lecherous playlist got up and wiggled to the podium.

I leaned over and whispered in Jackie's ear. "Who's that?"

"Victoria Polanski," Jackie said. "But Sophia calls her Slick."

"Why?"

Jackie smirked. "Because Victoria hates it."

The microphone crackled. "Slick" Victoria dabbed a hanky at her mascaraed eyes. "Freddy and I were very close," she said. "Nobody knew it, but we were secretly engaged."

"What?" I gasped. I leaned into Jackie. "What would she be doing with an old man like Freddy?"

"I heard a rumor at the nursing home that he was quite the lady killer," Jackie said. "Maybe the tide turned."

"Huh?"

"A lady killer got killed by a lady," Jackie said. "Classic gold-digger move."

"What do you mean?"

"Right out of the playbook," Jackie said. "Marry a rich old man, give him a bath, put him in a draft. Only this time, she went all Snow White on him."

"Excuse me, but that woman looks *nothing* like Snow White."

Jackie laughed. "That's for sure. But it looks like she knows her way around a poisoned beach apple, don't it?"

I stared at the woman still gushing tears at the podium. Slick looked like she knew her way around a stripper pole, too, if you asked me.

Huh. I wonder how much Freddy Sanderling had in his bank account...

Chapter Fifty-One

After the memorial service for Freddy was over, everyone lined up for coffee and desserts. Gloria Martinelli was first in line, so I stayed tucked behind Jackie and Aunt Edna. I kept a wary eye on the acorn assassin until she'd settled down at a table with her back turned toward us and began gnashing her mountain of food like a wood chipper at a sawmill.

"Did you see that piece of work?" Aunt Edna said, nodding toward "Slick" Victoria Polanski as she walked by us, her plate stacked with brownies. "I've seen better looking diamond rings in a bubblegum machine."

"So you think her jewelry's fake?" I asked.

My aunt huffed. "Dorey, it's as real as those boobs peeking out of her dress."

A tall, slim man with a head of frizzy, Bozo-like hair walked slowly along the line of people waiting for food. I noticed he was handing out something.

"Is that Neil Neil's husband?" Jackie asked.

"Not unless he's had some plastic surgery that went horribly awry," I said. "But he *does* have a cleft chin."

When the man got to us in line, he shot us a smile that was even faker than Slick's boobs.

"Ferrol Finkerman, attorney at law," he said. "Have a card. You never know when an injustice will occur."

"I think one just has," I said. "This is someone's funeral. Have some respect."

"Are you kin to Frederick Sanderling?" Finkerman asked.

"No."

"Beloved friend?"

"Err ... no."

"Then what are *you* doing here?"

My face reddened.

Finkerman smirked. "Uh-huh. That's what I thought."

Before I could think of a comeback, the ambulance chaser was already three guests down the line.

"Hold my place," Jackie said.

"Where are you going?" I asked.

"To introduce that jerk to Slick. Those two are made for each other."

I could hardly argue with that.

***

Our plates laden with pastries, the three of us headed for the table furthest away from Gloria Martinelli. As we sat down, Jackie picked up a cannolo. I recognized Morty's signature banana pudding inside.

"Don't eat that!" I whispered. "What if it's poisoned?"

"Gimme a break," Aunt Edna said. "We're too young to be targets for this old-folks scheme."

I studied the women for a moment. Jackie's pewter hair was in soft curls that hadn't been in style since Betty White played Rose on the *Golden Girls*. Come to think of it, Aunt Edna looked a lot like Bea Arthur.

Geez. Maybe reality and TV are the same thing ...

"Uh, right," I said. "But I think this could be more like a Russian-roulette situation."

"They got gambling going on?" Jackie asked.

"Gambling with people's lives," Aunt Edna said, and slapped the cannolo out of Jackie's hand.

"Well look who's here." I turned my attention to Dr. Mancini. "Why would he be attending Freddy's service?"

"To make sure Neil and his husband don't spend too much on the service?" Jackie asked.

It was as good a guess as any. And, unfortunately, that's all I had so far. Guesses.

I glanced around at all the silver hair and realized one head was missing. Sophia. She'd played us to get out of Shady Respite early. Maybe she's playing us again. I swallowed a knot in my throat.

Maybe that guy in the hoodie was hired by Sophia herself! Or Jackie and Aunt Edna. Geez! Maybe I'm being set up by the whole Family right this very second!

"What'cha thinking about, Dorey?" Aunt Edna asked.

I nearly gasped. "Oh. Uh ... nothing."

My aunt's left eyebrow was an inch higher than her right. "Don't look like nothing to me."

"Where's Jackie?" I asked, suddenly paranoid. She'd disappeared from her chair while I'd been lost in thought.

"Right here," she said, towering over me. "Take these and guard them with your life."

Jackie pressed a lumpy napkin into my hand. Was there a gun in there? A poison tree frog? At this rate, anything seemed possible.

"I wanna try a poppy seed muffin," Jackie said, and turned toward the buffet.

"What did we just say about—" I called after her. But it was too late. Jackie was already at the pastry table. I looked down at my hand as the napkin slowly unfolded.

Inside was a pair of dentures.

O. M. G.! Did she steal these from Freddy?

"Excuse me for a moment," I said to my aunt, then got up and made a beeline for Freddy's casket. I was about to slip the dentures inside when someone foiled my plan.

"What are you doing?" McNulty asked.

I quickly palmed the dentures. "Uh ... what do you mean?"

"I thought you'd be busy trying to get your friend Kitty off the hook."

"We are," I grumbled. "We're certainly not here for the free food."

"Right," McNulty said. "Well, take my advice. Don't try the poppy seed muffins."

I thought of Jackie and nearly choked. "Why? Are they poisoned, too?"

McNulty eyed me funny. "No. The little seeds get caught between your teeth."

"Oh." I smiled weakly. "Of course."

McNulty folded his arms across his chest. "I've got my eye on you, Diller. And your friends here, too."

"But we didn't do anything. I swear. And Kitty didn't either."

"You two desecrated this man's corpse," McNulty said, nodding toward Freddy as he lay in his coffin.

I winced. "Besides *that*, I mean."

"Listen to me, Diller. You need to step aside and let me conduct my own investigation into Sanderling's death. Can you do that?"

I looked down at his shoes. "Yes, sir."

"If I find you're meddling again, I can arrest you for tampering with an active investigation. Then you and Kitty can be cellmates."

I looked up at him. "But we've got the big party tomorrow!"

McNulty's eyes narrowed. "What party?"

Aww, crap!

"Uh ... my birthday party." It wasn't a lie, technically.

Suddenly, Jackie was beside me. "Our Dorey here turns forty tomorrow."

"I see," McNulty said. "Well, happy birthday. But one slip up Diller and you may find yourself celebrating it inside a jail cell."

Chapter Fifty-Two

"Great. Just great," I said as I drove the Kia out of the parking lot of the Neil Mansion. "Now McNulty suspects me even *more*. He told me one little slip-up and I'll be celebrating my big day in the big-house."

"Look on the bright side," Jackie said, and shot me a grin with her re-installed dentures.

"Bright side?" I asked.

"At least you got out of there without being beaned over the head by Gloria Martinelli."

I sighed. "I guess. But do me a favor, Jackie. Don't ever hand me your dentures again."

"But I didn't want any poppy seeds to get caught in them."

"Put them in your purse next time."

She cocked her head. "I'm not carrying a purse."

"Geez. Put them in your pocket then."

"I don't have any—"

"You know what?" I said, eager to change the subject. "After what I saw at the service, I think Neil Neil and Dr. Mancini for sure have a thing going on."

"Mancini's gay, too?" Aunt Edna asked.

"No. But they're both in love with money."

Jackie laughed. "What man ain't?"

"Brady," Aunt Edna said.

"Brady!" I gasped. "I forgot about him!"

"*I* didn't." Aunt Edna patted my knee. "Don't worry, Dorey. While you were busy being Miss Detective, I called him. We got it all worked out for him to drop by our place later."

"Whew." I breathed a sigh of relief. "Look. Before we meet up with him, there's some stuff I want to know."

"Like what?" Jackie asked.

"Like what you two think of the other suspects. You know. The ones on Sophia's list."

"You mean Victor the Vulture?" Aunt Edna asked.

I nodded. "You said he deals with dead bodies. Could he be poisoning people to get more business?"

"Naw," Aunt Edna said. "He makes bodies *disappear*. Not show up to funerals."

"Edna's right," Jackie said. "Besides, from what I hear, Victor's got more business than he can handle."

My eyebrows shot up an inch. "Excuse me?"

"Never mind." Aunt Edna shot Jackie a dirty look in the rearview mirror. "It ain't Victor."

"Then who?" I asked. "What about that Humpty Dumpty guy?"

"Humphry Bogaratelli," Aunt Edna said.

"Why would he do it?" Jackie asked. "The creep's got plenty of money, thanks to his sticky fingers."

"Maybe his tastes have changed," Aunt Edna said. "Maybe he's developed a hankering for *power* to go along with his dough."

I nodded. "That's what I was thinking. Look, Aunt Edna. I know you have a thing for Morty. But you have to face reality. That day at the bakery—could Morty have been chipping in cash for Humpty to pay for a hit on Sophia?"

"No!" Aunt Edna groaned and reached for her purse. "I need another Tums."

I frowned, then glanced in the rearview mirror. Jackie was shaking her head at me, running a bony finger across her throat. I got the hint and backpedaled. "But what do I know? It's probably somebody else."

"My money's on that old gasbag Gloria Martinelli," Jackie said. "She sure has it out for *you*, Dorey."

I grimaced. "Don't remind me."

"And there's bad blood between her and Sophia," Jackie added.

"True," I said. "But the woman is no pro at hiding her feelings. If Gloria wanted to have a showdown with Sophia, she would've done it while they both were at Shady Respite."

"Who says they didn't?" Aunt Edna said, chewing her antacid tablet.

Jackie patted Aunt Edna's shoulder. "Not me."

I pursed my lips. "If that's true—"

"I think it's that red-headed tramp at the funeral," Aunt Edna said. She spat out her name. "Slick Vicky. What a piece of work. That bimbo is Freddy's fiancé? I don't buy it." She shook another Tums out of the bottle. "Let me tell you, Dorey. It ain't just *men* who love money."

"I know that."

Aunt Edna popped the Tums into her mouth. "Here's a theory for you, Miss Detective. What if that ditz ordered those poisoned lemon bars for Freddy, but told the delivery guy the wrong room number?"

I sat up straight in the driver's seat.

Huh. Right now, that's as good a theory as any.

***

As I unfastened my seatbelt in front of Palm Court Cottages, Aunt Edna grabbed my arm.

"Dorey. You familiar with that expression, 'A girl's gotta do what a girl's gotta do.'?"

I thought about the time handsy Arthur Dreacher had summoned me to his trailer in the back lot of the studio at two in the morning. I'd armed myself with a mouthful of pea soup, then spewed it all over myself when he opened the door. My fake *Exorcist* impression had earned me the whole night off, Dreacher-free.

"I'm familiar with the term," I said.

"Good." Aunt Edna hauled herself out of the passenger seat. "When Brady comes over tonight, he might need a little persuasion, if you catch my drift."

I climbed out of the Kia and shut the door. "Not exactly."

"You like Brady, don't you?" she asked.

"Uh ... yeah, sure."

"We may need you to use your feminine wiles to help him see things our way."

"Wait a minute. Are you pimping me out?"

"It ain't pimping if you really like him. Besides, Brady's a good boy."

I frowned. "And you think I'm a bad girl?"

"No. Just use the assets Mother Nature gave you. Tease him a little. You don't gotta do nothing you don't want to do. Think of it as practice."

I blanched. "*Practice?*"

"Yeah. For your acting career. You got that big audition tomorrow, right?"

"Yes, but—"

Aunt Edna locked eyes with me. She looked tired and sad. "You care about Kitty, don't you?"

I cringed. "Sure."

"Well, she needs you. *We* need you."

I gulped. I've never been needed before. Tossed aside. Ignored. Taken advantage of. But never *needed*.

"Just be nice to Brady, that's all I'm saying," my aunt said. "Just flutter your Bambi eyelashes and find out what he knows. We only got tonight and tomorrow morning to figure this thing out. And while you're at it, see if maybe he'd be willing to help us get Kitty out of jail so she can come to the party."

My eyes grew wide. "You mean bust her out?"

"Yeah." Aunt Edna winked. "But on a *technicality*."

"Oh. Okay."

"Thanks, Dorey. But listen. Whatever you do, don't tell Brady about the Family. Capeesh?"

I nodded. "Capeesh."

Aunt Edna gave me a big bear hug, then hollered after Jackie, who was up the path a few steps ahead of us. "Jackie! Help our girl get dolled up a little! And you two come up with a cover story."

"I'm on it, Capo," Jackie said, turning back toward us.

"So it's all settled," Aunt Edna said. "Now, I'd better get a move on."

"Where are *you* going?" I asked.

"To make dinner. It's past five o'clock, already, for crying out loud!"

Chapter Fifty-Three

I guess it was my turn to take one for the CGCN team.

Kitty had confessed to the desecration of Freddy's corpse on the condition that I would go free. Aunt Edna had reluctantly faced the possibility that her old flame Morty could be involved in a plot with Humpty to kill Sophia. And Jackie? Well, I was convinced she was willing to do whatever it took to protect her Family.

Was I?

As I checked my look in the mirror, the lyrics to Bruce Springsteen's *Dancing in the Dark* ran through my mind.

I wanna change my clothes, my hair, my face.

Jackie's "makeover" for my date with Officer Brady was nothing less than stunning—but it the worst possible way. The sleeveless white shirt she'd insisted I wear bore enough sparkling rhinestones to cause an epileptic seizure. She'd also plumped my hair to epic volume with half a can of hairspray—and coated my eyelids with enough "smoky eye shadow" to start a forest fire.

I closed my eyes and took a deep breath.

Okay, Doreen. You can do this. Channel your inner Vicky Polanski.

I sighed.

Who am I kidding? Even Slick *didn't look* this *trampy.*

***

"Thanks for picking me up," I said, leaning into the open driver's window of Brady's Ford F-150. "I didn't know where else to turn."

"Uh ... no problem," he said to my cleavage.

I glanced around, tugged the hem of my too-short skirt, and whispered, "Listen, if anyone asks, we're on a date, okay?"

Brady's eyebrow shot up. "Okay, but—"

"Hold that thought." I pressed a fake fingernail to his lips. "Let me get in first."

I hobbled in stilettos over to the other side of the truck. One of my spike heels caught in a crack between the bricks lining the street. I yanked it free, then tugged opened the passenger door.

"This was the only way I could get out of there without them suspecting me," I said, spoon-feeding Brady the cover story Jackie and I'd come up with.

"I see." Brady watched me climb into the cab of his truck with all the grace of a drunken she-goat.

"So," he said. "Do you usually sleep over on a first date?"

I blanched. "I beg your pardon?"

Brady smirked. "I'm a trained observer. I couldn't help but notice the luggage."

"Oh." My cheeks caught flame. I grabbed my old suitcase off the road—a prop Jackie had insisted I take along. God only knew why. At least she'd left it unpacked. I lugged the old brown case onto the floorboard beside my feet. "It's not what you think."

"No?" Brady smirked. "Too bad."

"What?"

He laughed. "So, Ms. Diller. What's going on?"

"Don't ask. Just drive."

***

The hot cop turned left on Ninth Street and pulled up to what he said was one of his favorite haunts. The Dairy Hog.

The place was a complete dive.

Oozing the ambiance of an abandoned gas station, the Dairy Hog was the kind of hole-in-the-wall place where, during daylight hours, street urchins and bigwigs sat elbow-to-elbow and munched suspiciously red hotdogs at giant wooden picnic tables—tables selected because they were too heavy to steal. During nighttime hours, however, the Dairy Hog lost most of its charm.

I crinkled my nose. "What a dump."

"Not at all." Brady opened the driver's door and climbed out. "This is the perfect place."

"For what? A homicide?"

"Only if you order the fish sandwich," he quipped.

"Why in the world would you take me here?" I asked, trying to get out of the truck without being arrested for indecent exposure.

"Because here, no one will think twice about a cop talking to a prostitute."

"Prostitute?" I balked, wobbling on my heels as I followed him across the potholed asphalt.

"My bad." Brady stopped in front of the dive's walk-up order window. "That wasn't the look you were going for?"

"No!" I tugged at my skin-tight orange mini skirt. It was actually one of Jackie's old tube tops. "I was trying to look like I was going on a date with you." I stared at the spot where my stomach bulged the stretchy orange fabric. "Geez. I think I've put on a few pounds thanks to Aunt Edna's cooking."

Brady grinned. "I can see how that could happen." He turned to the guy in the order window. "Two dogs, Dairy style, and two chocolate milkshakes."

"You got it," the guy said.

Brady turned to me. "Hope that's okay with you. It's the most edible stuff on the menu. Unless you think the calories might make you pop a seam."

I punched him on the arm. "Ha ha."

We grabbed our food and found an empty spot at the end of one of the picnic tables.

"Sorry to dump all this on you, Brady. But if I didn't tell someone, I think my head would have exploded."

"Like your dress?"

I frowned. "One more crack like that and *you'll* be the one with your life in danger."

"Your life's in danger?" he asked, suddenly serious.

"Yes. No. I don't know!"

"From who? Your aunt and Jackie? Did they threaten you with a cane or something?"

I slumped in my chair. "It's ridiculous, I know. I ... I just can't decide whether to get out of here or stay."

"What's so bad about staying? From what you've told me, your life in L.A. was no pleasure cruise."

"No. But it seemed less ... I dunno ... dangerous."

Brady laughed. "Dangerous?"

I scowled. "You know what, trying to talk to you was a big mistake. Just take me back home."

I turned back toward the truck. Brady's hand softly gripped my upper arm.

"I'm sorry, Doreen. It's just hard to take you seriously in that getup."

"I know. I ... I'm only doing this because I care about my family."

"I can tell." Brady let go of my arm. "Look, give me another shot, okay? I promise I'll take you seriously."

I looked up at him with Bambi eyes.

I didn't have to fake them.

I sniffed and said, "Okay."

Chapter Fifty-Four

"I can definitely see why you needed a reality check," Brady said after listening to me spill my guts about ... well ... *everything*. "Like I said before, the women in your family are in possession of some truly exceptional imaginations."

My family.

Brady's words caused a lump to form in my throat.

"Yes, they *are* my family," I said, my spine stiffening. "And I believe this isn't their imagination. Not all of it, anyway."

Brady slurped his chocolate shake through a straw and set it down on the wooden picnic table. "You really think Sophia's life is in danger?"

"Yes! That's what I've been trying to tell you." I wiped mustard from my chin with a cheap paper napkin. "Someone tried to poison her with a machine ... a mancini ... a mansion ... a *beach apple*."

"Beach apple?" Brady's eyebrow shot up. "Is that anything like a road apple?"

I shot Brady some side eye.

He laughed. "Be honest. You didn't drink another Long Island iced tea before you came here, did you?"

"No!" Frustration boiled inside me. "*Manchineel*. That's it."

"That's what?"

"The name of the poison Kitty said was in the lemon bars. We tried to explain it to Sergeant McNulty, but he put her in jail instead!"

"Oh." The humor left Brady's face. "I'm sorry. I didn't know it had gone this far."

"Well, it has." I frowned and stared at my half-eaten hotdog.

Brady reached across the table and took my hand in his. "Doreen, why would someone want to kill a harmless little old lady like Sophia?"

"So they can take over the Fa—"

I choked on my own words.

Crap! I can't tell Brady about the Family!

"uh ... her *money*," I blurted.

Brady's eyebrows rose a notch. "So Sophia's loaded?"

Well, she's loaded with something, that's for sure.

I nodded. "I know it sounds crazy, but I'm worried whoever is trying to kill her may try again at the Coliseum tomorrow night."

"In Rome?"

"No. On Fourth Avenue. That's where they're holding her birthday party."

"Oh. But why *then*?"

"To keep her from turning a hundred."

Brady's brow furrowed. "I'm not following you. Why would they care about that?"

I chewed my lip, trying to come up with a reason that didn't involve mafia hitmen. I shrugged. "How should I know?"

"Is it because of the Collard Green Cosa Nostra thing?" Brady asked.

I nearly fell off the picnic bench. "You know about that?"

He laughed. "I bought Jackie a beer once."

"Oh." Relief washed through me. "Look. It's a real thing. Mob men are lining up to do Sophia in!"

Brady's shoulders straightened. "Why?"

"Because Sophia says they're like hermit crabs. They all need bigger shells."

"Excuse me?"

I shook my head. "Forget it. You think I'm nuts, just like my aunt and Jackie, don't you?"

"No." He smiled softly. "Well, not completely. But I don't get the crab reference."

"Whoever knocks off Sophia gets to be the new head of the ... *you know*. But if she lives to be a hundred, she can name the new leader herself."

"Ah. And McNulty thinks Kitty wants to take over?"

I shook my head. "He doesn't know about the whole Sophia thing. He nailed Kitty on desecration of a corpse."

Brady choked on his milkshake. "What?"

"Look. That's not important right now. What I know for sure is that Kitty didn't want to kill Sophia. She doesn't want her job. Believe me, none of us do."

"Are you sure about that?"

My nose crinkled. "Being head of the Cosa Nostra and walking around with a price on your head? No thanks."

Brady smirked. "Don't be so dramatic, Doreen. I've seen trailer park kids that were more dangerous than the CGCN gang."

"Really?" I chewed my bottom lip. "Well, then, there's your answer, Brady. *We're not killers.* If any of us wanted to be the new head of the family, why would we be working so hard to keep Sophia alive?"

"In hopes she'll name one of you to the role?"

I frowned. "No. We take care of her because she's family. And we keep her alive because despite her being a cranky old cuss we ..."

"We what?" Brady asked.

I looked up at him. "We love her."

Brady locked his brown eyes with mine. "Sounds like you've integrated pretty well into the clan, Ms. Diller."

I blanched.

Geez. I guess I have.

"So, your love for Sophia is what's driving you to seek my help?" Brady asked.

"Yes, I guess so," I admitted. "But not just me. Aunt Edna and Jackie want your help, too. It was their idea." I looked down at the sparkles on my shirt. "So was this horrible outfit."

Brady blew out a breath. "Thank goodness. I was worried about that."

"Could you can it with the jokes, please? If someone kills Sophia, we're worried her replacement could be somebody horrible. Like Sammy the Psycho."

Brady blanched. "The cheese-curd guy? He's *real*?"

"My Family sure seems to think so." I grabbed Brady's hand. "I'm worried her birthday bash could turn into a bloodbath!"

Brady shook his head. "Look, Doreen. If you want my opinion, I don't think there's going to be a shootout at the Coliseum. But I agree, something could be up with the poisoning thing. Otherwise, why would McNulty have arrested Kitty?"

"Exactly my point! I didn't mean to dump all of this on you, but I couldn't go to McNulty, now could I?"

"No, I guess not."

"Can you help us?"

Brady pursed his lips. "I'll check into it."

"No! That's just it, Brady. There's *no time* left to check into it! The party's tomorrow!"

"Then how can I possibly help you?"

"Come with me to the party. As my date."

"What exactly do you see me doing for you at the party?"

"You know. Keeping an eye out for us." I shrugged. "You can kind of be Sophia's bodyguard. You can bring your gun, can't you?"

Brady stiffened. "I can't exactly go shooting suspects for you, Doreen. We need to gather proof of intent."

I frowned. "How are we supposed to do that?"

"By recording incriminating statements."

My eyebrows shot up. "You mean by wearing a wire? Like that stray dog Jackie saw?"

"No," Brady said. "This time, the wire would be real."

Chapter Fifty-Five

I couldn't remember walking from Brady's truck to Aunt Edna's apartment. Or how I ended up staring at pink globs floating around in the lava lamp atop the old, yellowing French Provincial bureau in the spare bedroom where I slept.

I only remembered it wasn't a walk of shame.

Officer Brady had kissed me goodnight. Or maybe I'd kissed him. Either way, neither of us had objected.

After that, my mind had gone blank.

And now, here I was, staring at the gooey pink shapes rising and falling inside a globe full of mysterious liquid. I don't know how long I'd been standing there, but slowly I became aware of my surroundings.

Down the hall, I could hear Aunt Edna softly snoring. I turned toward the bed. In the pink glow of the lamp, I saw my pajamas laid out neatly for me next to my pillow. On the bedside table, a plate of cookies and a glass of milk sat waiting for me. The last time someone had done that for me was ... never.

Suddenly, my heart felt way too big for my chest. I sniffed back a tear and picked up a cookie. Beside the plate was a handwritten note on a neatly folded piece of pink paper.

Dorey honey,

I was worried you didn't get enough to eat. I hope you had a nice evening with B, and that he was a gentleman.

Sleep well,

Aunt Edna

P.S. I talked to Kitty. She said to tell you natives used the sap to poison their arrows.

"What the?" I muttered.

I set the note down and grabbed my toothbrush from the bureau. As I did, I caught a glimpse of myself in the mirror. I nearly screeched with terror.

I'd forgotten all about Jackie's makeover.

One brown eye and one pale-blue one stared back at me from dark, skeletal sockets, thanks to the brown eyeshadow Jackie's applied all the way to my eyebrows. My lacquered hair was the size of a frizz-ridden basketball.

Dear lord! I look like a zombie that just stuck its finger in a light socket!

As I stared at my hideous visage, a sudden thought melted my horrified expression into a dreamy smile.

And Brady had kissed me anyway.

***

After peeling off Jackie's sparkly top and tube-top mini skirt, I took a long, hot shower to remove every last trace of my stint as a low-rent femme fatale. I slipped on the pajamas so lovingly laid out for me and climbed into bed.

Suddenly, I realized I wasn't alone.

Something hard poked me in the elbow.

"Ack!" I yelped, then scrambled out of bed and flipped on the light.

Lying in the covers was Kitty's leather-bound poison journal. I picked up Aunt Edna's note and read it again.

> *P.S. I talked to Kitty. She said to tell you natives used the sap to poison their arrows.*

I sat down on the bed and picked up the journal. What was Kitty trying to tell me? We already knew the poison came from the Manchineel tree. Did she think someone was going to use a bow and arrow at the party? It seemed implausible. But then again, this *was* Florida.

I flipped through Kitty's hand-painted plant journal until I found the one I was looking for. The Manchineel.

I studied every entry Kitty had made next to the illustration of the sad-looking little tree-bush. Sure enough, the last note was about how the Carib Indians had poisoned their arrows with the toxic sap from the apple-like fruits, and used it to bring down small prey like birds, squirrels, and rabbits.

What had Kitty meant by this?

I thought about last night, when I'd been guarding Sophia at her cottage. Kitty had been messing around in the garden in the dark. She could've easily gone into her greenhouse and taken the fruits from the Manchineel tree. She could've staged the cut padlock to make it look like a robbery.

My eyes grew wide.

Is that why she never found the time to show me the greenhouse? Is she trying to throw me off her scent by giving me false clues as a pretense to helping?

Helping.

The word echoed in my head.

Wait a minute. Why wasn't anyone watching Sophia tonight? Had that whole guard-shift thing last night been a ploy to get me to stay inside Sophia's place so the three of them could hatch their poisonous scheme without my interference?

Am I being taken advantage of again? Duped like a fool by people pretending to love me?

A soft knock sounded on my door.

"Who is it?" I hissed.

The doorknob jiggled.

Then, before I could get up, a hand holding a shotgun forced its way inside.

Chapter Fifty-Six

"Get out!" I yelled, and hurled Kitty's poison journal at the intruder. It banged against the wall, missing its target.

"Geez," a familiar voice said. "You really need to work on your aim."

"Jackie!" I yelped, my eyes moving from the shotgun to her face. "Are you going to shoot me?"

"What? Heck, no, Dorey!" She leaned the shotgun on the wall. "I just came to check that you got home safe."

"Oh." I swallowed against the thumping in my throat. "Yeah. I'm okay. What are you doing walking around with the shotgun?"

"Guard duty. Tonight there was only me and Edna to take shifts watching Sophia. With you being ... you know ... *busy with Brady*, we figured you'd be exhausted. Edna went to bed early so she can work the midnight to six."

"Oh." I slumped back in my bed, ashamed I'd thought they might be plotting against me. *Again.*

Jackie's head cocked to one side. "What's wrong, kid?"

What isn't?

"I ... uh .... Nothing."

"You sure?"

"Why was Kitty's book in my bed?"

"Oh." Jackie laughed. "That was me. I thought it'd make good deadtime reading."

My nose crinkled. "You mean *bed*time reading?"

"Naw. Who can read when they're asleep?"

"I guess you're right." I felt the tension in my face slip away. Jackie's unique way of looking at the world was growing on me. "Jackie, can I ask you a question?"

"Sure, kid."

"Why do you keep unpacking my suitcase?"

She chuckled. "Why else? Because I want you to stay. That's why I had you take your suitcase along on your date with Brady. So you couldn't pack it without me knowing. I figured you wouldn't take off without your stuff."

I shook my head softly. "But why would you care if I stayed or not?"

Jackie's eyes grew wide. "Are you kidding? We love you, Dorey."

I bristled against the kindness Jackie was showing me. The vulnerability she displayed made me squirm with discomfort. Telling her I loved her back would be a sign of weakness, wouldn't it?

Damn, early programming dies hard.

"And we need you," Jackie said. "But more than that, *you* need *us.*"

I frowned. "Why would *I* need *you all*?"

"Everybody needs somebody to watch their back." Jackie sat on the edge of the bed. "Take me, for instance. If it wasn't for Edna, I'd probably be living in the streets."

I gulped. In a way, I was in the same boat. "Me, too," I admitted.

Jackie studied me. "I thought you were a famous movie star back in L.A."

I laughed bitterly. "Hardly. If I don't get this job Kerri's offering me at Sunshine Studios tomorrow, I'll be so broke I'll have to cash in my plane ticket and get a new career in fast-food delivery."

Jackie winked. "Well, then, I hope you don't get it."

I frowned. "What?"

"Only so you'll stay, I mean." She reached over and patted my hand. "Otherwise, break an arm."

I smiled. "Thanks."

Jackie stood up. "Now get some shuteye kid. In the morning, you can tell us all about the plan you and Brady came up with to save Sophia."

I gulped. "Right."

Jackie turned to go, then glanced around the room. "Where's your suitcase? Did you use the goodies I packed inside?"

"What goodies?"

"You know." She waggled her eyebrows. "The naughty nighty and the packs of 'protection.'"

I grimaced. "No. I'm not that kind of girl."

"Playing hard to get, eh? I like your style, kid." Jackie grinned at me, then clicked off the light and disappeared like a shadow.

Suddenly, I was so wide awake I was certain the whites of my eyes were glowing in the dark.

I'd accidently left my suitcase in Brady's truck.

Holy crap! Please, Brady, please. Whatever you do, don't open that suitcase!

Chapter Fifty-Seven

I was at the Coliseum in Rome, wandering among the ancient stone columns and arches. Dressed in a cop's uniform, I was wearing a wire frying basket atop my head like a rectangular helmet.

A sudden movement at my feet made me look down. The ground was swarming with hermit crabs. Instinctively, I knew they were acting suspicious. I reached for my service weapon.

It was a wooden mallet.

I raised my mallet in the air like Thor's hammer and took off in pursuit of the orange crustaceans running amok like miniscule hoodlums.

I followed a gang of them through a stone arch and cornered them by the base of a broken column. As I prepared to play Whack-a-Mole with the culprits, I spied something that made me freeze in place.

Holding court on a throne-shaped boulder was the biggest hermit crab I'd ever seen. Atop its flat, triangular head was a tinfoil turban.

As I crab-walked cautiously toward it, the turban grew larger with every step I took. Suddenly, the aluminum headdress split open like a fully-cooked Jiffy Pop. Out of the crack, a claw emerged.

The claw gripped the slit in the foil and ripped away a chunk of...

"Dorey? You okay?"

My eyes flew open. Aunt Edna was standing over me.

"Wha?" I mumbled, and raised up in bed on one elbow.

My aunt's eyes were full of concern. "You were groaning. I thought maybe Brady fed you a bad meatball or something."

"Huh? Oh." I blinked the sleep from my eyes. "No. Just a weird dream."

Aunt Edna smiled tiredly. "Well, time to rise and shine. I'm making something special for breakfast."

"What?" I asked.

"Eggs benedict. With fresh crab meat."

***

When I got dressed and stumbled to the dining room, Aunt Edna was at the table setting out a gravy boat full of hollandaise sauce for the eggs benedict breakfast she was making.

"What's the occasion?" I asked, reaching for the coffee carafe.

She grinned. "Your birthday, Dorey. Or don't you celebrate it no more?"

"Oh." I shrugged. "Ma never made a big deal out of it."

Aunt Edna frowned. She looked exhausted. Then I remembered she'd been up since midnight, watching Sophia's cottage.

"Can I help you with something?" I asked. "You need me to go get Sophia?"

"Nah, Jackie's doing it. So, how'd it go with Brady last night?"

I grimaced. "Okay, I guess. I didn't have to ... *you know*."

Aunt Edna eyed me funny. "I *meant* did you two work out a plan for making sure Sophia's balloons don't get popped tonight?"

I felt my cheeks heat up. "Oh. Yes. He's going to the party with me. As my date."

Aunt Edna shot me an arched eyebrow. "*That's* your plan?"

"He'll also be carrying a concealed firearm."

"Uh-huh. Well, it sure would be good if we could tell him who to aim it at, wouldn't it."

I winced. "I know. All we know for sure is what kind of poison was used to kill Freddy. And if we don't figure out who took those beach apples from Kitty's greenhouse, she's in big trouble."

Aunt Edna let out a big sigh. "Tell me something I *don't* know."

"Look, Aunt Edna. I need to be honest with you. I saw Kitty wandering around in the garden the night before last. She could've taken the apples herself. Are you sure she didn't want to get rid of Sophia and be the new godmother of the CGCN?"

Aunt Edna's back stiffened. "Yes, I'm sure. I've known Kitty Corleone for over thirty years."

"Then why didn't she want to show me her greenhouse?"

"She *did* want to. She just ran out of time. McNutsack showed up before she could give you the tour."

I chewed my bottom lip. "Okay. But if you don't suspect her, why did you leave me that note about Kitty saying natives poisoned arrows with the sap?"

"Why else?" Aunt Edna said. "Because Kitty *asked* me to. I'd tell you to talk to her yourself, but she already used up her one phone call. And believe me, the police were listening to every word we said to each other."

I blew out a frustrated breath. "I'm just trying to follow every lead."

"I get that. But look, Dorey. Around here, we watch after each other. Whoever messed with those lemon bars, it ain't Kitty. Go point your poison arrows at somebody else."

"Believe me, I'd like to. But McNulty told us the Manchineel is so rare it would take a botanist like Kitty to even recognize it."

Aunt Edna rested a tired hand on my shoulder. "Dorey, I dunno what you had happen to you growing up with Maureen and being an actress in L.A. and all, but around here, we don't eat our own young. Drop it with Kitty. If I can't trust her, I can't trust nobody."

The tired, sad, earnest look on my aunt's face made me feel like a heel. "I'm sorry. I'm just trying to make sure nobody gets hurt."

"I know that, kid. But that ain't the way the world works. No matter what choice you make in this life, you hurt somebody doing it."

I grimaced. "So what are we supposed to do? *Nothing?*"

"No. You just live your life the best you can and try to do the least damage to the ones you love."

My eyes filled with tears. I hugged my aunt. "I meant to thank you for the cookies. And your note. And for caring about my birthday."

Aunt Edna patted me on the back. "You're welcome. Now, Miss Detective, you keep on snooping around. But stay out of *our* doghouse, okay?"

I nodded. "Okay. You know, I looked through Kitty's journal last night, but I couldn't find any other clues."

Aunt Edna locked eyes with me. "Maybe she wants you to look harder."

"At what? The plant itself? It's so homely, nobody would give it a second glance."

"Are you talking about me?" Jackie asked.

She came slowly into the dining room, Sophia on her arm. Jackie's outfit of the day was a lime-green top and orange-and-white striped pants. She looked like she'd just been mugged by a circus tent.

Aunt Edna frowned. "What's up with that outfit?"

"What?" Jackie balked. "It matches my cheerful personality. Plus we're celebrating somebody's big day today."

Aunt Edna winced and shook her head. "Dorey, you wouldn't happen to still have those big sunglasses of Jackie's, would you?"

Chapter Fifty-Eight

The crabmeat benedict was delicious. The conversation, however, turned out to be a little harder to swallow.

We were running out of time to figure out who the poisoner was, and to get Kitty out of jail. So I kind of threw caution to the wind and went for broke.

"Sophia, I mean Queenpin, why did you choose Freddy Sanderling for your taster?"

"If Kitty were here, she'd tell you why," Sophia said.

"Well, that's just it," I said. "She isn't here. That's why I need to know why you chose Freddy."

"Dorey's only trying to help," Aunt Edna said.

Sophia sighed. "I didn't choose Freddy. *Kitty* chose him. She said when it comes to determining a poison's effectiveness, size matters."

I crinkled my nose. "What do you mean?"

"Kitty said we needed to test the food on someone about my size. Someone with a similar digestive constitution."

"Oh. That makes sense. The poison might not have been lethal for someone bigger and stronger."

Sophia gave me the evil eye. "You saying I'm not strong?"

I shook my head. "Not at all. I meant you made a good point. When it comes to choosing poisoning victims, *size matters*."

"Also helps when picking a few other things," Jackie quipped.

"Poor Kitty," Aunt Edna said. "We gotta figure this out and get her out of the slammer. Otherwise, she's gonna miss your party, Queenpin."

Sophia frowned. I wasn't sure if it was because Kitty wouldn't be there, or she'd miss out on another gift.

"Okay," Sophia said, drawing her shawl around her shoulders. "Let's put our heads together on this. I'd like to hit the century mark without wearing a target on my back."

"Where do we start?" Jackie asked. "We got no solid proof of nothing."

"What about this blister on my lip?" Sophia said, pulling down her lower lip for our viewing pleasure. "Freddy tried to poison me with a kiss!"

Aunt Edna sighed. "It's probably just the acid from the tomatoes in the caprese salad."

Sophia scowled. "That old goat."

"Be glad it isn't poison ivy," I said, then squirmed in my seat.

Jackie elbowed me. "Hey. Did you know a goat can eat poison ivy with no problem?"

I frowned. "For real?"

"Yeah." Jackie laughed. "I guess that means Freddy wasn't an old goat after all."

"Freddy was just a stooge," Aunt Edna said. "Somebody used him to try and get to you, Queenpin."

"Maybe," I said. "But he could've been poisoned as part of a scheme to sell expensive funerals."

"That isn't it," Sophia said.

Aunt Edna turned to Sophia. "So, who do you think is behind it?"

She frowned beneath her silver turban. "I'd put my money on Gloria Martinelli."

"The acorn lady?" Jackie asked. "Why?"

"Jealousy," Sophia said. "She was always giving me the evil eye because the men liked me better. But then again, they always have."

"Kitty told me that poisoning was a covert business," I said. "Not to disagree with you, your Queenpin, but Gloria Martinelli doesn't strike me as the stealthy type. Her attacks on me were about as inconspicuous as a dumpster fire."

"You don't know her like I do," Sophia said. "Gloria is a hands-on kind of woman. She likes to do her own dirty work."

"Then why wasn't she on your list?" I asked.

Sophia scowled. "What list?"

"The one in your robe pocket," I said.

Sophia locked her cat eyes on me. "You been going through my things, Miss Busybody?"

"No," Aunt Edna said. "We found the list when we picked up your stuff from Shady Respite."

"What list?" Sophia repeated.

"You know," Aunt Edna said. "The one that had Morty, Ventura, Humpty Bogart, Dr. Mancini and Gordon on it."

Sophia's scowl softened. "Oh."

"Were those your list of suspects?" I asked.

"Why would you think that?" Sophia said.

"Are you saying they *weren't* suspects?" I asked.

Sophia's face puckered. "What is this? Some kind of interrogation?"

"No!" Aunt Edna kicked my shin under the table.

I knew I was asking too many questions, but Kitty's life was at stake here!

"Listen here," Aunt Edna said, glaring at me. "Like I told you before, Morty wouldn't hurt a fly."

"But I saw him at the bakery," I said. "When Morty handed Humpty a bag of cash."

"Geez, enough about that," Aunt Edna said. "That money was to help pay for renting out the Coliseum tonight, okay?"

"Oh." I grimaced. "But what about Humpty?"

"That jerk wasn't in town when Freddy got poisoned," my aunt said. "The dirtbag took a trip to the rat's mouth."

"Oh." I wanted to know what rat's mouth was a mob euphemism for, but as angry as Sophia was, I was afraid if I asked, I might end up there myself.

"What about Ventura?" Jackie asked. "Could he be trying to do you in, Sophia?"

"Poisoning ain't Victor's style," Aunt Edna said. "He deals with bodies that are already dead."

Sophia stared at me. "Victor doesn't need to drum up business. He's got all that he can handle."

"So I've heard," I said. "What about Dr.—"

"Don't you dare say a word about Dr. Mancini," Sophia growled at me. "The man's a legend in my eyes."

"Fine." I threw my hands up. "I'm only trying to help clear Kitty and keep you safe tonight."

"That's right," Jackie said. "Cut the newbie a little slack."

"What did you say?" Sophia growled.

"Your Queenpin," I said, "if these guys aren't people you suspect of trying to kill you, then who were they?"

Sophia shrugged and adjusted her shawl. "A girl can dream about getting married again, can't she?"

I nearly fell out of my chair. "You want to get married?"

"Hell, no," Sophia said. "I meant for Edna."

Aunt Edna gasped. "What?"

"It ain't over till it's over," Sophia said.

Aunt Edna's face softened. She shot Sophia a small smile. "Oh. So, who's Gordon?"

Sophia's lips formed a crooked grin. "A new fragrance I saw on TV. It's supposed to drive the men wild."

Jackie snorted.

Aunt Edna swore under her breath. "Mother of pearl! What am I gonna do with her?"

Sophia's grin disappeared. "Speaking of driving the men wild, who's going to press my outfit for tonight?"

"I'll do it," Jackie said. She stood and picked up her empty plate.

"Wait a minute," I said. "I still have questions."

"I bet you do," Sophia said sourly.

"Like what?" Jackie asked.

"Like who let the delivery guy in at Shady Respite? And what about Sammy the Psy ... err ... I mean, your son, Queenpin?"

"What about him?" Sophia grumbled.

I didn't want to upset the old godmother any more than I already had. The last thing I wanted was to give her a heart attack six hours before her shindig.

I winced out a smile. "Will he be coming to your party?" Suddenly, a sharp pain shot through my shin. Aunt Edna had struck again.

"You in charge of the headcount or something?" Sophia barked. "Jackie, take me back to my cottage."

"Yes, ma'am." Jackie helped Sophia to her feet.

As they left the room, I rubbed my shin and turned to Aunt Edna. "Is Sammy going to be at the party?"

She grimaced. "I don't know. But stop talking about him already. It's bad luck!"

I grabbed my aunt's arm. "But I need to know if Brady and I should be on the lookout for him tonight."

"Sammy don't exactly send me his agenda, Dorey. For all I know, he could be standing at the door as we speak."

Bam! Bam!

Loud knocking commenced on the front door.

"I'll get it," Jackie called out from the living room.

"No!" Aunt Edna hollered. "Jackie, don't answer that!"

Chapter Fifty-Nine

"Who is it?" Aunt Edna asked.

She, Jackie, and Sophia were huddled up behind me. I appeared I'd been assigned to take another one for the team.

"Is it Sammy?" Jackie whispered.

I grimaced, then cautiously took a peek through the peephole in the front door.

"It's Brady," I said, then sighed with relief along with the others.

"Thank goodness," Aunt Edna said. "Go ahead and let him in."

"Hi, Brady," I said as I opened the door. The handsome cop was standing there with a bunch of dark-red roses in one hand, my suitcase in the other.

Jackie laughed. "So, you moving in, Romeo?"

"What?" Brady looked at the flowers. "Oh. No. This is—"

"Red roses. How romantic," Aunt Edna said. "Those for Dorey?"

Brady grimaced. "Um. I found them lying on the doorstep. I'm afraid they aren't from me."

"Huh. Well, come on in." Aunt Edna took the roses from Brady and opened the small envelope stuck to them with a plastic pick. Her face turned pale.

"What's it say?" Jackie asked.

Aunt Edna's hand fell to her side. "Hope you liked the curds."

I gasped. "Sammy sent them?"

"Hold on," Sophia said. "We don't know that for certain. All we know is that whoever sent them knows about the cheese curds, too."

"Aww, geez!" Aunt Edna said. "Red roses mean death."

"No they don't," Jackie said. "They mean love."

"Po-*tay*-to, po-*tot*-o," Sophia grumbled.

Brady frowned. "What's that supposed to mean?"

"Nothing." Aunt Edna folded the note back up. "These flowers must be a birthday gift for Sophia. Brady, come have a cup of coffee. Dorey, don't you need to be getting ready for your big audition?"

"Oh, crap! Yes, I better get going."

"Will you be needing this?" Brady asked, holding up my suitcase.

I cringed. "I hope not." I snatched the ugly brown bag from his hand. "Uh ... you didn't look inside, did you?"

He shrugged. "I'm a trained detective."

My brow furrowed. "Is that a yes or a no?"

Brady smirked. "Let's just say I'm prepared to fulfill my duties, and apparently you are too."

Fan-freaking-tastic.

I spun on my heels and headed for my bedroom. I needed to drop off the case and brush my teeth.

I suddenly had a very bad taste in my mouth.

***

"Take the Kia," Jackie said as I emerged from the bedroom dressed for my audition.

I wasn't sure what role to expect, so I kept my wardrobe simple. A pair of black slacks, a white shirt, and a pair of sensible sandals. I'd also lavished on a full set of makeup.

"Thanks." I glanced around the room.

"Brady's gone," Jackie said, then grinned. "I'll keep my fingers crossed."

"For my audition?"

"Nope. That the Kia starts."

"Thanks. I'll take it." I yanked open the front door.

"Good luck, Dorey!" Aunt Edna called out from the kitchen.

I turned and hollered, "Thank you!" I took a blind step out the door and suddenly found myself tumbling sideways onto the concrete porch.

"Ouch!" I yelped, rolling onto my knees.

"What happened?" Jackie asked.

I shot an angry glance back at the cottage. Piled up along the porch were five cardboard boxes. Whatever jerk had delivered them had put one right on the front door mat.

"I tripped on those fakakta boxes!" I hissed.

"What's going on?" Aunt Edna bellowed, bolting from the kitchen with the shotgun in her hand. Her eyes glued on me, she didn't see the boxes either. She tripped and fell on the ground beside me.

"Oh, no!" I scrambled over to her. "Are you okay?"

"Crap. I think I sprained my ankle," she grumbled. "Who sent the fakakta boxes?"

"That's what I want to know," I said.

Jackie leaned over a box. "Looks like they're from L.A."

"Geez." I shook my head. "I guess Sonya met Johnny Depp after all."

"Huh?" Aunt Edna grunted.

"Nothing." I turned back to her. "I'm *so* sorry. This is all my fault!"

"Horse hockey," my aunt said. "Now, get up and get going to your interview. I'll be fine. Jackie will take care of me."

"But—"

"I got this," Jackie said. "Go on. This is your big day, Dorey. We'll be okay."

I cringed. "Are you sure?"

"Yeah." Jackie squatted next to Aunt Edna. "I'll get her to her feet when she's ready."

I chewed my lip. "Well ... okay. But leave the stupid boxes where they are. I'll take care of them when I get back."

"Will do," Jackie said.

Aunt Edna winced out a smile. "Go get 'em, Dorey."

I took a step toward the street. Guilt washed over me.

Am I wrong to leave them here?

"Go!" Aunt Edna said.

"Okay, okay!" I turned and headed down the path, not at all sure I was making the right decision.

Universe, I need a sign.

If the Kia starts, I'll go to the audition. If it doesn't, I'll stay and help.

I turned the key in the ignition.

The Kia started right up.

Chapter Sixty

"What are *you* doing back?" Aunt Edna asked as I walked into her cottage. She was sprawled out in the hideous old brown recliner, a bag of frozen peas on her ankle.

"The Kia won't start," I lied.

"Cripes," Jackie said, walking into the room. "Lemme have a whack at that thing."

I shook my head. "No. I'm not going. I already left a voicemail for Kerri at the studio. It'll all work out."

Or it won't.

"You sure?" Jackie asked. "I can call a taxi for you. Or maybe Brady—"

"No," I insisted. "I don't think I could concentrate anyway. You know, with Kitty in jail and now Aunt Edna out of commission. You were right, Jackie. You guys need me."

And I need you.

My words, even though unspoken, caused a strange, warm feeling to envelop my heart. It was both exhilarating and a bit frightening. I smiled at the two women, and suddenly noticed how tough, yet vulnerable they were. Just like me.

Huh. Maybe it isn't Aunt Edna's food I've become addicted to after all.

Aunt Edna smiled through her pain. "But Dorey, missing your audition would mean you've already taken *two* for the team."

I thought it was three ...

I shrugged. "Talking to Brady wasn't that bad. And I'm sure Kerri will understand. Besides, Family is a lot more important than some acting role. If we don't find out who's trying to kill Sophia, both she and Kitty are in big trouble." I spotted the roses sitting in a vase on the coffee table. "Any idea who sent those?"

Aunt Edna winced. "I didn't want to say nothing, but it looks like both the flowers and the cheese curds were probably from Sammy."

I nodded. "So he's definitely alive, like we suspected."

"Pretty sure." Aunt Edna adjusted the frozen peas on her swollen ankle.

Jackie chewed her bottom lip. "You think that means Sammy's coming to the party, or is he still in Idaho?"

Aunt Edna shook her head. "Who knows? Sophia sure isn't gonna spill the beans on where he is. He could be in New York, New Jersey, or the new deli down the street."

I blanched. "You think Sammy is *here*? In St. Petersburg?"

"He's Italian, and it's his mother's centennial birthday. Why would he miss it?" Aunt Edna asked.

"So he's here," I said.

Aunt Edna blew out a sigh. "I'd bet on it."

Chapter Sixty-One

I hauled the boxes containing my junk from L.A. into my room and checked my cellphone. I had less than four hours to figure out who was trying to kill the CGCN matriarch, and save my Family from her psycho son.

Awesome.

I searched through my purse for the little yellow book I'd come to depend on for guidance. It wasn't anywhere to be found. After rifling through my entire room, I padded back to the living room. Jackie was trading the soggy bag of peas on my aunt's ankle for a frosty bag of frozen collard greens.

"Have either of you seen my *Hollywood Survival Guide*?"

Jackie cocked her head. "What do you need that for?"

"For ideas on how to deal with this situation," I said. "What's going to happen if Sammy takes over as Kingpin?"

"God forbid!" Aunt Edna said, and crossed herself.

I crumpled into the brown recliner beside her. "I don't know what to do!"

My aunt reached out and laid a hand on my knee. "You're part of the Family now, Dorey. You don't gotta do everything on your own anymore."

I gulped back a knot in my throat. "So, you two have some ideas?"

Jackie shook her head. "Not a one."

***

With no answers forthcoming from my aunt or Jackie, I went to the world's best source for accurate information. The internet.

As my fingers hovered over the keyboard on my laptop, I hit my first snag. What should I search for? How to deal with a psycho?

I typed that phrase in the browser and got 6,734,923 results.

You've got to be kidding me.

472

I glanced through the first dozen or so, but they didn't seem very helpful. Joining the witness protection program seemed implausible before six o'clock.

Now what?

I couldn't exactly call the police, file a restraining order, or tell Sophia to make her son stay home. I slapped my laptop closed. It tipped sideways and slid off kilter.

What the?

I picked up my computer and finally discover something useful—underneath was the little yellow book I'd been searching for.

Yes!

Like a madwoman, I thumbed through the *Hollywood Survival Guide.* Tip #366 seemed to fit the bill. *When life gives you lemons, make a grenade.*

I marched back into the living room and announced, "We're going to need weapons."

"For the party tonight?" Jackie asked.

"No," Aunt Edna said. "For our trip to the moon."

"You can't go," Jackie said. "You got a busted ankle!"

"It's only sprained. And yes, I'm going. I'll use Sophia's wheelchair. She don't really need it anyhow. It's just for show."

Jackie blew out a breath. "Really? I thought that—"

"Ladies," I said, clearing my throat. "We need to focus on how we can find and apprehend whoever might try to kill Sophia tonight, hopefully before they actually do it. Brady's going to have his gun. We need weapons, too."

"I got a new can of Raid," Jackie said. "Amazon just delivered it yesterday."

"A can of Raid?" I said. "Really?"

Jackie shrugged. "Everybody's got their weapon of choice, Doreen. I hear yours is cuticle scissors."

"Hilarious," I said. "What's the best weapon for taking down a bad guy?"

"Your brain," Jackie said. "If you use the old noodle, you never have to get into the soup in the first place."

"Well, it's a little late for that," Aunt Edna said. "The pot's already about to boil over."

I winced. "That's what I'm afraid of."

"Aww, don't worry so much," Jackie said. "It's your birthday."

"Yeah. Another lousy birthday," I grumbled. "Ma always thought they were bad luck."

"Not around here," Aunt Edna said. "Here, birthdays are always good luck."

My upper lip snarled. "I hope you're right. Because boy are we ever gonna need it."

Chapter Sixty-Two

It was D-Day at the lemonade stand—or, more accurately, the Coliseum on Fourth Avenue.

I wasn't packing lemon grenades, but I *was* packing—thanks to Jackie Cooperelli.

"I put the shotgun in your suitcase," Jackie said, pulling my ugly brown bag out of the back seat of the Kia. "Just *in case*. Get it?"

I frowned. "Why in the world would you—"

"Hello *Officer Brady*," Aunt Edna said loud enough for even Jackie to get the hint.

I turned around. Brady was right behind me, eyeing my suitcase. "You didn't tell me this was another actual *date*," he said. "You packing those thirty-eight caliber panties again?"

"No." The only heat I was packing was my flaming cheeks. "Am I the only one taking this seriously?"

"Sorry," Brady said. "What's with your eyes? They match tonight."

"I put a contact lens over the wonky one."

"Why?"

"So she can keep an eye out for Sammy!" Jackie quipped.

"Can it already," Aunt Edna said. "Jackie, help me into the wheelchair." She turned to me and Brady. "You two help Sophia inside, would you?"

"Of course." Brady leaned in and whispered, "Here we go."

"I sure hope you know what you're doing," I whispered back."

"You don't trust me?" he quipped.

"I have to. Besides you, I'm all alone in this mess and I don't have a clue what to do next."

"Looks like your family trusts you," he said, glancing over at them. "Maybe you should start trusting them back."

***

"Quite the crowd," I said to Sophia as she and Brady walked, arm in arm, toward the lights of the Coliseum.

I was a few steps behind them, talking to Aunt Edna as Jackie pushed her in Sophia's wheelchair. As we and the other geriatric partygoers formed a crowd in front of the entry doors, I got this weird vibe—as if I were an extra in *Night of the Living Dead II*.

"Geez, Louise!" Aunt Edna complained. "You'd think they'd have a special entrance for people in wheelchairs."

"They do," Jackie said, nodding toward a line to our left. "It starts way back over there."

"Are all these people, you know, *Family*?" I asked.

"No," Aunt Edna said. "Only about thirty are. The rest I invited from here and there. I didn't want Sophia to realize how small the Family has shrunk to."

"Here and there?" I asked.

"Ah-ha!" Jackie said. "*That's* why you had me post those flyers at all the senior centers!"

***

Fifteen minutes later, we'd managed to swim across the gray sea of old humanity and make it to our reserved table by the stage. Glancing around, compared to the rest of the crowd, Brady and I looked like we'd just teleported here from a mothership sent from the future.

"Would you just look at all these BENGAY Bozos and Geritol gals?" Sophia complained as she settled into her seat.

"You wanted a big party," Jackie said. "I voted for a night with the Chippendales."

"Brady and I are going to walk around and keep a close eye on the crowd," I said.

"Uh-huh." Jackie winked. "I heard there's a kissing booth behind the exit doors."

Brady smirked. "I'll be scanning the crowd for weapons, while Doreen tries to glean information from people's conversations."

"Eavesdropping, eh?" Aunt Edna nodded approvingly. "A tried and true tactic." She looked at her table mates and sighed loudly. Sophia was picking lint off her black shawl. Jackie was counting the peppermints in a bowl at the center of the table. "Well, get going," she said. "You sure as heck aren't going to pick up anything useful at *this* table."

"Hold on," Sophia said. "You think somebody's gonna confess to you because you're young and hot?"

"No," I answered. "But if L.A.'s taught me anything, it's how to tell if somebody's full of it."

Sophia chuckled. "Good on you, kid. Hey, don't forget. The mafia is like a hot fudge sundae. Only room for one nut on top."

"That reminds me," I said. "Stay away from sweets, and keep an eye out for anything suspicious." I cupped my hands to my mouth and whispered, "Or psycho."

"Got it," Aunt Edna said.

"Thanks. And Aunt Edna? Please, stay here at the table with Sophia. If something goes down, we need to be able to find you two in a flash."

"What about me?" Jackie asked, dropping the mints back into the bowl.

"I want you to keep an eye on anyone or thing coming out of the kitchen," I said.

She shot me a thumbs up. "You got it."

Sophia frowned. "Excuse me, young miss. But who died and made *you* Capo?"

"*I* did," Aunt Edna said. "I mean, I didn't die. But I gave Dorey a, you know, *temporary* position. Only until I can walk again tomorrow."

"Humph," Sophia said. "Well, then, if anything happens to me tonight, I blame *you*, Doreen."

I blanched. "But how could it be my fault? I—"

"I didn't say it was your fault," Sophia said. "I only said I was going to blame you for it."

My nose crinkled. "What?"

Sophia let out a huge sigh. "Geez. I'm getting too old for this gig. I used to have wiseguys clipped. Now, look at me. I'm clipping coupons for Depends."

The Queenpin looked up at me and flicked a ghostly wrist. "What are you waiting for, already, Miss Hotshot? Go make your bones."

Chapter Sixty-Three

Brady and I took Jackie's advice and slipped out the exit doors. Soon, Brady had his hand under my silk blouse. But it wasn't a romantic rendezvous. He was clipping a recording device to my bra.

"There," he said. "That ought to do it."

It sure did. Just ask my lady parts.

"You ready?" he asked.

"What?" I gulped.

"To do this thing." He shot me a serious look. "If you hear anything even slightly suspicious, please don't do anything stupid. Come and get me first."

"Of course," I said, tucking my blouse back into my skirt.

"All right then. Let's go."

***

After weaving back and forth through the crowd and around the grounds of the Coliseum, Brady and I returned empty handed to the table reserved for the guest of honor. I never realized how hard it was to find something when you didn't know what you were looking for.

As we walked up, I heard Sophia and Aunt Edna groan in unison. From the sound of it, Jackie must've just laid another rotten egg of a joke. I was grateful I hadn't been around to hear it hatch.

"How elegant you all look," Brady said, pouring on the charm. Being the youngest, best-looking man in the room *and* dressed in a tuxedo, he didn't have to pour much for our cups to runneth over. "You three certainly are gracing the place."

"More like *dis*gracing it," Sophia said. "Look at the three of us. I'm old as dirt. Edna fell in the dirt. And Jackie's dumb as dirt." She shook her head and scowled. "And nobody's even asked me to dance."

"You took the words right out of my mouth," Brady said. "May I have the next dance, please, Queen Sophia?"

The old lady's chin rose an inch. She shot Brady a smile. "The next waltz. I don't do any of those crazy Latin dances like the one on now."

"As you wish." Brady kissed her pale, liver-spotted hand. "It will be my pleasure."

Geez. Turn off the tap, Brady. Even I'm starting to swoon ...

"Ha!" Jackie laughed, killing the moment. "Look at that guy out there. He can really dance the flamingo."

"Flamenco," I said.

I glanced over at the dancefloor and spotted a familiar nest of red frizz that could only belong to Ferrol Finkerman, ambulance-chaser at law.

What could that funeral-hustling jerk be doing here?

Then I answered my own question.

Drumming up business.

My eyes narrowed in disgust, causing my contact lens to shift halfway off my pale-blue iris.

Not good.

"Uh ... I've got to go to the restroom," I said, cupping my hand over my eye.

"Itchy?" Jackie asked.

"What? No!" I said, mortified. "A little trouble with my contact lens, that's all."

"I'll go with you," Brady said.

I didn't argue. I might've taken a few for the team lately, but poor Brady had already taken at least ten tonight alone.

"I just heard from the clerk at the station," Brady said as we walked toward the restrooms. "He couldn't do anything to get Kitty released. He said McNulty wouldn't allow it."

"Why not?" I asked, frowning.

"I don't know. My buddy says there's a named suspect in the file, but it's not Kitty Corleone."

"Then who is it?"

"I can't say."

I cringed. "Does it start with Sammy and end in Psycho?"

Brady shook his head. "Like I said, I can't say."

My eyes flew open. "Is it *me?*"

"I can't say."

"*Why not?*"

"Because I don't know. He wouldn't tell me."

"Oh." I winced and wiped my eye.

"You know, you kind of look like you've got a lunar eclipse going on in your eye."

"Gee," I said sourly. "I bet you say that to *all* the girls."

Brady laughed.

I turned and headed for the ladies room door. "See you on the other side."

***

As I tried to shift my contact lens back to its proper position over my iris, the vanity lights above the bathroom mirror flickered. Startled, I lost my grip on the contact lens. It tumbled from my hand.

"Great," I grumbled, and searched around on the counter for it. I spied it in the sink. "Thank goodness!"

As I reached for it, the lights flickered again, and kept flickering like a black light at a disco party.

"Are you kidding me?" I said aloud.

But in a flash, the contact lens ended up being the least of my worries. As the lights flicked on and off, I spotted something in the niche between the two stalls.

It was a pair of mismatched eyes—and they were staring right at me.

Sammy the Psycho was here!

Chapter Sixty Four

I flew out of the ladies room and slammed right into somebody. Thank goodness it turned out to be Brady, or I'd be paying for somebody's hip surgery.

"Saw him!" I gasped.

"Who?" Brady asked.

I nearly collapsed. Brady grabbed my upper arms and held me steady.

"What is it?" he asked.

"Face! Man!" I gasped. "Sammy!"

"In the ladies room?"

"Yes!"

He let go of me and ran into the women's restroom, but came right back out a few seconds later.

"There's nobody in there, Doreen."

"What?" I ran back into the restroom, Brady right on my heels. He was right. It was empty.

I shook my head. "I know he was in here."

"Well, there's a small window above the tampon dispenser. But the guy would have to be Spiderman to get out that way."

"I saw him with my own two eyes!" I insisted. "Am I going nuts?"

"No," Jackie said. "Sammy's like the wind. He can disappear at will."

"Did you follow us over here?" I asked.

Jackie scoffed. "No. Last time I looked, this was a free-to-pee country. And when you're my age, you make sure and buy the express pass."

As I stood there, dumbfounded, Jackie looked us up and down and grinned. "Doing it in a public restroom, huh? Maybe I should add that to my bucket list."

Chapter Sixty-Five

Just when I thought the worst possible thing had already happened, Shirley Saurwein, reporter for the *Beach Gazette*, came flouncing through the entry door to the Coliseum.

Oh, crap.

"What's with the face?" Aunt Edna asked.

I nodded toward Shirley, who was wearing a skin-tight red dress that perfectly matched her pin-up-girl lipstick.

"Oh, geez," Aunt Edna said. "That woman has more issues than *Time* magazine."

"I only wish her fact-checking was as good as her wise-cracking," I said, as the snarky bleach-blonde made a beeline for our table.

"Well, if it isn't Miss Fancy Pants," Saurwein said, cracking her gum. She glanced at my crotch. "How's things down under? Still *itching* to make your big break?"

My eyebrows met my hairline. "How did you—?" I glanced across the table. "Jackie!"

"Sorry." Jackie cringed guiltily. "Hey, to change the subject, did you know iguanas taste like chicken? It says so on this flyer here." She waved a yellow slip of paper at us. "They eat them like crazy down in Central America."

"Where'd you get that?" I asked.

"From the lady with the big lizard. Here she comes now."

I turned to see Melanie the pet therapy lady come walking toward us in a red dress identical to Shirley's.

I shook my head. "Lemme guess. Big sale at Walmart?"

"Ha ha," Shirley said. "At least I don't wear animals or old lady sunglasses for accessories."

My contact lens down the drain, I'd had to resort to wearing Jackie's glaucoma glasses again. I pushed them higher up the bridge of my nose and took another look at Melanie. Her iguana, Iggy, was slung around her shoulders like a wrinkly, threadbare mink stole. My nose crinkled as she approached. Then I heard something squeak.

"What the—" I looked down and saw she was wearing expensive red loafers.

"I guess when you're nearly six feet tall, you don't need heels," Shirley said. "Lucky you."

"Thanks," Melanie said.

Wait a minute. I'd seen those shoes before. "Ha!" I sprang up from my chair and screeched at Melanie. "It was you!"

"What about me?" Melanie asked.

I heard a click. Saurwein had just pushed a button on her micro-recorder. She hoisted her camera, her big eyes pools of liquid gossip.

"Yeah, what about her?" Saurwein said, egging me on.

Thrown off my game for a second, I stuttered. "I ... I heard you, Melanie. In the bathroom at Shady Respite."

"Ha! I'll alert the media," Saurwein snorted. "Oh, wait. I'm already here. Farts at eleven!"

"Shut up, Shirley!" I swallowed hard, hoping the knot in my throat would go fortify my backbone. "You ... you were plotting with Gloria Martinelli," I said to Melanie. "I heard you!"

"Plotting?" Melanie asked, crinkling her nose at me. "Plotting *what*?"

"Yeah, plotting what?" Saurwein echoed. "She run out of toilet paper or something?"

"No!" I grumbled. "I heard you tell Gloria that if she'd done what she was told, she'd have gotten out sooner. And that some big cheese wasn't happy about it. Are you two helping Dr. Mancini poison people?"

Melanie's eyebrows shot up. "Geez. And I thought *Gloria* was delusional."

Saurwein snickered and started clicking off shots with her camera.

I scowled. "If I'm delusional, then explain yourself!"

Melanie shrugged. "All right, I will. I was talking with Gloria because she was using her umbrella as a cane. If she'd have used her walker instead, like the doctor said, then she'd have gotten out sooner. He'd just told her so himself."

"Oh." I wilted, suddenly wishing I could be like that lizard on her shoulder and blend into the woodwork.

Melanie shook her head. "You got some kind of imagination, lady."

"It runs in our family," Jackie said proudly.

Shirley Saurwein hooted. "Ha! I can't wait to write up this one!"

I scowled. "What are you doing here anyway, Melanie?"

I invited her," Sophia said.

My jaw fell open. "*You?*"

"Yes, me." Sophia hitched up the sides of her shawl. "It's my party, isn't it? Besides, that lizard of hers has more personality than most of those old coots in that stupid nursing home."

"Thank you, Sophia," Melanie said, walking over to the Queenpin. "Just for that, I think Iggy wants to give you a kiss."

"Bring it." Sophia puckered up for a smack on Iggy's lizard lips.

"Gross!" I hissed.

Melanie spun on her loafer heels to face me. "What's your problem? Iggy and I are working hard to change the minds of reptile-haters like you."

I blew out a breath. "So I've heard."

"Here you go, Dorey," Jackie said. She smiled and reached across the table to hand me the yellow flyer. I didn't take it.

"Melanie, do you have any more of those petition forms on you?" Sophia asked.

The lizard lady shook her head. "No. Not today. This is *your* special day. That's why Iggy's wearing his special birthday hat. Say happy birthday, Iggy!"

Melanie held the iguana out for Sophia to pet. My nose crinkled.

"What's amatta you?" Sophia asked, stroking the iguana's head. "Everybody loves Iggy."

Jackie leaned over and asked Aunt Edna, "What'd she say that lizard's name was?"

"Iggy. You know, like Iggy Pop."

Jackie frowned. "Iggy popped somebody?"

Aunt Edna shook her head. "Tomorrow, for sure we get you a Miracle Ear."

Chapter Sixty-Six

I took off Jackie's glaucoma glasses and stared at my reflection in the bathroom mirror. I'd lost my contact down the sink, and just accused an animal rights activist of conspiring to kill people at an old folks' home.

I was batting a total goose egg.

"What an idiot I am!" I said to my reflection. "I mean, can I get any more incompetent?"

As if in reply, the bathroom lights flickered twice. As they did, I came face-to-face with my own utter stupidity.

Staring at me from between the bathroom stalls were those wonky eyes again. Only they didn't belong to Sammy. They were my own reflection in the stainless-steel tampon dispenser.

I looked around for a rock to crawl under.

Is it physically possible to flush yourself down the toilet?

***

It took fifteen minutes for my face to fade from fire-engine red back to a reasonably normal flesh tone. I slapped Jackie's glasses on and headed back to the party. At least I knew Sammy the Psycho wasn't running wild. Who needed *him* when I was around to fill the position?

As I emerged from the restroom, I spotted Melanie leaning over a table full of old men. It wasn't hard to spot her red dress in a room full of gray suits. Then I noticed the clipboard in her hand. An old man was signing something clipped to it. Then he handed her some cash.

What the?

I marched over to Melanie. "This isn't the time or place to be collecting for your stupid cause!"

"No?" Melanie said. "Better go tell Sophia that."

"I will!"

"Wait," she said, and turned the clipboard over for me to see. "It's a birthday card for Sophia. I'm collecting for her centennial gift."

Again I wished I could morph into the scenery like a chameleon.

I cringed. "I'm sorry."

Then, mercifully, before I could dig myself deeper into the hole, someone yelled, "It's time for the cake!"

***

"Where's Brady?" Aunt Edna asked.

"Good question," I said. "I haven't seen him since Saurwein got here."

Aunt Edna looked over my shoulder. "Ah. There he is."

I turned and walked over to meet Brady, who'd come through the front door. "Where have you been?"

"I saw you talking to those two women in red. I wanted to hear what you were saying, so I went out to my car and listened in on the recording."

My eyes nearly doubled. "You heard all of that?"

"Every word."

"When did you turn it off?" I asked, trying not to whimper.

"I haven't."

Something deep inside me curdled like sour milk. "I need a drink."

Brady smirked. "Where's a Long Island iced tea when you need one?"

At this point, I'd settle for a bottle of Ripple.

Chapter Sixty-Seven

"Here it comes," Jackie said, rising from her chair as Morty and Humpty rolled a huge birthday cake up to our table on a catering trolley.

The three-foot-tall confection was white and tiered, like a wedding cake. Silver swags of icing adorned the edges. Sugary purple plums and green icing leaves hung from the swags, and completely covered the top layer. In a word, it was gorgeous.

Flutes of bubbly were passed around the table. As I took my glass, I noticed the other randomly invited guests were beginning to circle us like vultures. I hoped it was because they smelled something sweet, and not dead.

"A toast," Morty said, raising his glass.

"Hold up a second," Saurwein said, bending over between Sophia and the cake. "I need to change my film."

"This is *my* day," Sophia said. "Get the hell out of the way, you two-bit gossip-monger."

Morty grinned. "To Sophia, the sweetest angel left on Earth."

"Here, here," we said.

I tipped my glass back and guzzled the booze down in one big gulp.

"You're not worried you'll be incapacitated?" Brady whispered in my ear.

"Nope," I said. "You can't incapacitate something that was never capacitated in the first place."

He laughed. "Don't be so hard on yourself. You screwed up with Melanie. So what? You were just looking out for your family. I admire that."

I looked up at him. "You do?"

"Sure. I ... um .... Oh, look. They're cutting the cake."

"Who wants to do the honors?" Morty asked, holding up a knife.

"Oh, I will!" Melanie called out.

"Come on over, then, beautiful lady," Morty said.

Aunt Edna grunted. "Huh. Morty always was a sucker for a floozy."

"Here, hold this," Melanie said.

Before I could react, she'd plopped her purse on the table in front of me and her five-pound lizard had taken up residence in my lap.

"What the?" I grumbled. But there was no time to object.

"To Sophia's centennial!" Morty said, then everyone applauded as he and Melanie sliced a piece of cake from the top layer like two giggling newlyweds.

Aunt Edna popped a Tums into her mouth and chew it savagely.

"Here you go, Sophia," Melanie cooed, handing her a slice of cake. "The plum piece belongs to you!"

Sophia smiled serenely. "You bet your bottom butt cheeks it does."

"Hold up a minute," Jackie said, springing to her feet. She sprinted over to the cake. "There's one more plum on there than there outta be."

"What are you talking about?" Morty said. "I put ten on there. One for each decade."

"I know," Jackie said. "But look. There's still ten on the top."

Morty shrugged. "What's your point?"

"There's ten on the top, and one on Sophia's plate," Jackie said. "Now, I'm no mathematician, but that adds up to eleven."

"She's right!" Aunt Edna turned to me. "Dorey, what color are those beach apple fruit things?"

"Yellowish-green."

Aunt Edna took the slice of cake from Sophia and rubbed her finger on the plum. Yellow peeked through the layer of sugar icing. I gasped.

"What's going on here?" Sophia asked. "Can't a person have a piece of cake in peace anymore?"

"Eat that and you'll be resting in peace," I said. "That's a Manchineel fruit. I'm certain of it."

Aunt Edna shook her head. "Morty, how could you?"

"But ... I didn't," he said.

I pointed a finger at the woman in red. "Melanie put it there!"

"Geez. Not this again!" Melanie said. "I gotta say, I'm beginning to feel a bit persecuted here, Doreen. You don't like iguanas. You don't like me. Maybe you don't like Sophia, either. You trying to take over the Family or something?"

"No!" I yelled.

But as I looked around, I realized that more than a few Family members were eyeing me suspiciously.

Chapter Sixty-Eight

"Look, I'll humor you, Doreen," Melanie said. "Would I feed a poison fruit to my darling Iggy?" She took the knife and cut the suspicious plum on Sophia's plate in half. Then she walked over to me and popped the piece into the iguana's open mouth.

Dear god. I've stepped in it again!

Sophia shot me a look. "Now, can I eat my cake, or you want to take that over *that*, too?"

Melanie shook her head. "Go on, Sophia. Enjoy your cake. This woman's nuttier than a squirrel."

Squirrel.

Suddenly, my mind began to swirl. Like a jigsaw puzzle swept up in a tornado, snippets from the past five days began twirling and colliding and interlocking in my mind.

Squirrels. Rabbits. Indians poisoned their arrows with beach apples to kill small prey.

Size matters when choosing a poisoning victim.

Iguanas are small prey. They taste like chicken. They eat them like crazy in Central America.

If iguanas are so tasty, why didn't the Indians shoot them with their Manchineel arrows?

"You okay, Dorey?" Jackie asked.

"Huh?" I glanced at Jackie's striped pants.

Stripes.

The stripes on Iggy's tail. Goats can eat poison ivy with no ill effects.

"That's it!" I yelled, springing to my feet.

I glanced around. Everyone was staring at me like maybe someone should fit me for a straightjacket.

"That's nice, Dorey," Aunt Edna said softly, patting my shoulder. "Now sit down and we'll get you a nice cup of—"

"There's only one animal immune to the Manchineel's poison," I blurted. "And it's the striped iguana!"

"Huh?" Jackie grunted. "Why would Iggy want to kill Sophia?"

In the split second while we were distracted by Jackie, Melanie dove for the other half of the plum on Sophia's plate. Fortunately, Brady was quicker on the draw.

"I don't think so," he said, grabbing Melanie's wrist. "That little plum is going in an evidence bag."

"That's crazy," Melanie said. "What do I have to gain from killing this old coot?"

"Old coot?" Sophia hissed. "After I gave you twenty bucks and signed your petition? On my own birthday, no less!"

I eyed Melanie. "I thought you didn't bring that petition."

I grabbed the clipboard sticking up out of her purse.

"I told you already," Melanie said. "It's a birthday card for Sophia."

"Right." I lifted up the card. Behind it was a petition on animal rights. "What's this, then?" I asked, and waved the clipboard in the air.

"It's not against the law to fight for animal rights," she said.

"No. But it proves you're a liar."

"That's not against the law either," she hissed. "Unless you're on the witness stand."

"Maybe not. But I'm pretty sure forgery is." I held up the clipboard for everyone to see.

A hole had been cut through the petition form where the signature line was. I flipped the page over. Beneath it was a power of attorney form. And the latest victim to sign Melanie's bogus form was none other than Doña Sophia Maria Lorenzo herself.

Chapter Sixty-Nine

The evidence against Melanie was strong enough to earn her a pair of silver bracelets and a free ride to Sergeant McNulty's guest house. After Brady told McNulty what had happened, he agreed to release Kitty immediately.

"Thank you so much, Brady," I said.

He smiled. "You know, you really amazed me tonight. But thanks to *you*, I've now got a mountain of paperwork to do." He winked at me. "Could you and Kitty catch a taxi home?"

"Oh, sure. No problem."

"Good." He looked up. "Oh, speak of the devil."

"You figured out my clue about the iguana!" Kitty said, rushing to give me a hug in the lobby of the police station.

"It took me a while. Why did you have to be all 'Indians and arrows' cryptic about it?"

Kitty pulled her pink purse up higher on her shoulder and glanced around. "I had to. The cops were listening. If I told them I thought an iguana kissed Sophia and gave her that blister on her lip, they'd have locked me in the looney bin."

"You know, there was a moment tonight when I thought I might be going there myself." As I hugged Kitty again, my brain suddenly slammed on the brakes. I locked eyes with Kitty. "Wait—that's what your clue was about?"

***

On the ride home, I filled Kitty in on what she'd missed at Sophia's centennial party. "As it turned out, there were no hermit crabs with tommy guns. Just crabby old people with swollen gums."

Kitty laughed. "Wow. You make me sorry I missed it."

"You know, if you hadn't had the gumption to collect those samples from Freddy's throat, we might never have figured out the source of the poison, or Melanie's scheme to defraud the folks at Shady Respite."

Kitty shook her head. "Forging people's signatures on powers of attorney so she could bilk them out of their belongings. How low can you go?"

"I know, right?"

She shook her pink-haired head. "Melanie seemed so nice."

"You talked to her?"

"Yes. Before you showed up in our lives. I ran into her while I was stuck doing my tour of duty with Sophia at Shady Respite. Melanie said she was really into tropical plants, like me. She's even got a greenhouse in Boca Raton. She told me to drop by and see it some time. And I told her to do the same." Kitty's mouth fell open. "Oh, my word. I even gave her my address."

"Well, that explains what happened to your beach apples."

Kitty shook her head. "I guess you just never know, do you?"

"Nope."

"Oh, that reminds me. Who did Sophia name as heir to her throne?"

My mouth fell open. "You know, in all the commotion, I think everybody forgot about it. We were just glad to have foiled Melanie's plans and that Sophia was still alive."

Chapter Seventy

When we arrived back at Palm Court Cottages, the little glowing lights above the picnic table were on, but the table was bare. Kitty and I made our way along the path to Aunt Edna's door.

"Hey, Kitty! Hey, Dorey!" Jackie said as we entered the 1970s time warp that was Aunt Edna's living room. She shoved a cardboard box the size of a microwave at me.

"What's this?" I asked.

"One of those boxes you got today. I just happened to notice it was from Maureen." She grinned. "Looks like your ma sent you a birthday present!"

I took the box and frowned. "If she did, it'd be the first one."

"What?" Kitty gasped.

I shrugged. "Like I said, Ma thought birthdays were bad luck. I never even knew what a birthday was until I got invited to a party for the next-door neighbor's kid."

"Geez," Jackie said.

"Well, first time for everything!" Kitty said with way too much enthusiasm. "Go on! Open it up!"

"Hold on," Jackie said. "Let me get a knife to cut the tape. Or do you have your cuticle scissors handy?"

"Ha ha. Hurry up!"

Jackie disappeared, then returned a few seconds later with Aunt Edna trailing behind her.

I took the knife and sliced through the packing tape. Inside the box was a jumble of stuff, none of it wrapped.

"These are all my childhood things I left at Ma's," I said. "Why would she send me this?"

"I thought this might happen," Aunt Edna said.

"What would happen? Is Ma ditching me for good?"

Aunt Edna came and sat beside me on the couch. "It ain't like that. Not exactly."

I frowned. "Then exactly how is it?"

"Remember when I told you we were like a bunch of Prince Charles's, waiting for Sophia to die to take over the throne?"

I gasped. "Did Sophia *die*?"

"No. She just went home to get out of her girdle."

"Oh."

"The point is, your ma was like Wallace."

"What?"

"Maureen was a commoner. The kind of gal a prince shouldn't marry."

I shook my head. "What are you talking about?"

"Your ma got knocked up by somebody she shouldn't have been involved with. A big-wig we couldn't trust. That's why she moved so far away, and never kept in touch. To keep you a secret. To keep you safe."

"Safe from what?" I grumbled. "Love?"

"Don't say that." Aunt Edna patted my back. "Maureen is a regular woman, just like us. She ain't no superhero. She hid you from the Family because back then, if they'd found out, well, who knows what would've happened. She would've been a tramp, and you a bastard. She tried to make the most of it, but she resented having to give up her life for you. You can understand that, can't you?"

"Not really. But it does explain a lot."

"Maureen did you a favor, never telling you. So you could lead a normal life."

"Normal?" I scoffed. "That's rich. So who is this guy, or am I not supposed to know?"

"I ain't the one to say," Aunt Edna said.

"Who is?"

"Maureen."

I scowled. "I knew when you told me she went to Alaska that it was a lie. Ma hates the cold."

"You're right," Aunt Edna said. "She ain't in Alaska, Dorey."

"Then where is she?"

"No telling. Her phone's been disconnected. She's in the wind."

Chapter Seventy-One

"In the wind?" I asked. "What does that mean?"

Aunt Edna shook her head. "Only Maureen knows."

A knock sounded at the door. A woman's voice called out, "Let me in!"

Ma?

I sprinted to the door and flung it open. Sophia came hobbling in.

She looked around. "Where's the cake, already?"

"Right behind you," a man said.

Morty and Humpty Bogart came in, each carrying a torta alla panna heaped high with whipped cream.

"Finally," Sophia said. "A *real* Italian birthday cake."

"Sorry," Morty said. "I couldn't exactly make one of these to feed a hundred people."

A smile crooked Sophia' lips. "That's how many came?"

"A hundred and seventeen," Jackie said. "If I count you."

"Not bad." Sophia reached for the cake in Morty's hand. "So let's cut that thing, Morty. I'm starving."

"Not this one," Morty said. "Humpty's got yours. With bananas and blueberries, just like you like. This one's for Dorey."

My eyebrows ticked up a notch. "For *me?*"

"Yep," Morty beamed. "Underneath all this hand-beaten cream is a mound of the most delectable strawberries I could find."

"Strawberries," Sophia huffed. "I don't like things with little seeds. They get caught in your dentures."

"Me either," Jackie said, taking Sophia's arm. "Come on, let's all go celebrate in the courtyard, where there's room for everybody."

***

"You didn't think we forgot about you, did you Dorey?" Aunt Edna asked as I sliced my first official birthday cake.

"I didn't dare get my hopes up," I said. "Ma never called today, did she?"

Aunt Edna shook her head.

"And my son never came to *my* party," Sophia said. "You don't see me all down in the dumps."

"He sent you flowers," I said.

"Humph," she grunted. "Did he? Nobody signed the card." She scooped up a forkful of her cake. "Red roses. Death or love. I got neither tonight."

"You got love," Aunt Edna said. "From *us*. So did you, Dorey."

"What's this I hear about love?" a man's voice called out from the shadows. Brady walked into view carrying two bouquets of yellow roses.

"For you," he said to Sophia, handing her a bunch and kissing her on the cheek. "And for you, Doreen." Brady kissed me on the cheek and whispered, "Happy birthday." His breath sent shivers down my spine.

"Yellow roses mean happiness, new beginnings, and friendship," Kitty said. "How wonderful!"

Wonderful? I noticed love wasn't in there anywhere. Still, this was my best birthday ever, and I was happy to have any or all of the other things the yellow roses meant.

"I guess it's time for gifts," Aunt Edna said.

"Yes!" Sophia said. "Where are they?"

"Um ... you got yours already, Doña Sophia," Kitty said. "We blew quite a bit on your party."

"And Dorey here saved your life," Aunt Edna said. "What more gift do you want?"

"Eh," Sophia grunted. "I'd love to have my old bladder back."

Everyone laughed, their smiles lit by the warm glow of the overhead lights. The moment felt like a delicious group hug.

"So, here we go," Aunt Edna said. "Presents for Dorey."

"What?" I said.

"Here's mine." Aunt Edna shot me a smile. "Room and board for six months, and linguini for life."

"Are you serious?" Tears welled in my eyes.

"You bet'cha."

"This is from me," Jackie said. She handed me an unwrapped cell phone.

"But this is *my* phone," I said.

"Read the text."

I glanced down at the display. There was a text from Kerri.

Tomorrow at 10:30. Last chance. I mean it this time. Oh, and happy birthday!

"How did she know it was my birthday?"

Jackie grinned. "A little birdie told her."

"Here, this is from me!" Kitty said, handing me a wrapped gift.

I tore into it. It was a beautiful, leather-bound journal.

"I thought you might want to write down your observations," Kitty said. "You may not be on the big screen yet, but you've got a great talent for seeing the big picture."

My heart swelled to near bursting. "Thank you all! And you, too, Morty. For the cake. It's delicious."

"You're welcome." Morty shot me a wink. "Strawberries are *my* favorite, too."

"Geez," Aunt Edna hissed.

"Sophia," Kitty said. "Sorry I missed your party. I heard you didn't name an heir to your throne."

"Hey, it's a woman's prerogative to change her mind," the Queenpin said. "And the day ain't over yet."

"Women." Humpty laughed. "I hope you don't think we're all after your pot of gold, Sophia."

"I ain't worried about you," Sophia said. "You'd be out of your depth in a paddling pool."

"Well, I don't want the job," Kitty said. "The only crown I wear came with a matching root canal. No thanks."

"Don't look at me," Aunt Edna said. "I'm up to my elbows in macaroni as it is."

Sophia's cat-green eyes surveyed us one by one, until her eyes fell on me.

"Dorey, it's good to see you coming up in the ranks. You're no soft, coddled egg."

"Uh ... thank you," I said.

"Hard boiled." Sophia nodded. "That's what this organization needs."

Aunt Edna nudged me with her elbow. "Remember when we gave you the flip-flops and told you that you've got big shoes to fill?"

I gulped. "Uh ... yes."

"What we need is fresh blood," Aunt Edna said. "Youth."

"You got that right," Sophia said. "Around here, forty years old is barely out of diapers."

My mouth went dry. "You want *me* to be the new Queenpin?"

Aunt Edna and Sophia burst out laughing. After a quick pause, Jackie, Morty and Humpty joined in.

"No," Aunt Edna said, wiping tears from her eyes. "We want you to take over as the Doña's personal assistant."

"What?" I gasped. "Why me?"

Aunt Edna put a hand on my shoulder. "After what you told us you had to do for those celebrities back in L.A., we figured you have the perfect skills for the job." She leaned in and whispered in my ear. "Besides, if I have to do it for one more day, I might lose it."

"Well, if Dorey isn't gonna be the new Queenpin, who is?" Jackie asked.

"Me," Sophia said. "Anybody got a problem with that?"

"Not me," Kitty said.

Everyone at the table shook their heads.

Sophia smiled and adjusted her silver turban. "So then, it's settled."

***

After the guys left and the dishes were washed, I said my goodnights and padded back to the spare bedroom where I'd been staying.

Where I *would* be staying.

As I changed into my pajamas and climbed into bed, there was a soft knock on the door.

"You decent in there?" Aunt Edna asked.

"Sure. Come on in."

She peeked her head inside. "It's nice to see somebody using that bed. You know, you never did say whether you were gonna take the job as Sophia's assistant."

"How could I turn it down, given your glowing recommendation?"

Aunt Edna laughed. "Sophia ain't that bad."

"Maybe not." I shook my head. "I didn't realize Sophia was such a co-median."

"You wouldn't unless she likes you."

"Sophia *likes* me?"

"We all do. Face it, Dorey. You're one of us."

I winced. "Because of the eye?"

"No. Because it's in your blood."

"Like Ma?" I said sourly.

Aunt Edna sat down on the edge of the bed. "Our Family is *our* people, Dorey. No matter how much we hate each other, we love each other more."

I looked down at my hands. "I guess."

Aunt Edna stood. "Now, don't stay up too late. You've got a busy day tomorrow."

I looked up. "As Sophia's assistant?"

"At your audition."

"Oh. Yeah."

Aunt Edna shot me a smile, then closed the door behind her. The warm glow I felt as she left had nothing to do with the pink lava lamp on the bureau.

I smiled softly, remembering Tip #53 in my *Hollywood Survival Guide. When you come to a fork in the road, pick it up and use it to eat cake.*

I didn't know if my future would turn out to be filled with angel's food or devil's food. But I'd just picked up my fork and eaten my own, bona fide birthday cake with it.

The first one ever.

And the way I figured it, taking care of Sophia couldn't be anywhere near as bad as clipping Arthur Dreacher's toenails.

Ma's starting her life over. So am I. I hope wherever she is, she's somewhere warm.

I didn't mean it *that* way.

I picked up the beautiful journal Kitty had given me, then cracked it open and wrote down my first observation.

Humpty Bogart has a cleft chin.

Book Three: Almost a Dead Ringer

Prologue

Not long ago I, Doreen Diller, was a complete nobody.

Man, those were the good old days.

Ever take a trip inside the trunk of a Chevy Caprice? I don't recommend it. You see, three weeks ago, I played a crazy-eyed psycho killer on a low-budget TV serial. It aired on a Friday. By Monday morning, I'd already been called out as a murderer and hit over the head by an umbrella-wielding old woman.

The thing is, nobody told me that there's no escaping the public—or that in this digital age, no one seems to be able to tell the difference between entertainment and reality anymore.

I cannot overestimate how much this can totally screw up your life.

As an actress who failed to make it to the big screen in Hollywood, I don't know what being famous feels like. But being *infamous*? Well, it's like being stalked 24-7 by a clown carrying a mud pie with your name on it.

So if you've ever thought about becoming a serial killer—or even playing one on TV—take my advice.

Wear a really good disguise.

And don't let them use your real name.

Chapter One

The newspaper landed with a thump on the dining room table, right next to my bowl of Lucky Charms.

"Read it and weep," Aunt Edna said, shuffling past in her fuzzy slippers. She chuckled to herself as she took a seat across the table from me.

The paper was St. Pete's local tabloid, the *Beach Gazette*. My aunt had folded it to an article about Sophia's big party at the Coliseum downtown last night.

Twelve hours ago, the matriarch of the little-known southern branch of the mafia known as the Collard Green Cosa Nostra had turned 100 in style—if you considered narrowly escaping death to be stylish. And from what I'd learned so far about the gang of elderly mob ladies I was currently living with, I was pretty certain they *did*.

Sharing the same birthday as Sophia, I'd also turned a year older yesterday—only my odometer had clicked over to forty. I squinted at the newspaper. The only thing certain about my future was the need for bifocals ...

The article in the *Beach Gazette* was entitled, "*The Hundred Games.*" The headline was spot-on, considering Sophia's age and the underhanded shenanigans that had gone down last night. But it irked the stew out of me that the article's annoying author, Shirley Saurwein, had been clever enough to think of it.

The sarcastic, loud-mouthed, bleach-blonde reporter was quickly becoming my least favorite acquaintance *ever*. And as a gal who'd tried for 15 years to make it to the big screen in L.A., the list of scumbags I knew was longer than a trip up the Nile in a leaky canoe.

I scanned the newspaper article. Saurwein had made no mention of my heroic deeds in saving Sophia's life during last night's soiree. Or how I'd uncovered a scheming crook trying to defraud seniors of their life savings. Instead, Saurwein had decided to focus on clichés about Florida's growing glut of "golden years" seniors with nothing but time on their hands and complaints in their mouths.

I had to hand it to her, though. The photo Saurwein had published to accompany her story drove home her point like a spear gun to the gut. She'd caught Sophia, our reining Godmother, glowering like an angry gargoyle at the two people cutting her centennial birthday cake.

The Queenpin's thin-lipped, Grinch-like scowl creased the lower half of her ancient, pasty face. Her catlike green eyes bulged with fury beneath the shiny silver turban she wore like a Jiffy Pop crown.

I pursed my lips. Sophia's tragic/comic visage reminded me of the absurd, bubble-headed aliens in *Mars Attacks*.

Well played, Saurwein. Well played.

I snickered, then caught myself. I glanced up at Aunt Edna.

"What's so funny?" she asked, peering at me over the rim of her coffee cup. A cultural relic from the 1970s, the only thing my aunt was missing were pink curlers in her hair.

"Nothing," I said, then set the paper down and picked up my spoon. "Well, at least it wasn't *me* caught in Saurwein's crosshairs this time. I think I might've made it through this whole 'turning forty thing' without any damage after all."

Aunt Edna raised a silvery eyebrow. "You sure about that?"

I frowned. "What do you mean?"

"Turn the paper over."

I did—and nearly choked to death on a mouthful of magically delicious cereal. Unfortunately, Saurwein's caustic article continued beyond the fold. The second part of it was punctuated by a photograph of me that was just as odd and unflattering as Sophia's.

I stared at the image of myself wearing Jackie Cooperelli's old-lady glaucoma sunglasses. I'd donned them to hide my spooky, pale-blue left eye from the public. But that wasn't what galled me about the photo.

During the party, I'd been stuck holding one of the guest's therapy animals—a grayish-green iguana the size of a wiener dog. Saurwein had captured the lizard and me both glowering into the camera like a pair of infuriated dimwits.

Even worse, my downturned mouth exactly mirrored the iguana's. The only difference was, *I* had lips. Well, at least more lips than that *lizard*, anyway.

Argh!

My grip tightened on the paper. I took a deep breath, then steeled myself as I read the caption Saurwein had written beneath the cringe-worthy photograph.

> *Younger hunger. Some seniors have forgotten how to age grace-fully. Apparently, they're ready to do just about anything for at-tention—including, sadly, trying to look glamorous well beyond their expiration dates. Hitting a new low, accessories to attract attention now appear to include the exploitation of exotic pets.*

I gritted my teeth and hissed, "That woman is a menace to society!"

Aunt Edna smirked and shrugged her mannish shoulders. "Every-body's gotta have goals in life, Dorey."

My mouth fell open. As I waited for my brain to get with the pro-gram and spew forth a snarky retort, a different voice beat me to the punch.

"Morning, you two!" Jackie, Aunt Edna's ever cheerful sidekick, poked her pewter-haired head into the dining room. Wearing a flower-print shirt loud enough to bust an eardrum, she wagged her eyebrows playfully. "Brace yourselves, ladies. I've got the other birthday girl with me."

Jackie disappeared, then reappeared a moment later with Sophia on her arm. The rail-thin Godmother hobbled in, her silver turban slightly askew.

I snatched up the newspaper. "Did you see this?"

"Yes," Sophia said. She eased herself into a chair across the table from me. "Jackie. Coffee. Now."

"I'm on it," Jackie said. Springing into action like a soldier on a life-or-death mission, she scurried into the kitchen.

"What's so golden about the golden years?" Sophia muttered, pick-ing lint from her black shawl. "My hair is silver and my butt's turned to lead."

My upper lip snarled. "At least *you* weren't upstaged by a freaking *iguana*."

Jackie returned with two mugs of coffee. She handed one to Sophia, then patted my shoulder. "Aww, Dorey. You got to learn to take things with a stain of salt."

"Jackie's right," Aunt Edna said, ignoring yet another classic Jackie malapropism. "Don't let sourpuss Saurwein get to you. She's just jealous. So, you ready to start your new job today?"

Jackie cocked her head at me and grinned. "Oh, yeah! You're taking care of Sophia from now on."

"*Her* taking care of *me*?" Sophia scoffed. "More like *I'll* be taking care of *her*." The ancient woman jutted her pointy chin toward me. Her thin lips curled slyly. "I'm going to make Doreen my pet project."

Aunt Edna leaned my way and whispered, "Better pray they're merciful at the kill shelter."

"So, young Doreen," Sophia said, eyeing me through her bejeweled bifocals. "Are you ready for lesson number one?"

"Um ... I can't right now," I said. "I have an audition this morning downtown. At Sunshine City Studios. If I miss it a third time, Kerri Middleton will have my head."

Sophia scowled. "And who says *I* won't if you go?"

"I do," Aunt Edna said. "Doreen made this lady Kerri a promise, Doña Sophia. And we CGCN women keep our promises."

Sophia sighed. "Fine. When will you return?"

I shrugged. "I don't know. It depends on whether they want me for the part or not."

Aunt Edna smiled and raised her coffee cup. "Well, here's to hoping those studio folks give our Dorey here an offer she can't refuse."

"This ought to help even the odds," Jackie said, handing me a baseball bat.

"What's this for?" I asked.

Jackie beamed. "So's you can break a leg, kid. What else?"

Chapter Two

Achieving stardom in the acting biz was kind of like getting pregnant. Everybody was quick to congratulate you when you got the good news, but they had no idea how many times you'd gotten screwed before it finally happened.

Unfortunately, I'd yet to find real success as either an actress *or* as a girlfriend—much less somebody's mother. But this morning I was feeling pretty lucky just the same.

When I started out for my audition at Sunshine City Studios, The Toad, Jackie's ancient green Kia, had fired up on the first try. Usually the rusty green beast required a solid beating of its solenoid to get the engine to crank. But now, as I sat clutching the steering wheel, the car was shaking and purring like an asthmatic lion.

That had to be a good sign, right?

I smiled, shifted into reverse, and pulled away from Palm Court Cottages. Last night's performance—saving Sophia's life—had earned me six months free rent and all the linguini I could eat. I hoped my next performance at Sunshine City Studios would earn me enough to take care of the rest of my living expenses. If not, I'd have to start sewing my own clothes. Aunt Edna's pasta was going straight to my thighs.

Since I hadn't needed to apply "encouragement" to The Toad's solenoid, I was, for once, actually running ahead of schedule. I took this as yet another good sign—especially considering I'd been a no-show for my last two auditions with Kerri Middleton.

In all fairness, neither incident had actually been my fault. In both cases, my delinquency had been due to circumstances beyond my control.

The first time, I'd lost track of the hour while prying open a dead guy's jaws in a nursing home morgue. (Long story.) The second time? Well, let's just say I'd put the needs of the many above the needs of the few.

Me, of course, being the few.

MARGARET LASHLEY

But in the end, it had all worked out. While I'd been chasing down a murderer, the elderly former mob molls of the CGCN had managed to convince Kerri Middleton to give me a third chance at bat. In return, I'd promised Kerri I'd take whatever role Sunshine Studios had to offer.

For once in my life, things had ended in a win-win situation.

I smiled and hit the gas. Maybe my luck was finally turning around.

Chapter Three

I tugged nervously at the hem of my skirt as I picked my way down the cracked sidewalk along Central Avenue in downtown St. Petersburg, Florida.

Sunshine City Studios was in a red-brick building repurposed from an abandoned dry-goods store. It sat in the middle of an old-fashioned, main-street type section on Central Avenue. To either side of the studio were an eclectic mix of small, glass-storefront boutiques, trendy coffee shops, and tiny mom-n-pop diners.

Like me, St. Petersburg was in the throes of remaking itself. All around the old town, shiny, new high-rise condos were sprouting up like bamboo shoots. The towers appeared to be in competition with each other, vying to see which one could poke its head highest into the blue sky in hopes of affording its inhabitants a glimpse of nearby Tampa Bay.

The outward flashiness of the new "city residences" was in stark contrast to the dirty windows and grungy storefronts of their faded, aged neighbors—lingering reminders of how the city had been floundering just a short time ago.

As I nervously straightened the collar of my white silk dress shirt, the similarity to my own situation wasn't lost on me.

Since my mid-twenties I'd tried to make it as an actress in Los Angeles. I'd failed miserably. Then, after a decade and a half of doing the worst grunt-work imaginable, I'd finally caught a break. Like an angel from heaven, Kerri Middleton had called and offered me a role in a six-part, low-budget TV series called *Beer & Loathing* being filmed at the beach here in St. Petersburg.

Well, Kerri had *actually* only offered a role to soap-opera heartthrob Tad Longmire. Being his personal assistant at the time, I'd come along to cater to his every whim. How was I to know that fate would step in for me—and in the most unusual way imaginable?

As it turned out, I owed my big acting break to cheap rubber, dirt, and desperation.

***

During filming *Beer & Loathing*, the original killer, an inflatable shark, had popped. With no budget or backup plan, production had slammed to a standstill.

While we'd all wracked our brains trying to figure out what to do next, wind had blown sand in my eye. I'd been forced to take out the contact lens I normally wore to hide my wonky pale eye.

Marshall Lazzaro, the young director on set, had caught a glimpse of my mismatched peepers. Out of time, money, and any better ideas, Marshall decided my "spooky cool" eyes would make me the perfect replacement psycho killer. He'd hired me on the spot.

I'd landed my first speaking part. But throughout filming, I'd had to hide behind a stupid rubber mask. And my voice had been electronically disguised. But hey, everybody had to start somewhere, right?

Unfortunately, it wasn't long before fickle fate had stepped in again—this time to ruin things for me. Right after filming wrapped on *Beer & Loathing*, someone stabbed Tad Longmire to death, *for real* this time.

With the star of the show suddenly "indisposed," the sixth and final episode had to be rewritten. Believe me, no one was more shocked than me when, in the final minutes of the very last episode, my unmasked face—and wonky eyes—were revealed as the mysterious psycho killer who'd stabbed Tad's character to death.

After that? Well, all heck had broken loose.

People from all over the place began calling the cops, reporting that I'd actually murdered Tad Longmire—*because they saw me do it on TV.*

Even though I was eventually cleared of all charges, some people's minds could not be unmade—not even, I suspected, some within my own new mob family. More than one of the GCGN molls considered me a "made woman." And the only way you get made in the mob was ... well, to whack, cut, pop, ice, clip, hit, burn, or put a contract out on somebody.

Anyway, like the city of St. Petersburg itself, I was now on the verge of putting my less-than-fabulous past behind me. Today, I was moving on with my life. I had a *real* audition. And this time, it was no twist of fate. I'd been chosen for my talent!

As I walked toward Sunshine City Studios, I was jittery with excitement. To calm myself, I took a deep breath and ran down my mental checklist.

> *Contact lens in to conceal my pale eye? Check.*
> *No stains on my blouse, jacket, or pencil skirt? Check.*
> *Hair and makeup intact? Check.*

I marched up to the faded red door of the studio and knocked loudly, with confidence and purpose.

Move over, Mr. DeMille. I'm more *than ready for my close-up!*

As I waited for the door to open, I clicked my high-heels together for good luck.

Hey, it worked for Dorothy in *The Wizard of Oz*, didn't it?

Chapter Four

I was ready for my close-up, but apparently Mr. DeMille was not. Nobody answered the door at Sunshine City Studios.

My confidence deflating faster than a shot-down Chinese spy balloon, I reached up to knock on the door for a third time.

Had Kerri decided to stand me up this time, to get even? Was this whole audition just some perverse joke on me?

I bit my lower lip and pounded on the door. Suddenly, the door opened wide. A tall, slender, elegant woman in her mid-fifties beckoned me in with a graceful swoop of her hand.

"You're early," Kerri Middleton said. "I wasn't expecting that."

I winced. "Sorry. It's just—"

"Water under the bridge." Kerri winked a hazel eye at me and tucked a lock of silver hair behind her ear. "Here's to hoping three's the charm, eh?"

I sighed with relief. "Yes!" I grabbed her hand and shook it. "Thank you so much for giving me a third chance. I promise, whatever you need, I'm your gal!"

She grinned. "Good. I'm holding you to that. Shall we go and meet your new costar?"

I grinned. "Yes, of course! Do I know him or her?"

"You might. Follow me."

Kerri turned and marched down the hall, her heels clicking on the polished hardwood floor.

I followed her to the studio's familiar waiting room. It was a cozy sitting area furnished with a teal couch and two white leather chairs. I pictured Tad Longmire sitting languidly in one of them, looking bored and put out to have to be there.

I sucked in a deep, calming breath and thanked my lucky stars that my days of babysitting that spoiled man-child were over. Still, I wished it hadn't ended the way it did.

"Doreen?" Kerri asked.

I spun around to face her. "Sorry. Just lost in thought."

Kerri nodded as if she understood. "Doreen, I want you to meet Eddie Houser, your costar."

I glanced over at the paunchy, middle-aged man walking up to me and felt some of the starch go out of me.

"Nice to finally meet you," he said, reaching out a ruddy hand to shake mine.

"Thank you," I said, trying not to focus on the gold eyetooth gleaming inside his mouth.

The man grinned at me from beneath a black cowboy hat and a thick, wooly moustache that could've been lifted from the prop room of *Smokey & the Bandit*.

His face seemed hauntingly familiar.

But not in a good way.

Chapter Five

"Where have I seen you before?" I asked the man in the ten-gallon cowboy hat and fifty-cent moustache. "Wait. Did you play the father in *Joe Dirt*?"

The man laughed. "No. But thanks for the compliment. You probably saw me on TV, just like I saw you. Hey, where's that wonky eye of yours, psycho killer?"

I frowned. "Contact lens."

"Gotcha." He grinned and said, "Hey, watch this!"

To my surprise, he pulled a pair of finger guns from imaginary holsters on his hips, then popped off a couple of silent shots. "Figured out where you saw me yet?"

I smiled weakly. "Sorry, still not ringing a bell."

Kerri cleared her throat. "Doreen, let me introduce you to Eddie Houser of … Crazy Eddie's Used Cars."

Instantly, my mind swirled with images of old sedans, their windshields covered with painted-on prices that were riddled with fake bullet holes.

My mouth fell open. "You're the guy who's always shooting down high car prices."

"Ha!" Eddie laughed. "You got that right, little lady. And you're the weird-eyed killer who slashed Tad Longmire to death in *Beer & Loathing*!"

I crinkled my nose. "I didn't *actually* kill him, you know."

"Right." Eddie winked salaciously. "Between you and me, whether *you* did him in or it was somebody else, I'm glad Longmire's gone."

My eyes grew wide. "What? Why?"

"My wife had a crush on that ne'er-do-well rascal," Eddie said. "Around here, I'm used to being top dog. So, thanks for getting rid of my competition, so to speak."

"Huh?" I grunted.

Eddie slapped me on the back. "That's what gave me the idea to hire you in the first place. I figured if you could get rid of my rivals in *that* department, you could help me with my *business* competition, too."

I turned to Kerri, my eyes pleading. "What's he talking about?"

"I need a new shtick," Eddie said.

Kerri stifled a wince. "Um ... Mr. Houser is hoping to ... uh ... ride the wave of publicity from your role on *Beer & Loathing*."

"Get it?" Eddie said, slapping me on the back again. "*Ride* the wave?"

"No, I don't." I stepped out of slapping range. "What is it exactly that you want me to do?"

"Be my hired killer," Eddie said. "You and that wonky eye of yours. Bust it out, and lets you and me get busy slashing prices to the bone!"

I nearly swallowed my tonsils.

This must be how a bug feels when it hits the grille of a Mack truck.

I closed my eyes and tried to compose myself. Like that poor, hapless bug, there was no escaping what fate wrought for it, or for me. A promise was a promise.

Where's a Mack truck when you need one?

I opened my eyes, forced a smile at Eddie, and glanced over at Kerri. "Awesome. When do we start?"

Kerri winced again. "I'm afraid that, you know, since you missed your first two auditions, we're in kind of a time crunch."

My nose crinkled. "What do you mean?"

Eddie took a step toward me and put his hammy hand on my shoulder. "She means, little lady, that you need to get yourself all gussied up *right now*. We'll be shooting at my car lot on US 19 in half an hour."

***

As I stumbled out the back door of Sunshine Studios, Kerri and Leslie, the young, blue-haired makeup girl I'd met filming *Beer & Loathing*, shoved me into a white van.

The van's engine was already running. At the wheel was Marshall, the young producer and owner of the studio.

"Good to see you Doreen," the handsome, 20-something blond man said. He grinned at me from behind aviator shades as I bounced onto the back seat with all the grace of a thrown garbage bag.

"Uh, you too," I managed to say as Leslie slid into the bench seat beside me, blocking my escape.

Kerri climbed into the front passenger seat and slammed the door. "Step on it!"

"You got it," Marshall said, and hit the gas. The van lurched forward.

"Am I being abducted, or what?" I asked.

"We're just in a time crunch," Kerri said. "And to be honest, business has been slow, Doreen. Not to mention we got stiffed by a couple of deadbeats. I know this isn't ideal, but we can't afford to lose this client."

I nodded. "Okay. I made you a promise. I'll do whatever it takes."

"Thank you." Kerri sighed with relief. "Now, let's get you prepped."

My nose crinkled. "Prepped?"

Leslie shoved a wardrobe bag into my lap. "Get into this outfit while I tease your hair."

I gulped. "Here? In the van?"

"It's either change in here or in the bathroom at Crazy Eddie's," Kerri said. "Trust me. The van is the choice you want to make."

I grimaced and zipped open the bag. "Um ... these jeans are a size six."

"That's what it said in your portfolio," Leslie said. "Five feet four, 115 pounds, size seven shoes, size six pants.

"Oh, sure." And I was—a month of eating Aunt Edna's pasta ago. "Here goes."

I stripped off my pencil skirt and heels. Then, trying not to grunt like a pig, I squeezed into a pair of jeans tighter than a tourniquet. Surviving that, I traded in my silk blouse for a Daisy Duke shoulder-less top.

"How do I look?" I asked, barely able to breathe.

Kerri turned and looked me up and down. "Better get out the filets, Leslie."

"The what?" I asked.

"On it." Leslie bent over and dug through her huge bag of props. "Here we go." She pulled out two pieces of flesh-colored rubber the size and shape of large chicken breasts. "Here. Stick these in your—"

"I know where they go," I said, snatching them from her hands. Be-grudgingly, I shoved the rubber boobs into my bra.

"Eddie likes cleavage," Leslie said, then twisted her face in disgust. "Now, lean your head toward me so I can start teasing your hair."

Kerri shook her head. "Sorry, Doreen. The only thing Eddie likes better than big boobs is big hair."

I blew out a breath.

And the only thing I like less than playing a bimbo is clipping ugly old Arthur Dreacher's toenails.

Chapter Six

It had all happened so fast, it was still a blur. Or maybe it was just that those stupid jeans had cut off the circulation to my brain ...

"Come on," Leslie said, tugging me out of the van. "And watch the hair!"

I climbed out and caught a glimpse of myself in the van's side mirror. Blue eyeshadow glimmered all the way to my eyebrows. A fake mole loitered just above my lips, which had taken on the hue and shine of candied apples. My brown hair was the size of a beach ball.

"Who am I supposed to be?" I asked. "The leading lady in *Hairspray*?"

"Daisy the Price Slasher," Leslie said, handing me a rubber knife the length of a windshield wiper. "Remember, your motivation is to slash prices to the bone."

"Seriously?" At this point, my only motivation was to keep my personal dignity from meeting its own untimely death. But I had a sinking feeling that ship had already sailed.

"Come on," Leslie said, tugging me by the elbow. "We'll put the stilettos on you once we get you across the parking lot."

"Okay, okay!" I held my head high and followed her past rows of old, dented cars on their last legs. It certainly wasn't a glamourous gig. But the good news was, nobody could possibly recognize me in this ridiculous getup.

***

If it were physically possible to die of embarrassment, I'd have never made it all the way over to the rusty blue Ford Escort parked in the middle of the lot at Crazy Eddie's Used Cars.

"Places, everybody," I heard Marshall yell as I tugged on the leopard-print high-heels.

"Nice," Eddie said as I fastened the buckles.

Creep!

When I stood up, Eddie's greasy smile evaporated. The shoes make me almost six inches taller than him, and he seemed none too pleased about it.

"Here, take this," Leslie said, handing me my rubber knife. "Now, stand next to Eddie by the windshield of the blue Escort."

I hobbled over to Eddie, feeling like a magician's bubble-headed assistant. I definitely needed rescuing from "the denim trousers of death."

"Ready, little lady?" Eddie asked, twitching his dime-store moustache.

I shot him a fake smile. "Ready as I'll ever be."

"Remember your lines?" Kerri asked.

I nodded. "Take that, you beastly prices."

"With a bit more enthusiasm?" she asked.

"I'm saving it for the real thing," I said.

"Fair enough." Kerri nodded at Marshall. "We're ready when you are."

"Okay, ready, set, action!" Marshall yelled.

Leslie slapped down the top of the clapboard. "Price Slasher, take one!"

I was surprised to see that Marshall was not only directing, he was manning the camera as well. Money must've really been tight, just like Kerri had said. Marshall zoomed in on Eddie as the used car salesman hucksvered out his spiel.

"Howdy, folks!" Eddie tipped his black hat. "Now, when the little lady says she wants a new car, but you're short on cash, who you gonna call?" Eddie shrugged his shoulders and held his palms open wide. "Eddie Houser, that's who!"

"Bring your better half on over to Crazy Eddie's Used Cars. I'm sure we can make a deal. After all, I'm a sucker for a pretty face. Ain't that right, Daisy?"

"Oh, yes, Eddie!" I gushed, giving the camera a gander at my fake cleavage.

Eddie waggled his eyebrows. "So Daisy, how about you show the good folks out there how deep we slash those car prices?"

"You got it, handsome Eddie dear." I raised my rubber knife over the windshield of the dented, Ford Escort. "Take that, you beastly prices!"

Suddenly, I felt a hand grab my left butt cheek and squeeze.

"What the!" I gasped and swung around. As I did, the edge of my rubber blade skimmed across the neck of the fast-handed pervert.

"Argh!" Eddie bellowed. He grabbed his throat with both hands and stumbled backward.

"Oh, hell!" I screeched. "Mr. Houser! Are you all right?"

He looked up at me and grinned, causing his gold tooth to glint in the sun. "Ha ha!" he laughed. "I'm fine, darlin'. But I got you good, didn't I?"

"Cut!" Kerri yelled.

"No kidding," Marshall said.

I glowered at Eddie. "Excuse me, but you had no right to grab me like that!"

"Oh, come on," Eddie said. "I just wanted to get you to open up those crazy eyes of yours a little wider."

I scowled. "Believe me, my eyes are *wide open*." I turned to Kerri. "I quit!"

I turned to go, but tripped on my stilettos. Kerri caught me by the elbow. "Please," she whispered in my ear. "You can't quit, Doreen. You promised."

I snorted steam through my nostrils. "Fine. But one more take and that's it. And if he grabs my butt again—"

"He won't," Kerri said. "I'll make sure of it."

"Awe, that's too bad," a woman's voice sounded from behind me. "I kinda liked it."

I whirled back around on my stilettos and nearly toppled over again. My mouth twisted into a snarl. "Shirley Saurwein! What the hell are *you* doing here?"

Saurwein laughed and twirled a lock of platinum blonde hair between her fingers "I was just driving by and happened to catch a glimpse of you coming out of that van."

She cracked her gum and nodding toward the Sunshine Studios vehicle. "I thought maybe you'd been kidnapped. Or is this a new look for you?"

"We're shooting a commercial," I grumbled. "This outfit is for my character."

"Oh yeah?" she quipped. "Who you supposed to be? Daisy Duke or Bride of Frankenstein?"

Chapter Seven

I slid into the backseat of the van, unfastened the button on my anaconda jeans, and gasped in a lungful of air. I rubbed the red ring encircling my waist. My face had to be just as crimson beneath the quarter-inch-thick layer of makeup it was smothering under.

"Geez, Kerri!" I grumbled as the van pulled out of the lot at Crazy Edie's Used Cars. "Daisy the Bimbo Price Slasher? Whatever happened to us making a difference for women with our film projects?"

Kerri cringed. "Sorry, Doreen. But sometimes you have to eat your vegetables first."

I blew out a breath. "I get that. But at this point, I'm beginning to think I'm doomed to be a lifelong vegetarian."

Kerri shot me a sympathetic smile. "Come on. It wasn't *that* bad, was it?"

My eyebrows met my teased hairline. "Not that bad? Whatever possessed you to think of *me* for this role anyway?"

"I didn't. Eddie Houser did. After seeing you on *Beer & Loathing*, he called me saying he'd pay a pretty penny to get you."

I sat back in my seat. "I sure hope he paid more than that."

Kerri grinned. "He did. But that's not the best part. Doreen, do you know what this means?"

I shot her a sour look. "That I have enough pennies to buy a veggie burger *and* fries?"

Kerri's nose crinkled. "No. I mean, well, yes. But it means something else, too."

"What?" I grumbled.

"It means you've got a *fan base*, Doreen. That's worth something, isn't it?"

I chewed my lip. "I guess. What's my take in this, anyway?"

Kerri smiled. "Five hundred dollars up front, plus five percent of all the extra profits for the next month."

"Studio profits?" I perked up. "That's really nice of you, Kerri. Thanks!"

"Not *our* profits," Kerri said. "Eddie's used-car sales profits. He's banking on a return on investment from his ads. It's his way of incentivizing you to want them to be successful, too. Pretty shrewd, eh?"

"For a lecherous dirtbag?" I groused. "Yeah, I guess. Anyway, at least it's all over with." I lifted my butt from the van's bench seat and started yanking off the merciless jeans.

Leslie grabbed my arm. "You can change when we get back."

"Are you kidding?" I balked. "I might not survive that long." I tugged the jeans halfway down my hips and scowled. "Why is it that we women have to do all this crap to try and be attractive, while men do pretty much *absolutely nothing*?"

Kerri bit her bottom lip. "I don't know. Sometimes I think we women do it to ourselves."

I peeled the legs of my painted-on jeans down to my knees and plopped my butt back onto the seat. "We're supposed to be perfect—not to mention *hairless*. Meanwhile, men walk around like bipedal apes. They don't even bother to cut their hair or shave their faces anymore!"

Kerri sighed. "That's one of the reasons I gave up dating." She shook her head. "We get what we put up with nowadays. And beards and cigars were the last two straws for me."

"You've got a point," Leslie said, swiping her blue bangs from her forehead. "See this? I got this new piercing on my eyebrow last week. My boyfriend Jeremy didn't even notice." She flopped back onto the bench seat beside me. "All he cares about is microbrews and his razor scooter. If I left him, I don't think he'd even notice until the beer in the fridge ran out."

"Hey, that's not fair," Marshall said, eyeing us from the rearview mirror.

"It's not?" Leslie said. "Prove me wrong."

Marshall winced. "Well, you know Jeremy better than I do."

"I sure do." Leslie glared at Marshall, then shot me a crooked purple eyebrow. "See? Told you."

I sighed and handed her the rumpled jeans. "Wouldn't it be awesome if the roles were reversed?"

"What do you mean?" Leslie asked.

"You know. That it was the *men* who had to be perfect, and all we women had to do was show up."

"Come on," Marshall said. "You women demand way too much attention from us. Anyway, Doreen, you should be getting plenty of it after this spot airs."

I grimaced.

Yeah. That's what I'm afraid of…

***

As I drove home in The Toad, I glanced through the windshield and up at the sky, hoping a meteor would come hurtling down and put me and the Kia both out of our misery.

Who had I been kidding, thinking I was going to be offered a serious acting gig?

The Kia and I were both well past our prime. And just when I'd thought my acting career had sunk as low as it could go, I'd been forced to do the *bimbo limbo*.

I glanced in the rearview mirror at my makeup-free face, still ruddy from a good scrubbing in the Studio's bathroom sink. I cringed. Crow's feet were coming in for a landing around the corners of my eyes.

I blew out a breath. Whatever happened to the fresh-faced young woman full of piss and vinegar? The woman who'd been eager to fight the good fight against sexist portrayals of women in the media?

I know what happened.

I'd just traded her in for five hundred bucks and five percent of the profits on a lot full of dented Ford Escorts.

I scanned the sky through the windshield again. Still no meteor.

I hit the steering wheel with my fist and groaned.

"Argh!"

Not only had I kowtowed to the Hollywood clichés, I'd gone and forged new ground in objectifying women as weak-minded, simpering idiots.

And to top it off, that blasted Shirley Saurwein had seen me do it.

Chapter Eight

As I shifted the Kia into park in front of Palm Court Cottages, I envisioned the next edition of the *Beach Gazette* lying on the lawn.

In my mind's eye, the entire front page would be an image of me dressed as Daisy the "Bimbo" Price Slasher. The headline above it would scream out in big bold letters: *Doreen Diller, Still Unmarried and Unemployable at Age 40, Single-Handedly Slays the Feminist Movement.*

I groaned and I kicked open the car door.

"What's wrong?" Jackie asked, appearing out of nowhere. "Don't tell me somebody broke *your* leg!"

"What?" I grumbled, slamming the car door. Then I remembered she'd given me the baseball bat for luck. "Oh. No legs were broken. Just my spirit. And I broke that all by myself."

"Aww." Jackie slung a skinny arm across my shoulders. "Didn't go well? Don't you worry, kid. I know just the cure for that. A nice, steaming bowl of Edna's linguini Alfredo. Come with me."

I trailed behind the wiry, silver-haired woman like a child doomed for a dose of castor oil. As I trudged into Aunt Edna's apartment, I was surprised to discover the 1970s brown-and-avocado time capsule didn't smell like pasta sauce—or even Lemon Pledge, for that matter.

"Is Aunt Edna sick?" I asked.

"Nope." Jackie nodded toward the dining room. "Just busy. She's got her *own* job, you know."

"Really? I didn't know that."

"There's a lot you don't know about us yet," Jackie said as we entered the dining room.

Aunt Edna was standing beside the dining table talking on the wall phone—an ancient, dull-green landline with enough curly cord dangling from the handset to hog-tie three people.

"Call you back," my aunt said when she saw us, then quickly slammed the phone back into the cradle hanging on the wall. She grabbed a small notebook off the dining table and stuffed it into her apron pocket.

"Geez! What happened, Dorey?" my aunt asked as her eyes darted to the mop of teased hair atop my head. I'd tried to contain it with a scrunchy, but ended up looking like a fried Kewpie doll instead. "Don't tell me you got electrocuted!"

"No such luck," I said, flopping into a dining chair.

"Dorey's got the morbs," Jackie said. "I can tell by the infliction in her voice."

"In*flection*," Aunt Edna said, shooting Jackie a look.

"I told Doreen it's nothing your pasta Alfredo can fix," Jackie said.

Aunt Edna wiped her hands on her apron. "Well, it sure can't hurt. Let me fix you a plate."

"I'm not hungry," I said.

My aunt nearly tripped on her own feet. "What? You got a fever?"

"No, but I *am* burning mad." I crossed my arms over my chest and sulked. "Why is it that when a woman turns forty, she's considered washed up?"

Aunt Edna frowned. "Only in some circles, Dorey."

"Yeah," Jackie said. "Only the circles full of squares."

Aunt Edna started to scold Jackie, then stopped and cocked her head at me. "For once, Jackie's right. The only people who think 'women of a certain age' are has-beens are the ones too stupid to see beyond surface beauty. And you know what? In a way, it's a blessing."

"A blessing?" I scoffed. "What's so great about being over the hill?"

"Plenty." Aunt Edna put a hand on my shoulder. "I'm not saying you're past your prime, Dorey. But me and Jackie sure ain't gonna win any beauty contests no more."

Jackie beamed and elbowed my aunt. "You got *that* right, Edna."

Aunt Edna blew out a breath. "You don't gotta be *that* enthusiastic about it, Jackie."

"Enthusiastic about what?" I asked. "Being undesirable?"

Aunt Edna frowned. "I didn't say nothing about being undesirable."

I frowned. "Then what *are* you saying?"

Aunt Edna shrugged. "What I mean is, once beauty is off the table, everything else is wide open."

I cocked my head. "Huh?"

My aunt sat down in the chair beside me. "Some people have beauty for a while, Dorey. And some never have it. If you ask me, beauty is a burden. A curse, even."

I sat up in my chair. "I don't follow."

"Men know how to *work* beauty," Aunt Edna said. "They know how to manipulate you with it. But if you ain't got it, you ain't susceptible to their bull crap. In fact, you can turn the tables on them."

I studied my aunt. "What do you mean?"

Aunt Edna reached into her apron pocket and pulled out the notebook. She opened it to a page and shoved it at me. "See this list of guys, here?"

I glanced at the names of about a dozen men she'd written down. "Yeah. So what?"

Aunt Edna grinned slyly. "Every month, these guys send me money, hoping to hook up with me."

I nearly fell out of my chair. "What?"

Aunt Edna's face puckered. "Don't look so surprised. With the right incentive, any man can be yours for the taking."

Jackie winked. "You mean, 'any man can be taken.'"

"Same thing," my aunt said.

"Wait a minute," I said. "Are you having *sex* with these guys for *money*?"

Aunt Edna laughed. "No way!"

"She's more like their pen pal while they're in the pen," Jackie said. "Get it?"

"These guys are in j...jail?" I stuttered.

Aunt Edna laughed. "Yep. And these creeps ain't never getting out. Even if they did, they'll never find me. I have them send the money to a post office box downtown."

A weird mixture of horror and fascination and admiration and envy swirled inside me. "What do these guys get in return?"

"Something to brag to their cellmates about," Aunt Edna said.

"Let's just say Edna sends 'em a kiss to build a dream on," Jackie said.

I shook my head. "What are you talking about?"

Aunt Edna fanned through the pages of the notebook. A picture of a brunette bombshell in a one-piece bathing suit fell onto the table.

I snatched it up. "Whoa! Is that Elizabeth Taylor?"

"Nope." Aunt Edna beamed and pointed a thumb at her chest. "That's me, forty-eight years ago."

"You?" I gasped.

"Careful, Dorey." Aunt Edna showed me her palm. "If you say 'What happened?' I ain't gonna take it too well."

I shook my head. "No. What I meant was, I can't believe you sent them a *real picture of you*! Did you tell them your real name, too?"

"What kind of Reuben you think she is?" Jackie said. "Edna made up a name. It's a real doozy, too."

Aunt Edna wagged her eyebrows. "Liz Barker."

I eyed her skeptically. "How'd you pick that name?"

"On account of you ain't the only one who ever thought I looked like Elizabeth Taylor," Aunt Edna said.

"And Barker?" I asked.

"Because that was my mother's maiden name."

"Edna's grandmother was Arizona Donnie Barker," Jackie said.

My brow furrowed. "Who?"

Aunt Edna stared at me, slack jawed. "You playing with me, Dorey?"

"No. I swear."

My aunt frowned. "You really don't know?"

My eyes darted between the two women. "Know what?"

"Who Arizona Donnie Barker was," Jackie said.

I winced. "Um ... should I?"

Aunt Edna shook her head. "She was only the most famous female criminal in history."

"Oh." I smiled apologetically. "Sorry. Honestly, I've never heard of her."

"For crying out loud!" Aunt Edna moaned. "J. Edgar Hoover himself said she was 'the most vicious, dangerous, and resourceful criminal brain of the last decade.'"

"Give her a break, Edna," Jackie said, putting a hand on my aunt's shoulder. "That was a lot of decades ago."

Aunt Edna sighed. "I guess so. You know, in 1960, they even made a movie about my grandmother."

I grimaced. "I wasn't even *born* then."

My aunt hung her head. "Geez Louise. From America's most wanted to the dustbin of history." She elbowed her friend. "I guess we'll all end up there one day, hey Jackie? Some of us sooner than others."

I winced. "I'm really sorry, Aunt Edna."

My aunt locked her sad eyes with mine. "Dorey, my grandmother was Ma Barker, public enemy number one back in the 1930s."

My eyebrows shot up. "Hold on a second. Do you mean Ma Barker as in, *Ma Barker's Killer Brood*?"

Aunt Edna's lips hitched up into a tentative smile. "You've heard of the movie?"

"Heard of it?" I gasped. "I actually auditioned for the remake!"

Aunt Edna grinned. "No kidding!"

Jackie laughed. "What did I tell you, Edna? Dorey's got Barker blood running through her veins. Ha! You owe me fifty bucks."

"Can it," Aunt Edna grunted. "Dorey, you'd be perfect for the role. In fact, you kinda look like her."

"Uh ... thanks," I said. "So this dating service thing. You're actually stringing along a bunch of crooks for cash?"

Aunt Edna shrugged. "In a manner of speaking."

"How many have you got on the line?" I asked.

Jackie smirked. "A *Baker's* dozen. Get it?" She slapped me on the back. "Kinda ironical, considering Edna ain't had a date since she and Morty broke up."

Aunt Edna scowled. "Jackie, ain't it time for you to take some cyanide tablets or something?"

"Hold on." I turned to Jackie. "Are you in on this, too?"

"No way." Jackie laughed. "The way I see it, life is better without a man mucking things up."

I smirked. "You can say *that* again."

"Okay. Life is better without a—"

The phone rang. Aunt Edna jumped up, snatched the receiver from the wall, and pretended to club Jackie over the head with it. Then she spoke into the phone, pretty as punch.

"Hello? Oh, well yes, sir. Hmm. Let me see if she's available." Aunt Edna put her hand over the speaker and shot me a quizzical look. "Some guy asking questions about you."

I thought about Eddie Houser and grimaced. "Tell whoever it is, I'm not interested," I whispered, then winked at Jackie. "Like you said, I don't need some guy mucking up my life."

Aunt Edna nodded, and slid her hand from over the mouthpiece. "Sorry, Officer Brady, Dorey says she's not—"

"Hold on!" I yelped.

I sprang from the chair and snatched the phone from Aunt Edna's hand. The smug look on her face needed no translation.

"Careful," she whispered as I put the phone to my ear. "We wouldn't want some man mucking up your life now, would we?"

Chapter Nine

"What was that all about?" I heard Officer Gregory Brady ask as I held the receiver of Aunt Edna's old landline phone to my ear.

I picked at the flocked wallpaper on the dining room wall. "Don't ask."

He laughed. "Well, I certainly wouldn't want to muck up your life now, would I?"

I grimaced. "You heard that?"

"I did. Care to elaborate?"

I glanced over at Aunt Edna and Jackie. The pair were busy doing nothing as they loitered within earshot, eavesdropping in on every word Brady and I said to each other.

"Not at the moment," I said.

"The vultures circling, I take it?" Brady asked.

"Flap, flap."

Brady chuckled. "Here's an idea. Why don't you tell me all about it over an early dinner?"

I turned my back to the two elderly mob ladies and whispered, "Fine. As long as it's not that low-rent dive you took me to last time."

"The Dairy Hog?" Brady laughed. "Like I said, I wouldn't want to muck up your—"

"Stop!" I hissed. "Say another word, and you can forget about picking me up at six."

Brady must've taken me literally. His answer was a dial tone. I untangled myself from the curly phone cord and hung the receiver back on the wall.

"So, you two going out or what?" Jackie asked, pretending to dry a plate with a dishtowel.

I smirked. "Either that, or Aunt Edna didn't pay the phone bill."

"Huh?" my aunt grunted, snatching the plate from Jackie.

"Nothing." I sighed. "Look, it's been a long, strange day already, and it's barely past three o'clock. I'm going out for a walk to clear my head."

"Good idea," Aunt Edna said. "Just keep an eye out for Sophia. She's pretty eager to teach you a lesson."

I blanched. "What did *I* do?"

"Nothing," Jackie said. "You're her new assistant, remember? You gotta learn the ropes. And take my word for it. Sophia likes to give out just enough of it so's you can hang yourself."

My nose crinkled. "Thanks for the warning."

As I turned and took a step toward the front door, my aunt crossed herself, plucked the phone from the wall, and mumbled something under her breath.

It sounded like she said, "Mother Mary, have mercy on her soul."

***

With only a few hours before Brady was to pick me up, I didn't have the time or desire to get caught in Sophia's web. The way I saw it, that creep Eddie Houser had taught me enough lessons for one day.

With extreme caution, I stuck my head out of Aunt Edna's front door and peeked around. The coast was clear, so I headed outside and into the courtyard—a colorful jungle of palms, crotons, and plants I couldn't name.

The tropical courtyard was surrounded by five single-story detached apartments that made up Palm Court Cottages. The place was a little slice of old Florida, and was the exact opposite of my ugly, high-rise tract apartment back in L.A.

Eager to burn off some nervous energy with a walk, I snuck along the paved path toward the street, keeping an eye out for Sophia. I was almost to the street when my attention was suddenly drawn to faint grunts and groans coming from the azaleas beside one of the cottages.

What the heck?

I took a few steps closer. I could hear huffing and puffing. I spotted something pinkish-tan moving up and down in the azalea bushes.

You've got to be kidding me. All I need to top off this crap-shoot of a day is to spot a couple of wrinkly old love birds having a quickie in the dirt.

I grimaced, focused my eyes on the sidewalk, and picked up my pace. I was almost past the hedges when, all of a sudden, a head popped up from between the leaves. It belonged to an elderly woman. Her cheeks were as pink as the floppy hat atop her head.

"Kitty!" I gasped at the CGCN's resident gardener, scientist, and maker of sketchy potions. "What in the world are you doing behind the hedges?"

"Pulling weeds. What else?" Kitty grunted and worked her way up off her knees to standing. She gripped a garden spade in one hand, a drooping dandelion in the other. Her pink T-shirt read: *Botany Plants Lately?*

"How'd the audition go?" she asked.

I glanced down at the ground. "I don't want to talk about it."

"Oh. I see." She shot me a soft smile. "You should take up gardening, hon. You can't lose with gardening."

"What do you mean?"

"Just look at this monster!" Kitty held up the dead dandelion as if it were the prize catch of the day. At its leafy base protruded a taproot the size and shape of a white carrot.

"Uh ... nice one," I said.

"Isn't it?" Kitty grinned at me like Jack Nicholson in *The Shining*. "Ah! It's so satisfying to rip these buggers out by the roots. It's like pulling somebody's head off with the spine attached."

I stifled another grimace. "Right." My thoughts flashed back to how, last week, Kitty had made me hold open a dead guy's jaws so she could swab his throat.

Fun times ...

"Oh, look!" Kitty exclaimed.

I blanched. "What? Is there a dead guy in the bushes?"

"No. Even better!" Kitty used the dandelion's root to point at an azalea bush. "See there? It's a loveliness of ladybugs!"

My nose crinkled. "A loveliness?"

She beamed at me from under her pink visor. "That's what a group of ladybugs is called. You know, like a gaggle of geese? A pod of dolphins?"

"Oh." I leaned over and watched a "loveliness" of red, pill-shaped dots swarming around on the leaves.

"They eat aphids," Kitty said. "Suck the life right out of them."

"Nice to know."

"That's why they're red, I suppose. In nature, red means danger."

"And the spots?" I asked.

She shrugged. "Just a bit of bling, I guess. They *are* ladies, after all."

I frowned. "Not *you*, too."

She cocked her head. "What do you mean?"

"Never mind." I took a step toward the street. "I gotta go. I was just heading out for a walk."

"Catch you at dinner!" she called after me.

"Not tonight. I'm meeting with Brady."

Kitty beamed. "Oh, a date!"

"Not a date. A meeting."

"Well, in case you change your mind about that, I've got plenty of bling we can dress you up with!"

I forced a smile. "Thanks. I'll keep that in mind."

I turned and marched down the sidewalk, suddenly more nervous than I was perturbed.

Was it a date?

When it came to Brady, I was never sure.

Since I'd arrived in St. Petersburg less than a month ago, the handsome police officer had helped me out of two scrapes with the law—and had kissed me once in the moonlight.

All three times, I'd found myself completely out of my depth.

I chewed my lip and picked up my pace. Even so, I had the feeling that no matter how fast I went, there was no way I could outrun what lay in wait for me just around the corner.

Chapter Ten

I stared into the mirror hanging above the old, yellowing French Provincial bureau in my Aunt's spare bedroom—the one I now called home.

What should I wear to dinner with Brady?

Should I try to look attractive? Or should I try to look like I didn't try to look attractive?

I closed my eyes and shook my head.

Geez. Maybe Kerri's right. We women do *do this to ourselves.*

I'd come home from my walk as sweaty as if I'd been inside a Finnish sauna. Florida in June definitely wasn't for sissies.

A cold shower had cooled down my body, but not my heart. It was still racing in my chest. Was it pulsing wildly because I was going to see Brady soon? Or was it because I was still boiling mad over being duped into playing Daisy the Price Slasher?

I unwrapped the towel from around my wet hair and slathered on some conditioner. I hoped it had enough strength to undo Leslie's professional-strength tease-job.

Now, if only they made a lotion that could tame moods ...

I combed through my wet hair, glad to see it was beginning to relax, even if I couldn't. As I set the comb down, I spied my little yellow *Hollywood Survival Guide* lying next to the pink lava lamp.

"What sage advice do you have for me today?" I asked as I picked it up.

I closed my eyes, flipped through the pages blindly, and stopped at a random page. I opened my eyes to find that the *Guide*, like some Tinsel-Town Ouija Board, had landed on Tip #666.

> *Dress for the part you expect to play—unless, of course, you're expecting.*

The glib words hit me in the face like a clown's cream pie.

What role did *I want to play? Not just with Brady, but my whole life?*

As I stared blankly at the glowing globs of goo floating around in the lava lamp's mysterious pink liquid, a glimpse of something yellow reflected in the glass. I turned and saw the vase of yellow roses on the nightstand beside my bed. Brady had given them to me last night for my birthday.

I walked over to the bed and sat down next to the nightstand. Kitty had told me yesterday that yellow roses meant happiness, new beginnings, and friendship. If that message hadn't been ambiguous enough, Brady had also given Sophia an identical bunch.

What was I supposed to make of that?

I blew out a sigh. When it came to matters of the heart, I abhorred mixed signals. I'd had my fill of them from my mother, my ex boyfriends, and pretty much everyone I ever met in L.A.

I plucked a yellow rose from the vase and twirled it in my fingers. Hopefully, Brady would be straight up with me about his feelings tonight. If not, I was going to nip our yet-to-blossom romance right in the bud.

Chapter Eleven

I'd taken a chance on romance. I'd worn an off-the shoulders white blouse and snug—but not excruciating—jeans. Brady had looked pleased when he saw me. And I'd been just as pleased when he'd parked his black F-150 in the street next to Sundial, an open-air shopping and entertainment plaza in downtown St. Pete.

Brady had opened the truck door for me. He'd also led me up the escalator to the outdoor deck of an upscale seafood restaurant. When we were seated, he'd pulled out my chair for me. And when our waiter had appeared, Brady had taken charge, ordering a bottle of wine and a dozen raw oysters.

It was definitely a date.

***

"And that's when she told me her grandmother was Ma Barker," I gushed to Brady, feeling giddy after a glass of red wine and a couple of oysters.

"Seriously?" Brady asked. His handsome smile faded a notch. "*The* Ma Barker?"

I nodded. "Yes. The very same. You don't believe me?"

"It's not that." Brady set his glass of wine on the table and smirked. "Just keep in mind, Doreen. This is the same woman who told me she saw Mongo the Monkey Boy on TV."

I choked on a sip of wine. "What?"

"While I was waiting for you to get ready, your aunt told me she'd seen a guy she used to know on the Channel 22 news." Brady shook his head. "I figured she had to be joking. I mean, who would have a nickname like Mongo the Monkey Boy?"

I thought about some of the other people my aunt and her friends hung around. Victor "the Vulture" Ventura, who could make bodies disappear. Victoria "Slick" Polaski, the red-headed bombshell who'd claimed to be Freddy Sanderling's fiancé at his funeral. And, of course,

Sammy the Psycho, Sophia's psycho killer son with a penchant for cheese curds.

I shrugged and smiled at Brady. "Gee, I really couldn't say."

He waggled an eyebrow at me. "Couldn't? Or won't?"

I played dumb. "I've never heard of this monkey boy, I swear. Maybe he's one of my aunt's boyfriends."

Brady's eyebrow went still. "One? How many does she have?"

I laughed. "About a dozen. Just old-school, snail-mail romances. But they're not real."

"What do you mean?"

"You know," I said, twirling a lock of brown hair in my fingers. "They exchange letters, but they never actually meet."

Brady's casual demeanor took on a more serious tone. "Why would they never meet?"

"Uh ..." I shifted my gaze to my wine glass.

Crap. I've said too much. Dang it, cabernet!

"Well," I fumbled, nervously tapping a finger on my wine glass. "On account of ... it could be because the men are ... uh ..."

"Incarcerated?" Brady asked.

I cringed and looked up at him. "Maybe."

Brady shook his head. "Poor Edna. Do you know if these guys are bilking her for money?"

I glowered at myself for ratting out Aunt Edna. Then realized Brady had it all wrong. It was more like the other way around.

"I don't know," I said. Which, technically, wasn't a lie.

Brady's brow furrowed. "Doreen, your aunt could be the victim of a lonely hearts scam."

"Really?" I pretended to gasp. "Is that illegal?"

"Yes. Last time I checked. I need to talk to her about it."

"No. Let me," I blurted. "She might be ... you know ... embarrassed. We women have our pride."

"But she could—"

"I tell you what," I said. "I'll ask my aunt if these guys are trying to get money from her. I promise I'll let you know if she's been duped and wants to press charges, okay?"

"Okay." Brady shook his head softly. "It's a crime, you know."

"This lonely hearts club band thing?" I asked.

"No. I mean, yes. But that wasn't what I was referring to. I meant it's a crime what love does to people. It makes them do crazy, desperate things."

I shot Brady my best doe eyes. "Are you speaking from experience?"

Brady pursed his lips. "Listen, Doreen. I didn't want to get together with you to talk about your aunt."

I smiled coyly. "You didn't?"

"No. I wanted us to meet so we could discuss what went down at Sophia's party last night."

"Oh."

My racing heart slammed on the brakes. "Was that only last night?" I asked, trying to hide my disappointment. "It seems like that happened ages ago. I guess times flies when you're not having fun."

"What?" Brady asked, busy pulling a notepad from his shirt pocket.

"Nothing." I reached for my wineglass and drained it. As I set it back on the table, I noticed Brady was smiling at me.

"You really did amaze me," he said.

I stifled a belch. "I did?"

"Yes. The way you figured out that it was Melanie who trying to con those old folks at Shady Respite out of their life savings. And then you go and top it off by foiling her plan to poison Sophia. That's like hitting a double header, Doreen!"

"Thanks."

Nothing like a sports analogy to win a woman's heart...

Brady laughed. "You're a real prize fighter. The way you kept coming back for more, even after Melanie shot you down over and over again for making false claims and amateur mistakes—"

I frowned and refilled my wine glass. "Is there a point to all this?"

Brady cocked his head. "I thought I just made it. It's *you* who gets the credit for figuring out the case."

I shrugged. "Thanks. But I already knew that. So, is that why you wanted to see me?"

Brady nodded. "Yes. I figured I at least owed you dinner for that."

Great.

I raised my wine glass. "Well, consider the debt paid. And thanks again for the yellow roses you gave me and Sophia."

"Another token of my appreciation." Brady clinked his glass against mine. "Your work broke the case. Now mine is just getting started."

"What do you mean?" I asked, then gulped my wine and imagined beating him over the head with a bunch of yellow roses.

Brady grinned. "I'm the one who has to wade through the mountains of paperwork. I've been working on the case since seven this morning."

"Sorry to ruin your day," I said sourly.

Brady's brow furrowed. "I didn't mean it that way."

I stabbed an oyster with a little fork. "What way *did* you mean it?"

"What I meant is that I'm proud of you, Doreen. You're a one-woman *tour de force*. After interviewing Montoya, I—"

"Montoya?" I asked.

"Melanie Montoya. That's the con-woman's name—her *real* one, that is. I went through her personal effects and found four different IDs with her picture on them. And that notebook she had? It contained signed powers of attorney from at least a dozen other elderly victims she was planning on duping into giving her control of their assets."

I grimaced. "That many?"

Brady nodded. "That may be just the tip of the iceberg." He shook his head. "What kind of cold heart takes advantage of people in nursing homes who have no one around to stick up for them?"

"The same kind that uses innocent animals to sneak into their hearts—then into their wallets."

Brady nodded solemnly.

I gulped half a glass of wine for courage, then began my own line of questioning—about where our relationship was headed.

"Speaking of hearts ..." I said.

But Brady wasn't listening. He was staring off into space, probably consumed with thoughts about the next sporting reference he could "compliment" me with.

Annoyed, I let the rest of my question drift off, just as his attention had. Apparently, I wasn't as interesting to him as football, or Melanie Montoya, the heartless scammer.

Speaking of heartless ...

I shook my head and studied the handsome cop sitting across from me. Brady was about the same age as me. In society's view, he was a man in the prime of his life. I, on the other hand, was well past *my* prime. As the world saw it, my worth was unraveling faster than a Walmart sweater.

Life is so unfair.

"More wine?" the waiter asked, startling both me and Brady out of our unshared daydreams.

"Yes, please," I said.

"Not for me." Brady put a hand over his glass. "I'm driving."

The waiter drained the last of the bottle into my glass. I snatched it up.

"I was just thinking—" Brady said.

"Let me guess," I interrupted. "About baseball, or the case?"

"The case." He shook his head. "I'm not convinced Montoya could've pulled all this off on her own."

"I agree," I said, reluctantly.

Brady looked surprised. "You do? Why?"

"Because she doesn't have a cleft chin." I slugged back more wine.

Brady's brow furrowed. "Excuse me?"

I sighed. "Sophia told me the person who delivered the poisoned lemon bars to her room at Shady Respite had a cleft chin."

Brady nodded. "Right. But couldn't they've just been a hired delivery person?"

"I guess. But somebody had to let this delivery person into the nursing home after visiting hours."

"Unless they worked there." Brady leaned back and drummed his fingers on the table. "Or they could've arrived earlier, hid out, and waited until the coast was clear to deliver the cookies."

I shot him a sour, tipsy smile. "You're really good at shooting down my ideas. Are you like, a trained sniper or something?"

Brady laughed. "No. It's just the way we work here at the station."

I slammed my wine glass on the table and crossed my arms over my chest. "In case you haven't noticed, we're not 'here at the station,' Brady."

He locked eyes with me. "I'm not trying to prove you wrong, Doreen. I'm only trying to look at all the plausible explanations."

I blew out a breath. "Yeah. I know."

I only wish that one of those plausible explanations was that we were here because you fancied me.

"Let's say this delivery person was in on it," Brady said, oblivious to my plight. "Do you have any ideas as to who it might be?"

I gave up my lost cause. For Brady, this was a business meeting, nothing more. "Yes," I said. "It's probably a guy."

"Why do you say that?"

I swallowed the knot of anger in my throat. "Sophia said whoever it was had a deep voice, and used a pompous, high-brow tone. I thought it might've been Neil Neil from Neil Mansion funeral home, but he doesn't have a cleft chin. Neither does his partner."

Brady nodded. "So, who does?"

"Have a cleft chin?" I asked.

"Yes."

"A lot of people. In fact, approximately 25.9% of the population. Cleft chins are the most common in people with European, Middle Eastern, and Southern Asian ancestry."

Brady raised an eyebrow. "Sounds like you've been doing some homework."

I shrugged, feeling a bit woozy. "A little."

"Anybody fit this bill that I should be aware of?

I hiccupped and leaned in toward him. "Yes. Humpty Dumpty. I mean Humphrey—"

Brady burst out laughing. "Good one, Doreen." He shook his head and grinned. "You really had me going there for a minute. Let me guess. Is this Humpty Dumpty guy the father of Mongo the Monkey Boy?"

Oh no he didn't!

My last nerve snapped. Brady had chosen the wrong day to make me the butt of yet another man's joke.

"How would I know?" I hissed at him. "Why don't you ask my Aunt Edna?"

Brady picked up his wine glass and winked at me. "Well, like you said, I wouldn't want to embarrass her."

I glared at him like an angry mother bear. "Is that all you needed from me? If so, I want to get out of here."

Brady's goofy grin vanished. "What about dinner?"

"Now!" I said, and banged my fist on the table.

"Um ... sure. If that's what you want."

I scowled. "It is."

"Okay. Wait here. I'll get the check."

As soon as Brady left, I slugged down the rest of my wine and glared at all the stupid, happy couples walking around hand-in-hand in the courtyard below.

I chided myself. What a fool I'd been to think Brady would consider me girlfriend material.

Suck it up, Doreen. You've made it this far on your own. You don't need Brady, or anyone else for that matter. The only person you can depend on in this world is yourself.

I spotted Brady's truck parked along the street and dreaded the tension-filled ride home that awaited me. As people strolled by the F-150, I noticed one had stopped and was now staring up at me. I tried to make out his or her face, but the hoodie they wore shaded their eyes and nose.

As I stared down at distant figure, the person held up something shiny. He or she thrust it toward me, then turned and disappeared into the crowd. Whatever had been in their hand had glinted in the streetlamp light like a knife blade.

And whoever it was, man or woman, had a distinctive cleft chin.

"You ready?" Brady asked.

Startled, I gasped and whipped around to face him.

"What's wrong?" Brady asked.

"Nothing!" I scrambled up from my chair. "Nothing you need bother to take seriously, at any rate. Let's go."

Chapter Twelve

I sat up in bed and nearly screamed. My pajamas were stained with blood! Then I realized it wasn't blood. And I wasn't wearing pajamas. I was still wearing the white shirt from last night. And it was splattered with wine.

I nearly gasped.

Last night!

There wasn't enough red wine in the world to erase the memories of the catastrophe that would forever be emblazoned in my memory banks as "The Sundial Disaster."

I blew out a breath and wondered, was it just me? Or was it normal for a woman's world to implode the moment she turned forty? After all, that's what Hollywood films always told us would happen.

Even so, the word "implode" didn't do justice to the 24 hours I'd experienced since turning the big four-oh.

For starters, I'd been upstaged by an iguana in the daily news. Then I'd nearly been cut in half by a pair of jeans. My hair had been teased to within an inch of its life. Crazy Eddie Houser had grabbed my ass. And I'd humiliating myself along with all of womankind by playing Daisy the bimbo used-car price slasher.

But that had just been Act One.

Act Two had been my disastrous date with Brady.

He'd probably never talk to me again.

I rubbed my pounding forehead and tried not to think about it. But I couldn't help myself. The memories from last night kept surging back like a bad case of acid reflux.

***

Instead of having Brady take me straight home, I'd insisted he drop me off at a convenience store a few blocks from Palm Court Cottages. He'd wanted to accompany me inside, but I'd gone and pulled the FCP-card.

546

I'd told Brady I'd needed to buy some feminine care products—and I wanted to do it alone.

As I'd climbed out of his truck, I'd practically begged Brady to leave. I'd argued that I'd be fine walking home by myself. (I'd planned to arm myself with a huge bottle of wine.) But as I'd sorted through the alcohol on offer in the store, I could see Brady waiting patiently for me in the parking lot.

Brady's "chivalry" had forced me to change my plans. Instead of buying a decent bottle of cabernet, I'd had to resort to purchasing a cheap box of wine the shape of a family-sized carton of tampons. In hindsight, I suppose Brady had done me a favor—I'd planned to guzzle the wine, and it was a lot harder to chip a tooth on cardboard than on glass.

Anyway, after I'd left the store, Brady and I'd exchanged a few words in the parking lot. Exactly, which words I couldn't recall. I only remembered that I'd refused to get in the truck with him. Eventually, he'd given up and let me have my way.

A vague recollection made me cringe.

Had I kicked his truck as he'd pulled away?

I blew out a tired sigh, then leaned across the bed and dragged my laptop to my side. The movement set off a base drum pounding inside my skull. I groaned, then powered up the computer and opened a search browser.

According to Google, the odds of winning the PowerBall lottery were one in 195 million. Meanwhile, the odds of being struck by a meteorite were nearly 800 times higher, at 250,000 to one.

I snapped the computer shut. With neither my salvation nor my demise as eminent as I'd hoped, I resigned myself to slogging through another day.

I pinched the bridge of my nose in an attempt to ease my aching head. It didn't work. I put aside the computer and fumbled for the leather-bound journal on my nightstand. The beautiful notebook had been a birthday gift from Kitty. She'd encouraged me to write down my observations in the journal. Kitty thought I had a knack for "seeing the big picture."

I'd definitely proved her wrong yesterday.

I sighed and opened the journal to the first page. The night before last, I'd scrawled a note on it, right after my own little birthday celebration was over.

Humpty Bogart has a cleft chin.

I rummaged around in the nightstand drawer for a pen. I had a few choice observations about turning forty I wanted to jot down. As my fingers wrapped around an ink pen, a knock sounded on my bedroom door.

"Up and at 'em, Dorey," Aunt Edna's voice rang out. "Coffee's ready, and so is Sophia."

I slumped back onto the pillows.

Oh, crap. I'd forgotten all about Sophia.

***

I pulled a coffee mug from my aunt's kitchen cupboard. The inscription on it read:

Good morning. I see the assassins have failed.

I shook my head and muttered, "Man, I can't catch a break."

"What's that?" Jackie asked strolling into the kitchen. Dressed in a screaming yellow shirt and matching pants, she looked like an overgrown banana Popsicle.

"Nothing," I said, shielding my eyes from the glare of her clothing. I filled my mug with coffee. "Did you see the paper this morning?"

"Which one?" Jackie asked.

"The *Beach Gazette.*"

"Nope. It only comes on Wednesdays and Saturdays, kiddo."

"Oh. Thanks."

Bleary-eyed, I did the math in my head. Today was Thursday. Crazy Eddie's ads didn't start airing until tomorrow. And thanks to Jackie, I now knew the progeny of Saurwein's poison pen couldn't possibly go to print until Saturday. That meant I still had around 24 to 48 hours before the rest of my life turned into complete dumpster juice.

"Big day, eh?" Jackie asked as I passed the carafe of coffee to her.

"What do you mean?"

"Your first day as Sophia's new assistant."

I winced.

Make that 24 to 48 seconds *until my life hit Dumpsterville.*

"Don't remind me," I said, grabbing a box of Lucky Charms from atop the fridge. The sight of the grinning leprechaun on the box only curdled my already sour mood.

Lucky Charms? Since when?

I shoved the cereal box back on top of the fridge and took a giant slurp of coffee.

"You're gonna need your strength," Jackie said. "Top off your cup?"

"Please."

Jackie filled my assassin cup, then I dutifully followed her glowing yellow pantsuit into the dining room.

"Morning," Aunt Edna said as Jackie and I took our places at the table next to her and Sophia. I noticed that, besides her silver turban, the ancient Queenpin was dressed all in black.

"Morning, Sophia," I quipped. "Whose funeral is it?"

Sophia's green cat eyes narrowed in on me. "I don't know. I haven't decided yet."

I glanced over at Aunt Edna. She smirked at me from behind the rim of her coffee cup. "Time to earn your keep around here, Dorey. There ain't no such thing as a free lunch, you know."

"Don't you mean free breakfast?" Jackie asked.

"It's a figure of speech," Sophia grumbled, then turned and studied me. "So, young Doreen. Are you ready for lesson number one?"

I smiled weakly. "Sure. Let me go put on my flip-flops and I'm all yours for the day."

***

After scrounging my pink rubber sandals from the closet, I turned around to find Aunt Edna standing over me.

"What's up?" I asked.

"Just wanted to tell you not to worry, Dorey."

"Worry?" I asked, suddenly full of dread. "Should I be worried?"

"No." She patted me on the back. "You're gonna be fine. Sophia can be tough, but remember, you come from a long line of mobsters who were even tougher."

I frowned. "You mean like Mongo the Monkey Boy?"

Aunt Edna's face went pale. "You know about Monkey-Faced Mongo?"

"Sure. He was on the Channel 22 news, right?"

"Yeah." Aunt Edna grimaced and rubbed her palms on her apron. "He's one of my uh ... pen pals, Dorey. He ... uh, got out of prison a couple of days ago."

"What?" I gasped. "I thought you said those guys would never get out."

"Not legally," Aunt Edna said. "He ... escaped."

I took my aunt's hand. "But he ... he can't *find you*, right?"

Aunt Edna winced.

"Right?" I asked again.

"Doreen!" Jackie yelled from another room.

Aunt Edna's eyes grew wide. "Don't tell Sophia about ... you know."

"The lonely hearts scam you're running?" I said, inching my feet into the pink flip flops.

Aunt Edna's worry lines softened. "Yeah. Not a peep, okay?"

Jackie burst into the room and grabbed me by the arm. "Come on, Dorey. We gotta go. Now!"

"What's the rush?" I asked.

"Sophia needs to get back to her place. Her bladder ain't what it used to be."

Aunt Edna shook her head and sighed. "Neither is mine."

Chapter Thirteen

"Take it easy, I'm not a racehorse," Sophia grumbled as I helped her along the path to her apartment.

"Why don't you use that fancy wheelchair of yours?" I asked, tightening my grip on her elbow.

"And look like a weakling?" She tugged at the black shawl draped over her shoulders, even though it was nearly ninety degrees outside. "Besides, my hip is fine."

"Is that because the fracture healed, or because you never had one to begin with?" I quipped.

"That's my private business, young lady," Sophia snarled. "And you'd be wise to keep clear of it."

I grimaced. "Yes, ma'am."

"Getting old sucks," Sophia muttered as she unlocked the door to her cottage and slowly stepped inside. "My shoulders are always freezing and my feet are hot as coals." She hung her shawl on a hook on the wall, then hobbled over to the couch and flopped into it.

"I thought you had to go to the bathroom," I said.

"I told Jackie that so I could escape her idiotic jokes."

My eyebrow rose a notch. "Well played. So, where do we start? With the mafia lessons, I mean."

"Eager," Sophia said, eyeing me up and down. "I like that. Well, we start with lesson *numero uno*, of course. 'The Family always comes first.'" She smiled at me. "But you already proved that at my party the other night."

"I did?" I asked.

Sophia picked up the TV remote. "You saved my life from that fruit fly with the iguana. I remember the lizard's name. Iggy. But what was hers?"

"Melanie Montoya. At least, that's what Brady told me last night." I winced at the thought of our meeting gone awry. "Brady said Montoya had a bunch of fake IDs on her. And a stack of power of attorney forms with scammed signatures on them."

Sophia nodded. "Not a bad scheme, actually. That hustler would probably be a fat cat if she didn't eat alone."

"Eat alone?" I asked.

"Get greedy." Sophia clicked the TV on. "If this dame had shared a piece of her action with the Family, she might still be in business. With a scam like that, you need backup."

"So you don't think she ran the con all by herself?"

"Nah. She had the charisma, but not the brains."

I chewed my bottom lip. "That's what I was thinking, too."

Sophia shrugged. "Eh, what does it matter now? She got pinched. The cops caught themselves a fish. No need for them to keep baiting the hook anymore, is there?"

"But if someone else was involved, shouldn't we—"

"Excuse me, Doreen. You forget what side of the fence you're on? You're a member of the Collard Green Cosa Nostra, not the St. Petersburg police force."

"I know. It's just that—"

"Basta! Enough already! Do you need to relearn lesson number one?"

I pursed my lips. "No ma'am. The Family always comes first."

"Good. Now, time for lesson number two. 'Cleanliness is next to godmotherliness.'"

I cocked my head. "Excuse me?"

Sophia threw her arm in the air. "Clean up this place!"

I blanched. "What?"

"Get to it. You can start by taking out the trash."

"Sorry. Is that a euphemism for—"

Sophia shook her head. "Geez. The can in under the kitchen sink cupboard, already."

"Oh. Right."

I walked into the kitchen and took the lid off the trash can. To my surprise, it was full of paper Starbucks coffee cups. I pulled out the liner and placed a clean one in the can. Then I toted the dirty bag into the living room, where Sophia was busy watching *Wheel of Fortune*.

I held up the sack. "I take it Aunt Edna still doesn't know you're drinking Starbucks coffee instead of hers?"

"That's not Starbucks," Sophia said. "It's ScarBux. The new place down the street. They got free delivery, too. The guy's here like clockwork every morning at 5:30."

Chapter Fifteen

With all hopes of a love life spiraling down the drain, it was only fitting the Universe would have me spend the rest of the afternoon cleaning Sophia's bathroom.

After all, we were both washed up.

I'd no sooner scrubbed the tub clean when Sophia came in and announced she wanted to take a bath.

"Be careful," I warned. "It's so squeaky clean you might slip. I wouldn't want you to fall in and drown."

"Not a chance. I always keep one of these handy." She patted a package of adult diapers.

"What?" I asked, then immediately regretted it.

"These things can be used as flotation devices," she said.

I almost asked her how she knew that, but decided I desperately didn't want to know.

"Well, I'll leave you to it." I made a hasty exit, closing the door behind me. I was pretty sure that Sophia was crazy. But the old Queenpin was right about one thing—getting older sucked.

While Sophia puttered in the bathroom, I finished up the last of my chores by putting clean sheets on her bed. Stripped bare, I noticed her bed had two mattresses stacked atop each other. I laughed to myself. Sophia was as prickly as a cactus while she was conscious. Apparently she was just as touchy while she slept.

The Mafia madam was part *Princess and the Pea*. Or was it Princess and the *Pee*?

After amusing myself with that little gem, I got back to work. Given the amount of dust I'd found under Sophia's bed, I decided to give the mattresses a good whacking with the broom. After that, I vacuumed them, along with the rug. Finally, I put on the clean sheets, straightened the bedspread, and plumped the cushions.

I stood back and admired my work.

After this, there's no way Sophia can call me a sloth again.

With my list of chores dutifully completed, I went back and listened at the bathroom door. The water was still running.

"Everything okay in there?" I asked through the door.

"Fine. Now just let an old woman soak, would you?"

"You got it." I smiled, rubbed my hands together, and made my own clean getaway.

I had my own chores to do—including laundry. But when I got back to my room, the heap of dirty clothes were gone. I spied them hanging in the closet. Even my wine-stained white shirt, which I'd given up for dead, had been cleaned, pressed, and hung neatly away.

Gee. A girl could get used to this ...

***

For once, I was grateful that Aunt Edna served dinner promptly at four o'clock every afternoon. After getting Sophia fed and settled back into her cottage, I was off the hook for the rest of the evening.

Hmm...maybe that was her strategy all along.

I joined the other three ladies in the dining room. They were enjoying their evening ritual—playing cards and gossiping around the dining table.

"Pull up a chair," Kitty said, dealing me in. "You're one of us now."

"Thanks," I said. "And whoever did my laundry? I appreciate it."

"That was me." Aunt Edna elbowed. "Comes with the rent."

I grinned. "How'd you get all those stains out of my shirt?"

She shot me a look. "You really have to ask?"

"So when are you and Brady going out again?" Jackie asked.

I looked at my cards and sighed. "Never."

Jackie's eyes grew wide. "What happened?"

"I screwed things up. I thought it was a date. But it turns out, Brady just wanted to discuss Sophia's case."

"Oh." Aunt Edna laid her cards down on the table.

I cringed. "I got angry about it. Then I got a little drunk. I think I might've kicked his truck."

"His shiny F-150?" Aunt Edna asked.

"In my defense, he compared me to a prize fighter and a baseball double-hitter."

Aunt Edna shook her head. "Men. The only game they got nowadays is on ESPN."

"What did Brady want to know about Sophia?" Kitty asked.

I shook my head. "Nothing. He asked me if I thought anyone else could be involved in the plot to poison her. I said Humpty Bogart, then before I could explain that was a nickname, Brady laughed at me."

"Grrr," Kitty grumbled. "Nothing I hate more than when a man laughs at me!"

I smirked sourly. "What about when he grabs your ass?"

Aunt Edna's mouth fell open. "Brady grabbed your ass?"

"No." I scowled. "That dirtbag Eddie Houser did. The guy I shot the commercial for."

"Geez, Dorey," Kitty said. "Things don't work out for you and guys. First Tad. Now Brady. Eddie better watch his step."

"You aren't kidding." I grumbled.

Jackie closed her fan of cards. "Guys. Who needs 'em?"

"You've got a point there," Kitty said. "Why involve Brady? We can work on this case ourselves."

"Yeah," Aunt Edna said. "So, Dorey, why do you think Humpty's caught up in all this?"

I chewed my lip. "Because the guy Sophia saw delivering the cookies has a cleft chin. And Humpty has a cleft chin. But then, you said he couldn't have made the delivery because he was visiting the rat's mouth."

Kitty and I locked eyes. "What's that mean, Edna?" Kitty asked.

"What does *what* mean?"

"Visiting the rat's mouth," I said. "Is that mob speak for something?"

Aunt Edna frowned. "No. That's just what I call Boca Raton. I only meant Humpty couldn't have done the drop because he was out of town in Boca, that's all."

"Oh." I slumped in my chair.

"Wait a minute," Kitty said. "That Melanie character told me she had a greenhouse in Boca Raton. I bet that's where she grew the poisonous manchineel fruits."

"I guess the cops will find out when they search the place," Jackie said.

"Maybe they will, maybe they won't," I said. "We caught Melanie red-handed with the poisonous fruit. What need do the police have to search the greenhouse for more?"

Kitty pursed her lips. "Hmm. Maybe the cops don't need to, but whoever was working with her just might—if they plan on destroying the evidence, that is."

"Or gather up more fruits and try to finish the job," Aunt Edna said.

We all exchanged glances.

Aunt Edna frowned. "So when Humpty went to Boca, you think he could've been going to visit Melanie at her greenhouse?"

"It's possible," I said. "Sophia told me she thought Melanie was too dumb to come up with the scheme all on her own. I agree."

"Kinda sketchy if you ask me," Jackie said. "Lots of people go to Boca. And lots of people have cleft chins."

"True enough," Aunt Edna said. "But what's the harm in asking Humpty for a little more information?"

"We might spook him," I said. "We could put a tail out on him and see what he's up to."

"In the Kia?" Aunt Edna said. "That thing sticks out like one of Jackie's outfits."

"Ask Morty to do it," Kitty said.

Aunt Edna scowled. "We don't need guys messing this up. We can handle this ourselves."

"Why not?" I said. "After all, this *is* Family business."

Kitty smiled and laid down her hand. "All for one, and one for all!"

"Like the four Mouseketeers!" Jackie said.

"Musketeers," Aunt Edna said.

"What?" Jackie cocked her head. "So, you saying I shouldn't order us some Minnie Mouse hats?"

Aunt Edna rolled her yes. "Yes. That's exactly what I'm saying."

"Ooh," Kitty cooed, rubbing her hands together. "The only thing I like more than proving a man wrong is proving him guilty."

"I dunno," I said. "I like proving them wrong more."

Kitty laughed. "Who am I kidding? So do I."

Aunt Edna smiled coyly. "Jackie, put a pot of coffee on. We got some man-splaining to do."

Chapter Sixteen

In the moonlight, I could make out the shadowy figure of someone in the hoodie walking toward me. My heart involuntarily skipped a beat. I was standing in the dark in front of Sophia's cottage at 5:29 in the morning. I had to give it to them—the ScarBux delivery person was right on time.

"I'll take that," I said as he drew closer.

"Who are *you*?" a man's voice asked.

"I'm helping out the elderly woman who lives here."

"Sophia?"

My shoulders stiffened. "You know her name?"

"Sure!" the youthful sounding voice under the hoodie said. "I hope she's okay. She's such a sweetheart."

My nose crinkled. "Are you sure you've got the right address?"

He laughed and handed me a paper sack. "That'll be ten bucks even."

"Ten bucks for a cup of coffee?"

"For *two* cups."

"Oh." I gave the guy a twenty. He handed me back a five and five ones. I smirked and gave him back two bucks.

He grinned. "Thanks. Same time tomorrow?"

"Sure."

He turned to go. "Tell Sophia I said hi."

"Okay. What's your name?"

"Chase."

"Right. Will do, Chase."

As Chase turned and sprinted back to his car, I noted that he looked like your ordinary, average, athletic young man. He was probably in his early twenties. And one more thing—Chase was utterly devoid of a cleft in his chin.

My mind flashed back to the stranger standing in the street at Sundial—the one who'd jabbed at me menacingly after my disastrous non-date with Brady. He or she was probably just some drunk loser, or some young punk checking for unlocked doors in hopes of scoring some spare change.

I shrugged it off. Whoever they'd been they probably hadn't even been looking at me. I shook my head softly.

What is it with all these hoodies nowadays, anyway?

The aroma of fresh coffee snagged my wandering attention. I peeked inside the ScarBux sack. Sophia had called in a double order. I smiled. Maybe she didn't think I was such a sloth after all.

I pulled out one of the cups, punched in the lid's sipper hole, and took a taste. The coffee was so strong and bitter it made my face pucker.

Yuck. Now I know how Sophia powers up that bad attitude of hers ...

I climbed the three steps leading up to the front porch of the Queen-pin's cottage and slipped the key into the lock. Slowly, I opened the door and tiptoed into her apartment, trying not to make a sound. The way I saw it, the longer the old lady slept, the shorter my day with her would be.

I set the sack with the other coffee on the kitchen counter. Suddenly, the ceiling lamp flicked on like a floodlight, blinding me where I stood.

"It's about time," a cranky voice grumbled.

Squinting in the harsh light, I made out the visage of Doña Sophia hobbling into the kitchen in her bathrobe. It was the first time I'd seen her without her silver turban. No wonder she wore it. Her hair was as thin on top as a desperate man's comb-over.

"Why are you drinking my coffee?" she growled.

"What?" I fumbled. "No. I ... uh ..."

"Both of those are for *me!*" Sophia snatched the cup from my hand. "A sloth *and* a thief," she muttered. "What am I going to do with you?"

Fire me?

Please?

***

After pouring Sophia's bootleg ScarBux into a real cup and saucer, I settled her on the couch. Then I made her bed to the sounds of *Wheel of*

Fortune blasting on the TV. Mercifully, my first order from the old lady was to check on breakfast. I was happy for the break.

I marched over to Aunt Edna's to find her sitting at the dining room table looking haggard as she sipped her own mug of coffee.

"Morning," I said. "You look tired."

She waved my comment away like it was a pesky fly. "I was up a little last night. I couldn't stop thinking about what you said. You really think Humpty could be trying to poison Sophia?"

I shrugged. "I don't know. It's just a theory. But one thing I know for sure, Sophia's ready for her breakfast now. For an old lady, she's sure got a heck of an appetite."

"Don't I know it. Hey, wait a minute. I know. Why don't I make her breakfast in bed? That way we can discuss this Humpty matter with Kitty and Jackie without Sophia horning in."

"Sounds good to me."

"Me, too," Jackie said, appearing from around a corner.

Aunt Edna hauled herself up from the table. "If Melanie really *was* working with Humpty or somebody else, we need to keep a sharp eye on anything Sophia eats. They could still be trying to poison her."

"What's to worry about?" Jackie asked, following her into the kitchen. "Since Sophia ain't in the nursing home no more, we control every morsel she eats, and every sip she takes."

I grimaced. "Uh ... except for one."

Aunt Edna's eyes narrowed in on me. "What are you talking about, Dorey?"

I cringed. I hated to be a snitch, but this was important. Besides, Sophia already thought I was a sloth and a thief. What did it matter if she added rat to my list of attributes?

"Coffee," I said. "Sophia gets coffee delivered every morning."

"What?" Aunt Edna dropped the spoon in her hand. It clattered to the kitchen floor.

I bent down to pick it up. "Uh ... sorry. Sophia gets her morning coffee delivered from ScarBux." I flinched as I added, "She thinks it's better than yours."

"Excuse me?" Aunt Edna growled, her face lighting up like a red balloon. She picked up her rolling pin.

I showed her my empty palms. "Hey, I don't agree with her. I tried the stuff this morning. That ScarBux crap is as bitter as p ..."

My face dropped an inch. "Poison."

The three of us exchanged glances.

Aunt Edna shook her head. "If that doesn't ... How long have you known?"

"Only about a week," I said. "Sophia swore me to silence about it."

"An Omertà?" Aunt Edna whacked her palm with the rolling pin. "She made you take an oath of silence about her stupid ..." She gritted her teeth and glared at me like a bulldog. "I should whack—"

"I'm sorry!" I blurted. "At the time, I didn't think it was important. But I do, now. Please. Don't hit me with that!"

"Huh?" Aunt Edna glanced down at her hands and seemed to suddenly realize she was brandishing her rolling pin like a lethal weapon. She tucked it in her apron and hugged me. "Dorey, I'd never whack you with my rolling pin. Now Sophia, on the other hand—"

"Uh, shouldn't we be getting that coffee away from Sophia?" Jackie asked.

Aunt Edna let go of her bear hug on me and began barking orders. "Dorey! Get back over there right now and get that crappy coffee away from Sophia. Then take it over to Kitty to test. Go! Now!"

"But how?" I asked. "Sophia nearly bit my head off when she found out I took a sip."

"That's *your* problem," Aunt Edna said. "I've got breakfast to make."

Jackie put a hand on my shoulder. "We can double-team her, Dorey. Do a little switcheroo."

"What do you mean?"

Jackie winked. "Just follow my lead."

"Hard not to, considering you look like a traffic light in that red shirt and green pants," I quipped.

"Hey, in my day, I could stop traffic another way, if you catch my drift."

"Would you two get out of here, already?" Aunt Edna grumbled.

Jackie grabbed the half-full coffee carafe from the kitchen counter and headed for the front door. As I followed behind her, I saw Aunt Edna open the fridge and rub her hands together. Her expression was pure evil genius.

"So the Queenpin don't like my coffee, eh?" I heard my aunt mutter to herself. "Well, this morning she's getting a special breakfast in bed. And I know just what to make. Eggs Benedict-Arnold."

Chapter Seventeen

Jackie's coffee switcheroo had worked. While Sophia watched the news with a cupful of Aunt Edna's coffee, my aunt got busy preparing the Queenpin's "special breakfast."

What made it special, I didn't want to know...

Meanwhile, Jackie was standing watch like a red-and-green beacon outside Kitty's front door, while Kitty and I got busy testing the ScarBux coffee in the secret laboratory Kitty had in her spare bedroom. If Dr. Frankenstein had been a woman, she'd have been Kitty Corleone.

"Hmm, none of the usual suspects," Kitty said, peering through pink lab goggles at the clear, plastic thingy she was holding up to the light. Inside the plastic cube, different colored stripes ran up and down like a bar chart.

"What do you mean?" I asked.

Kitty frowned. "If this coffee was poisoned, it wasn't cyanide, arsenic, or even manchineel."

I chewed my bottom lip. "Hopefully, for Sophia's sake, it wasn't poisoned at all."

Kitty pursed her lips. "It's looking that way. But I've got to run some more tests before I can call it safe." She set the plastic testing kit on the concrete lab counter and turned to me. "Dorey, you've been working with Sophia for the past couple of days. Has she mentioned any complaints?"

My right eyebrow rose an inch. "Are you kidding me?"

Kitty laughed and rolled her eyes. "I mean beyond her usual grumblings. You know, weird stuff."

I crossed my arms. "She said I was a sloth and a thief. Does that count?"

"Naw. She calls everybody that. I mean, did she say anything about *herself.* You know, body aches, constipation, diarrhea, gas, that kind of thing?"

I grimaced. "No."

Thank goodness.

"Huh," Kitty grunted.

"Oh, wait. I remember Sophia saying the other day that her hair had gone silver and her butt had turned to lead."

Kitty laughed. "Sounds like Sophia, all right. Did you notice any stains or powder residue on her clothes or bedsheets when you changed them?"

"Uh ... no. But I wasn't exactly looking for any."

"Right." Kitty reached for a blue bottle on one of the lab shelves. "Why would you, when she's always wearing that ratty old shawl of hers, right? It's like her security blanket or something."

"Huh. That reminds me. Yesterday morning after breakfast, Sophia was hanging up her shawl and complained that her shoulders were always cold and her feet were hot."

Kitty rubbed her lips with her index finger. "Hmm. That could just be poor circulation. At any rate, until further notice, no more ScarBux for the Queenpin."

I blew out a breath. "Great. I can't wait to break the news to her. She'll probably put a hit out on me."

Kitty shot me a smirk. "Hey. Good thing you only took a tiny sip of that coffee. If it had been laced with cyanide, you'd already be dead."

***

After serving Sophia her "special breakfast" and fluffing up the couch cushions, I went back to Aunt Edna's and joined the three mob molls sitting around the breakfast table.

"I still have a few tests to run, but as far as I can tell, the coffee isn't being poisoned," Kitty said.

"Not even with them fruits?" Jackie asked.

Kitty shook her head. "Not even with beach apples."

"Why would anyone want to poison Sophia now anyway?" Jackie asked, setting down her coffee cup. "She ain't got no money."

"Maybe not," Aunt Edna said. "But she's still got the power. Sophia still ain't named her heir. So that means the position for new head of the Family is still up for grabs."

My mind flashed to a horde of gangsters in pinstripe suits with Tommy guns lining up to become the next leader of a bunch of old ladies who were in bed by 9:30. I snickered.

"What's so funny?" Aunt Edna asked.

I straightened up in my chair and scrambled for something to say. "Nothing. I ... uh ... I just wish I could prove to Sophia that she's wrong about me. I'm not a sloth or a thief. Can you believe she called me lazy, even after I hit the mattresses for her, for crying out loud?"

Aunt Edna stared at me. "Sophia told you to hit the mattresses?"

I shook my head. "No. I took the initiative. See? I'm no sloth. I did it while she was in the shower."

"You and who else?" Kitty asked.

I shrugged. "Nobody. What? You all don't think I can hit a couple of mattresses all by myself? Geez! What kind of wimp do you people think I am?"

"That ain't what we're saying, right ladies?" Aunt Edna said.

Kitty and Jackie nodded. "Right."

I glanced at the gaudy gold cherub staring down at us from the clock on the wall. It was half past nine. "Oh, crap. I've got to get ready and go."

"Where to?" Jackie asked.

I sprang up from my chair. "I've got an appointment with Crazy Eddie." I shook my head. "Believe me, it's the last thing I want to do, but a contract's a contract. I can't get out of it."

"Uh-huh," Aunt Edna said. "Crazy Eddie, eh?"

"Yeah." I laid my breakfast dishes in the sink. "It'll all be over with today. Then, with any luck, things will get back to normal."

"Right," Aunt Edna said.

I turned back around from the sink to see the three women staring at me. "Oh! Hey, can one of you take care of Sophia this morning?"

"Take care of her?" Kitty asked.

"Yeah. Go get the breakfast dishes? And tell Sophia I'll be back before she even notices I'm gone. Hopefully, she won't mind. Tell her I'm doing this for the Family. We could use the money, right?"

"Sure," Aunt Edna said.

"I'll watch Sophia until you get back," Jackie said.

I smiled. "Thanks, Jackie."

Jackie nodded. "Sure thing. You can count on me."

I grinned like the Cheshire cat. "I'll show Sophia I'm not lazy. I'm ... *scrappy.*"

"You ain't scrappy, kid," Aunt Edna said.

I frowned. "I'm not?"

My aunt shook her head. "No. Scrappy means you settle for scraps. From what I see, you're after the whole enchilada."

I grinned. "Thanks. I'm trying."

Chapter Eighteen

Just when I thought I'd survived my showdown with the tourniquet jeans of death, they'd gone and made a second attempt on my life.

"Kerri, you owe me *big time* for this," I grumbled through the bathroom door at Crazy Eddie's Used Cars.

"For the jeans, or the bathroom?" she asked.

"Both," I hissed.

I leaned against the sticky, mustard-colored wall to brace myself, then sucked in my stomach and forced the button on the waistband closed. Cinched nearly in half, I peered in the cracked mirror at my teased hair and makeup.

Ugh! I don't know what I did in a past life to deserve this, but I sure hope I don't do it again.

No longer able to breathe for more reasons than one, I burst through the bathroom door in full Daisy-the-Price-Slayer regalia. I waved a hand in front of my face. "Whew! That place ought to be labeled a biological hazard zone."

Kerri cringed. "Sorry. After this, you're off the hook, I promise." She grabbed my elbow to support me as I wobbled like a newborn colt in the six-inch stilettos.

"I'd better be." I stared past a couple of cheap office desks through a wall of plate glass windows. Outside in the car lot, a gigantic inflatable gorilla stared back at me. Balloons and banners festooned every junker car I could see.

"Eddie sure pulled out all the cliché stops for this one, didn't he?" I quipped.

Kerri whispered in my ear, "You haven't even seen the clowns or the corndog cart yet."

My upper lip snarled. "Speaking of corndogs, I'd like to stick one right up Eddie's—"

"I get the picture," Kerri said. "You ready?"

"Lead the way. The sooner we get started, the sooner this car crash will be over."

571

Kerri stopped in front of the exit door and turned to face me. "Have you seen the commercial yet?"

"No." I swatted a lock of afro hair away from my face. "And I hope I never do."

"I've got it right here on my phone. Maybe it'll get you more ... *in the spirit.*"

"Fine."

Kerri clicked her phone and handed it to me. As I watched the video play on the display, whatever dignity I had left shriveled up and blew away like a dung ball in the Sahara.

"So, you feel in character now?" Kerri asked.

"Sure."

If that character's Arnold Schwarzenegger and we're about to film The Terminator ...

***

I batted an errant balloon away from my face and followed Kerri into the fray of used cars, carny workers, and chaos. She stopped short in front of a small crowd of people.

"What a sad-sack circus this is," I grumbled, nearly running into the back of her. "This dump is the last place I want to be."

"Uh ... Doreen," Kerri said. "I want you to meet Eddie's wife, Kareena."

I laughed, "As in *careening* out of control?"

"It's Kareena with a *K*," a woman's gravelly voice said.

I gulped. So much for making a good impression. But then again, Kareena wasn't that impressive, either. The middle-aged woman was too tan, too red-headed, and too old for her outfit. A moment earlier, she'd been puffing Virginia Slims and talking to someone with a microphone. But now her beady eyes were locked on me.

"I take it you're that psycho killer chick Eddie hired," she said, a sneer creasing her hard face. She lit another cigarette off the burning end of her last one. "You don't want to be here? Too bad. We paid you. You're ours for the next two hours."

"So nice to see you again," Kerri said, stepping between us. "Everything looks so ... festive! Where's Eddie?"

Kareena's face shifted from haughty to annoyed. "I dunno. He ain't showed up yet." She shot me a nasty look. "Hey, bimbo chick. You two got something going on I don't know about?"

"No, ma'am!" I blurted.

"Ma'am!" Kareena screeched. "Who you callin' ma'am?"

"Take it easy," a young man standing beside her said. He put a hand on Kareena's shoulder. "I'm sure she only meant it as a sign of respect."

I nodded too rapidly. "Yes, he's right. I only meant it like that. I swear."

"Hi, I'm Racer," the guy said. "Eddie's son."

"Something ain't right," Kareena said. "Eddie wouldn't miss this shindig for the world." She laughed bitterly. "Mr. Top Dog's always got to mark his territory." She eyed me with suspicion and disgust. "When's the last time you saw him?"

"Wednesday, when we shot the commercial," I said.

Kareena's laser glare shifted to Kerri. "And you?"

"Same for me," Kerri said. "But I talked to him briefly yesterday, and sent him a copy of the commercial for his approval."

"That so, eh?" Kareena said. She put her hands on her hips, causing a cascade of twinkling gold bangles to collide at her wrists.

I studied Kareena's jaded face. Suddenly, I realized she had a cleft chin. So did her son, Racer!

I took a step away from Kerri and was about to go call Aunt Edna with the news when I noticed that the guy selling corndogs also had a cleft chin. So did the clown handing out balloons.

Ugh! What's with all the cleft chins nowadays?

I turned back around and nearly groaned. Some guy in the bad suit was walking up to us. He also had—you guessed it—a cleft chin.

So much for that *clue.*

"Hey, where's Eddie already?" he asked.

"If I knew, Brad, don't you think I'd have dragged him here by now?" Kareena said.

"Uh, who's gonna run the raffle to win the hundred dollar gift certificate for Scooters Wings & Dings?" Brad asked.

Kareena rolled her eyes. "Seeing as you're our top salesman, I'm putting you in charge."

"What does Eddie say?" Brad asked.

"Eddie ain't here, you dimwit!" Kareena screeched.

"Um ... excuse me," I said. "Brad, when did you see Eddie last?"

"Yesterday afternoon." Brad pulled at his collar with his index finger. "We got a trade-in. A lime-green Nissan Cube. Eddie took it out for a test drive."

"When did he come back?" I asked.

"I don't know. I took off early yesterday." Brad cupped his hand like a visor over his eyes and scanned the parking lot. "I don't see the Cube. Maybe he took it home last night."

"Taking a strange one home," Kareena grumbled. "Sounds like Eddie, all right."

I turned to Kareena. "When did Eddie get home last night?"

She glared at me from beneath her cherry-red bangs. "How should I know? We ain't lived together for over six months now."

"Oh, I'm sorry," I said, dancing inside with joy. "I guess that means this whole 'shindig' is cancelled, then. What a shame."

Kareena snorted. "Not on your life, toots. Me and Eddie had our differences, sure. But we had *one* thing in common. We always demanded our money's worth."

Chapter Nineteen

A torrent of sweat streamed down my back. At the moment, it was taking all the acting talent I could muster not to stab someone to death.

Kerri had abandoned me for another appointment just as people were arriving at Crazy Eddie's Used Cars in droves. The problem was, most of them weren't customers. They were women—angry women with picket signs. Signs with Eddie Houser's name on them and a pig face crossed out inside a red circle.

While I totally concurred with the sentiment, it couldn't be good for business. Five percent of nothing was ... *nothing*.

"How can you humiliate yourself like that?" one of the woman shouted at me as I stood next to a rusted out Chevy Malibu, pointing my rubber sword at its "Crazy-Eddie-Low" price sticker.

My face grew hot. My arm went limp. "Uh ... it's just a job."

I looked away from the woman and made a half-hearted attempt to slash the price on the windshield. I knew right then I'd sunk the absolute lowest a human could go without becoming a politician.

"Come on, you can do better than that," a voice rang out.

I recognized it immediately. It belonged to Shirley Saurwein.

Seriously, Universe?

I ground my molars and looked up at the sky.

Come on, stupid meteor!

"If you're looking for salvation for your dignity, that ship has sailed," Saurwein said.

I glared at her and hissed, "What are *you* doing here?"

Saurwein grinned and cracked her gum between her bright-red lips. "You kiddin'? I wouldn't miss this encore performance for the world. Where's Eddie? I could use some juicy soundbites from that idiot."

I scowled. "Eddie's a no-show."

Saurwein's blonde eyebrow ticked up a notch. "You don't say."

"He probably skipped town," I quipped. "After meeting his wife, I could hardly blame him."

"Hey!" a woman shouted from the growing mob of picketers. "Aren't you that reporter from the *Beach Gazette*?"

Saurwein stuck her chin out and smiled. "Yours truly."

"I thought so," the woman growled. "Your portrayal of women in that rag is almost as bad as Eddie's in that commercial!"

"Yeah," another woman yelled. "Those two poor little old ladies you smeared in the last issue. What's wrong with loving an iguana, anyway?"

"Last I heard, there's laws against bestiality," Saurwein yelled back, then laughed.

Someone in the crowd hollered a string of obscenities, punctuated by hurtling a half-eaten corndog right at Saurwein. I smirked as the greasy projectile hit the brassy reporter right above the crotch of her white pants.

"Very funny," Saurwein hissed. She grabbed a tissue from her pocket and swiped at the mustard stain commemorating the corndog's inaugural landing. "Anybody throw anything else at me and I'll have the lot of you arrested for assault!"

The women glared at us. We glared back. The parking lot standoff lasted about a minute, until the corndog hurler said, "Come on, ladies. Let's not waste any more time with these pathetic examples of womankind. Let's take our protest to the streets."

After quite a few choice facial and finger expressions aimed our way, the gang of picketers turned and headed toward the sidewalk running along US 19.

I shook my head at Saurwein. "I can't believe I'm saying this, but I think I owe you one."

"More than one," Saurwein said. "I counted fourteen of those broads."

I fidgeted with the rubber chicken filet squashing my left boob. "Hey. Do you know what time is it?"

"Five minutes to two. Why? You got a hot date with Jethro Bodine?"

"Ha ha." I scowled. "No. In five minutes, my time is up."

Saurwein smirked. "I think your time's been up for a few years now, honey."

I gritted my teeth. "That's not what I—"

"I know. But geez, Diller. You make it so easy."

***

"Where do you think you're going?" Kareena asked as I slammed the driver's door on The Toad.

"You got your two hours' worth," I said. "I'm getting out of here before those women over there start throwing Molotov cocktails." I turned the key in the ignition. Nothing but click.

Crap! Why now?

I popped the hood latch, grabbed the socket wrench, and kicked open the door.

"Hey, what are you doing?" Kareena growled as I climbed out. I turned to see she'd pulled a small pistol from her bra and had it pointed right at me.

"What?" I squealed. "I ... I was just going to bang on the solenoid."

"Like you 'banged' Eddie?"

My face twisted with disgust. "No offense, but Eddie Houser is the last person on Earth I'd want to bang."

Kareena glared at me. "You think you're better than us? That me and Eddie are just two-bit used-car hustlers? Well, let me tell you something, missy. Every single car in this lot is better than that hunk of junk you're driving."

I hoped Kareena's aim with a gun wasn't as good as it was with an insult. I gathered up the last of my gumption and said, "You know, Kareena. You're absolutely right. Sorry for the confusion. Just let me get this hunk of junk started, and I'll be on my way."

"Humph. You should trade that thing in. I've got a nice Plymouth Breeze in the back lot that—"

"Thanks," I said, whacking the Kia's solenoid. "Maybe another time. One when you're not holding me at gunpoint."

"Oh. Sure."

Kareena tucked the pistol back into her left bra cup, then began to pull something out of the right one. I held my breath, wondering if she was going to pull out a switchblade and finish me off. She took a step toward me.

"What are you doing?" I asked, tightening the grip on the socket wrench.

"Here," she said, whipping out a business card. "Take my card. I'll make you the best price in town."

Numb with shock, I took the card.

Kareena grinned and slapped me on the back. "You can't do better than Crazy Eddie's. I guarantee it."

I shook my head.

Unbelievable. This woman's got more balls than Willy Loman.

As Kareena turned and walked away, a thought made me swallow a knot in my throat.

Geez. I hope this isn't a remake of Death of a Salesman.

Chapter Twenty

I was halfway home when I realized I was being tailed.

Ever since I'd left Crazy Eddie's and turned off US 19 onto 22nd Avenue North, a blue Ford Taurus with tinted windows had been ducking around traffic, keeping a low profile as it stayed about a football field length behind me.

My mind went haywire with paranoia.

Who could be after me? Kareena? One of those ladies at the protest? Humpty Bogart? Sammy the Psycho? The cleft-chin guy from Sundial? Brady?

I glanced in the rearview mirror again and chewed my bottom lip. What was wrong with my life that I could easily name half a dozen people who might want to knock my lights out?

I sped through the yellow light at the intersection of 22nd Avenue and 16th Street. Two blocks down, I took a right on a side street, then worked my way back to Palm Court Cottages, zigzagging every couple of streets just to be sure I wasn't being followed.

Keeping an eye out for the blue Taurus, I circled the block before finally pulling in and parking in front of Aunt Edna's place. As I climbed out of the Kia, a car caught my eye. But it wasn't the blue Taurus. It was a lime-green Nissan Cube parked two spaces down.

What the?

Still dressed like Daisy the Price Slasher, I kicked off the stilettos and hobbled barefoot over to the ugly, neon-green box of a car. The windows were tinted dark, making it hard to see inside.

I tried the door handle. It opened. The car was empty—except for the blood splatter covering pretty much the entire front seat compartment.

"Hell!" I screeched, then lost my balance and nearly fell head first into the grisly scene. My right hand caught the driver's headrest. I grabbed it and pushed off, propelling my torso out of the car. I stared at the scene for another second, then quickly slammed the door.

Panic shot down my spine. Was that *Eddie's* blood? What the hell was his car doing in front of my place?

The rattle of an engine made me look up. Half a block away, a blue Taurus was heading my way. I couldn't make out the driver through the darkened windshield. Scared witless, I stood, paralyzed, as the car drew nearer, then stopped right in front of me.

The driver's side window went down a few inches. I saw the glint of something metal. Then a flash.

"Don't shoot!" I screamed.

Chapter Twenty-One

"What the hell's going on, Diller?" Saurwein called out from the blue Taurus. She rolled the driver's side window down a couple more inches, aimed her camera, and took another shot of me.

"Argh!" I growled, anger eclipsing my panic. "Why are you following me?"

Saurwein shrugged. "Because you always make such an interesting subject. That, and my in-laws are staying with us. Believe me, I'm in no hurry to get home."

"Well, I don't care—"

"Hey, what's with the blood?" Saurwein asked.

"Blood?"

"Yeah, the red stuff all over your hands."

I looked at my bloody palms and nearly screamed again. I willed myself to keep calm.

"Oh ... I ... uh ... I fell down wearing those stupid stilettos. Scraped my palms up pretty bad."

"Uh-huh."

I scowled. "You know what, Saurwein? You following me home has got to be against the law. Stalking. Harassment. Something. Unless you leave me alone this instant, I'll figure out a way to charge you with something."

"Uh-huh," Saurwein grunted. She snapped another picture of me, then put her camera away and eyed me up and down. "You know what, Diller? You should get some sun."

"Sun?"

"Yeah. Because in my book, right now you're looking shadier than shit."

***

I made sure Saurwein was gone, then I scrambled into the azalea hedges lining Aunt Edna's house.

What in the world is Eddie's car doing here? Should I call the cops? Should I tell Aunt Edna?

I crawled on hands and knees behind the hedges and over to the garden spigot. I was barely able to keep it together until I could wash off whoever's horrible blood was on my hands.

I turned on the rusty tap and rubbed my palms together under the stream of lukewarm water. Mesmerized and horrified, I stared at the ground as the reddish water seeped into the soil below the spigot.

Suddenly, I felt a hand on my shoulder.

"What'cha doing, Dorey?" Jackie asked, kneeling beside me.

"Yaaugh!" I squealed. "How do you do that?"

"Do what?"

"Sneak up on people like that."

Jackie stood up and shrugged. "It's a gift."

I turned off the tap and hoisted myself to standing. "I'm uh ... just washing up. I—"

"Come inside," Jackie said calmly. Her boney fingers curled around the back of my neck. "We've been waiting for you."

Chapter Twenty-Two

I was sitting on my hands in Aunt Edna's "good chair." It was a brown, vinyl recliner that had probably made its advertising debut on *The Lawrence Welk Show*.

Across the room, perched on my aunt's olive-green couch, sat my aunt, Kitty, and Jackie. They stared at me like a trio of Judge Judies. I couldn't help but notice all the velveteen curtains had been drawn shut.

Under their narrow-eyed scrutiny, I began to fidget—and wonder if the ancient Barcalounger I was sitting in had come with an electrocution switch. I prayed the chair was too old to have come with a remote. A quick scan of the women's hands showed they were empty. But their faces were full of worry.

"Uh ... what's wrong?" I asked, forcing a twitchy smile.

"You seem to be taking matters into your own hands now, Dorey," Aunt Edna said. "Were you gonna fill us in on the plan?"

"The plan?" I asked. "What plan?"

Aunt Edna's face grew taut. "It ain't proper protocol, Dorey. Maybe you didn't know no better, being so new to the garbage business and all. But you should've gone through the proper channels before you went and hit the mattresses with Eddie Houser."

"What?" I balked. "I didn't sleep with Eddie Houser! Gross!"

"Who's talking about screwing the guy?" Jackie asked. "I'm confused here."

"You and me both," I said, turning back to my aunt. "Why are you saying I'm sleeping with Eddie Houser?"

"I ain't," Aunt Edna said. "I'm talking about *hitting the mattresses*, Dorey. You told us yourself. Don't deny it."

"Well, sure," I said, relieved they didn't think I'd killed the guy. "What's the big deal?"

Jackie's eyes grew wider. "What'd you use? A bat?"

"No. A broom."

Jackie cringed. "Ouch."

My brow furrowed. "What else was I supposed to use to beat the dust off Sophia's old mattresses?"

The women's faces went slack.

Kitty cleared her throat. "Doreen, *hitting the mattresses* means starting a war with a rival clan."

I gulped. "It does? I didn't know that."

"What did you think it meant, then?" Kitty asked.

I scooted to the edge of the Barcalounger. "What I just said. You know, to beat the dust out of Sophia's mattresses."

Aunt Edna shook her head slowly. "And I suppose you also didn't know that Eddie Houser was a known associate of Humphrey Bogaratelli, either."

"What?" I felt the air drain from my lungs. "No. I didn't."

"Huh," Kitty said.

I grimaced. "Look. All I did was go see Eddie to—"

"We know all about it, Dorey," Aunt Edna said, cutting me off. "Amateur move, just leaving the body out there to be found."

"Body?" I gulped. "You mean ... in that Nissan? You saw his body?"

"Yeah," Jackie said. "And you didn't do the deed with no cuticle scissors this time, that's for sure."

My shoulders slumped. "But I ... I didn't ..."

"You don't gotta worry about it," Jackie said. "We took care of it."

My eyebrows jumped up an inch. "You three got rid of Eddie's body?"

"Not us," Aunt Edna said. "We called Victor to do it. We look out for our own around here." Aunt Edna's eyes narrowed in on mine. "So, you looking out for *us*, too?"

"I ... I ..."

Aunt Edna sighed. "Dorey, Dorey, Dorey. You vying to be the new Queenpin, or what?"

I nearly fell out of the Barcalounger. "What? No! Why would I? Listen. This is all a big misunderstanding."

Jackie laughed. "Well, that ain't no consolation to Eddie, now, is it?"

I shook my head in dismay. "Why would I kill Eddie? You just told me he's part of the Family!"

"You don't got to be outside the Family to be *outside the Family*, if you know what I mean," Aunt Edna said.

"A traitor's a traitor," Kitty said.

"Why'd you kill him?" Aunt Edna asked. "Is Eddie working with Humpty to poison Sophia? Or maybe they're in cahoots to steal from the Family Fund?"

"Humpty's been eatin' alone for a long time," Kitty said, rubbing her chin. "You thinking maybe Eddie was his secret lunch partner?"

I stared at the three ladies in disbelief. "I ... I don't know."

Aunt Edna chewed her bottom lip. "Either way, you could've just stirred up a hornet's nest, Dorey. We need to take this to the consigliere."

"The what?"

"The *consigliere*," Kitty said. "The Family adviser. He's supposed to be consulted before decisions that big are made."

"Oh." My mind flashed to some horrible old man in a wheelchair, ready to put his lit cigar out in my eyeball.

"Who's the consigliere?" I asked.

"Morty," Jackie said.

"But first, we've got a few loose ends to tie up," Kitty said.

"Uh ... loose ends?" I squeaked.

"Yeah," Jackie said. "We couldn't find the weapon. What'd you do with the broom?"

"I didn't kill Eddie with a broom!" I said.

"So you was lying?" Jackie asked. "Ah. You used the bat, didn't you?"

My jaw went slack. "The bat?"

"Yeah. The baseball bat I gave you," Jackie said. "Where is it?"

"Uh ... it's still in the Kia."

Aunt Edna shook her head and blew out a breath. "Another amateur move."

***

"So this is what you used to bust Eddie up with, eh?" Jackie said, pulling a bloody baseball bat from the trunk of The Toad.

I stared at the bat in horror. I'd been driving around all day with that thing in the trunk! "I ... I—"

"Louisville Slugger," Kitty said, examining it with a pink-handled magnifying lens. "A classic."

"Bag it," Aunt Edna said, glancing around. "We got to get rid of the evidence. Pronto."

"I'm on it," Jackie said.

Kitty held open a black garbage bag. Jackie dropped the bat inside.

"Now what?" Kitty asked, pulling the bag's string tight.

"We go see Morty," Aunt Edna said. "Jackie, you stay with Sophia. We don't need her knowing about this. Capeesh?"

Jackie nodded. "You got it, Capo."

"Good. Kitty, you come with us. Shove the bat under the driver's seat. Doreen, you drive."

"But I ..." I stuttered.

"No more excuses," my aunt said, dropping the keys into my palm. "You made this mess. You gotta do your part to clean it up."

Unable to figure out where to even begin to try and explain, I gave up and nodded. I climbed into the driver's seat and turned the key in The Toad's ignition.

Nothing but click. *Again.*

"Well, that makes two dead in one day," Kitty quipped.

"This ain't funny," Aunt Edna said, handing me the socket wrench. "You know the drill, Dorey. At least we know *that* for sure."

"Fine," I said. "I'll do it. I just wish you'd given me time to change. These jeans are killing me."

"Now you know how Eddie felt," Aunt Edna said.

What?

I climbed out of the Kia, unlatched the hood, and got busy beating the life out of the solenoid. I didn't need any motivation to perform the act.

Aunt Edna thinks I'm a murderer. That I'm trying to take over the Family! She hates me! How could this get any worse?

Then, as if a magic genie had granted my wish, I instantly saw how it could get worse.

A police cruiser was headed our way. And behind the wheel was Officer Gregory Brady himself.

Chapter Twenty-Three

"Car trouble, ladies?" Brady asked as he slowly steered his police cruiser up beside The Toad until his window was even with Aunt Edna's.

"We're fine," Aunt Edna said. "Dorey's taking care of it."

"Is that so." Brady inched the cruiser forward until he spotted me hiding behind the raised hood. His grin evaporated.

"Nothing happening here," I said, my voice at least an octave above normal. I forced a trembling smile. "I mean, nothing that we can't deal with on our own. You know, all by little old selves."

Little-old selves? Really, Doreen?

My heart thumped so loud I was sure he could hear it. I tried to whack the solenoid again, but my fumbling fingers lost their grip. I watched in horror as the socket wrench clattered onto the brick street as if in slow motion. When Brady got out of his patrol car, my heart nearly came out of my mouth.

No, no no!

"Go try the ignition again," Brady said coolly as he bent down beside me and picked up the wrench. "I'll hit the solenoid if it won't start."

"Uh ... thanks." If I'd had a tail, it would've been tucked between my legs. "Sorry if I scratched your truck."

"Seriously?" Brady shook his head. "That's the best apology you've got?"

My mouth fell open. "What else should I—"

But Brady wasn't having it. He just stared at the engine. "Go give the ignition another turn so we can both get out of here. Okay?"

I nodded, and slunk back into the driver's seat. I tried the key. The traitorous Kia purred to life like a newborn kitten.

"You ladies really should consider getting a new vehicle," Brady said, his handsomely stern visage appearing beside Aunt Edna's window. He handed my aunt the socket wrench.

"Right you are, Officer Brady," Aunt Edna said. "Now all we need is the money to buy one. Maybe we'll get lucky and it'll fall out of the sky."

I held my breath.

Along with a meteor, please. A giant one.

Brady smiled and gently slapped the bottom of Aunt Edna's window with his palm, as if to put an end to the conversation. "Now you all please, try to stay out of trouble, would you?"

"We will!" Kitty gushed. "Thank you, Officer Brady!"

Brady's eyes met mine as if to say, "Especially *you.*" I looked away, shifted into drive, and hit the gas, leaving him in a belch of black smoke.

"Whew!" Kitty said. "Good thing you didn't use that socket wrench on Eddie, or you'd be on your way to jail right now, Doreen."

"Yeah," Aunt Edna said. "And good thing Jackie wasn't with us, or we'd all be heading straight for the slammer." Aunt Edna locked eyes with me. "You remember the way to Morty's Bakery, don't you Dorey?"

I nodded. "Yes."

"Good. I'm gonna count rosary beads until we get there."

"Why? You didn't do anything wrong."

"I aided and abetted, Dorey. I threw out the empty wine bottle Jackie found under your bed. I washed all them red stains out of your shirt."

I shook my head. "But that was just wine."

"Don't you get it?" Kitty said. "You went pulled another Sammy on us, Doreen. You know, like when you got drunk and killed Tad Longmire."

"What?" I gasped. "No I didn't!"

Did I?

Chapter Twenty-Four

I pulled the old Kia into the parking lot of a run-down strip center, then found a spot near the storefront window emblazoned with the words, *Morty's Bakery*.

"Let me do the talking," Aunt Edna said, grabbing her pocketbook and opening the passenger door. "You've already dug a deep enough hole for yourself."

"Yes, Capo," I said.

Aunt Edna shot me some side eye. "That had better be sincere. You're gonna need every friend you got on this one, Dorey."

"She's right, young lady," Kitty said. "Things aren't looking to bright for you, Sunshine."

***

"And that's when we spotted the body in the car," Aunt Edna said as the four of us stood in the back room of Morty's Bakery.

By this point, I was so bewildered I had no problem keeping my mouth shut. Worried that I'd actually killed Eddie in a drunken rage, neither my mouth nor my brain were in working order.

"Well, technically, *I* was the one who found him," Kitty said. "While I was clipping the azaleas, I spotted blood stains at the bottom of the Nissan's driver's door. Hard to miss against that godawful lime-green chassis."

"What time was that?" Morty asked, pulling a little red book out of his front pocket. He eyed me up and down, but didn't say a word about my trashy hair, makeup, or skin-tight jeans. No wonder he was the consigliere. The man was a pro.

"Sometime between 10:00 and 10:30, I think," Kitty said.

Aunt Edna nodded. "Sounds right. It couldn't have been more than half an hour after Dorey here told us she was hitting the mattresses, and her first "appointment" was with Eddie Houser."

Morty glanced at me. His bushy eyebrows ticked up a notch. "The girl works quick."

"Maybe, but not *that* quick," Kitty said. "From the looks of the stiff, I'd say he'd been there at least overnight. Maybe longer."

Morty exhaled through his big, red nose. "You saw the body then, Kitty. You sure it was Eddie?"

Kitty nodded. "Yeah. But not by his ugly mug. After Doreen here got done with him, his own mother wouldn't recognize him."

"So how do you know it was Eddie?" Morty asked, scratching his head with a meaty finger.

"I'll show you how." Kitty popped on some pink rubber gloves and opened the black garbage bag lying on the counter. "Take a look for yourself."

"A bloody baseball bat?" Morty frowned. "What? You already run the DNA or something?"

"No. Better." Kitty turned the bat an inch. "Look closer."

Morty squinted through his bifocals, then shook his head. "I'll be."

I stepped forward for a closer look myself. There, imbedded in the head of the baseball bat was a shiny hunk of gold. My knees began to knock.

"Looks like Eddie's eyetooth, all right," Morty said. "Okay, so the body's his." He turned to me, his eyes angry and suspicious. "Why'd you do it?"

"Go easy on her," Aunt Edna said. "She was sloppy, yeah. But this is her first job for the Family."

I burst into tears. "I didn't do it! I swear!"

Aunt Edna wrapped an arm around me. "Morty, we think our girl pulled a Sammy. She got drunk and can't remember a thing. Jackie found the baseball bat in the trunk of the Kia. She could've been driving around with it for days."

Morty shook his head. "Geez."

"I also found this beside the body," Kitty said, shoving some papers at Morty.

He grabbed them and flipped through them. "What is all this?"

"A contract," Kitty said. "Doreen did a commercial for Eddie's car lot. He was trying to sell her that Nissan Cube for a discount, instead of giving her five percent of the profits like he promised."

Morty locked eyes with me. "That tick you off, Doreen?"

I shook my head wildly. "No. I didn't even know about the contract. This is the first time I've heard of it. I swear!"

"You seem to swear a lot," Morty said, taking off his bifocals.

I cringed. "I didn't kill Eddie, I swea ..."

"What if the kid isn't lying," Kitty asked. "If you ask me, she's too smart to be driving around with the murder weapon."

"Unless she didn't remember nothing about it," Aunt Edna said.

"Or somebody planted it on her," Kitty said.

Morty rubbed his eyes. "Well, if *she* didn't kill Eddie, who did?"

"Maybe it was a message job from Humpty," Kitty said.

"A message job?" I asked.

Kitty nodded. "Yeah. You know. A bullet in the mouth sends the message that you talk too much. A bullet in the eye, you saw too much. A bullet to the groin—"

"I get it," I said. "But whoever killed Eddie didn't use bullets."

"No, they used that thing right there," Morty said, nodding toward the bloody baseball bat.

"So, what kind of message could that mean?" I asked.

"Besides that *you* did it?" Morty said.

I cringed. "Yes. Besides that."

Morty eyed me up and down. "Maybe it was Sammy saying it's your turn at bat."

My eyes grew wide. "What?"

"Or maybe it was his way of warning Humpty to keep away from his girl," Aunt Edna said.

Kitty nodded. "Like father, like daughter."

I suddenly felt the world closing in on me "What are you saying?"

Aunt Edna laid a hand on my shoulder. "I didn't want you to find out this way, Dorey, but Sammy's your father."

Chapter Twenty-Five

I now knew how Luke Skywalker felt—but I didn't have *The Force* behind me. I had *The Family*.

Sammy the Psycho is my father? This can't be happening!

The backroom of Morty's Bakery began to spin. I wobbled on my stilettos. I was about to keel over when Aunt Edna caught me by the arm.

"Steady, Dorey."

I shook my head in dismay. "Is that why my mother hated me?"

"Maureen didn't hate you Dorey." Aunt Edna patted my arm. "She just kept a little distant. She had her reasons."

"And now she's disappeared," I said.

Aunt Edna nodded. "Maureen's in the wind."

I moaned, and burst into tears. "Sammy killed her!"

"No, Hun," Kitty said. "You got it all wrong. Maureen's where she always wanted to be. She's *with Sammy.*"

"What?" I sniffed. "Why? How? Where are they?"

"We can't tell you, because nobody knows," Aunt Edna said. "And nobody will, unless they want us to. Doreen, you've got to understand something. Don't believe everything you hear about Sammy, okay?"

"What do you mean?"

"I can't say. Only that Sammy and your ma waited forty years to be together. Who are we to deny them their chance at happiness?"

"But why did they have to wait?" I asked.

"For a lot of reasons," Morty said. "But we ain't got time for that now."

"The biggest reason was they were waiting for you to come into your own," Aunt Edna said, putting an arm around my waist.

"Come into my own?" I gasped. "You mean, be a killer like Sammy?"

"Yeah," Morty said.

"But I *can't* be!" I squealed. "Before I came here, nothing like this ever happened to me!"

"It takes women more time to gather up enough rage at the world to turn homicidal," Kitty said. "That's a proven fact. Why else would most serial killers be men?"

"Yeah, blame it on the men," Morty said sourly. "It's always *our* fault."

"Look, Morty," Aunt Edna said. "We came to you for advice. So give us some!"

"Okay, fine." Morty opened his little red book. "Where's the car? We've got to get rid of it."

"In front of our place," Aunt Edna said.

Morty nodded, and ran an index finger down a page in the book. "Okay, I'll call my cousin at the scrapyard."

"Thanks, Morty." Aunt Edna nodded toward the bat. "And could you get rid of that?"

"Yeah." Morty sighed. "I'll put some feelers out, too. See who knows what about what's already gone down."

"We've got to keep a close eye on Humpty," I said. "He's got to be involved in this somehow."

Aunt Edna nodded. "Doreen thinks Humpty was in on that scheme to poison Sophia on her birthday. Maybe he's tired of skimming off the Family Fund and wants to get his hands on the whole wad."

"I wouldn't put it past him," Morty said. "I never have liked that guy. I'll put a tail on him."

"Thanks, Morty" I said. I broke free of my aunt and Kitty and hugged him. He patted my back stiffly, then pushed me away.

"Now for Pete's sake," he said. "You ladies go home and lock your windows and doors."

"Why?" I asked.

He scowled at me. "Because when you start hitting the mattresses, Dorey, *everybody's* a target."

***

On the drive home, Aunt Edna kept glancing in the side-view mirror.

"Anybody tailing us?" Kitty asked.

"No. Not yet, anyway," Aunt Edna said.

"We've got to find the real killer," I said. "Why didn't you mention the coffee, Aunt Edna?"

"Because there's nothing to tell," she said. "Kitty said it wasn't poisoned. And Sophia swore you to secrecy about it. There's no need to let Sophia know we're on to her. If she knew we knew, no telling what kind of 'chores' she might have in store for you."

"Oh. Thanks."

"You really think I killed Eddie?" I asked.

"It don't matter either way, Dorey. You're Family. If you did it, you did it for *us*. We love you no matter what."

A lump the size of an egg pressed down on my tonsils. I couldn't speak. When Aunt Edna reached over and gently patted my thigh, it was all I could do not to break down and sob.

Chapter Twenty-Six

"That was Morty on the phone," Aunt Edna said, tucking her cellphone back into the big, brown pocketbook on her lap. She turned and glanced at Kitty in the backseat of the Kia. "The guy with the tow truck is on his way."

Kitty nodded. "Let's hope he gets there before the cops do."

Aunt Edna touched my arm. "Better step on it, Dorey."

"Yes, ma'am."

Speeding down Fourth Street toward Palm Court Cottages, my mind swirled with a mishmash of contradicting thoughts. What *really had* happened to Eddie? Had I clubbed him to death in a drunken rage? Or had someone else beaten me to it?

Maybe it was one of those angry women with picket signs. Or an old customer Eddie had swindled. Perhaps his wife Kareena? There certainly hadn't seemed to be any love-loss there.

Or maybe it really *was* me.

Drunken Doreen in the Nissan Cube with a baseball bat.

As I passed an old man at a bus stop in shorts and a wife-beater T-shirt, the thought of being back in LA clipping Arthur Dreacher's toenails began to take on a certain allure ...

"I'm telling you, you can't convict without a body," Aunt Edna's voice burst through my thought bubble. How long she and Kitty had been arguing, I couldn't say.

"Sure you can," Kitty said. "It's just a little harder, that's all. DNA evidence is the new smoking gun. It's like the hand of God pointing a finger right at you."

"Even so, I'm glad the body's gone," Aunt Edna said. "*And* the bat. Once the blasted car is off our street, we're home free."

"And there it goes now," Kitty said, pointing toward a tow truck passing us in the opposite lane. The rig was hauling a lime-green, cube-shaped car. The driver shot us a thumb's up as he sped by.

While I watched the Nissan on the tow truck disappear in the rearview mirror, a boulder lifted off my shoulders.

I didn't know if that was a good sign, or a bad one.

The only thing I knew for sure was, I was in this mess up to my ultra-teased hairline.

***

As I turned onto the street in front of Palm Court Cottages, an avalanche of boulders fell back on top of my shoulders.

A cop car and a forensics van was parked right in front of the apartments.

I recognized the cop—a tall, slim, black man. He was none other than Sergeant McNulty. My molars pressed together. Sergeant McNulty had it out for me. Every time I turned up next to a dead body, he blamed me. Go figure?

I cringed. "Aww, crap."

"McNutsack," Aunt Edna muttered. "This ain't good."

"Stay calm," Kitty said, putting a hand on my shoulder from the backseat. "Just keep driving like nothing's happening."

I tried to do as Kitty commanded, but people were everywhere. On-lookers lined the streets, pointing and gawking at something in front of the apartments.

"What are they looking at?" I asked.

"I dunno," Kitty said. "Something by the curb."

"Keep going," Aunt Edna said. "We're almost to his car."

Slowly, I cautiously steered the Kia, weaving through the crowded scene at a snail's pace. As we passed McNulty's police car, I was about to breathe a sigh of relief when a fat guy in gym shorts and a T-shirt started crossing the road right in front of us. He couldn't have walked slower if he were going backward.

"Geez. Of all the luck," I grumbled, nervously chewing my bottom lip as the guy slowly blundered along. Just as he reached the center of the road, he dropped his water bottle. He bent over to pick it up, lost his balance, and toppled over head first onto the brick street.

"Ouch," I said. "Should I go help him?"

"No. Stay in the car!" Aunt Edna hissed. "Don't worry about him. Don't look like he uses that head of his much, anyway."

Time seemed to stand still as we held our breath and watched the guy slowly grunt and huff his way to his feet. It was then I noticed he had a cleft chin.

Seriously, Doreen? Maybe Aunt Edna's right. I'm as looney-toons as my father.

"He's clear," Kitty said. "Punch it!"

"Right." I was about to hit the gas when a pair of knuckles banged on the window right by my head. I turned and felt a quarter of my life-force drain away.

"Diller, is that you?" McNulty asked.

I glanced in the mirror at my candy-apple lips, bozo hair, and fake beauty mark. "Yes. Unfortunately, it's me," I muttered under my breath.

"Roll down your window," McNulty demanded. "Where are you going?"

My guilty brain curdled like cottage cheese. "Um ... just ... yeah. You know."

McNulty lowered his mirrored sunglasses and glared at me. "No, I *don't* know, Diller, or I wouldn't be asking."

"We're looking for a parking space, officer McNut ... uh," Aunt Edna said.

"What's going on, officer?" Kitty blurted.

"Big pool of blood by the curb," McNulty said. "You ladies know anything about it?"

"No, sir," Kitty said.

"Aww, for the love of," Aunt Edna hissed.

I turned away from McNulty toward Aunt Edna. She was staring out the passenger window toward the apartments. Suddenly, I saw what she saw.

Jackie was hoofing it down the garden path toward us. Still dressed in that blazing red shirt and green pants, she kept dragging a boney finger across her chicken-neck throat like a doomed member of a *Star Trek* landing party.

"Real subtle, that one," Kitty muttered, then slumped back into her seat.

By some Christmas-in-June miracle, McNulty apparently hadn't noticed Jackie. He continued his line of questioning. "So you're saying you don't know nothing about the blood on the curb?"

"Did an animal get hit by a car?" I asked.

"Don't know yet." McNulty glanced around inside our vehicle. "But I have reason to believe it's more serious than that."

"You do?" I said, trying not to squeal.

"Yes, I do." McNulty pulled out his cellphone. "Someone called in an anonymous tip about the blood being human. Then I received this video."

I gulped. "Video?"

McNulty shoved his cellphone in my face. Playing on the display was an outtake from the commercial I shot with Kerri at Crazy Eddie's Used Car Lot.

There I was, in the same Daisy the Price Slayer outfit I was donning yet again today. I watched the screen as I swung that stupid rubber sword and accidently hit Eddie in the neck with it. Eddie grasped his throat and fell backward. The video cut off.

I groaned inside. It had all been a joke. But it appeared Eddie was going to have the last laugh.

"That was just us goofing around at a commercial shoot on Wednesday," I said.

"Is that so." McNulty eyed me, then Aunt Edna and Kitty. "Can anyone corroborate your story?"

I nodded. "Yes, sir. Kerri and Marshall at—"

"I can," Jackie said. She jutted her pointy chin at McNulty. "That clip there is totally bogus. Everybody knows that ain't the way Houser got whacked."

Chapter Twenty-Seven

"So, just exactly how *did* Eddie Houser 'get whacked?'" McNulty asked Jackie. He held a pen to his notepad, ready to record the moment our ship was torpedoed.

I groaned, already hearing the handcuffs clinking shut around my wrists. As I awaited my inevitable incarceration, Aunt Edna grabbed a life raft and started bailing.

"Jackie, you been watching too much TV again," my aunt said, climbing out of the car. "Sorry, officer. The old gal's got dementia. She's always getting Eddie Houser mixed up with *Doogie Howser, M.D.*" She elbowed Jackie in the ribs. "Ain't that right, Jackie?"

"Uh ...," Jackie said. Unable to lie, her narrow face creased with confusion. Apparently, Jackie still didn't realize she'd just spilled a pot of baked beans big enough to bury us all the way to Boston.

"See, officer?" Aunt Edna said, shaking her head. "Just look at that dumb, confused expression. She definitely forgot to take her meds again this morning."

"I mean, who in their right mind would wear that outfit?" Kitty said, climbing out of the backseat. She took Jackie's other elbow. "She thinks she's an elf. We better get her back into her apartment before she wanders off again."

"Yeah," Aunt Edna said, and started tugging on Jackie's elbow.

"Hold on," McNulty said.

Kitty winked at him and whispered, "Yesterday, she kept asking where Pat was. She thought she was Vanna White. We better get her inside. Those diapers aren't getting any fresher, if you catch my drift."

A horn honked behind us. The Kia was blocking the street.

"Fine, go," McNulty said. "But Diller, get your car out of the street. Then you and I need to talk."

***

I led McNulty beyond the prying eyes of the crowd on the street, over to the picnic table in the center of the tropical courtyard. Aunt Edna had offered to bring us iced tea, but I was glad when McNulty turned her down. All we needed was to have another body to get rid of.

"Play the video again," I asked McNulty. "I want to show you something."

He plucked his phone from his breast pocket and loaded the video.

"Take a good look," I said. "You can see in the background that the video was filmed at the car lot. Like I tried to explain earlier, I can get Kerri and Marshall at Sunshine City Studios to send you the rest of the clip. You'll see Eddie Houser was just pulling a prank on me. I swear, he was alive and kicking when I left the lot."

McNulty tucked his phone back into his pocket. "Why would he pull a prank like that?" He crossed his arms and studied me like a puzzle he was trying to figure out.

"Because he's a jer ... Jersey native, I think. Pranking is in their blood."

"Uh-huh. Speaking of which, if that blood on the curb turns out to belong to Eddie Houser, you can bet I'll be back here before you can say 'Jersey Devil.'"

"Yes, sir."

McNulty's phone rang. He took the call. "I see," he said, then hung up. "Well, the blood on the curb is no mutt's. It's human."

I gasped. It was no act.

"You don't mind if we search your premises, do you," McNulty said. It wasn't a question.

My heart began humping in my throat. "No. Of course not."

"Good. I'll send a couple of officers out now."

***

I barely had time to get out of the Daisy Duke Jeans of Death and scrub the makeup off my face before I heard a knock at the door.

"Remember what we talked about," Aunt Edna said. "There ain't no evidence inside the house. So there's nothing to worry about."

"Right." I chewed my thumbnail. "Nothing to worry about, except the trunk of the Kia where the bloody bat was."

Aunt Edna patted me on the shoulder. "Don't worry! We're gonna make the Kia disappear during the search."

"Then you better get going." I handed her the keys.

"Leaving now. Out the back door."

"Be sure and get Jackie out of here, too," I whispered.

Aunt Edna shot me a look. "You think this is my first rodeo? Now relax. Breathe. You got this, Dorey."

I nodded. "Okay. I'll call you when the coast is clear."

The knock sounded at the door again.

Aunt Edna patted me on the shoulder, then turned and headed through the kitchen toward the back door.

Calling on everything I'd learned from years of acting classes, I prepared for the performance of a lifetime. , Channeling my inner Doris Day, I smoothed my hair and dress, then plastered on a smile and opened the door.

"Diller?" the cop said.

Doris caught a cab to a liquor store.

I glared at the cop. "Brady. Why did McNulty send *you* to search our place? Isn't this some kind of conflict of interest or something?"

"Why would it be?" Brady said. "I have no personal interests here."

And with that bullet to the heart, I stepped aside and let him in.

Chapter Twenty-Eight

While Brady ransacked my aunt's apartment, I flopped into the Barcalounger and surfed the internet for cheap ways out of the country. On Craig's list, some guy named Lefty was looking for a cook to serve on a junket cruise down to Bogota and back.

What the hell? My goose is probably cooked, anyway.

I was about to type Lefty an email when Brady shouted out my name. "Diller! Bedroom!"

If only...

I hauled my butt out of the chair and padded to my bedroom.

"What's this?" Brady asked, holding up my leather journal.

"That's personal!" I said, then scrambled to snatch it out of his hands. "It was a birthday gift from Kitty!"

Brady held the book over his head, out of my reach. "Sit down, Diller."

My face as hot as the surface of the sun, I flopped onto the edge of the bed and crossed my arms. "What?"

Brady opened the journal and read from it aloud. "Humpty Bogart has a cleft chin?"

"Yes," I huffed. "I tried to tell you that the other night."

"I thought you were making it up," Brady said. "Humpty Bogart?"

"It's a nickname for Humphrey Bogaratelli." My shoulders slumped. "But it doesn't matter anymore. Turns out, every Tom, Dick, and Harry in St. Pete has a cleft chin."

"Who's Bogaratelli?"

I frowned.

A slimy bagman bilking the Collard Green Cosa Nostra out of their ill-gotten gains.

"He's a money manager for my aunt," I said. "I thought he might be involved with Montoya in trying to poison Sophia, okay?"

"Why didn't you tell me?"

"I tried! But you were too busy laughing at me about it."

"Laughing at you? I didn't."

"You asked me if Humpty Bogart was the father of Monkey-Faced Mongo. Remember?"

Brady frowned. "I thought it was Mongo the Monkey Boy."

"Whatever! Can I have my journal back now, please?" I made a grab for the notebook. Brady was quicker.

"Not so fast." Brady turned a page in the journal and started reading aloud. "What's wrong with Brady? Forty and not married. Some kind of power-hungry perv? What a baby, getting all pissed at me over a scratch on his bumper! Any man who loves his truck more than me can go to—"

"I wrote that in a moment of anger!" I blurted.

"So that's why you defaced my truck? You think I'm a power-hungry pervert?"

I closed my eyes and tried to clear my head. At this point, my mouth was a shovel, busily digging my grave. I opened my eyes and said, "I don't want to talk about it. You said this wasn't personal."

Brady shook his head and snapped the journal shut. "Geez, Diller. This is my payback for not laughing at your joke? You're a real hothead. Especially when you've been drinking. My advice? Don't drink anymore. And don't date."

***

Relegated to the Barcalounger while Brady finished his search of my aunt's cottage, I pecked out a note to Lefty on my laptop. I was about to press *send* when Brady called my name again.

"Diller! Laundry room."

I set down my laptop and dragged myself to the small nook off the kitchen that housed the washer and dryer. Brady was standing there holding a pair of sopping-wet jeans.

The Daisy Duke jeans. Aunt Edna must've tossed them into the wash.

"Are these yours?" he asked.

"Well, yes. But technically they belong to the Studio."

"Why are you washing your clothes now, during a police search? In my line of work, this is called trying to get rid of evidence."

"Seriously?" I scowled. "I voluntarily submitted to this search, remember? In my line of work, that's what we call Friday night laundry. Why are you persecuting me, Brady?"

"I'm not persecuting you. I'm trying to help you."

My eyebrows rose and inch. "Help me? By *incriminating* me?"

"Look, Doreen. I asked for the assignment to search your place."

"Why?"

"Because you have this uncanny knack for incriminating *yourself*. I thought I could shield you. Listen to your explanations and sort things out." He looked down at the sopping jeans. "But even *I* find this hard to explain away."

"Size six jeans?"

"No. The bloody fingerprint on the back left thigh."

"What?" I gasped. "It's ... it's probably just ketchup from a corndog."

"Seriously?" Brady shook his head. "That's the best excuse you can come up with?"

"But—"

"I'm going to have to take these in evidence." Brady slipped the jeans into a plastic bag. "You'd better pray this isn't blood. And that if it is, you better pray even harder that it doesn't match that pool of blood on the curb outside."

At a loss for words, I simply nodded.

"And Doreen? Don't go anywhere. As of this moment, I'm having McNulty place you under house arrest."

Chapter Twenty-Nine

"The coast is clear," I said into my cellphone as I peeked through the living room curtains. Officer Brady was leaving down the courtyard path.

"Good," Aunt Edna said. "It's too late to get dinner started. We're picking up takeout on the way home. You got a hankering for anything?"

Yeah. A fast boat to China.

I sighed. "How about Chinese?"

"You got it. See you in a bit."

"No hurry. Believe me, I'm not going anywhere."

I hung up the phone and flopped into "the good chair." Utterly dejected, it occurred to me that somehow I'd managed to star in a 3-D disaster movie of my own making.

One—the disastrous *date* with Brady. Two—the disastrous *death* of Crazy Eddie. And three—my disastrous fate as the *daughter* of Sammy the psycho.

I shook my head in disbelief. My whole Family thought I was a next-generation psycho killer. Even worse, I was seriously beginning to think they might be right. I'd have asked the Universe what else could possibly go wrong, but as of late I'd come to believe that was a trick question ...

***

"You've hardly touched your Peking Duck," Aunt Edna said as we sat around the dining room table digging through cardboard cartons from Lucky Duck Chinese Restaurant. "What's wrong?"

"Maybe it's because I feel like a *sitting* duck," I said, picking at my food with a pair of chopsticks. "Now even *Brady* thinks I killed Eddie."

Aunt Edna frowned. "Huh. Brady's always been on our side."

"That's because up to now, we haven't gotten our hands this dirty," Kitty said.

Jackie examined her fingernails. "My hands ain't dirty. I used Lysol."

I glanced from face to face at each of the three little old ladies who'd worked so hard to cover a killer's tracks—possibly *my* tracks. They didn't deserve this mess.

I pushed my chair back and stood up. "Thanks for all your help, ladies. But I'm not hungry. I need to be alone for a while."

"You go ahead, Dorey," Aunt Edna said. "We'll be here for you when you're ready to talk."

I nodded. "Thanks."

As I turned to go, a knock sounded at the front door.

"I'll get it," I said. "I'm already up."

"If it's the cops, don't let them in without a warrant," Kitty said.

"Right." I headed for the front door and yanked it open, ready to deliver a speech about our rights as citizens of the United States. But to my surprise, no one was there. Instead, a bouquet of white flowers lay on the doormat.

"Relax! It's just flowers," I called out, then picked them up and carried them into the dining room.

"Who're they for?" Jackie asked. She elbowed Aunt Edna. "Maybe they're from one of your 'pen pals.'"

"Can it," Aunt Edna grumbled.

"What's the card say?" Kitty asked.

I set the flowers on the table and plucked the small envelope from the plastic pick poking from the bouquet. I opened it, swallowed hard, and read the handwritten note out loud.

"It says, 'You're dead to me.'"

Chapter Thirty

"Who could've sent the flowers?" I asked, staring wide-eyed at the trio of elderly mob molls.

"Monkey-Face Mongo?" Jackie asked, ribbing Aunt Edna.

Aunt Edna winced. "Crap. I forgot about him."

I chewed my bottom lip. "Do you think he might have tracked you down to get his money back? Or *worse*?"

Aunt Edna shook her head. "Marco Telleroni ain't the brightest bulb in the box. Still, he *is* a made man, so he's bona fide to make a hit."

"You think he killed Eddie?" I asked.

"I was thinking more like him wanting to kill me," Aunt Edna said. "But Marco would send a message first. You know, to let me know he was on to me."

I waved the note in the air. "And you don't think 'You're dead to me.' is a message?"

"It's a message, all right." Aunt Edna took the note from me and studied it. "But it probably ain't Marco. All the words are spelled right."

"Somebody else could've written it for him," Kitty said.

"Maybe." Aunt Edna glanced around at each of us. "But these flowers could've just as easily come from Humpty Bogart for Sophia."

"How do you figure that?" Jackie asked.

"Maybe he's trying to scare her into a heart attack or something, since the poison didn't work."

"We're not even sure it's Humpty trying to poison her, or if *anybody* is at this point," I said.

"Then who?" Kitty asked.

I grimaced. "Brady. He made it pretty clear this afternoon that our relationship was dead in the water."

"Brady?" Aunt Edna said. "Nah. I can't believe that."

"What about Eddie's family?" Kitty asked. "They could've sent them. They probably heard it through the grapevine by now."

"Heard what?" I asked.

"That you started a clan war and killed Eddie," Kitty said.

I winced. "How would they have heard about that?"

Aunt Edna and Kitty's eyes darted toward Jackie.

"Why you lookin' at me?" Jackie said. "I didn't tell nobody nothing." She made a sour face and pulled the shoulder of her red shirt. Elves don't gossip. Even Santa knows that."

"These flowers are white chrysanthemums," I said, picking up the bouquet. "Kitty, what do those mean?"

Kitty shook her head. "What do you think, Dorey? They mean *death*."

"Oh." My already clattering heart fell to my knees. I felt dizzy and nauseated.

"You okay?" Kitty asked.

"Yes. Uh ... I'm going to my room for a while. I need to rethink my life while I've still got a life to rethink."

***

I sat on the edge of my bed and stared at the cardboard boxes stacked against the wall. It was hard to believe only three days had passed since the cartons containing my old life back in LA had arrived on Aunt Edna's doorstep. With everything going haywire around me, I hadn't had time to unpack them.

I frowned and wondered what Sonya, my old roommate back in South Park, was up to. We'd both been grunts at a Hollywood production studio.

A smile curled my lips as I imagined Sonya running around like mad, trying to appease whichever celebrity dictator she'd been assigned to tonight. I envisioned her trying to catch a fitful nap in a dirty cot in the corner of the production studio. I could almost hear Sonya grunting as she squeezed a witchy prima donna into full-body Spanx ...

I sighed with envy. That ship had sailed. My eyes focused back on the boxes against the wall.

At least when I go to prison, I won't have to repack.

On that cheery note, I got up off my duff and picked up the package from my mother. I'd opened it on my birthday three days ago, hoping she'd sent me a gift. Instead, the box had been crammed with my baby pictures and childhood stuff.

Junk Ma didn't want anymore.

Like a stupid moth to a flame, I opened the box again. Lying atop the pile of painful memories was a picture of me and Ma in a park outside Snohomish.

My heart burned with anger and pain as Aunt Edna's words sounded in my head. "Your ma and Sammy waited forty years to be together. Who are we to deny them their chance at happiness?"

What about my *happiness? Didn't you care about me at all, Ma?*

Rage surged through me. I hurled the box against the wall. Photos, toys, eyepatches, and junk scattered everywhere.

I shook my head. I'd just created yet *another* mess I had to clean up.

Good going, Doreen.

Limp with hopelessness, I bent down and picked up the empty box. As I started tossing stuff back into it, a flash of color caught my eye.

An envelope had been taped to the inside bottom of the box.

A teal-colored envelope labeled, *To Doreen.*

Chapter Thirty-One

Dear Doreen,

By now, you know the truth. Sammy Lorenzo is your father. I'm sorry I didn't tell you earlier, but I had my reasons. Before you hate me for it, please give me a chance to explain.

Harvey Lorenzo (Sophia's husband) had big plans for his sons, Saul and Samuel. Saul towed the line. But Sammy had plans of his own.

He and I fell in love. Harvey bitterly disapproved of me. I wasn't the mob moll darling he had in mind for Sammy. But by the time Harvey put the hammer down, you'd already been conceived.

Harvey was as brutal as he was handsome. He threatened to do Sammy in. He started spreading lies about Sammy being a drunk and a rage killer. But his scheme backfired. Instead of ruining Sammy, his reputation only grew.

Everyone began to fear Sammy more than they feared Harvey. And in the Family, fear is the same thing as respect. Harvey became enraged and obsessed with punishing Sammy for making a fool out of him—even though he'd done the dirty work himself.

Sammy had no choice but to disappear. And that meant you and I had to, as well. Sammy didn't want us to live in fear of the mob coming after us. So before I started showing and Harvey put two and two together, Sammy set us up in that house in Snohomish, as far away from Florida as we could get.

The plan was for Sammy to go to Wisconsin and work as a mechanic until things cooled off. But they never cooled off. Rumors started to spread that Sammy had gone rogue and joined a rival Family. The truth was, all Sammy wanted was a peaceful life for the three of us. But Harvey wouldn't let him go.

When you were about to turn four years old, Sammy wrote me saying he thought he'd been found out. Not long afterward, Sammy sent me a news-paper clipping about Harvey and Saul dying in a car accident near Mani-towoc.

Doreen, Harvey and Saul had been hunting for Sammy. To exterminate him.

I don't know if the car crash was really an accident or not. Sammy never told me, and to be honest, I never asked. I didn't want to know. If Sammy killed his father and brother, it was to save us. So how can I hold it against him?

After the accident, RICO agents really turned up the heat on mafia families. The campaign to get Sammy got shoved to the back burner. But believe me, there are still people who hold grudges out there, running free.

Sammy feels it's still not safe to show his face, much less mine. If he did, it might stir up things again. People might want to reopen the accident investigation. Who knows what they'd uncover with today's technology? I don't want to take the risk—for your sake, and Sammy's.

Thankfully, as far as I know, Harvey and Sophia never found out about you. I only told Edna. My dear sister put her life on the line for us. She invented a cover story about me getting a job and moving to Detroit. She also kept the story alive about Sammy being a killer, so people would be afraid to go after him and find us in the process.

Edna's never wavered from her story. Ever. Don't ask her to, Doreen. She'll tell you when the she feels the time is right.

I never told you any of this before because I didn't want you to get caught up in the Lorenzo "Family business." At least, not until you were old enough and wise enough to decide for yourself what you wanted. And you are now.

I've watched you come into your own, Dorey. And I'm proud to say you're the most determined, persistent, and irascible person I've ever known—except maybe for your father. And Sammy's just as proud of you as I am. I thought you should know.

Now for the hard part. Doreen, I know I didn't show you the kind of love you deserved. But you have to understand, I lived in constant fear that Sophia would find out about you and take you away from me. You were like a present I couldn't keep.

As a result, I'll admit I never really bonded the way I should have with you. I shielded my heart for fear of it breaking when they finally took you away. It was wrong. I know that now. And even though they never found us, I fear you got damaged in the process anyway. That's my fault. And I'm sorrier about it than I can express here.

Sammy and I stayed apart for forty years to protect you. He worked hard to pay for you and me to live in isolation. I hope the sacrifice we both made shows you how much you mean to us.

But time isn't on our side any longer. We're both getting old. We knew if we didn't get together now, well, maybe we never would. And what would be the point of living any longer?

Then, when you called me to say you were in St. Petersburg, Florida, you were practically on Edna's doorstep. I took it as a sign, Doreen. And now, with you living there with Edna, I'm not worried so much anymore. Not about Sophia or the mob coming after me and Sammy, anyway.

But let me warn you of this: If Sophia figures out her niece is actually Sammy's daughter, there's no telling what might happen. I believe she, like a lot of people, blames Sammy for Harvey and Saul's death. And as I've explained, the need for revenge runs deep with the Lorenzos.

I can't help you with money or muscle, Doreen. Sammy and I have little of either. But we can give you our love. And one other thing—leverage. Two secrets I've kept safe for forty years. With Sammy at my side, I've got all the protection I need now. So I'm passing them on to you.

My darling daughter, it's totally your call how to use this information. Just remember, whatever you do, I'll always love you, no matter what. And so will Sammy.

Be brave,

Ma

I turned to the next page of Ma's letter and gasped.

I wasn't exactly sure what to do with the information she'd just given me. But thanks to Ma, I'd just been forewarned—and fore*armed*.

Chapter Thirty-Two

As I re-read my mother's letter, the missing pieces to my life—and my heart—began to fill themselves in.

I felt like the *Grinch* when his heart suddenly grew 10,000 times bigger. I felt like James Garner in *The Notebook*, when his wife finally recognized who he was. I felt like Julia Roberts in *Erin Brockovich*, when she got fed up with all the bull-crap in the world and started kicking people's butts.

I'd swear I actually felt my spine grow stronger.

I'm tired of always paying the price but never getting any of the glory. I'm sick to death of being at the whim of other people!

I folded the precious letter and tucked it into my shirt pocket. Fortified with Ma's pure love and her dirty secrets, I was no longer willing to cower in a corner and wait for the world to strike me down.

"Meteors be damned!" I said, and marched straight back to the dining room.

"You hungry now?" Aunt Edna asked. "We saved you some egg rolls."

"No. I want something else."

"What?" Aunt Edna asked. "Linguini?"

I crossed my arms and straightened my shoulders. "An Omertà. What I'm about to say doesn't leave this room. Capeesh?"

"Sure, Dorey," Aunt Edna said. "You okay with that, ladies?"

Jackie and Kitty nodded.

"Good." I locked eyes with Aunt Edna. "I want you to call Morty and invite him to breakfast tomorrow morning at six o'clock sharp."

"What for?" Kitty asked.

"Because," I said defiantly. "We're going to start beating the mattresses again. *For real* this time."

Aunt Edna choked on a mouthful of chow Mein. "Are you serious?"

I gave her one short nod. "Yes. *Dead* serious."

"Uh, who died and left you in charge?" Jackie asked, pointing a chopstick at me.

I shot her my best evil grin. "Nobody. *Yet.* But the first person on my list is Doña Sophia Maria Lorenzo."

Chapter Thirty-Three

It was 5:25 a.m. I was standing in the dark courtyard in front of Sophia's apartment, waiting on cute, hoodie-headed Mr. ScarBux to arrive.

As part of my plan, I'd figured I should stick to the routine, so Sophia wouldn't get suspicious. But little did she know, delivering her coffee was the last grunt work I expected to ever do for the old Queenpin.

Tucked inside my shirt pocket was my ticket to freedom—and to Sophia's potential demise.

"Good morning," I said as the hooded figure drew nearer.

"Morning," he said, a smile appearing above his cleft-less chin. "Here's your order."

I handed him twelve bucks. "Thanks."

"Oh, and here's some more sugar." He reached into his jacket pocket and pulled out a plastic baggie full of sugar packets.

"A baggie full?"

Chase shrugged. "The old lady likes her sugar."

"Right." I took the packets and watched him go. I turned around and nearly swallowed my tonsils. Someone was standing in the dark a mere two feet from me.

"Jackie!" I gasped. "What are you doing up so early?"

"I wanted to see if you were really gonna murderize Sophia."

"What?"

"Death by sugar," Jackie said. "Pretty clever."

"What are you talking about?"

"Sophia's diabetic. That stuff could kill her."

"Oh." I stared at the baggie of packets. "You know what, Jackie? I've got a feeling you may be right."

Jackie shrugged. "We'll, I ain't no doctor, but I seen one on TV."

I smiled and crooked my elbow around hers. "Come with me, Sherlock."

Arm in arm, we walked the few paces over to Kitty's cottage. Jackie tapped softly on the front door. A moment later, Kitty appeared, dressed and ready for our 6 a.m. meeting, except for the pink rollers in her hair.

"What's up?" she asked.

"This," I said, holding up the baggie of packets. "If I'm right, these things are full of poison. Could you run some tests, then meet us over at Aunt Edna's?"

"Sure." She held up the packets. "ScarBux?"

"It's a new coffee joint," I said.

"Hmm," Kitty said. "I've never heard of it."

***

While Jackie replaced the coffee in the paper ScarBux containers with fresh brew from Aunt Edna's coffee carafe, I pulled out my laptop and searched the internet.

"There's no mention of ScarBux," I said.

Jackie shrugged. "You said they were new."

"Yeah," I said. "Even so, if they went to the trouble to print cups and packets with their logo on them, they're market savvy enough to be online. Nowadays, the internet knows about everything."

Jackie cringed. Her eyes darted around the room. "*Everything?*"

"Everything. ScarBux has got to be a front. I'm sure someone really *is* trying to poison Sophia."

"You mean besides you?"

"Argh!" I groaned. "Jackie, for the millionth time, no! It's not *me*."

"Then who?" Aunt Edna asked, walking into the kitchen.

I pursed my lips. "I don't know yet. Maybe that cute little ScarBux kid isn't so cute after all."

"You want we should have somebody run him down?" Aunt Edna asked.

"No. We don't have time for that. We can lay in wait for him tomorrow. In the meantime, put another pot of coffee on. It's gonna be a long morning."

I grabbed the refilled ScarBux cups.

"I can take them to Sophia," Jackie said, tossing the used coffee filter in the garbage.

"No," I said. "I'll do it. I've got something I need to discuss with the Queenpin anyway."

Aunt Edna put a hand on my shoulder. "Listen, Dorey. She's just a little old lady."

"Don't worry. I'll be bringing her back here alive. I promise. I need her for my plan to work." I smiled. "I need *all* of you."

"What plan you talking about?" Jackie asked.

"I'll explain everything as soon as Morty gets here. I've just got one loose end to tie up first."

"Here," Jackie said, handing me a zip-tie. "Fresh from the box."

Chapter Thirty-Four

As I stepped halfway into Sophia's front door, someone reached out and snatched the bag of ScarBux coffee out of my hand. Startled out of my wits, I let loose a string of obscenities.

"You kiss your mother with that mouth?" Sophia asked, digging into the paper sack. "Where you been? You're late."

"Geez, Sophia!" I gasped. "You scared me half to death. Sorry I'm three minutes late. I was busy saving your life again."

"Oh, yeah?" she said, plucking a cup from the bag. "How can I ever thank you?"

I scowled. "How about by dying?"

Sophia snorted. "You mean like when Edna put enough Metamucil in my breakfast to blow me up?" She took a sip of coffee from the paper container. "Ugh. You switched these again." She shook her head. "You want to kill me? One more sip of this shlock and Edna will have beaten you to the punch."

Sophia shoved the sack holding the other coffee into my hands. "You know the routine," she said, then hobbled over and flopped onto the couch.

I headed for the kitchen to fetch her royal pain-in-the-Queenpin a *real* cup and saucer. When I returned, she was staring at me like a hungry lioness.

"You really want me to die, young Doreen? I knew you were ambitious. But are you really ruthless enough to bump off a defenseless old lady?"

I frowned and took the ScarBux coffee container from her gnarled hand. "I didn't mean *really* die." I transferred the coffee from the container to her ceramic cup. "I meant that I want you to *pretend* to be dead."

"Oh." Sophia scowled at the cup of coffee I handed her. "First my hair falls out. And now my taste buds are being tortured to death. What's left worth living for anyway?"

I smirked. "Go ahead. I know about the sugar."

Sophia eyed me with keen interest. "You seem to know a lot. Maybe more than you should." She reached between the sofa cushions and pulled out a baggie of ScarBux sugar packets.

"Ha! I thought so!" I snatched the baggie from her hands. "That stuff could be killing you!"

"Double crosser!" Sophia hissed. "You know something, Doreen? At my age, I don't give a flip if sugar does me in. Food is the last of life's pleasures that I've got left."

I dangled the baggie in front of her. "Are you saying you no longer have a taste for revenge?"

The old woman's thin lips curled upward. "I didn't exactly say *that*."

"Good. Hold on a moment." I walked over to the front door and opened it a crack. "Jackie?"

Jackie appeared from the shadows. "Present and accounted for."

"Take these over to Kitty." I handed her the baggie of sugar packets. "Tell her to test them separate from the others."

Jackie nodded. "You got it."

I closed the door and walked back over to Sophia. She was fiddling with the TV remote and muttering under her breath.

"Now, my dear Queenpin, I need you to pretend to die."

She looked up, her cat-eyes narrow slits. "Why should I? So you can be the boss?" She banged the remote against the arm of the sofa. "It's undignified to mock the dead."

"Don't consider it mocking the dead. Consider it a test drive. You'll get to see what your deluxe funeral at Neil Mansion looks like. And you'll get to see who shows up and what they say about you."

Her brow furrowed below her silver turban. "I'll be there?"

"Yes."

Sophia's wrinkly face puckered. "No way. I'm not getting in a coffin until I'm good and dead."

"Then you can be one of the mourners. An old friend from Sicily, perhaps? Think of it. You can find out what people *really* think of you. Maybe then you'll have enough information to choose your new heir."

The old woman scowled. "And what about the money for my *real* funeral?"

I smirked. "When that time comes, I don't think money is going to be a problem. Do you?"

"I see." Sophia's green eyes sparkled. "You're running a scam. Who's the mark?"

I chewed my bottom lip. "To be honest, I'm not sure. That's what I'm trying to find out. But if you don't cooperate, *you'll* be the patsy, for sure. I'm pretty sure someone's still actively trying to poison you."

Sophia shrugged. "Somebody's always trying to get me, one way or the other. I'm used to it."

"Aren't you tired of always having to look over your shoulder?"

Sophia sighed. "If it isn't me, it has to be *someone*. When I name an heir, that curse gets put on *their* head."

I shot the old woman a sympathetic smile. "Is that why you haven't named anyone?"

Sophia pursed her lips. "Look, Miss Know-It-All. I plan on going on living for as long as I can. So Edna and the others can live in relative peace. Capeesh?"

I shook my head. "Don't you get it, Sophia? There won't ever *be* peace until we find out who's willing to kill to be the new head of the family. I want to fake your death to see who comes out of the woodwork to claim your throne."

"No," Sophia grumbled. "I won't do it. If things go wrong, it could bring hell down on my girls."

I crossed my arms. "It *won't* go wrong. And you *will* do it."

Sophia smiled smugly. "You can't make me."

I pulled a fragile, yellowed slip of paper from my pocket. "You sure about that?"

Sophia glared at the paper in my hand. "What is that?"

"It's your original birth certificate. From Sicily."

Sophia's smug expression evaporated. "Where'd you get it?"

"That's not important right now. What *is*, is the fact that you're only ninety-six."

Sophia's droopy face fell an inch lower. She shook her head. "I *told* Harvey that would come back to haunt us one day. He made me lie about my age so we could get married. I was only sixteen." She stared at her gnarled hands. "He made me do a lot of things I didn't want to do."

"I had a feeling that might be the case. I wouldn't ask you to do this unless I really needed you to. For the Family."

Sophia glared at me. Her ancient, green eyes were an unreadable, shifting storm.

I thought about how she'd headed the Collard Green Cosa Nostra alone for the past thirty-five years. She'd buried her husband and her son. And she'd burned for over three decades with the belief that her only other child, Sammy had killed Saul and Harvey. Who would I have been in the face of all that?

I knelt down in front of Sophia. "With all due respect, your Queenpin, you are a living legend. It would be a travesty for you to lose your status as the oldest mafia leader in history."

Sophia scowled. "What are you talking about?"

"If your true age is made known, you'll become the laughing stock of the entire mafia. Do you want to be forever thought of as a demented old woman who doesn't even remember how old she is? And what will that do to the Family? We threw you a centennial party that was a complete sham. That alone will surely make us the joke of every other mafia family for decades to come."

Sophia sat there limp, but didn't say a word.

I touched her foot as a sign of respect. "You already scammed the Family, Sophia. This is your chance at redemption."

She glared at me. "And if I go along with your plan?"

"You and I keep this whole conversation between us, and the birth certificate disappears."

"Humph." Sophia wrapped her shawl a little tighter around her shoulders. "Omertà?"

"Omertà." I got up off my knees, kissed her hand, and offered her a tentative smile. "Act now, and I'll even throw in some new batteries for the TV remote."

Sophia's hard face cracked into a smirk. "Blackmail, Doreen? I didn't think you had it in you. Let me hear the rest of this plan of yours."

"Most certainly, your Queenpin. Come with me."

Chapter Thirty Five

My teeth were about to sink themselves into one of Morty's delicious, banana-pudding filled cannoli, when Kitty burst into the dining room.

Like kittens following a ball of string, Morty, Aunt Edna, Jackie, Sophia, and I all turned and stared at the resident potioneer. She was standing before us, huffing and puffing like an asthmatic puffer fish.

"You were right, Doreen!" Kitty gasped, her cheeks as pink as her shirt. "The sugar packets were laced with thallium!"

"Thallium?" I asked. I eyed the cannoli in my hand and set it back on my plate.

"Yes ... thallium." Kitty sucked in another lungful of air. "The poisoner's poison. Colorless ... odorless ... tasteless ... and bloody brilliant."

"How can that be?" Sophia asked, her cat eyes narrowed to slits. "I've been using those sugar packets for weeks."

Kitty gulped in a huge breath. "That's just it. The ones in the older baggie between the couch cushions only had trace amounts of thallium on them. But the new batch you and Jackie brought over earlier were covered with it."

"The rats upped the dosage," Morty said.

"Exactly." Kitty locked eyes with Sophia. "If you—or any of us—had touched them, we'd be on our way to the hospital right now. Or even the morgue."

"How did you know to test for thallium?" I asked.

"The symptoms you told me about," Kitty said. "Slow doses over time create symptoms similar to other illnesses. Hot feet. Hair loss. Pain in the joints."

"Got all three," Sophia said. She grimaced and pulled her shawl tighter. "Am I done for?"

"No." Kitty smiled softly at Sophia. "That's the good part. You're still breathing, so there's an antidote. Prussian Blue."

"You got any of that?" Aunt Edna asked.

"Of course." Kitty waved a small jar with a black lid. "What? You guys think I'm an amateur?"

"Hold on," Sophia said. "Has that stuff got any side effects?"

"Besides making you not die?" Kitty asked. "Well, constipation, maybe. And if you take enough, your sweat might turn blue."

Sophia shrugged. "Eh, nothing I haven't lived through before."

"Good. Sit tight. I'll run go make you a dose right now." Kitty took a step toward the kitchen, then turned back toward us and shook her head. "Sophia, you should be glad it wasn't oleander or rosary pea. If it had been, right now you'd be Snow White—minus the Prince Charming."

Sophia sighed. "Take it from me. Prince Charming isn't always what he's cracked up to be."

***

"I don't get it," Morty said while Kitty mixed up a dose of Prussian Blue for Sophia. "Why poison the sugar packets and not the coffee?"

"I thought about that myself," I said. "What it comes down to is proof."

Morty poured everyone another round of coffee. "Proof?"

I bit into a cannolo. "Yes," I mumbled through a mouthful. "There is no real ScarBux store. I looked it up. It doesn't exist. So the ScarBux sugar packets aren't available to anyone but the poisoner."

"So?" Jackie said. "I don't get it."

I licked banana cream from my lips. "Well, if their plan was to kill Sophia and take over as head of the Family, they'd need proof they were responsible. If they put the poison in the *coffee,* the evidence of where the thallium came from would be ambiguous."

"Who're Ambi and Gus?" Jackie asked.

I shook my head. "What I mean is, if the thallium was in the coffee, *anyone* could have said they put it there. But since it's on the ScarBux sugar packets, no one else but the poisoner would have them. They're indisputable proof."

Morty shook his head. "*Family* law is above the law. We'd have to let this jerk take over."

"Exactly," I said. "I think that's why they poisoned Sophia slowly. They hoped we wouldn't figure it out until it was too late. A swing and a miss with a big dose would've outed their game, and put a price on *their* head instead of Sophia's."

"Okay, say you're right," Aunt Edna said. "What do we do now?"

I smiled smugly. "My plan is to let them think they've won. We're going to stage Sophia's death."

"You're gonna make a play out of it?" Jackie asked.

I pressed my molars together. "No. We're going to hold a fake funeral and see who shows up with the sugar packets."

Morty rubbed his chin. "That could actually work."

I smiled. "Thanks."

"I guess that makes sense," Aunt Edna said. "But honestly, who would want to take over the CGCN? We're just a motley little crew now."

"I can think of two reasons right off the bat," I said. "One, to build it back up. And two, for the money."

Aunt Edna frowned. "Money? We ain't got no money."

"What about The Family Fund?" Jackie asked.

Morty grimaced. "I checked the bank balance last week. Believe me, it's not enough to kill for."

"Here she is," Kitty announced, helping Sophia back into the dining room. "Come on, Sophia. Show them! Please?"

"All right already," Sophia grumbled. She plopped down into a chair and stuck out her tongue. It was as blue as Papa Smurf's.

Jackie guffawed. Aunt Edna cackled. Morty snorted. And Kitty and I burst into belly laughs. Even the Queenpin herself couldn't help but snicker.

As we all fought to compose ourselves, Aunt Edna wiped tears of laughter from her eyes. "Well, we may be a broke-ass crew, but at least we can still laugh."

"Oh, we're not broke," I said. "Are we, Sophia?"

Sophia's snicker dried up. "What?"

I patted the yellowed paper tucked in my shirt pocket. The birth certificate wasn't the only secret Ma shared with me. "Do you want to tell them, or should I?"

Sophia sighed. "Fine. I'll tell them."

Chapter Thirty-Six

"So that's the plan," I said. "Everybody on board with it?"

All around the table, heads nodded.

"Then it's settled," I said. "Not a word of this to anyone. Only the other Family players we need to help pull this off. Can I get an Omertà?"

One by one, Morty, Aunt Edna, Jackie, Kitty, and, finally Sophia, repeated the mafia pledge of silence. "Omertà."

I nodded. "Good. Now, everybody get to work."

"I'll call Victor," Morty said. "And put some feelers out about Scar-Bux."

"I'll call Neil Mansion," Aunt Edna said. "I'll get the funeral arrangements set for noon tomorrow."

"Tomorrow?" Sophia grumbled. "Why so quick?"

"Hey, it's summer, remember?" Aunt Edna said. "You ain't getting any fresher. You're like Nosferatu. We gotta get you into the ground before you turn to dust. Besides, wouldn't you like to ruffle persnickety Neil Neil's feathers? He hates surprises."

Sophia grinned. "Yeah. Okay. So what do I do? Die of poisoning like a sick, old bird?"

"No," I said. "The fake coroner's report will say you died of natural causes."

"Why?" Kitty asked. "I thought the whole point was to get the poisoner to step up and take credit for their work?"

"That's just it," I said. "Not being acknowledged should enrage the poisoner. Tell me. Do you know a man alive who doesn't expect a gold star for every little thing he does?"

"You make a good point," Aunt Edna said, shooting Morty some side-eye.

Morty grumbled. "Go ahead. Blame the men again."

"But what if it's not a man?" Jackie asked.

"It still works," Morty said. "Hell hath no fury like a woman scorned."

I grinned. "Touché."

623

"So, what about me?" Sophia repeated. "Do I just lay out in a coffin here like an expired slab of olive loaf?"

"No. We don't have time for a wake," I said. "It'll be a closed casket, too. But we *do* need you to lay low so you can't be spotted. That means you can't leave Edna's cottage until I give the word."

Sophia scowled. "Where am I gonna sleep?"

I glanced over at my aunt. "You can bunk with Aunt Edna."

"Nothing doing," Aunt Edna said. "This is *your* plan Dorey. Sophia bunks with *you*."

"But I don't have a TV in my room," I argued. "How's she gonna watch *Wheel of Fortune*?"

"Yeah?" Sophia said.

"No problem," Aunt Edna said. "I'll put my TV in your room, Dorey."

Sophia grunted. "Humph. Good to know I'm so deeply treasured."

"Now, don't get all riled up Sophia," Kitty said. "You need to rest." Kitty winked at me. "I'll get your room ready and watch over Sophia. I'll make sure she gets her antidotes on schedule. The Prussian Blue should work miracles in no time."

"Miracles, huh?" Jackie said. "Like raising Lavoris from the dead."

"*Lazarus*," Aunt Edna said. "Lavoris is a mouthwash."

"What?" Jackie frowned. "You telling me I've been drinking a capful of that stuff every morning for twenty years for *nothing*?"

Aunt Edna shot me a look. "Maybe *that's* what did it."

"Did what?" Jackie asked.

I stifled a smirk and slapped on a serious face. "Jackie, you're vital to this operation."

She cocked her head. "I am?"

"Yes. You're holding the lynch pin."

Confusion lined Jackie's narrow brow. "Uh ... I don't think I got one of those."

Aunt Edna and I exchanged glances.

I took Jackie by the hand. "What I *mean* is, it's your job to get the word out that the Queenpin suddenly dropped dead this morning. Right after drinking a cup of coffee."

"Oh." Jackie beamed at Sophia. "It would be my pleasure."

Sophia frowned, shook her head, then aimed her sour gaze at me. "What about *you*, Miss Bossy Pants. What are *you* gonna do?"

I grimaced. "Believe me, I saved the worst job for myself."

My plan to out Sophia's poisoner was flawless—except for one huge fly in the ointment.

Brady.

Somehow, I had to convince him I wasn't a rage-drunk, a vengeful vandalizing jerk, and a homicidal maniac.

No biggie.

Chapter Thirty-Seven

I checked my look in the mirror. Following Kitty's advice, I'd donned a pink blouse she'd lent me.

According to Kitty, the shirt wasn't just pink. It was "drunk-tank pink." The exact rosy hue law enforcement painted holding cells to calm inmates.

How Kitty knew this, I didn't ask. I only hoped it worked its charms on cops, too. Based on my last couple of conversations with Brady, I was going to need all the calming effects I could get.

After slipping into a pair of jeans and some pink kitten heels, I said a prayer to St. Jude, patron saint of lost causes, and headed for the living room. Aunt Edna was perched in the good chair, perusing the Neil Mansion Funeral's casket brochure.

"Have you called them yet?" I asked.

"Getting ready to. Want to make sure they give Sophia the works, like she paid for."

"What does it matter?" I asked.

Aunt Edna's eyebrow ticked up. "Until Sophia's really dead, we've still got to live with her."

"Point taken."

Aunt Edna scowled and shook her head. "I can't believe Sophia was holding out on us. All these years I've been running that stupid lonely hearts scam because I thought we were low on cash. Meanwhile, there she was over there, sitting on a wad of cash."

"Well, like you once told me, you can't expect to know all the Family secrets all at once."

"If you're trying to get on my good side, it's not working," Aunt Edna said.

"Sorry. Hey, did you ever figure out where those flowers came from?"

"My guess? Probably the same place as the ScarBux sugar packets."

I pursed my lips. "You're probably right. Okay if I borrow the Kia?"

"Sure. Where you going all dressed up?"

"To see Brady. We need him for the plan."

"You think you can trust him?" she asked.

"I have to. You think you can trust Morty?"

Aunt Edna blew out a sigh. "I have to."

My brow furrowed. "You two used to be an item. What happened between Morty and you?"

"He thought I did something I didn't do."

"What?"

Aunt Edna frowned and shook her head. "He accused me of stepping out on him. I couldn't believe he would think I would do something so low."

"You couldn't convince him otherwise?"

"Why should I *have* to?" Aunt Edna snapped.

I winced. "So what happened?"

"You got eyes, don't you? It ruined things between us, Dorey."

"What did?"

"Pigheadedness."

"Oh." I chewed my bottom lip. "On whose part?"

Aunt Edna sighed. "On both of ours."

***

I took off to make amends with Brady. But I didn't get far. I'd no sooner driven The Toad a block from Palm Court Cottages when a siren sounded. Behind me, blue-and-red lights began flashing. I groaned.

I can't get busted now! How will the plan go on without me?

I watched through the rearview mirror as the cop climbed out of his cruiser.

It was Brady.

He marched toward me, his handsome face as hard and steely as that half-robot policeman in *RoboCop.*

I rolled down the window. My heart fluttered in my chest. It was do or die time. Literally.

"You're supposed to be under house arrest!" Brady barked as he reached my window.

I cringed and bit my lip. "I know."

Come on, drunk-tank pink! Do you thing!

"But you didn't say *which* house," I said, trying to sound both humble and like a damsel in distress.

"What are you talking about?" Brady growled.

Thanks a lot, stupid pink shirt.

I took a deep breath and just went for it. "Brady, you and I both know that if I don't do something to clear my name from the Eddie Houser suspect list, I could end up living in this car, on the lam. So, technically, the Kia could be considered my house, right?"

Brady shook his head. "Doreen, sometimes your logic ... *defies logic.* You know I can't just let you break the law."

"I'm not asking you to."

"Then what are you asking?"

"For a chance to explain. Give me ten minutes and I'll give you the truth."

"About what?"

"About everything."

Chapter Thirty-Eight

"First off, I want to apologize about your truck," I said, smiling tentatively at Brady from the passenger seat of his police cruiser. "I was angry that you didn't take me seriously about Humpty Bogart. And ..." I winced. "I'd been drinking."

"Yes, you had. Polished off almost a whole bottle of wine by yourself."

I pursed my lips. "I'm trying to apologize, here."

Brady's hard face softened. "Right. Sorry."

"Anyway, when you blew me off by laughing at my suggestion, I kind of ... *lost it*. I'm sorry that in my anger I accidently scratched your truck."

"Accidentally?" Brady said. "*That's* what you call it when you scratch the word PIG into the side of someone's truck?"

My mouth fell open. "What? I didn't do that! I only kicked your bumper."

I think.

"What? You didn't scratch the word PIG into my truck's passenger door panel?"

I shook my head. "No! How could I? When would I have had the opportunity?"

Brady chewed on that for a moment. "So you really didn't—"

"No. I swear!"

Brady frowned. "If you didn't, who did?"

"How should I know? *You're* the cop. Shouldn't you ..." I stopped mid-sentence. "Wait a minute. It could've been the guy I saw waving a knife at me while you paid the check."

"What?" Brady practically squealed. "You saw a guy with a knife and you didn't bother to mention it?"

I bit my bottom lip. "Well, I *think* it was a guy. And it *could've* been a knife. I couldn't see their face. They were wearing a hoodie and standing by your truck."

"And you're just telling me this now?"

My shoulders stiffened. "Yes. It's the first time you've given me a chance to explain anything without cutting me off first."

629

Brady sighed. "Fair enough."

I reached over and touched his hand. "Sorry about your truck."

He nodded. "Sorry about you getting tangled up in another homicide investigation."

"I didn't do *that*, either."

We both smiled and shook our heads. Then, as if on cue, we simultaneously laughed.

"How do you keep getting into these messes?" Brady asked.

I shook my head again. "I dunno. Just lucky, I guess."

"Me, too." Brady's brow furrowed. "Why would some random person scratch the word PIG on my truck? How would they even know I'm a cop?"

My right eyebrow rose an inch. "Are you kidding? Everything about you screams cop, Brady."

"It does not."

"Cop haircut. Cop body language. Cop attitude."

"Oh, really? How about this?" Brady leaned across the seat and kissed me hard on the mouth. "Do I *kiss* like a cop, too?"

I smirked. "I can't say. You're my first policeman. But I *can* say this. You kiss better than Tad Longmire. And way better than the guy who works the drive-thru at the In-N-Out Burger in LA."

Brady shot me a sideways smile. "Nice to know I'm not at the bottom of your list, Diller."

I grinned and leaned in to kiss him again. But as I did, the playful sparkle in Brady's eyes disappeared.

"Now, tell me about that pool of human blood McNulty found on the curb outside your apartment, Diller. How did you know it was Eddie Houser's?"

Chapter Thirty-Nine

Brady shook his head and took a slurp of his Dairy Hog milkshake. "And here I was, thinking they were just a bunch of harmless little old ladies."

"They *are*, Brady." I set down my chili dog. "They didn't *kill* Eddie. They just found him and called somebody to remove his body. They only did it to protect me."

"Protect you from what?"

I shot him a look. "Myself. Okay? You know my track record for this type of thing. I'm the queen of self-incrimination."

Brady nodded. "Okay. But you said they found Houser inside a car."

"Yes. A Nissan Cube the color of Kermit's keister."

"What happened to the car?"

"They had it ... uh ... removed."

"I see. Along with the murder weapon?"

"No, we took that to—"

"Hold on," Brady said, showing me his palm. "We?" He shook his head. "Doreen, this is *so* not good. Perhaps I should remind you that you have the right to remain silent?"

I locked eyes with Brady. "I appreciate that. But Brady, I don't have anything to hide. Somebody's trying to *frame* me. They took the baseball bat out of the Kia, killed Eddie with it, then put it back in Aunt Edna's car to make it look like I did it."

"The killer put the bat *back* in the ..." Brady's eyes bore into mine. "Let me get this straight. You're telling me someone drove Houser to your apartment and he just sat there patiently in the Nissan while they got out, stole the bat from your car, then came back and bludgeoned him to death right in front of your place? And then the killer simply put the baseball bat back in your car and went on his merry way?"

I winced. "Well, not exactly."

Brady blew out a breath. "Thank you."

I stared intently into Brady's eyes. "I think Eddie drove himself to my place and was ambushed."

Brady's brow furrowed. "What exactly would Houser be doing at your place, anyway?"

"He wanted to give me a discount on the Nissan. As payment, instead of the profit-sharing scheme I'd originally agreed to."

"Wait a minute. You talked to Houser before he was murdered?"

"No. All that stuff was spelled out in the contract lying next to his body."

Brady pinched the bridge of his nose. "And where is this contract now?"

I winced. "Uh ... I don't know."

"Putting that aside for the moment, do you have any idea who would want to kill Houser?"

"I'd say pretty much anyone who ever met him. He was a pig."

Brady's face puckered. "As in P-I-G?"

I grimaced. "Unfortunate use of the descriptive."

"Right," Brady said. "We need to narrow the suspects down from the entire human population. Do you have any idea who would want to kill Houser and frame *you* for it?"

I thought about it for a moment. "No. I mean, generally, I'm a nice person."

Brady laughed. "This isn't not a personality contest, Diller. Innocent people get framed all the time. That's why we call it getting framed. So, do you know anyone who might have it out for you?"

"Maybe Humpty Bogart? I mean, *Humphrey Bogaratelli*? Or someone I pissed off by doing that sexist commercial for Eddie's car lot? Or wait ... maybe whoever scratched PIG into your car?"

Brady frowned. "Would any of them have access to the Kia?"

"Probably. Jackie drives it a lot. She never locks the doors."

Brady blew out a breath. "So anyone could have taken the bat out of your car."

I nodded. "Yeah. Pretty much."

"Doreen, answer me this, would you?"

"Sure." I raised the hotdog to my mouth. "What?"

"What were you doing with a baseball bat in your car in the first place?"

"Oh. Jackie gave it to me. For good luck."

"Yeah? How's that working out for you?"

I shrugged. "I don't know yet."

"Argh! Doreen, why are you so ... so ..."

"Unlucky?" I asked.

Brady shook his head.

I raised the hotdog to my mouth. "Ridiculous?"

"Yes, but no."

I took a bite of hotdog. Mustard squirted onto my shirt. "Disaster prone?"

"No." Brady pursed his lips. "The word I'm searching for is ... irresistible."

My mouth full of hotdog fell open. "Are you serious?"

Brady shook his head softly. "Unfortunately, yes. Against all my better judgement, I can't stop thinking about you."

"Wait a minute." I swallowed and wiped my mouth with a paper napkin. "You're not worried I'm a killer?"

"No."

My heart skipped a beat—in a good way. "But what about the bloody thumbprints on the jeans you stole out of my washing machine?"

"*Confiscated*," Brady corrected. "And no, I'm not worried about them. It turns out, the prints were actually ketchup with a little cornmeal and old fryer grease mixed in."

"Ketchup from a corndog. *Told* you."

"Yes, you did."

I grinned and took a savage, celebratory bite from my hotdog.

Brady shook his head. "Only you, Doreen. Only you."

***

After a make-out session in Brady's squad car in an alley behind the Dairy Hog, I filled Brady in on my plan to fake Sophia's death and entrap the person poisoning her.

"Who knows?" I said between lip-locks with the handsome cop. "Maybe we'll catch Eddie's killer in the process."

Brady stopped kissing me. "You think they're related?"

I shrugged. "Maybe. Aunt Edna told me Humpty and Eddie might've been working in cahoots to steal from the Family Fund. Maybe their partnership went south."

"Louisville Slugger south." Brady said. "It makes sense."

"Hey, now that we've kissed and made up, I just wanted to say that I can see how you thought the name Humpty Bogart was a joke. But believe me, if my hunch about him is right, he's definitely no one to be taken lightly. That's why I need your help with my plan."

Brady pursed his swollen lips. "Like I told you before, I can't do anything illegal to help you, Doreen. I'd lose my job. *And* it's against my principles."

"I'm not asking you to do anything you haven't done for my aunt and her friends before. Just hang around the apartments in plain clothes tomorrow. Keep an eye out on the property while we're at the funeral."

"Do you think the women are in danger?"

"No, I don't think so. Whoever was trying to do Sophia in thinks that mission's been accomplished."

"Then why do you want me to watch the place?"

"Because if my scheme goes according to plan, someone's going to try and break into Sophia's cottage during her funeral service and make off with the Family Fund. And when they do, I'll need you to be there to aid in the apprehension."

"Aid in the apprehension?" Brady frowned. "Does that mean you don't plan on being at the apartments?"

I chewed my lip. "I haven't decided yet."

"Geez, Diller. This plan of yours seems to have a few holes in it."

I nodded. "Yeah, but you can't account for every little thing, now can you?"

Brady sighed. "I suppose not. Anything else you need me to do?"

I smiled and kissed Brady. "Well, since you asked, in about a half an hour, we're going to be carrying Sophia out in a body bag. Your police cruiser at the scene would add a nice touch of authenticity."

Brady shook his head. "I had a feeling I was going to regret this."

"Which part?"

Brady smirked. "I haven't decided yet."

Chapter Forty

When we pulled up to Palm Court Cottages in Brady's police cruiser, operation "Sophia the Stiff" was already well underway.

A black hearse was parked where the Kia normally stood. Two men were huffing and puffing down the garden path, hauling a black body bag toward the street.

I recognized the meaty, ex-prize-fighter face of one of the men. It was Morty. The tall and lanky one had to be Victor the Vulture. After all, he was the one who made bodies disappear. Looking like the love child of Lurch and Elvira, Victor seemed born for the job.

Trailing behind the men were Kitty, Aunt Edna, and Jackie. Each was putting on an academy award performance worthy of Shirley McClain in *Terms of Endearment*.

I laughed out loud. Jackie heard me. She looked up and beamed a Poligrip smile, followed by a thumb's up.

Brady shook his head. "I'm assuming Sophia isn't really in that body bag?"

I smirked. "I thought you said you wanted to know as little about this as possible."

"Right. But if her life is at stake—"

"She's not in the bag."

"What is?"

"Believe me, you really don't want to know."

***

I was sitting on Aunt Edna's green velvet couch complimenting Jackie, Kitty and Aunt Edna on their acting skills when Morty came through the front door.

"The 'body of evidence' is in transit," he said, then smiled at me. "Nice touch having Brady's cruiser park outside."

"Thanks." I smiled at the four elderly mobsters. "Phase one of Sophia the Stiff is officially complete. But Morty, I thought you were going with Victor."

"I was. But I thought I'd better stick around. While he and I were loading the hearse, I spotted a couple of suspicious vehicles cruising around."

"Wow," Kitty said. "Word of Sophia's demise has already hit the streets."

I shot Jackie a thumb's up. "Good work."

She grinned. "I do what I can."

"I do, too," Aunt Edna said, somewhat grumpily. "In case anyone's interested, the funeral's all set for noon tomorrow." She smiled smugly. "Neil Neil wasn't too keen on the idea, but after promising to book my own funeral if he pulled off this one for Sophia, he changed his tune pretty quick."

"Excellent," I said.

Aunt Edna shot a look at Sophia. "I ordered the works for myself."

Sophia scowled beneath her silver turban. "I hope you didn't skimp on the hor d'oeuvres for tomorrow. I don't want people thinking I went cheap."

"I got it all taken care of," Morty said. "You'll have a shrimp tower as tall as a mountain, and a spread that could make the cover of *Southern Living*."

Sophia smiled smugly and rubbed her gnarled hands together. "I can't wait to see the looks on their faces."

"You're gonna be there?" Jackie asked. "I thought you were gonna be dead."

"She is," I said. "But Sophia's coming as her old friend visiting from Sicily. She'll wear a black veil to cover her face."

"Oh." Jackie cocked her head. "What's your friend's name?"

Sophia's face puckered. "Brunhilda. Okay?"

"Huh," Jackie said. "I thought she was from Sicily, not Austria."

Sophia shook her head and looked at me. "I still can't decide if that's her personality, or some kind of disorder."

"Moving on," I blurted. "With the transfer done, we need to keep Sophia out of sight and hope the funeral goes off without a hitch. Jackie, who do you think will show up?"

Jackie shrugged. "Everybody. People have been waiting a hundred years for Sophia to croak."

I hazarded a quick glance at Sophia. She looked as if her turban were about to explode.

"Uh ... Morty!" I said. "I was wondering if that other bag man who works with Humpty might show his face tomorrow."

"Vinny Zamboni?" Morty said. "Not likely. Victor told me he picked up Vinny's body three days ago. It's still on ice waiting on an autopsy."

"That's a crying shame," Jackie said.

"Speaking of crying," Sophia said, eying us with aggravation. "I hope you gals put on as big a waterworks show as you did today when I really *do* kick the bucket."

"Of course we will," Kitty said.

"'Cause I'll still be watching," Sophia said. "You can count on it." The old woman straightened in her seat and tugged on her shawl. "So, now on to more important matters. What's for lunch?"

Chapter Forty-One

I was at the Texaco when it happened.

The ever-ravenous Sophia had demanded fried chicken and collard greens for lunch. The only place in town that met Aunt Edna's standards was a food truck in the parking lot of the Texaco on Ninth Street.

So while the others dug through their closets assembling outfits for the funeral tomorrow, I volunteered to pick up the fried chicken—on stern orders from my aunt not to get suckered into buying the corn on the cob.

I'd just paid for our massive lunch order and was sinking my teeth into a mushy, tasteless ear of over-boiled corn when someone snuck up behind me and beaned me over the head.

"Ow!" I yelled, then dropped the corn and whirled around. Glaring at me from behind inch-thick, horn-rimmed glasses was a short, elderly woman somewhere between the ages of 70 and 800.

"Murderer!" she hissed, waving an empty Coke bottle in the air like a club.

I rubbed the rising knot on the back of my head. "Geez, lady. I didn't kill Tad Longmire. It was *pretend*. It was only a show on TV!"

"What are you talking about?" the old woman growled. "I'm talking about the viral video on TakTok. Thanks to you, I missed out on Crazy Eddie's deal of a lifetime on a Dodge Durango!"

"What?"

The old woman in a house dress and orthopedic shoes took another swing at me. I took a step toward the Kia. She took a step to block my way.

"Where do you think you're going?" she hissed.

Geez. That must've been one great discount on that Durango.

My path to the Kia currently inaccessible, I tightened by grip on the sacks of fried chicken and did the only thing I could think of. I ran like an idiot to the side of the Texaco and lock myself in the washroom.

For an eternity lasting about five minutes, I tried not to touch anything or breathe in the smelly air. Suddenly, a knock sounded on the door.

"Occupied," I yelled.

"I gotta pee!" a woman's muffled voice yelled back. "Are you coming out anytime in the next century?"

I grimaced. "Is there an old lady out their wielding a Coke bottle?"

"What?"

"I said, is there an old lady out their wielding a Coke bottle?"

"Uh ... no. Why?"

I flung open the restroom door and sucked in a deep breath. "Thanks. It's all yours," I said to the woman. Then I realized it was Shirley Saurwein.

I looked up at the heavens. "Seriously?"

"Seriously what?"

My gaze returned to the bleach-blonde bane of my existence. "What are you doing here?"

She glanced at the paper sacks in my hand. "Same as you. They've got the best chicken in town. You eating for eight now? Don't tell me you're gonna be the next octamom."

"Ha ha." I rubbed the knot on my head and began walking past her. "And just for the record, I had nothing to do with how that place smells."

"Yeah," she cracked. "I bet you say that to *all* the ladies."

I took another step. Suddenly, two-and-two came together in my head. I whirled back around. "Wait a minute. Was it you who released that video of me slashing Eddie Houser's neck with that stupid rubber knife?"

Saurwein grinned and waggled her eyebrows. "Oh. So you've seen my work."

I gritted my teeth. "Yes."

"Pretty good, eh? It's up to 237,000 views!" Saurwein squealed in delight. She flipped through her cellphone and shoved the screen in my face. "Look. It even beat out the alligator riding an ATV."

"Geez, Saurwein!" I hissed. "Don't you realize how harmful those videos can be? Thanks to the new '*digital age*,' people can't tell the difference between reality and entertainment anymore."

"I know!" She wagged her eyebrows. "And *I'm* cashing in on it!"

I glared at her. "Unbelievable!"

"It sure is!" Saurwein waved her phone at me. "You probably don't know this, Diller, but it's a biological fact that the human brain can't tell the difference between real events and pixels on an electronic screen. The poor saps can't help themselves!"

I didn't have a gun, so I shot the sketchy reporter a sneer instead. "Believe me, Saurwein, that's no consolation to the victims when they get knocked in the head by an old lady armed with a Coke bottle."

"Oh, is *that* what this is all about?" Saurwein shrugged and cracked her gum.

I blew out a breath. "I guess I should thank you for not printing a picture of me slashing Eddie on the cover of today's *Beach Gazette*."

Saurwein frowned. "Don't thank me. That was my game plan. You, slitting Eddie's throat, right next to the article about how the guy suddenly disappeared. But my stupid editor started yammering some nonsense about slander and yellow journalism, so your pic didn't make the cut. Plus, I needed to let the heat die down."

"The heat?"

"My editor's been getting a few angry calls from some disgruntled women."

"Gee, I wonder why?" I shook my head. "You know, Saurwein, we women should work *together*, not tear each other apart."

"Oh. Sorry, Diller. I didn't realize you're a woman." Saurwein winked at me. "Here's a tip on the house. Whatever you're using to get rid of your moustache? It ain't working."

"Arrgh!" I growled. "Why do you hate me?"

Saurwein shot me a pair of pouty lips. "Aww. I don't hate you, Diller. But when it comes to local tabloid news, you're top of the food chain right now."

"How do I get off your food chain?"

"Three ways. Die. Leave town. Or pray some other poor sap even more pathetic than you crawls out from under a rock."

An evil grin curled my lips. "What if I could give you a scoop? Something way tastier than me?"

Saurwein's right eyebrow crooked. "I'm listening."

Chapter Forty-Two

Good thing I put swearing in the car alone in the same category as the calories in broken cookies. Neither counted. I'd just made a pact with a devil in red lipstick. I only hoped it didn't come back to haunt me.

As I slammed on the brakes and cursed out a red traffic light, my cellphone rang. It was Brady. My heart fluttered.

"Hey," I said, trying to sound casual.

"Hey, yourself. Just calling to say hi, and to give you a heads up."

"Heads up?"

"An escaped prisoner was spotted in the downtown St. Pete area about an hour ago. I thought you should know."

"Why? Should I interview them as a potential cellmate?"

"No. I told you, I believe you. You didn't kill Eddie."

"Then why—"

"The convict's name is Marco Telleroni. Aka, *Monkey-Face Mongo*. It turns out he's real."

"I know. My aunt told me. He's one of her ... uh ..."

Crap!

"Diller!" Brady gasped. "Is this guy your aunt's prison pen pal?"

I cringed. "Yes. Does it say in his file why they called him Monkey-Face Mongo?"

"No need to. The mugshot says it all."

I laughed.

"This isn't a joke, Doreen. They guy was serving life for murder. You should talk to your aunt. Make sure she's not being swindled by this con-man."

"Maybe she's the one swindling *him*," I said. "You ever think about that?"

"Either way, it would be wrong."

"I say if Aunt Edna can con guys like these back, they had it coming."

"*Guys* like these? How many are there?"

I cringed again.

Double crap!

"I don't have an exact count ..."

"Doreen, no one deserves to be preyed upon."

"Yeah? Well men like that take advantage of women all the time."

"An eye for an eye leaves us all blind and toothless."

I scowled. "Who died and appointed you the new Yoda?"

I heard Brady blow out a breath. "I'm just worried about you and the other ladies, that's all."

The tone in his voice made *me* worry, too. "Brady, my aunt and her friends have been taking care of themselves for longer than we've been alive."

"That's my point, Doreen. They're old. They're not as invincible as they may think they once were."

"I get it," I said. "I promise I'll talk to Aunt Edna when I get home."

"Where are you?"

"I just left the chicken place at the Texaco."

"Oh. Nice. They have the best chicken in town. I may stop by there myself."

"If you do, here's a heads up for *you*. Don't order the corn on the cob."

"Everybody knows that."

"And one other thing. Watch out for old ladies with Coke bottles."

"What?"

"Don't ask." The red light turned green. "I gotta go."

***

After stuffing ourselves with fried chicken and collard greens, I joined Aunt Edna in the kitchen for a TUMS chaser.

As we both crunched on a couple of chalky tablets, we washed up the dishes and talked about Mongo, Morty, and life's other relationship mysteries.

"Could Mongo have sent the flowers?" I asked, rinsing a plate in the sink. "Do you think he could've found out where we live?"

Aunt Edna's brow furrowed. "Mongo's got connections. He could find out anything he wanted to." She snatched the plate from me and began drying it with a dish towel. "Do me a favor, Dorey. Don't say any-thing to the other women about it."

"Why not?"

"It might ... uh ... scare them."

"More the reason they should know." I scrubbed the grease from an-other plate. "Maybe it would be good for Morty to stay with us tonight. To have some muscle around. You know, as reinforcement."

"He can't." Aunt Edna placed the dried plate in the cupboard atop the others. "Morty's pulling an all-nighter to get the catering for the fu-neral done."

I shot her a soft smile. "Sounds like he really cares."

She shrugged. "He's been good to us."

"Then why not rekindle the flame?" I handed her the final plate to dry. "Why not go out with Morty again?"

She shook her head. "It's too late. I've let myself go. Look at me. I've gained twenty pounds since Morty and I last went out."

"Is that *all*?" Jackie asked, peeking around the corner.

Aunt Edna shot her nosy sidekick some serious side eye. "Too bad I ain't like Jackie here, who has the amazing butt."

Jackie stepped into the kitchen and twisted around to get a gander at her backside. "I do?"

"Yeah," Aunt Edna said. "Every time you walk away, I can't help but think, 'What an ass.'"

Jackie beamed. "Thanks, Edna."

***

After Aunt Edna chased Jackie out of her apartment with her rolling pin, the two of us went and sat in the living room to finish our chat while Sophia was in the restroom.

"There's more to Mongo than you're letting on, isn't there?" I asked, sitting down on the sofa.

Aunt Edna grimaced from her perch in the Barcalounger. "He used to be sweet on me."

"What happened?"

Her eyebrow crooked upward. "Have you seen his face?"

"Uh ... no."

"Let me put it this way. You ever watch *BJ and the Bear*?"

"The show with the truck driver and the chimpanzee?"

"Yeah. Well, Mongo looks like the one who ain't driving."

"Looks aren't everything," I said.

"No, they ain't. But you gotta draw the line somewhere. Mine is you gotta look like a member of the human race."

I laughed.

"See?" Aunt Edna said, scowling. "That's what I'm afraid of. If the other women knew Mongo was sweet on me, I'd never live it down."

I snickered. "I get it. Mum's the word."

"Thanks. You know, Dorey, when I was younger, I always hoped something good would happen to me. Now I just hope whatever crappy thing happens will at least be amusing."

"But Brady told me Mongo was no laughing matter."

My aunt's eyes doubled in size. "You told him about us?"

"Only that he was one of your lonely-hearts scam guys."

"You told him I was running a lonely-hearts scam!"

I winced. "Not exactly. He thinks you're the *victim* of the scam, not the one running it."

Aunt Edna shook her head. "I'm not so sure which is worse."

"If Mongo does find you, what do you think he'll do?"

"I dunno. But right now, we've both got other things to worry about."

I sighed. "You're right. I think I'll call Brady and ask him to keep an eye on the place overnight."

"Oh. I was talking about dinner. With all this commotion, I haven't had time to get to the grocery store."

Chapter Forty-Three

"What is this? A hamster?" Sophia complained as Aunt Edna set her dinner in front of her.

"It's quail," Aunt Edna said. "They were on sale. I bought them before I found out you were actually Granny Warbucks."

"Humph," Sophia grumbled. "There isn't enough meat on this thing to keep a cockroach alive."

"At least it's not a rat," Kitty said, removing a pink visor from her head. "Did you know Queen Elizabeth was once served a gibnut while she was in Belize?"

"A gibbon?" Jackie asked.

"No," Kitty said. "A *gibnut*. It's a member of the rodent family."

My upper lip snarled. "Well, let's hope we catch the rodent who's been infesting *our* Family tomorrow."

Kitty smirked coyly. "Speaking of rats. Edna, have you heard anything more about Mongo?"

Aunt Edna choked on a sip of iced tea. "No. Thank heavens. Listen. I've learned my lesson. No more lonely hearts clubs for me. Real *or* fake."

"What about Morty?" Kitty asked. "There's still a chance there, isn't there?"

"Yeah," Jackie said. "I think Morty's still got the hots for you, Edna."

"No he ain't." Aunt Edna scowled. "That spark went out years ago. Sophia's right. When you get old, *food's* the only real pleasure you got left."

"Of course I'm right," Sophia said, stabbing her fork at the tiny bird carcass on her plate. "But now I'm beginning to wonder about *that*, too."

"Aww, come on, Aunt Edna," I said, nudging her. "Morty seems like a nice guy to me."

Aunt Edna blew out a breath. "I dunno. The whole idea of dating again is ... *horrifying*. I think I'd rather go to jail."

"I can't argue with you," Kitty said. "I don't think there's any bigger blow to a woman's ego than being dumped by an old geezer whose portrait should be hanging in the comb-over hall of fame."

Jackie laughed. "I remember that guy. Gary, right?"

Kitty shook her head. "Yes."

"What about that guy Blane?" Jackie asked. "He seemed okay. Or was that just the toupee talking?"

Kitty rolled her eyes. "Blane *did* put some good money into his bridgework. I'd give him that. But solid dentistry isn't enough to build a relationship on."

"Jackie, whatever happened to Walter?" Aunt Edna asked. "He had a kind of infectious smile."

"Turned out to be herpes," Jackie said. "Nope. I say the best man to date is the pizza delivery guy."

I nearly dropped my fork. "What? Why?"

Jackie shrugged. "Because you know right off the bat he's got a car, a job, and a pizza."

Sophia shook her head. "Listen to you all! You youngsters still have it made. At my age, the best a woman can hope for is a little hair on the guy's head and a mouth that doesn't look like it's harboring some kind of disease."

I elbowed Aunt Edna. "Morty's sounding pretty good about now, eh?"

She sighed. "I dunno. I think he's more into young chicks like you, Dorey."

"If he is, he's too late," Jackie said. "Dorey's sweet on Brady."

"I am not!"

Jackie wagged her eyebrows. "Then why was you two doing the mush-mouth pretzel in his squad car this morning?"

My mouth fell open. All around the dining table, every face turned and smirked at me.

I cringed. "You saw that, huh?"

"Me and everybody else who passed you two on the sidewalk. Including Benny here." Jackie leaned down and patted the ancient pug lying in wait for table scraps. "And you wanna know something?"

I grimaced. "Not really."

"Benny here didn't get a single whiff of deadbeat, did you, girl?"

"Huh," I grunted. "Well, I guess that's something."

"So, are you and Brady an item?" Kitty asked.

I shrugged. "I don't know yet."

Sophia jabbed her fork in my direction. "Does he play the guitar?"

I cocked my head. "I don't know. Why?"

Sophia's green eyes locked on mine. "I'm always leery of anything with strings attached."

"Me, too," Jackie said. "I can't stand raw celery."

Aunt Edna threw her hands in the air. "*Food*, I'm telling you! It's all we've got left!" She shook her head. "What's a person to do when eating becomes the best thing they got going in their life?"

"Easy," Jackie said. "Get a better life."

***

After dinner, Sophia, Aunt Edna, and I retired to the living room to watch TV. After a riveting round of *Wheel of Fortune*, Sophia announced she was ready for bed.

My bed.

With her bunking in my room, I'd been relegated to the couch. I suppose that's why I found it so disconcerting when the old Queenpin farted into the cushion where my head would soon lie.

"Hey, look," Aunt Edna said, flipping through the *TV Guide*. It says here your show's on tonight, Dorey."

"What show?" I asked.

"*Beer & Loathing*."

"Gee. I can't wait," I groaned as I helped Sophia to her feet.

Aunt Edna clicked the remote to Channel 22. I watched warily as the opening scene of *Beer & Loathing* came on the screen. Playing serial killer Doreen Killigan had been the highlight of my pathetic acting career. Still, even *I* wasn't that keen on watching it again.

I took Sophia by the arm. "Come on, off to bed."

Suddenly, the show was interrupted by breaking news.

"Wait. What's that about?" Sophia asked.

We stood and stared at the TV set as a couple of standard-issue news anchors came on the screen.

"The police have issued a be-on-the-lookout warning for escaped fugitive, Marco Telleroni," the woman anchor said. "He was serving a life term for murder, and is considered armed and dangerous."

A picture of Telleroni's mugshot flashed full screen, accompanied by the anchorman's voiceover. He warned viewers, "If you see this fugitive, please report any and all information immediately to the local authorities."

"Ha!" Sophia cackled. "Who are we supposed to call? The police or a zookeeper?"

Chapter Forty-Four

I grumbled and turned over on the velveteen couch.

Go to sleep, Doreen!

Between smelling the ghosts of Sophia's farts and imagining Mongo's monkey face peeking in the windows, I was having a hard time nodding off.

But when someone tapped lightly on the front door, I knew I wasn't just making it up.

My heart began thumping in my throat. I bolted upright and scrambled for a weapon. Aunt Edna's figurine of St. Christopher would have to do. Holding it in my fist like a knife, I tiptoed to the front door and peeked through the peephole.

I nearly fainted with relief. It was Brady.

I cracked opened the door to find the handsome cop wearing dark jeans and a black T-shirt. His hair was slicked back like The Fonz on *Happy Days*.

"What are you doing here?" I whispered.

He glanced at the statuette in my hand. "Answering your prayers, apparently."

"What?" I glanced down at poor St. Christopher. "Ha ha."

Brady grinned. "You asked me to come over, remember? So as soon as I got off shift, I got a shower and headed over."

"Oh. Right."

His dark eyes twinkled playfully. "I figured I could keep an eye on the place just as well from the inside as the outside, don't you think?"

I chewed my bottom lip. "I dunno. What if Mongo shows up?"

Brady smirked. "And what? Catches us monkeying around?"

I laughed. "Shut up and kiss me."

He grinned. "I thought you'd never ask."

***

I woke up at the crack of dawn. Oddly, I thought I smelled bacon frying.

Dang. Maybe it's true. Food really is one of the last pleasures in life.

But it wasn't *the* last one. Not for *me*, anyway. I smiled coyly, remembering last night.

Then I *totally freaked*, remembering last night. Brady had spent the night here with me!

I heard a toilet flush. I sat up on one elbow and spotted Brady's shoes tucked beside the old Barcalounger.

Holy crap! Brady's still here!

I scrambled off the couch and met him in the hallway. He had on his jeans, but no T-shirt. Those washboard abs looked strikingly familiar ...

"Brady!" I whispered, tugging him by the arm. "You have to get out of here! Quick!"

He grinned. "Can I at least get my shirt back first?"

I looked down. I was wearing it. "Double crap."

I heard the coffee machine begin to perk. Before I could say a word, Aunt Edna peeked around the corner.

"So, is lover boy staying for breakfast?" she asked. "I'm making my famous egg-noodle quiche."

My face flamed as red as a thousand suns.

Brady laughed. "Sure, Mrs. Barker. I'd love to stay."

Aunt Edna smiled. "Good. I'll set another place at the table."

As my aunt disappeared back into the kitchen, Brady pulled me to him and kissed me on the nose.

"Hey, Diller. You ever get the feeling we're like Hansel and Gretel, only the house is made of linguini?"

"Yeah."

All. The. Time.

***

As I sat at the breakfast table with Brady and my Italian mob family, I felt like Cher in *Moonstruck*. Here we all were, biding our time, waiting for whatever fate would soon befall us.

Mercifully, the conversation had kept to casual morning greetings—along with a few smirks and furtive, darting eyes. As for the

Queenpin, Sophia seemed oblivious to the handsome newcomer sitting at the table. Her nose was buried in the Sunday edition of the *Tampa Bay Times*.

"Nothing!" she hissed, then tossed the crumpled newspaper aside.

"What are you talking about?" Aunt Edna asked.

"I didn't make the front page," Sophia grumbled. "Not even the obits."

Aunt Edna sat her coffee cup down. "That's because I didn't post one."

Sophia's cat eyes narrowed. "Why not?"

Aunt Edna shot her a look. "Because you're not *really dead*!"

"Humph." The Queenpin's glare switched over to me. "Where's my ScarBux?"

Seriously?

"Sorry," I said. "The guy didn't show up this morning." Just as I'd expected.

"Why not?" Sophia grumbled.

I shrugged. "Probably because he thinks you're dead."

Sophia chewed on that a moment, then tugged the ends of her shawl together and grumbled, "Can't depend on anybody nowadays."

Brady squeezed my hand under the table and whispered, "Is she always this feisty?"

I smirked. "Only when she's conscious."

"All right, everybody, breakfast is a wrap," Aunt Edna announced. She stood and began gathering up empty plates. "It's time to get going. We've got a big day ahead."

"That's right," Jackie said. "Especially you, Sophia. This is the day you drop dead."

Sophia glared at Jackie. "If only I could say the same about you, Jackie, I could die a happy woman."

Jackie grinned. "Well, ain't that nice."

Chapter Forty-Five

"Double up on the gauze," I said to Kitty. "We don't want anyone recognizing her."

"Got it." Kitty added another layer of netting on Sophia's black veil. "How's this?"

"Geez," Sophia grumbled, waving a hand in front of her face. "I can hardly see through this thing. I might walk into a wall or something."

"You won't," Kitty said. "One of us will be by your side at all times, to make sure you're safe." Kitty winked at me and whispered, "And to make sure she doesn't let the cat out of the bag."

"I'm only blind, not deaf," Sophia said. "And it's *Jackie* you've got to worry about spilling the beans. Not *me*."

"Yes, Brunhilda," Kitty said, shooting me another wink.

Sophia shook her head. "Why did I pick that stupid name?"

"I kind of like it," Kitty said sweetly. She looked at me and mouthed the words, "Suits her to a T."

"What?" Sophia asked.

As if on cue, Aunt Edna barged into my bedroom. For the last two nights, my quarters had been taken over by Sophia as her sleeping chambers. This morning, my tiny pink bedroom was serving as the makeup and wardrobe department for act two of my plan—the fake funeral.

"Well, how do I look?" Aunt Edna asked. She'd tweezed her eyebrows, done her hair and makeup, and was donning a black silk dress that fit tight in all the right places.

I barely recognized her.

"Wow!" I said. "You look amazing!"

"You think?" she asked. "Kitty found this thing is the back of my closet. I haven't worn it since the Kennedy administration. Is the fur-lined cape-let too much?"

I shook my head. "No. Very Jackie O, if you ask me." I looked her up and down. "Full body girdle?"

Aunt Edna frowned. "How'd you know?"

I laughed. "Experience. All the celebrities wear them. And right now, you look a lot like one. Elizabeth Taylor, to be exact."

Aunt Edna's cheeks tinged rose. "I haven't heard that in a while. Are you just pulling my chain?"

I grinned. "Absolutely not."

"What do *you* think, Sophia?" Aunt Edna asked.

"How should I know?" the old woman grumbled, picking at her veil. "I couldn't see an *avalanche* coming through this thing."

"Edna, you never looked better," Kitty said. She beamed at her friend. "Necessity may be the mother of *invention*, but the mother of *reinvention* is romance. Believe me. You're gonna knock 'em dead at the funeral."

"Who's Edna gonna kill?" Jackie asked, appearing out of nowhere. She was dressed in a purple pantsuit quite possibly made from an old *Barney the Dinosaur* pelt.

"*Nobody*," Kitty said. "Edna's gonna win Morty over in this outfit. I'm telling you, one look and the man will be on his knees begging for another chance."

Aunt Edna frowned. "I wouldn't be so sure about that. Morty's no masochist, after all."

"What are you talking about?" Jackie said. "I seen him at mass last Sunday!"

***

I was in Aunt Edna's bedroom fixing a loose thread in the hem of her dress when Jackie popped her purple-hatted head in the doorframe and scared the bejeebers out of me.

"Hiya!" she announced, then slipped the rest of her wiry frame into the room.

"Geez, Jackie!" I squealed. "Give us some warning, would you? We're all kind of jumpy today."

"Sorry. I just wanted to let Edna know that Morty called. He said everything's all set."

Aunt Edna chewed her bottom lip. "Okay. Thanks, Jackie. Do me a favor? Go make sure Sophia isn't up to something?"

"On it, Capo." Jackie saluted, looking like an ancient stewardess for Flintstone Airways, and disappeared again.

I trimmed the loose thread at the bottom of Aunt Edna's dress. "Can I ask you something?"

My aunt shook her head. "Please. No more about me and Morty, okay? My nerves are shot as it is."

"No. That's not what I wanted—"

"You and Brady?" She shook her head at me. "I like him. Why are you wearing pants, Dorey? You should show him a little leg while you still got good gams."

I frowned. "I've got things to do today that a lady doesn't do in a dress, okay?"

Aunt Edna's tweezed eyebrow arched. "You don't say. So what did you want to ask me about?"

"What? Oh. It's about *Jackie*. I was wondering how she can be so ..."

"Addle brained and still drive?"

I laughed. "Well, that, too. But what I really want to know is how she can be so *stealthy*. That woman can pop up out of nowhere, and disappear just as quick."

"Oh." Aunt Edna shrugged. "Practice, I guess. It sure ain't camouflage. You've seen how she dresses. Jackie's outfits are loud enough to be charged with disturbing the peace."

I grinned. "True enough. So how does she do it?"

Aunt Edna adjusted her mink hat in the mirror. "I guess when you're wearing the opposite of camouflage, you learn other ways to blend into the crowd."

***

"Wow! You ladies look beautiful," Brady said as Aunt Edna, Jackie, and Kitty paraded in front of him in their fancy funeral attire. "You all remind me of how my mom used to get us dressed up for Easter."

"Aww, that's sweet," Kitty said. "I guess with me in pink and Jackie in purple, we look like a couple of jellybeans."

Brady grinned. "No. You all look lovely. Especially you, Mrs. Barker." He wagged his eyebrows at her. "May I say, va-va-va-voom?"

"You may." Aunt Edna smiled shyly. "And call me Edna. By the way, Brady. I didn't want you to go hungry while you was watching the place. I made you some sandwiches to tide you over. They're in the icebox, along with a pitcher of iced tea and a whole apple pie."

Brady shot me a glance. "What? No *gingerbread*?"

"Gingerbread?" Aunt Edna cocked her head. "You like gingerbread?" She patted Brady's hand. "Next time, I promise. I'll have gingerbread."

I smirked at Brady. My cellphone buzzed. "Oh. My ride's here. I gotta go. See you all at the service, 12:30 sharp!"

"Why are you leaving so early?" Brady asked, following me to the front door.

I shrugged noncommittally. "I've just got a few little things to put into place before the crowds show up."

"Should I go with you?"

"No. I have plenty of reinforcements at the funeral home. Besides, nothing's going to happen there. It's all going to happen *here*, during the funeral service. That's why I need you to stay here with them until they're all safely underway."

Brady nodded. "Who's driving them?"

"Jackie." I glanced over at the skinny, septuagenarian dressed like a purple dinosaur. "Maybe you should say a prayer to St. Christopher, while you're at it."

"Who?"

"St. Christopher. The patron saint of travelers."

Chapter Forty-Six

As I approached the blue Ford Taurus, through the tinted window I could see Shirley Saurwein chewing her gum like a bottle-blonde cow.

"This had better be good," she said as I climbed into the passenger seat. "I'm missing a gopher race in Ruskin for this."

"It'll be worth it." I strapped on my seatbelt. "You'll see."

Saurwein hit the gas. "So you really think there's gonna be a mob showdown at your granny's fake funeral?"

"Doña Sophia Maria Lorenzo isn't my granny."

Wait a minute. Yes she is.

"So what's your connection with these gangsters, anyway?" Saurwein asked.

"Long-lost relatives."

She cackled. "You come to Florida for a visit, and they turn out to be mobsters. You just can't catch a break, can you Diller?"

I frowned. "I'm hoping to catch more than *a break* at the funeral, like I told you."

"Right. Some old mobster's just gonna show up and claim to be king of the Cornbread Cosa Nostra." Saurwein shook her head. "Diller, you may not be the dumbest chick in the world, but you better pray she doesn't die."

"There it is, up ahead," I said, pointing to an eggplant-colored Victorian mansion right off the interstate.

Saurwein hooked a right into the nearly empty parking lot of Neil Mansion Funeral Home. "I hope you're expecting a bigger crowd than this," she said, shifting into park. She grabbed her camera from the floorboard.

"You're going to have to leave that behind," I said. "It's too ... *obvious.*"

"What?" Saurwein hissed. "How am I supposed to get anything on video?"

"I've already got a professional crew on it. They're going to hide in the fake palms behind the casket and record the whole event. If anything juicy turns up, you've got first dibs."

Saurwein scowled. "There *better* be, for your sake, Diller. Or you're going right back to the top of my menu as *Jerk du Jour*."

"Believe me, there will be." I looked her up and down. "Thanks for wearing the black dress and orthopedic shoes. Now, just do everything like I say, and this could be the day your journalism career hits the big time."

***

"What am I supposed to do in here?" Saurwein asked.

"Just look dead. In case somebody takes a peek."

I smirked. I had to admit, closing the coffin lid on Saurwein was like living out a fantasy that'd been knocking around in my head since the day I'd first met her. The sour, slightly frightened, distrustful look on her face as I covered it with a veil was one I'd savor until I took it to my *own* grave one day.

"Who's the woman in the coffin?" Kerri asked as walked over to her.

"Her? Just a problem I'm putting on layaway. Thanks for coming out and doing this for me so last minute."

"No. Thank *you*." Kerri cringed. "I owe you one after all that Crazy Eddie business. Plus, work's been slow. We're glad for the opportunity."

Kerri cupped her hand to her mouth and nodded in the direction of the young blond man setting up a camera tripod behind a screen of fake palms. "Marshall actually had to take a job as a DJ to pay the rent on the studio. Poor guy. He's been working day and night."

I frowned in sympathy. "I'm sorry things have been so slow. What about the money from the Crazy Eddie gig?"

Annoyance creased Kerri's normally pleasant face. "His wife Kareena refuses to pay us. In fact, she blames us for getting the public riled up. She says that's why someone killed Eddie. She's even threatened to sue us!"

"What?" I shook my head. "Geez. What a mess."

"I'm sorry," Kerri said. "This is *our* problem, not yours." She tried to put on a cheerful face. "So, what do you want us to do, exactly?"

"Well, mainly just stay up front here hidden behind all these fake palms and record whatever happens at the funeral."

"You want us to *hide*?"

"Well, yes. I don't want people getting stage fright, or acting weird because they know they're being recorded."

Kerri nodded. "I get that."

"Good. Now, tell Marshall to try and get headshots of everyone who comes in. And keep the camera panning around on the attendees, in case anything hinky goes down."

"Hinky?" Kerri asked.

"Yeah."

"What do you mean by—"

"Oh!" I blurted. "I gotta go. I need to talk to this guy coming in."

***

"Morty!" I said, sprinting over to meet the weary-looking baker standing at the front entrance to the funeral suite. I glanced at the sign-in table decorated with flowers and a picture of Sophia back in her heyday. "Nice. Is everything in place?"

"Yeah. We're good to go."

"Great." I hugged his neck. "You look good in a suit."

He grinned. "Thanks. Looks like we've got the same tailor."

I glanced down at my black pants and tennis shoes. "I know. But I need to be able to make a run for it in case things go down."

Morty sighed. "Don't we all."

"Good point." I glanced around. "Okay, let's get this show on the road, shall we?"

"Hold up a sec."

"What?"

Morty's eyes twinkled softly, looking out of place in his rugged, prize-fighter face. He smiled and nodded toward the sign-in table behind me. "Looking at you next to that picture of Sophia, I gotta say, you're a dead ringer for her at that age. Well, all except for the eyes. You've definitely got Sammy's eyes."

My heart fluttered. "You knew Sammy?"

"Yeah. And I've heard all the stories."

I looked down at my shoes again. "About him turning into a killing machine when he got drunk."

"Yeah." Morty reached out and touched my chin, then gently lifted it until my eyes met his. "But those were just gossip, Dorey. Sammy was a good man. Honest. The only problem he had was that he had too much integrity to make a good mobster. You know, Brady kind of reminds me of him, in that way."

My eyes brimmed with tears. "Really?"

"Yeah." Morty shook his head softly. "Sammy was head over heels about Maureen. He'd do anything for her." Morty locked eyes with me. "He *did* everything for her. *And* you."

"I want to know more," I said. "What about my mom? What was she like?"

"I'll tell you later. But right now, we've got a killer to catch, don't we?"

Chapter Forty-Seven

I breathed a sigh of relief when I saw the rusty old Kia pull into the funeral home parking lot at exactly 12:30. So far, my plan was running like clockwork. I rushed over to The Toad and yanked open the driver's door.

"You're right on time," I said, then found myself being licked in the face by Benny the pug. "What'd you bring the dog for?" I asked, wiping doggy saliva from my cheek.

"I couldn't leave her all alone at the apartments." Jackie climbed out of the driver's seat with the ancient old pug tucked in her arms. "Benny's too blind to find the doggy door anymore. Plus, she gets scared when she's left by herself."

"Uh ... okay." I felt uneasy, sensing a slight hitch might be developing in my plan. I scurried over to the passenger door to help Sophia out.

"I can do it," Sophia grumbled. "I'm not an invalid!"

"My Queenpin," I said, "from this point forward, no talking, please. At least, not in English. You're Brunhilda from Sicily, remember? We can't have your cover blown."

Sophia obliged by rattling off something in Italian.

"What did she say?" I asked Aunt Edna as she and Kitty climbed out of the back seats.

Aunt Edna shook her head. "Believe me. You don't want to know."

***

With Sophia on my arm, we entered the main door of Neil Mansion Funeral Home. Morty was waiting for us at the reception table. When he saw Aunt Edna, his practiced smile hit a glitch.

"Edna?" he asked, his mouth unable to shut.

"What?" she grumbled. "You sayin' you don't recognize me?"

Morty grinned. "I do *now*." He held out a crooked elbow. "May I escort a lady to her seat?"

A few steps behind my aunt, Jackie started to say something. Kitty slapped a hand over her mouth.

"You may," Aunt Edna said, and took Morty's arm. The pair smiled at each other, then began to make their way down the aisle toward the front of the suite reserved for Sophia's funeral.

"All the way up front," I called to them. "I reserved the first row for us."

"I don't see anybody here," Sophia complained, peeking out of her veil as we headed up the aisle.

"It's early," I said. "I wanted you in place before anyone else showed up."

Sophia grunted. "Humph. I'd say, 'We'll see about that,' but I'm as blind as a bat with this fakakta veil on."

I patted her gnarled hand. "Don't worry about that. Like I told you, we're recording everything. You'll get to see it all later." I sat Sophia down in the front row. "Now, please. No turning around and glaring at people. If you do, you could jeopardize the whole operation."

Sophia replied in Italian. Whatever she said, I figured I didn't want to know.

***

At a few minutes to one o'clock, Neil Neil, the oddly named owner of Neil Mansion, made his way to the podium. The crowd was sparse. I was glad Sophia couldn't see.

Maybe I should've had Jackie spread gossip about the free food afterward ...

I noted a few familiar faces from Sophia's centennial birthday party. It seemed like an eternity ago, but shockingly, I counted a mere *five days* since the event. Even so, I couldn't place the names of the stranger anymore. I guess that old saying was true; babies and seniors mostly all looked alike.

There were a few attendees, however, who stood out from the crowd. I instantly recognized the tall, Lurch-like visage of Victor Ventura. He and Morty had carried the fake body bag to his hearse. And, of course, Morty himself. He was sitting beside Victor with his eyes glued on Edna, a goofy grin on his face.

There was also a skinny guy with a big nose and frizzy red hair who looked vaguely familiar. He'd been at the funeral of Freddy Sanderling last week. Freddy had been Sophia's food taster at the nursing home. He'd also been one of the seniors scammed by that iguana-toting Melanie Montoya.

I frowned, trying to remember the guy's name. He'd told me he was an attorney. He'd even given me his business card. I tried to picture it in my mind. His name was something weird.

Fargo? Ferris? Ferrolman?

"A-*hem*," Neil Neil said, startling me as he loudly cleared his throat into the podium microphone. "Thank you all for coming today on such ... *short notice.*"

On those last two words, Neil Neil shot me and Aunt Edna some serious side-eye. Then the persnickety funeral director went on to deliver an overtly snarky speech about Sophia's life. It was peppered with puns such as "her un*time*ly demise," and "her *short time* with us," leaving me in no doubt as to how put-out he felt for having to arrange such a hasty funeral.

"I'll conclude with this *brief* word," Neil Neil said. "Though *short* in stature, Sophia Lorenzo will be remembered for a *long time.*" He nodded his head curtly, then said, "I'll now turn the microphone over to anyone who would like to say a few *timely* words. Afterward, everyone is invited to retire to the salon for refreshments."

Neil took a step away from the podium. A female voice rang out from the back of the room.

"I've got something to say!"

I turned my head and spotted a woman in the back row waving her hand like a kid in class who desperately needed to pee. I hadn't noticed her come in. But when she stood and approached the podium, the busty, auburn-haired woman in a clingy red dress seemed hauntingly familiar.

"Not this chick again," I heard Aunt Edna mutter.

I elbowed Jackie. "Is that—?"

"Victoria Polaski," Jackie said.

I grimaced. "The one Sophia calls Slick?"

"The very one."

As Slick wiggled past us in the aisle, Benny growled in Jackie's arms. I frowned.

That can't be a good sign.

The microphone crackled as "Slick" blew her nose into it, then dabbed the same hanky at her thickly mascaraed eyes. "Scotty and I were very close," she whimpered. "Nobody knew it, but we were secretly engaged."

"What kind of horse hockey is this?" Sophia yelled.

Startled, Neil Neil scrambled forward and took the microphone from Slick. "Um, excuse me, *Miss Scarlet*. This is the funeral for *Sophia Lorenzo*. Scotty McBride's funeral is going on in the next suite over."

"Oh." Slick sniffed and looked down her powdered nose at us. "Oops. My bad." Her crocodile tears evaporated. She smiled, curtseyed, and waved at us like a two-bit starlet at a low-budget movie premiere.

"What a piece of work," Aunt Edna said, scowling and shaking her head.

As Slick flounced past us down the aisle, Benny started barking her little pug head off. "I told you she smells deadbeats," Jackie said, smiling down at Benny like a proud mama.

"One thing's for sure," Kitty said. "Slick sure got *Edna* seeing red."

I glanced over at Aunt Edna. Her face was the color of a ripe tomato. "Red," I said absently.

The color of danger.

I leapt up out my chair. "Excuse me. I've got to go!"

"What?" Kitty asked. "Why?"

"No time to explain. Stay here with the others." I scooted to the end of the row and sprinted halfway down the aisle.

But that was as far as I got.

Out of nowhere, a figure came barreling right for me. It was someone I hadn't planned on.

Not even in Plan C.

Chapter Forty-Eight

I stood frozen in the aisle as Monkey-Face Mongo hurtled toward me. Dressed in a gangster's pinstripe suit, he cradled a long, narrow box under one arm. A box the perfect size and shape to house a Chicago typewriter—aka a Tommy gun.

As Mongo drew nearer, I could see the lunatic gleam shining from his semi-primate eyes. "Ack!" was all I managed to utter as Mongo rushed toward me, tearing open the box.

"Edna!" he yelled. "Edna Barker! Where are you?"

Mongo swooshed past me, flinging the empty box behind him. "Edna! I know you're in here!"

As if in slow motion, I watched my aunt stand and turn around to face the escaped convict.

My voice failing me, I mouthed the word, "No!" Then I noticed something that made my heart melt.

Aunt Edna didn't look frightened. She smiled at me softly, then shifted her gaze to Mongo as she worked her way to the aisle. The calm, resolute expression on her beautiful face told me she'd resigned herself to her fate.

"I'm right here, Marco," Aunt Edna said.

Mongo stopped in his tracks. "Ah! There you are!" He rushed up to Edna and shoved something at her. "This is for you!"

I caught a flash of red.

Oh my god! Is that a bayonet?

My voice cracked as I screamed, "No!"

Then, as if my single word had the power of a .45 caliber bullet, I saw Monkey-Face Mongo go down on one knee.

"Marry me, Edna!" he said. "I can't wait no longer!"

My own knees almost buckled. The bayonet wasn't a bayonet. It was a dozen long-stemmed red roses. I stared, dumbfounded, as my aunt held them in her hands like a bridal bouquet.

Marco Telleroni didn't want to murderize my aunt. He wanted to *marry* her!

"Hold on there just a minute!" Morty's voice boomed from the dead silence of the funeral suite.

Mongo turned around. "Is that you, Morty?"

"You're damned right it's me!"

"Well, you're too late!" Mongo said as Morty marched toward him. "All these years, you had your chance with Edna here. But like a fool, you wasted it!"

For a moment, the two men glared at each other, nose-to-nose, like a pair of feuding mountain gorillas.

"Men, please!" Aunt Edna said. A coy smile curled her lips. "Continue."

Taking his cue, Morty took a swing at Marco. He missed and fumbled sideways. As he struggled to regain his balance, Marco scrambled to the podium.

Mongo grabbed the microphone and sneered at Morty. He opened his mouth and was about to say what I figured would be some rather unflattering words about Morty.

But the grizzled old baker never gave him the chance. A right hook sent Mongo's bridgework flying. The two seized hold of each other and grappled and scuffled around until they both fell to the ground.

Mongo dropped the microphone. It tumbled to the floor beside them, amplifying every grunt and groan the two men made as they wrestled around. Realizing they were on mic, the two men lost focus and struggled back to their feet.

That's when someone yelled, "Call the police!"

Mongo's eyes grew wide. He turned and scanned the crowd to see who might be dialing the cops. Morty seized the opportunity and clocked Mongo on the side of his primate noggin. Knocked out cold, Mongo tumbled backward, striking the coffin like a 250-pound sack of potatoes.

Knocked off its pedestal, the coffin careened to the floor and burst open. Shirley Saurwein came rolling out. Either she was unconscious or she was a damned good actress. She came to rest lying face down in the ugly red carpet.

"Look at that!" someone yelled. "Sophia sure has let herself go!"

***

"Has anybody seen Kerri?" I asked, scrambling around in the ensuing mayhem. Morty had Mongo pinned into a corner, tying his arms behind his back with his own necktie. Neil Neil was running around, shrieking in panic, looking as if he's just escaped from prison himself.

"Kerri?" I shouted into the crowd.

"Is that the name of the woman in red?" a man's voice asked behind me. I turned around and came nose-to-nose with the frizzy-haired attorney from Freddy's funeral.

I frowned. "What are *you* doing here?"

He smirked. "Not *this* routine again. Don't you remember? I'm an attorney. Just looking to drum up a little business."

He handed me his card. I read it aloud. "Ferrol Finkerman. You just don't give things a rest, do you?"

He raised an auburn eyebrow. "You either, apparently. What's your dealio?"

"Dealio?"

"Yeah. Your scheme. Your game." Finkerman rubbed shoulders with me. "Maybe we can work together."

I snarled. "Over my dead body!"

"How poetic." Finkerman shrugged. "Have it your way. You're not my first turn-down of the day."

"What?" I gasped. "Are you harassing these people?"

"Me?" Finkerman looked taken aback. "Compared to that redhead's act, I'm the Pope. That gal might not be too bright, but she's sure got herself a clever manager."

My brow furrowed. "What are you talking about?"

"After she brushed me off, I heard her leaving a message for someone on her cellphone." Finkerman laughed. "Whoever it was didn't take her call. Boy, she ripped him a new one."

"Did she happen to say anyone's name?"

"No. But based on the choice terms of endearment she used, I'd bet it was her soon-to-be-ex-husband."

Chapter Fifty

"Who're your pals here?" Humphrey Bogaratelli asked, training his revolver on us.

"Uh ... they're my brothers," I lied.

"One black, one white, eh? Your mamma must've gotten around."

"I got it!" a male voice rang out from the courtyard.

That's when I realized the figure in the hoodie was a man. He was slowly working his way down the garden path, dragging a duffle bag stuffed to the gills.

"Look, you've got the cash," I said. "Just leave. Nobody's stopping you."

"Hold up a sec," Humpty said. "It was *you* who tipped me off about the mattress, wasn't it. Why'd you do it?"

"I just wanted you to leave Sophia alone. She's old. She'll die soon enough."

Humpty's pudgy face lost its smugness. "I thought she already *did*."

"Oh." I swallowed hard. "About that ..."

"Come on, Dad!" the young man called out. He brushed the hoodie aside. Sweat streamed down his face. "I need your help. It's too heavy!"

"Hold on!" Humpty yelled. "Can't you see I'm a little busy here?"

"But Dad!"

Annoyed, Humpty took a glance toward his son.

"Go," McNulty whispered.

All of a sudden, everything around me became a blur of motion. A gunshot rang out. I could feel the heat of the bullet as it passed mere inches from my face. I heard a metallic *clink*. Then a man yelped.

What the hell's going on?

By the time I could get my bearings, Brady was on top of Humpty, pinning him to the ground.

"Damn it, Racer!" Humpty yelled. His hand that had been aiming the revolver at us was now empty and bleeding.

I heard a vehicle engine start. I scrambled off my knees and stood up. Over the hedges, I saw the young man running toward the van. McNulty was on his tail, about five yards behind him.

"I've got this guy," Brady said. "Go help McNulty!"

Without thinking, I grabbed Humpty's gun from the ground and ran after McNulty. I heard a shot fire and a tire blowout. As I stepped into the road for a better view, I spotted the white van barreling right for me.

Unable to get my feet to move, I stood my ground, squeezed my eyes almost shut, and shot at the van until the gun emptied.

As the smoke cleared, I heard another gunshot—and another tire blow. A sharp creak pierced the air as the back end of the van sunk a foot. Smoke began billowing from the front grille, then the engine died. The van stalled out and rolled to a stop in the middle of the road six feet in front of me.

Through the blown-out windshield, I made out the face of the person behind the wheel. It was Kareena Houser. A Virginia Slim hung limp from the corner of her open mouth. In the passenger seat beside her sat another familiar face. Her other son, the ScarBux delivery kid named Chase.

We stared at each other, all too stunned to move. My mind began to whir as it put pieces together like a jigsaw puzzle.

"Some help here," I heard McNulty groan.

"Nobody move!" I yelled, suddenly coming back to life. I trained the empty gun on the van as I cautiously made my way to the side of the vehicle. McNulty was limping alongside it. Blood was running down his pant leg.

"McNulty!" I gasped. "What happened?"

"A bull gored me, Diller. What do you *think*? Call an ambulance!"

***

"Shot in the butt," McNulty said as he was wheeled into the ambulance on a stretcher. "Why is it always the sergeant who gets it in the end?"

"You're gonna be all right," the EMT said. "Looks like the bullet passed clean through without hitting any major arteries."

"But it's still going to be a pain in the ass, isn't it?" McNulty said, his eyes locked with mine.

"Oh, you'll feel it all right," the EMT said. "Just as soon as the morphine wears off."

McNulty shook his head. "You just can't stay out of trouble, can you Diller?"

I winced out a sympathetic smile. "Sorry."

"You'll be okay, Sarge," Brady said.

"I suppose," McNulty said.

Relieved, I gawked in wonder at the flashing lights and cops surrounding Palm Court Cottages. I looked up at Brady. "You guys really have each other's backs, don't you?"

"We have to." Brady turned to McNulty. "I'll come check on you at the hospital as soon as we get these people booked."

"You do that," McNulty said. "And bring Diller with you."

"Why?" I asked.

"You shot me. You're going to have to deal with that."

Chapter Fifty-One

"I think I know what happened," I said to Brady as he drove us to the police station. "It all makes sense now."

Brady shook his head. "Well, that makes one of us. Fill me in. Who was the woman driving the van?"

"Kareena Houser. Eddie Houser's wife."

"The dead guy? How's *she* tied up in all this?"

"By blood. Those two young men with her are her sons, Racer and Chase."

Brady shook his head. "No wonder they turned to a life of crime."

"Yeah. It gets better. The kids aren't Eddie's. They're Humphrey Bogaratelli's. The young guy in the hoodie called Humpty 'Dad.' You heard him yourself."

Brady hooked a left onto Fourth Street. "So Bogaratelli was messing around with Kareena on the side and Eddie found out about it?"

"Yes. I think they were able to keep their affair under wraps for a long time. But when Eddie found out, they decided he had to go. Humpty whacked Eddie and tried to frame me for it."

"Why?"

"As far as I can figure, he needed the money."

"But I thought you said Humpty was in control of the Family Fund."

"He was. For over thirty years. But having three wives uses up a lot of cash."

Brady nearly wrecked the patrol car. "Wait. *What?*"

"Three women," I said. "I figured it out when I was talking to Ferrol Finkerman at the funeral."

"Ferrol who?"

"Long story. Not important right now. Anyway, you know how you and I thought Melanie Montoya had a partner in scamming those old folks in the nursing home? Getting them to hand over control of their assets by signing powers of attorney?"

Brady shot me a glance. "Yeah."

"Montoya's partner had to be *Humpty*. With power of attorney over Sophia, they could grab all the assets she had *legally*. We foiled their plans, so they had to switch up their game."

"Okay," Brady said. "But how—"

"The way I figure, Humpty is either married to Melanie or shacking up with her. He was always going down to Boca Raton. She's got a place down there. It's a lot easier to hide another wife if she's out of town, right? Plus, why would she drive all the way from Boca to bring therapy animals to a nursing home in St. Pete?"

"And this Ferrol guy told you all this?"

"No." I shook my head. "You missed the big fireworks at the funeral. At the end of the service, this piece of work named Victoria Polanski went up to the podium and started running the same fake fiancé scam she did at Freddy Sanderling's funeral. Only she got the *wrong* funeral."

"What?"

"Yeah. Finkerman told me he heard her on her cellphone blessing out some guy for not answering his phone. He told me it sounded to him like she was talking to her *soon-to-be ex-husband.*"

"And you think that soon-to-be-ex was Humpty ... I mean Humphrey Bogaratelli?"

"It sure fits his M.O. Find a woman dumb enough and greedy enough to help him run his scams. And he seems to have a thing for redheads."

"Melanie is blonde," Brady said.

"Bottle job. Anybody can tell that. Take a look at her roots next time you pass her jail cell."

"So let's say you're right. Humpty's running a shell game with three different women. Why should it blow up now?"

"Two reasons. Okay, everything's been running smoothly for years. Humpty's got it made, having these women do his dirty work. He thinks he's untouchable. So he ups his game."

"How?"

"He has Eddie start helping him with things. Aunt Edna told me she thought Humpty and Eddie might've been working in cahoots to steal from the Family Fund."

"Seriously?" Brady shook his head. "Who *isn't* in on this?"

"I know, right? Anyway, Humpty's all of a sudden more and more in the picture, hanging around Kareena and the kids. Maybe Eddie starts to notice things."

"What kind of things?"

"That maybe Kareena likes Humpty too much. Or that now that Racer and Chase are young men, Eddie spots a family resemblance, only it's not to *him.*"

"I see." Brady chewed his bottom lip. "Or maybe one of those boys slipped up and called Humpty 'Dad.' They don't seem like the brightest bulbs in the carton."

"Exactly. Maybe Kareena and Humpty get nervous. They start worrying Eddie's going to put two and two together and come up with TNT."

"Huh?"

"Blow his top. Seek revenge. So together, Humpty and Kareena conspire to get rid of Eddie before he can get rid of either of them."

"And the second thing?" Brady asked. "You said you had two reasons why you thought the gig was up for Humpty."

"Oh. The Family Fund. Morty told me Humpty had drained it dry. He needed a big score if he was going to keep his shell game running."

"Thus the money in the mattress," Brady said.

I smiled. "Bingo."

Brady pulled into the police station and parked. "That all makes sense, Doreen. But why would Humpty try to pin Eddie's murder on you?"

"I dunno." I unbuckled my seat belt. "But that's what I'd like to find out."

Chapter Fifty-Two

"Please," I whined. I'd followed Brady through the police station all the way to booking, but he wouldn't let me go with him to the interrogation room. "Give me a few minutes with Kareena. I think I know how to get her to talk."

"She's already told Officer Daniels she won't talk to a cop."

I smiled. "I'm not a cop. I'm a rival. And if I know Kareena like I think I do, she just might be spoiling for a catfight."

Brady frowned. "Doreen, I'm not going to let you sit alone with a murder suspect."

"I won't be alone. You'll be behind the glass watching, and I'll be armed with a pack of Virginia Slims."

"I dunno."

"Gimme one crack at her, Brady. If you do, I'll tell you who scratched PIG into the side of your truck."

Brady pursed his lips. "Okay. You got five minutes."

***

"I knew it!" Kareena said, sucking on a Virginia Slim like it was going to save her soul. "I knew Humpty was gettin' some strange with a chick down in Boca Raton. Lousy cheater."

That's rich, considering you were married to Eddie.

"Melanie wasn't the only one," I said.

"What?" Kareena eyed me up and down. "I guess you'd know all about that, wouldn't you? You've been trying to break up my marriage since you laid eyes on Eddie."

"Excuse me?" I said.

"I saw Eddie making eyes at you. Squeezing your ass during that stupid commercial. And I found a copy of that contract on his desk. He was gonna give you a Nissan Cube." Kareena snarled and shook her head. "That's Eddie's classic MO. Give a girl a free ride, then pull the wool over her eyes."

"So he's done this before?" I offered her another cigarette.

Kareena grabbed it and let out a long sigh. "Since we first got hitched. You were just the last in a long string of trashy bimbos. You know, the whole ironical thing about this is, we'd have had a legit fortune if it weren't for his wandering eye."

Ironical? What about your own?

"That must've hurt," I said. "But believe me, I wasn't going to take Eddie's deal."

Kareena cocked her head. "You were gonna do it for *free*?"

"What? No. I mean ... I have a *boyfriend*. I wouldn't cheat on him."

"Oh. You mean the pig? He's kinda cute. You know, for a pig."

"Er ... so Kareena, who killed Eddie?"

Kareena sighed and stamped out her cigarette butt. "Racer did it." She shook her head. "Humpty filled him with tales about how he knew where this fortune was hidden. That all they had to do was go steal it, and we could all leave Eddie's stupid used car business behind."

"Where was the fortune?"

"Some old lady hoarder had it," she said. "He didn't tell us who. Humpty had tried to get the old lady to die so he could get it without nobody knowing about it. He'd planned it for months. But then last week, he told me something went wrong. He had to adjust the plan."

"What plan?"

"To kill the old lady and get her fortune," Kareena said. "Pay attention!"

"Sorry." I offered her another cigarette. She took it.

"Humpty told Racer about the setback. That it might take a few more weeks to get things in place. But Racer, our oldest, ain't the most patient kid in the world. He and Eddie never got along. He was tired of having to work at Eddie's car lot. He thought it was degrading. So when Humpty told us his plans were gonna take longer than he thought, Racer lost it."

"He killed Eddie."

"Yeah. He told Humpty. He blew a gasket! But Humpty told Racer not to worry. He'd make it all go away. And he did. The next day, you showed up for that stupid sale of the century at the car lot, and Eddie didn't."

"Humpty set it up to make it look like I murdered Eddie. Why?"

Kareena smiled cruelly. "Because I told him to. He needed a patsy, and I needed revenge."

***

"Geez, Diller. I've got to hand it to you," Brady said as I walked out of the room with Kareena. "You really got that woman to open up."

I smiled smugly. "Weren't expecting a full-blown confession, eh?"

"Well, at this point, Kareena's only pointed the blame at her son and Humpty. We're going to need some corroborating evidence to make it stick. Any ideas?"

"Yeah. Ask her other son, Chase."

Brady cocked his head. "Ask him *what*, exactly?"

"Have him tell you about ScarBux."

Chapter Fifty-Three

After assembling a list of questions for Brady, it was my turn to sit behind the mirror and watch as Brady interviewed a terrified young man who was barely out of his teens.

The youngest offspring of Kareena Houser and Humphrey Bogaratelli appeared totally unaware of his parents' criminal intents.

"How did you get involved in ScarBux?" Brady asked.

Chase fiddled with his fingers and chewed his bottom lip. "Dad told me I needed a part-time job to start building experience. You know, to put on a job application."

"Sure," Brady said. "That makes sense. So, why ScarBux?"

"It was Dad's idea. He actually started the company. He wants ... *wanted* me to be an entrepreneur."

"How did the company work?"

"Dad made the coffee in the morning, and I delivered it."

Brady nodded. "So, what kind of hours did you work?"

Chase shrugged. "Not many. I have morning classes at the junior college. I didn't have time to find customers. Dad found me my first one."

"The old woman at Palm Court Cottages?"

"Yeah. Sophia." Chase looked up at Brady, his eyes brimming with tears. "I didn't know we were going to rob her!"

"It's okay," Brady said. "You're not being charged with that. I'm just trying to find out about ScarBux."

"I thought it was legit," Chase said. "Dad had cups printed up and everything."

"What about the sugar packets?" Brady asked.

"Dad bought them at a restaurant supply store. He had a rubber stamp made. I stamped the name on the packets and left them to dry. Dad put them into baggies for me to give to the old lady."

"How long have you been delivering coffee to her?"

"A couple of months."

"Good. Now, Chase, do you happen to still have any of the sugar packets?"

"Dad told me to throw them all away. He didn't need them anymore."

"Oh," Brady sighed.

Chase shrugged. "But I forgot." He reached into a pocket and pulled out a baggie of packets. "Is this what you're looking for?"

"Yes, it absolutely is," Brady said.

As I'd instructed, Brady let the baggie lie on the table untouched. He shot me a covert thumbs up. Then he turned to the frightened young man and said, "Thanks, Chase. That's all for now."

***

681

"Good work," I said to Brady, meeting him in the interrogation room after Chase left. "Just as I suspected, ScarBux was another one of Humpty's scams."

A lab tech arrived suited up with rubber gloves.

"Take those for testing," Brady said. "Handle them carefully."

"You got it." As the tech picked the baggie up with a pair of tongs, Humpty passed by in handcuffs on his way to booking.

"Hey, Humpty!" I said, shooting him a grin. "Look what we found. We'll be sure to test them for thallium."

Humpty glanced at the packets. His pudgy face went pale. "Those aren't mine. I'm being framed!"

"Gee," I said. "I wouldn't have any idea how *that* feels."

***

"So who scratched PIG into my truck?" Brady asked. We were sitting at his desk eating Dairy Hog hamburgers and filling out a mountain of paperwork big enough to give a Billy goat indigestion.

"Racer," I said, sucking down a sip of vanilla milkshake. "I saw him in the street at Sundial. When he pulled that hoodie off in the courtyard today, I was sure it was him."

Brady shook his head. "But why?"

"You're asking *me* why criminals do the things they do?"

Brady laughed. "Good point."

I shrugged. "Actually, I think it might've been jealousy. Kareena thought Eddie and I were having an affair. He grabbed my ass, you know."

Brady frowned. "Good thing he's dead."

I grinned. "Jealous, are we?"

Brady blew out a breath. "I'm too tired to be jealous. Now, help me concentrate." He turned over a form he was filling out. "According to the evidence report, the money seized in the duffle turned out to be mostly ones and fives wrapped around stacks of blank paper."

I smirked. "You don't say."

Brady shot me a look. "Humpty's treasure hunt turned out to be worth less than three hundred dollars."

"That's a crying shame."

"Doreen, the banknotes are going to have their serial numbers traced. If they're part of a bank heist or something, that could open up a whole new can of worms for your family."

I pictured me and the other mob molls sitting around Aunt Edna's dining table sipping tea, eating snickerdoodles, and wrapping the fake money bundles with small notes Morty had brought us from his bakery business.

"I'm not worried about that," I said.

The look of relief on Brady's face was precious. "Good. So answer me this one last thing. Why thallium? And why sugar packets?"

I shrugged. "As my Aunt Edna always says, "Revenge is a dish best served in a disposable container."

Chapter Fifty-Four

"You got home late last night," Aunt Edna said, poking her head into my bedroom.

"Yeah. Thanks for the clean sheets. And for getting Sophia out of my bed."

"Oh, that was the easy part." Aunt Edna laughed. "When she saw the new memory foam mattress being delivered, she practically stampeded over me to check it out."

I grinned. "I wish I'd been there to see it."

"Oh, from what I hear, you saw *plenty* yesterday. Now get dressed and come to breakfast. We're all dying to hear how everything turned out."

***

"Seriously? Humpty had *three wives*?" Kitty nearly spilled her coffee. "The man looks like a boiled egg with legs!"

"What a trio of bimbos *they* had to be," Sophia said. "I don't think even Oscar Mayer could swallow that much baloney. Still, it's a shame ScarBux was a sham. Humpty could sure make some good coffee."

I glanced over at Aunt Edna. She didn't appear to have heard Sophia's slight. She was too busy gazing into Morty's eyes while he returned the favor.

"I hate to break up a pair of love birds," I said. "But Morty, you told us Humpty nearly emptied the Family Fund trying to cover his own expenses. How come we kept receiving enough money to get by on?"

Morty shrugged. "It's a mystery."

Aunt Edna's mouth fell open. "It was *you*, wasn't it? *You* paid the rent and kept a roof over our heads!"

"Hey," Sophia grumbled. "I coughed up a few bucks as needed, too, you know. Not all those bills were traceable."

"The truth is, this place has been paid off for years," Morty said. "I was going through some papers in Humpty's car last night. The mortgage on Palm Court Cottages is free and clear. And it's in Sophia's name."

"Geez," I said. "If Humpty had managed to get that power of attorney, we'd all be out on the street. He'd have sold this place right out from under us."

"I guarantee it," Morty said.

"Well, Humpty won't have to worry about food and shelter where he's going," Jackie said. "I only hope there's worms in his porridge, like in *Shawshank Redemption*."

I grinned at Jackie. "Precisely."

Morty laughed. "You know, while I was waiting for the cops to come take Mongo away, he told me Humpty framed him for murder."

My nose crinkled. "Really? Wouldn't it be the ultimate karma if fate made them cellmates?"

"It sure would," Sophia said. "Humpty wanted to have big money. Turns out he only had a big mouth. Let's see how that works out for him in prison."

"Speaking of money, it's Monday," Kitty said. "Has anyone checked the Family Fund account?"

"I'll do it." Morty pulled out his cellphone. "That body bag full of bills Victor deposited at the bank Saturday should have registered in our new account by now." He grinned and wagged his eyebrows. "I think we just might be looking at a tidy sum."

"Hey, look at all the zeroes!" Jackie said, peeking over his shoulder.

Morty's jaw dropped. "There's *only* zeroes. The account's *empty*."

"Awe, geez!" Aunt Edna said. "Don't tell me we've been conned ourselves!"

"*Now* I think I know who sent the flowers," Kitty said, shaking her head. "Victor Polanski, you dirty, double-crossing dog!"

Chapter Fifty-Five

"I can't believe Victor would do that!" Morty said. "He told me I had nothing to worry about. That I could trust him!"

"How could you make such an amateur mistake, Morty?" Aunt Edna said. "Smart people don't tell you how smart they are. Rich people don't tell you how rich they are. Honest people don't tell you how honest they are. Only con men do!"

"Humpty needed all that money to support his girlfriends and wives," Jackie said. "Maybe Victor has a whole harem, too!"

Kitty shook her head in disgust. "And he had the nerve to show up at your fake funeral, too, Sophia! That smirk on his face. I should've known he was up to something!"

"It's all dirty money," Sophia said. "From a Federal bank heist. If Victor tries to use them, he'll be busted faster than a cheap party balloon. That's why I never spent the dough in the first place."

"But why let us try to deposit it, then?" Aunt Edna asked.

Sophia smirked and adjusted the silver turban on her head. "Because I knew it would never make it to a bank. Look around! Haven't you all noticed? Everybody we know is a con man!"

Kitty sighed. "I guess you're right."

"I *know* I'm right," Sophia said. "Besides, I was tired of sleeping on that lumpy mattress. Thirty years was enough."

Aunt Edna frowned. "I'm glad you can make jokes, Sophia. But it's not funny. We're broke."

"No we're not." Morty smiled. "We own the apartments. Given today's inflation, they're worth at least a half a million bucks."

"We could take out a home equity line on them," I said.

"No need for that." Sophia stood and started toddling toward the living room. "What are you all waiting for? Follow me."

The old Queenpin took up position in the "good chair"—Aunt Edna's ugly old brown vinyl recliner. "Gather round," she said as we filed in. "I've got something I want to tell you."

Morty opted to stand. We four ladies squeezed together into the olive-hued velveteen couch.

Sophia's cat-green eyes sparkled. "Now, what I'm about to tell you is my *last* secret."

"What was the first one?" Jackie asked.

Sophia rolled her eyes. "Pay attention. You're gonna like this. Especially you, Edna."

Aunt Edna's eyebrow rose with suspicion. "What do you mean?"

Sophia grinned like a Sphinx. "I'm finally granting you permission to get rid of this hideous chair."

"What?" Aunt Edna gasped. "I mean, thank you. I've been wanting to for thirty years! But why? Why *now*?"

"Because we're about to bust it open like a piñata," Sophia said. "There's a couple hundred grand in gold coins stuffed inside this bad boy."

Chapter Fifty-Six

I was on my way out the door when my phone rang. It was the call I'd been waiting for.

"Shirley Saurwein," I said smugly. "How's it hanging?"

"What's the meaning of this?" she hissed over the phone.

"I have no idea what you're talking about."

"The video of me passed out by the coffin!" Saurwein screeched. "Dear god. Whose *dentures* are those anyway?"

I stifled a laugh. "All I know is I heard a rumor about some two-bit reporter who faked her own death to try and make the national headlines. Poor dear passed out, pissed herself, and lost her dentures in the process. But like I said. It's just a rumor. The actual video hasn't been released yet."

"You wouldn't."

"Wouldn't what?" I asked sweetly.

"Unbelievable!" Saurwein hissed. "Blackmail? You really *are* related to the mob, aren't you, Diller?"

"All I want is to live in peace. How about you?"

"Ha," Saurwein laughed bitterly. "So you decided to answer the call of your family. Too bad it's 'Scam Likely.'"

"Hey, you're the one who taught me that the best way to make a lasting impression is with a sledge hammer."

Saurwein blew out a sigh. "Touché. Be seeing you Diller."

I smirked. "Not if I see you first."

I clicked off the phone.

"Who were you talking to?" Jackie asked, appearing out of nowhere with Benny in her arms.

"Oh, just a big nobody." I opened the front door and took a step outside.

"Where you off to?" Jackie asked.

I cringed. "I've got to go see a man about a bullet hole in his butt."

Jackie grinned. "I hate when that happens."

Chapter Fifty-Seven

"You ready?" Brady asked, meeting me outside the hospital room where Sergeant McNulty lay—though probably not on his back.

I cringed. "I guess so. I shot McNulty in the ass, Brady. What's he gonna do to me? Press charges?"

Brady shot me a sympathetic smile. "I don't know."

I blew out a breath and took a step toward McNulty's room. "Come on, let's get this over with."

"Nope. He wants to see you alone." Brady grimaced. "Good luck."

"Thanks." I pushed open the door. McNulty was lying on his side in the hospital bed. An IV drip ran to a vein in the crook of his elbow.

"Diller," he said, his voice husky and dry.

I rushed to his side. "I'm *so sorry*, Sergeant McNutly! I didn't mean to shoot you! I've never even fired a gun before!"

"No kidding," he quipped.

I winced. "You know, I normally lead an ordinary, mundane life. It's just that lately, it's been ... you know ... sprinkled with moments of life-threatening madness."

McNulty chuckled, then winced from the effort. "So we have that in common."

"Like I said, I'm so sorry—"

"It's okay, Diller. It was an accident. Things like this happen."

My mouth fell open. "So you've been shot before?"

McNulty locked eyes with me. "Never."

I cringed again and looked around. "Is there anything I can do for you? Water? Bedpan?"

"Yes." McNulty struggled to sit up. "Quit pretending, Diller. You're no actor."

I felt punched in the gut. "Thanks."

"I'm just being honest. The way I see it, you're like a feral mutt."

"Excuse me?"

"Like the dogs we take in for K-9 school." McNulty took a sip from a cup with a straw in it. "All you need is some discipline and training, and you have the potential to be transformed from a public nuisance to a contributing member of society."

I frowned. "Are you on morphine?"

McNulty laughed. "I got something for you. In that bag on the chair over there."

"Really?" I went over to the chair. The top half of a book peeked out from a paper sack. It read, *Survival Guide.* "What is this?" I asked. "A survival guide for prison?"

"No. Take it out of the bag."

I pulled the book from the sack. The full title read, *Survival Guide for Police Recruits.*

"You ever consider joining the police academy, Diller? A class starts next Tuesday."

"Huh?" I nearly fell on the floor. "What about my police record? Or all those times you arrested me?"

McNulty shrugged. "You were cleared every time. And to be honest, I'd rather have you on *our* side than theirs."

My jaw went slack. "Are you serious?"

McNulty grinned through a wince. "You've definitely got the chops for it. Now beat it, Diller. I need my beauty rest."

"Yes, sir. Get well soon, Sergeant McNutly."

"McNulty."

"Sorry." I walked out the door and closed it behind me. Then a thought hit me.

Wait a minute. I have the chops *for it? Did McNulty just insult me?*

I smiled. That had to be a good sign.

Chapter Fifty-Eight

"So you really don't mind going to the Dairy Hog again for lunch?" Brady asked as we pulled into the parking lot of the dive restaurant off Ninth Street.

"No. But I have a confession to make. I think the secret ingredient in their vanilla shakes might be crack."

Brady studied me with all seriousness. "You know, I've suspected the same thing for a while now."

I grinned. "And yet you keep coming back."

"What can I say? It's the crack."

I laughed. "Can you believe McNulty wants me to try out to become a policeman?"

"Absolutely. You're a natural, Doreen."

I frowned. "I am not."

"Sure you are. Stop shooting yourself in the foot."

"Ha ha."

Brady took my hand. "I didn't mean to make a joke. What I mean is, all you lack is confidence. Honestly, I think that's why you didn't make it as an actress."

"Ouch."

"That came out wrong. Doreen, confidence comes from trusting yourself."

"Like you do?"

"Yes. Like *I* do." Brady shot me a grin. "You know, you're already the talk of the police station."

My face flushed. "I am? What are they saying?"

"Mostly jokes. But believe me. Cops only kid you if they like you."

My nose crinkled. "What kind of jokes?"

"Well, nowadays, whenever a suspect gets caught wearing a ridiculous disguise, they call it "Doing a Diller.""

"Arrgh!" I groaned. "So what you're saying is that fame finally found me, and that fame is a real butthole."

Brady laughed. "Doreen, whether you choose to be an actress, a cop, or whatever, some nut will always be after your Lucky Charms." He squeezed my hand. "It might as well be me."

***

After a vanilla-crack milkshake and a quick make-out session with Brady, I ditched him for a date with a banana cream cannolo.

"There you are," Aunt Edna said as I came through the door. "Morty's here for dinner, and he brought dessert."

I grinned. "I was hoping he would."

"Which one?" my aunt asked. "Come for dinner, or bring cannoli?"

I hugged her neck. "Both."

"Thanks." She grinned and swatted me on the butt with a dishtowel. "Now go get cleaned up for dinner. I'm making your favorite!"

"Which one?"

She winked. "Both."

***

As I was washing up in the bathroom, I thought I heard my cellphone buzz. I dried my hands and went back to my bedroom. In the pink light of the lava lamp on the bureau, I saw a message blinking on my phone.

I clicked it. An oddly familiar voice waivered over the speaker.

"Doreen? Hi. It's Delores Benny. Are you in town? I have a small part in this movie I'm working on. You'd be my spinster housekeeper. Call me ASAP."

Suddenly, the warm, comforting feeling of my life falling into place here in St. Petersburg felt blasted to pieces by a nuclear bomb called Hollywood.

A decent part? Why now?

Feeling torn, I called the only person who I thought would understand.

"Kerri?" I said into my cellphone.

"Doreen! Hi! How'd the 'insurance video' work out?"

"Perfect. My lifetime policy is locked in. Thank you so much!"

"Glad to hear it. Anytime."

I chewed my bottom lip. "Listen, can I ask you something?"

"Sure."

"I got a call from Hollywood. About a part in a movie."

"Oh. Well, that's good news, isn't it?"

"Two weeks ago, I'd have sold my right kidney for a call like that."

"But not now?" Kerri asked. "What's changed?"

"Everything and nothing. Being a former news anchor, you know what it's like. The biz is completely cutthroat. And even if you make it, you're only as good as your last gig. Being a flop is worse than death. Death you can live down."

"All true," Kerri said. "So what are you asking?"

"Why *now*? Why would the universe send me this role now that my life is ... well, worth living?"

"You know," Aunt Edna said. "Morty's right, Dorey. When you get that certain expression on your face, you're a dead ringer for Sophia in her early days."

"I knew it!" Sophia said. "You're my granddaughter, aren't you?" She laid down her knife and fork. "That's it. I'm naming my new heir right now!"

Kitty gasped. "You are?"

Sophia's green cat eyes darted from face to face. "I've put this off as long as I can. What we need around here is somebody who hasn't committed the M word yet."

"Murder?" Jackie asked.

"No," Sophia grumbled. "*Medicare.*"

"Well, that rules *us* out," Aunt Edna said.

The Queenpin turned her gaze to me. "Young Doreen. You've saved my life twice, now."

I shook my head. "I couldn't have done it without the help of everyone here."

"Maybe not," Sophia said. "But I've been waiting thirty years for someone with enough gumption to blackmail me."

"Seriously?" Kitty said.

Sophia raised a fork in the air like a scepter. "Well done, Doreen. I choose *you* to follow in my footsteps. You want the job?"

I swallowed a dry knot in my throat. A few days ago, I had felt like a total loser with no prospects. But now, in this moment, I felt like a champion with a world of choices laid out before me. I liked this new feeling. I liked this new *me.*

"Um ... I'm honored, Sophia," I said. "Really, I am. But I'm not ready—"

"I'm a reasonable woman," Sophia said, cutting me off. "I know answers aren't always black and white. You don't have to tell me today, Doreen."

"Thank you."

"But don't wait too long," she warned, shooting me a wink. "Someone else might beat you to it."

I nodded. "Fair enough. But, just to be clear, either way, I'm not wearing that turban. Capeesh?"

Laughter burst out around the table. A hopeful giddiness filled the air. As I glanced from face to face, I saw no signs of anger or envy in any of my new found family. Only acceptance. And love.

And maybe a hint of relief.

I drank it in.

This must be what home feels like.

As we ate and drank under the soft yellow lights strung in the courtyard above our heads, I couldn't say what the future held for any of us. The only thing I knew for sure was this:

People are never who you think they are. Especially yourself.

The End

***

Thanks so much for reading ***Almost a Dead Ringer***, the final book in the *Doreen Diller Humorous Mystery Trilogy*.

I hope you enjoyed it, along with the whole series. If so, I'd love it if you would take a few minutes to leave a review. I appreciate every single one! Here's a handy link to the page on Amazon:

https://www.amazon.com/dp/B0BMZCB4S9

Ready for more laughs and twisty mysteries?

Already jonesing for more Doreen Diller and the gang? Well, you never know which of your favorite characters might drop by in my brand new "Val Fremden Strikes Back" series! Click the link below to check out *That Time I Kinda Killed a Guy*, the first book:

https://www.amazon.com/dp/B0C2VZT3LM

Check out my Author Page on Amazon and discover what else I've been up to:

https://www.amazon.com/author/mlashley

While you're there, be sure to follow me so you won't miss out on my next new release or book sale. Thank you so much for being a fan. You totally rock!

More Mysteries by Margaret Lashley

Freaky Florida Investigations
https://www.amazon.com/gp/product/B07RL4G8GZ
Val Fremden Midlife Mysteries
https://www.amazon.com/gp/product/B07FK88WQ3
Val Fremden Strikes Again
https://www.amazon.com/dp/B0C2VZT3LM
Doreen Diller Humorous Mystery Trilogy:
https://kdp.amazon.com/en_US/series/W34F3Z8FNY5
Mind's Eye Investigators
https://www.amazon.com/gp/product/B07ZR6NW2N

About the Author

Why do I love underdogs?

Well, it takes one to know one. Like the main characters in my novels, I haven't led a life of wealth or luxury. In fact, as it stands now, I'm set to inherit a half-eaten jar of Cheez Whiz...if my siblings don't beat me to it.

During my illustrious career, I've been a roller-skating waitress, an actuarial assistant, an advertising copywriter, a real estate agent, a house flipper, an organic farmer, and a traveling vagabond/truth seeker. But no matter where I've gone or what I've done, I've always felt like a weirdo.

I've learned a heck of a lot in my life. But getting to know myself has been my greatest journey. Today, I know I'm smart. I'm direct. I'm jaded. I'm hopeful. I'm funny. I'm fierce. I'm a pushover. And I have a laugh that lures strangers over, wanting to join in the fun.

In other words, I'm a jumble of opposing talents and flaws and emotions. And it's all good.

I enjoy underdogs because we've got spunk. And hope. And secrets that drive us to be different from the rest.

So dare to be different. It's the only way to be!

All my best,

Margaret

Made in United States
Orlando, FL
14 March 2024

44732372R00388